T0375814

Medieval French Interlocutions

YORK MEDIEVAL PRESS

York Medieval Press is published by the University of York's Centre for Medieval Studies in association with Boydell & Brewer Limited. Our objective is the promotion of innovative scholarship and fresh criticism on medieval culture. We have a special commitment to interdisciplinary study, in line with the Centre's belief that the future of Medieval Studies lies in those areas in which its major constituent disciplines at once inform and challenge each other.

Editorial Board (2024)

Peter Biller, Emeritus (Dept of History): General Editor
Tim Ayers (Dept of History of Art)
Henry Bainton: Private scholar
K. P. Clarke (Dept of English and Related Literature)
K. F. Giles (Dept of Archaeology)
Shazia Jagot (Dept of English and Related Literature)
Holly James-Maddocks (Dept of English and Related Literature)
Richard McClary (Dept of History of Art)
Harry Munt (Dept of History)
Jessica N. Richardson (Dept of History of Art)
L. J. Sackville (Dept of History)
Elizabeth M. Tyler (Dept of English and Related Literature): Director, Centre for
    Medieval Studies
Hanna Vorholt (Dept of History of Art)
Sethina Watson (Dept of History)
J. G. Wogan-Browne (English Faculty, Fordham University)
Stephanie Wynne-Jones (Dept of Archaeology)

All enquiries of an editorial kind, including suggestions for monographs and essay collections, should be addressed to: The Academic Editor, York Medieval Press, Department of History, University of York, Heslington, York, YO10 5DD (E-mail: pete.biller@york.ac.uk)

Details of other York Medieval Press volumes are available from Boydell & Brewer Ltd.

Medieval French Interlocutions
Shifting Perspectives on a Language in Contact

Edited by
Thomas O'Donnell, Jane Gilbert and Brian J. Reilly

THE UNIVERSITY *of York*

YORK MEDIEVAL PRESS

© Contributors 2024

All rights reserved. Except as permitted under current legislation no part of this work may be photocopied, stored in a retrieval system, published, performed in public, adapted, broadcast, transmitted, recorded or reproduced in any form or by any means, without the prior permission of the copyright owner

First published 2024

A York Medieval Press publication
in association with The Boydell Press
an imprint of Boydell & Brewer Ltd
PO Box 9, Woodbridge, Suffolk IP12 3DF, UK
and of Boydell & Brewer Inc.
668 Mt Hope Avenue, Rochester, NY 14620-2731, USA
website: www.boydellandbrewer.com
and with the
Centre for Medieval Studies, University of York

ISBN 978 1 914049 14 9

A CIP catalogue record for this book is available from the British Library
The publisher has no responsibility for the continued existence or accuracy of
URLs for external or third-party internet websites referred to in this book, and
does not guarantee that any content on such websites is, or will remain, accurate
or appropriate

In memory of
Simon Gaunt
trailblazer, interlocutor, friend

Contents

List of Illustrations	ix
Contributors	xi
Acknowledgements	xii
List of Abbreviations	xiv

Introduction   1
Thomas O'Donnell, Jane Gilbert and Brian J. Reilly

1. Our Language and the Others: Old French Glosses in Berekhiah Ha-Naqdan's *Uncle and Nephew* and *Commentary on the Book of Job*   27
   Ruth Nisse

2. From Liutprand of Cremona to Robert de Clari: Wonder and the Translation of Knowledge Before and After the Crusader Conquest of Constantinople   47
   Teresa Shawcross

3. Mixed Metaphors, Mixed Forms: Across Medieval Hebrew and French Prosimetra   89
   Isabelle Levy

4. Deeds and Dialogue from a French-Irish Medieval Cultural Sphere   115
   Máire Ní Mhaonaigh

5. The Presence of French in German Courtly Literature *c*.1200   137
   Mark Chinca

6. Marco Polo and the Multilingual Middle Ages   159
   Sharon Kinoshita

7. Romancing Allegory: Theories of the Vernacular in Outremer   179
   Uri Zvi Shachar

8. 'Dize en la estoria francesca': The Circulation of Francophone Matter of Antiquity in Medieval Castile (*c*.1200–1369)   197
   Clara Pascual-Argente

9. Anxiety in the Contact Zone: The Debate of the Body and the Soul in late-medieval French and Occitan poetry   219
   Catherine Léglu

VIII Contents

10. The Uses of French in Medieval Wales 237
Georgia Henley

11. In Between Dutch and French: Multilingual Literary Patronage of
the Flemish Nobility in the Fifteenth Century 253
Bart Besamusca and Lisa Demets

12. Sicilian Multilingualism and Cosmopolitan French 269
Karla Mallette

Bibliography 293
Index 345

Illustrations

Introduction, Thomas O'Donnell, Jane Gilbert and Brian J. Reilly

0.1.   A Necker Cube. Courtesy of Brian J. Reilly   2

2. From Liutprand of Cremona to Robert de Clari: Wonder and the Translation of Knowledge Before and After the Crusader Conquest of Constantinople, Teresa Shawcross

2.1.   Constantinople, Great Church of the Holy Wisdom, Southern Gallery balustrade, graffito, tenth to eleventh centuries (?). Courtesy of Hermann Junghans, CC BY-SA 3.0 DE https://creativecommons.org/licenses/by-sa/3.0/de/deed.en, via Wikimedia Commons   53

2.2.   Avranches, Biblothèque patrimoniale, MS 236, fol. 97v, eleventh century (?), detail. Courtesy of the Commune nouvelle d'Avranches   58

2.3.   Auxerre, Bm, MS 212, fols. 133v–134r, twelfth century (?), detail. Creative Commons Licence 3.0. https://creativecommons.org/licenses/by-nc-sa/4.0/deed.fr. Courtesy of the Bibliothèque municipale d'Auxerre   58

2.4.   Paris, BnF, MS fr. 24376, fol. 8v, fourteenth century. © Bibliothèque nationale de France. Courtesy of Gallica.fr   61

2.5.   Munich, Bayerische Staatsbibliothek, MS Clm 6388, fol. 48r, tenth century. CC BY-NC-SA 4.0 Licence. https://creativecommons.org/licenses/by-nc-sa/4.0/deed.en   62

2.6.   Munich, Bayerische Staatsbibliothek, MS Clm 6388, fol. 85r, tenth century. CC BY-NC-SA 4.0 Licence. https://creativecommons.org/licenses/by-nc-sa/4.0/deed.en   66

2.7.   Oxford, Bodleian Library, MS Canon. Misc. 378, fol. 84r, 1436. CC-BY-NC 4.0 Licence. © Bodleian Libraries, University of Oxford   70

2.8.   Vatican City, Biblioteca Apostolica Vaticana, MS Ross.702, fol. 32v, fifteenth century. © Biblioteca Apostolica Vaticana   72

x ILLUSTRATIONS

2.9. Copenhagen, Det Kongelige Bibliotek, MS GKS 487, fol. 122v (p. 258), fourteenth century. © Det Kongelige Bibliotek   74

2.10. Madrid, Biblioteca Nacional de España, MS Graecus Vitr. 26–2, fol. 172v, twelfth century, detail. CC-BY Licence. Courtesy of Wikimedia Commons   75

2.11. Turkey, ancient column with nest of Mediterranean White Storks. © Richard Billingham. Courtesy of Dreamstime.com   76

2.12. Cambridge, Trinity College Wren Library, MS O.17.2, fol. 13, sixteenth century. CC BY-NC-SA 4.0 Licence. https://creativecommons.org/licenses/by-nc-sa/4.0/deed.en. © Master and Fellows of Trinity College, Cambridge   80

2.13. Cambridge, Trinity College Wren Library, MS O.17.2, fol. 12, sixteenth century. CC BY-NC-SA 4.0 Licence. https://creativecommons.org/licenses/by-nc-sa/4.0/deed.en © Master and Fellows of Trinity College, Cambridge   81

2.14. Washington, Dumbarton Oaks, black and white photograph, twentieth century. Courtesy of Dumbarton Oaks, Trustees for Harvard University, Washington, D.C. Photo by Slobodan Ćurčić   81

2.15a–b. Princeton, Firestone Library, Special Collections, Numismatics Collection. Coin: 9864. With permission of Firestone Library, Princeton University   83

2.16a–b. Paris, Archives nationales de France – Site de Paris, J//419 no 5. Chrysobull, Paris, March 1268   84

2.17. Paris, Archives nationales de France – Site de Paris, J//409 no 2. Charter, June 1247   85

8. 'Dize en la estoria francesca': The Circulation of Francophone Matter of Antiquity in Medieval Castile (*c*.1200–1369), Clara Pascual-Argente

8.1. Santander, Biblioteca de Menéndez Pelayo, M-558, fol. 22r, *c*.1360–80, detail. © Biblioteca de Menéndez Pelayo, Ayuntamiento de Santander. Image courtesy of Ricardo Pichel   211

The editors, contributors and publisher are grateful to all the institutions and persons listed for permission to reproduce the materials in which they hold copyright. Every effort has been made to trace the copyright holders; apologies are offered for any omission, and the publisher will be pleased to add any necessary acknowledgement in subsequent editions.

Contributors

Bart Besamusca	Utrecht University
Mark Chinca	University of Cambridge
Lisa Demets	Ghent University
Jane Gilbert	University College London
Georgia Henley	Saint Anselm College
Sharon Kinoshita	University of California, Santa Cruz
Catherine Léglu	University of Luxembourg
Isabelle Levy	Columbia University
Karla Mallette	University of Michigan
Máire Ní Mhaonaigh	University of Cambridge
Ruth Nisse	Wesleyan University
Thomas O'Donnell	Fordham University
Clara Pascual-Argente	Université Toulouse II, Jean Jaurès
Brian J. Reilly	Fordham University
Uri Zvi Shachar	Ben-Gurion University
Teresa Shawcross	Princeton University

Acknowledgements

The thinking behind this volume – as well as many of the individual papers – was first developed as part of the conference *Medieval French without Borders*. This conference was originally scheduled to take place at Fordham University's Lincoln Center campus on the weekend of 21–22 March 2020 as the 40th Annual Conference of the Center for Medieval Studies at Fordham University. The Covid-19 Pandemic necessitated that the conference be postponed to 20–21 March 2021, and then be reimagined as an online event featuring pre-circulated videos, new abstracts, online discussion panels and three plenary lectures. The editors of this volume would like to thank, first, all the participants in the online conference, who gave their energy and excitement to the online discussion; all the presenters, chairs and respondents, who readily agreed to experiment with the new format and, without exception, produced brilliant work during a difficult time; and our generous colleagues Sarah Kay, Maryanne Kowaleski and Elizabeth M. Tyler, who organised *Medieval French without Borders* alongside us (twice!). It would have been impossible to imagine the conference, or this volume, without their shared efforts and ideas and their friendship.

Thanks are also due to the faculty, staff and students at the Fordham Center for Medieval Studies whose work made the conference possible, especially Alberto Ayala, Grace Campagna, Frances Eshleman, Mikayla Fenley, Michael Innocenti, Chloe Knupp, Camila Marcone, Matthew Maresca, Ashley Newby, Anna Paczuska, Alex Pisano and Christian Stempert. Scott G. Bruce, Christina Bruno, Laura K. Morreale and Nicholas L. Paul shepherded the Conference from conception to completion. Christina deserves special thanks for her unerring advice and her extraordinary good humour.

We are pleased to record our gratitude to the organisations and individuals who offered funding for the 2021 conference: Melissa Labonte, interim Dean, and the late Tyler Stovall, Dean, of Fordham's Graduate School of Arts and Sciences; Eva Badowska, Dean of Fordham's College of Arts and Sciences; Maura Mast, Dean of Fordham College at Rose Hill; Laura Auricchio, Dean of Fordham College at Lincoln Center; and George Z. Hong, Chief Research Officer at Fordham's Office of Research. Maryanne Kowleski and Mary C. Erler offered funding out of their own research grants. The Conference was co-sponsored at Fordham by the Center for Jewish Studies, the Orthodox Christian Studies Center and the Program in Comparative Literature; at

New York University, by the Department of French Literature, Thought and Culture; and at the University of Southern Denmark and the University of York, by the Centre for Medieval Literature, housed jointly at both institutions.

Funding for the publication of the volume was provided by a Fordham University Manuscript and Book Publication Award, administered by Fordham's Office of Research, and by grants from Fordham's Faculty Research Expense Program, administered by the Departments of English and Modern Languages and Literatures at Fordham. Without this generous support, the publication of the volume would have been impossible.

We were fortunate in the support of the editors and production staff at Boydell and Brewer and York Medieval Press. We would like to thank Caroline Palmer, Laura Bennetts, Elizabeth McDonald and Pete Biller. They were always receptive to our questions and ideas – not to mentionthat they were also very patient! We are happy to acknowledge here the volume's anonymous reviewers; their thoughtful advice improved the volume in countless ways.

Many other people generously lent us their time and resources while we worked on this volume. We would like to thank Tihana Abiala, Andrew Albin, Carole Alvino, Susanna Barsella, Christopher C. Baswell, Mary Bly, Keith Busby, Martin Chase, Labelle De La Rosa, Marilynn R. Desmond, Shonni Enelow, Mary C. Erler, Maria Farland, Thelma Fenster, Marisa Galvez, Miranda Griffin, Elias Holmquist, Julie C. Kim, Kerri Maguire, Chaney Matos, Beth Munnelly, Nahir I. Otaño Gracia, Nina Rowe, Joshua Byron Smith, Cristiana Sogno, Luke Sunderland, Magda Teter, MonaLisa Torres-Bates, Hannah Weaver, Jocelyn Wogan-Browne and Suzanne Yeager. The expertise of the librarians at Fordham University Library, the New York Public Library, UCL Library Services and Universiteitsbibliotheek Gent was indispensable.

Both Brian and Tom would like to thank Fordham University for the Faculty Research Fellowships that supported their work on this project. Tom did further work on the volume while on a teaching exchange at Ghent University, and he would like to thank his hosts there, especially Stef Slembrouck, Andrew Bricker, Marco Formisano, Wim Verbaal and Jeroen Deploige. Jane would like to thank University College London for sabbatical leave and teaching relief in the 2021–22 academic session and Fordham University for kindly hosting her during this time on a Medieval Fellowship. We are grateful to one another for all the interlocutions and, even more so, the chats.

Finally – and most of all – we are deeply grateful to the contributors to the present volume. We feel very lucky to have had the opportunity to work with you.

Abbreviations

AND	W. Rothwell et al., ed., *Anglo-Norman Dictionary*, https://anglo-norman.net
BL	British Library
Bm	Bibliothèque municipale
BnF	Bibliothèque nationale de France
Lang Cult	J. Wogan-Browne, C. Collette, M. Kowaleski, L. Mooney, A. Putter and D. Trotter, ed., *Language and Culture in Medieval Britain: The French of England, c. 1100–c. 1500* (York, 2009)
MFLCA	J. Gilbert, S. Gaunt and W. Burgwinkle, *Medieval French Literary Culture Abroad* (Oxford, 2020)
MFLCOF	N. Morato and D. Schoenaers, ed., *Medieval Francophone Literary Culture Outside France: Studies in the Moving Word* (Turnhout, 2018)
ODNB	*Oxford Dictionary of National Biography*
PC	A. Pillet and H. Carstens, *Bibliographie der Troubadours* (Halle, 1933)
PL	Jacques-Paul Migne, ed., *Patrologia Latina* (Paris, 1844–65)
T-L	A. Tobler and E. Lommatzsch, *Altfranzösiches Wörterbuch* (Berlin, 1925–)
UN	Berekhiah Ha-Naqdan, *Dodi ve-Nechdi (Uncle & Nephew)*, ed. and trans. H. Gollancz (Oxford, 1920)

Introduction

Thomas O'Donnell, Jane Gilbert and Brian J. Reilly

The Necker Cube illusion captures well the experience of reading medieval literature: a nest of lines printed on a flat page pops out into a three-dimensional object upon inspection (Figure 0.1). More precisely, though, the illusion does not produce just a single object: shift your perspective and the cube pops out elsewhere, revealing different dimensions to an object you thought you had seen in full.

Medieval French Interlocutions: Shifting Perspectives on a Language in Contact takes the perceptual shift as a metaphor for the work of the diverse essays in this collection. The objects of study that we think we know well reveal new dimensions when others help us shift our perspectives. The object we consider here is the rapid expansion of French language use over the course of the Middle Ages. This expansion was both geographical, as French gained status in many places across western Eurasia and the Mediterranean, and social, as the language was adopted by new groups for new purposes. Although this expansion has been a subject of scholarly inquiry for some years, critical work too often remains defined by canonical texts, well-known controversies and conventional framings. We challenge some of these persistent perspectives in this volume by gathering contributions from a group of interlocutors who approach medieval French from very different disciplinary and theoretical directions and who offer new perspectives on the use of French in medieval contact zones, in particular. Their work reveals dimensions of French use in the Middle Ages that have been neglected by scholars of French up until now, and which provoke us to look anew at French, as well as other languages in contact with one another in the medieval world. A key message of this volume is that the meaning of medieval French, particularly the French used in such contact zones, can never be grasped by one model alone, and a full understanding of medieval French requires the changes in focus that interlocution makes possible.

Medieval French contact zones

Coined by Mary Louise Pratt in reference to the contact of Spanish and Andean cultures, *contact zone* originally referred to 'social spaces where cultures meet, clash,

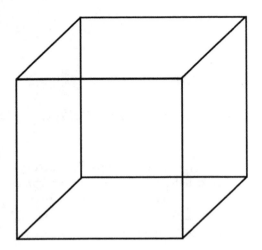

0.1. A Necker Cube. Courtesy of Brian J. Reilly.

and grapple with each other, often in contexts of highly asymmetrical relations of power'.[1] Such 'social spaces' can be sought in geographically defined regions where representatives of speech communities lived side by side, as happened in medieval Flanders, or across a wider area, as when the exponents of elite Irish learning repeatedly encountered French-speakers on their travels abroad or at home (due to the arrival of English settlers after 1169). The contact zone has been a generative term of art in the study of the Middle Ages, a time when opportunities for contact were provided by commerce, travel, dynastic marriage, warfare and other pursuits.[2] The contact zone is an especially useful concept for thinking about French-language writing during a period in which French-speakers were prominent players in networks that linked northern Europe to the Mediterranean and Asia.[3] Such networks helped create the contact zones – such as between French, Latin, Welsh and English in Wales; between French, Dutch and Latin in the Low Countries; between Greek, Latin and French among the western visitors to and settlers in Constantinople; and so on – considered in the chapters in this volume. The importance of these contact zones for the material preservation of much French-language literature ought not to be underestimated: the medieval

---

[1] M. L. Pratt, 'Arts of the Contact Zone', *Profession* (1991), 33–40 (p. 34).
[2] Medievalists have broadened the use of the contact zone to cover more than colonial and postcolonial contexts. See, for example, J. Hsy, *Trading Tongues: Merchants, Multilingualism and Medieval Literature* (Columbus, 2013); S. Niiranen, 'Apothecary's Art as a Contact Zone in Late Medieval Southern France', in *Multilingualism in the Middle Ages and Early Modern Age: Communication and Miscommunication in the Premodern World*, ed. A. Classen (Berlin, 2016), pp. 207–32.
[3] *MFLCA*, pp. 14–17.

transmission of many major French-language works depends on texts copied or composed in England, Italy, the Low Countries and the crusader lordships of the eastern Mediterranean.[4] In addition, through its constant concern for spaces and times both within and beyond the historical kingdom of 'France', medieval French literature frequently restaged contact zones textually and imaginatively.[5]

One feature of the contact zones studied by Pratt was what she called *autoethnography*: discourses of self-description emerging from less dominant groups within a contact zone produced 'in response to or in dialogue with' the language and culture of dominant groups and 'intended to intervene in metropolitan modes of understanding'.[6] In those medieval contact zones where it was used extensively, French is frequently figured by scholars as one such 'dominant' language and culture, which others adopted or transformed in order to address a wide public.[7] Looking at French this way (from 'inside' French Studies, as it were) illuminates the means by which French language and culture were already being projected across Europe and the Mediterranean in the pre-modern period. Equally important, we believe, is to ask whether and how those in contact zones figured French for themselves – irrespective of demonstrable French 'influence'. We therefore invited our contributors to help us shift our perspectives on medieval French: what did medieval French look like to its neighbours within medieval contact zones? And further: how could the answer to that question help us rethink the dynamics of medieval contact zones themselves?

Inside out

In extending these invitations, we kept in mind Jacques Derrida's dictum about the nature of the (impossible) absolute invitation: 'Une invitation laisse libre, sans quoi elle devient contrainte' ('An invitation leaves [the invitee] free,

[4] S. Lefèvre and F. Zinelli, 'La France, jardin d'acclimatation pour la francophonie médiévale?', in *En français hors de France. Textes, livres, collections du Moyen Âge*, ed. F. Zinelli and S. Lefèvre (Strasbourg, 2021), pp. 1–31 (pp. 6–9).

[5] As Sharon Kinoshita notes, her book *Medieval Boundaries: Rethinking Difference in Old French Literature* (Philadelphia, 2006) 'began with the curious realization that many of the best-known works of medieval French literature take place on or beyond the borders of "France" or even the French-speaking world' (p. 1).

[6] Pratt, 'Arts', p. 35. For the 'dialogism' of key examples of medieval (auto-)ethnography, see S. A. Khanmohamadi, *In Light of Another's Word: European Ethnography in the Middle Ages* (Philadelphia, 2014).

[7] *MFLCA*, pp. 11–20; S. Gaunt, *Marco Polo's 'Le Devisement du Monde': Narrative Voice, Language and Diversity* (Cambridge, 2013), p. 110; K. Busby and A. Putter, 'Introduction: Medieval Francophonia', in *Medieval Multilingualism: The Francophone World and Its Neighbours*, ed. C. Kleinhenz and K. Busby (Turnhout, 2010), pp. 1–14 (p. 2); A. Butterfield, *The Familiar Enemy: Chaucer, Language, and Nation in the Hundred Years War* (Oxford, 2009), p. 11.

otherwise it becomes constraint').[8] To leave our interlocutors free, we have had to accept that the presence of French within medieval contact zones was sometimes an intrusion or a form of linguistic or cultural tourism. In some cases, the perception that medieval French was culturally or politically preeminent in a certain area might be nothing but a flattering illusion for modern scholars of the language. The literature and cultural forms associated with French were not emulated or admired everywhere they appeared, and literary phenomena now seen as evidence of French influence can also sometimes be explained by local traditions. For example, the absence of extensive French writing in medieval Sicily might shock modern observers familiar with the history of Norman and Angevin settlement on the island and accustomed to French's elite status in northern Europe. But, as Karla Mallette demonstrates below, the choice of Sicilian authors *not* to use French reflects the island's place at the crossroads of entrenched cosmopolitan languages like Arabic, Greek and Latin as well as Sicilians' own robust awareness of their language as a vehicle for prestigious, aulic expression, on the models of Occitan or Arabic – *not* of French.

The Sicilian choice against French also reveals the fragility of our own assumptions about the prestige of French, based largely on the study of England and northern Italy. Post-medieval consolidations of French and 'European' culture within Paris and its environs also distort our judgments about the nature of French and its relationships within the kingdom of France itself. As Catherline Léglu explores in her chapter, the perceived 'exceptionality' of Occitanian literature, which both elevates Occitan as a field of study and saddles it with so much political and cultural baggage, relies in part on an arbitrary judgement of what characterises (or ought to characterise) the European mainstream. Meanwhile, the linguistic thought of the high medieval Jewish scholars who incorporated French-language words into their commentaries and scientific treatises, which Ruth Nisse explicates in her chapter, offers a compelling alternative to French as the dominant language of Christian invaders and crusaders. For the famous Jewish exegete Rashi, it was instead 'our language', connecting Jewish communities across Europe and available as a tool for studying and teaching God's law.

Derrida further reminds us that, although it might be free, 'l'invitation doit être pressante, non indifférente' ('the invitation must be pressing, not indifferent').[9] Ours is indeed pressing: the study of medieval language contact, and of French in contact specifically, needs the points of view contained in the following pages.

---

[8] J. Derrida, *Passions* (Paris, 1993), pp. 35–6, translated into English as 'Passions', trans. D. Wood, in *On the Name*, ed. T. Dutoit (Stanford, 1995), pp. 3–34 (p. 14).

[9] Derrida, *Passions*, p. 36; 'Passions', trans. Wood, p. 14.

The 'autoethnography' described by Pratt concerned the self-representation of an indigenous Andean to a colonial Spanish audience; autoethnographies are a self-representation by the colonised 'other' using a mixed idiom.[10] The essays contained here extend Pratt's insight by offering not so much autoethnographies but rather 'heteroethnographies' of medieval French. That is, they turn the ethnographic gaze back onto medieval French and its users. French, in its many varieties, is seen 'from the other side', or rather, from a series of 'other sides' that are not typically considered in narratives of French literary history. These 'heteroethnographies' allow the perceptual shifts that pop out new dimensions for medieval French Studies to acknowledge: foreground becomes background, and vice versa. At the same time, our contributors' arguments have the power to shift perspectives within their home fields.

In conversations with our contributors, we always risked rephrasing our invitation as a kind of demand to turn from their concerns to our own: tell us more about Old French! But the freedom of invitation must allow for non-response. When viewed from an 'other side', the French language may be less dominant, less present in contact zones than the common scholarly cosmopolitan image of French might suggest. By contemplating contact producing minimal imitation or appropriation and by sometimes highlighting contact zone texts that are indifferent to their reception in the French-speaking cities and courts of northwestern Europe, our interlocutors demonstrate the limitations of that image. What emerges is an understanding of not so much a 'French without borders', which had been the title of the conference that originated most of the essays collected here, as French in 'other places'. The views from the contact zones of this book also show us the other sides of our disciplines' borders – often elsewhere than we think them to be. When studying the particular 'ideological and cultural freight' that French bore for medieval users in specific contexts, those of us who work in disciplines where French looms large must be careful not to over-emphasise it at the expense of other choices.[11]

Créolisation in the contact zone

As we edited this volume, we came to see another provocative model for medieval contact zones in Édouard Glissant's thinking about the relation between different languages and cultures in the contemporary period. Despite his work with medievalist Alexandre Leupin, Glissant has received relatively little attention within medieval French Studies, but his notions of *créolisation*

[10] Pratt, 'Arts', p. 35.
[11] Gaunt, *Marco Polo*, p. 28.

and *multilinguisme* have much to offer medievalists.[12] In his formulation, *créolisation* is a process of cultural transformation brought about by exchange in a manner that is 'imprévisible' ('unforeseeable') and whose disparate elements 's'intervalorisent' ('intervalorise' one another).[13] *Créolisation* implies a processual becoming which is unsystematic and unpredictable (*étant* rather than *être*).[14] Glissant develops his ideas out of his knowledge of the Creole languages of the francophone Caribbean, whose lexis, phonology and syntax derive from several varieties of French, Cariban and African languages. Crucially, Glissant argued that the composite culture of the modern Caribbean was a result of the forced mixing of people and languages in the 'open boat' of the slave ship. But he claims for *créolisation* a deeper and wider history. For Glissant, 'presque toute langue à ses origines est une langue créole' ('almost every language is at its origins a Creole language'), including French. That is: before linguistic standardisation and its association with a delimited territory and state, medieval French was 'une langue composite, née de la mise en contact d'éléments linguistiques absolument hétérogènes les uns par rapports aux autres' ('a composite language, emerging from contact between entirely heterogeneous linguistic elements').[15]

Without insisting on the validity of Glissant's claim as a scientific description of Gallo-Romance or claiming that the movement of peoples in early medieval Europe held equivalence with the transatlantic slave trade,[16] we believe that

---

[12] See especially É. Glissant with A. Leupin, *Les entretiens de Baton Rouge* (Paris, 2008); English version É. Glissant, *The Baton Rouge Interviews, with Alexandre Leupin*, trans. K. M. Cooper (Liverpool, 2020) and a monograph by Leupin: *Édouard Glissant, philosophe. Héraclite et Hegel dans le Tout-Monde* (Paris, 2016); English version *Édouard Glissant, Philosopher: Heraclitus and Hegel in the Whole-World*, trans. A. Brown (Albany, 2021). Glissant's work is used extensively by Marisa Galvez: 'Unthought Medievalism', *Neophilologus* 105 (2021), 365–89; and Galvez, 'Review Essay', *H-France Forum* 16:4 (2021), issue focusing on Z. Stahuljak, *Médiéval contemporain. Pour une littérature connectée* (Paris, 2020), accessed 24 February 2023, https://h-france.net/wp-content/uploads/2021/09/Stahuljak3.pdf. H. Solterer offers a different approach in 'A Timely Villon: Anachrony and Premodern Poetic Fiction', *New Literary History* 52 (2021), 311–34.

[13] É. Glissant, *Introduction à une poétique du divers* (Paris, 1996), hereafter *Introduction* (F), pp. 15, 18–19; English version *Introduction to a Poetics of Diversity*, trans. C. Britton (Liverpool, 2020), hereafter *Introduction* (E), pp. 6, 8.

[14] *Introduction* (F), p. 28; *Introduction* (E), p. 14.

[15] *Introduction* (F), pp. 21, 20; *Introduction* (E), pp. 10, 9.

[16] The most sustained argument in favour of a creole theory of French linguistic origins is conducted by S. S. Mufwene; see 'The Emergence of Creoles and Language Change', in *The Routledge Handbook of Linguistic Anthropology*, ed. N. Bonvillain (London, 2015), pp. 345–68. Mufwene argues against 'creole exceptionalism' (p. 360); Mufwene, 'L'émergence des parlers créoles et l'évolution des langues romanes.

Glissant's description of *créolisation* as a process of cultural transformation through the combination of disparate elements offers an inspired model for describing the development of medieval French language and literature. The early written traces of French (among other medieval European languages) show a constitutive heterogeneity and openness that defy such binary oppositions as internal/external or endogeneous/exogeneous. Early French writings display their contacts with languages, discourses and idioms at many different scales. As Martin Glessgen and others argue, the written language's initial formation as well as its later standardisation were the products of varying, complex interactions with Latin, with local spoken dialects and with other written languages or idioms.[17] There is not, there has never been, a 'French' – whether oral or written – that is not composite. Moreover, French is not exceptional in this: in Glissant's account no language can claim a special privilege as non-creole.

We should beware, of course, of making French, however creolised, into a standard-bearer of political 'diversity' or 'tolerance'. Glissant argues that all early literary monuments of what he calls 'les communautés ataviques' ('atavistic cultures') work to present their chosen language as primary, unitary and God-given: for him, the *Bhagavad Gita*, the Hebrew Scriptures, Egyptian Book of the Dead, Mayan *Popol Vuh* and *Chilam Balam*, classical antique and

---

Faits, mythes et idéologies', *Études créoles* 33 (2016), n.p., accessed 24 February 2023, https://doi.org/10.4000/etudescreoles.525. For Mufwene, the reasons why the European Romance vernaculars are traditionally considered to be 'languages' whereas such modern vernaculars as Haitian creole or Dominican creole are termed 'creoles' 'paraissent être nationalistes dans le premier cas et racistes dans le second' ('seem to be nationalist in the first case, and racist in the second') ('L'émergence des parlers créoles', n. 19). He points nevertheless to the significant historical difference that the Romance languages developed where populations speaking substratum languages resided in their own territories, whereas the modern vernaculars developed out of interactions in territories that were 'foreign' to both: 'L'émergence des parlers créoles', n. 2.

[17] The dominance of England in early instances of written French is only the most famous example. See M. Glessgen, 'La genèse d'une norme en ancien français au Moyen Âge: mythe et réalité du "francien"', *Revue de Linguistique Romane* 81 (2017), 313–97 (p. 345). Glessgen helpfully reviews the state of scholarship on the emergence of a standard French in the later Middle Ages. For pluralising views of medieval French, see also *MFLCA*, pp. 10–11; S. Lusignan, 'Le français médiéval: perspectives historiques sur une langue plurielle', in S. Lusignan, F. Martineau, Y.-C. Morin and P. Cohen, *L'introuvable unité du français. Contacts et variations linguistiques en Europe et en Amérique (XIIe–XVIIIe)* (Quebec, 2011), pp. 45–65; D. Trotter, '"Une et indivisible": Variation and Ideology in the Historiography and History of France', *Revue roumaine de linguistique* 51 (2006), 359–76; M. Careri, C. Ruby and I. Short, with the collaboration of T. Nixon and P. Stirnemann, *Livres et écritures en français et en occitan au XIIe siècle. Catalogue illustré* (Rome, 2011), pp. xxii–xxxviii.

medieval epics (including the *Chanson de Roland*) all partake in the same defensive mythologisation in the face of communal threat.[18] His call for attention to the specific inequalities operating in different contact situations is important for our historical work, and his insistence on keeping in sight the ideal equality of all the elements in a composite culture prompts us to attend to phenomena that might otherwise be considered minor or insignificant.[19]

The essays in this volume illustrate certain correspondences between medieval Europe and processes that Glissant detects in the modern world, where 'les continents "s'archipélisent", ... se constituent en régions par-dessus les frontières nationales' ('the continents are turning themselves into archipelagos, ... they are forming themselves into regions across national frontiers'), becoming 'des îles, mais des îles ouvertes' ('islands, but open islands'). Glissant is keen to rescue local or minority languages from the 'enfermement' and 'repli sur soi' often attributed to (or imposed on) them in recent centuries, representing them instead as dynamic and creative, in contact and in process.[20] Much of this will chime with those working on medieval local cultures that have multiple, profound and wide-reaching networks.

Glissant advocates what he calls *multilinguisme* as an ethical and political response to modern *créolisation*. In his formulation, *multilinguisme* does not require the acquisition of multiple languages; indeed he rejects what Rey Chow would later call a 'neoliberal attitude towards multilingualism'.[21] Rather, *multilinguisme* is an ethical awareness of and openness to other languages based in a relational ontology. It requires that different languages 's'entendent à travers l'espace, aux trois sens du terme entendre: qu'elles s'écoutent, qu'elles se comprennent et qu'elles s'accordent. Écouter l'autre, les autres, c'est ... mettre [sa propre langue] en relation' ('agree with each other across space, in the three senses of "s'entendre": they must listen to each other, understand each other, and get on well with each other. Listening to the other, to the others, means ... putting [one's own language] in relation').[22] *Multilinguisme* opposes standardisation, ideological monolingualism, cultural purification and their myths; in its rhizomatic world-view, all languages are networked and entangled,

---

[18] For the distinction between cultures, see *Introduction* (F), pp. 59–61; *Introduction* (E), pp. 37–8. On epic: *Introduction* (F), pp. 33–9, *Introduction* (E), pp. 19–23. On the ideal of a new, non-exclusionary epic: *Introduction* (F), pp. 67–8 and 78–9; *Introduction* (E), pp. 42–3, 50–1. For a similar assessment of historiography: *Introduction* (F), pp. 61–4; *Introduction* (E), pp. 39–40.

[19] Especially *Introduction* (F), pp. 16–23; *Introduction* (E), pp. 6–11.

[20] *Introduction* (F), p. 44; *Introduction* (E), p. 26.

[21] R. Chow, *Not Like a Native Speaker: On Languaging as a Postcolonial Experience* (New York, 2014), p. 31.

[22] *Introduction* (F), p. 44; *Introduction* (E), p. 26.

mutually necessary to each others' well-being while – indeed, by – remaining distinct, particular and grounded in the places where they are used. *Multilinguisme* may be most dramatically manifest in macaronic texts, but for Glissant, its spirit is best realised in practices of translation.[23] Indeed, it has much in common with Derrida's *monolinguisme de l'autre*, which undermines, for instance, nationalist or identitarian ideas about language hegemony by insisting on every language's internal fractures.[24] Like Derrida's *monolinguisme*, Glissant's *multilinguisme* highlights how ideas about language are deployed politically, and how both political deployments and languages themselves inspire (and repel) desire and fantasy. Glissant's *multilinguisme*, however, brings into focus unpredictable, even anarchic aspects of medieval language histories quite unlike Derrida's concern with standardisation and purism (which would find their greatest fruition in post-medieval centuries).[25] For, although *multilinguisme* and *créolisation* are firmly grounded in the contact zones of Antillais history and geography, languages and cultures, we also recognise elements of these practices in medieval receptions and productions. This is as Glissant intends, we believe: he presents the Antilles, so peripheral to any map or history focused on metropolitan France, as itself an alternative universal model, thus upending the Eurocentric worldview that notoriously established itself in the post-medieval period. Since these Antillais-based universals do not conform to the exclusive model espoused by atavistic cultures but are inclusive of particularities, exceptions and nuances of difference – 'islands, but open islands' – we are emboldened to find room in them for the many ways and contexts in which French was used across and beyond Europe in medieval times.

Two familiar 'islands': French in northern Italy and England

In order to understand the relations of language within, between and beyond the 'open islands' of medieval Europe, we took care to look beyond the contact zones with French in northern Italy and England. Existing accounts of French in those areas, although excellent, have so structured our understanding as to be part of the dominant disciplinary discourse of medieval French. We wished to draw attention to the ways in which French was written also 'in the

---

[23] *Introduction* (F), pp. 45–6; *Introduction* (E), pp. 27–8.

[24] J. Derrida, *Le monolinguisme de l'autre, ou la prothèse d'origine* (Paris, 1996); English version: *Monolingualism of the Other; or, The Prosthesis of Origin*, trans. P. Mensah (Stanford, 1998).

[25] Examples of medievalists deploying Derrida's *monolinguisme* are *MFLCA*, pp. 25–8, 98–9; E. Campbell and R. Mills, 'Introduction: Rethinking Medieval Translation', in *Rethinking Medieval Translation: Ethics, Politics, Theory*, ed. E. Campbell and R. Mills (Cambridge, 2012), pp. 1–20; Gaunt, *Marco Polo*, pp. 78–112.

presence of 'other language varieties, to borrow another phrase from Glissant.[26] Nevertheless, the shifts in perspective provided by this volume bring out new dimensions in those contact zones we think we know well. Work in recent decades on French in Italian contexts has highlighted the importance of the nobles, merchants and professionals of city-states in the northern regions of Lombardy, the Veneto, Emilia-Romagna and Tuscany.[27] Whereas formerly, the local idioms might be regarded as incompetent efforts to ape the French of France (whatever that might be), consensus now regards 'Franco-Italian' as a sophisticated, polymorphic *koine*.[28] This Franco-Italian *koine* mapped, in ways that would advance northern Italian interests, a large and transnational contact zone centred on, but not limited to, the Mediterranean Sea.

Work on Franco-Italian is an important corrective to those who seek in medieval usage some mythical purity and autonomy – an original monolingualism or atavism – of what would eventually become 'national' languages such as French or Italian. However, Sharon Kinoshita's essay in this volume shows how much further the methodology of the perceptual shift can carry our understanding of the multilingual situations in which French took part. A passage in the *Devisement du monde* which claims that the young Marco Polo learned four languages at the Mongol court offers an opportunity to explore the multilingual framework within which Marco, his father and his uncle operated in the East. When communicating in Mongol circles, the Polos did not use any variety of

---

[26] 'Je parle et surtout j'écris en présence de toutes les langues du monde', *Introduction* (F), p. 39 ('I speak and above all I write in the presence of all the world's languages', *Introduction* [E], p. 23).

[27] For an expanding corpus of digital texts and studies of French associated with northern Italy and northern Italians see the collaborative project *RIALFrI – Repertorio informatizzato antica litterature franco-italiana*, accessed 7 October 2023, https://www.rialfri.eu/. Different northern Italian contexts are discussed in Gaunt, *Marco Polo*; A. Cornish, *Vernacular Translation in Dante's Italy: Illiterate Literature* (Cambridge, 2013); L. Sunderland, *Rebel Barons: Resisting Royal Power in Medieval Culture* (Oxford, 2017); Gruppo Guiron, *Il ciclo di Guiron le courtois*, accessed 24 February 2023, https://guiron.fefonlus.it/; and the contributors to *The Arthur of the Italians: The Arthurian Legend in Medieval Italian Literature and Culture*, ed. F. R. Psaki and G. Allaire (Cardiff, 2014). On the Angevin *Regno* in southern Italy, see, among others, *The Italian Angevins: Naples and Beyond, 1266–1343*, ed. J. Gilbert, C. Keen and E. Williams, special number of *Italian Studies* 72 (2017), and the classification, discussion and bibliography at *French of Italy*, accessed 24 February 2023, https://frenchofitaly.ace.fordham.edu.

[28] On *koine* ('a form of a language that develops as a supralocal norm … entailing the levelling [or generalization] of a range of forms from a variety of dialects') and *scripta* (designating 'specifically written practices, which may develop independently of spoken forms') as complementary terms, see *MFLCA*, pp. 8–9.

French: only on Marco's return to Italy was his narrative couched in Franco-Italian, a decision presumably made with his collaborator, the experienced Arthurian romance writer Rustichello, as a way to turn the narrative towards a specific target audience and to frame it relative to familiar discourses. But nor, apparently, did the Polos use the languages that a modern Western reader might expect, like Chinese, Mongolian or Arabic. The prominence of these languages today obscures more likely candidates for the Polos' attention, such as Turkic (Uighur or Cuman) or Persian. The *Devisement* is written in a variety of French, but 'in the presence of' many other languages. Kinoshita's account thus shows how classifying the *Devisement* as either 'French' or 'Franco-Italian' risks effacing Polo's journeys and contacts, which exceed modern Eurocentric mindsets.

The contact zones of medieval England have for a long time provided further prominent examples of French usage outside the medieval kingdom of France.[29] As such, features associated with 'the French of England', *mutatis mutandis*, have come to seem normal for the use of French carried to other parts of the medieval world. These include an expectation that the French used by those outside the French kingdom should be linguistically distinct, in the manner of 'Anglo-Norman' or 'Anglo-French'; an association of French with boundary-crossing elites, such as those who appeared in England following the Norman Conquest or the arrival of the Plantagenets; and an assumption that French should 'compete' with native and neighbouring languages, in the manner described by many scholars of Old and Middle English.[30] Such assessments about the French used in England reflect institutional concerns of English Studies and French Studies, but the assumptions underlying them do not stand up to scrutiny. The use of French by residents of England was hardly limited to the learned, chivalric or administrative functions of cosmopolitan elites (as is discussed below), and the linguistic exceptionality

---

[29] Lefèvre and Zinelli, 'La France', p. 3. On the use of French in England, see J. Wogan-Browne, T. Fenster and D. W. Russell, ed., *Vernacular Literary Theory from the French of England: Texts and Translations, c.1120–c.1450* (Cambridge, 2016); C. Baswell, C. Cannon, J. Wogan-Browne and K. Kerby-Fulton, 'Competing Archives, Competing Histories: French and Its Cultural Locations in Late-Medieval England', *Speculum* 90 (2015), 635–700; *The French of Medieval England: Essays in Honour of Jocelyn Wogan-Browne*, ed. T. Fenster and C. P. Collette (Cambridge, 2017); *Lang Cult*; Butterfield, *Familiar Enemy*; M. D. Legge, *Anglo-Norman Literature and Its Background* (Oxford, 1963); and the materials gathered at *French of England*, accessed 4 April, 2023, https://frenchofengland.ace.fordham.edu.

[30] T. W. Machan, 'French, English, and the Late Medieval Linguistic Repertoire', in *Lang Cult*, pp. 363–72; Butterfield, *Familiar Enemy*, provides a nuanced account of the rivalry and exchange between French and English that makes any simple concept of competition untenable.

of 'Anglo-Norman' or 'Anglo-French' has been frequently overstated both now and during the Middle Ages.[31] Moreover, outside England, the local power and prestige of French-speakers did not produce the same pattern of widespread French use as they did among the English. As the studies in this volume by Máire Ní Mhaonaigh, Georgia Henley, Karla Mallette, and Bart Besamusca and Lisa Demets all show, the enduring presence of French-speaking cosmopolitan elites in Ireland, Wales, Sicily and the Low Countries did not suffice to establish the same sort of preeminence for French in those places that the language gained in England. Taking the 'French of England' as the paradigm for French use outside the historic boundaries of the *langue d'oïl* makes French's differing impact in those places seem exceptional when in fact all these distinct patterns, including those in England, require explanation – and explanations that go beyond the contestation of ethnicity and class or the ambition to high cultural performance. The typical image of French pitted against English also misrepresents the extensive collusion between users of French and users of English in shaping England's medieval cultures and occludes the *other* languages in the English kingdom – most of all Latin, but also varieties of Norse, Welsh, Cornish, Irish, Dutch and Hebrew. Users of these languages possessed their own versions and views of French and shaped the language's place within England's 'linguistic repertoire'.[32] Any of these languages might, in certain contexts, assert its claims of preeminence over French.[33] In setting aside the 'English' model of a French-language contact zone in conversation with other specialisms we hope to access new dimensions of the 'French of England' itself in the context of England's composite medieval cultures. In keeping with Glissant's *multilinguisme*, the meanings of French to its users in England were unpredictable – still less should they be universalised to other contact zones.

---

[31] D. Trotter, '*Deinz Certeins Boundes*: Where Does Anglo-Norman Begin and End?', *Romance Philology* 67 (2013), 139–77; Butterfield, *Familiar Enemy*, pp. 55–65; A. M. Kristol, 'Le début du rayonnement parisien et l'unité du français au moyen âge. Le témoignage des manuels d'enseignement du français écrits en Angleterre entre le XIIIe et le début du XVe siècle', *Revue de linguistique romane* 53 (1989), 335–67. For a strong account of Anglo-Norman as an 'independent member of the extended family of Medieval French dialects', see I. Short, *Manual of Anglo-Norman*, 2nd edn (Oxford, 2013) (quotation from p. 11).

[32] B. O'Brien, *Reversing Babel: Translation Among the English During an Age of Conquests, c.800 to c.1200* (Newark DE, 2011).

[33] T. O'Donnell, 'Talking to the Neighbours', *High Medieval Literature*, ed. E. M. Tyler and J. Wogan-Browne (Oxford, forthcoming).

Revising perspectives

Although our contributors write from their own disciplinary backgrounds, our project as a whole enters into a dialogue with rich bodies of research within the study of medieval French and of other medieval languages and literatures. A traditional approach to medieval French takes the boundaries of metropolitan France (the modern 'Hexagon') as its framework – whether that approach works within or across those boundaries, and whether those boundaries are modern or medieval. We may call this approach, often-criticised but persistent, Hexagon Studies. The cosmopolitan and regional languages used in the medieval kingdom of France have long been discussed by specialists.[34] Such work has often been fed by a political imperative either to integrate an overlooked culture and population into the French national story, or to resist such integration; in either case, the Hexagonal framework dominates. Recent projects investigating the wide range of cultural sources drawn upon in medieval French-language compilations, such as wisdom literature or narrative anthology manuscripts, testify to contacts with a still wider range of languages.[35] However, with the notable exceptions of scholarship on Occitan and Latin, these discussions of Hexagonal contact zones have generally had regrettably little impact on the mainstream of medieval French studies.

A complementary development has been the interest in the differences perceptible between varieties of the French language. Although sometimes still corralled by regional or national interests, the potential for such scholarship to point further afield is demonstrated by Picard studies. The Picard *scripta* is associated with places within the kingdom of France, but it cannot be adequately described within a framework of national boundaries and national cultural politics. In the first place, Picard's heartland lay across the border between the kingdom of France and the Empire (including the towns and courts of Artois, Brabant, Flanders, Hainault, Liège, Namur, Ponthieu, Vermandois),

---

[34] Examples of notable work include: for Hebrew, K. A. Fudeman, *Vernacular Voices: Language and Identity in Medieval French Jewish Communities, Jewish Culture and Contexts* (Philadelphia, 2010); for Norse, E. Ridel, *Les Vikings et les mots. L'apport de l'ancien scandinave à la langue française* (Paris, 2009); for Arabic, M. R. Menocal, *The Arabic Role in Medieval Literary History: A Forgotten Heritage* (Philadelphia, 1988) and S. Amer, *Crossing Borders: Love between Women in Medieval French and Arabic Literatures* (Philadelphia, 2008); and for Occitan, C. Léglu, *Multilingualism and Mother Tongue in Medieval French, Occitan, and Catalan Narratives* (University Park, 2010) and E. Zingesser, *Stolen Song: How the Troubadours Became French* (Ithaca, 2020), esp. pp. 1–36.

[35] See, for instance, the work on short verse narratives contained in miscellany manuscripts done by the international, HERA-funded project, *The Dynamics of the Medieval Manuscript: Text Collections from a European Perspective*, accessed 24 February 2023, https://dynamicsofthemedievalmanuscript.eu/.

where local Romance and Germanic usages met.[36] In the second, Picard forms also often appear within other forms of written French in Ireland, Britain, northern and southern Italy and the eastern Mediterranean. The presence of Picard *scripta* outside Picardy seems to reflect the mobility of people and goods and sometimes to signify affiliation with one or more far-reaching supralocal networks, whether mercantile, ideological, religious, kin-based or literary.[37]

Hexagon Studies have also been complemented in recent decades by a fruitful interest in varieties of medieval French and their users 'outside France'. A well-known example of such varieties of French originating elsewhere and entering into France is Franco-Italian, used by Brunetto Latini in his *Trésor* as well as in Polo's *Devisement*.[38] Attention to such varieties within medieval French literature and culture challenges the traditional assimilation of the French language to 'France' (whether medieval kingdom or modern state and territory); diversifies and decentres the study of medieval French – in particular, away from Paris, the Île-de-France and outdated ideas about *francien*; and insists that French literary history be written transnationally as well as transregionally.[39] Sylvie Lefèvre and Fabio Zinelli note that such work has not been much conducted in France itself in recent decades, but point to an older history represented by scholars like Paul Meyer and Édith Brayer, who were more open to French

[36] According to C. T. Gossen, *Grammaire de l'ancien picard*, rev. edn (Paris, 1976), pp. 27–9, the heartland of the Picard dialect corresponds to the modern *départements* of the Somme, the northwest of the Pas-de-Calais and the north of the Oise and of the Aisne (p. 29). In-depth discussion of the variety's use is provided by S. Lusignan, *Essai d'histoire sociolinguistique. Le français picard au moyen âge* (Paris, 2012). The *Multilingual Dynamics of Medieval Flanders* project led by Bart Besamusca (2018–23) has significantly enhanced understanding of the interactions between Dutch, Latin and Picard French in the southern Low Countries; accessed 24 February 2023, https://multilingualdynamics.sites.uu.nl/.

[37] *MFLCA*, pp. 18–19. On the mobility and spread of Picard to Britain and Ireland, see Butterfield, *Familiar Enemy*, pp. 60–1; Joffroi de Waterford, *The French Works of Joffroi de Waterford: A Critical Edition*, ed. K. Busby (Turnhout, 2020); Kristol, 'Début'. On its spread in Outremer, see L. Minervini, 'Le français dans l'Orient latin (XIIIe–XIVe siècles). Éléments pour la caractérisation d'une scripta du Levant', *Revue de linguistique romane* 74 (2010), 119–98; C. Aslanov, *Evidence of Francophony in Mediaeval Levant: Decipherment and Interpretation (MS. Paris BnF copte 43)* (Jerusalem, 2006); C. Aslanov, *Le français au levant, jadis et naguère. À la recherche d'une langue perdue* (Paris, 2006).

[38] A. Cornish, 'Translatio Galliae: Effects of Early Franco-Italian Literary Exchange', *Romanic Review* 97 (2006), 309–30 (p. 324).

[39] Against the traditional centralising ideology, see the works cited in n. 17, and *La régionalité lexicale du français au Moyen Âge*, ed. M. Glessgen and D. Trotter (Strasbourg, 2016).

beyond the kingdom's or Hexagon's borders.[40] In the United States, Fordham University has established digital projects on French outside of France under the leadership of scholars such as Thelma S. Fenster, Laura Morreale and Jocelyn Wogan-Browne. The Fordham 'French of England', the 'French of Italy' and the 'French of Outremer' projects integrate non-Anglocentric approaches within English-language scholarship and promote these language varieties as objects of rigorous study for literary scholars, historians, and historians of art.[41]

On the other side of the Atlantic, two major team research projects led by the late Simon Gaunt directly confront the persistence within medieval French studies of 'the retrospective lens of the national literary histories associated with modern nation states', question the heuristic value of national boundaries when studying the Middle Ages and reject a core-periphery model of French in favour of network analyses (on which more below). The project *Medieval French Literary Culture Outside France* (2011–15), funded by the Arts and Humanities Research Council, aimed to sketch a literary history focused on 'fragments of the histories of places, people, objects, communities, and networks that used French literary culture without its ever becoming "national" for them'.[42] *The Values of French Language and Literature in the European Middle Ages* (2015–20), funded by the European Research Council, vastly deepened the earlier project's work on a single textual tradition, the *Histoire ancienne jusqu'à César*. Its achievements included exhaustive work on text and manuscript circulation that showed how in important instances, 'loin d'être le centre reconnu de la culture littéraire francophone à cette époque, la France n'en est … qu'une étape' ('far from being the acknowledged centre of Francophone literary culture at the time, France was only … one staging post').[43] Moreover, it reflected on large questions of the relationships that may pertain between language and identity, and specifically on the role played by French in the emergence during the medieval period of a transnational, supralocal European

[40] Lefèvre and Zinelli, 'La France', pp. 3–4.

[41] *French of England*, accessed 24 February 2023, https://frenchofengland.ace. fordham.edu/; *The French of Italy*, accessed 24 February 2023, https://frenchofitaly. ace.fordham.edu/; *French of Outremer*, accessed 24 February 2023, https:// frenchofoutremer.ace.fordham.edu/. See also the related volume, *The French of Outremer: Communities and Communications in the Crusading Mediterranean*, ed. L. K. Morreale and N. L. Paul (New York, 2018).

[42] *MFLCA*, p. 247. The project website, accessed 24 February 2023, is at http:// medievalfrancophone.ac.uk. See also the associated volume, *MFLCOF*.

[43] S. Gaunt, 'Texte et/ou manuscrit? A propos de *l'Histoire ancienne jusqu'à César*', in *En français hors de France*, ed. Zinelli and Lefèvre, pp. 35–57 (p. 37).

identity.[44] Knowledge of the different varieties of medieval French within and beyond the Hexagon has allowed scholars to reconceptualise the boundaries of medieval French Studies as a series of internal and external contact zones.

An important impetus for looking beyond the Hexagon has come from postcolonial literary studies, which have significantly revised perspectives within medieval studies over the past few decades. Postcolonial work on the Middle Ages has explored both the *longue durée* history of pre-modern colonialism and the 'long-standing intimacies of colonialism and medievalism' within the modern period in order to uncover structures of domination and othering during the Middle Ages.[45] Such efforts are not politically neutral: Ananya Jahanara Kabir and Deanne Williams demonstrated in an early anthology that 'critiques of colonialism work in tandem with critiques of modernity'.[46] Within the present collection, the critical and ethical reorientations made possible by postcolonial studies compel the reconsideration of the connections between medieval and modern contact zones, most evidently in the contributions made by Teresa Shawcross, Sharon Kinoshita and Karla Mallette. Even when our authors do not engage explicitly with questions of the postcolonial, shifts in perspective made possible by postcolonial scholarship expose the absence of a single, unified French in the Middle Ages, and cast light instead on French(es) that recall Glissant's terms of *créolisation* and *multilinguisme*.

Both Hexagon and postcolonial studies can, in some cases, suggest an opposition between centre and periphery that is often unrepresentative of the complex circulation of people, objects and ideas within and beyond medieval Europe.[47] Network studies is one device to which scholars have now turned to describe these movements better and to represent the power of 'marginal' places. Networks reorganise both the time and the space of the contact zone by allowing us to follow habitual chains of transmission and to record the waxing and waning of plural 'centres', many of which may register only insignificantly on a modern map. Networks have taken an important place alongside 'communities' and 'identities' as frameworks for analysis. As Wendy Hui Kyong Chun, building on Benedict

---

[44] 'About the Project', *The Values of French*, accessed 24 February 2023, https://tvof. ac.uk/about.

[45] M. R. Warren, *Creole Medievalism: Colonial France and Joseph Bédier's Middle Ages* (Minneapolis, 2011), p. xxxi.

[46] *Postcolonial Approaches to the European Middle Ages*, ed. A. J. Kabir and D. Williams (Cambridge, 2005), p. 2.

[47] On the centre-periphery model implied by some models of postcolonialism and by the concept of *francophonie médiévale* in particular, see Lefèvre and Zinelli, 'La France', pp. 1–6. For arguments in favor of the concept of 'medieval francophonia', see Busby and Putter, 'Introduction'.

Anderson's famous 'imagined communities', argues, an important continuity between these frameworks is the role played by imagination: '[n]etworks are *imagined* – they are not simply or directly experienced'.[48] Chun's point speaks not only to the ways in which networks functioned for medieval people, but also to how scholarship today imagines medieval networks. A welcome new way of thinking about flexible, scalable connections has entered critical discourse, allowing us to overcome classificatory barriers that many find stale: 'Networks are imagined as *glocal* collectives that create seemingly direct, traceable trajectories between the local and the global, the social-historical and the psychical, the collective and the individual, as well as the technical and the social'.[49]

Network studies have already made it possible to rethink old commonplaces in the study of the circulation of French language and literature in medieval Europe and the Mediterranean. As mentioned earlier, French has enjoyed an image within scholarship as the international medieval language of courtliness and chivalry. This image paid implicit homage to the lifestyles of the nobility and royalty of France and to circles of learning centred in Paris. The view has now been substantially revised: at least until the fourteenth and fifteenth centuries – and even afterwards – the aspirations for which French was a vehicle might have little to do with Paris or the kingdom of France. Modern interest in network thinking inclines us to regard certain kinds of elite text and manuscript as instances of globalising discourses put to local uses. Expressions in French of such discourses – notably courtliness, chivalry, universal history, apocalyptic and encyclopedic – often travelled particular routes, such as from Flanders to Outremer (for example, the *Histoire ancienne*) or from England to Italy (Rustichello da Pisa claims that his *Arthurian Compilation* is based on a book in French lent to him by the future Edward I on his way to the Holy Land). Their networking potential was activated not only via journeying, but by processes of copying, translation, imitation, composition, compilation and quotation, whether in French or in other languages, that might happen at any point along the route as well as at the destination.[50] Such processes might also be

---

[48] W. H. K. Chun, 'Imagined Networks: Digital Media, Race, and the University', *Traces 5: Universities in Translation: The Mental Labour of Globalization*, ed. B. de Bary (Hong Kong, 2009), 341–54 (p. 346). For Anderson's concept, see his *Imagined Communities: Reflections on the Origin and Spread of Nationalism*, rev. edn (London and New York, 2006).

[49] W. H. K. Chun, 'Networks NOW: Belated Too Early', *Amerikastudien/American Studies* 60 (2015), 37–58 (p. 43).

[50] *The Values of French* blog documents numerous detailed studies of *Histoire ancienne* manuscripts changing as they travel; see, for instance, R. M. Rodríguez Porto, 'A Crucial Episode in the History of Medieval Book Illustration: The *Histoire ancienne*

triggered by people encountered unexpectedly, who exported the material to still other locations. Seeing medieval French as dominant in the networks in which it played a part is one way of imagining those networks. Our contributors present others. Clara Pascual-Argente, Mark Chinca, and Bart Besamusca and Lisa Demets show that experiments with different strategies for re-using Old French texts or manuscripts were attempts to resituate the practitioner or sponsor in relation to networks, which were more likely to function multilingually than monolingually and which might have a very wide and very particular reach. In such cases, prestige might flow through French instead of pooling in it.

A second notable imagining of the networks of medieval French has attended to the language's humbler uses and has conversely put into question French's 'elite' status for its many users. In Ireland, Britain, Italy and the eastern Mediterranean, as well as in the kingdom of France and the Low Countries, French was used by mariners, small tradesmen and rural administrators 'not as a [sign of] social grace or literary ornament, but as a mundane tool in the world of work'.[51] Documentary sources show French being employed to name commodities, to negotiate agreements, to articulate good business customs and to record transactions in both widely spaced and highly localised networks. French allowed mariners working their routes in the North Atlantic and the Mediterranean to communicate with one another and with officials and business

---

in Italy', *The Values of French Blog*, December 19 2018, accessed 24 February 2023, https://tvof.ac.uk/blog/crucial-episode-history-medieval-book-illustration-histoire-ancienne-italy; M. T. Rachetta, 'Evolving Texts and Evolving Witnesses', *The Values of French Blog*, April 24 2017, accessed 24 February 2023, https://tvof. ac.uk/blog/evolving-texts-and-evolving-witnesses. For an account of late medieval European literature that takes itineraries as its starting point, see D. Wallace, ed., *Europe: A Literary History, 1343–1418*, 2 vols. (Oxford, 2017). For Rustichello's *Arthurian Compilation*, see F. Cigni, 'French Redactions in Italy: Rustichello da Pisa', *The Arthur of the Italians: The Arthurian Legend in Medieval Italian Literature and Culture*, ed. F. R. Psaki and G. Allaire (Cardiff, 2014), pp. 21–40 (23).

51 W. Rothwell, 'Sugar and Spice and All Things Nice: From Oriental Bazar to English Cloister in Anglo-French', *Modern Language Review* 94 (1999), 647–59 (p. 650); L. Minervini, 'What We Know and Don't Yet Know about Outremer French', in *The French of Outremer*, ed. Morreale and Paul, pp. 15–29 (pp. 19–20). French was used as a language of record in Angevin Italy in the thirteenth century, which might indicate a wide dissemination, but these records are overwhelmingly associated with the royal treasury and seem to reflect the habits of the court rather than Neapolitan society more broadly: C. Lee, 'That Obscure Object of Desire: French in Southern Italy', in *MFLCOF*, pp. 73–100 (p. 88). For some examples of French-language documents associated with northern Italians, see 'Indice dei testi', *RIALFrI*, accessed 7 October 2023, https://www.rialfri.eu/rialfriPHP/public/index/index.

INTRODUCTION   19

associates at their ports of call.[52] Further inland, French was needed by monks, nuns, townspeople and rural nobility in some contact zones to administer households, to manage servants and to adjudicate disagreements.[53] The use of French in the kitchen to work out the accounts or dockside to haggle over lading fees does not itself imply cosmopolitan desires or strong feelings of identity.

The 'material' life of French in workaday documents and outside elite cultural circles also demonstrates the unpredictable and complex 'intervalorisation' of languages within medieval contact zones, in ways that recall Glissant's *créolisation* and *multilinguisme*. Even in documents where French is the dominant grammatical code, the frequent appearance of words and phrases in Latin or another vernacular make it plain that business was conducted in the presence of many different forms of speech and writing.[54] Such *multilinguisme* is at the heart of a text like Walter de Bibbesworth's *Tretiz*, a French-language manual for household administrators. The English glosses that regularly accompany Bibbesworth's text are usually understood as a kind of trot but equally they might demonstrate the need for household managers to command a wide vocabulary in *both* English and French.[55] Polyglossia also shaped the lexicon of labourers' French in ways very different from the varieties cultivated by elites. Even as she argues for a major role for French in maritime communication, Maryanne Kowaleski points out that the lexicon of seafaring was widely shared between the languages of the medieval North Atlantic, and French boating jargon borrowed heavily from Germanic languages; one seaman's French might be heard by another as English or Dutch.[56] It can be difficult, moreover, to extrapolate the

[52] M. Kowaleski, 'The French of England: A Maritime *Lingua Franca?*' in *Lang Cult*, pp. 103–17; D. A. Trotter, 'Italian Merchants in London and Paris: Evidence of Language Contact in the Gallerani Accounts, 1305–8', in *On Linguistic Change in French: Socio-Historical Approaches. Le changement linguistique en français: aspects sociohistoriques. Studies in Honour of R. Anthony Lodge. Études en hommage au Professeur R. Anthony Lodge*, ed. D. Lagorgette and T. Pooley (Chambéry, 2011), pp. 209–26.

[53] R. Britnell, 'Uses of French Medieval English Towns', *Lang Cult*, pp. 81–9; M. Oliva, 'The French of England in Female Convents: The French Kitcheners' Accounts of Campsey Ash Priory', *Lang Cult*, pp. 90–102.

[54] L. Wright, 'Bills, Accounts, Inventories: Everyday Trilingual Activities in the Business World of Later Medieval England', in *Multilingualism in Later Medieval Britain*, ed. D. A. Trotter (Cambridge, 2000), pp. 150–6; Rothwell, 'Sugar and Spice'.

[55] T. Hinton, 'Anglo-French in the Thirteenth Century: A Reappraisal of Walter de Bibbesworth's *Tretiz*', *Modern Language Review* 112 (2017), 855–81 (pp. 868–74); P. Knox, 'The English Glosses in Walter de Bibbesworth's *Tretiz*', *Notes and Queries* 60 (2013), 349–59.

[56] Kowaleski, 'French of England', pp. 114–15, and D. A. Trotter, '*Oceano vox*: You Never Know Where a Ship Comes From: On Multilingualism and Language-Mixing in

minutiae of language use from the records before us: not only do scribes write in one language when they speak another, but the use of conventional shorthands, abbreviations and suspensions frequently makes the identity of the language on the page ambiguous.[57] So even though the presence of French in the language of working people is undeniable, it is far from obvious that medieval people imagined their networks to be uniquely or even primarily 'French-speaking', as modern scholarship often presents them. Such is certainly the case in later medieval Wales and Flanders, where the ability to move between different languages was more sought after than just the acquisition of French and where an individual's choice to use French (or not) cannot be easily explained in terms of status or nationality. The jump from utilitarian French, imposed by the material conditions of medieval economic life, to scientific, encyclopedic and even lyric expressions could be a short one. Bibbesworth again provides a ready example. The same labour-oriented and mixed lexis are used in *The Tretiz* as in his lyric *tençon* with Henry de Lacy, earl of Lincoln, in which Walter draws on the specialist vocabulary of farming to counter the young earl's views on those courtly interests, *par excellence*: love and Crusade.[58]

The links proposed in scholarship between network studies, trade and globalisation are not incidental. The envisaging of networks as intrinsically open, relational, multiple, mobile, heterogeneous, deterritorialised, free and empowering is, as Chun points out, intimately involved in 'the emergence, management, and imaginary of neoliberalism, in particular to its narrative of individuals collectively dissolving society'.[59] Networks, in other words, are creatures of affect, imagination and politics. We need in our own practice to be alert to how unconscious or occluded desires, ideologies and affiliations play into the building or resisting of connections.[60] Our contributors demonstrate such sensitivity when describing how communications networks in which medieval French played a part were imagined or experienced differently in particular contexts. For instance, Shawcross demonstrates that the wide-eyed wonder evinced by writers in French describing Constantinople before the Fourth Crusade is not the 'spontaneous' response to the ancient capital that it claims to be, but a repetition of statements and ideas found in Greek-language texts written in Byzantine

---

Medieval Britain', in *Aspects of Multilingualism in European Language History*, ed. G. Ferraresi and K. Braunmüller (Amsterdam, 2003), pp. 15–33.

[57] Wright, 'Bills, Accounts, Inventories'.

[58] Hinton, 'Anglo-French', pp. 877–8.

[59] Chun, 'Networks NOW', p. 37. 'Networks, as opposed to communities, emphasize flow, movement, and the constant adding and pruning of connections; they emphasize relations rather than identities' (Chun, 'Imagined Networks', p. 346).

[60] *MFLCA*, pp. 194–242.

interests with the aim of magnifying imperial prestige and restricting visitors' access. During the Fourth Crusade and its aftermath, this 'wonder' discourse will be translated into a new reality of conquest and domination. Clara Pascual-Argente's essay, meanwhile, highlights several networks between Castile and centres of French literary production during the later Middle Ages in Acre and southern Italy that were realised in Castilian translations of *romans d'antiquité*. While such connections are certainly comprehensible in terms of commercial contact, Pascual-Argente suggests that the appeal of *romans d'antiquité* from these places rested instead on the association that elites in such places crafted between ancient empire-building and their own self-image. The selection and use of these texts were not just a reflex of French 'cosmopolitanism', in other words, but the manifestation of a Castilian desire to bind their own expansionist policies with analogous chivalric projects elsewhere in the Mediterranean.

High-profile publications have emphasised how French travelled along trade routes and trading links that opened up perspectives beyond western Europe.[61] There is, sometimes, a celebratory tone to the modern imagining of medieval trade, as if we believed that travel for commerce broadens the mind while that undertaken for pilgrimage or crusade narrows it; that whereas the former construes those whom the traveller encounters as potential collaborators, the latter frames them as only allies or enemies. Slave trading is just one example of how trade itself can damage or kill; we can also point to dangerous trade wars of the Middle Ages and today as political acts. As one recent commentator on US foreign affairs puts it: 'We need to realize that economic warfare truly is a kind of warfare, and it can and does kill'.[62] As an axiom of modern neoliberal political ideology, trade's supposed 'openness' cannot be cleanly distinguished from, or assumed to be superior to, the ideals and ideologies that sent medieval people travelling across the known world for religious reasons.[63] It is not only that trade often inspires warfare: the Venetian-sponsored sack of Zara as a way for the Fourth Crusaders to pay their shipping debt is a clear example, the sack of Constantinople by the same crusaders a more arguable one.[64] The

[61] Wallace, ed., *Europe*; Gaunt, *Marco Polo*; Hsy, *Trading Tongues*.

[62] D. Larison, 'Sanctions are Targeted Warfare, and They do Kill', *Responsible Statecraft*, September 16 2022, accessed 24 February 2023, https://responsiblestatecraft.org/2022/09/16/sanctions-are-targeted-warfare-and-they-do-kill/.

[63] On the complex relations between US multiculturalism, capital and politics, and on that multiculturalism's reception both in and of Latin America, see the classic essay by G. Yúdice, 'We are *Not* the World', *Social Text* 31/32 (1992), 202–16. Chun, 'Imagined Networks', is a recent intervention.

[64] Christopher Tyerman offers a polemical review of recurrent criticisms of crusading in historiography over the centuries in *The Debate on the Crusades, 1099–2010* (Manchester, 2011).

cosmopolitanism of the medieval merchant-adventurer is hardly incomparable to the attitudes motivating the colonial encounters between Spain and the Americas analysed by Pratt in 'Arts of the Contact Zone', and to ideologies of expansionist 'discovery' and 'civilisation', in general.[65] An emphasis on trade and trade routes can also obscure the fact that there are other kinds of mobility, and other kinds of contact zone: for instance, forced movement of Jews from Iberia as discussed here by Isabelle Levy, often resulting in untraceable contact.[66] Meanwhile, the absence of clear literary evidence of exchange with French in Sicily (Mallette) and the mediated connections between French and Irish in Ireland (Ní Mhaonaigh) cannot be taken as evidence of non-contact; rather, they are effects of the contact that did take place, which was simply different from experiences elsewhere.

Finally, the studies here offer yet another opportunity to reconsider the concepts of the 'vernacular' in medieval literary history. During the central Middle Ages, when scribes begin to represent the spoken romance languages differently from Latin, they use *roman* to designate local language varieties used by laity over fairly restricted areas.[67] By the later Middle Ages, French was considered in many places an appropriate vehicle for learning, court life and the law, in both writing and in speech; in this later period, French might have indeed functioned as a 'common language' uniting both the learned and unlearned, which Fiona Somerset and Nicholas Watson identified as a key feature of medieval vernacular languages.[68] As a language detached from a

[65] J. Derrida, 'L'autre cap: mémoires, réponses et responsabilités', in *L'autre cap. Suivi de La démocratie ajournée* (Paris, 1991), pp. 11–101. Translated into English as *The Other Heading: Reflections on Today's Europe*, trans. P.-A. Brault and M. B. Naas (Bloomington, 1992). On cities and agriculture as indices of civilisation and justifications of European civilising missions, see R. Waswo, 'The History That Literature Makes', *New Literary History* 19 (1988), 541–64, and *The Founding Legend of Western Civilization: From Virgil to Vietnam* (Hanover NH, 1997).

[66] On the ethical and political challenges that minimal or non-existent historical records pose to historians, see especially S. Hartman, 'Venus in Two Acts', *Small Axe*, 12.2 (2008), 1–14, and M.-R. Trouillot, *Silencing the Past: Power and the Production of History* (Boston MA, 1995).

[67] M. Selig, 'L'église et le passage à l'écrit du vernaculaire dans le Nord de la France au XIe siècle', in *The Church and Vernacular Literature in Medieval France*, ed. D. Kullman (Toronto, 2009), pp. 15–34; M. Banniard, *Viva voce. Communication écrite et communication orale du IVe au IXe siècle en Occident latin* (Paris, 1992); R. Wright, *Late Latin and Early Romance in Spain and Carolingian France* (Liverpool, 1982).

[68] 'Preface: On "Vernacular"', in *The Vulgar Tongue: Medieval and Postmedieval Vernacularity*, ed. F. Somerset and N. Watson (Philadelphia, 2003), pp. ix–xvi (pp. ix–x). See also Wogan-Browne, Fenster and Russell, ed., *Vernacular Literary Theory*, pp. 401–413; C. M. Waters, *Translating Clergie: Status, Education and Salvation in Thirteenth-Century*

definite locality but without the same associations as Latin, French was suitable for elite individuals who wished to signal their cultural and social attainments and to communicate across wide distances.[69] Yet even here, the value of French to its cosmopolitan users could remain tied to 'local' origins in surprising ways. For example, French was certainly a language of learning for Flemish noble readers at the end of the Middle Ages, but – as Besamusca and Demets show – Dutch was being used in very similar ways by the very same families, who were intensely focused on local networks connecting town, country and court, within a single county. As Uri Zvi Shachar shows in his analysis of Cypriot and Egyptian writers, French could appear to some individuals in the multiconfessional Mediterranean as an entirely appropriate vehicle for revelation precisely because of its status as a minority language 'out of place'. Meanwhile, Ruth Nisse invites us to consider how French could occupy a learned function alongside Aramaic as an accessory for scriptural interpretation for Jewish scholars like Rashi and Berekhiah ha-Naqdan. Moving between and across opposed conceptual poles like the cosmopolitan and the local, sacred and secular, affected and authentic, at home and displaced, medieval French use prefigures and embodies the relational character of the vernacular and the cosmopolitan in the postcolonial world, which must always be 'transforming, retreating, advancing, and shapeshifting in relation to the uneven system of languages and cultures it inhabits and refracts'.[70] The shifting status and cultural associations of medieval French, according to time or place, mean that the language does not become explicable through vernacularity so much as it exposes that concept's unresolved complexities.

Vernacular Texts (Philadelphia, 2016), pp. 6–13, and S. Lusignan, *La langue des rois au Moyen Âge. Le français en France et en Angleterre* (Paris, 2004), pp. 163–85. For contemporary references to French as a language spoken by people outside the elite, see Busby and Putter, 'Introduction', pp. 2–4 (England, Flanders and Italy), and Aslanov, *Le français au Levant* (Outremer).

[69] F. Zinelli, 'Inside/Outside Grammar: The French of Italy Between Structuralism and Trends of Exoticism', in *MFLCOF*, pp. 31–72. Pollock has suggested that early medieval vernaculars, having acquired some of the traits of 'cosmopolitan' Latin in the course of becoming written but still tied to specific territories, ought to be compared to the 'cosmopolitan vernacular' that he has described emerging in South Asia, but even this paradoxical reformulation does not capture the geographic and social penetration of a language like medieval French. S. Pollock, *The Language of the Gods in the World of Men: Sanskrit, Culture, and Power in Premodern India* (Berkeley, 2006), pp. 437–67, and S. Pollock, 'The Cosmopolitan Vernacular', *Journal of South Asian Studies* 57 (1998), 6–37.

[70] C. Kullberg and D. Watson, 'Introduction: Theorizing the Vernacular', in *Vernaculars in an Age of World Literatures*, ed. C. Kullberg and D. Watson (London, 2022), pp. 1–24 (p. 21).

Conversations

The interlocutions printed in this volume began as presentations and discussions at the international conference *Medieval French without Borders* organised by the volume's editors, along with Sarah Kay, Maryanne Kowaleski and Elizabeth M. Tyler, and hosted by Fordham University's Center for Medieval Studies in March 2021. Over a series of subsequent workshops during which our contributors further refined their arguments, they sustained their dialogue not just with French Studies but, more consequentially, with each other on topics of fundamental importance for understanding medieval language and literature. These conversations provide several pathways for readers to encounter these arguments beyond the loosely chronological arrangement of the essays.

Across the collection we hear about the ways that formal properties of language and literature, such as prosody or genre, bear witness to contact as well as about the ways that contact creates new aesthetic possibilities. Chinca's essay reveals different ways in which 'presences of French' in German texts could function, whether to produce 'aspectual shifts' caused by its sudden interruption into the text for humour or irony; to call attention to 'language as a system which overdetermines and exceeds the intentions of speakers who believe they master its codes'; or even to give the German audience the feeling of being 'strangers in their own language'.[71] The essays by Besamusca and Demets, on bilingual French-Dutch text collections in Flanders, and by Léglu, on Occitan renditions of the debate between the body and the soul, demonstrate the ways that formal exchange could unify literary traditions frequently seen to be at odds with one another in modern scholarship. Levy's essay traces the flow of literary practices related to metaphor across linguistic traditions in the western Mediterranean; nevertheless, such 'formal manoeuvring ... challenge[s] both ... formal and fictional boundaries'. Even when encounters between vernacular literatures exposed limits to their idioms, Shachar argues that such patent 'linguistic imperfection and dependence' offered a new ground for claiming universality and authority. Ní Mhaonaigh reminds us that preexisting formal traditions may go unrecognised post-contact, challenging us to reconsider what we heard as source and echo, while Mallette gives us a 'counterexample' to French's influence on genre in the lack of trace in Sicilian histories of Sicily.

Such formal innovations were sometimes facilitated by translation, and for most of our contributors the process and effects of translation were major

---

[71] Chinca's discussion of 'aspectual shifts' really got us talking and inspired our use of 'perceptual shifts' as a guiding metaphor for this Introduction. We note this, with thanks, as an example of the conversations the essays below have generated for us.

concerns. Adaptations across genres, discourses and milieus as well as across languages shape and are shaped by specific contact zones. Specific discussions of medieval thinking about translation will be found in the contributions of Levy, Shachar, Nisse and Pascual-Argente. The essays by Henley and Ní Mhaonaigh take a complementary approach and show how interpreters played key roles in shaping the event and memory of contact on the edges of England's first empire in Wales and Ireland. A related concern is transliteration – that vanishing-point of translation into the 'alienating' pole identified by Lawrence Venuti. Medieval writers' fascination with the challenge of how to render foreign sounds receives particular attention, as well, in the essays by Kinoshita and Shawcross. In Nisse's essay, we hear how this challenge could become a formal tool for Jewish scholars wishing to demonstrate that French was, after all, 'our language'. In the Middle High German translations explored by Chinca, translators were not faced with the need to change writing systems, but they could still exploit the differences between languages through complex puns and neologisms.

Some contributors deepen our understanding of the relationship between language and experiences of the local, which goes beyond mere affirmation of 'original' identities or resistance to French as an outsider. Besamusca and Demets reveal how late medieval Flemish authors and collectors drew on French and Dutch together to foster a wide array of interests and to anchor themselves in the multilingual elite of the county. The cases of post-conquest Ireland and Wales, discussed by Ní Mhaonaigh and Henley, respectively, bear comparison for the evidence they provide, in a much earlier period, for a rich exchange between French and local languages that could assimilate French to local needs without invalidating the claims of any language to importance in the wider world. Like Occitan, explored here by Léglu, Welsh and Irish were venerable high-status languages with strong claims to prestige and importance independent of their contact with French. This might account for the apparently 'eccentric' development of these literatures in contact with French, when compared to areas of English, Dutch and Italian language-use (but why should those constitute the norm?), where French established itself as a dominant language for learning and government (although English too was used for these purposes in England well into the twelfth century). The case of Sicily, which, like England, saw several waves of subjugation by French-speaking elites, demonstrates yet another possibility, where a local vernacular assumes importance only after French has withdrawn and never seems to have looked to French for models at all. As Mallette explains, Sicilians set French set aside in favour of cosmopolitan languages like Latin and Arabic, and Sicilian assumed the role (played in England, Flanders and northern Italy by French) of a language for local history and self-representation.

Other contributions here engage with the claims made for languages as vehicles for translocal communication and signification in the various guises of cosmopolitan, sacred or imperial languages. Even as Sicilians rejected French as a cosmopolitan language in favour of Latin and Arabic, users of other languages sought out French as a language for imitation but on a limited number of topics: courtly romance and epic in the case of Middle High German-speakers (discussed by Chinca) and narratives of ancient nobility in the court of Castile (detailed by Pascual-Argente). Other essays reveal the complex situation of French when used as a cosmopolitan language, within a wide array of other cosmopolitan languages. Franco-Italian may have conveyed Rustichello's narrative of Marco Polo's travels across western Europe, but Kinoshita rightly emphasises that Rustichello was representing the very different multilingualism of the Mongol Empire, in which French had very little authority at all. And the French appearing in the Hebrew works of medieval Jewish exegetes and scientists, analysed by Nisse, attained its authority from several sources: by analogy with ancient Jewish practices of translation from Hebrew into Aramaic; by its association with local Jewish communities as a shared language; and, perhaps most of all, by its difference from Latin, whose Christian associations disqualified it as a language for Jewish learning. In the eastern Mediterranean, users of French contended with linguistic values different from the Latin-dominated west. As Shachar explains, thinkers here developed new justifications for the use of French to communicate authoritative knowledge, based not on grammatical perfection or purity but on its own dependence on other languages for truth and its motley origins as a newcomer – very unlike the model of the cosmopolitan vernacular theorised by Pollock, which attains its position by imitating cosmopolitan forms and ideologies.[72] These chapters reveal not only the encounter between languages within contact zones but confrontations between competing ideas of language; the new possibilities such confrontations generate are not always easy to assimilate to theoretical models developed within the study of French alone.

These are just some of the conversations that we found most generative for rethinking the nature of French in contact, and we hope that readers will find threads of discussion to follow across the volume. In that spirit, we extend to readers the same invitation to seize the opportunities our contributors provide for shifting perspectives on medieval French in contact – and to respond with interlocutions of their own.

[72] Pollock, 'Cosmopolitan Vernacular'.

1

Our Language and the Others: Old French Glosses in Berekhiah Ha-Naqdan's *Uncle and Nephew* and *Commentary on the Book of Job*

Ruth Nisse

Berekhiah Ha-Naqdan's *Uncle and Nephew* represents any number of contact zones, real and imaginary: between Christian and Jewish epistemologies in science and religion, West and East, and the spaces of territory, travel and diaspora. The most pertinent ones for this volume, however, are the porous boundaries between languages. This chapter will examine how Berekhiah's French glosses in his *Commentary on the Book of Job* and the scientific-philosophical dialogue *Uncle and Nephew* draw on two distinct rabbinic and medieval theories of language and translation. The first is the use of vernacular words and phrases, called *le'azim* ('foreign languages', here: 'glosses') in Hebrew biblical exegesis, narrowed to a focus on Rabbi Solomon ben Isaac of Troyes (Rashi) and his northern French followers' translation of Hebrew and Aramaic words and phrases into French as an aspect of *peshat* or 'plain meaning'. This movement marks a transformation of French from their spoken language into the limited written form of words in Hebrew letters. Berekhiah subsequently extends these glosses in his own commentary. The second is his own idiosyncratic approach to French and Latin in *Uncle and Nephew*. Both examples are based on ancient ideas of multiligualism that evolve, in the late eleventh and early twelfth centuries, into Rashi's linguistic triangulations of Hebrew, Aramaic, and French. Berekhiah reworks this method for the very different triangle of Hebrew, Latin, and French. Other languages such as Greek, Arabic, and Hebraico-German ('Ashkenazi' in Hebrew) also occasionally inform both of these particular modalities of Jewish translation.[1]

---

[1] All references to the Targums and to commentaries on the Bible by Rashi, Ibn Ezra, and other exegetes are taken from the full edition of the Rabbinic Hebrew Bible *Mikra'ot Gedolot 'Ha-Keter'*, 24 books in 21 volumes, ed. Menachem Cohen (Ramat Gan, 1992). All translations of Rashi on the Torah are from *Pentateuch with Rashi's Commentary*, ed. and trans. M. Rosenbaum and A.M. Silbermann (London, 1929–1934) (https://www.sefaria.org/Rashi_on_Genesis.1.1.1?lang=en), unless

28   RUTH NISSE

Berekhiah Ha-Naqdan (*c*.1130s–1220?) is one of the most linguistically complicated Northern European Jewish writer of the twelfth century. He translated works freely from Latin into Hebrew, notably Adelard of Bath's *Quaestiones naturales* (*c*.1120) as *Dodi ve-Nekhdi* (*Uncle and Nephew*) as well as several fables from the *Romulus* collections and a few from Avianus in his masterpiece, *Mishlei Shuʿalim* (*Fox Fables*). He also translated from French some of Marie de France's fables as part of *Fox Fables* and an Old French lapidary as *Koʾakh ha-Avanim* (*Virtues of the Stones*).[2] In addition to these extraordinary transfers of the scientific and literary trends of his day, he wrote other Hebrew works, including the Job commentary that, in part, follows the methods and translations of the Northern French school of exegetes. Rashi's younger contemporary Joseph Kara, his grandson Rashbam, Eliezer of Beaugency, and Joseph Bekhor Shor were the main translators of hundreds of biblical and rabbinic Hebrew and Aramaic words and phrases into Hebraico-French. The descendant of an illustrious rabbinic family of this time and place, Berekhiah cites his father R. Natronai and uncle R. Benjamin as prominent biblical interpreters as well.[3] His son Elijah compared him to Solomon in wisdom and claimed that Berekhiah had written commentaries on the entire Bible; if so, only the text on Job has survived.[4]

---

otherwise noted. Translations of the Babylonian Talmud are by A. Steinsaltz, from *The William Davidson Talmud* (https://www.sefaria.org/texts/Talmud/Bavli).

[2] For a convincing hypothetical biography and timeline of Berekhiah's works, see Tamás Visi, 'Introduction', in *Berekhiah Ben Natronai Ha-Naqdan's Works and Their Reception*, ed. T. Visi, T. Bibring, and D. Soukup (Brepols, 2019), pp. 7–28.

[3] A. Grossman, 'The School of Literal Jewish Exegesis in Northern France', in M. Sæbo, ed., *Hebrew Bible/Old Testament: The History of Its Interpretation*, 3 vols. (Göttingen, 2000), I, 320–71.

[4] *A Commentary on the Book of Job*, ed. W. A. Wright and trans. S.A. Hirsch (London, 1905). For a description of the manuscript (Cambridge, Cambridge University Library MS Dd 8, 53) and arguments for Berekhiah's authorship of the commentary, see J. Olszowy-Schlanger, 'Livre de Job avec le Commentaire de Berakhyah ben Natronai ha-Naqdan', in *Savants et Croyants: Les Juifs d'Europe du Nord au Moyen Age*, ed. N. Hatot et J. Olszowy-Schlanger (Ghent, 2018), pp. 134–5. As a measure of its influence, there is a second version of the commentary in the text and margins of the Job section of the famous Hebrew-French-German Leipzig Glossary. On the transmission of Berekhiah's commentary and its relation to manuscripts of Rashi's Job Commentary, see J. Penkower, 'The End of Rashi's Commentary on Job: The Mss and the Printed Editions', *Jewish Studies Quarterly* 10 (2003), 18–48. Penkower notes the 'intense preoccupation with Job among the French Exegetes of the 12th–13th centuries' at p. 21. For Elijah's celebration of his father, see N. Golb,

Uncle and Nephew (1160s), Berekhiah's version of Adelard's *Quaestiones*, loosely follows the original form of a dialogue between the eponymous relatives.[5] It is a unique work, the earliest medieval Hebrew translation by several decades of a Latin scientific text. It also stands out for being written among the Jewish communities of either northern France or England rather than among the prolific Arabic-to-Hebrew scientific translation centres in Provence, and it continues to vex interpreters.[6] It is possible that some of Rashi's followers in *peshat* exegesis, the *pashtanim*, may have read Latin in order to write their polemics against Christianity; perhaps they and their students included the handful of Berekhiah's readers who would have understood his provocative ideas about translation itself expressed in this odd philosophical work. Adelard's text itself was on the cutting edge of science in northwestern Europe, a list of questions on natural philosophy, medicine, and cosmology in the form of a contentious dialogue between the author and his stubborn nephew. In this partly fictional account, which dramatises a conflict between the conservative teaching of the Church and the newly-recovered 'secular' sciences, the author has traveled to the East to study with 'Arab Masters' while his nephew has stayed in the famous cathedral school at Laon. In fact, while it is likely that Adelard traveled to Antioch, the *Quaestiones* reflect no Arab sources – only the Neoplatonism of the contemporary schools of Salerno and Chartres. When he translates from Adelard's Latin into Biblical and Rabbinic Hebrew in *Uncle and Nephew*, however, Berekhiah collapses his opposition of religious and scientific knowledge, and for the most part erases the conceit of an argument between the two characters. He crucially replaces Adelard's notional Arab science with the alternate fiction that the entire text was originally composed in Arabic.[7] In Berekhiah's version, the Spanish 'sage' Abraham ibn Ezra's Arabo-Greek science, taken from his biblical commentaries, often overshadows Adelard's original sources.

 The Jews of Medieval Normandy: A Social and Intellectual History (Cambridge, 1998), pp. 324–33.

[5] Berekhiah Ha-Naqdan, *Dodi ve-Nechdi (Uncle & Nephew)*, ed. and trans. H. Gollancz (Oxford, 1920) (henceforth *UN*). For Adelard's text, life and sources, see *Adelard of Bath's Conversations with his Nephew*, ed. and trans. C. Burnett (Cambridge, 1998).

[6] G. Freudenthal, 'Arabic and Latin Cultures as Resources for the Hebrew Translation Movement', in *Science in Medieval Jewish Cultures*, ed. G. Freudenthal (Cambridge, 2012), pp. 74–105.

[7] As Tamás Visi, among others, has shown, Berekhiah's claims to know Arabic are completely fictional. T. Visi, 'Berechiah ben Natronai ha-Naqdan's *Dodi ve-Nekhdi* and the Transfer of Scientific Knowledge from Latin to Hebrew in the Twelfth Century', *Aleph* 14 (2014), 9–73.

The foundation of Hebrew translation, as practiced by Rashi and subsequent exegetes, including Berekhiah, is the Aramaic bible of the Targums. Translations dating from the rabbinic period, the Targums are in most cases literal, but also include additional information or interpretation. Although several survive, the two canonical Aramaic texts are Onkelos on the Torah and Jonathan on the Prophets; Targums exist for most of the other books of the bible as well, including Job.[8] In some surviving medieval manuscripts, including the famous English manuscript Codex Valmadonna 1 (now held by The Museum of the Bible in Washington, DC), the Targums accompany the Torah, weekly haftarah readings from the prophets, and the five scrolls, with a Hebrew verse directly followed by its Aramaic translation.[9] This layout facilitates the crucial Talmudic formula to read the Torah 'twice scripture and once Targum' for private study of the weekly Torah portion. If the Hebrew and Aramaic were originally heard by the audience as a kind of 'interlinear' reciprocal translation in ancient synagogues when Aramaic was the local spoken language, the manuscripts blend the two languages together in one continuous bilingual scripture.[10] This structure brings out the relation between the Aramaic Targum and its Hebrew source as simultaneously linguistic difference and similarity, a transfer of meaning, and a change in aspects of comprehension.

Rashi's concept of French as part of an overall vocabulary of commentary is an innovative addition to the foundation of the traditional Aramaic. Indeed, it constitutes a new theory of translatability as a form of interpretation. Berekhiah later enthusiastically took up and extended this concept, especially in *Uncle and Nephew*, which, like *peshat* commentaries, incorporated *le'azim*, French glosses in Hebrew letters. The culture of Rashi's and Berekhiah's French glosses is defined spatially by the shifting territories of Jewish diaspora in medieval Europe and temporally by a larger conceptual trajectory of diasporic languages that emerges after the Second Temple period. For example, French dialects as they appear in Hebrew texts reflect the Jewish communities of northern France

[8] The best reference work is P. V. M. Flesher and B. Chilton, *The Targums: A Critical Introduction* (Waco, 2011).

[9] J. Olszowy-Schlanger, 'Hebrew Books' in *The European Book in the Twelfth Century*, ed. E. Kwakkel and R. Thomson (Cambridge, 2018), pp. 159–74. The manuscript is now Washington, Museum of the Bible MS 858 but I will refer to the manuscript by its familiar name, Codex Valmadonna 1. Link to MS: https://collections.museumofthebible.org/artifacts/32220-codex-valmadonna-i

[10] S. D. Fraade, 'Rabbinic Views on the Practice of Targum and Multilingualism in Jewish Galilee of the Third–Sixth Centuries', in *The Galilee in Late Antiquity*, ed. L. I. Levine (Cambridge MA, 1992), pp. 253–86 (p. 257). Cited by K. Fudeman, *Vernacular Voices: Language and Identity in Medieval French Jewish Communities* (Philadelphia, 2010), pp. 122–3.

and England – the spaces shared with Christians. At the same time, these local vernacular languages operate within Hebrew commentaries and other genres as part of a trans-historical ordering of knowledge in the Diaspora. The *le'azim* in *peshat* biblical commentaries are a subset of a small body of medieval 'Hebraico-French' texts, as Kirsten Fudeman, in her field-defining work *Vernacular Voices* calls the entire diasporic language of French written in Hebrew characters. She identifies thirteen biblical exegetes who use French glosses, and three further religious texts; eight extant long glossaries and several fragments; seven bilingual poems; and four bilingual medical, magical and culinary texts.[11] The mirroring Hebraico-French and Hebrew versions of the Troyes elegies, commemorating the martyrs of 1288, are singular literary productions.[12] An anonymous commentary on Song of Songs with 36 *le'azim*, *The Way of Lovers*, has recently been published with much attention to the French.[13] These French texts, from the twelfth to the fourteenth centuries, used the written 'mother tongue' for a variety of purposes within Jewish communities, communicating between learned and less-learned audiences, teachers and pupils, and men and women.

Although Rashi's term for such uses presents French as the language 'foreign' to Hebrew (*la'az*), he also calls French *leshonenu*, 'our language' as opposed to Hebrew, the *lashon ha-qodesh*, 'holy language' (by contrast, Ibn Ezra calls Hebrew *leshonenu* as opposed to his own vernacular Arabic).[14] Its status as a specifically Jewish vernacular in this formulation – analogous to ancient vernacular Aramaic in certain ways – allows Rashi to interpret some difficult passages of Job through French culture. In a particularly imaginative example (Job 5:23), for the mysterious 'For you will have a pact with the rocks in the field (*'avnei ha-sadeh*)/ And the beasts of the field will be your allies', he interprets the rocks as the Mishnaic Hebrew *'adnei ha-sadeh* (m. *Kilayim* 8.5)

---

[11] Fudeman, *Vernacular Voices*, pp. 156–8.

[12] Fudeman, *Vernacular Voices*, pp. 86–8.

[13] *The Way of Lovers: The Oxford Anonymous Commentary on the Song of Songs (Bodleian Library, MS Opp. 625)*, ed. and trans. S. Japhet and B. D. Walfish (Leiden, 2017). See C. Aslanov, 'The Old French Glosses of an Anonymous *Peshat* Commentary on Song of Songs', *Jewish Quarterly Review* 109 (2019), 38–53.

[14] Rashi's French glosses on the Bible and Talmud are collected in M. Catane, *Otsar Leazei Rashi* (Jerusalem, 1988). For a reading of Rashi's use of *leshonenu*, see M. Banitt, 'La Langue Vernaculaire Dans Les Commentaires de Raschi', in *Rashi 1040–1990: Hommage à Ephraim Urbach: congrès européen des études juives*, ed. G. Sed-Rajna (Paris, 1993), pp. 411–18. See, for example, Rashi on I Samuel 9:17. An example of Ibn Ezra's use of the term is in his commentary on Psalms 37:23.

32   RUTH NISSE

('man-like beasts of the fields') with the gloss גרוליש (*garols*) – 'werewolves'.[15] At the lexical level, the literal biblical interpreters strove to create intrinsic connections between Hebrew and French. Menachem Banitt, and more recently Fudeman and Cyril Aslanov, have identified the ways in which these commentators tried to make French translations align with Hebrew words as paronyms or calques. Fudeman points to Joseph Kara's translation in Isaiah 44:13 of the hapax שרד (*sered*: either a 'stylus' or a 'saw', as Rashi reads it) as *serre* ('saw') – a paronym.[16] Similarly, Banitt notes Rashi's translation of אצילות (*'atsilot*) in Jeremiah 38:12 and the alternate form אצילים (*'atsilim*) in Ezekiel 13:18 as the similar-sounding *aiselles* ('armpits').[17] Aslanov works through a complicated calque in Eliezer of Beaugency's ingenious translation of לבתך (*levatekha*) (Ez. 16:30), a hapax meaning 'your heart' as *ta corine*; this *la'az* is only previously attested in old French with the meaning of entrails, but the gloss aligns the Hebrew word for heart (*lev*) with a word derived from old French *cuer*.[18] Fudeman further notes examples of 'code-switching' in Joseph Kara's commentaries where he combines Hebrew and French grammar in a single word or phrase or words from both languages. The most striking example of the latter is from the commentary on Isaiah 66:18 which he begins in French (up to *doneid*) and ends in Hebrew: 'Ba'ah be-l[a'az]: ço me fera avenir et tu ma'[s] doneid SHE-AQQWBBAṢ ET KOL HA-GOYIM WE-HA-LESHONOT U-VA'U WE-RA'U ET KEVODI – (In french: that will make me approach; and you have allowed me TO GATHER [LIT. THAT I WILL GATHER] ALL NATIONS AND TONGUES, AND THEY WILL COME AND SEE MY GLORY).'[19] The sentence itself enacts the reconciliation of different language-speakers and the possibility of transparent

---

[15] The word, in the form גארלוש (*garelos*), is also found in the Leipzig Glossary. See *Le Glossaire de Leipzig*, ed. M. Banitt, 4 vols. (Jerusalem, 1995–2005), III, 1288–89. See AND, *garulf*. Citations of Rashi's Commentary on Job are from *Mikra'ot Gedolot 'Haketer': Job*, ed. Cohen. Translations of Rashi's *Commentary on Job* are from R. A. J. Rosenberg, *Job: A New English Translation* (New York, 1995). All French glosses from the Bible are in the form in which they appear in *Haketer*.

[16] K. Fudeman, 'The Old French Glosses in Joseph Kara's Isaiah Commentary', *Revue des études juives* 165 (2006), 147–77 (pp. 172–3). Rashi translates it as 'a saw called *doloire* in French' – also not a 'saw', but rather an 'adze'.

[17] Banitt, 'La Langue vernactulaire', p. 416. See AND, *essele*.

[18] C. Aslanov, 'Le Français de Rabbi Joseph Kara et de Rabbi Eliezer de Beaugency d'après leurs commentaires sur Ezekiel', *Revue des études Juives* 159 (2000), 425–46. There is a similar calque in *The Way of Lovers*: '*acorajas mei*' glossing לבבתני ('you have ravished me') (Song of Songs 4:9). The word *accorajer* is a calque derived from *corage* ('state of mind', from *cor*, 'heart'), meaning 'encourage'. This is a new meaning to line up with the Hebrew לב ('heart'). Aslanov, 'Old French Glosses', p. 42.

[19] Quotation and translation from Fudeman, *Vernacular Voices*, pp. 52–3.

understanding in the prophet's vision of a messianic future. These examples all demonstrate that one aspect of *peshat* commentary is to bring French, Rashi's *leshonenu*, the spoken language, closer to the holy tongue linguistically, even as the commentary as a whole also positions French as 'foreign', a translation that necessarily remains in Hebrew script.

Berekhiah, an exponent of Rashi's methods, includes fifteen *le'azim* in his Job Commentary, mostly taken from earlier exegetes. He cites a wide range of sources, from the Aramaic Targums to the Babylonian Talmud to Rashi and Joseph Kara, to his own father and uncle, and above all, to his favorite biblical interpreter and natural scientist, Abraham ibn Ezra, the exponent of literal-linguistic commentary.[20] In an example of direct borrowing, he takes a convoluted paronym from Rashi at Job 21:24: *'atinav mal'u halav u-moakh 'atsmotav yeshuqeh* ('His pails are full of milk/ The marrow of his bones is juicy'). Taking *'atinav* as 'his breasts', 'a place for fat/milk', and winding through Rashi's discussion of olive presses (b. Menachot 86a), he translates the word as *tetins* (טיטינש).[21] While the Job Commentary was composed after *Uncle and Nephew*, the two texts provide a dialogue of sorts on the status of Jewish languages and on what the very term 'Jewish languages' as written and spoken might mean. *Uncle and Nephew* also contains much biblical commentary in the form of elaborations on Adelard's scientific conclusions.

The Targums, as the *pashtanim* used them together with the French glosses, provide another model of how vernaculars relate to Hebrew in hermeneutic practice and in the transmission and temporality of sacred texts. Writing about their original role in third to sixth-century Galilee, Steven Fraade has located the Targums within a larger rabbinic understanding of multilingualism as history. Aramaic is closest to Hebrew but still not as sacred as the Holy Language; nevertheless, various rabbinic texts consider it not only holy, but a language of revelation.[22] Other midrashim put Aramaic in the context of other languages: for example, the idea that God spoke at Sinai in four languages

---

[20] On Ibn Ezra as a literal exegete, see U. Simon, 'Abraham ibn Ezra' in M. Sæbo, ed., *Hebrew Bible/Old Testament: The History of Its Interpretation*, 3 vols. (Göttingen, 2000), I, 376–87. For a discussion of his multilingualism, see E. Viezel, 'Abraham Ibn Ezra's Commentary on Job 2:11', *Hebrew Union College Annual* 88 (2017), 113–57.

[21] *Commentary*, ed. Wright and trans. Hirsch, p. 63 (Hebrew Section) and p. 147 (English Section). Rashi's commentary on this verse is: 'In Hebrew *'atinav*. This is the language of the Mishnah (Menahoth 86a): "He packs it (*'oteno*) in the olive press." They gather the olives together, and their oil forms globules and gathers in its midst in order to be ready when he presses it in the press, and that vessel in which they gather it in order for its oil to gather within it is called *ma'atan*. Here too, his milk and moisture and fat are called *'atinim, tetins* in *la'az*.'

[22] Fraade, 'Rabbinic Views', pp. 269–73.

(Hebrew, Aramaic, Greek, and Latin) or 70 (the number of all human tongues). As Fraade characterises this strand of rabbinic thought: 'To translate a text of Scripture into one of these languages may be thought of not so much as a distancing from Sinai as a return.'[23] In these midrashim, the unilingual written text is understood by means of multilingual interpretation. This discussion supports Fraade's larger point that the original Palestinian synagogue audiences who heard the weekly shabbat service with the traditional 'twice scripture and once Targum' were not strictly dependent on the oral Aramaic translation to understand the Torah read from the scroll. The bilingual approach, at the time, was for those who understood both languages; Hebrew and Aramaic, heard together, were dependent on each other to produce meaning through the work of ongoing renewal.[24]

Contrary to Fraade's image of the early Palestinian synagogues, Rashi famously asserted that the Targums were meant to serve women and uneducated men, and that Aramaic is the vernacular language of the Babylonians.[25] By the twelfth century, there was a debate among Talmud scholars about the status of the spoken 'twice Hebrew, once Targum' in northern European communities where nobody knew the Aramaic language. Given this reality, some advocated either an 'updating' of Aramaic to the local spoken language or for both Aramaic and the local vernacular to be read on shabbat. Other authorities rejected the current vernacular as a replacement for Aramaic, but considered Rashi's biblical commentary, with its numerous French glosses, as a possible substitute or addition. These disputes show the theoretical distinction between the Targum, as read, and a potential French version. The two can never be precisely equivalent as translated scripture, but they both relate to Hebrew as artefacts of diaspora. For some, Aramaic, although linguistically similar to Hebrew, comes to represent a loss of cultural continuity, and French a possibility of recovery in that loss. By Berekhiah's time, Aramaic had become almost solely a language of study and interpretation, conceptually linked to French as a site of historical change in opposition to Hebrew.[26] The status

[23] Fraade, 'Rabbinic Views', p. 268.

[24] Fraade, 'Rabbinic Views', pp. 273–6.

[25] In his commentary on b. Megillah 21b, Rashi explains that the Targum was intended for an uneducated audience. For the repercussions of this idea in the Middle Ages, see J. Penkower, 'The Process of the Canonization of Rashi's Commentary on the Torah' (Hebrew), in *Study and Knowledge in Jewish Thought*, ed. H. Kreisel (Beersheva, 2006), pp. 123–46.

[26] Penkower, 'The Process', pp. 138–45. See also A. Houtman, 'The Role of the Targum in Jewish Education in Medieval Europe', in *A Jewish Targum in a Christian World*, ed. A. Houtman, E. van Staalduine-Sulman, and H.-M. Kirn (Leiden, 2014), pp. 81–98; and E. Kanarfogel, 'Schools and Education', in *Cambridge History of Judaism, Volume 6: the*

of French as a supplementary written language of interpretation is clearly different from the canonical status of the Aramaic Targums, yet they intersect in a theory of multilingual reading.

Rashi cites the Targums frequently in his biblical commentaries to determine the meaning of a Hebrew term in its context. He occasionally accompanies the Targum's explanation with a French equivalent. For example, on Exodus 9:17, *'odekha mistolel be-ami*: 'Understand this as the Targum does: you tread down my people (Aramaic *kvishat be be-ami*). The Hebrew word *mistolel* is of the same derivation as *mesilah*, which we render in the Targum by "a trodden path" (Aramaic *'orakh kvisha*); in French (*be-la'az*): *chalcier* (קלק״ר וּבְלְעַז)'.[27] Here Rashi uses Targum Onkelos in order to clarify the exact sense of 'to tread' in this place, adding a French equivalent that supports the reading in a double translation.[28] The effect is a harmonizing of temporal distance; the alignment of the two languages, past and current, affirms the meaning of the Hebrew in a continuous process of reading. Rashi's interpretation of Exodus 9:17 continues to his much more common methods of drawing the meaning of Hebrew words from other biblical passages and analyzing grammatical rules, but here he privileges the place of 'our language', the mark of local identity as a translation of both the holy language and the possible next-holy language.

In Job 24:6, Rashi uses Targum Jonathan together with French in an attempt to figure out a hapax in an unusual expression: 'and the wicked gather the plants of the vineyard,' Hebrew *kerem rasha yelaqeshu*. He writes, in full: 'And [from] the vineyards of others these wicked men take their fruit, *esfroitant* (אשפרוייטנט) in French. They take their *leqesh*. *Leqesh* is an expression of a growth of produce (*tsemakh pri*), as in (Amos 7:1) at the beginning of the shooting up of the grain, which [Targum] Jonathan renders *tsimuakh* – growing. And so did Rabbi Eleazar establish (in the Hoshanah "Soil from curse") produce (*leqesh*) from

---

Middle Ages: The Christian World, ed. R. Chazan (Cambridge, 2018), pp. 393–415. On Rashi's use of the Targum, including its relation to the French glosses, see E. Viezel, 'Targum Onkelos in Rashi's Exegetical Consciousness', *The Review of Rabbinic Judaism* 15 (2012), 1–19.

[27] Catane, *Otsar Leazei Rashi*, p. 6, transliterates the word קלק״ר as the French *chalcier*. See T-L for *chauchier* (II, 321–2), 'to tread' or 'to trample', cited in the forms 'calcherent' and 'calcanz' in the twelfth-century *Oxford Psalter* and *Cambridge Psalter*, respectively. See also the AND for the forms *chaucher, calcher, calcer*.

[28] Usually taken metaphorically, as 'to oppress': the JPS translation of Ex. 9:17 is 'Yet you continue to thwart my people, and do not let them go!' See M. Sokoloff, *A Dictionary of Jewish Palestinian Aramaic of the Byzantine Period*, 3rd edn (Ramat Gan, 2017), pp. 266–7.

36   RUTH NISSE

locusts.'[29] Rashi's process of interpretation shows many things, not least the frustrations of reading Job, with its plentiful hapaxes and confusing grammar. As in the Exodus interpretation, he begins with a triangulation. First he translates the Hebrew *yelaqeshu* with an unusual French word that would appear to mean literally 'take away fruit', but he then moves on to Amos 7:1 for the meaning of the noun *leqesh* itself with the Targum's Aramaic for growing crops. The French word is the most immediate possible translation in this reading process, but it must be backed up with the Aramaic translation (*tsimuakh laqish*) of a different aspect of a similar Hebrew word from scripture (*tsemakh*). Neither is complete without the other, given the uncertainty of the entire text's meaning. Rashi is compelled by the ambiguity to offer a further instance of *leqesh* in a liturgical work by the early medieval poet Eleazar Kallir, but his first approach is through an alignment of languages, a potential coherence in the present moment that might shed light on one of many difficulties in Job.

Berekhiah builds on Rashi's modes of interpretation in his engagement with both Aramaic and French in his Job Commentary. To cite an example, 32:4–5: 'Elihu waited out Job's speech, for they were all older than he.' In Hebrew: *Ve-Eliahu ḥikah et-Iyov bi-devarim ki zeqanim-hemah mimenu leyamim*. Rashi himself glosses the word *ḥikah* ('he waited') with the Mishnaic Hebrew *himtin*. Berekhiah, however, explains that 'the Targum [to Job] translates *ḥikah* as *matan*, from which the language of the sages, *matun* ('slow' or 'careful'); *atendre* (אטנדרא) in French.'[30] In this case, the trilingual translation has three components: Hebrew to the Targum's Aramaic to later Talmudic Aramaic and finally to French. In Berekhiah's process, two historical layers of Aramaic mediate between Hebrew and the current vernacular language. The two forms of Aramaic, also frequently cited by Rashi, operate both in terms of translatability of semantic range and their place in the hierarchy of rabbinic authority. Hebrew and French words can be recognised in this case as roughly equivalent in exegesis because of the Aramaic recovery of meaning in

---

[29] For *esfruitier* in Rashi's sense of 'steal fruit', see T-L III, 1060; the word was previously read as *esfroijerent* by Catane, *Otsar Leazei Rashi*, p. 71.

[30] *Commentary*, ed. Wright and trans. Hirsch, pp. 92 (Hebrew) and 215 (English). Rashi explains *ḥikah* with Mishnaic *hamtin*. See M. Jastrow, *A Dictionary of the Targumim, The Talmud Babli and Yerushalmi, and the Midrashic Literature* (Philadelphia, 1883–1903) for examples of the adjective *matun/ metuna* in the sense of 'slow', 'careful', 'patient' (https://www.sefaria.org/ Jastrow%2C_%D7%9E%D6%B8%D7%AA%D7%95%D6%BC%D7%9F_II.1?lang =bi&with=all&lang2=en). See T-L, I, 629–33 for this sense of *atendre*, attested in the *Vie de saint Alexis*. See also AND for *atendre* in the early twelfth-century *Cambridge Psalter*.

the past, the 'language of the sages' – a language at once vernacular, sacred, and linguistically close to Hebrew.

Another example shows Berekhiah's negotiation of multilingualism when faced with a particularly obscure verse from Job (13:27): 'That You put my feet in the stocks/ And watch all my ways,/ Hemming in my footsteps?' In Hebrew: *Ve-tasem ba-sad raglai ve-tishmor kol-'arkhotai, al-shoreshei raglai tithaqeh*. Confronted with the difficulties of the words themselves and the previous interpreters, Berekhiah sets Rashi against Ibn Ezra. Rashi's gloss makes use of both French and German *le 'azim* as well as Talmudic Aramaic in order to clarify the sense of Job's restraints: 'in the stocks Hebrew *be-sad*. In Aramaic (b. Pesachim 28a): "The one who makes the stocks (*sadana*) sits in his own stocks (*be-sadanei*)." [This is] a large [block of] wood in which the prisoners' feet are inserted, *sipa* (ציפא) in French and in the Askenazic language *astok* (אשטוק).'[31] Berekhiah cites Rashi's understanding of stocks without the glosses and then refers to Ibn Ezra for the 'true' literal sense of *sad* and a completely different translation that instead agrees with the alternate Aramaic of the Targum to Job's *shiya* ('plaster' or 'lime'): 'the plain meaning may be that *sad* is like *sid* ('lime'); like a man who throws lime, or flour, or dust round his house or his rooms in order to trace the footsteps of anyone who may come there; and he marks all his paths, and the footsteps become known, and wherever he turned from there, and he pursues and overtakes him if he comes there on another night, compare (Ps. 56:7): "they mark my steps."'[32] Banitt has noted that among other astonishing aspects of this dialogic exegesis, Ibn Ezra's translation of *sad* as 'lime', much elaborated by Berekhiah, is remarkably close to the famous flour-trap scene in Béroul's *Roman de Tristan*.[33] While this reading or listening matter would be unlikely for Ibn Ezra, it would be perfectly in keeping with Berekhiah's attention to Marie de France and Anglo-Norman lapidaries. This long account of a plaster-trap may indeed be a kind of signature of Berekhiah's secular literary interests in a commentary that in general is not terribly innovative – and a sharp cultural turn, beyond the use of glosses, to engagement with an entire French romance. The commentary

---

[31] Catane, *Otsar Leazei Rashi*, p. 69, transliterates צייף as Old French *cep*, but Haketer corrects Rashi's word to ציפא (*sipa*). See *Mikra'ot Gedolot 'Haketer': Job*, ed. Cohen, p. 98. 'Ashkenazic' אשטוק (a stok?) is what we might call Old Yiddish.

[32] *Commentary*, ed. Wright and trans. Hirsch, pp. 41 (Hebrew) and 94 (English). On the traditions that inform Ibn Ezra's interpretation, see *El Comentario de Abraham Ibn Ezra al Libro de Job: Edición Crítica, Traducción y Estudio Introductorio*, ed. and trans. M. Gómez Aranda (Madrid, 2004), p. 110.

[33] M. Banitt makes this observation about Frocin's flour-trick in the *Roman de Tristan* in his Introduction to *Le Glossaire de Leipzig*, I, p. 152.

RUTH NISSE

demonstrates Berekhiah's mastery of his most eminent predecessors' glosses, but also his reluctance, whether explicit or implicit, to choose among them and the competing languages.

Both Rashi and Ibn Ezra make use of multilingualism – the latter with Arabic as well as Aramaic – to underline their own temporal situation in relation to an occasionally incomprehensible Hebrew. Ibn Ezra somewhat outrageously suggested that Job had actually been written in a different language, and that its version of Hebrew was a translation. Berekhiah receives Job as an anthology of interpretations, including one by his uncle Benjamin, and two by his father. This most peculiar book of the bible perhaps attracted his already-honed sense of dialogue and strategic uses of le'azim from *Uncle and Nephew*. He emphasises in particular the actual stakes of translation: Aramaic, French, and German all have a place in Jewish exegesis, and all reflect the diasporic subject, the exegete of the linguistic contact zone. Even if, as is frequently claimed, French mainly serves to explain 'lost' Biblical Hebrew words to other medieval readers, in these examples it is clearly not the primary purpose of the language. *Ḥikah* in Job 32:4 is not an especially obscure Biblical word and Berekhiah first offers two Aramaic translations before *atendre*. Rashi's *garols* ('werewolves') is a vernacular elaboration of a rabbinic Hebrew interpretation of biblical rocks, and, therefore, they represent the insertion of a fanciful Mishnaic field-being and a French folk-literary figure into the murky landscape of Job 5:23. The French glosses in these cases serve the more theoretical aim of inscribing the current spoken Jewish language into scriptural reading as a kind of living Targum, able, once written down, to assume a place in a bilingual and trilingual dialogue about the sacred texts at the level of the word. Like the traditional, fixed Targum, written in a language no longer spoken but read by all learned Jews, it has a relation to Hebrew that exists and changes in time.

At this point, a short excursus on the problem of 'unclean' birds in the 1189 English Codex Valmadonna 1 will illustrate the necessary connections between Hebrew, Aramaic and French as the living language.[34] This manuscript, of the multilingual type described earlier, includes parts of the Torah with alternating Hebrew and Aramaic verses from Targum Onkelos; the weekly readings from the prophets; and the five scrolls with Targums. In the far left margin of fol.72r (most of the text of Leviticus 11), the scribe has listed fourteen of the unclean

---

[34] *The Only Dated Medieval Hebrew Manuscript Written in England (1189 CE) and the Problem of Pre-explusion Anglo-Hebrew Manuscripts*, ed. M. Beit-Arié with appendices by M. Banitt and Z. E. Rokéaḥ (London, 1985). See also Fudeman's detailed linguistic discussion of this manuscript and a thirteenth-century French glossary of birds and other animals in *Vernacular Voices*, pp. 109–115.

birds from verses 13–19 in Hebrew together with the corresponding French terms. His names mostly follow the order of the biblical text, from *nesher/*Aramaic *nisra/ègle* (אייגלא), 'eagle'; to *tinshemet/*Aramaic *bavta/çuète* (צואיט), 'owl'; to the final bird, *shalakh*, which the scribe translates as *malve* (מאלבא), 'seagull', and refers to the Aramaic from Onkelos for the explanation: 'a bird that draws fish from the sea (*shalei nuna*).'[35] Parenthetically, Banitt points out that *malve*, while rare at this time, appears in the form *mauve* in Marie de France's *Isopet*.[36] This page shows the interaction of the three languages in a practical aspect of interpretation, the halakhic importance of figuring out the exact birds that are forbidden to eat. Unknown birds are subject to rabbinic methods for determining cleanness in the Talmud; the named ones are just clean or unclean.[37] The work of interpretation involves all three languages – Holy, historical and also holy, and current. The hierarchy emphasises temporality of signification. The Targums are ancient and fixed explanations of the bible, the work of sages, but French is fluid and without entirely stable meanings. The names of all of the birds are written on this page in alternating Hebrew and Aramaic; but for the scribe, this problem demands current knowledge of the environment. The Aramaic terms and the French are directed toward the same problem of deciphering this part of the Torah, culminating in the nebulous sea bird vaguely defined by Onkelos and understood as the local gull. The French names of these unclean birds are not identical in rabbinic Torah commentaries, given the difficulty of aligning languages with observed nature. In many cases they are similar, but really reflect the distinct strategies of the exegetes. This list, for instance, differs considerably from Rashi's canonical French glosses in his commentary on Leviticus.

The mid twelfth-century *Uncle and Nephew* closely follows the historical moment of the first generation of French glossators. Berekhiah, their heir, nevertheless often favors and cites competing interpretations from Ibn Ezra's works, with their keen interest in Neoplatonism and natural science. In *Uncle and Nephew*, Berekhiah turns his attention not to exegesis but to a secular and

---

[35] There is a reproduction of the manuscript page, plate 4 at the end of *Only Dated*, ed. Beit-Arié: it includes most of Leviticus 11: 13–19, showing the list of birds in the margin.

[36] M. Banitt, 'Appendix 1: The Glosses, 29–31', *Only Dated*, ed. Beit-Arié, pp. 29–31. According to Banitt 'we find *malve* in the twelfth century only in the writings of Anglo-Norman authors such as Marie de France and Philippe de Thaun', p. 31. The word is found in Marie's *Isopet* in the fable 'L'Aigle, l'autour et la grue': 'Dunc [la'] d la maue respondue' (l. 35). Marie de France, *Les Fables*, ed. C. Brucker, 2nd edn (Paris, 1998), p. 306.

[37] B. Ḥullin 62 and Fudeman, *Vernacular Voices*, pp. 109–15.

40 RUTH NISSE

hitsoni or 'external' text to imbue it with many references to the Bible and a very different interplay of languages. As in the Job commentary, he names himself as the author, here directly as 'Berekhiah ben Natronai'. The triangulation in this text is between its original or source language – Latin – Hebrew, and the occasional French words; Aramaic, Greek, and (Pseudo-)Arabic are also all essential to the author's scheme. Berekhiah's central idea of translation is that Adelard's Latin ('the writing of the *goyim* [the nations]', here: Christians), which he creatively identifies as already translated from Arabic, while useful, must be 'purified' from 'the hand of the foreigner'.[38] He is writing in the Holy Language, which excels all others. As the language of Rome, Latin cannot wholly become a Jewish language – or a language of Jewish culture. Yet, as in the rabbinic midrash, Sifre Deuteronomy 343, that includes Latin, along with Aramaic and Greek, in the revelation at Sinai (as the 'language of war'), it is certainly part of the Jewish narrative going back to Rome's origin with Esau.[39] Following this narrative, Berekhiah translates Adelard's debased language into a Hebrew idiom that occasionally employs French terms as a means of marking fissures in the text's multiple languages. If Latin is the language of Christian scholars, French, understood as *leshonenu*, 'our language', becomes the common vernacular in an exploration of newly framed 'natural questions'. Berekhiah may well have discussed this new science in French with Jews and Christians alike, yet French words in the text function as polemic rather than clarification. The handful of *le'azim* in *Uncle and Nephew* do not work to recover senses of terms, as they do, alongside the Targum, in Rashi's biblical commentary; rather, they open the possibility of a substitute for Latin. Among Berekhiah's French glosses are – in Hebrew characters – *melancholien* (15), *estomac(a)* (17–18), *perles* (56), and *folderon* (59). In the most prominent and curious case (57), Berekhiah repeats the translated formula '*qerakh* ("ice") called *grele*' for the substance of 'hail' five distinct times in his brief discussion of lightning and thunder.[40]

---

[38] *UN*, pp. 10 (Hebrew) and 16 (English).

[39] Cited by Fraade, 'Rabbinic Views', p. 267.

[40] *Uncle and Nephew* is textually challenging: there are four surviving manuscripts, all from the fifteenth or sixteenth century. In *UN* Gollancz published Munich, Bayerischer Staatsbibliothek, Cod. Hebr. 42 as the main text and the shorter Oxford, Bodleian Library Bodleian MS Opp. 181 (which also has different, more conventional *le'azim*). Visi has examined all of the manuscripts and concludes that the 'long' Munich manuscript and related parts of a third Leiden manuscript represent the closest text to Berekhiah's original in 'Berechiah ben Natronai ha-Naqdan's *Dodi ve-Nekdi*', pp. 32–6.

Berekhiah's first *la'az* in *Uncle and Nephew* is a translation of the Latin *melancholica*, which, as Adelard explains, is a 'Greek expression' used by scientists 'que Greca appellatione phisici melancholica vocant.'[41] The context is a discussion of animals who are cold and chew the cud (i.e. ruminants), for example oxen, deer, and goats. Berekhiah translates the word as animals 'called cold, and the *goyim* call them *melancolien* (מילקנין).'[42] Later in the same chapter, he says that 'medical doctors call them *melancolien*.'[43] Although the word is one of the French forms for 'melancholy' and would be understood by Berekhiah's readers, it also invokes two other cognates, the Latin *melancholica*, which is itself Adelard's translation of the Greek *melancholikos*. In this multilingual text, French is not brought closer to the Holy Language through paronyms or calques, but instead attached to the older languages of the *goyim*, the peoples of the world. Nevertheless, while foreign and inherently lower than revealed Hebrew, Latin and Greek are, as Berekhiah marks them, essential languages of science. He could clearly read Latin well enough to convey much of Adelard's essentially Neoplatonic collection of ideas about microcosm and macrocosm to Jewish readers. Remarkably, he could also understand and even theorise the subtle movement of languages outside of Hebrew. Greek is the root of the word and concept of 'melancholy', which then becomes Latin and French with little change. From there, Berekhiah writes it as a *la'az*, in Hebrew letters. The temporality of this term for black bile and coldness in humans as well as animals is part of the historical scientific trajectory of the *goyim*, from Greece to Rome to current-day France or England; Berekhiah's translation is an appropriation and improvement of these languages in the time of Jewish diaspora. Even though *Uncle and Nephew* is a translation of Latin, Berekhiah's Hebrew exists both within and outside of its external sources.

Berekhiah's next *la'az*, *istumaka* or *estomad(a)*, is linguistically ambiguous. In the same discussion of animals' digestive systems, he extends Adelard's scientific discourse by introducing a fifth language – Aramaic. The passage concerns why birds have no stomach, but rather a gizzard. He translates the word for Adelard's *stomachum* as איסתומכא (*istumaka*), not actually French as written, but Aramaic, taken from the Talmud, on the laws of slaughtering

---

[41] *Adelard of Bath*, ed. Burnett, pp. 104–05.

[42] As written, the word מילקנין would be the nonexistent 'meilakanin'; Gollancz amended it for the obvious context on p. 14 (Hebrew). Old French *melancolien* is the closest to the corrected form.

[43] *UN*, pp. 14–15 (Hebrew) and 22 (English). See AND for the form *malencolien/melancolien*, attested in the early thirteenth century for the zodiac sign of Taurus and in a slightly later medical text on the humours.

animals and distinguishing kosher from non-kosher (b. Ḥullin 50b).[44] Although it is somewhat unclear from the rabbis' discussion, *istumaka* seems to have the meaning of the inner rumen or opening of the rumen here; Rashi comments 'I have heard *istumaka* in French (*be-la'az*), but I don't know what it is.'[45] Although the precise nature and context of Rashi's uncertainty about the French word that he heard (presumably *estomac*) is unknown, Berekhiah's use of the term *istumaka* – four times in a short discussion of birds – emphatically demonstrates both the similarity and diffusion of languages. Berekhiah, likely familiar with Rashi's link between the Aramaic term and the French *estomac*, takes the two words' similarity into a theoretical realm. The Greek *stomachos* (only implicit here) is the root of both the Aramaic *istumaka* and Latin *stomachum*; the French *estomac* comes from Latin, but is still a quasi-cognate with the Aramaic. Berekhiah offers the two indisputably Jewish languages, together with three indeterminate ones. The rabbis permitted translation of scripture into Greek; Latin is Berekhiah's own source for this material; and French is the language that connects him, and Rashi before him, to the culture of the Christians as well as to contemporary local Jews. The passage and Rashi's gloss also demonstrate the lack of precision and clarity that comes with the evolution and meeting of languages: Berekhiah uses the word *istumaka* for the stomach that other animals (*behemot*) have, but birds do not. For animals' and humans' stomachs in the preceding passage on melancholy, he uses the common Hebrew word *beten*. The dynamic of Berekhiah's apparently unnecessary use of Aramaic in his text recalls Eran Viezel's explication of Rashi's account of a forgotten and revived language. In his commentary on b. Qiddushin 49a, Rashi affirms that that the Targum was given at Sinai, which entailed a circuitous historical trajectory from Moses to the return to Zion, when Ezra read Aramaic to the people, to the fall of the Second Temple and the time of Yavneh, the new centres of rabbinic study and law where Onkelos

---

[44] *Adelard of Bath*, ed. Burnett, pp. 109–11. *UN*, pp. 16 (Hebrew) and 24 (English). For French *estomac*, see T-L III, 1406.

[45] In the only other place the word appears in the Talmud, it refers to a human body: the edge of the ribs near the heart (b. Av. Zar.29a). Rashi on Ḥullin 50b:

איסתומכא דכרסא - אני שמעתי איסתומכ''א בלע''ז ואיני יודע מהו

See Catane's discussion about the similarity of the two words in *Otsar Leazei Rashi*, p. 159, and M. Sokoloff, *Dictionary of Jewish Babylonian Aramaic*, p. 54. See Jastrow, *Dictionary*, on the understanding of 'stomach' as the covering of an organ (https://www.sefaria.org/Jastrow%2C_%D7%90%D6%B4%D7%A1%D6%B0%D7%AA%D6%B9%D6%BC%D7%95%D7%9E%D6%B0%D7%9B%D6%B8%D7%90.1?ven=London,_Luzac,_1903&lang=bi&with=all&lang2=en)

is said to have reconstructed the 'lost' Targum.[46] Berekhiah takes the radical position of applying something like this sacred temporality to his own new theory of translation. *Uncle and Nephew* is written in the Holy Language, with Adelard's Latin (itself supposedly a translation from Arabic) 'purified' and reconstructed with biblical prooftexts and commentaries. Berekhiah's translation is a project of recovery, with the aim of raising Adelard's knowledge into a superior realm, not only in terms of language but current practice. When Berekhiah replaces a section of Adelard's discussion of the soul with Ibn Ezra's from his *Commentary on Ecclesiastes* – composed in Hebrew – he recuperates Neoplatonism, in a perfected tongue, for a Jewish audience.[47] The multilingual *le'azim*, *melancolien* and *istumaka*, punctuate Berekhiah's text, revealing the temporality outside of Hebrew as an inherent aspect of the entire recasting of science and its terminologies.

All of the remaining French words in *Uncle and Nephew* concern thunderstorms and their consequences. The most straightforward of Berekhiah's glosses is '*Margoliot*, translated into *la'az* as *perles* (פיירלש)', an attempt to use French to explain Adelard's oysters who, when they hear thunder, leave their work and hide. It (mis)translates Adelard's *conche marine*: 'shellfish [who] abandon their shells, leaving their pearls (*gemmas*) unfinished.'[48] Possibly Berekhiah had never considered oysters and thunder together, and added the French word to further explain the situation to his confused readers. Berekhiah's next chapter asks 'Where does the ice (*qerakh*) called *grele* (גריילא) come from after thunder?'[49] Some of what Adelard says about hail during thunderstorms is as follows: 'We have sometimes seen, too, such hailstones that their blows have killed brute animals and some people. What then? Surely they should have been called *pieces of ice* rather than hailstones.'[50] He then goes on to describe how sheets of ice descend to the lower realms and become hail. Berekhiah, in his translation, repeats the word *grele* several times for effect, which may clarify a specific form of ice as hail (which, following Adelard, he calls *petotei qerakh* – 'morsels of ice'), but it also presents a polemical response to Latin by supplying an alternate version of

---

[46] Viezel, 'Targum Onkelos', pp. 13–14.

[47] R. Nisse, *Jacob's Shipwreck: Diaspora, Translation, and Jewish-Christian Relations in Medieval England* (Ithaca, 2017), pp. 77–87.

[48] *Adelard of Bath*, ed. Burnett, pp. 202–03; *UN*, pp. 41 (Hebrew) and 59 (English). See AND for *perle*, found in twelfth-century Anglo-Norman lapidaries.

[49] *UN*, pp. 42 (Hebrew) and 61–2 (English).

[50] *Adelard of Bath*, ed. Burnett, pp. 204–05.

one of Jerome's Vulgate translations.[51] Hail, after all, is not an obscure concept in Hebrew; it is one of the ten plagues that God visits upon the Egyptians, and the word *barad* appears no less than seventeen times in Exodus 9–10. The French *la 'az 'qerakh* called *grelé*, then, effectively uses French to obscure Adelard's Latin word for hail, *grando*, the Vulgate's translation of *barad* in Exodus.[52] Fudeman conceptualises this kind of substitution by interpreting Joseph Kara's choice of *haleine* to translate two distinct Hebrew words for 'breath' (or 'soul' or 'spirit') in Job literally (*ruakh* in 7:1 and 9:18; *neshama* in 26:4) as a possible way to 'counter' Jerome's translation of these words as the metaphorical *spiritus* in the Vulgate.[53] While the stakes are more consequential for spirit than hail, *le 'azim* are a way to circumvent Latin words that could constitute Christian exegesis or even come close. Berekhiah, like Kara, repeats the French translation but for emphasis rather than multiple glosses. While he uses the more common word *barad* in a later chapter on atmospheric forces, Berekhiah here subverts this prominent and obvious biblical translation into meteorological words that seem to struggle for equivalence.

Adelard continues with a discussion of thunderbolts: besides the fiery kind, 'sometimes from their throes a stone is born, which is called *ceraunium* by the Greeks, and named "a splitting thunderbolt" by the Latins [Greek *keraunos*, via Isidore of Seville]. Sometimes only the air is struck by it: this is called "a tearing thunderbolt".'[54] Berekhiah translates: 'If the clash is slight and weak through the contact, there issues something of the nature of stone, which Greek scholars call *serlion* (צרליון), shaped like the stag and ram, and it breaks the ice.' Rather than continue with Adelard's discussion, he turns immediately to a relevant passage from the Book of Job:

> So explain the wise men. But I the copyist, say: we find it explained in scripture thus: 'Out of whose womb came the ice (*kefor*)? And the hoary frost (*qerakh*) of heaven, who has given it birth?' (Job, 38:29) This is what God said to Job, and without these words, he would not have known it.

For Berekhiah, Adelard's Greek provides a new opportunity to put Hebrew – his own and the biblical language – into dialogue with French and Latin – plus the language of 'the Greek scholars.' In the voice of the inquiring Nephew, he earlier uses the *la 'az foldrin* (פולרדין) for the scary noise of

---

[51] *UN*, pp. 42 (Hebrew) and 61–2 (English).

[52] See Rashi's use of *gresle* as a gloss for *barad* (hail) in Ps. 148: 8.

[53] K. Fudeman, 'The Linguistic Significance of the Le'azim in Joseph Kara's Job Commentary', *Jewish Quarterly Review* 43 (2003), 397–414 (p. 400).

[54] *Adelard of Bath*, ed. Burnett, pp. 206–07.

a kind of thunderbolt that he himself has experienced, corresponding to Old French *foudrien* or *fuildrin*.[55] The entire sequence defines limits: there is no available Latin or Hebrew word for the thunderbolt-stone itself, so Berekhiah leaves it as the distorted-Greek *serion*.[56] He winds up the entire section with the limits of scientific authority itself. He, the scribe, knows more than the Greek wise men, because he also interprets Hebrew scripture – in particular, Job with its wealth of meteorological references. Rashi glosses *qerakh* as *glace* in this passage of Job, making the French translation part of the Divine lesson. *Keraunos* may have been been distorted through transmission by other scribes to the point that its meaning is uncertain, but in the language of the bible the question of its creation ideally remains stable. Greek, in this brief appearance, is the language of ancient knowledge and historically prior to Latin. Like French, it is a *la'az*, foreign in Berekhiah's text – distinct from, and subordinate to, Job's theophany in the transcendent Holy Language.

Berekhiah's vision of multilingualism comes into focus in his two works taken together: the Job Commentary locates him within the intellectual currents of late twelfth-century France and England as a follower of the *pashtanim,* producing Hebrew meaning through the Targums and the French of the *le'azim,* the current language in a sense of diasporic continuity. *Uncle and Nephew,* however, is a radical departure into the languages of other people, a work in which Latin is essential for Jewish knowledge yet just the most immediate, after French, among a constellation of other languages. Latin is derivative of Greek, not holy like Aramaic, and in the text at hand, not even the original language. In reality, however, Berekhiah must have taken pains to obtain a manuscript of Adelard's recent work; even as he seeks to marginalise Latin through linguistic interventions, its value is obvious as the basis of his free translation and interpretation. The French glosses are crucial elements of both works' concepts of language. In the Job commentary, Berekhiah follows Rashi's work of recovery and invention, the inclusion of the current time and local space in a Hebrew and Aramaic text; the ultimate goal of translation is to bring the French language, at once foreign and ours, *leshonenu,* closer to Hebrew. Even if attenuated from Rashi's project, Berekhiah's French words

---

[55] 'There is no noise like the noise of the thunder called *foldrin.' UN*, pp. 43 (Hebrew) and 63 (English). These adjectives are the closest forms of *foudre* in T-L, III, 2178–80. For *fuildrin,* see AND, *fuildrin*; for *foudrien,* see *foudrien, DEAFpré Online,* ed. F. Möhren and T. Städtler, accessed 29 Jan 2023, https://deaf-server.adw.uni-heidelberg.de/lemme/foudre#foudrien

[56] Jane Gilbert suggested to me that the French *cerf* ('stag') could possibly be the *ser* in the enigmatic *serlion,* supposedly shaped like a stag and ram.

mark his contemporary identity. In *Uncle and Nephew*, by contrast, the *le'azim* reveal the developments of language itself. The French glosses – French concealed in Aramaic in the case of *istumaka* – push Latin to its limits and extend Adelard's own multilingualism with the addition of the holy languages. French in this Hebrew text is no longer *leshonenu*, but only the most recent mode of language. Berekhiah's only real language, as he declares by name, is Hebrew. French is instrumental in its historicity; Latin is challenged by previous languages, but also by the present.

2

From Liutprand of Cremona to Robert de Clari: Wonder and the Translation of Knowledge Before and After the Crusader Conquest of Constantinople[1]

Teresa Shawcross

In the high summer of 1203, as the fleet of the Fourth Crusade passed through the Dardanelles and began to make its way up the Sea of Marmara towards the Bosporus, the soldiers aboard the cogs, galleys and horse-transports caught sight of the imperial capital: Constantinople. To those who drew near to it under canvas, the fabled city, 'rich in renown', appeared on the horizon as 'triangular in shape' – its outline resembling that of the sail of another ship, or perhaps an island.[2] While two of the city's sides jutted out into the water, the third – as the troops would soon discover – was linked to a vast hinterland of

---

[1] The research presented here was made possible by the award of a Visiting Fellowship at CRASSH of Cambridge University. A substantial debt is also owed to Nicholas Paul, Laura Morreale and the other collaborators in the *French of Outremer* project housed in the Center for Medieval Studies at Fordham University, as well as to Thomas O'Donnell and the other organisers of the 'French Without Borders' conference held virtually at Fordham in 2021. Finally, thanks are due to the editors of the volume for inviting this contribution. In conformity with the conventions of the volume as a whole, quotations in this study from French texts are reproduced then translated, while passages from texts in other languages (e.g. Latin, Old Norse) are translated only. However, the Greek that is embedded in western texts is reproduced in the original form in which it is preserved in the manuscript tradition. This means that Greek words are sometimes rendered in the Greek alphabet and at other times transliterated into the Latin alphabet.

[2] Odo of Deuil, *De Profectione Ludovici VII in orientem*, ed. and trans. V. G. Berry (New York, 1948), p. 62; *The Chronicle of Morea*, ed. J. Schmitt (London, 1904), pp. 36–8 (v.333); E. Malamut, *Les Îles de l'empire byzantin, VIIe–XIIe siècles*, 2 vols. (Paris, 1988), II, 613–21.

48   TERESA SHAWCROSS

gardens, arable land cultivated by plough and harrow, and 'groves planted with beautiful pines and laurels' ('vergers plantez de pins e de lorers beaus').[3]

The Constantinople that lay before the crusaders was an impressive place: a cosmopolitan city that provided the focal point for far-flung commercial networks and attracted visitors of many languages and ethnicities. All routes, whether of brine or dirt, led here from the Balkans, the Black Sea and the Mediterranean – converging on the formidable fortifications and arched gates, where they became a series of broad, colonnaded avenues crossing spacious squares and circuses before terminating at the milestone, the Milion, at the very heart of the urban plan. Nearest the sea, towering over the manmade anchorages and natural estuary that made up the city's harbours, stood the gigantic complex of the Great Palace, the Church of the Holy Wisdom and the Hippodrome. Of great age – and noted for their unparalleled collections of relics and other treasures – these resplendent edifices were the focal point of civic and religious ceremonial. At the opposite end of the peninsula, resting against a protuberance in the land walls, was a second lofty complex, the Vlacherna Citadel, known for its elegance and its skilful construction. This acted as the main residence of the imperial family as well as the main location of the ordinary business of government. The city presented an urban landscape replete with fountains, statues, and columns 'looming like massive giants'. Its skyline shimmered and soared, with all available surfaces seemingly having been made to ripple with marble, glint with mosaics or glow with burnished metals. Towers, bridges and imperial eagles all gleamed. Exteriors of 'incomparable loveliness' were surpassed only by interiors decorated in 'varied hues' with lavish materials arranged with such artistic subtlety they created the impression of immeasurable beauty. The cumulative visual effect was nothing if not stunning.[4]

---

[3]   Odo of Deuil, *De Profectione Ludovici*, pp. 62–4; Повѣсть времаньныхъ лѣтъ (*Povest' vremennych let*), trans. S. H. Cross and O. P. Sherbowitz-Wetzor (Cambridge MA, 1953), pp. 65–8; *Le Pèlerinage de Charlemagne*, ed. G. S. Burgess (Edinburgh, 1998), p. 18 (v.265).

[4]   É. Legrand, 'Description des œuvres d'art et de l'église des Saints Apôtres de Constantinople: poème en vers iambiques par Constantin le Rhodien', *Revue des études grecques* 9 (1896), 32–65 (p. 46). For the physical aspects of Constantinople, see: J. Harris, *Constantinople: Capital of Byzantium* (London, 2007); N. Necipoğlu, *Byzantine Constantinople: Monuments, Topography and Everyday Life* (Leiden, 2001); C. Mango, *Studies in Constantinople* (Aldershot, 1993); *Constantinople and its Hinterland: Papers from the Twenty-Seventh Spring Symposium of Byzantine Studies, Oxford, April 1993*, ed. C. Mango, G. Dagron, and G. Greatrex (London, 1995); R. Janin, *Constantinople byzantine* (Paris, 1964).

Constantinople was not just a 'beautiful and excellent' city. It was 'rich' ('riche') and 'redoutable' ('vaillant') – 'of all other cities the sovereign queen' ('la vile qui de toutes autres estoit souverainne'), as one observer arriving with the crusader fleet noted.[5] In the two main surviving narratives known as the *Conqueste de Constantinoble* that related the approach of the crusader fleet, the authors – the Champenois Geoffroy de Villehardouin, marshal of one of the main contingents of the fighting forces, and the Picard Robert de Clari, a more humble knight – depicted their comrades gazing on 'the grandeur of the city' ('le grandeur de le vile'). Coming within striking distance and readying to anchor, the men from Flanders, Champagne, Blois, Picardy, Lombardy and the Veneto, we are told, stared long and hard. Overawed by what they found before them, they could scarcely credit the veracity of what their eyes were telling them. They had not believed a place 'like this could exist anywhere on earth'. So filled with wonderment were they that there was no man among them who did not feel 'his flesh quiver' ('n'i ot si hardi qui la char ne fremist').[6] The narratives treated the crusaders' arrival at the gates and subsequent breaches of the fortifications as if these constituted an unprecedented encounter with a wholly unknown entity that eluded habitual understanding. It was as if Constantinople were a place that had only at that very moment been discovered.

The insistence on novelty was, of course, disingenuous. To be sure, the familiarity with Constantinople of westerners may not have been that of a native courtier or emperor who was accustomed to seeing 'at every hour' without ever 'leaving the palace' all the 'new inventions' assembled there for his delectation.[7] But over the previous three hundred years, the city had increasingly acted as a magnet for large numbers of those who, 'drawn from

---

[5] Fulcher of Chartres, *Historia Hierosolymitana (1095–1127)*, ed. H. Hagenmeyer (Heidelberg, 1913), pp. 176–7; Geoffroy de Villehardouin, *La Conquête de Constantinople*, ed. J. Dufournet (Paris, 2004), p. 102; *Pèlerinage de Charlemagne*, ed. Burgess, p. 18 (v.262).

[6] Geoffroy de Villehardouin, *La Conquête de Constantinople*, p. 102; Robert de Clari, *La Conquête de Constantinople*, ed. J. Dufournet (Paris, 2004), p. 106. For the reaction of the crusaders, see D. E. Queller and T. E. Madden, *The Fourth Crusade and the Conquest of Constantinople* (Philadelphia, 1997), pp. 137–40; R. Macrides, 'Constantinople: The Crusaders' Gaze', *Travel in the Byzantine World*, ed. R. Macrides (Aldershot, 2002), pp. 193–212; J. Phillips, *The Fourth Crusade and the Sack of Constantinople* (London, 2004), pp. 144–5.

[7] Constantine Manasses, *Constantini Manassis breviarium chronicum*, ed. O. Lampsides, 2 vols. (Athens, 1996), I, 281–2.

almost every nation' of western Europe, were commonly 'called Franks'.[8] Diplomatic missions were routinely sent to the Byzantine Empire, and many tens of thousands of westerners intent on pilgrimage or trade had passed through Constantinople – a significant portion of whom made the city their home. Moreover, one did not need to rely on first-hand experience since one could also access information about the urban landscape 'from afar' ('de luign'). Set descriptions of encounters with the great metropolis were already a well-established part of the western literary repertoire. Initially composed in Latin, then gradually also in Old French, a series of writings across a range of genres had not merely enumerated the wonders of an urban landscape but also presented a clearly-defined range of reactions to those wonders.[9]

This study's aim is to highlight some of the strategies used by western texts to portray the imperial capital. After introducing and analysing the descriptions of the sights and sounds of Constantinople in works composed from the mid tenth to the late twelfth century – works ranging from travelogues that purported to relate the facts to overtly fictionalised accounts – it turns to texts from the early thirteenth century in order to determine the degree to which they conformed to earlier practices. As we shall see, authors had recourse to specific rhetorical figures by which they insisted that the means of expression available to them could not adequately evoke the place whose characteristics they were trying to convey to their readership. Authors also displayed a tendency to reproduce words and phrases either in the Greek alphabet or transliterated into the Latin alphabet – sometimes, but not always, accompanying the terms in question with a translation or other semantic gloss. The employment or avoidance in specific passages of code-switching, borrowing and other forms of interaction between languages served to convey a range of effects. Emphasising solidarity or difference, such strategies allowed both author and readers to explore issues of identity and define power relations.[10]

---

[8] Walter Map, *De nugis curialium*, ed. and trans. M. R. James, rev. R. Mynors (Oxford, 2002), p. 178; K. N. Ciggaar, 'Une description de Constantinople dans le Tarragonensis 55', *Revue des études byzantines* 53 (1995), 117–140 (p. 119); C. Rapp, 'A Medieval Cosmopolis: Constantinople and its Foreigners', in *Constantinople as Center and Crossroad*, ed. O. Heilo and I. Nilsson (Istanbul, 2019), pp. 100–15.

[9] *Pèlerinage de Charlemagne*, ed. Burgess, p. 24 (v.386). On the concept, see C. W. Bynum, 'Wonder', *American Historical Review* 102 (1997), 1–26.

[10] For approaches to Greek in Western Europe during the Middle Ages, see B. Bischoff, 'Das griechische Element in der abendländischen Bildung des Mittelalters', *Byzantinische Zeitschrift* 44 (1951), 27–55; and W. Berschin, *Greek Letters and the Latin Middle Ages: From Jerome to Nicholas of Cusa* (Washington, D.C., 1988).

In the Latin and French texts describing the Byzantine Empire that were produced in the tenth, eleventh and twelfth centuries, language-mixing was identified as an asymmetrical endeavour, with Greek representing the tongue of the politically and socially dominant group, and Latin and French belonging to the subordinate group. This mixing signalled the acknowledgement on the part of those employing it that they had not become fully acculturated but instead found themselves caught suspended between two cultural systems. Moreover, much of the material that made up the content of these texts can be shown not to have originated in the authentic first-hand observations of travellers, but rather to have been taken from official guides produced and disseminated by the Byzantines themselves. Western authors often displayed little independence in their transmission and interpretation of this material, instead contenting themselves with halting and imperfect word-for-word renditions of their sources. The resulting domination by the discourse of the host culture belied assertions by westerners that theirs was a high degree of linguistic fluency and social insight enabling them to converse with the emperor and his court and be treated as near equals.

The corpus that was created before the thirteenth century under the influence of eastern models was not merely known to the participants in the Fourth Crusade but also fundamentally shaped the content and organisation of the narratives they produced. Yet this intertextual web remained unacknowledged following the conquest. Instead, the chronicles in the French vernacular composed during the initial decades of the thirteenth century presented themselves as having been created in a spirit of triumphalism out of a virgin discourse uncorrupted by any earlier attempts to come to grips with Byzantium. This permitted responses that had previously been impossible. The originality of genre and language – the group of narratives that are known as the *Conqueste de Constantinoble* are among the very first examples we have of histories composed in prose in French – permitted the chronicles ostensibly to begin anew, erasing the traumatic memory of earlier encounters and allowing the negotiation of a more satisfying relationship with the city. What the crusaders undertook was not the destruction and abandonment of the imperial capital and consequent dismantling of the imperial provinces into a series of smaller independent kingdoms and principalities, but rather a redistribution of property, moveable possessions and other resources that were carried out while preserving intact the overarching imperial framework. The new regime would increasingly articulate a sense of intimacy with its surroundings. Through the performance and recording of ritual, it would define the process less as a gradual one of assimilation than as the recovery of an intuitive, visceral form of understanding allegedly surpassing that of the indigenous inhabitants, whose

TERESA SHAWCROSS

traditions were co-opted and whose authority was discredited. By framing the invasion and installation of an occupying regime as an act that sought to erase the influence of corruption and restore the integrity of the Byzantine Empire, the narratives composed by the crusaders sought to monopolise interpretation and establish claims of moral superiority.

Feelings of wonder

On a normal day in the mid twelfth century, a citizen out on a stroll in Constantinople would have expected to cross paths with western visitors, with whom he might casually chat for several minutes regarding their place of origin and the experiences they had had during their journey, before getting to the point and enquiring whether it was their ambition to stay and number themselves among the half a million inhabitants of the vast and teeming metropolis.[11] Indeed, these foreigners, who included pilgrims, diplomats, mercenaries and merchants, did often seek to settle. Different ethnic groups had been assigned specific districts, with the 'Lombards', the 'English', the 'Varangians', the 'Dacians', the 'Amalfitans' all having 'their own places of residence'.[12] Certain of these groups, such as the Venetians, had been for over a hundred years the beneficiaries of privileges granting them the use of wharves and warehouses where they could unload and store merchandise, of inns and houses where they could live and transact business, of mills where flour could be ground, and of churches where masses could be said.[13]

---

[11] H. Hunger, 'Zum Epilog der Theogonie des Johannes Tzetzes', *Byzantinische Zeitschrift* 46 (1953), 302–307 (pp. 304–5).

[12] Ciggaar, 'Tarragonensis', p. 119.

[13] Fulcher, *Historia Hierosolymitana*, p. 176 (I.viii.9); *Urkunden zur älteren Handels- und Staatsgeschichte der Republik Venedig mit besonderer Beziehung auf Byzanz und die Levante vom neunten bis zum Ausgang des fünfzehnten Jahrhunderts*, ed. G. L. F. Tafel and G. M. Thomas, 3 vols. (Vienna, 1856–7), I, 43–54, 95–8, 109–24, 150–167, 175, 179–204 (nos. 23, 43, 50–1, 62, 67, 70–2); D. M. Nicol, *Byzantium and Venice: A Study in Diplomatic and Cultural Relations* (Cambridge, 1988), pp. 60–1, 77–8, 97–102, 106–8, 116–17, 121. See D. Jacoby, 'The Venetian Quarter of Constantinople from 1082 to 1261: Topographical Considerations', *Novum millennium: Studies in Byzantine History and Culture, dedicated to Paul Speck*, ed. C. Sode and S. Takács (Aldershot, 2001), pp. 153–70; M. E. Martin, 'The Chrysobull of Alexius I Comnenus to the Venetians and the Early Venetian Quarter in Constantinople', *Byzantinoslavica* (1978), pp. 19–23; H. F. Brown, 'The Venetians and the Venetian Quarter in Constantinople to the Close of the Twelfth Century', *The Journal of Hellenic Studies* 40 (1920), 68–88; compare with C. Desimoni, 'I Genovesi ed i loro quartieri in Constantinopli nel secolo XIII', *Giornale ligustico di archeologia, storia, e belle arti* 3 (1876), 217–74.

2.1. Constantinople, Great Church of the Holy Wisdom, Southern Gallery balustrade, graffito, tenth to eleventh centuries (?). Runes attributed to a member of the palatine Varangian Guard. Transcribed as [...] FTAN [...]TR[...]SAL[...]IA[...]A[R?] and thought to have once read 'Halfdan carved these runes'. Creative Commons Licence 3.0. Courtesy of Wikimedia Commons.

The status of these communities remained nonetheless precarious and the foreigners who comprised them were well aware that they lived within the empire on sufferance. Despite being required to declare their loyalty to the emperor at regular intervals, such displays did not fundamentally change their status. They remained interlopers whose right to residency could be abruptly revoked. They could, at any time, find their goods confiscated and their persons rounded up and either banished or massacred. Such threats hung constantly over resident foreigners, with their fears being heightened by the arrests of 1171 and the pogrom of 1182.[14] On one occasion, at least 10,000 Venetians were rounded up in the capital and provinces. Their doge back in Venice proffered a resistance that proved to be entirely ineffectual, receiving for his pains a public dressing-down from the emperor, who warned him that 'no-one, not even someone representing the greatest powers on earth, makes war' with the Byzantines 'with impunity'. Those who had entertained, however briefly, the thought that they 'could match the strength' of the Byzantines had only revealed their 'stupidity' and made themselves into 'a general laughing stock'.[15] During another attack directed against westerners, a few Genoese, Venetians and others of maritime origin scrambled to board their ships to leave, but the majority, unable to flee in time, either perished in the flames

---

[14] K. N. Ciggaar, *Western Travellers to Constantinople: The West and Byzantium, 962–1204* (Leiden, 1996), pp. 33, 34, 75, 183, 231; C. Brand, *Byzantium Confronts the West* (Cambridge, MA, 1968), pp. 15–12, 31–42; T. Madden, *Enrico Dandolo and the Rise of Venice* (Baltimore, 2003), pp. 50–6, 80–2; Nicol, *Byzantium and Venice*, pp. 98–100.

[15] John Cinnamus, *Ioannis Cinnami epitome rerum ab Ioanne et Alexio Comnenis gestarum*, ed. A. Meineke (Bonn, 1836), p. 285.

when their places of residence were set on fire, or were dragged outside and 'put to the sword', or otherwise died 'under excruciating torture'.[16]

Even when not directly imperiled, westerners living and working in Constantinople were marginalised. While some sought to make their mark by inscribing their names in the marble revetments of the galleries of the Church of the Holy Wisdom at the city's centre ('[H]alfdan [carved these runes]', or 'Árni m[ade these runes]'), these carvings constituted little more than graffiti: furtive, half-legible scratchings more redolent of a puerile attempt at the subversion of authority than an indication of meaningful integration within the regime (Plate 2.1).[17] This relegation of foreigners to the periphery of society was given voice in writings that portrayed Constantinople not only as a highly desirable place to live, but also one whose very desirability prompted feelings of disorientation and even a kind of paralysis. Descriptions of 'wondrous things' and 'wondrous sights' formed 'in a wondrous fashion' that produced in the beholder a 'stupefaction of the mind' had become a standard feature of western accounts of the city.[18] An anonymous travelogue from the eleventh century rehearsed in what became established as conventional terms its author's amazement upon arrival in a Constantinople full of 'innumerable temples of marble' with 'gold depictions inside' and 'lead roofs covering them', 'palaces that were also of marble and had similar lead roofs', as well as 'likenesses of quadrupeds and birds and all other types of creatures that had been formed with artifice in a most wondrous manner out of bronze and metal'.[19]

One of the earliest examples of these western writings was the tenth-century memoir of an embassy to the imperial court composed in Latin

[16] Walter Map, *De nugis curialium*, ed. and trans. James, rev. Mynors, 178; Nicetas Choniates, *Nicetae Choniatae historia*, ed. J. A. van Dieten, 2 vols. (Berlin, 1975), I, 171–2, 251; *Willelmi Tyrensis Archiepiscopi chronicon*, ed. R. B. C. Huygens, 3 vols. (Turnthout, 1986), II, 1020–1.

[17] E. Svärdström, 'Runorna i Hagia Sofia', *Fornvännen* 65 (1970), 247–9; M. G. Larsson, 'Nyfunna runor i Hagia Sofia', *Fornvännen* 84 (1989), 12–14; J. E. Knirk, 'Runer i Hagia Sofia i Istanbul', *Nytt om runer 14* (1999), 26–7.

[18] K. N. Ciggaar, 'Une description anonyme de Constantinople du XIIe siècle', *Revue des études byzantines* 31 (1973), 335–54 (p. 338), and 'Une description de Constantinople traduite par un pèlerin anglais', *Revue des études byzantines* 34 (1976), pp. 211–68 (pp. 245, 263). The idealisation of Constantinople in medieval western culture is discussed in: G. Heng, *Empire of Magic: Medieval Romance and the Politics of Cultural Fantasy* (New York, 2003), pp. 9–10; W. Burgwinkle, 'Utopia and its Uses: Twelfth-Century Romance and History', *Journal of Medieval and Early Modern Studies* 36 (2006), 539–60; R. Devereaux, *Constantinople and the West in Medieval French Literature: Renewal and Utopia* (Cambridge, 2012).

[19] Ciggaar, 'Tarragonensis', pp. 119–28.

by Liutprand, bishop of Cremona. Liutprand's account, known as the *Antapodosis*, recounted at some length an audience and a banquet, as well as other scenes from the palace, dwelling in particular on the various kinds of magic performed at court. The author described in detail the imperial throne, which was 'of immense size' and 'marvellously fashioned'. Guarded by 'lions' of gold 'who beat the ground with their tails and gave a dreadful roar with open mouth and flickering tongue', this throne was said to have levitated suddenly during audiences, at one moment being 'a low structure' and at another rising 'high into the air'.[20] Of both a visual and aural nature, the special effects were carefully timed by the hosts so that, following the entrance of an ambassador and his performance of the act of obeisance before the throne, 'the lions begin to roar, and the birds [...] begin to sing' and the other 'beasts' stand 'upright', while, at his departure, 'the lions subside and the birds stop singing' and the 'beasts sit down in their places'.[21] Furthermore, an atmosphere of anticipation was cultivated by officials during the approach and entrance of the delegation. The very portals to these extraordinary palatine spaces featured doors that did not creak or grind in the fashion usual elsewhere, but instead when opening performed 'a tuneful song' whose words could be recognised as celebrating the ruler within ('the song says: "Glory of rulers! O Emperor! O King!"').[22]

By the twelfth century, texts in Latin giving information regarding the arrival and reception of foreigners had been joined by texts in French containing more overtly fictional content. These included lengthy poems, such as the *Pèlerinage de Charlemagne* and the *Chanson de Girart de Roussillon*, telling of the feats of Charlemagne or Charles Martel and their companions. The poems recounted stories of these men's initial sighting of Constantinople, then their meeting outside the walls with the emperor and his court, their passage through the gates, their arrival and reception at the palace, and their establishment in lodgings. The buildings the Franks entered were repeatedly presented on a superhuman scale: they were said to be constructed with huge spans of vaulting and massive supports of marble, decorated with revetments and mosaics of precious stones, equipped with furniture that was constructed of gold and silver, and strewn with soft furnishings of silk and velvet. One

[20] *Opera omnia Liudprandi Cremonensis*, ed. P. Chiesa (Turnhout, 1998), p. 149.

[21] Constantine VII Porphyrogenitus, *De ceremoniis aulae byzantinae libri duo*, ed. J.J. Reiske, 2 vols. (Bonn, 1829–1840), II, 568–9; J. Trilling, 'Daedalus and the Nightingale: Art and Technology in the Myth of the Byzantine Court', in *Byzantine Court Culture from 829 to 1204*, ed. H. Maguire (Washington, 1997), pp. 217–30.

[22] P. Magdalino, 'The Bath of Leo the Wise and the 'Macedonian Renaissance' Revisited: Topography, Iconography, Ceremonial, Ideology', *Dumbarton Oaks Papers* 42 (1988), 97–118.

56   TERESA SHAWCROSS

palace, instead of being anchored to the ground by a foundation, was alleged in the *Pèlerinage* to 'revolve slightly and often' ('turner e menut e suvent') when it was struck by a 'breeze or other wind' ('bise ne altre vent'). Emphasis was put on the city's relationship with the supernatural. Inanimate objects were apparently endowed with qualities normally the preserve of living creatures. Among the wonders listed were two figures 'cast in copper and metal' ('[d]e quivre e de metal tregeté') so skilfully wrought that they could move and emit sounds such that 'you would swear they were completely alive' ('ço vus fust viarie que tut fussent vivant').[23]

Through such accounts, Constantinople was presented as a place where one's ordinary purchase on the external world was loosened. It was a place where visitors had the solid ground suddenly pulled from under them – so that they fell down and remained prostrate, their disorientation rendering them unable to do anything but cover their heads and cry out in abject terror.[24] It was not merely that the roaring golden lions around the imperial throne reminded diplomats of all that their people would face should the might of the empire be unleashed: the 'terrifying' lions and other monsters that were mounted on the prows of Byzantine warships and that spewed forth the unquenchable curtain of flame that was known as 'Greek Fire'.[25] Rather, constant conjuring by imperial necromancers ('nigromanz') made, we are told, 'the images of great things appear as signs' ('signs par samblances granz aparer') in the sky above the city. Whereas, for the emperor who ordered them, such spectacles constituted 'courtly games' ('jous corteis') put on for his amusement, for foreigners they were 'strange games' ('jous estrains').· Including uncanny feats such as raising 'a tempest of rain' ('tanpez plover'), these spectacles were meant to provide an intimation of the exercise of authority by the imperial regime over the cosmos, reinforcing the westerners' total subordination.[26] Forbidden any knowledge of the secrets of the wonders before them, these westerners were denied the tools that might permit them to advance from the position of inferiority to which

---

[23] *Pèlerinage de Charlemagne*, ed. Burgess, pp. 22–4 (vv.334–399); L. Polak, 'Charlemagne and the Marvels of Constantinople', in *The Medieval Alexander and Romance Epic*, ed. P. Noble, L. Polak and C. Isoz (New York, 1982), pp. 159–171 (p. 164).

[24] *Pèlerinage de Charlemagne*, ed. Burgess, p. 24 (vv.385–99); see also the reference to 'pavor' in *La Chanson de Girart de Rousillon*, ed. M. de Combarieu du Grès and G. Gouiran (Paris, 1993), p. 56 (v.215).

[25] Anna Comnena, *Annae Comnenae Alexias*, ed. D. R. Reinsch and A. Kambylis, 2 vols. (Berlin, 2001), I, 350.

[26] *Chanson de Girart de Rousillon*, ed. de Combarieu du Grès and Gouiran, 56 (vv.203–22).

they had been relegated. They remained entirely dependent upon the whims of their hosts. Moreover, the exposure of visitors to a collection of strange sights and sounds was intended to inspire 'special fear' and 'admiration' not only in those who observed the phenomena directly but also in those who merely received reports of them.[27]

The Inadequacies of language

'I neither know nor can tell', admitted the anonymous author of one twelfth-century travelogue concerned with Constantinople. Another stated: 'I cannot … enumerate, nor do I know. I cannot write …' Such confessions of incapacity underscored the notion that arrival in the Byzantine capital entailed contact with something that was not only beyond westerners' ordinary knowledge, but also beyond their ordinary articulateness. The frequent use of rhetorical figures such as *aporia* and *admiratio* (as well as *epimone, amplificatio* and, conversely, *paralypsis, adynaton*) emphasised the fundamental inexpressibility of what was being described. 'It is exceedingly difficult' to convey in words what is to 'be found there' another author declared, adding that the reality 'surpasses anything I can say about it'. The sights of the capital were such, according to yet another author, that 'no-one, to be sure' could give a 'satisfactory account'.[28] Authors claimed to have made efforts to overcome their aphasia through the acquisition of the rudiments of the language of the empire. One individual stated that he had studied 'Greek letters and the Greek language'. Another explained that his family had arranged an immersive course of study for him, underwriting the costs of tuition. The texts even coined a neologism, 'grecolonon', by which they designated a person who knew something of 'the Greek language'.[29] Such was said to be the effect of Constantinople upon people that it 'led us to transform even our discourse'.

Statements of this type on the part of western authors regarding the pursuit of Greek learning through participation in formal instruction or personal study are borne out by contemporary practices. A number of manuscripts from the eleventh and twelfth centuries contain lists of words and phrases that were first given in Latin and then translated into Greek (Plates 2.2–3). Content included greetings ('Good day to you: *calos ymera si*') and salutations ('May God grant you many years: *Poli coron pissem na se o theos*; God save you! *Calo*

---

[27] Constantine VII Porphyrogenitus, *De ceremoniis*, ed. Reiske, II, 568–9; Trilling, 'Daedalus and the Nightingale', ed. Maguire, pp. 217–30.

[28] Ciggaar, 'Pèlerin anglais', pp. 245, 263 and Ciggaar, 'Anonyme', p. 338; Odo of Deuil, *De profectione Ludovici*, pp. 64–5; Fulcher, *Historia Hierosolymitana*, p. 177.

[29] Ciggaar, 'Tarragonensis', 125; *Opera Liudprandi*, ed. Chiesa, pp. 207–8.

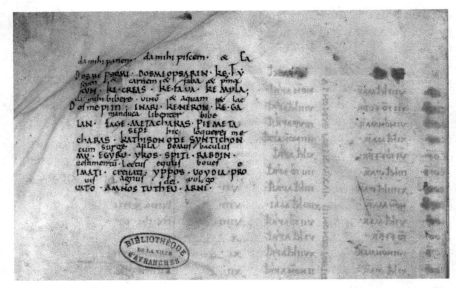

2.2. Avranches, Bibliothèque patrimoniale, MS 236, fol. 97v, eleventh century (?), detail. Latin-Greek wordlist. Courtesy of the Commune nouvelle d'Avranches.

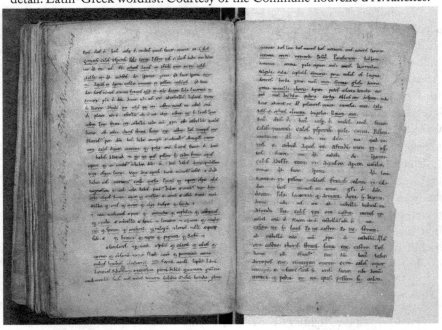

2.3. Auxerre, Bm, MS 212, fols. 133v–134r, twelfth century (?). Beginning of a Latin-Greek wordlist copied multiple times in different hands. Creative Commons Licence 3.0. Courtesy of Bibliothèque municipale d'Auxerre.

sosis e o theos'). There were also words for 'horse' ('YPPOS'), 'bed' ('CREUATI'), 'house' ('SPITI') or 'mansion' ('YKOS'), 'clothing' or 'shirt' ('IMATI'; 'imati mou'); requests for directions (e.g. 'Tell me, where is the castle: *Si levis, po ne castro?*'; 'Which is the road to the castle: *Pourze strata oto castro?*'); orders of food and drink (e.g. 'Give me bread: *DOSME PSOMI*; give me fish: *DOSME OPSARIN*; and cheese and meat and fava and apples: *KE TYRYN KE CREAS KE FAVA KE MYLA*. Give me wine and water and milk to drink: *DOS ME PIIN INARI KE NERON KE GALAN*'); and other simple and useful words and phrases (e.g. 'Monday: *dextera*, Tuesday: *triti...*'; 'head: *cephalis*, eyes: *obmatia*: nose: *miti*'). One sequence concerned a commercial transaction during which buyer and seller haggle ('Do you have anything to sell: *Equis tipote que amna pulissem?* [...] I have. Do you want to buy: *Esquo. Celis nagorassem?*, etc.'). Some were concerned with religion (e.g. 'Lamb of God: *AMNOS TUTHEU*'; 'Bless me, Father, Mother: *Eblois em despota, rcda!*'). The most advanced word lists also include instructions for phrases to be used in order to ask after the Byzantine emperor ('What do you hear from the Greek emperor: *ti aquis to apeto vasilio romeco?*'; 'What is the emperor doing: *ti pissem vasilios?*') – and ascertain whether he was favourably disposed towards westerners and likely to reward them ('Is he good to the Franks: *Francis calom?*'; 'What good things has he given: *ti kalo docem?*').[30]

The content of these lists overlaps substantially with the Greek found in Latin and French literary works. For example, in the case of *Florimont*, a late twelfth-century *roman* by Aimon de Varennes telling the story of the origins of the Macedonian kings and written as a prequel to the *Roman d'Alexandre*, a rather incongruous attempt is made to transliterate the Greek phrases of greeting and appreciation belonging to a low register and to explicate them in French as if they were being used in the imperial court (e.g. '*Galimera, vassilio!* .../ Iseu welt dire em fransois/ Que boen ior eüsse(nt) li rois' ['This means in French:/ "May the king have a good day!"']; '*Matoteo/ Qalo tuto vasileo!*/ Iseu veult dire en fransois/ Se m'aïst Deux, boins est li rois' ['This means in French:/ "By God, but this is a truly good king!"']; '*O theos offenda*

---

[30] Avranches, Bibliothèque patrimoniale, MS 236, fol. 97v; Auxerre, Bm, MS 212 (179), fols. 134v–135v. See W J. Aerts, 'The Latin-Greek wordlist in MS. 236 of the Municipal Library of Avranches, fol. 97v', *Anglo-Norman Studies* 9 (1987), 64–9; W J. Aerts, 'Froumund's Greek: an analysis of fol. 12v of the Codex Vindobonensis Graecus 114, followed by a comparison with a Latin-Greek wordlist in MS 179 Auxerre fol.137v ff.', in *The Empress Theophano*, ed. A. Davids (Cambridge, 1995), pp. 194–209 (pp. 203–8); L. Delisle, 'Notes sur quelques manuscrits de la Bibliothèque d'Auxerre', *Le Cabinet historique* 23 (1887), 11–15; K. Ciggaar, 'Bilingual Word Lists and Phrase Lists: For Teaching or For Travelling?', in *Travel in the Byzantine World*, ed. R. Macrides (Aldershot, 2002), pp. 165–78 (pp. 165–8).

calo/ Salva *cuto vassilleo*!/ En fransois dit: Deus, boin signor,/ gardeis hui cest empereor!'" ['In French this means: "Good Lord God/ Guard this emperor today!'"]) (Plate 2.4).[31] Other texts address the emperor in a far more decorous fashion (e.g. 'φιλάνθροπε βασιλευ'), praising him for his charitable treatment of supplicants.[32]

In addition to concerning themselves with the basics of communication during receptions by the imperial regime, the texts also seek to give a sense of the peculiarities of the physical environment of the capital and the reactions it elicited. Eleventh- and twelfth-century Latin compositions mention by their Greek names the city's religious sites (e.g. 'Church of the Mother of God called in Greek *tistheotochu*'; 'Church *Pantocratori*, which is "of the Omnipotence of God"'), objects (e.g. 'most admirable image which in Greek eloquence is called *ycona*'; see also 'gold *ycona*', 'marble *ycona*', '*ycona* of the Mother of God' and '*lampades* of gold and silver'), and people ('one hundred *metropolos*, that is, archbishops').[33] The most extensive example however, was that of Liutprand's Latin *Antapodosis*, which embeds almost two hundred lexical items transcribed in or transliterated from Greek, the majority of

---

[31] Although the manuscript branch represented by Paris, Bn F, MS fr. 15101 (see fols. 6v, 7r, 13r) and London, BL, Harley 4487 is superior in other respects, Paris, BnFrance, MS fr. 24376 (see fols. 5r, 8v), which belongs to the other manuscript branch, nonetheless often appears to contain the most accurate readings of these passages as far as the Greek is concerned. See also Aimon de Varennes, *Florimont: Ein altfranzösischer Abenteuerroman*, ed. A. Hilka [and A. Risop] (Gottingen, 1932), pp. 30–1, 54 (vv.1303–86, 693–6, 713–16); http://digiflorimont.huma-num.fr/flsite/florimont.html# [last accessed 13th April 2022]; J. Psichari, 'Le Roman de Florimont: Contribution à l'histoire littéraire – étude des mots grecs dans ce roman', in *Études romanes dédiées à Gaston Paris le 29 décembre 1890 (25e anniversaire de son doctorat ès lettres)*, ed. 'par ses élèves français et ses élèves étrangers des pays de langue française' (Paris, 1891), pp. 507–50; A. Risop, 'Ungelöste Fragen zum Florimont', in *Abhandlungen Herrn Prof. Dr. Adolf Tobler zur Feier seiner fünfundzwanzigjährigen Thätigkeit als ordentlicher Professor an der Universität Berlin von dankbaren Schülern in Ehrerbietung dargebracht* (Halle, 1895), pp. 430–63; L. Harf-Lancner, 'Le Florimont d'Aimon de Varennes: un prologue du *Roman d'Alexandre*', *Cahiers de civilisation médiévale* 147 (1994), 241–53 (pp. 241–5).

[32] *Opera Liudprandi*, ed. Chiesa, p. 15. That the unceremonious tone adopted in *Florimont* need not reflect ignorance but might be deliberate is suggested by the fact that 'Franks' were recorded as flouting protocol during their reception at the imperial court and instead insisting upon informality in their relations with the emperor in order to assert the superiority of their own 'pure' race and 'noble' ancestry. See Anna Comnena, *Comnenae Alexias*, ed. Reinsch and Kambylis, I, 316.

[33] Ciggaar, 'Tarragonensis', pp. 121, 122, 123, 125, 127, and Ciggaar, 'Anonyme', pp. 339–40.

2.4.   Paris, BnF, MS fr. 24376, fol. 8v, fourteenth century. Aimon de Varennes, *Florimont*. The word 'grego' in the bottom left margin marks two expressions derived from Greek and transliterated into Latin characters: 'Calimera uasileo' and 'sirtes kalo'. Other manuscripts have readings such as: 'Garismera vassileo', 'Galimera vassilio' and 'sartiscalo', 'serticalo'. © Bibliothèque nationale de France. Courtesy of Gallica.fr.

2.5.   Munich, Bayerische Staatsbibliothek, MS Clm 6388, fol. 48r, tenth century. Liutprand of Cremona, *Antapodosis*. Greek words and expressions are inserted in browner ink in blanks left in the manuscript. These are sometimes reproduced in full in Greek characters, then transliterated and translated (e.g. 'πτοχος ptochos i. pauper'), and at other times they are simply transliterated. CC BY-NC-SA 4.0 Licence.

FROM LIUTPRAND OF CREMONA TO ROBERT DE CLARI   63

which are nouns (Plate 2.5).[34] Many of these words concern locations in the city and the palace ('το χρυσοτρικλινον'). The name 'Magnaura' of one reception hall is glossed as the Greek for 'Fresh Breeze', while the name 'Decanneacubita' of another is said to mean 'Nineteen Couches'.[35] Further words give imperial titles ('δεσποτην', 'βασιλέα'), indicate the relationship of members of the imperial family to the emperor (e.g. 'pater vasilleos'), or designate the offices held by important courtiers (e.g. 'δομεστικον μεγαν', 'δελονγαρην της πλοως', 'parakinumenon') or the ranks of the other members of the elite (e.g. 'magistros', 'patricios', 'logothétin', 'éparcon', 'protospathários', 'spathários', 'spatharocandidátos').[36] Similar preoccupations can be found in French texts. For example, *Florimont* tries to gloss the meaning of πρωτοσέβαστος, which was a title that was almost exclusively reserved within the imperial hierarchy to be granted to eminent foreigners, often vanquished enemies transformed into allies: 'A la cort a l'empereor/ Cil qui aprés lui sont posé/ *protosabato* sont nome/ Proto dist en fransois: premier/ Et sabato por: ostoier' ('In the emperor's presence/ Those who stood before him [after being defeated]/ were called *protosabato*;/ *Proto* means in French "first"/ And *sabato* for "steward"').[37]

These works in Latin and French often followed a script dictated by the host culture and were themselves translations or paraphrases. Western travelogues opened their descriptions of Constantinople with claims of personal testimony: 'Now will be described what we saw with our eyes'.[38] However, that the assertion made in Latin by at least one traveller in the opening sentence of his text that he and his companions were eye-witnesses was false is betrayed by the word-for-word reproduction of a statement from a Greek model. 'Vidimus Constantinopolim illam egregiam civitatem miro et ineffabili opere fundatam, in qua vidimus...' was derived from Ἑωράκαμεν τὴν Κωνσταντινούπολιν ἐκείνην τὴν ἐξοχωτάτην πόλιν θαυμαστῷ καὶ ἀτιμήτῳ ἀπὸ παλαιοῦ ἔργῳ

---

[34] *Opera Liudprandi*, ed. Chiesa, pp. 5–6, 8–16, 35–6, 41, 45–6, 49–50, 68, 77–9, 82, 84–6, 88–9, 97–10, 131–2, 136–7, 147–50; J. Koder, 'Liutprand von Cremona und die griechische Sprache', in J. Koder and T. Weber, *Liutprand von Cremona in Konstantinopel* (Vienna, 1980), pp. 15–70.

[35] *Opera Liudprandi*, ed. Chiesa, pp. 147–8.

[36] *Opera Liudprandi*, ed. Chiesa, pp. 9, 11, 79, 80.

[37] Paris, BnF, MS fr. 15101, fol. 94v and Paris, BnF, MS fr. 24376, fol. 62v; see also Aimon de Varennes, *Florimont*, ed. Hilka and Risop, p. 426 (vv.10824–10,828) and Psichari, '*Roman de Florimont*', p. 536; for Greek names in this work, see P. Simons, 'Naming Names: Onomastics, Etymologies and Intertexts in Aimon de Varennes' *Florimont*', *Neuphilologische Mitteilungen* 113 (2012), 457–85.

[38] See, for example, Ciggaar, 'Tarragonensis', p. 119

64   TERESA SHAWCROSS

τεθεμελιωμένην, ἐν ᾗ εἴδομεν...'. Likewise, 'Vidimus ibi clavum Domini et spineam coronam...' was derived from Εἴδομεν [...] τὸν ἧλον ᾧ ἐσταυρώθη ὁ δεσπότης ἡμῶν Χριστὸς καὶ τὸν ἀκάνθινον στέφανον...'[39] The enumerations of relics that Latin texts claim were found in particular churches did not so much rely on first-hand experience as adapt pre-existing Greek texts:

Iuxta autem ipsam ecclesiam est aecclesia sancte Mariae Dei genitricis. Supra autem altare ipsius aecclesiae est posita argentea archa et iacet intus vestimentum sanctae Mariae Dei genitricis. In dextera autem parte altaris sunt reliquiae sanctarum mulierum quae quesierunt Christum in monumento portantes ungenta in sepulturam eius. In atrium autem foras ipsius ecclesiae est ecclesia sancti Iacobi apostoli, suptus autem ipsius ecclesie in cripta iacet sanctus Iacobus frater Domini, et sanctus Zacharias propheta, pater sancti Iohannis baptistae et sanctus Symeon qui suscepit Dominum et sancti Innocentes.	Τὴν ἁγίαν Σορὸν τὰ Χαλκοπρατεῖα Ἰουστῖνος καὶ Σοφία ἔκτισαν οἱ καὶ τὸν ναὸν ἀνοικοδομήσαντες. [...]. Ἐκεῖνε δὲ ἀπόκειται ἡ τιμία ζώνη καὶ ἡ ἐσθὴς τῆς ἁγίας Θεοτόκου, τὸ δὲ ἅγιον ὠμοφόριον ἐν Βλαχέρναις. Ἀνήγειρεν δὲ καὶ τὸν ἅγιον Ἰάκωβον ὁ αὐτὸς βασιλεὺς καὶ τέθηκεν ἐν τῇ σορῷ τῶν ἁγίων Νηπίων τὰ λείψανα καὶ τοῦ ἁγίου Συμεὼν τοῦ Θεοδόχου καὶ τοῦ προφήτου Ζαχαρίου καὶ τοῦ ἁγίου Ἰακώβου τοῦ ἀδελφοθέου καὶ ἐν τῇ ἁγίᾳ Σορῷ εὐωνύμως μὲν τοῦ ἁγίου Ἰωάννου Προδρόμου τὰς τρίχας, δεξιὰ δὲ τὰ σώματα πάντα τῶν ἁγίων μυροφόρων γυναικῶν[40]

The sources behind these types of borrowings appear to have belonged to a genre of texts in Greek collected together at the imperial court and handed down to us under the common title of *Patria*. The *Patria* formed a guidebook

---

[39] Ciggaar, 'Anonyme', p. 338–9; T. Martínez Manzano, *Konstantinos Laskaris. Humanist, Philologe, Lehrer, Kopist* (Hamburg, 1994), pp. 118–19. That the Latin is the original and the Greek the translation is possible, but seems unlikely. The Latin reads: 'We saw Constantinople, that excellent city founded on wonderful and ineffable works, in which we saw...' and 'We saw there the Nail of the Lord and the Crown of Thorns...'.

[40] Ciggaar, 'Pèlerin anglais', pp. 223–4, 249; *Scriptores originum Constantinopolitanarum*, ed. T. Preger, 2 vols. (Leipzig 1901–7) II, 263. The Latin text can be translated as: 'Next to this church is the holy church of Mary, the Mother of God. And above the altar of this church is placed a silver reliquary, inside which lies the raiment of the holy Mary, the Mother of God. And on the right side of the altar are the relics of the holy women who sought out Christ in the tomb, bringing ointments for his burial. In the courtyard outside this church is the church of St James the Apostle, and in the crypt inside that church lies St James, the brother of the Lord, and St Zacharias the prophet, the father of St John the Baptist, and St Simeon who received the Lord, and the Holy Innocents.'

on the patrimony of the empire – and especially the history and monuments of the imperial capital. Its earliest elements date to the period from the sixth to the eighth centuries, but the tenth and twelfth centuries saw new compilations and revisions that appear to have circulated widely.

Where both the original Greek and Latin translation have survived, it is possible to compare the two in detail. In other cases, the source has been lost, but its existence can be inferred from the unidiomatic grammar and syntax of its calqued derivative. An attempt was made, for instance, in one unattributed Latin text to render the weak adversative Greek particle δέ despite the fact that Latin does not have a similar locution. Elsewhere, an anonymous author explicitly acknowledged the derivative nature of his work in a postscript: 'All these things have been translated [..] into Latin from Greek'. [41] Yet another Latin text contended that its unidentified author, when he had attempted to learn Greek, had 'heard and seen written by many' the content he now sought to convey 'briefly and succinctly'.[42] The texts surviving in French similarly emphasised that whatever merit they may have had was derived from the memory they preserved of the content of a Greek original that had been seen and examined. Aimon de Varennes described the process as one whereby the 'story' ('l'istoire') first had been transferred from Greek into Latin, and afterwards put into 'the French language' ('en la langue de fransois') so that it had been made into 'the romance' ('le romans') that readers now had before them.[43]

Through constant recourse to an eastern vocabulary and genre, western texts drew attention to the fact that it was impossible for them to achieve an independent assessment of the realities their writers observed. For example, Liutprand of Cremona foregrounded the limitations of his own means of expression by stating he had felt compelled, when asked by the emperor to evaluate his visit to Constantinople, to admit ruefully that he could not do so because he 'did not know' what was 'the most marvellous'. His choice to reach in his reply not for the word *mirabilius*, but for *thaumastoteron* (Plate 2.6), only served to underscore the insufficiency of his interpretative skills and draw attention to the gulf that separated him from his surroundings ('Cumque me ignorare quid mihi *thaumastoteron* edicerem...').[44] Despite professing a dedication to the task of language acquisition, men such as he

[41] Ciggaar, 'Pèlerin anglais', pp. 214, 263.

[42] Ciggaar, 'Tarragonensis', p. 125.

[43] Paris, BnF, MS fr. 24376, fols. 1r and 78v; Paris, BnF, MS fr. 15101 is acephalic; Aimon de Varennes, *Florimont*, ed. Hilka and Risop, pp. 1–2, 361–2 (vv. 14–32, 9213–16); D. Kelly, 'The Composition of Aimon de Varennes' *Florimont*', *Romance Philology* 23 (1970), 277–92.

[44] *Opera Liudprandi*, ed. Chiesa, p. 149.

2.6. Munich, Bayerische Staatsbibliothek, MS Clm 6388, fol. 85r, tenth century. Liutprand of Cremona, *Antapodosis*. The ultimate line of this page contains the word 'thaumastoteron' (the more marvellous), which is glossed as 'mirabilius'. CC BY-NC-SA 4.0 Licence.

had not been exposed even to the introductory educational curriculum of the Greek classics taught to young boys in Byzantium. They consequently struggled with literary allusion when they encountered it. When faced with a tag ('διότι οὔτε στόμα οὔτε γλῶττα αὐτὰς ἀριθμῆσαι δύναται') that could be traced back to specific Homeric lines ('πληθὺν δ᾽ οὐκ ἂν ἐγὼ μυθήσομαι οὐδ᾽ ὀνομήνω/ οὐδ εἴ μοι δέκα μὲν γλῶσσαι. δέκα δὲ στόματ᾽ εἶεν'), they did not attempt to offer a translation, but instead skipped over the locution and moved on to less demanding content.[45] In this, they conformed to the expectations of the host culture, which, highlighting westerners' inability to 'read and have knowledge of the epic verses' of the twin masterpieces of the *Iliad* and *Odyssey*, concluded that these westerners were strangers to the foundations upon which contemporary eloquence was built – and therefore scarcely better than 'unlettered barbarians' who maintained themselves in 'ignorance even of the alphabet'.[46]

The establishment of assumptions regarding the inherited character of cultural capital meant that, by the end of the twelfth century, the marvels of Constantinople had established a reputation for being both so impressive and so alien that they were untranslatable into a western framework. Such attempts as had been made fell far short of the mark, for the transpositions of Greek into Latin and later into French contexts rarely involved more than a handful of words and expressions. Renditions of this content tend to be characterised by grammatical mistakes, false etymologies and spurious glosses. The impression is of authors who would sometimes display awareness that their skills in Greek were severely limited, but who nonetheless sought either to convince themselves – or delude their readership – regarding the extent of their fluency. One Latin author acknowledged that, although he had carried out his task 'as best' he 'could', the result could not but be lamented as 'most miserable' and inadequate.[47] Other Latin authors, by contrast, presented themselves as able to interpret the alien and render it, if not completely transparent to the intellect, at least accessible ('*thaumastoteron*, that is, "most marvellous'"). Authoritatively glossing words and phrases ('δεσποτία σοῦ η αγια, that is, "your holy dominion'"), they claimed to have derived special insight into the workings of high politics in Byzantium and to be able to presume to be on familiar terms with the

---

[45] Ciggaar, 'Anonyme', p. 338: 'neither the mouth nor the tongue can enumerate them'; Homer, *Iliad*, ed. and tr. A.T. Murray and W. F. Wyatt, 2 vols. (Cambridge MA 1999), I, 96–7 (II, vv.488–9): 'the multitude I could not tell or name, not even if ten tongues were mine and ten mouths').

[46] Nicetas Choniates, *Nicetae Choniatae Historia*, ed. Van Dieten, I, 653.

[47] Ciggaar, 'Pèlerin anglais', pp. 214, 263.

68 TERESA SHAWCROSS

emperor – and therefore secure favourable treatment for their compatriots.[48] In this, they targeted audiences that invariably consisted of the western elites for whom they claimed to be acting not only as commentators, but also as power brokers who could navigate the situation on the ground.[49]

Claiming such status entailed writing about imagined scenarios in which the Byzantines were receptive to western overtures, accommodated themselves to western desires – and shared or even ceded power. Aimon de Varennes dramatised the envisaged exchange, declaring that his hero's clumsy salutation in Greek received a response in the same language from the emperor that sought to welcome the foreigner in a friendly fashion and put him at ease ('Li rois respont: "*Certis calo!*"/ .../ Vuelt dire: " Bien soiés venu"' ['The King responds, "*Certis calo!*"…which means "Welcome!"']).[50] Another author described the disposition and generosity of the emperor's officials as favourable ('What type of man is the general: *Pios antropos ene estraiget?* By God, he is good: *Maten cetu, calos.* [...] You should go, he will be good to you: *Na ipas, pissem si calon, Franc*'). A basic word list had westerners being offered food and drink, and being encouraged to sit by their hosts and converse with them: 'Please eat: FAGE METACHARAS; Please drink: PIE METACHARAS; Sit you here and chat with me: KATHISON ODE SYNTICHON MV.'[51] Indeed, some passages in the literature that present the Franks treating the Byzantines unceremoniously could have been intended to convey an impression of boldness rather than ignorance. Certainly, real-life visitors to Constantinople were recorded in the mid twelfth century as actively having set out to flout protocol and insist upon informality during their reception at the imperial court. By means of such conduct, westerners attempted to defend their 'pure' race and 'noble' ancestry. By claiming the right to be on first-name terms with the emperor, they sought to indicate that they were the equals of any eastern potentate.[52]

---

[48] *Opera Liudprandi*, ed. Chiesa, p. 13.

[49] A. M. Small, 'Constantinopolitan Connections: Liudprand of Cremona and Byzantium', in *From Constantinople to the Frontier: The City and the Cities*, ed. N. S. M. Matheou, T. Kampianaki and L. M. Bondioli (Leiden, 2016), pp. 84–97; K. Leyser, 'Ends and Means in Liudprand of Cremona', in *Communications and Power in Medieval Europe*, ed. T. Reuter (London, 1994), pp. 125–42; H. Mayr-Harting, 'Liudprand of Cremona's Account of his Legation to Constantinople and Ottonian Imperial Strategy', *English Historical Review* 116 (2001), 539–56.

[50] Paris, BnF, MS fr. 15101, fol. 13r and Paris, BnF, MS fr. 24376, fol. 18v; Aimon de Varennes, *Florimont*, ed. Hilka and Risop, 54 (vv.1304–08).

[51] Aerts, 'Latin-Greek Wordlist', pp. 65–6.

[52] Such interpretations of the Franks' apparent lack of manners were suggested by the Byzantines themselves. See Anna Comnena, *Comnenae Alexias*, ed. Reinsch and Kambylis, I, 316.

On the eve of the Fourth Crusade, poems produced in the francophone world repeatedly recounted the story of a bold Frankish knight who had travelled to Constantinople and there ravished the emperor's daughter, achieving by means of his possession of her body supremacy over the empire and proving the inherent superiority of his people. In both *Girart de Rouissillon* and the *Pèlerinage de Charlemagne*, for instance, initial displays of power by the Byzantine emperor avail him nothing, we are told, for he is forced to surrender up his daughter in the one story to a Frankish king, Charles Martel, who then marries her, and in the other story to a Frankish baron, Oliver, who proceeds to bed her 'thirty times' ('.xxx. feiz') without even observing the niceties of wedlock.[53] The fantasy articulated in the texts was one in which westerners would obtain access to imperial wealth, satiate their sexual appetites with women from the imperial family – and even rule over imperial territory – at minimal cost to themselves. The fact that these ambitions remained largely unfulfilled through negotiation meant that the only option that remained available to westerners was that of preparing themselves to become conquerors. Observing the conduct of the 'Franks', the Byzantine court historian Anna Komnene declared in her *Alexiad*, an account of the reign of her father and emperor, Alexios I (r.1081–1118), that they were always on the lookout for an opportunity to 'fulfil their dream of taking the great city' in order to 'dethrone the emperor, and themselves assume power'.[54] Articulating these exact ambitions, the hero of one French chanson de geste declares that he wants 'the domain' ('l'onor') of Byzantium and is not afraid to take risks in order to gain it.[55]

After the conquest

By the thirteenth century, that conquest of the Byzantine Empire was finally underway. As the victorious crusaders advanced through the streets of the capital in 1204, they encountered monuments of various types and repeatedly stopped in their tracks, their attention arrested ('s'en merveillierent molt durement, et se merveillierent molt'). Here was another wondrous sight, they declared breathlessly, according to de Clari's *Conqueste de Constantinoble*, here

---

[53] *Chanson de Girart de Rousillon*, ed. Combarieu du Grès and Gouiran, p. 54 (vv.182–7); *Pèlerinage de Charlemagne*, ed. Burgess, pp. 40–4, 50 (vv.683–734, 852–7); T. Shawcross, 'The Seduction of Constantinople', *The French of Outremer: Communities and Communications in the Crusading Mediterranean*, accessed 13 April 2022, https://mvstconference.ace.fordham.edu/frenchofoutremer/conference-program/.

[54] Anna Comnena, *Comnenae Alexias*, ed. Reinsch and Kambylis, I, 299, 309, 411–12; Robert de Clari, *Conquête*, ed. Dufournet, pp. 142–4.

[55] *Chanson de Girart de Rousillon*, ed. Combarieu du Grès and Gouiran, p. 48 (v.112).

URBS CONSTANTINOPOLITANA NOVA ROMA.

2.7.   Oxford, Bodleian Library, MS Canon. Misc. 378, fol. 84r, 1436. Bilingual
Latin-Greek manuscript containing a representation of the city of Constantinople
emphasizing the Church of the Holy Wisdom (Haghia Sophia) and the triumphal
column of Justinian topped by the emperor's equestrian statue. CC-BY-NC 4.0 Licence.
© Bodleian Libraries, University of Oxford.

'another wonder' ('une autre merveille'), and here 'an even greater wonder' ('une greigneur merveille'). There were all around them so very many 'great wonders' ('grans merveilles') that needed to be admired! They gawped at the Golden Gate, the Vlacherna Palace, Great Palace, the Hippodrome and the Church of the Holy Wisdom. They squinted up at triumphal columns. One of these, they noted, was made of marble drums bound with copper and iron, and capped with a large capital upon which rested the statue of a man 'cast in copper on a large horse' also 'of copper' ('jeté de coivre, seur un grant cheval de coivre'). Their gaze was drawn to other sculptures 'of men, women, horses, bulls, camels, bears, lions and many other types of beasts', all 'cast in copper' ('d'ommes et de femmes et de chevaus et de bués et de cameus et de ors et de lions, et de molt de manieres de bestes getees de coivre').[56] Over the previous millennium, as is attested by the archaeological and documentary record, Constantinople had seen the erection of perhaps as many as five hundred monumental structures. A significant proportion were statues that had been transferred there at Constantinople's founding from 'all the cities of the West and East by Constantine the Great' and especially 'from Rome'; others had been added subsequently.[57] They had memorialised the long history the empire had claimed for itself (e.g. The Judgement of the Goddesses by Paris; The Suckling of Romulus and Remus by the She-Wolf; The Oracle Received by Octavian Augustus on the Eve of His Victory at Actium). They also had celebrated in allegorical fashion essential qualities associated with imperial might (e.g. The Eagle Vanquishing the Snake).[58]

Particularly prominent had been the images of emperors displayed on walls, boards, banners and plinths. The most impressive of these imperial likenesses had been the bronze statues raised up on the tall marble columns (Plates 2.7–8).[59] Instead of an ordinary structural function, such columns

[56] Robert de Clari, *Conquête*, ed. Dufournet, pp. 174–8, 180–2; S. Kinoshita, *Medieval Boundaries: Rethinking Difference in Old French Literature* (Philadelphia, 2006), pp. 139–75.

[57] *Scriptores originum Constantinopolitanarum*, ed. Preger, II, 189; G. Dagron, *Constantinople imaginaire: études sur le recueil des* Patria (Paris, 1984), pp. 136–7, 146–7.

[58] Nicetas Choniates, *Nicetae Choniatae historia*, ed. Van Dieten, pp. 558–9, 648, 650–1; C. Mango, 'Antique Statuary and the Byzantine Beholder', *Dumbarton Oaks Papers* 17 (1963), 53–75 (p. 55); T. Shawcross, 'The City as an Archive of Speaking Statues: Language, record-keeping and memory in the Middle Byzantine Empire', in *Anekdota: Festschrift für Albrecht Berger*, ed. A. Riehle, I. Grimm-Stadelmann, R. Tocci, and M. Vučetić (Boston and Berlin, 2023), pp. 661–81.

[59] *Scriptores originum Constantinopolitanarum*, ed. Preger, II, 138, 159, 178, 181–2, 184–5, 205; P. Magdalino and R. Nelson, 'The Emperor in Byzantine Art of the

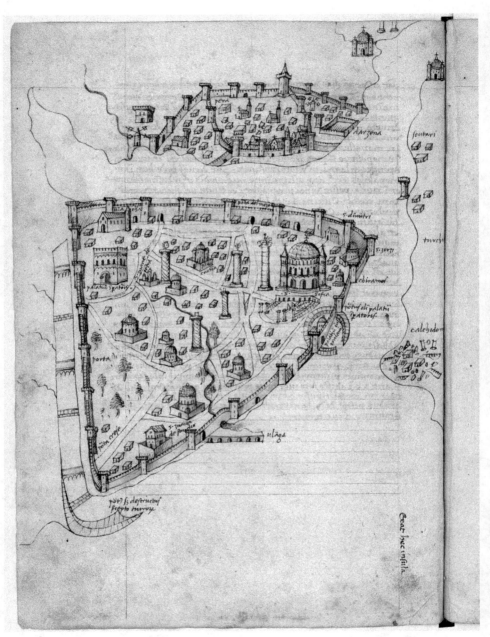

2.8. Vatican City, Biblioteca Apostolica Vaticana, MS Ross.702, fol. 32v, fifteenth century. Buondelmonti, *Liber insularum archipelagi*. This map of Constantinople depicts one monumental column with an equestrian statue, one column with another imperial statue, and at least two historiated columns. © Biblioteca Apostolica Vaticana.

had had a metaphysical purpose. Inhabiting the region next to the heavens, the emperors of metal who had stood at the columns' summit had acted as a lightning-rod for the transfer of a divine charge downwards into earthly affairs. These emperors had looked out triumphantly across the urban and country districts of the immediate vicinity towards the distant horizon, surveying an empire with pretensions to a rule so universal it had extended to the bounds of the earth. The sculpted representations and their living embodiments of the imperial office had been understood by the Byzantines to form a unity, with each existing in and through the other so that whatever was seen in the image should also be seen in the emperor, and – vice versa – whatever was seen in the emperor should also be seen in the image. Thus, emperors had been expected to remain seated on their thrones in an impassive and unruffled manner even in crisis so that their posture gave them the appearance of having been 'wrought by the chisel, or made perhaps of copper or cold-forged iron' and consequently rendered them reminiscent 'of model statues whose forms expert sculptors had carved'. To tell an emperor 'You go about here [...] as a living and moving statue' had been to praise him. Only a man who bore a 'perfect resemblance' to the formal image that constituted 'his species and his form' could be considered to have subsumed his personality to his calling – and therefore be worthy of ruling.[60]

In trying to make sense of the city that lay before them, authors belonging to the crusader army turned for explanations to the native imperial lore of the Byzantines as it had already been mediated for them by an established western literary tradition. Faced with an urban landscape about which they had read and been told so much before they sailed up the Bosporus, the crusaders initially set about locating within that landscape what they expected to find there. We should not take statements in texts such as that of de Clari that 'the Greeks said' ('disoient li Griu') or 'the Greeks attested' ('tesmongnoient li Griu') as necessarily referring to real-life conversations held in the streets between the conquerors and conquered after the fall of the capital.[61] Instead, when de Clari depicted the war chariot that had traditionally been used in imperial victory

---

Twelfth Century', *Byzantinische Forschungen* 8 (1982), 123–83.

[60] Geoffroy de Villehardouin, *Conquête*, ed. Dufournet, p. 175; Michael Psellus, *Michaelis Pselli chronographia*, ed. D. R. Reinsch (Berlin, 2014), pp. 14–15, 22–3; Anna Comnena, *Comnenae Alexias*, ed. Reinsch and Kambylis, I, 441; P. Lamma, 'Manuele Comneno nel panegirico di Michele Italico (Codice 2412 della Bibliotheca Universitaria di Bologna)', in *Atti dell'VIII congressio internazionale di studi bizantini*, 2 vols. (Palermo, 1951), I, 397–408; W. Regel, *Fontes rerum byzantinarum*, 2 parts (St Petersburg, 1892–1917), I, 244–5.

[61] Robert de Clari, *Conquête*, ed. Dufournet, pp. 168–70, 176–8, 208.

Il auoit ailleurs en le chite vne por
te q on apeloit le mantiau dor : seur
chele porte si auoit vn pumel dor · q estoit
fait par tel encantement q li grui disoient
q autant come li pumax i fust caus de
touniourie ne carroit en le chite. Seur
chu pumel auoit · j · image iere de cou
ure qui auoit vn mantel dor a fasle si
le tendoit auant seur sen brach · Et
auoit lettres escrites seur lui q disoient
q tout chu fait li ymages q manient
en coustantinoble · j · an · doiuent auoir
mantel dor aussi come iou ai.

Ailleurs en le chite a vne autre
porte · q on apele porte doree. Se
chele porte auoit · ij · olifans ieres de
coure q si estoient grit q chestoit vne
fine muelle. Ichele porte nestoit on
q ouuerte · deuant la q li empe reue
noit de bataille · q q il auoit de q q se
Quar q reuenoit de bataille q il auoit
iere de q q se dont si uenoit li clergies
de le chite a pchession en iere l'empereur.
si ouuroit on chele porte · se li aueno
on vn ire dor · q estoit aussi fait come vu
cars a · iiij · roes. q on apeloit ire. En cel
iiij chu ire auoit vn haut siege · Et se
le siege auoit vne caiere · Et encor le
caiere auoit · iiij · colombes qui portoient
· j · halstade q a omroit le caiere · qui
sanloit q il fust tout dor · si estoit li empe
enchele caiere tout coronet · si entroit
enchele porte · si le menoit on seur chu
curre q grant goie q grant feste dusqs en
sen palais.

En le chite auoit · j · autre muelle
q il auoit vne plache q pc estoit du
palais de louke de lion · q on apeloit les

Jne l'empereur. Ichele plache si a bien ar
baleestee q remue de lonc q pies dune de
le. Entor chele plache si auoit · vij · xxx ·
de gret ou · xl · La ou li grui montoient
p esſwarder les Jus · Et p reseure ches
de gret si auoit · vne logue mte comtes.
q mlt nobles ou li empe q l'empeeris
se seoient quar on juoit · Et li autre
haut home · q les dames se iauoit · ij ·
Jus en sanle. quar on juoit · q se wagio
ient en sanle. li emperes q l'empeeris
q li vns tes Jus guieroit imege de lautre.
Et tout chu enseme q les grit esgardoient.
Du lonc de chele plache si auoit vne
masiere q bien auoit · xv · pies de haut.
q · x · de le. de seure chele masiere si auoit
il · ymages · comes q de femes. q de che
uaus. q de bues q de cameus. q de ors.
q de lions. Et de mlt de manieres de be
stes gerees de coure · q si estoient vn
fares · q si natureement formees q il na
si bon maistre en paienisme ne en cre
stiente q seust vne pture · ne si bien
former ymages · come chil ymages estoi
ent forme. Et soloient cha en arriere
guier p encanteure · Mais ne juoient
mais mehu · Et chel grui l'empereur · esgar
doient li franchois auuelle quar il les uirent.

Il auoit ailleurs en le chite vne
autre muelle. li auoit · ij · ymage
ieres de coure en forme de feme · si bien
faites · q si natuemt · Et si beles q trop.
Si mi auoit cheluy naie bien · xx · pies
de haut. Si tendoit li vne de chel ymages
se main porocidine · Et auoit lettres es
tes seur lui q disoient · de vers ocidente
venront chu qui costent. q q iront · Et
li autres ymages tendoit main en vn vilai

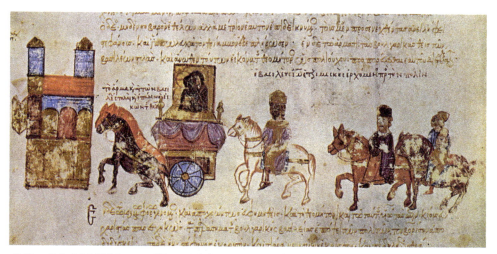

2.10. Madrid, Biblioteca Nacional de España, MS Graecus Vitr. 26–2, fol. 172v, twelfth century, detail. John Skylitzes, *Synopsis of Histories*. Depiction of a triumphal procession approaching the Golden Gate of Constantinople, with the emperor John Tsimiskes advancing on horseback. The imperial war chariot and its trappings ('τὸ ἅρμα καὶ τῶν βασιλέων στολαί') precede him carrying an icon of the Virgin Mary and the Christ Child. CC-BY Licence. Courtesy of Wikimedia Commons.

processions in Constantinople (Plates 2.9–10) as a peculiar vehicle 'of gold' that was 'constructed a bit like a four-wheeled cart' ('un curre d'or qui estoit ausi fais comme uns cars a quatre roes, que on apeloit curre') and contained 'a throne [which] was surrounded by four columns whose canopy cast shade upon it' ('le caiiere avoit quatre colombes qui portoient un habitacle qui aombroit le caiiere'), he was borrowing from similar descriptions found in chansons de geste and *romans d'antiquité* of conveyances associated not only with the Greek emperor, but also with legendary rulers from Greece's remoter past.[62] De Clari seems to have recalled the account in the *Pèlerinage de Charlemagne* of the Emperor Hugo who is to be found at the entrance to Constantinople driving a contraption that superficially resembles a 'plough' ('carue arant'), but whose wheels, axles and blades were all made of 'gleaming pure gold' ('Les cunjungles en sunt a or fin relusant,/ Li essués e les roes e li cultres arant'), and whose main component was a 'suspended golden seat' ('caiiere [...] d'or suzpendant') covered with a canopy of 'fine grey cloth' ('bon paile grizain'). Other accounts that may have influenced him included that in the *Roman d'Alexandre* of the marvellous throne – part chair, part basket, and part chariot – to which griffins were yoked, as well as in the *Roman de Thèbes* of the chariot of gold, ivory and chrysoprase drawn by zebras whose hooves did not touch the ground. These last two vehicles

[62] Robert de Clari, *Conquête*, ed. Dufournet, pp. 170, 178; *Pèlerinage de Charlemagne*, ed. Burgess, pp. 18–20 (vv.280–301).

2.11. Turkey, ancient column with nest of Mediterranean White Storks.
© Richard Billingham. Courtesy of Dreamstime.com.

FROM LIUTPRAND OF CREMONA TO ROBERT DE CLARI 77

respectively are said to have taken the ruler Alexander up to the heavens and the sorcerer Amphiaraus down to hell.[63] Similarly, the procedure by de Clari or his amanuensis of transcribing the word εἰκών ('*ansconne*') and explaining it as meaning 'image' ('l'*ansconne* [...], un ymage de Nostre Dame que li Griu apeloient ensi' ['the *icon* [...], an image of Our Lady, which the Greeks call by this name']) did not represent actual observation of the material culture of the Byzantines. Instead, it deployed a cliché found in earlier travelogues, where references to icons were used as shorthand to indicate a specific ethno-religious context (e.g. 'most admirable image which in Greek eloquence is called *ycona*').[64] Even such apparently general statements as 'the Greeks attest that two parts of the wealth of this world is in Constantinople and the other third is scattered throughout the rest of the world' ('Et si tesmongnoient li Griu que les deus pars de l'avoir du monde estoient en Coustantinoble et le tierche estoit esparse par le monde') can be shown to echo earlier textual antecedents (e.g. 'There is so much gold and silver here that it is said and believed that a third, or, according to some, half of the wealth of the world can be found in this place, while others assign fully two thirds to Constantinople and only one third to the rest of the world').[65]

Yet, while much of what the crusaders saw appeared only to confirm for them the preconceptions that they had brought with them, there were other things, such as the detail of the 'nests of ten herons' ('dis aires de hairons') they spied on top of one monument, whose existence had indeed been previously unknown

---

[63] *The Medieval French* Roman d'Alexandre. *Vol. II: Version of Alexandre de Paris, Text,* ed. E. C. Armstrong, D. L. Buffum, B. Edwards, and L. F. H. Lowe (Princeton, 1938), pp. 253–357 (vv.4914–5098), but note also the numerous visual images of this episode found sculpted on ecclesiastical complexes and in other contexts across Europe: C. Frugoni, *Historia Alexandri elevati per griphos ad aerem, origine, iconografia e fortuna di un tema* (Rome, 1973); *Le roman de Thèbes*, ed. and trans. F. Mora-Lebrun (Paris, 1995), pp. 169–70, 340–56 (vv.2119–49, 5042–5309).

[64] Robert de Clari, *Conquête*, ed. Dufournet, p. 146; Ciggaar, 'Tarragonensis', p. 122 (see also pp. 121, 123, 125, 127); Copenhagen, Royal Danish Library, MS GKS 487, fol. 117r (p. 247). The word εἰκών or εἰκόνα, however, is not transliterated into French according to the conventions that had already been established for Latin, but rather according to those that would be increasingly attested in Italian. So as to impress upon the reader the foreign origins of the term being transliterated, the many different Greek graphemes – i.e. not only iota (ι), but also eta (η), ypsilon (υ), and digraphs such as epsilon + iota (ει) and omicron + iota (οι) – that iotacism reduced to the phoneme /i/ – were customarily all represented in Latin by means of the letter *y*, which itself had been a late addition to the Roman alphabet. For the presence of Greek in Latin texts, see W. Berschin, 'Greek Elements in Medieval Latin Manuscripts', in *The Sacred Nectar of the Greeks: The Study of Greek in the West in the Early Middle Ages*, ed. S.A. Brown and M.W. Herren (London, 1988), pp. 85–104.

[65] Robert de Clari, *Conquête*, ed. Dufournet, p. 170; Ciggaar, 'Tarragonensis', p. 119.

78   TERESA SHAWCROSS

to them (Plate 2.11).[66] Such seemingly insignificant details play a crucial role in the accounts that would be written of the conquest. Their dissonance created an opportunity for a new reckoning, opening up the possibility of re-engaging with the physical landscape and re-interpreting it along different lines. This process required the application of the organising power of western calculative technologies – that is, it entailed a representation of the environment through acts of quantification that explicitly referred back to the crusaders' own subjectivity and therefore necessitated their physical presence. De Clari suggests that Constantinople was only revealed to him and his compatriots when they started counting and measuring everything. They determined, for instance, that one of the city's palaces had five hundred chambers, while another had three hundred chambers, and a church had two hundred hanging chandeliers of silver each with twenty-five lamps. Increasingly, the crusaders calculated the dimensions of objects and distances with reference to units of measurement provided by their weapons and, above all, their own bodies. A square in which games were held had an open space that was one-and-a-half crossbow shots long. Some of the columns were as thick as three times the length of a man's arm and as high as fully fifty times the span of a man's outstretched arms. Every part of the city might now be not merely touched but grasped – its secrets studied and mastery over it established.[67]

The Greek guidebook to the patrimony of the empire, the *Patria*, had insisted that the monuments of Constantinople were to be understood as not merely commemorative but also prophetic. These monuments had served for the Byzantines as sites where they could collectively imagine their manifest destiny. The most important of the statues representing emperors, a sculpture of Constantine the Great, had been erected in the centre of the city atop a column that was expected to last as long as the world itself. When the sea would rise to engulf all creation, the Column of Constantine, it was thought, would alone remain above the surface of the waters after all else disappeared.[68] Although this particular column was plain, others were historiated. Beneath the statues of emperors, indeed, spiralling friezes that unfurled like scrolls were believed to record all the events that had already happened, set out all the events that were currently happening, and foretell all the events that would happen until the end

---

[66] Robert de Clari, *Conquête*, ed. Dufournet, p. 178; but note *Scriptores originum Constantinopolitanarum*, ed. Preger, I, 11, discusses the banishment of 'the race of storks' from the city.

[67] Robert de Clari, *Conquête*, Dufournet, pp. 170–80; on the politics of measuring in the medieval Mediterranean, see E. Lugli, *The Making of Measure and the Promise of Sameness* (Chicago, 2019).

[68] *The Life of St. Andrew the Fool*, ed. L. Rydén, 2 vols. (Uppsala, 1995) II, 276–8; L. Rydén, 'The Andreas Salos Apocalypse: Greek Text, Translation and Commentary', *Dumbarton Oaks Papers* 28 (1974), 197–261 (p. 222).

of time. Some of these monuments bore inscriptions explicitly stating not only 'why they were raised', but also 'what they signify' – and even listing the 'names of the rulers until the end of ages'.[69] This double function of the statues as oracles as well as public memorials informed the Byzantines' view of them as precious and holy talismans the vandalism of which was tantamount to high treason and sacrilege punishable by the forms of death reserved for the most serious crimes perpetrated against the state. One statue rendered this conflation of treason and vandalism explicit. A sculpture of the hung, drawn and quartered corpse of a man found guilty of seditious action against his emperor, it also had inscribed on it the injunction: 'Let him who disturbs the monuments be delivered to the gibbet!'[70]

The crusaders responded to such traditional interpretations by contending that the Byzantines had not properly understood the statues' message. Such had been the Byzantines' lack of acuity, according to de Clari, that they had not realised that on the friezes of the historiated columns 'the conquest by the French was written and portrayed, and the ships with which they attacked and through which the city was taken' ('cheste conqueste que li Franchois le conquisent i estoit escrite et pourtraite, et les nes dont on assali par coi le chités fu prise'). Only after the walls of the city had been breached, de Clari contended, did its inhabitants go and look again at the columns, noticing for the first time the inscriptions that had been written 'on the ships' predicting that from the West there 'would come a people [...] who would conquer Constantinople' ('les letres, qui estoient escrites seur les nes pourtraites, disoient que de vers Occident venroient une gent [...] qui Constantinoble conquerroient').[71] Referring to the Column of Theodosius or the Column of Arcadius, whose height continued to dominate the urban landscape, the crusaders sought to discredit and amend the cultural memory that previous regimes had associated with these civic monuments. Focusing on specific representational details verifiable by observers, such as the depiction of warships or of armed troops on the columns (Plates 2.12–14), the conquerors presented themselves as the sole possessors of the correct interpretation of the scenes' meaning.

This argument may have derived strength from the fact that the Byzantines were aware that the inscriptions on some of the monuments were written in Latin ('Roman letters') rather than in Greek. Moreover, sources such as the *Patria* had often discussed the betrayal by local rulers of the custody of the state with which they had been entrusted. Emperors had wrecked the monumental landscape of the capital despite the protestations of that landscape's inhabitants (e.g. 'she [the

---

[69] *Scriptores originum Constantinopolitanarum*, ed. Preger, II, 176, 178, 184, 191, 206, 230.

[70] *Scriptores originum Constantinopolitanarum*, ed. Preger, I, 34–5; Robert de Clari, *Conquête*, ed. Dufournet, pp. 182–4.

[71] Robert de Clari, *Conquête*, ed. Dufournet, pp. 180–2.

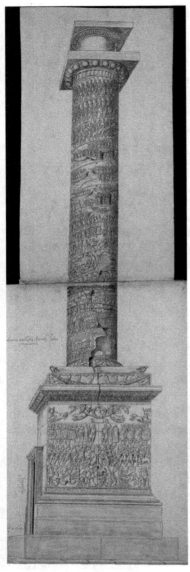

2.12. Cambridge, Trinity College Wren Library, MS O.17.2, fol. 13, sixteenth century, detail. Freshfield Album. Depiction of the Column of Arcadius. CC BY-NC-SA 4.0 Licence. © Master and Fellows of Trinity College, Cambridge.

empress Euphrosyne] removed the limbs from other statues and beheaded some with hammer blows'). Indeed, in a perversion of the correct order of things, imperial effigies had taken to toppling down suddenly and slaughtering citizens (e.g. 'this statue [of the emperor Constantine] fell from the column and caused the death of the men and women who happened to be there'). That such occurrences – of which a notable example had occurred in 1106 – were 'improper' had been highlighted by the fact they were accompanied by inauspicious omens (e.g. 'About the third hour, it became dark and a violent [...] wind blew [...] for a comet [...] appeared [...] and then stayed').[72]

The conquerors, for their part, claimed to have been destined to liberate the city from its false rulers and rescue its monuments – and by extension the empire itself – not merely from defilement but from the very threat of annihilation. Initially planning to execute the last Byzantine emperor by hanging him as a traitor, the crusaders decided that 'high justice' ('haute joustice') would be better served if the captive were taken to a great column – which was, de Clari and de Villehardouin explained, 'towards the centre' of Constantinople ('en Costentinoble en mi la vile') and 'one of the tallest and most finely constructed of marble they had ever seen' ('une des plus hautes et des mieulz ouvrees de marbres qui onques fust veüe d'eulz') – and 'made to leap down' ('le fist saillir aval') from there in the sight of all the people. The deposed ruler was duly forced to climb to the top of the column and thrown over the edge, falling 'from such a

[72] *Scriptores originum Constantinopolitanarum*, ed. Preger, I, 22, 138–9, 181, 198, 221, 278; Nicetas Choniates, *Nicetae Choniatae Historia*, ed. Van Dieten, p. 519.

2.13. Cambridge, Trinity College Wren Library, MS O.17.2, fol. 12, sixteenth century, detail. Freshfield Album. Depiction of the Column of Arcadius. CC BY-NC-SA 4.0 Licence. © Master and Fellows of Trinity College, Cambridge.

2.14. Washington, Dumbarton Oaks, black and white photograph, twentieth century. Image of a fragment of the fourth-century Column of Theodosius in Istanbul. Courtesy of Dumbarton Oaks, Trustees for Harvard University, Washington, D.C. Photo by Slobodan Ćurčić.

82   TERESA SHAWCROSS

height that as soon as he touched the ground every bone in his body was broken'
('chaï de si hut que, quant il vint a terre, il fu touz esmiez').[73] This regicide appears
to have been intended by the crusaders as a symbolic ritual by which past wrongs
could be righted, reversing the ruination of the empire perpetrated by the previous
regime. It was furthermore identified by de Villehardouin as the fulfilment of a
prophecy, since the column from which execution was carried out was said to have
borne on it depictions of 'figures of various kinds, carved in the marble', including
'one representing an emperor falling headlong' ('en cele coulombe dont il sailli
aval, avoit ymages de maintes manieres ouvree ou marbre; et entre les autres en y
avoit une qui estoit labouree en forme d'empereeur, et cele si chaï contreval'). In
carrying out this signal form of justice, the executioners asserted that they had
responded to 'a great wonder' ('une grant merveille') encoded as prophecy in the
physical environment surrounding them, by themselves engineering the 'wonder'
('la merveille') and making it actuality.[74]

In the wake of this execution, the conquerors were said to have instituted an
elaborate programme of processions and other ceremonies in order to establish
their guardianship of the urban landscape. Some were rites of passage such as
coronations, marriages and lyings-in-state that occurred only from reign to reign.
Others, including receptions, banquets, church services, sporting events and even
levées and couchées, recurred in more regular annual, weekly or daily cycles. By
these means, the crusaders sought to occupy imperial buildings and monuments,
and render routine their own presence there. The inauguration and coronation of
Baldwin I in 1204 (d.1205) was followed by further coronations of emperors, such
as of Henry in 1206 (d.1216) and Robert in 1221 (d.1228), and of empresses,
such as Agnes in 1207 (d.1207/8). Henry celebrated his marriage 'with joy and
great splendour' ('a grant joie et a grant enneur'). He is also recorded taking part
in stational processions on feast days, such as that to the Church of Our Lady of
Vlacherna to mark the anniversary of the Purification of the Theotokos.[75]

---

[73] Robert de Clari, *Conquête*, ed, Dufournet, pp. 204–6; Geoffroy de Villehardouin, *Conquête*, ed. Dufournet, pp. 204–6; B. Hendrickx and C. Matzukis, 'Alexios V Doukas Mourtzouphlos: His Life, Reign and Death (?–1204)', Ἑλληνικὰ 31 (1979), 108–32.

[74] Geoffroy de Villehardouin, *Conquête*, ed. Dufournet, pp. 204–6.

[75] Robert de Clari, *Conquête*, ed. Dufournet, pp. 184–90; Geoffroy de Villehardouin, *Conquête*, ed. Dufournet, pp. 178, 262, 289–90; compare with G. Dagron, *Priest and Emperor: The Imperial Office in Byzantium*, trans. J. Birrell (Cambridge, 2007), pp. 84–114; M. McCormick, 'Analyzing Imperial Ceremonies', *Jahrbuch der österreichischen Gesellschaft für Byzantinistik* 35 (1985), 1–20; M. McCormick, *Eternal Victory: Triumphal Rulership in Late Antiquity, Byzantium and the Early Medieval West* (Cambridge, 1986), 131–230; A. Cameron, 'The Construction of Court Ritual: The Byzantine Book of Ceremonies', in *Rituals of Royalty. Power and Ceremonial in Traditional Societies*, ed. D. Cannadine, and S. Price (Cambridge, 1987), pp. 106–36; and A. Beihammer, 'Comnenian Imperial Succession and the Ritual World of Niketas Choniates's *Chronike Diegesis*', in *Court*

2.15a–b. Princeton, Firestone Library, Special Collections, Numismatics Collection. Coin: 9864. Latin imitative issue billon trachy, Constantinople, thirteenth century. Obverse: Christ standing; legend: 'IC XC'. Reverse: Emperor; legend: 'ωΔC| Τω ΠΟΡ'. Copied from coinage originally issued by John II Komnenos (r.1118–43). With permission of Firestone Library, Princeton University.

It was perhaps a final irony that the concerted effort by 'a people' from the west with 'iron hauberks' ('une gent [...] a costeles de fer') to display their ownership of the Byzantine Empire – an effort delineated by de Clari in his native French vernacular – resulted in the rejection of precisely that vernacular in favour of a return to the Greek of the indigenous population.[76] The coins struck by the crusaders not only imitated earlier iconography, but reproduced inscriptions in Greek that included the words 'ΔΕCΠΟΤΗC' (i.e. despot) and 'ΠΟΡΦΥΡΟΓΕΝΝΗΤΟC' (i.e. porphyrogennitos), and even the names of dead emperors from the previous Komnenian dynasty (Plates 2.15a-b).[77] Similarly, the charters they issued bore seals that depicted crusader emperors in eastern imperial regalia – dressed in the *loros* and crowned with a closed crown with lappets – and that were inscribed in Greek (Plates 2.16a-b).[78] Thus, the legend

---

Ceremonies and Rituals of Power in Byzantium and the Medieval Mediterranean, ed. A. Beihammer, S. Constantinou and M. Parani (Leiden, 2013), pp. 159–202.

[76] Robert de Clari, *Conquête*, ed. Dufournet, pp. 106, 136, 178–84; T. Shawcross, 'Conquest Legitimized: The Making of a Byzantine Emperor in Crusader Constantinople (1204–1261),' in *Byzantines, Latins, and Turks in the Eastern Mediterranean World after 1150*, ed. J. Harris, C. Holmes and E. Russell (Oxford, 2012), pp. 198–204.

[77] Franscesco Balducci Pegolotti, *La pratica della mercatura*, ed. A. Evans (Cambridge MA, 1936), 287–9; A. Stahl, 'Coinage and Money in the Latin Empire of Constantinople', *Dumbarton Oaks Papers* 55 (2001), 197–206 (pp. 199–200).

[78] G. Schlumberger, F. Chalandon, and A. Blanchet, *Sigillographie de l'Orient latin* (Paris, 1943), pp. 168–173; *De Oorkonden der Graven van Vlaanderen (1191–Aanvang 1206)*,

2.16a–b. Paris, Archives nationales de France – Site de Paris, J//419 no 5. Chrysobull, Paris, March 1268. Golden seal of Baldwin II depicting the emperor dressed in a Byzantine-style crown and *loros* (obverse) and referring to him as 'ΔΕCΠΟΤΗC' and 'ΠΟΡΦΙΡΟΓΕΝΝΗΤΟC' (reverse).

on the seals of Henri I (r.1206–16) contains the titles '*ΔΕΣΠΟΤΗΣ*' (despot) and '*ΑΥΤΟΚΡΑΤωΡ*' (autokrator). Born and nurtured in Constantinople, Baldwin II (r.1228–61/73) was in the habit of referring to himself in addition

---

Part I, ed. W. Prevenier (Brussels, 1966), p. 476; R. Chalon, 'Trois bulles d'or des empereurs belges de Constantinople', *Revue de numismatique belge* 17 (1861), 384–8 (p. 384); J. Longnon, 'Notes sur la diplomatique de l'empire latin de Constantinople', in *Mélanges dédiés à la mémoire de Félix Grat*, ed. É.-A. van Moé, J. Vielliard and P. Marot, 2 vols. (Paris, 1949), II, 3–18 (p. 12); B. Hendrickx, 'Les Institutions de l'Empire Latin de Constantinople (1204–1261): Le Pouvoir impérial (L'empereur, les régents, l'impératrice)', *Βυζαντινά* 6 (1974), 85–154 (pp. 130–3).

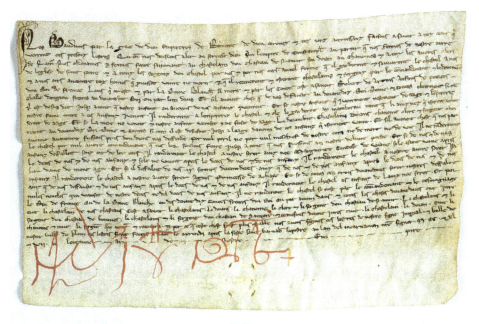

2.17. Paris, Archives nationales de France – Site de Paris, J//409 no. 2. Charter, June 1247, with subscript with the date in the Byzantine manner and the emperor's signature in Greek written by Baldwin II in his own hand using cinnabar ink. The seal formerly affixed to the document depicts the emperor in a Byzantine-style crown and *loros*.

as 'ΠΟΡΦΙΡΟΓΕΝΝΗΤΟC' (i.e. porphyrogennitos), meaning 'born in the purple' – an appellation indicating birth in the special chamber in the Great Palace where for centuries empresses had repaired for their lying-in.

Indeed, Baldwin, who signed official documents in subscripts in cinnabar ink with his name and the month and year calculated in the Constantinopolitan manner, knew how to write Greek in a confident cursive (Plate 2.17). By contrast, his grasp of his ancestral tongue displayed the limited vocabulary, imperfect grasp of grammar and halting diction that was typical of a second-generation emigré and was considered by native speakers back in France to be so rudimentary as to appear infantile.[79] Responding to the sexual politics of pervasive narratives about the entertainment of western knights by the

---

[79] For studies on the subject of acculturation and language use by modern immigrant communities and other bilinguals, see U. Weinreich, *Languages in Contact: Findings*

daughters of the imperial house in Constantinople, an anonymous chronicle – the *Récits d'un ménestral de Reims* – offered by way of contrast the sober reception accorded at Marseille to the Latin emperor of Constantinople by the queen regent of France. The chronicle explained that Blanche granted Baldwin II an audience during which she gave him a great deal of good counsel – only to discover that the 'words' with which he responded to her were silly and 'immature' ('et le trouva enfantif en ses paroles'). The impression the queen dowager gained of the emperor displeased her 'greatly' ('et li deplaisoit mout'), the text explained, 'for the maintenance of an empire needs a very wise and energetic man' ('car à empire tenir convient mout sage homme et viguereus').[80] The reader is encouraged to draw the inference that the crusader claimant to the legacy of Byzantium lacked the potential to become a model of knightly masculinity.

Conclusions: Novelty and wonder in the thirteenth century

The early thirteenth-century narratives of the Fourth Crusade and its conquest of Constantinople and the Byzantine Empire composed by Geoffroy de Villehardouin and Robert de Clari were among the very first works of history written in prose in the French language. Their creation was undoubtedly influenced by the ambitions of the crusading movement, begun in 1095, to occupy the eastern Mediterranean. As such, these narratives can be considered watersheds in the ongoing creation of a canon that proclaimed the cultural supremacy of the colonisers over those whom they colonised. The alleged novelty of the experience was underscored by the adoption of an original literary genre for its recounting. And yet, as I have argued here, these works of historiography in Old French cannot be properly analysed unless they are considered together with other texts from which they are in fact descended. Some of these texts were also composed in Old French (albeit in verse) – while still others were composed in Latin and, crucially, in Greek. Unless we acknowledge that the content and form of the group of vernacular histories known as the *Conqueste de Constantinoble* were deeply indebted to sources originating in the east of which westerners were already well aware by the end of twelfth century, we run the risk of missing the distinctive way in which these narratives of conquest undertook to accomplish an act of cultural

---

and Problems (The Hague, 1979); and F. Grosjean, *Life with Two Languages: An Introduction to Bilingualism* (Cambridge MA, 1982).

[80] *Récits d'un ménestral de Reims*, ed. N. de Wailly (Paris, 1876), p. 225; Shawcross, 'Conquest Legitimized', p. 201.

appropriation and refashioning. Nor will we be able to evaluate the extent to which that enterprise ultimately proved successful.

Wonderment of the type westerners claimed to experience when they attempted to engage with the physical and imaginary landscape of Constantinople was identified by contemporary thinkers with a particular response, largely physiological, but also emotional and intellectual, that was triggered by amazement at the sensible appearance of something unusual, great and portentous. Wonderment, argued theoreticians such as the thirteenth-century scientist and philosopher Albertus Magnus, manifests itself in the body through a constriction and suspension of the heart. While on a superficial level this response of wonder is 'something like fear in its effect on the heart', it in fact constitutes a different phenomenon, for it springs from a 'longing to know' that which appears to be strange – a longing that is acutely felt and needs to be fulfilled. He who wonders feels a compulsion to acknowledge his puzzlement, confess his ignorance and coarseness and declare an earnest wish to be enlightened. This means that wonderment is essentially 'the movement of the man who does not know but is on his way to finding out, who is getting at the bottom of that which he wonders and determining its cause'.[81] Moreover, as the thing that initially eluded and alienated the wonderer seems to change before his scrutiny, gradually becoming more approachable and familiar, he finds that he is engaged in what is in fact an act of submission that should be apprehended not as one-way but rather as reciprocal. To set out to acquire and possess knowledge is also to allow oneself to be potentially so profoundly affected by that knowledge that one is possessed by it.[82] Thus, and ineluctably, one may be turned from a native speaker of French into a native speaker of Greek – with all the transformation of one's identity this linguistic shift entails.

Of course, in the process one both gains something and loses something. What has seemed supernatural ends up by becoming banal. As de Clari lamented, the statues 'formerly were accustomed to play by enchantment, but now never play' ('et soloient cha en arriere giuer par encantement, mais ne juoient mais nient').[83] In time, the animation of the inanimate monuments of the Byzantine Empire ceased to belong to the realm of the uncanny, but could be explained away instead as a trick worked through the manipulation of the technology peculiar to automata. Within a couple of generations, for those who settled in the former territories of the Byzantine Empire, such as

---

[81] Albertus Magnus, *Alberti Magni opera omnia*, ed. A. Borgnet, 38 vols. (Paris: 1890–5), VI, 30–1.

[82] Geoffroy de Villehardouin, *Conquête*, ed. Dufournet, p. 102.

[83] Robert de Clari, *Conquête*, ed. Dufournet, p. 180.

88   TERESA SHAWCROSS

the family of Marco Polo, who referred to themselves with pride as inhabitants 'of Constantinople', the location of the wonderous was no longer to be found on the shores of a Bosphorus that had become their regular place of residence, but rather in distant Beijing – at the court of the Great Khan of the Mongols, Qubilai.[84] Yet such emigrés continued to want to believe in marvels and in magic – and to choose to write about them in French.[85] But, in order to do so persuasively, they had to set out for a new destination across the globe where they might exchange 'familiar things' for those 'unheard of'.[86] The foreignness of Greek words had receded before that of the Turkic (e.g. 'que sunt apelés *bargherlac*' ['which are called *bargherlac*']) and Mongolian (e.g. 'et s'appellent en lor langajes *gudderi*' [and they are called in their language *gudderi*']) that would now be embedded in French texts.[87] For the 'old' must give way to the 'new'. And that which has become 'natural' must be replaced by that which is still 'marvellous'.[88]

[84]   G. Orlandini, 'Marco Polo e la sua famiglia', *Archivio veneto-tridentinio* 9 (1926), 1–68 (p. 7); T. Shawcross, 'The Worldview of Marco Polo's *Devisament dou monde*: Commercial Marvels, Silk Route Nostalgia and Global Empire in the Late Middle Ages', in *Authorship, Worldview, and Identity in Medieval Europe*, ed. C. Raffensperger (Abingdon, 2022), pp. 142–70 (155).

[85]   Marco Polo, *Milione/Le Divisament dou monde. Il Milione nelle redazioni Toscana e franco-italiana*, ed. G. Ronchi (Milan, 1982), pp. 305–662; P.-Y. Badel, 'Lire la merveille selon Marco Polo', *Revue des Sciences Humaines* 183 (1981), 7–16; S. Marroni, 'La meraviglia di Marco Polo: L'espressione della meraviglia nel lessico e nella sintassi del Milione', in *I viaggi del Milione: Itinerari testuali, vettori di trasmissione e metamorfosi del Devisement du monde di Marco Polo e Rustichello da Pisa nella pluralità delle attestazioni*, ed. S. Conte (Rome, 2008), pp. 233–62.

[86]   Gervase of Tilbury, *Otia imperialia: Recreation for an Emperor*, ed. and trans. S. E. Banks, and J. W Binns (Oxford, 2002), p. 558.

[87]   Polo, *Milione*, ed. Ronchi, pp. 393 and 464.

[88]   Gervase of Tilbury, *Otia imperialia*, ed. and trans. Banks and Binns, p. 558.

3

Mixed Metaphors, Mixed Forms:
Across Medieval Hebrew and French Prosimetra

Isabelle Levy

Something unexpected occurs in the prose of medieval Hebrew and French prosimetra: as the poetry in some mixed-form compositions becomes increasingly meta-poetic and didactic, the prose, in turn, expresses metaphors typically rendered in verse, such as the beloved's eyes as twinkling stars. Such instances result in profoundly imaginative moments of formal manoeuvring that challenge both the formal and fictional boundaries of such compositions, and that likewise challenge the reader to revisit medieval Hebrew and French texts with a fresh comparative gaze. In this chapter, I draw on attitudes toward and treatments of metaphor to compare these unexpected moments in Hebrew prosimetra and French prosimetric or polymetric compositions of the same period, which seem to offer the only comparable treatment of what I call 'concrete metaphors'. Not to be confused with the didactic practice of turning verse to prose, for some medieval authors, the prosification of poetic metaphors expresses their idea of love as bound to poetic practice even when that love is articulated in prose.

The Hebrew prosimetra known as *maqamat* that form the focus of this inquiry into metaphor were composed in northern Spain by Solomon ibn Ṣaqbel (twelfth century) and Jacob ben El'azar (twelfth–thirteenth centuries). These authors drew on a hybrid of Arabic and Romance poetics and thematics. The Romance elements conceivably arrived via the troubadours, *trouvères* and Galician-Portuguese troubadours at the Iberian courts, though, as is the case for many plausible literary-historical contacts, no paper trail can verify such assertions.[1] The French works with similar treatments of metaphor include the anonymous *Aucassin et Nicolette*, Tibaut's polymetric *Roman de la poire* and Jean Renart's *Roman de la rose ou de Guillaume de Dole*. A comparison of the development of metaphor across traditions points to deeper literary and historical correspondences; viewing this kindred feature in medieval French literature alongside Jewish literary traditions

---

[1] H. R. Lang, 'The Relations of the Earliest Portuguese Lyric School with the Troubadours and Trouvères', *Modern Language Notes* 10 (1895), 104–16. For analysis and mapping of troubadour movement, see R. Harvey, 'Courtly Culture in Medieval Occitania', in *The Troubadours: An Introduction*, ed. S. Gaunt and S. Kay (Cambridge, 1999), pp. 8–27.

underscores the need to consider these traditions within a complex network of indistinct borders and many different languages and literary traditions, including Occitan, Hebrew and Arabic.[2]

Medieval Hebrew poetry

Before describing medieval metaphor theory across traditions and comparing uses of concrete metaphors, I first contextualise Jewish literary practices with background on the development of medieval Hebrew poetics in al-Andalus and its increasingly multifaceted trajectory in Christian Spain and southern France. In the prime period of intellectual flourishing in al-Andalus (*c.*950–1150), Hebrew was not a spoken language and was voiced only in prayer. Jews living under Islamic rule spoke colloquial Arabic day-to-day and studied a wide array of treatises in Arabic, many of which comprised translations and commentaries, via intermediaries, from Ancient Greek.[3] When writing their own such treatises on topics ranging from medicine to poetics, Jewish thinkers wrote in Judeo-Arabic – Arabic in Hebrew letters – since Hebrew was the first alphabet that educated Jews learned. But the language of poetry spurred a different innovation: inspired by the forms and themes of classical Arabic poetry, and more broadly by its vibrant secular intellectual culture (known as *adab*), the very same authors who wrote treatises in Judeo-Arabic devised a new Hebrew poetics in tenth-century al-Andalus, to the initial dismay of early detractors who feared blaspheming the Holy Tongue. Secular and sacred variations of this Hebrew poetry proliferated, all the while incorporating Arabic poetry's forms and quantitative metre, which was not a natural fit to

---

[2] Rina Drory urges the reader of medieval Hebrew literature to look for the 'hidden contexts' inherent in such compositions, even if this kind of speculation defies a notion of historical precision: 'The Hidden Context: On Literary Products of Tri-cultural Contacts in the Middle Ages' [Hebrew], *Pe'amim: Studies in Oriental Jewry* 46/47 (1991), 9–28. For recent scholarship that takes this crucial comparative approach, see S. Kinoshita, *Medieval Boundaries: Rethinking Difference in Old French Literature* (Philadelphia, 2006); K. Mallette, *Lives of the Great Languages: Arabic and Latin in the Medieval Mediterranean* (Chicago, 2021); and more specifically with respect to Jewish literature and its multivalent surroundings, J. P. Decter, *Iberian Jewish Literature: Between al-Andalus and Christian Europe* (Bloomington, 2007); D. Wacks, *Double Diaspora in Sephardic Literature: Jewish Cultural Production before and after 1492* (Bloomington, 2015); and R. Brann, *Iberian Moorings: Al-Andalus, Sefarad, and the Tropes of Exceptionalism* (Philadelphia, 2021).

[3] For a discussion of the Hebrew-Arabic diglossia, see R. Drory, '"Words Beautifully Put": Hebrew versus Arabic in Tenth-Century Jewish Literature', in *Genizah Research after Ninety Years: The Case of Judaeo-Arabic*, ed. J. Blau and S. C. Reif (Cambridge, 1992), pp. 53–63.

the Hebrew language; still, this style persisted beyond the time and space of al-Andalus and was adopted by Jewish poets unfamiliar with Arabic.[4]

In the two centuries following the florescence of Andalusi Hebraic poetry, Jewish authors continued to write secular and sacred lyrics in Hebrew using Arabic forms and metre. While the Hebrew lyric corpus of this period has traditionally been regarded as decadent and derivative, scholars are revisiting it now with a greater attention to its historical context: no longer based in al-Andalus, Jews grappled with different social and political realities and intellectual currents.[5] Some Jews and Christians in Christian Spain continued to speak Arabic into the thirteenth century (such Christians were known as Mozarabs), but Alfonso X, who embraced elements of Andalusi intellectualism and culture to his own ends, promoted the supremacy of Castilian. The undervalued writings born of these circumstances were shaped by encounters with shifting cultural contexts, from experimentation with Romance metre to shifting thematics.[6]

Sometime in twelfth-century northern Spain, Jewish authors began to experiment with Hebrew versions of the *maqama*, a collection of prosimetric stories typically featuring a narrator who recounts the adventures of his (anti-) heroic friend.[7] Invented by Badīʿ al-Zamān al-Hamadhānī (968–1008) in current-day north-eastern Iran, the Arabic *maqama* gained its reputation as showcase of scholarly erudition with the rapid spread of the collection by al-Ḥarīrī of Baṣra (1054–1122). Hebrew *maqamat* – which have been so termed due to their prosimetric structure – were not limited to the Arabic model; scholars have discussed various ways in which some of these Hebrew *maqamat* seem to draw on Romance literary motifs.[8] Of the extant Hebrew *maqamat*, only al-Ḥarizi's

---

[4] For a thorough explanation of these literary developments, see R. P. Scheindlin, 'Hebrew Poetry in Medieval Iberia', in *Convivencia: Jews, Muslims, and Christians in Medieval Spain*, ed. V. B. Mann, T. F. Glick and J. D. Dodds (New York, 1992), pp. 38–59.

[5] J. P. Decter 'Belles-Lettres', in *The Cambridge History of Judaism*, vol. 6, *The Middle Ages: The Christian World*, ed. R. Chazan (Cambridge, 2018), pp. 787–812 (p. 788).

[6] For an instance of use of Romance metre in Jacob ben Elʿazar's *Sefer ha-meshalim*, see I. Levy, *Jewish Literary Eros: Between Poetry and Prose in the Medieval Mediterranean* (Bloomington, 2022), pp. 14, 34 n. 29. In the early fourteenth century, Immanuel of Rome adapted the sonnet for use in Hebrew, which he wove into his *maqama* collection; for further reading on how he rendered the sonnet in Hebrew, see D. Bregman, *The Golden Way: The Hebrew Sonnet during the Renaissance and the Baroque*, trans. A. Brener (Tempe AZ, 2006).

[7] For history and contents of the Arabic and Hebrew *maqama*, see R. Drory, 'The Maqāma', in *The Literature of Al-Andalus*, ed. M. R. Menocal, M. Sells and R. P. Scheindlin (Cambridge, 2000), pp. 190–210.

[8] For scholarship on the Romance elements in *Sefer ha-meshalim*, see the following: J. Schirmann, 'Les Contes rimés de Jacob ben Eléazar de Tolède', in *Études d'orientalisme dédiés à la mémoire de Lévi-Provençal*, ed. R. Brunschvig (Paris, 1962), pp. 285–97; *Toledot*

92   ISABELLE LEVY

Taḥkemoni adheres to the Arabic precedent in form and content; other Hebrew compositions known as *maqamat* are replete with nods to various Romance practices, from their fixation on poetry to their unusual uses of metaphor.[9]

As just mentioned, al-Ḥarizi (1165–1225) was particularly intrigued by the Arabic model, having translated al-Ḥarīrī's *maqamat* from Arabic to Hebrew before creating his own Hebrew collection, the *Taḥkemoni*. When, like other educated Jews living in Christian Spain and southern France, al-Ḥarizi lamented the loss of Andalusi intellectualism, he did so via the *Taḥkemoni*, in the introduction to which he bemoaned the decay of the Hebrew language. Nor was he alone in this effort; a preoccupation with the status of Hebrew is the most compelling shared feature across al-Ḥarizi's *Taḥkemoni* and the other so-called Hebrew *maqamat*, such as ben El'azar's *Sefer ha-meshalim* and ibn Sahula's *Meshal ha-qadmoni*. These authors also shared an impetus toward translation: al-Ḥarizi translated Maimonides' *Guide of the Perplexed* from Judeo-Arabic into Hebrew, and ben El'azar rendered ibn al-Muqaffa''s Arabic version of *Kalila wa-Dimna* into Hebrew rhymed prose. Ben El'azar's choice of text exemplifies the intellectual currents in Iberia and southern France that shaped both Hebrew and Romance writers alike: in 1251, a year before he came to power, Alfonso X commissioned a translation of *Kalila wa-Dimna* into Castilian. Along with twinning translations are potential crossed paths at the courts: the Toledan ben El'azar might have encountered any number of the troubadours, trouvères and Galician-Portuguese troubadours who spent time singing at the courts of Alfonso VIII of Castile, Ferdinand III of Castile and León and Alfonso X of Castile, León and Galicia.[10] In addition to compelling temporal and geographic connections, uses of metaphor provide textual evidence of interactions among practitioners of various literary traditions.

---

ha-shira ha-'ivrit bi-Sfarad ha-noṣrit uvi-drom Ṣarefat [Hebrew], ed. J. Schirmann and E. Fleischer (Jerusalem, 1997), pp. 224–40; J. Schirmann, 'L'Amour spirituel dans la poésie hébraïque du moyen âge', *Lettres Romanes* 15 (1961), 315–25; R. P. Scheindlin, 'Sipure ha-ahava shel Ya'aqov ben El'azar' [Hebrew], in *Proceedings of the Eleventh World Congress of Jewish Studies*, ed. D. Assaf (Jerusalem, 1994), pp. 16–20; Decter, *Iberian Jewish Literature*; Decter, 'Belles-Lettres'; Wacks, *Double Diaspora*; I. Levy and D. Torollo, 'Romance Literature in Hebrew Language with an Arabic Twist: The First Story of Jacob ben El'azar's *Sefer ha-meshalim*', *La Corónica* 45 (2017), 279–304; Levy, *Jewish Literary Eros*.

9   Drory, 'The Maqāma', p. 206. Instead of using the term *maqama*, Dan Pagis refers to such texts as 'rhymed narratives' which 'should be examined individually' given their variety; 'Variety in Medieval Rhymed Narratives', *Scripta Hierosolymitana* 27 (1978), 79–98 (pp. 81, 83).

10   Lang, 'Portuguese Lyric School'. Matti Huss dates *Sefer ha-meshalim* sometime from the mid-1100s to the mid-1200s: 'Clarifications Regarding the Time and Date of Composition of *Sefer HaMeshalim*' [Hebrew], in *Meir Benayahu Memorial Volume: Studies in Talmud, Halakha, Custom, Jewish History, Kabbala, Jewish Thought, Liturgy, Piyyut, and Poetry in Memory of Professor Meir Benayahu z'l*, ed. M. Bar-Asher, Y. Libes, M. Assis and Y. Kaplan (Jerusalem, 2019), pp. 1021–56.

Metaphor in theory

A shared stake in Ancient Greek approaches to figurative language led literary critics across medieval Arabic, Hebrew and Romance cultures to engage metaphor as a topic worthy of detailed discussion. Equally crucial was the importance of biblical metaphor to Romance and Hebrew poetics and of biblical and quranic metaphor in Hebrew and Arabic composition.[11] Tenth- and eleventh-century Arabic literary critics wrote about metaphor in complex terms, which included considerations of *takhyīl* (make-believe) and *muḥākāt* (imitation or mimesis), drawn from Aristotle's μίμησις (mimesis): al-Fārābī connected poetry with *takhyīl* and *muḥākāt* in his *Kitāb al-Sh ʿir* (d. 950; *The Book of Poetry*), part of his commentary on the *Organon*.[12] A century later, considerations of metaphor by ibn Sīnā (Avicenna; d. 1037) and ʿAbd al-Qāhir al-Jurjānī (d. 1078) encompassed what Lara Harb describes as the evocation of wonder in the listener.[13] Others, notably al-Qāḍī al-Jurjānī (d. 1002; different from ʿAbd al-Qāhir al-Jurjānī), found fault with metaphors that went too far beyond the realm of logic: 'the goal is moderation and contenting [oneself] with what is close and known, limiting [oneself] to what is apparent and clear'.[14] Moderation, however, seems not to be the prevailing concern among authors of some Hebrew and French prosimetra and polymetres.

The Andalusi Jewish scholar Moses ibn Ezra (1055–post-1135) included a detailed discussion of metaphor in his early twelfth-century Judeo-Arabic treatise *Kitāb al-muḥāḍara wa-l-mudhākara* (*The Book of Discussion and Conversation*). The final twenty chapters of the text treat 'stylistic recourses to embellish poetry', and ibn Ezra dedicates the first of these to metaphor in an explanation that does not limit metaphor to the realm of poetry: 'One must know that, among all of the rhetorical devices that are necessary for whomever composes poetry and which beautify the words of whomever writes prose, the

---

[11] Some Arabic theoreticians were attuned to biblical poetics and metaphor, particularly converts from Judaism to Islam, such as Abū 'l-Barakāt al-Baghdādī: W. Heinrichs, 'Takhyīl: Make-Believe and Image Creation in Arabic Literary Theory', in *Takhyīl: The Imaginary in Classical Arabic Poetics*, ed. G. J. van Gelder and M. Hammond (Cambridge, 2008), pp. 1–14 (p. 9).

[12] Heinrichs, 'Takhyīl', pp. 5, 6. Of particular interest given the present context, Heinrichs was likewise a trailblazer in his consideration of the prosimetrum in Classical Arabic: see his 'Prosimetrical Genres in Classical Arabic Literature', in *Prosimetrum: Crosscultural Perspectives on Narrative in Prose and Verse*, ed. J. Harris and K. Reichl (Cambridge, 1997), pp. 249–75. For a parallel pioneering study of prosimetrum, see P. Dronke, *Verse with Prose from Petronius to Dante: The Art and Scope of Mixed Form* (Cambridge MA, 1994).

[13] L. Harb, *Arabic Poetics: Aesthetic Experience in Classical Arabic Literature* (Cambridge, 2020), p. 93.

[14] Al-Qāḍī al-Jurjānī, trans. and brackets Harb, *Arabic Poetics*, p. 40.

94   ISABELLE LEVY

metaphor is one of the most beautiful things one can use'.[15] But what exactly renders metaphor beautiful poses more of a challenge. The ineffable nature of figurative language demands a sufficiently complex explanation; ibn Ezra tackles this complexity by describing how metaphor would function as a tangible object: 'in dressing it in the clothing of metaphor, the word is left embellished in its ornament and its envelope becomes more delicate'. In conveying the kind of mastery required to implement metaphor properly, ibn Ezra takes a figurative approach to figurative language echoed in Walter Benjamin's notion of how 'the language of the translation envelops its content like a royal robe with ample folds' – metaphor and translation as linked forms of crossing.[16]

Ibn Ezra's subsequent textual examples are drawn from the Bible, the Qur'an, Arabic poetry, Hebrew poetry and ibn al-Mu'tazz's ninth-century Arabic treatise *Kitāb al-badi* (*The Book of Rhetorical Figures*), a work credited with initiating 'the study of poetics in Islam'.[17] Ibn Ezra's reliance on ibn al-Mu'tazz's early work on metaphor leads Mordechai Cohen to surmise that ibn Ezra's definition of metaphor 'suited his literary outlook by highlighting the imaginative capacity of metaphor', and Jonathan Decter likewise links ibn Ezra's consideration of panegyric in the *Kitāb* to al-Fārābī's notion of the 'imaginative faculty'.[18] Cohen further notes that ibn Ezra 'foreshadows the modern rejection of Aristotle's narrow linguistic definition in favor of a more comprehensive literary one'.[19] This 'return' to an earlier, broader notion that more readily embraces more creative metaphors is, in fact, fitting to the context of Hebrew prosimetra in the two centuries following ibn Ezra's writing.

Moses Maimonides (1135–1204) instead derived his definition of metaphor (the very definition that ibn Ezra seems to have moved beyond) from Aristotle via al-Fārābī: a 'borrowing' of a term and transferring it to 'designate something

---

[15] Moses ibn Ezra, *Kitāb al-muḥāḍara wa al-muḍākara*, ed. M. Abumalham Mas, 2 vols. (Madrid, 1986), I, 118v, ll. 6–8 (p. 243).

[16] W. Benjamin, 'The Task of the Translator', in *Illuminations. Essays and Reflections*, ed. H. Arendt, trans. H. Zohn (New York [1968] 2007), pp. 69–82 (p. 75).

[17] B. Lewin, 'Ibn al-Mut'azz', in *Encyclopaedia of Islam*, 2nd edn (Leiden, first published online, 2012), accessed 5 December 2022, http://dx.doi.org/10.1163/1573–3912_islam_SIM_3312.

[18] M. Z. Cohen, 'Ibn Ezra vs. Maimonides: Argument for a Poetic Definition of Metaphor (Istia'āra)', *Edebiyāt* 2 (2000), 1–28 (p. 2). J. P. Decter, *Dominion Built of Praise: Panegyric and Legitimacy among Jews in the Medieval Mediterranean* (Philadelphia, 2018), p. 172. See also the discussion in J. P. Decter, 'Panegyric as Pedagogy: Moses ibn Ezra's Didactic Poem on the "Beautiful Elements of Poetry"' (*maḥāsin al-shiʿr*) in the Context of Classical Arabic Poetics', in *'His Pen and Ink Are a Powerful Mirror': Andalusi, Judaeo-Arabic, and Other Near Eastern Studies in Honor of Ross Brann*, ed. A. Bursi, S. J. Pearce and H. M. Zafer (Leiden: Brill, 2018), pp. 65–93 (p. 71).

[19] Cohen, 'Poetic Definition of Metaphor', p. 2.

ACROSS MEDIEVAL HEBREW AND FRENCH PROSIMETRA 95

else'.[20] He would have likely balked at both ibn Ezra's embracing of metaphor as 'imaginary ascription' and the Hebrew *maqama*'s subsequent uses of metaphor. In his *Treatise on Logic* (*Maqāla fī sinā'at al-mantiq*), Maimonides writes that 'the metaphorical term is a name which in the original usage of the language came to denote, and to be fixed permanently in, a certain object, and afterwards it was given but not permanently to another object, e.g., the name "lion" given to one of the animal species, but sometimes also to a man of might...Poets may use many such terms'.[21] Maimonides drew examples of metaphor from the Bible and reasoned that metaphor was necessary in the biblical context because it could explain complex concepts in a way that was readily understandable and could thus 'persuade the people to obey God's directives'.[22] His notion of metaphor must be considered within the context of his view of poetry, which though seemingly expansive in theory, is actually quite limited, given his injunction against poetry that enlists Hebrew to profane ends and goads men to improper behaviour.[23]

Shem Tov ibn Falaquera (1223/28–post-1290) espoused an equally wary approach to figurative language that complemented his rejection of poetry in favour of unrhymed and unadorned prose. In *Sefer ha-mevaqesh* (*Book of the Seeker*), Falaquera describes sets of intellectual exchanges between the Seeker and the thinkers he encounters on his journey toward enlightenment, including an encounter with the Poet, who explains that metrical language allows poets 'to increase their metaphorical power and elegance, to feed man's imagining

[20] Cohen, 'Poetic Definition of Metaphor', pp. 5, 15.

[21] Moses Maimonides, *Maimonides' Treatise on Logic* (*Maqāla fī sinā'at al-mantiq*), ed. and trans. I. Efros (New York, 1938), p. 60. Cohen notes that what editor and translator Efros has translated as metaphorical literally means 'borrowed': 'Poetic Definition of Metaphor', p. 5.

[22] D. L. Roberts-Zauderer, *Metaphor and Imagination in Medieval Jewish Thought: Moses ibn Ezra, Judah Halevi, Moses Maimonides and Shem Tov ibn Falaquera* (Cham, 2019), p. 200, n. 51; for Maimonides' discussion of imaginative faculty as facilitating comprehension of prophecy, see Moses Maimonides, *The Guide of the Perplexed*, trans. S. Pines (Chicago, 1963), 1.17 (pp. 42–3). Thomas Aquinas similarly noted 'that poetry employs metaphors for the sake of representation, for this is something which naturally gives men pleasure. But sacred instruction uses metaphors because they are necessary and useful'; A. J. Minnis and A. B. Scott, ed., with the assistance of D. Wallace, *Medieval Literary Theory and Criticism c. 1100–c. 1375: The Commentary Tradition*, rev. edn (Oxford, 1988), p. 240.

[23] See Maimonides, *Guide of the Perplexed*, 3.8 (II, 435); Moses Maimonides, *Mishna 'im perush Rabenu Moshe ben Maimon*, ed. and trans. Y. Qa'fiḥ (Jerusalem, 1964), Avot 1:16. For a translation of the latter text, see J. T. Monroe, 'Maimonides on the Mozarabic Lyric (A Note on the *Muwaššaḥa*)', *La Corónica* 17.2 (1989), 18–32 (p. 20).

96   ISABELLE LEVY

soul which yearns to see beautiful things'.[24] What starts out as a prosimetrum, however, becomes a prose treatise: following his meeting with the Poet, the Seeker vows to renounce poetry, reasoning that 'those who practice it use only figurative and metaphorical terms, which are far from the truth'.[25]

On the medieval Latin side, the medieval arts of poetry were practical in nature, intended to instruct schoolboys in matters of language; rhetorical flourishes served as examples. Medievals did not consider Aristotle's *Rhetoric* from the standpoint of instruction in the arts of discourse but as a component of moral philosophy.[26] Metaphor is the first trope Geoffrey of Vinsauf discusses in his early thirteenth-century *Poetria nova* (*c.*1210), which he groups with simile as comparison (*collatio*): 'the third step is a comparison, which may be performed by a twofold principle, either covertly or openly, covertly and openly as signifying metaphor and simile, respectively'.[27] Concerned with proper implementation, Geoffrey notes that the poet should avoid 'forced metaphors' when transforming the subject so that 'whenever your meaning comes clothed in apparel of this sort, the sound of the words is sweet to the happy ear, and it soothes the inner mind with an unexpected delight'.[28] Figurative language of clothing again describes rhetorical figures.

Like Maimonides' and Falaquera's discourses, the discussion of metaphor by John of Garland (*c.*1195–1272) is inseparable from poetry, but rather than narrowing his definition, John's broad notion of formal possibility expands his notion of metaphor in his *Parisiana poetria de arte prosayca, metrica et rithmica*. John considers prose, verse and rhythmics as a single art and more broadly 'for treating any subject whatever', as he explains: 'The author teaches how to find, according to the categories of invention, the words, that is, nouns, adjectives, and verbs used both literally and figuratively, for any kind of composition, whether it be a legal or academic letter, an elegiac poem, a comedy, a tragedy, a satire, or a history'.[29]

While these Latin manuals were intended as teaching tools for school students, their slightly later vernacular counterparts, such as the early fourteenth-century Occitan *Leys d'Amors* attributed to Guilhem Molinier, were intended for

---

[24] Shem Tov ben Joseph ibn Falaquera, *The Book of the Seeker* (*Sefer Ha-Mebaqqesh*), trans. M. H. Levine (New York, 1976), p. 89.

[25] Falaquera, *Sefer Ha-Mebaqqesh*, trans. Levine, pp. 81–2. R. Brann, *The Compunctious Poet: Cultural Ambiguity and Hebrew Poetry in Muslim Spain* (Baltimore, 1991), pp. 124–36, esp. pp. 126, 135.

[26] J. J. Murphy, ed., *Three Medieval Rhetorical Arts*, paperback edn (Berkeley, 1985), p. xv.

[27] Murphy, ed., *Three Medieval Rhetorical Arts*, p. 42, trans. Kopp.

[28] Murphy, ed., *Three Medieval Rhetorical Arts*, p. 67; J. J. Murphy, 'The Arts of Poetry and Prose', in *The Cambridge History of Literary Criticism. Vol. 2: The Middle Ages*, ed. A. Minnis and I. Johnson (Cambridge, 2005), pp. 42–67.

[29] John of Garland, *Parisiana Poetria*, ed. and trans. T. Lawler (Cambridge, 2000), p. 3.

'use by practicing poets rather than by young learners of language'.[30] Even so, the Latin treatises would have been useful to those who composed in Latin and in vernacular languages: 'hence the inference is that vernacular facility may derive from Latin training.'[31] In his early thirteenth-century *Razos de trobar* (*Rational Principles of Poetic Composition*), Raimon Vidal de Besalú (fl. 1190–1213) offers readers 'the first poetic grammar and rhetorical treatise in any Romance language', but he does not mention metaphor.[32]

Slightly out of our temporal range but crucial for a full picture of the development of metaphor theories in Romance traditions is the anonymous (debatably authored by Dante) early fourteenth-century *Epistle to Can Grande della Scala*. The author reminds the reader that 'we perceive many things by the intellect for which language has no terms – a fact which Plato indicates plainly enough in his books by his employment of metaphors; for he perceived many things by the light of the intellect which his everyday language was inadequate to express'.[33] The notion of metaphor has moved from being one among a practicable list of potential rhetorical devices in the Latin treatises to a significant link to the world of the imaginary; theory and practice are merged here. Of course, the imaginary was already hard at work in practice, most conspicuously in medieval allegorical traditions, but the Romance-language theoretical articulation of the idea seems to emerge once Romance poetics had flourished and experimented with metaphor for centuries, as was likewise the case in preceding centuries in classical Arabic and Hebrew: theory reflects practice.

Hebrew prosimetra with striking metaphors

Solomon ibn Ṣaqbel composed the first extant Hebrew *maqama* in Christian Spain during the first half of the twelfth century. The text is known as *Ne'um Asher ben Yehuda* (*The Words of Asher, Son of Judah*); Jefim Schirmann and Ezra Fleischer both proposed that ibn Ṣaqbel's story was likely part of a larger

---

[30] Murphy, 'The Arts of Poetry and Prose', p. 61.

[31] Murphy, 'The Arts of Poetry and Prose', p. 67.

[32] E. Bou, 'Catalan Poetry', in *The Princeton Encyclopedia of Poetry and Poetics*, 4th edn, ed. R. Greene, S. Cushman, C. Cavanagh, J. Ramazani, P. Rouzer, H. Feinsod, D. Marno and A. Slessarev, pp. 211–13 (Princeton, 2012), p. 211. Translation of title is Sarah Kay's: *Parrots and Nightingales: Troubadour Quotations and the Development of European Poetry* (Philadelphia, 2013), p. 27. For the text and analysis, see E. W. Poe, *From Poetry to Prose in Old Provençal: The Emergence of the 'Vidas', the 'Razos', and the 'Razos de trobar'* (Birmingham AL, 1984); and Raimon Vidal, *The 'Razos de Trobar' of Raimon Vidal and Associated Texts*, ed. J. H. Marshall (London, 1972). For discussion of Raimon Vidal's treatise, see Kay, *Parrots and Nightingales*.

[33] Minnis and Scott, ed., *Medieval Literary Theory and Criticism c.1100–c.1375*, p. 468.

collection, corroborating its classification as a *maqama*.[34] The frame of *Ne'um Asher* certainly evokes the Arabic *maqama*'s narrator-protagonist scheme: Asher recounts an adventure he had as a youth which concludes when he is duped by his trickster friend, the Adulamite. The interior story contains a detailed allegory of love in which vapid Asher is educated in the arts of poetry and love by a refined lady: Asher wanders in a drunken stupor searching for 'gazelles' (the frequent term for the lady in medieval Hebrew poetry, stemming from both the Song of Songs and classical Arabic poetry) until a lady throws him an apple engraved with poems. By the time Asher realises he should have responded to her, she is gone; he wanders aimlessly, lamenting his foolishness, until a group of ladies promises to introduce him to the lady of the apple inside the harem. Once Asher is inside, an angry man chastises him for breaching the walls – until 'he' reveals himself to be one of the ladies. Asher's 'lady' then approaches but subsequently reveals *himself* to be Asher's old friend the Adulamite, who offers Asher his daughter in marriage. The frame of the story ends with the narrator's poem, which utterly undercuts the contents of the story: 'Enjoy my charming story, gentle friends,/ But don't be taken in by what you've heard./ A tale of lover's folly this, no more,/ A pack of lies – I made up every word!'[35]

Similarly, a few of the ten stories in Jacob ben El'azar's early thirteenth-century *Sefer ha-meshalim* (*The Book of Stories*) feature women who lead their muddled male objects of desire toward a state of spiritualised and poetic amorous enlightenment. Still, except for a brief autobiographical nod in the introduction in which ben El'azar champions the revivifying of Hebrew, his stories lack a consistent narrator's frame, leaving the entire collection in an allegorical haze.[36] In the sixth story, maiden Penina and her beloved Maskil

---

[34] J. Schirmann, 'Poets Contemporaneous with Moses ibn Ezra and Judah Halevi' [Hebrew], *Studies of the Research Institute for Hebrew Poetry* 2 (1936), 62–152; and E. Fleischer, 'Studies in Liturgical and Secular Poetry' [Hebrew], in *Studies in Literature Presented to Shimon Halkin*, ed. E. Fleischer (Jerusalem, 1973), pp. 183–204.

[35] Solomon Ibn Saqbel, 'Asher in the Harem', in *Rabbinic Fantasies: Imaginative Narratives from Classical Hebrew Literature*, trans. R. P. Scheindlin, ed. D. Stern and M. J. Mirsky (New Haven, 1998), pp. 253–67 (p. 264); Solomon Ibn Saqbel *Ha-shira ha-'ivrit bi-Sfarad uvi-Provans* [Hebrew], ed. J. Schirmann (Jerusalem, 1954) 1.2, 565, ll. 197–8.

שעו דודי יפי שיחי וטובו / ושמרו–נא לבל תנקשו בו: //
הלא הם לעגי עוגבים ומלים / אשר בדא דידכם מלבבו

[36] For discussions of allegory in *Sefer ha-meshalim*, see Decter, *Iberian Jewish Literature*, pp. 141–156; T. Rosen, *Unveiling Eve: Reading Gender in Medieval Hebrew Literature* (Philadelphia, 2003), pp. 95–102; I. Levy, 'Hybridity through Poetry': *Sefer ha-meshalim* and the Status of Poetry in Medieval Iberia', in *A Comparative History of Literatures in the Iberian Peninsula*, ed. C. Domínguez, A. Abuín González and E. Sapega, 2 vols. (Philadelphia, 2016), II, 131–7; T. Bibring,

ACROSS MEDIEVAL HEBREW AND FRENCH PROSIMETRA 99

encounter a giant, Cushan, whom Maskil defeats as much by physical strength as by Penina's coaxing of Maskil to gird himself for battle by reciting poetry. In the seventh story, two women, Yemima and Yefefiya (who fight dressed as men), duel over the affections of a young man, Yashefe. The ladies ultimately agree to share Yashefe and live out peaceful days instructing his sister in the arts of poetry. In the ninth story, a young man named Sahar leaves home to escape his father's grasp, finds himself shipwrecked outside of a harem; and Kima, the princess within, instructs him in the art of love poetry. Kima's father eventually consents to the marriage and dies soon after, leaving the lovers to continue their poetic quarrels as they rule as king and queen.[37]

Al-Ḥarizi's early thirteenth-century *Taḥkemoni* includes stories that touch on poetry and on love but none with the components of poetic instruction or ethical striving in love. One story in his collection echoes *Ne'um Asher*, as the narrator mistakes his old trickster friend for a tall, beautiful maiden; another recounts the brilliance of the great poets of Spain; and a third culminates in a marriage to a hag disguised as a beauty, whom the narrator murders at the story's close. While these canonical *maqamat* present the themes of poetry and love as they are treated in their Arabic counterparts, they do little to explain certain aspects of ibn Ṣaqbel's and ben El'azar's compositions, such as their seeming nods to courtly love and their unusual metaphors.[38] Given that the *Taḥkemoni* appeared around a century after *Ne'um Asher* and contemporaneous to *Sefer ha-meshalim*, al-Ḥarizi could have borrowed certain textual elements from ibn Ṣaqbel's work, though he seems to have avoided its unconventional metaphors.

'Fairies, Lovers, and Glass Palaces: French Influences on the Thirteenth-Century Hebrew Poetry in Spain – the Case of Ya'akov ben El'azar's Ninth Maḥberet', *Jewish Quarterly Review* 107 (2017), 297–322; and Levy and Torollo, 'Romance Literature in Hebrew Language with an Arabic Twist'. For allegory more generally in the Hebrew *maqama*, see Drory, 'The Maqāma', pp. 202–3.

[37] The characters' names are significant: *Penina* means 'pearl'; *Maskil*, 'wise'; *Cushan* is a name derived from the land of Cush (Habbakkuk 3.7); *Yemima* is 'the old one' or 'the one of the sea'; *Yefefiya* is 'the most beautiful'; *Yashefe* is the jasper stone; *Sahar*, the crescent moon; *Kima*, the Pleiades. In his *Iberian Jewish Literature*, p. 143, Decter comments on the allegorical meanings of names in *Sefer ha-meshalim*. For a translation of the story of Maskil and Penina, see T. Rosen, 'The Story of Maskil and Peninah by Jacob Ben El'azar: A Thirteenth-Century Romance', *Florilegium* 23 (2006), 155–72; for an analysis of the story of Sapir, Shapir and Birsha, see J. P. Decter, 'A Hebrew "Sodomite" tale from Thirteenth-Century Toledo: Jacob Ben El'azar's Story of Sapir, Shapir and Birsha', *Journal of Medieval Iberian Studies* 3 (2011), 187–202.

[38] For a discussion of what might be termed courtly love in these texts, see Levy, *Jewish Literary Eros*, chapter 2.

Chronology and geography: connecting Hebrew and French

While scholars have compared the spiritualised notion of love in these stories to Romance counterparts, specifically to *Aucassin et Nicolette*, metaphor offers an equally compelling point of entry, since the ways in which these authors use poetry and prose provide a glimpse into their visions of love poetics.[39] But tracing of influences or confluences in these works is unfortunately chronologically flawed: *Aucassin et Nicolette*, itself an anomaly, has dubious dating ranging throughout the thirteenth century, with *c.*1270 as the latest date proposed.[40] Ibn Ṣaqbel's *maqama* appeared roughly a century prior to *Aucassin et Nicolette*, Tibaut's *Roman de la poire* and Jean Renart's *Roman de la rose ou de Guillaume de Dole* (c. 1210–30).[41] These French prosimetra or polymetres are, nevertheless, rough contemporaries of *Sefer ha-meshalim*, a *maqama* that seems to refer knowingly to the plot and thematics of *Ne'um Asher*.

Such kindred literary treatments prove more convincing when paired with historical confluences, and *Sefer ha-meshalim*, *Aucassin et Nicolette* and *Guillaume de Dole* share more than the mixed form and metaphors in prose: Occitan is their natural go-between. If we momentarily put aside the other prosimetra in question and their seemingly inconsistent chronologies and geographies – *Ne'um Asher* is too early, the *Roman de la poire* too geographically disconnected – the remaining three offer compelling evidence: in addition to their chronological alignment in the early to mid thirteenth century, the fictional and parodic Languedoc setting of *Aucassin et Nicolette*, Jean Renart's quotations of Occitan lyric and ben El'azar's probable interactions with troubadours who visited the courts in northern Spain provide reasonable common ground. Accompanying these geographical confluences is a shared compositional landscape, in part exemplified via Occitan lyric and the innovative prose of the *vidas* and *razos*.[42]

---

[39] For comparisons to *Aucassin et Nicolette*, see Schirmann, 'Les Contes rimés de Jacob ben Eléazar de Tolède', p. 295; Scheindlin, 'Sipure ha-ahava shel Ya'aqov ben El'azar', pp. 17, 19; and Decter, *Iberian Jewish Literature*, p. 152.

[40] B. Blakey, 'Aucassin et Nicolette XXIX, 4', *French Studies* 22 (1968), 97–8.

[41] For comments on the dating of *Guillaume de Dole*, see Kay, *Parrots and Nightingales*, pp. 93, 418 n. 5.

[42] Kay remarks that *Guillaume de Dole*'s dating places it 'later than Raimon Vidal's grammar and *Abril issia*, and probably also after the composition of *So fo* and Uc's earliest *razos* and *vidas*. Its inclusion of troubadour quotations acquires additional resonance from the fact that its probable date range coincides with that of the Albigensian Crusade (1209–ca. 1229).' She concludes that 'situating Guillaume de Dole in this way nuances the traditional view of it as inaugurating French lyric insertion'; *Parrots and Nightingales*, pp. 93, 105. For further insights into Jean Renart's quotations of Occitan lyrics, see *Parrots and Nightingales*, chapter 5.

Although the mixed form was a mainstay among Jewish authors of medieval Iberia, prior to the twelfth century prose texts were composed in Judeo-Arabic, and Hebrew prose was a relatively new phenomenon.[43] Why did Jewish authors not adopt and adapt the *maqama* for use closer to its inception in Arabic? And why is al-Ḥarizi's *Taḥkemoni* the only Hebrew *maqama* that truly adheres to the narrative framework of the Arabic *maqama*? It is worth considering whether these difficult-to-classify Hebrew prosimetra are more closely attuned to their surrounding Romance literary environs than their formal characteristics indicate, particularly since Hebrew prose experiments appear when Jewish life in al-Andalus shifted toward Christian Spain and southern France/Occitania. The chronological overlapping of our Hebrew prosimetra with Occitan lyric and its *vidas* and *razos* helps elucidate the apparent hybridity of many Hebrew *maqamat*; after comparing metaphors in prose in the Hebrew and French prosimetra, I will offer some kindred instances from the *vida* and *razo* corpus as potential intermediaries.

Metaphor in practice

The following comparisons parse some of the unusual uses of metaphor in prose in the Hebrew *maqamat* and French prosimetra. I begin with metaphors about fruit, since these instances allow for a deeper consideration of the way in which such metaphors influenced the narrative structures of these polymetric and prosimetric compositions. Comparison of the beloved to fruit existed across traditions, from biblical and Ancient Greek and Roman precedents to contemporaneous Arabic, Hebrew and Romance applications. Accordingly, these fruit-as-beloved metaphors are a natural first step toward understanding unexpected uses of metaphor and can be expressed in two phases: first, a fruit can be a stand-in for the lover or beloved; second, the fruit itself can be an object that has poems inscribed on it, in which case the fruit's description takes on an ekphrastic quality in its representation of love. This secondary phase more firmly links the beloved to poetry, the verses on the fruit subsuming not only the beloved's representation but also the crucial connection between poetry and proper loving.[44]

The inscription on fruit is particularly at home in the Arabo-Andalusi sphere: al-Washshā' devoted a portion of his tenth-century treatise on eloquence to poems fit for inscription on a variety of surfaces, including apples

---

[43] For a discussion of shifting languages of composition among Jewish authors, see Drory, 'Words Beautifully Put'.

[44] For a discussion of metaphors that appear on various objects in Hebrew *maqamat*, see Levy, *Jewish Literary Eros*, chapter 3.

102 ISABELLE LEVY

and various other fruits.[45] This very phenomenon occurs in *Ne'um Asher* and in ben El'azar's story of Sahar and Kima when the beloveds throw apples engraved with poems at their prospective poet-lovers.[46] But the apple persists beyond this initial moment as a clever object and becomes a veritable player in the narrative when it remains as a physical embodiment of the more elusive human beloved. This increasingly complex use of fruit is evident in Asher's treatment of the apple and its effect on him: 'I took out the apple that she had thrown me, to read it again and to return to its beauty, and its verses stuck to my heart and crumbled it into meal'.[47] The 'she' who threw the apple is the beloved, but here she seems an afterthought, the mere conveyor of love and not its source, since the physical apple possesses control over Asher's heart. Asher returns to the apple repeatedly through the narrative: 'whenever my strength failed and my spirit diminished, I took the apple out on my hand, brought it to my nose, and sniffed its perfume to revive myself by its pleasures'.[48]

Kima, the beloved in the ninth story of ben El'azar's collection, likewise presents Sahar with an inscribed apple. Later in the narrative Kima's handmaiden refers to the apple when informing Sahar of his beloved's name: 'Kima is the name of your fair beloved, the owner of the apple anointed with the oil of myrrh'.[49] And once Sahar knows her name, he uses the apple to distinguish her from among her ladies in waiting: 'Who among you is my lady Kima, the creator of the lovely poem inscribed on the apple that was left beside the wall?'[50] Given the kindred

---

[45] Muḥammad ibn Isḥāq ibn Yaḥyā al-Washshā', *Kitāb al-muwashshā* (*Book of Eloquence*) (Beirut, 1965). For a translation into Spanish, see Muḥammad ibn Isḥāq ibn Yaḥyā al-Washshā', *El Libro del Brocado* [*Kitāb al-muwashshā*], trans. T. Garulo (Madrid, 1990). For a discussion of fruit poetry, see A. Schippers, 'Hebrew Andalusian and Arabic Poetry: Descriptions of Fruit in the Tradition of the "Elegants" or ẓurafā'', *Journal of Semitic Studies* 33 (1988), 219–32. Apples carried clear Edenic connotations particularly in the Christian sphere, but they were just as useful in the vernacular Romance context: Raimon Vidal includes the apple as an example of a 'substantive' word; for the text and commentary, see Kay, *Parrots and Nightingales*, p. 30.

[46] Scheindlin draws attention to the inscribed apple-as-beloved motif and recalls the similar occurrence in *Sefer ha-meshalim*: 'Asher in the Harem', p. 265 n. 11.

[47] Ibn Ṣaqbel, *Ha-shira ha-'ivrit*, ed. Schirmann, 1.2, 558, ll. 40–2:
הוצאתי את התפוח / אשר היה אלי שלוח / שבתי לקרותו /
וביפיו לחזותו / דבקו בלבי הבתים / ופתות אותו פתים

[48] Ibn Ṣaqbel, *Ha-shira ha-'ivrit*, ed. Schirmann 1.2, 560, ll. 83–4:
כאשר כשל כחי / וקצרה רוחי, הוצאתי את התפוח בכפי
והגשתיהו לאפי / הריחותי בשמיו / וחייתי במנעמי

[49] Jacob ben El'azar, 'Sipure ha-ahava shel Ya'aqov ben El'azar' [Hebrew], ed. J. Schirmann, *Studies of the Research Institute for Hebrew Poetry in Jerusalem* 5 (1939), 247–66, p. 250: ll. 88–9: הלא כימה / שם אהובתך הנעימה / בעלת התפוח / אשר בשמן המור משוח

[50] Ben El'azar, 'Sipure ha-ahava shel Ya'aqov ben El'azar', ed. Schirmann, pp. 252–3, ll. 141–2: מי מכם גברתי כימה / בעלת השירה הנעימה / החקוקה בתפוח המשלך בעד החומה For

presence of apples with engraved poems and the chronology of the authors, it seems likely that ben El'azar drew his inspiration from ibn Ṣaqbel's narrative.

Fruit likewise plays a courtship role in Tibaut's mid thirteenth century polymetric *Roman de la poire* (*Romance of the Pear*), a composition that seems to defy all aspects of classification, from genre to form. Though its title suggests it is a romance, it draws 'on tropes from troubadour and other love lyric'.[51] Its form consists of a complex array of mixed verse forms, including acrostics, octosyllabic couplets, refrains, additional 'stanzas of four twelve-syllable lines each, with internal and end rhyme' and some sixteen-syllable lines.[52] Lush illuminations accompany the text in one of its two extant manuscripts, Paris, BnF, MS fr. 2186. The composition shares significant parallels with both *Ne'um Asher* and ben El'azar's story of Sahar and Kima, from the lady's instruction of the poet-lover in the arts of poetry to the fruits as stand-ins for the lady. Following the elaborate prologue of the *Poire* in which the narrator envisions himself as various love-struck literary heroes, the lady hands him a pear from which she has taken a bite; as soon as he too takes a bite, he is in love.[53] While its expression of the fruit motif differs slightly from ibn Ṣaqbel's and ben El'azar's figurations, Tibaut's pear nonetheless recalls the same biblical passages, most likely the Edenic fruit (to which the *Poire* narrator refers, l. 453), with further representations in Song of Songs 2.3, 2.5, 4.3, 4.13, 6.7, 7.8, 7.9, 8.2, and Proverbs 25.11. Further, despite the pear's fixed metaphorical state within the narrative (it does not further influence the plot as does Asher's apple) its presence in the manuscript's illuminations suggests a more sustained impact: as the illustration of the lady's handing the pear to the narrator (fol. 15r) indicates, the pear embodies the beloved and is a symbol of the lover's heart.[54] The physical illustration of the pear-as-heart adds a new formal

---

a discussion of the apple in *Ne'um Asher* and *Sefer ha-meshalim*, see Levy, *Jewish Literary Eros*, pp. 97–8.

[51] L. E. Doggett, 'When Lovers Recount their Own Stories: Assimilating Text and Image Units in the Prologue of the *Roman de la Poire*, MS Paris BnF 2186', *Textual Cultures: Texts, Contexts, Interpretation* 11 (2019), 17–41. See Tibaut, *Le Roman de la poire*, ed. C. Marchello-Nizia (Paris, 1984), xvi–xviii.

[52] S. Huot, 'From *Roman de la Rose* to *Roman de la Poire*: The Ovidian Tradition and the Poetics of Courtly Literature', *Medievalia et Humanistica* n.s. 13 (1985), 95–111 (pp. 95, 109 n. 3). Given Huot's consideration within the tradition of the *Roman de la Rose*, see K. Lynch, *The High Medieval Dream Vision: Poetry, Philosophy, and Literary Form* (Stanford, 1988), p. 127, for a discussion of the metaliterary parsing of metaphor (and use of the word 'metaphor') in the *Roman de la Rose*.

[53] Tibaut, *Roman de la poire*, ll. 398–455.

[54] Paris, BnF, MS fr. 2186, fol. 15r: https://gallica.bnf.fr/ark:/12148/btv1b105065252/f33.item, accessed 2 October, 2023. For an overview of scholarship on the illuminations, see Doggett, 'When Lovers Recount their Own Stories' and H.

104   ISABELLE LEVY

dimension to the polymetric nature of the composition – it is concrete but also increasingly metaphorical, and thus analogous to the substantiated apple in the Hebrew *maqamat*.

The meanings accruing to the pear, made possible via mixed verse forms and illumination, do not make the meaning of the pear more accessible; instead, the additional formal components add additional layers of complexity to the figuration – a complexity that highlights the agency of the female beloved.[55] The beloved's tearing of the pear in the narrative and the illustration of her bestowing the pear-heart show her active role in narrative, much like the active function of Asher's and Sahar's ladies.[56] This fruit is not a single-use metaphor in poetry but rather constructs an intricate web of metaphorical meaning that spotlights women as active participants in generating love and the plot.

Nicolette's viol can be compared to the apples and pear belonging to the other ladies; though not a stand-in for her, it acts as an extension of her and directly facilitates her reunion with Aucassin. Far from the unresponsive object of the typical poet-lover's affections who, despite being bound to the confines of a rhymed and metred poem, causes the poet-lover emotional and physical distress, the ladies in these mixed-form compositions use their objects to secure the affections of their lovers, and in turn, their metaphorical instruments grant them vocal positions of narrative import.

Further, these women enact transformations – their own kind of metaphors – in order to influence the outcomes of their respective narratives: Nicolette dresses herself as a (male) minstrel, and one of the ladies-in-waiting (another metaphor or stand-in for the true beloved) in *Ne'um Asher* disguises herself as

---

Franco Júnior, 'Entre la figue et la pomme: l'iconographie romane du fruit défendu', *Revue de l'histoire des religions* 223 (2006), 29–70: 'La popularité croissante de la pomme dans ce rôle était peut-être aussi liée à sa forme arrondie et à sa couleur rouge, qui la rapprochait du cœur, organe où le christianisme et sa mystique liée au sang versé du Christ voyaient le centre de l'être humain' (p. 46).

[55] For further reading on images that accompany text, see A. Stones, *Gothic Manuscripts, 1260–1320* (London, 2013). Note that in this period, images also began to accompany Hebrew manuscripts as well: Guadalajara native Isaac ibn Sahula included captions to accompany woodcuts in the text of his 1281 Hebrew *maqama* collection, *Meshal ha-qadmoni* (*Story of the Ancient One*). For the text, translation, and reproduction of woodcuts, see Isaac ibn Sahula, *Meshal ha-qadmoni*, ed. and trans. R. Loewe (Oxford, 2004). Scholars have compared ibn Sahula's woodcuts to those that appear in the Galician-Portuguese *Cantigas de Santa María*, commissioned by Alfonso X, who ruled from 1221–84: see Loewe's Introduction, cxxiii–cxxvi; L. Mortara-Ottolenghi, 'The Illumination and the Artists', in *The Rothschild Miscellany*, ed. I. Fishof, 2 vols. (London, 1989), II, 127–251 (p. 127).

[56] For further analysis of the lady in the *Poire*, see H. Solterer, *The Master and Minerva: Disputing Women in French Medieval Culture* (Berkeley, 1995), chapter 2.

male. Similarly instrumental to the plot, Yefefiya and Yemima of ben El'azar's collection dress as male knights to fight for Yashefe's affections. Such disguises – transformations kindred to metaphor – are further signs of the beloveds' active roles. Their actions garner more substantive results than do those of the bickering components of the lover's inner self. These women's transformations prompt the instruction of their lovers; their metaphorical extensions are didactic.[57] In the context of a rhymed, metred poem – even a poem with dialogue or a poem with a refrain, such as a *muwashshah* – physical transformations and metaphorical representations of the beloved are not only confined to the metre and rhyme but also limited by the authority of the poetic 'I'. In the mixed form, however, these ladies and their transfigurations are crucial to the narrative progression, even if they are ultimately constructs of male authors.

The next set of metaphors moves from the bodily to the celestial: metaphors for the beloved's eyes are particularly conducive to comparison across literary traditions given the common Greco-Roman mythological contexts of stars, coupled with the widespread Aristotelian notion of the eyes as gateway to the soul. In *Ne'um Asher*, Asher does not at first see the lady's face but rather 'a star gazed from the windows, peeking from the corners, eyes winking at me, a hand gesturing'.[58] Thus, in this moment before the lady throws Asher the apple, ibn Ṣaqbel invokes in prose a metaphor drawn from Arabo-Andalusi poetry. While the comparison of the beloved to a star in the context of a rhymed, metred poem is expected, it likely had a startling effect in prose given the newness of ibn Ṣaqbel's endeavour; this composition was, after all, the first of its kind in Hebrew – or at least the earliest to survive. As Rina Drory noted, the Hebrew *maqama* was a natural home for fictional storytelling, since Hebrew, which was not used in day-to-day communication, was already somewhat obscure and far from the ordinary, waiting to be manipulated by authors whose readers would delight in their clever manipulations of biblical language.[59]

---

[57] Solterer notes the didactic intent of the female in the *Roman de la poire* and the *Dit de la panthère d'amours*: 'Both texts build on the *Roman de la rose* by combining the disputational model with the common pedagogical genre of the *ars dictaminis* (the art of correspondence). Their account of the disciple's efforts to compose a letter for a woman is thus designed as a school exercise. This exercise turns out to be an ordeal for the disciple', *Master and Minerva*, p. 64; see also pp. 72–4 for Solterer's discussion of how the narrator of the *Roman de la poire* learns how to write. This aspect of the female as a teacher of poetics is likewise the case in *Ne'um Asher* and in the seventh and ninth stories of *Sefer ha-meshalim*; see Levy, *Jewish Literary Eros*, pp. 68–72.

[58] Ibn Ṣaqbel, ed. Schirmann, *Ha-shira ha-'ivrit* 1.2, 557, ll. 22–3:

והנה כוכב משגיח מן החלונות / ומציץ מן הפנות / קורץ אלי בעינו / ומולל בימינו

[59] Drory, 'The Maqāma', p. 199.

106 ISABELLE LEVY

Roughly a century later, ben Elʿazar creates a more intricate version of the same metaphor in the prose of his ninth story: Sahar laments having been saved in a storm only to be captured by two men with bows and arrows who trap him in a net, as the narrator describes: 'He saw glowing faces and twinkling eyes, and two black warriors treated him bitterly, angrily shot arrows at him and concealed a trap for him, the archers finding him with their bow'.[60] Kima's twinkling eyes are both like stars and like warriors. Later in the rhymed prose narrative, the warriors' arrows return as physical objects, now substantiated threats to Sahar's heart and soul, which are 'crushed by arrows and divided': one of the ladies-in-waiting tells Sahar, 'Here are the arrows that tired you', and urges him to run toward the arrows, to which he responds, 'How can you send me to those who will kill me?' In the poem immediately following, Sahar bemoans the perilous state of his heart and soul.[61]

Ibn Ṣaqbel and ben Elʿazar both draw on a trope at home in the Arabo-Andalusi lyric context in which twinkling stars represented the beloved's eyes. In their formulations, the eyes serve as a synecdoche for the beloved and simultaneously refer to the lover's attraction to the beloved's soul. The twinkling eyes also provide a sense of the setting, their twinkling effect presumably evoking the image of a lady swaying behind the lattice wall that marks the harem entrance.

The beloved's eyes were equally at home across Romance traditions, from their frequent appearance in Occitan lyrics to their mention in *Aucassin et Nicolette*. Like Asher and Sahar, Aucassin also sees twinkling stars, but unlike the stars in the Hebrew *maqamat*, the stars he sees are literal. Still, Aucassin links these stars to Nicolette in the poem following, thus forging a joining of beloved and stars that the reader has likewise experienced in the Hebrew *maqamat*:

Et il garda par mi un trau de le loge, si vit les estoiles el ciel, s'en i vit une plus clere des autres, si conmença a dire. Or se cante.

Estoilete, jéte voi,
que la lune trait a soi;
Nicolete est aveuc toi,
m'amïete o le blont poil.
Je quid Dix le veut avoir

---

[60] Ben Elʿazar, 'Sipure ha-ahava shel Yaʿaqov ben Elʿazar', ed. Schirmann, p. 249, ll. 58–60. The story again refers to arrows in the prose passages that follow poems 8 and 25:
וירא והנה פנים נוצצים / ועינים מתלוצצים / ושם שני בני כושים חלוצים
וימררהו ורבו וישטמהו בעלי חצים / ויטמנו לו רשת / וימצאוהו המורים בקשת

[61] Ben Elʿazar, 'Sipure ha-ahava shel Yaʿaqov ben Elʿazar', ed. Schirmann, p. 253, ll. 158–60: מחצים מ חוצים;הנה החצים ממך והלאה; איך תשלחוני אל–הורגי

Across Medieval Hebrew and French Prosimetra 107

> por la lu... e de s... / ... / ... / ... /
> que que fust du recaoir,
> que fuisse lassus o toi:
> ja te baiseroie estroit.
> Se j'estoie fix a roi,
> s'afferriés vos bien a moi,
> suer douce amie.'[62]

The prose inspires a metaphor that the poetry subsequently propels into an increasingly abstract context, just as it elucidates the inner workings of the prosimetrum: contrary to what the audience might expect, the prose initiates a rhetorical complexity that the poetry advances. This plays out in a strikingly similar way in the Hebrew prosimetra, in which the poetry takes on a didactic function – instructing key characters in the art of poetry – while the prose conveys complex rhetorical phenomena.[63] Once prose can do what poetry has traditionally achieved, poetry is free to take on new roles.

Of course, *Ne'um Asher* and *Aucassin et Nicolette* might both be parodic texts – or partially parodic, since some of their contents might evoke moments of seemingly genuine courtliness when viewed apart from the narrative as a whole.[64] Their common use of parody might also explain the presence of this extended metaphor: if *Ne'um Asher* is a spoof, as the author claims in the closing epigram, and if *Aucassin et Nicolette* is a parody of courtly lovers, the preponderance of eyes dressed up as metaphorical stars would further add to the overwrought quality (and perhaps unexpected features) of these compositions.

The *Roman de la poire* contains a similar metaphor in its opening verses in which the narrator compares himself to various lovers, including his

---

[62] *Aucassin et Nicolette*, ed. M. Roques (Paris, 1977), pp. 27–8 (24.87–25.15). 'Gazing up through a gap in the foliage he saw the stars in the sky above, and observing one that was brighter than the others he started to address it. *Here it is sung.* 'Little star, I see you shine,/ Drawn towards the orb of night;/ Nicole is with you on high,/ My sweet love with tresses bright./ Methinks God wants her in the sky/ To be a [light at eventide/ And shed more lustre on the night./ Sweetest love, 'twere my delight/ Up the heavenly stair to climb,]/ Careless how I'd downward dive/ Could I but reach you on high./ How I'd kiss and hug you tight!/ Though I came of royal line/ You would be a fitting bride,/ Most sweet love mine!' *Aucassin et Nicolette*, in *Aucassin et Nicolette and Other Tales*, trans. P. Matarasso (Harmondsworth, 1971), p. 47.

[63] Levy, *Jewish Literary Eros*, p. 105. See Solterer, *Master and Minerva*, for a discussion of female didacticism in the French context.

[64] For a discussion of a moment in which *Aucassin et Nicolette* resists parody, see Kinoshita, *Medieval Boundaries*, p. 66; and for a possibly genuine expression of courtliness in *Ne'um Asher*, see Levy, *Jewish Literary Eros*, pp. 63–7.

comparison of himself to Cligès, of Chrétien's *Cligès*, whose beloved Fenice is struck by the painful and sweet arrows of Love.[65] The arrows do not come back in the course of the narrative but nonetheless appear in a set of tropes that furnishes the plot. Further, the accompanying illustration of villainous doctors who pour lead into Fenice's hand acts as an extension of Fenice's wounded state and enriches the text, just as verse and prose work together to create a deeper meaning in the mixed form.[66]

Finally, we come to fire and water – a set of metaphors that certainly exists across traditions; even so, their expression in the French compositions does not reach the extraordinary extreme achieved in the Hebrew prosimetra. Asher describes the flames of his love for the lady of the apple: 'My soul is trapped like a deer a doe has captured, her bow unswerving in its path, it won't stop until she releases it into my liver. She makes my innards burn and my heart is in flames'.[67] The ladies-in-waiting then hand Asher a poem from his beloved rebuking him for his folly in delaying a response to the apple poem. Asher recounts in prose: 'a fire burst into flames inside of me, my heart and my insides turned on me, my inner grief grew hot', only to be plunged into further danger when the ladies-in-waiting guide him to the following predicament: 'as soon as I passed through the door I was in fire and water…frightened, I tried to get back to dry land, but I could not. Terror gripped me'.[68] Asher survives this – barely – only to find his heart melting like wax when the lady-in-waiting (still dressed as a man) chastises him for his ignorance of the 'etiquette of nobles'.[69] Indeed, Asher's experiences with fire and water show his lack of courtesy. Put simply, he is out of his element, and in the narrative, the natural elements take advantage of his weakness.

In the ninth story of *Sefer ha-meshalim*, Sahar's liver, like Asher's, is burning. This was a frequent trope in classical Arabic poetics, stemming from the

---

[65] Tibaut, *Roman de la poire*, ed. Marchello-Nizia, ll. 61–2. For a discussion of these verses with respect to the accompanying drawing, see Doggett, 'When Lovers Recount their Own Stories', p. 24.

[66] For further analysis of the *Cligès* reference and accompanying image, see Doggett, 'When Lovers Recount their Own Stories', p. 38.

[67] Ibn Ṣaqbel, *Ha-shira ha-ʿivrit*, ed. Schirmann, 1.2, 560, ll. 78–80:
נפשי בפח צביה כצבי אשר נשבה, / דרכה קשתה באיתן ולא שבה
לבד כי לקרב עת אסיפתי / חצי נדודי / תשלח תוך כבדי / ואור תבעיר בקרבי ולבת אש בלבתי

[68] Ibn Ṣaqbel, *Ha-shira ha-ʿivrit*, ed. Schirmann, 1.2, 561–2, ll. 107–8:
ואש בקרבי מתלקחת / ונהפך עלי לבי נחומי / יחד נכמרו ורחמי
and 116–18:
עד אשר עברתי הדלת / ובאתי באש ובמים...ונבהלתי
וחתרתי / להשיב אל היבשה – ולא יכלתי / ותאחזני זלעפות

[69] Ibn Ṣaqbel, 'Asher in the Harem', trans. Scheindlin, 262. Ibn Ṣaqbel, *Ha-shira ha-ʿivrit*, ed. Schirmann, 1.2, 563, l. 146. ברית נדיבים

Arabic translation of Galen's medical treatise on the physiological effects of love in which Galen denotes the liver as the processing centre of sensations of lovesickness.[70] Even so, ben El'azar takes this symbol into unexpected territory: Sahar's beloved Kima *sees* this burning and expresses alarm in the prose.

There are potential analogues in *Aucassin et Nicolette* and Renart's *Roman de la rose ou de Guillaume de Dole*. Aucassin's father twice promises to engulf Nicolette in flames, but given that no one encounters an actual fire, these outbursts seem to be exaggerated prose expressions devoid of unusual rhetorical features. Still, the fire might possess an afterlife in the narrative when Nicolette plays with the possibility of being burned: she reiterates in prose and verse her lament that if she falls, she will be found and burned in a fire. Thus, while the outbursts of Aucassin's father serve as exaggerated expressions of anger that propel the effect of the composition, Nicolette's subsequent mention might signal a real threat. Even if Nicolette's reference to fire were parodic, this would nonetheless continue the metaphor in prose and poetry, now voiced by a different character. The protagonist in Renart's composition likewise expresses in prose the burning sensation of love, but this seems to be purely figurative: after the narrator explains that 'the fires of love were still burning', Guillaume laments that 'all this pain and suffering comes from my love of you'.[71]

---

[70] H. H. Biesterfeldt and D. Gutas, 'The Malady of Love', *Journal of the American Oriental Society* 104 (1984), 21–55. Franco Júnior discusses how the medieval Latin West substitutes the fig for the liver: 'Entre la figue et la pomme'. This is a fitting substitution, given that secular lyrics in the Arabic/Hebrew context are in some instances more overtly erotic and more directly achieve the desire of the poet-lover; the apple allows for more of an allegorical distancing. The fact that ibn Ṣaqbel and ben El'azar include both the liver and the apple is particularly revealing of their existences at literary crossroads. In his *Etymologies*, Isidore of Seville wrote the following about the heart: 'The word 'heart' (*cor*) is either derived from a Greek term, because they call it καρδία, or from 'care' (*cura*), for in it resides all solicitude and the origin of knowledge'. He writes the following about the liver: 'The liver (*iecur*) has this name because there the fire (*ignis*) that flies up into the brain (*cerebrum*) has its seat. From there this fire is spread to the eyes and to the other sense organs and limbs, and through its heat the liver converts the liquid that it has drawn to itself from food into blood, which it furnishes to individual limbs for sustenance and growth. Those who debate medical questions also maintain that the liver is the seat of pleasure and desire'. Isidore of Seville, *The Etymologies of Isidore of Seville*, trans. S. A. Barney (Cambridge, 2006), XI.i.118 and XI.i.125. For further instances in which medieval thinkers considered the heart and the liver, see Franco Júnior, 'Entre la figure et la pomme', p. 47.

[71] Jean Renart, *The Romance of the Rose, or, Guillaume de Dole*, trans. P. Terry and N. V. Durling (Philadelphia, 1993), p. 71. Jean Renart, *Le Roman de la Rose ou de*

Without perfect analogues in Romance or Arabic compositions, the Hebrew prosimetra present their readers with a conundrum. Their extended metaphors in prose about the liver (at home in the Arabic context) and fire and water (present across traditions) are objectively standard, but when placed across poetry and prose and carried by various characters, these metaphors become active players in the narratives; what ibn Ṣaqbel and ben El'azar evoke with these standard terms is highly unconventional. Although there is no extant introduction to ibn Ṣaqbel's *maqama*, subsequent Hebrew mixed-form compositions with varying contents, including *Sefer ha-meshalim*, the *Taḥkemoni* and *Meshal ha-qadmoni*, share a common desire in their introductions to revive the Hebrew language. Perhaps this drive is at work in these unusual extended metaphors in prose: repurposing biblical Hebrew with intentional creativity.

Razos: prose links

Metaphors found in the Occitan corpus touch upon similar themes: the fracturing of the body, in particular the anthropomorphised heart; the eyes and eyesight of the beloved; and the seemingly real physical danger of dying of lovesickness. All of these are expected in poetry and could be termed dead metaphors, but in the context of prose they are unusual, especially since the prose itself was unusual, as William Burgwinkle notes: 'Assuming that [the author of the *razo*] still expected these introductions to be performed (and one need only peruse the closing formulae of many of the texts to see that), what could have led him to compose in prose rather than in verse? Prose was surely an anomaly at this time; the *vidas* and *razos* are actually among the earliest vernacular examples of extended prose writing'. He then offers a plausible explanation: 'At its very inception, prose can be seen to be ideologically motivated, its role being to appropriate a body of culturally canonized founding texts from the exclusive dominion of another supposedly privileged signifying practice, namely verse, that is too closely associated with the dominant political order'.[72] A variation of this rings true in the Hebrew circumstance as well: as an unspoken language whose

---

Guillaume de Dole, ed. F. Lecoy (Paris, 2005), 3889; 3892–3893. 'Encor l'en ert li feus el cors'; 'Touz li pechiez et toz li maus es de vos'.

[72] W. E. Burgwinkle, *Razos and Troubadour Songs* (London, 2019), p. xxx. For further analysis of the purpose of the *vidas* and *razos*, see W. E. Burgwinkle, *Love for Sale: Materialist Readings of the Troubadour Razo Corpus* (New York, 1997), especially the Introduction. The earliest surviving razos appear in thirteenth-century manuscripts, but they refer to earlier razos that circulated in the western Mediterranean, both orally and in writing, before 1219. See E. W. Poe, 'The *Vidas*

compositions one might characterise according to Deleuze and Guattari's notion of a 'minor literature', Hebrew prose was a revolutionary step beyond poetry, perhaps owing its development in part to forced migration out of al-Andalus into territories in which Jewish authors confronted readers unequipped to read their Judeo-Arabic prose texts.[73]

In the following examples drawn from *razos*, the comparatively straightforward prose does little to conceal the strangeness of these metaphors, which exist amid the recounting of otherwise standard information. Such jarring metaphors evoke a range of reactions, from humour to wonder to concern for the poet's wellbeing. The text accompanying Bernart de Ventadorn's canso *Ara'm conseillatz, seignor* (PC 70.6) mentions what one might construe as an unusual metaphor in prose, when his lady opts to pursue the affections of another: 'con hom vencuz d'amor, qe miels li era q'el agues en leis la meitat qe del tot la perdes'.[74] In the *canso*, Bernart explains 'having half of her' as a measure to prevent his madness (ll. 28–30). Neither the prose nor verse explains the halving of the lady, but the repetition of the metaphor in the *razo* is striking, since it does not mirror the other bodily images of the poem, which focus on the lady's and poet's eyes. Of course, the 'half of her' implies an acknowledged agreement that another lover will share her, but the prose itself could have termed this differently than does the poem, in which the halving seems a more natural expression. The half of the body might be intended as humorous in the same way that certain aspects of *Ne'um Asher* and *Aucassin et Nicolette* are. It is also possible that the halving could represent the poet's hope of possession of an actual part of the lady, in which case it is a neat parallel to the lady-as-fruit phenomenon of the Hebrew prosimetra and the *Roman de la poire*. In the same vein, the halving could also resemble the fracturing of the self into metaphorical/anthropomorphised components; even though those were internal components of the self in the Hebrew prosimetra, they are kindred to the half-lady, who is certainly more conspicuous in prose than in poetry, as are extended conversations between the heart and soul.

---

and *Razos*', in *A Handbook of the Troubadours*, ed. F. R. P. Akehurst and J. M. Davis (Berkeley, 1995), pp. 185–197 (pp. 188–189, 194–195).

[73] G. Deleuze and F. Guattari, *Kafka: Toward a Minor Literature*, trans. D. Polan (Minneapolis, 1986).

[74] *Biographies des troubadours: textes provençaux des XIIIe et XIVe siècles,*, ed. J. Boutière and A.-H. Schutz (Paris, 1964), p. 30. 'like a man conquered by love, he realised that it would be better to have half of her than to lose all of her', Burgwinkle, *Razos and Troubadour Songs*, p. 6.

112   ISABELLE LEVY

Similarly, the razo accompanying Bertran de Born's *Domna, pos de mi no us cal* (PC 80.12) describes the following:

> E penset, pois qu'el non poiria cobrar neguna que'ill pogues esser egals a la soa domna, si['s] conseillet qu'el en fezes una en aital guisa qu'el soiseubes de las autras bonas dompnas e bellas de chascuna una beutat o un bel senblan o un bel acuillimen o un avinen parlar o un bel captenemen o un bel gran o un bel taill de persona. Et enaissi el anet queren a totas las bonas dompnas que chascuna li dones un d'aquestz dos que m'avetz auzit nomar per restaurar la soa domna c'avia perduda.[75]

The descriptions of particular attributes in the paired *sirventes* are entirely fitting to the context of poetry, and yet in prose, the effort to grasp particular attributes of individual ladies seems more realistic in its jarring evocation of fragmented people.

In the *razo* associated with Gaucelm Faidit's *No'm alegra chans ni critz agrada* (PC 167.43) and *Tant ai sofert longamen grant afan* (PC 167.59), Lady Audiartz entreats Gaucelm to bestow affections on her rather than on Maria de Ventadorn: 'Et En Gauselms Faiditz, quant auzit los plazers plazens qu'ela li dizia, e vit los amoros semblans qu'ela li mostrava e'ls dous precx qu'ela li fazia e'ill dizia, e'ls grans bes qu'ela li prometia, e vi las grans beutatz e las frescas colors, si fo si sobrepres d'amor qu'el perdet lo vezer e l'auzir'.[76] In another manuscript, Gaucelm 'fo si dolens qu'el volc morir', capturing a metaphor in prose that is much more at home in the lyric context and is analogous to Aucassin's overwrought lament in the *chantefable*.[77]

---

[75] *Biographies des troubadours*, ed. Boutière and Schutz, 75. 'And since he would not find another the equal of his lady, he decided that he should make one through a system of borrowing from each of the other good and beautiful ladies one trait of beauty: an expression, a warm welcome, a lovely way of speaking, beautiful composure, perfect height or an ideal figure. And so he went around asking all the good ladies to give him one of the gifts that you have heard me name in order to bring back to him the lady he had lost.' Burgwinkle, *Razos and Troubadour Songs*, p. 47.

[76] *Biographies des troubadours : textes provençaux des XIIIe et XIVe siècles*, ed. J. Boutière and A.-H. Schutz (Paris, 1964), p. 171. 'And Sir Gaucelm Faidit, when he heard about the pleasing pleasures that she was offering, saw the loving expression that she showed him, the sweet requests that she composed and recited, the magnificent good she was offering, and her great beauty and fresh colours, was so overtaken with love that he lost his sight and hearing.' Burgwinkle, *Razos and Troubadour Songs*, p. 136. The passage continues the loss of sensation by noting what he does 'when his sight and hearing returned'. Burgwinkle notes that 'these physical reactions to pain or pleasure are found elsewhere in the prose texts' and accordingly directs the reader to the *vida* of Jaufre Rudel (*Biographies des troubadours*, ed. Boutière and Schutz, p. 16), p. 138 n. 4.

[77] *Biographies des troubadours*, ed. Boutière and Schutz, p. 181. Gaucelm 'was in so much pain that he wanted to die.' Burgwinkle, *Razos and Troubadour Songs*, p. 144.

Kindred to the mortal distress expressed in the prose of both *Aucassin et Nicolette* and the ninth story of *Sefer ha-meshalim* is the following moment from the *razo* of Raimbaut de Vaqueiras associated with *Ara'm requier sa costum' e son us* (PC 392.2): 'Et el moria de dezirier e de temensa, qu'el no l'auzava preguar d'amor ni far semblan qu'el entendes en ella.' Lady Beatriz knowingly plays along: 'e denan era ben aperceubuda qu'el moria languen deziran per ella', and the following: 'mas enans qu'el mueira, si'll don conseill qu'el li digua l'amor e la volontat qu'el li porta.'[78] Burgwinkle notes that 'what is couched in erotic terms (desire, fearing, dying, loving) turns out to be another case of the poet being hired to sing the lady's praises', but even so, it is striking that the composer of the *razo* would use the same exaggerated terms to describe Raimbaut's dying state and Lady Beatriz's observations thereon, creating the conditions for the beloved to notice the lover's internal state of being.[79] Even if this brief concern is intended as a parody of the overwrought nature of poetry, it noticeably conveys a momentary concern for Raimbaut's wellbeing, particularly when compared to a similar metaphor in the companion poem, which refers briefly to the possibility of death if the lover does not obtain the beloved: 'Mas ben deu far tal ardit vostr' amans/ Moira per vos o n'aia benananssa'.[80] In the poem, the notion of dying comes across as a dead metaphor which will have very little effect on the audience and does not urge the reader to worry for the lover's wellbeing, as the immersed reader of ben El'azar's composition is likely to do. But the metaphor in prose achieves an extraordinary effect in both, whether the intent is parody or ethical enlightenment: the evocation of wonder.

Conclusions

The metaphors in the *razos*, coupled with their temporal and geographical links between the Hebrew *maqamat* and the French prosimetra, offer a compelling case for the transmission of such notions in prose. Such unexpected moments in prose point to a kindred effort across literary traditions – for indeed this

---

[78] *Biographies des troubadours*, ed. Boutière and Schutz, pp. 456–7. Raimbaut 'was dying of desire and fear, for he didn't dare ask her for her love or show any signs that he had any interest in her love.' Lady Beatriz, the object of his affections, 'had already noticed much earlier that he was dying, languishing with desire for her', and when he asks her advice about his feelings for an unnamed lady, she replies that 'rather than dying, I would advise him to tell her of the love and desire that he has for her.' Burgwinkle, *Razos and Troubadour Songs*, pp. 279–80.

[79] Burgwinkle, *Razos and Troubadour Songs*, p. 281 n. 3.

[80] 'But truly your lover must needs display such courage that he should die for your sake or attain bliss'. Raimbaut de Vaqueiras, *The Poems of the Troubadour Raimbaut de Vaqueiras*, ed. J. Linskill (The Hague, 1964), p. 147, l. 32, trans. 148.

was an effort: to use prose in new ways (or to use prose at all) required these authors to reconfigure existing notions of how, when, and why prose ought to express ideas, and, in turn, how to do so in the context of the mixed form. The same could be said of compositions such as the *Roman de la poire* that used a variety of distinct verse forms in unprecedented combinations. The particularly noticeable extremes in the prosified metaphors of the Hebrew *maqamat* are understandable, given the prevailing impetus across Hebrew *maqamat* to showcase the splendour of the Hebrew language – a trend that seems to evoke the idea, however anachronistic, of a proto-cultural Judaism.

Texts that comprised unalloyed prose were a rarity in medieval Hebrew of this period.[81] In its utter disavowal of verse, Falaquera's *Sefer ha-mevaqesh* is a particularly conspicuous example: Falaquera renounced poetry because his titular Seeker, having learned all that can be gleaned from personified Poetry, was ready to progress toward deeper philosophical understanding, which, according to the author's scheme, meant without poetry and without florid prose.[82] Elements traditionally associated with poetry no longer held value in Falaquera's framework. Yet, this could not be further from the endeavours of our authors from across literary traditions, who, in the same century as Falaquera, saw prose and the mixed form as capable of aesthetic, entertaining, and in some cases philosophical value beyond mere conveyance of plot – and others who saw the potential for parody in these very same concepts. With little precedent and great possibility, the newness of prose and the mixing of forms allowed authors of medieval Hebrew and French prosimetra and polymetres to experiment in ways that re-contextualised and revived metaphor to wondrous effect.

---

[81] Rhymed prose was considered prose in the classical Arabic and medieval Hebrew context and not a midway point between poetry and prose; see S. Leder and H. Kilpatrick, 'Classical Arabic Prose Literature: A Researchers' Sketch Map', *Journal of Arabic Literature* 23 (1992), 2–26.

[82] Brann, *Compunctious Poet*, pp. 126, 135.

4

Deeds and Dialogue from a French-Irish Medieval Cultural Sphere

Máire Ní Mhaonaigh

Introduction

Among the burgeoning vernacular literature in French from the late twelfth century is a verse chronicle written in Ireland towards the end of that century that bears witness to the existence of a vibrant French literary culture there not long after the English began to settle in Ireland from 1169, and King Henry II sought to incorporate the territory into his Angevin domain.[1] The poem in question, surviving incomplete and without a title in its single manuscript copy, concerns the recent incomers to Ireland, including the role in the invasion of the second Earl of Pembroke, Richard fitzGilbert de Clare, known as Strongbow, and his Irish father-in-law Diarmait Mac Murchada (Dermot McMurrough), king of Leinster.[2] With reference to these two protagonists, it is often referred to as 'The Song of Dermot and the Earl', but has been retitled *La geste des Engleis en Yrlande* in its most recent edition.[3]

---

[1] 'Normans', 'Anglo-Normans' and 'Cambro-Normans' are often used interchangeably with 'English' to describe the incomers to Ireland in this period; the descendants of Norman settlers in England identified as English by this point, as C. Veach has noted: 'Conquest and Conquerors', in *The Cambridge History of Ireland, Volume 1, 600–1550*, ed. B. Smith (Cambridge, 2018), pp. 157–81 (p. 157 and n. 1). French literary culture in Ireland has been expertly explored in K. Busby, *French in Medieval Ireland, Ireland in Medieval French: The Paradox of Two Worlds* (Turnhout, 2017), and I am very grateful to Professor Busby for his perceptive comments on the material presented here.

[2] The events of this period are briefly described in S. Duffy, *Ireland in the Middle Ages* (Dublin, 1997), pp. 111–33; and in more detail in M. T. Flanagan, *Irish Society, Anglo-Norman Settlers, Angevin Kingship: Interactions in Ireland in the Late 12th Century* (Oxford, 1989).

[3] G. H. Orpen, *The Song of Dermot and the Earl: An Old French Poem from the Carew Manuscript no. 596 in the Archiepiscopal Library at Lambeth Palace* (Oxford, 1892); E. Mullally, *La geste des Engleis en Yrlande: The Deeds of the Normans in Ireland: A New Edition of the Chronicle Formerly Known as the Song of Dermot and the Earl* (Dublin, 2002).

The growing power of Earl Strongbow, who was married to Diarmait's daughter Aífe (Aoife) and had claimed Leinster on the unexpected death of his father-in-law in 1171, as well as that of fellow magnates, prompted Henry to journey to Ireland towards the end of that year in an effort to exert control.[4] A number of Irish kings submitted to him, and he assembled many of his English subjects at a Christmas gathering in Dublin shortly after his arrival.[5] It has been suggested that the romance of *Horn* was performed on that occasion. Moreover, perceived resonances between the depiction of Horn and Strongbow have led to speculation that it was in fact specifically refashioned for that feast.[6] Concrete evidence one way or the other is lacking, but the composition of a lengthy poem on recent political events in a French literary milieu in Ireland less than two decades later points to the existence of a cultural sphere conducive to vernacular writing from the time significant numbers of English acquired land and power in what was to become for many of them home.

Two factors may have had a particular bearing on the development of this specific French literary hub outside France: Ireland's participation in the wider world of European learning, and especially in a Norman network, before the arrival of French speakers in significant numbers in the last quarter of the twelfth century. In addition, the culture within which these incomers settled had a long-established, centuries-old tradition of writing both in Latin and the Irish vernacular, directed and maintained by a secular and ecclesiastical ruling elite. In what follows, I will first address these twin considerations in presenting the context out of which a contact zone involving Irish and French emerged. Out of this interactive ambience, a dramatic versified account of contemporary events, written in French and featuring both Irish and English heroes and villains, came forth. Ireland's *Geste* as literary product and impulse will then be explored.

---

[4] Flanagan, *Irish Society*, pp. 79–136. T. M. Charles-Edwards suggests plausibly that Strongbow was initially offered Dublin rather than Leinster: 'Ireland and its Invaders, 1166–1186', *Quaestio insularis* 4 (2003), 1–34 (pp. 26–34).

[5] Flanagan discusses Henry's actions in Ireland, *Irish Society*, pp. 167–228.

[6] J. Weiss has argued that it was written for the occasion: 'Thomas and the Earl: Literary and Historical Contexts for the *Romance of Horn*', in *Tradition and Transformation in Medieval Romance*, ed. R. Field (Cambridge, 1999), pp. 1–13. K. Busby is more circumspect, noting that 'it is perfectly possible that *Horn* was read at Henry II's Christmas court at Dublin in 1171–2, much less likely that it was composed there, given time constraints': *French in Medieval Ireland*, pp. 168–9.

'The Franks of Ireland'

The earliest manuscript evidence for both Old Irish and Old French is found on the margins of Latin manuscripts of the eighth and ninth centuries.[7] By the time writing in the *langue d'oïl* was emerging in the ninth century, however, Irish had a relatively stable literary form, contemporary biblical and grammatical manuscripts preserving glosses and longer passages of prose and verse.[8] A greater diversity of material extant only in later manuscripts but bearing the linguistic hallmarks of earlier composition suggests that already in the seventh and eighth centuries, such topics as law and liturgy, grammar and genealogy, had been committed to vellum in vernacular ink.[9] This development took place in a bilingual learned environment, Latin providing the underlying matrix out of which vernacular experimentation came forth. As contributors to a Latinate intellectual milieu, Irish scholars were active participants in various learned centres across the Carolingian world.[10] Their continental footprint was visible early, the monasteries of Lagny-sur-Marne and Péronne (for example) having been founded by the seventh-century holy man, and later saint, Fursa, whose earliest missionary activities had brought him to East Anglia whence he travelled to northern Francia.[11] In the second half of the eighth century, a copy of a bilingual Latin-Irish homily dating to some decades earlier was included in a manuscript written for a bishop of nearby Cambrai and Arras, now Cambrai, Bm, MS

---

[7] A. Gautier discusses the rise of various European vernaculars, including Irish and French, in his 'Vernacular Languages in the Long Ninth Century: Towards a Connected History', *Journal of Medieval History* 47:4–5 (2021), 433–50.

[8] The earliest writing from Britain and Ireland is discussed by J. M. H. Smith, 'Writing in Britain and Ireland, *c.* 400–*c.* 800', in *The Cambridge History of Early Medieval English Literature*, ed. C. A. Lees (Cambridge, 2012), pp. 19–49, and M. Ní Mhaonaigh, 'Of Bede's 'Five Languages and Four Nations': The Earliest Writing from Ireland, Scotland and Wales', in *Cambridge History*, ed. Lees, pp. 99–119.

[9] T. Ó Cathasaigh, 'The Literature of Medieval Ireland to *c.* 800: St Patrick to the Vikings', in *The Cambridge History of Irish Literature, Volume 1: to 1890*, ed. M. Kelleher and P. O'Leary (Cambridge, 2006), pp. 9–31, and M. Ní Mhaonaigh, 'The Literature of Medieval Ireland, 800–1200: From the Vikings to the Normans', in *Cambridge History*, ed. Kelleher and O'Leary, pp. 32–73.

[10] See, for example, the essays in *The Irish in Early Medieval Europe: Identity, Culture and Religion*, ed. R. Flechner and S. Meeder (London, 2016).

[11] S. Harmann, 'St Fursa, the Genealogy of an Irish Saint – the Historical Person and his Cult', *Proceedings of the Royal Irish Academy* 112 C (2012), 147–87, and I. Warntjes, 'Die Verwendung der Volkssprache in frühmittelalterlichen Klosterschulen', in *Wissenspaläste: Räume des Wissens in der Vormoderne*, ed. G. Mierke and C. Fasbender (Würzburg, 2013), pp. 153–83 (p. 160).

679. Copying errors suggest that the scribe was not familiar with the Irish language, but nonetheless interest in the document was such that it was preserved between sections of an important collection of canon law, *Collectio canonum Hibernensis*, attributed to two seventh- or eighth-century Gaelic ecclesiastics.[12] In this way the earliest surviving passage of continuous Old Irish prose is preserved, written about 150 years before the Strasbourg Oaths of 842 provide glimpses of what Charlemagne's grandson Louis is said to have uttered in Romance.

In ecclesiastical and courtly contexts in which Irish and continental scholars mingled in the Carolingian period, Latin functioned as a lingua franca and in this intellectual environment, Gaelic learning had a significant place. This is evident in the prominent representation of the Irish script, Ogam, on a page of the late eighth-century manuscript, Bern, Burgerbibliothek, MS 207, written at Fleury, in the context of grammatical writing.[13] In the realm of scientific learning, specifically computistics (the reckoning of time), the considerable Irish contribution is witnessed in the early ninth-century codex, Laon, Bm, MS 442,[14] as well as in the tenth-century related manuscript, Paris, BnF, MS lat. 6400B.[15] Jacopo Bisagni has demonstrated the importance of Fleury and the Loire Valley in the transmission of this material in the ninth and tenth centuries.[16] This was also around the time in which philosophical thinking was shaped by the ninth-century theologian, Johannes, known to contemporaries as *Scottus* 'the Irishman' and who referred to himself as *Eriugena* 'of Irish birth'.[17] Before taking up his position at the court of Charles the Bald, he had been educated in Ireland where he would have encountered vernacular writing; a series of biblical glosses in Old Irish

[12] For discussion of the homily and references to the edition, see P. P. Ó Néill, 'The Background to the Cambrai Homily', *Ériu* 32 (1981), 137–48; see also G. Knight, 'Bilingualism in the *Cambrai Homily*', in *Movement and Mobility: Ideologies of Translation III*, ed. J. Odstrčilík (Vienna, 2021), pp. 104–19.

[13] R. Derolez, 'Ogam, "Egyptian", "African" and "Gothic" Alphabets: Some Remarks in Connection with Codex Bernensis 207', *Scriptorium* 51 (1951), 3–19 (pp. 3–11).

[14] The material in question was discovered by J. Bisagni who discusses this manuscript in his *From Atoms to the Cosmos: The Irish Tradition of the Divisions of Time in the Early Middle Ages*, Kathleen Hughes Memorial Lectures 18 (Cambridge, 2020), pp. 30–2.

[15] For a description of this manuscript, see J. Bisagni, 'Paris BnF MS Lat. 6400B', in J. Bisagni, ed., *A Descriptive Handlist of Breton Manuscripts, c. AD 780–1100*, accessed 3 February 2023, https://ircabritt.nuigalway.ie/handlist/catalogue/138.

[16] Bisagni, *From Atoms to the Cosmos*, pp. 32–4.

[17] For a brief introduction to him, see M. Herren, 'Ériugena, John Scottus', in *Medieval Ireland: An Encyclopaedia*, ed. S. Duffy (New York, 2005), pp. 157–9.

most likely written by him attest to the continuing influence of that training on his thought.[18] Other glossed manuscripts show how interest in Ireland's origins was being developed in Carolingian circles. By drawing specific correspondences between names in Irish pseudo-history and Orosius, as well as Isidore, scholars embedded aspects of Ireland's past in a Latinate learned milieu.[19] Vatican, Biblioteca Apostolica Vaticana, MS Reg.lat.165, located by Olivier Szerwiniack at Reims in the late ninth century,[20] and the roughly contemporary, Laon, Bm, MS 447, provide tangible evidence of this process at work.[21]

While Irish scholars highlighted links between their own origin narratives and canonical histories in continental circles, one specific Irish *grammaticus*, Moriuht, is portrayed as immoral, monstrous and other, in a satirical invective written in the first quarter of the eleventh century by Warner of Rouen, a prominent theme of which is the nature of learning and poetry.[22] Echoing the universal view of Ireland as a fertile land,[23] its non-Christian, unrefined, sexually-preoccupied people do not tend it properly, and so cannot take advantage of its riches.[24] The animal-like Moriuht is the embodiment of their vices; he may consider himself a rhetorician and a poet of the calibre of Homer and Virgilius Maro, but in reality 'he is lukewarm for learning,

---

[18] John Scottus Eriugena, *Glossae divinae historiae: The Biblical Glosses of John Scottus Eriugena*, ed. J. J. Contreni and P. P. Ó Néill (Florence, 1997), especially pp. 17–29 and 54–5.

[19] See M. Clarke, 'The *Leabhar Gabhála* and Carolingian Origin Legends', in *Early Medieval Ireland and Europe: Chronology, Contacts, Scholarship*, ed. P. Moran and I. Warntjes (Turnhout, 2015), pp. 441–79.

[20] O. Szerwiniack, 'Un commentaire hiberno-latin des deux premier livres d'Orose, *Histoire contre les païens*', *Archivum latinitatis medii aevi* 51 (1992–3), 5–137, and 65 (2007), 165–207; and O. Szerwiniack 'D'Orose au *LGÉ*', *Études celtiques* 31 (1995), 205–17.

[21] Clarke, 'The *Leabhar Gabhála*', pp. 454–5.

[22] Warner of Rouen, *Moriuht, A Norman Latin Poem from the Early Eleventh Century*, ed. and trans. C. J. McDonough (Toronto, 1995), pp. 5–7 (on date), on which see also E. van Houts, 'The Date of Warner's *Moriuht*', in her *History and Family Traditions in England and the Continent, 1000–1200* (Aldershot, 1999), pp. 1–6 (IIIb).

[23] Paulus Orosius, for example, notes that Ireland is quite close to Britain and smaller in area than it, but 'richer on account of the favourable character of the climate and soil' ('sed caeli soliquae temperie magis utilis'): *Pauli Orosii Historiarum Adversum Paganos Libri VII*, Corpus Scriptorum Ecclesiasticorum Latinorum 5 (Vienna, 1882), ed. K. Zangemeister, I.2.81; for discussion, see D. Ó Corráin, 'Orosius, Ireland and Christianity', *Peritia* 28 (2017), 113–24 (pp. 118–20).

[24] 'a populo non bene culta suo': Warner of Rouen, *Moriuht*, ed. McDonough, l. 30.

but hot-blooded for sex' ("Sum," canit, "Homerus, sum Maro Virgilius" ... Mineruę tepidus, sed Veneri calidus).[25] While this depiction may suggest he is fictitious, Moriuht could represent an actual rival scholar, possibly another schoolmaster at Rouen.[26] The competitor in question may have been Irish, though Warner's imaginary portrayal of his grotesque characteristics reflects contemporary ethnographic traditions, rather than lived experience, it might be assumed. Significantly, in a vernacular Irish poem cataloguing features of various different groups, based on a Latin tract, *De proprietatibus gentium* from about 900 CE, 'beauty and lust' ('ailli ocus etrad') are associated with the Irish or Gaels.[27] A common reference to *libido Scottorum* could underlie Warner's denunciation of Moriuht's ethnic kind.[28]

The vernacular poem in question, *Cumtach na nIudaide nArd* (*The Edification of the Noble Jews*),[29] is Middle Irish and so perhaps tenth- or eleventh-century in date.[30] The *ferocitas* ascribed to the Franks in the Latin source-text may be echoed in the obscure *frecraid* in Irish, as Patrick Wadden has noted.[31] The second trait accorded them, greed, is connected to Franks in a number of contemporary Irish sources.[32] It is applied to specific Frankish mercenaries in the service of an eleventh-century king of Leinster in the eastern part of Ireland, Diarmait mac Maíl na mBó, 'an avaricious kindred, greedy for old mead' ('fine chuindgeda, sanntaig senmeda').[33] These are likely to have been French-speaking Normans, to whom the term

[25] Warner of Rouen, *Moriuht*, ed. McDonough, ll. 99, 102.

[26] Warner of Rouen, *Moriuht*, ed. McDonough, pp. 40–1, and F. P. C. de Jong, 'Rival Schoolmasters in Early Eleventh-century Rouen with Special Reference to the Poetry of Warner of Rouen (fl. 996–1027)', *Anglo-Norman Studies* 39 (2016), 45–64.

[27] P. Wadden, '"The Beauty and Lust of the Gaels": National Characteristics and Medieval Gaelic Learned Culture', *North American Journal of Celtic Studies* 2:2 (2018), 85–104 (pp. 89–90, for text and translation).

[28] The Latin text is cited in Wadden, '"The Beauty and the Lust of the Gaels"', pp. 90–1.

[29] I use the translation of the wide-ranging term, *cumtach*, favoured by Wadden, '"The Beauty and the Lust of the Gaels"', p. 90; its meanings are set out in *The Electronic Dictionary of the Irish Language*, s.v. *cumtach*, accessed 3 February 2023, http://www.dil.ie/13903.

[30] Wadden, '"The Beauty and the Lust of the Gaels"', pp. 87–9.

[31] Wadden, '"The Beauty and the Lust of the Gaels"', p. 94.

[32] See P. Wadden, 'Some Views of the Normans in Eleventh- and Twelfth-century Ireland', in *The English Isles: Cultural Transmission and Political Conflict in Britain and Ireland, 1100–1500*, ed. S. Duffy and S. Foran (Dublin, 2013), pp. 13–36.

[33] Wadden, '"The Beauty and the Lust of the Gaels"', p. 94.

'Franks' (*Frainc*) was also applied.[34] Diarmait's own sustained involvement with trade and politics in England meant that he encountered Normans in that context also. His principal dealings were with Harold Godwineson and other members of his family, whom he had hosted in Dublin in the 1050s. And Harold's sons retreated across the Irish Sea to Diarmait after their defeat by Normans at the Battle of Hastings, using it as a base for subsequent attack.[35] Wadden has speculated that the negative portrayal of avaricious Franks in Diarmait's service may in fact reflect his experience as an ally of the anti-Norman house of Wessex.[36] This may have been the case, but encounters between Irish and Normans in the eleventh century and later were of many different hues.

To judge from the names of those involved recorded, Normans were among the participants in the Battle of Clontarf in 1014, fighting on the side of Leinstermen and Vikings against a retinue under the king of Munster, Brian Boru.[37] An entry on this conflict was included in the chronicle of Adémar of Chabannes, writing a decade or so after the encounter in 1025. It contains significant detail, alluding to the three-day duration of the battle and the drowning of Viking women and children.[38] Adémar may have had access to both written sources and oral testimony, while his own approach to history writing would also have coloured the account.[39] Nonetheless, the

---

[34] The Irish, Mainz-based universal chronicler, Marianus Scotus referred to Normans fighting at the Battle of Hastings in 1066 as *Franci*, using the term *Northmanni* 'Northmen' for Norwegians fighting at the Battle of Stamford Bridge in the same year: Wadden, 'Some Views of the Normans', p. 18, and see E. van Houts, 'The Norman Conquest through European Eyes', *English Historical Review* 110 (1995), 832–53.

[35] B. T. Hudson, 'The Family of Harold Godwinsson and the Irish Sea Province', *Journal of the Royal Society of Antiquaries of Ireland*, 109 (1979), 92–100; and M. Ní Mhaonaigh, '*Carait tairisi*: Literary Links between Ireland and England in the Eleventh Century', in *Adapting Texts and Styles in a Celtic Context: Interdisciplinary Perspectives on Processes of Literary Transfer in the Middle Ages, Studies in Honour of Erich Poppe*, ed. A. Harlos and N. Harlos (Münster, 2016), pp. 265–88.

[36] Wadden, '"The Beauty and the Lust of the Gaels"', p. 94.

[37] Norman names cited include Simon, Geoffrey and Bernard: see M. Ní Mhaonaigh, *Brian Boru: Ireland's Greatest King?* (Stroud, 2007), pp. 60, 67.

[38] Adémar of Chabannes, *Ademari Cabannensis Chronicon*, ed. P. Bourgain, Corpus Christianorum Continuatio Mediaevalis 129 (Turnhout, 1999), p. 173 (§55).

[39] Ní Mhaonaigh, *Brian Boru*, pp. 57–8; on Adémar as historian, see J. Gillingham, 'Ademar of Chabannes and the History of Aquitaine in the Reign of Charles the Bald', in *Charles the Bald: Court and Kingdom*, ed. M. T. Gibson and J. L. Nelson (Oxford, 1981), pp. 3–14.

record bears witness to continued broader interest in Irish affairs. Ireland's place in the wider Norman world is evident later in the same century in the extended cordial relations between Brian Boru's grandson, Tairdelbach Ua Briain (O'Brien), and William the Conqueror.[40] Ties across the Irish Sea encompassed trade and commerce, as well as secular and ecclesiastical politics at the time. A striking example of such links is the visitation to Tairdelbach by five Jews, perhaps from Rouen, bearing gifts in 1079.[41] His son, Muirchertach, was similarly well connected, exemplified in the arranged marriage between his infant daughter and the Norman Earl of Pembroke, Arnulf de Montgomery, who sought assistance from the Munster ruler in his struggles against William the Conqueror's son, Henry I.[42] It was during the period of Muirchertach's rule that an heroic biography of his great-grandfather, Brian Boru, was written, extolling him as glorious ancestor, triumphant over Vikings at Clontarf. His dynasty is lauded as 'the Franks of Ireland' in the narrative in question, *Cogadh Gáedhel re Gallaibh* (*The War of the Irish against Foreigners*), indicative perhaps of the positive manner in which Normans were viewed in the first decade or so of the twelfth century, Muirchertach dying in 1119.[43] By the last few decades of the century, Normans had settled in Ireland; their arrival in 1169 was associated with a later king of Leinster, Diarmait Mac Murchada, as we have seen. His appeal for assistance against rival Irish dynasts to King Henry II of England and his magnates formed part of a well-established pattern of transmarine contacts and collaboration, as the preceding snapshots of varying types of interaction have shown.

The means of communication involved in these interactions must have been diverse, drawing on the range of languages in use in what were cosmopolitan centres such as Dublin, Bristol and Rouen, including English,

---

[40] See B. T. Hudson, 'William the Conqueror and Ireland', *Irish Historical Studies* 29:114 (1994), 145–58.

[41] *The Annals of Inisfallen (MS. Rawlinson B. 503)*, ed. and trans. S. Mac Airt (Dublin, 1951), pp. 234–5 (1079.3).

[42] E. Curtis, 'Muirchertach O'Brien, High-king of Ireland, and his Norman Son-in-law, Arnulf de Montgomery, c. 1100', *Journal of the Royal Society of Antiquaries of Ireland* 6th ser., 11 (1921), 116–24; Ní Mhaonaigh, *Brian Boru*, p. 114.

[43] *Cogadh Gaedhel re Gallaibh: The War of the Gaedhil with the Gaill, or the Invasions of Ireland by the Danes and Other Norsemen*, ed. and trans. J. H. Todd (Dublin, 1867), pp. 160–1. On the date of the text, see M. Ní Mhaonaigh, 'The Date of *Cogad Gáedel re Gallaib*', *Peritia* 9 (1995), 354–77.

Irish, Welsh, Norse and French.[44] The importance of Latin as a medium can be glimpsed, for example, in the letters between Tairdelbach Ua Briain and his son Muirchertach, and successive archbishops of Canterbury, Lanfranc and Anselm,[45] as well as in twelfth-century Latin Lives of Irish saints directed at non-Irish audiences.[46] In writing his Life of Malachy around 1150 shortly after his subject had died, Bernard of Clairvaux refers to source material from Ireland, presumably in Latin, to which he had access.[47] Malachy was associated with the introduction of both the Cistercian and Augustinian rules to Ireland resulting in another important connecting strand between Irish and continental ruling elites.[48] The continued engagement of Irish scholars with European learning at an advanced level in this period is illustrated in the contents of Oxford, Bodleian Library, MS Auct. F. III 15, containing a copy of Calcidius's translation of Plato's *Timaeus* and an up-to-date synthesis of cosmographical and computistical theory. Glossed in Irish, it was written by an Irishman at Chartres in the first half of the twelfth century, as Pádraig Ó Néill has shown.[49] In an Irish context, this engagement with developing learned trends saw Latin and vernacular

[44] J. Crick, '"The English" and "The Irish" from Cnut to John: Speculations on a Linguistic Interface', in *Conceptualizing Multilingualism in Medieval England, c. 800 – c. 1250*, ed. E. M. Tyler (Turnhout, 2011), pp. 217–37.

[45] Lanfranc, *The Letters of Lanfranc, Archbishop of Canterbury*, ed. and trans. H. Clover and M. Gibson (Oxford, 1979).

[46] For a discussion of a pair of such Latin Lives, see D. Ó Corráin, 'Foreign Connections and Domestic Politics: Killaloe and the Uí Briain in Twelfth-century Hagiography', in *Ireland in Early Mediaeval Europe: Studies in Memory of Kathleen Hughes*, ed. D. Whitelock, R. McKitterick and D. N. Dumville (Cambridge, 1982), pp. 213–31, who places the author of the Lives in France and the Rhineland (p. 223); their significance is also discussed in D. Ó Riain Raedel, 'The Travels of Irish Manuscripts: from the Continent to Ireland', in *A Miracle of Learning: Essays in Honour of William O'Sullivan*, ed. T. Barnard, D. Ó Cróinín and K. Simms (Aldershot, 1998), pp. 52–67; and C. Etchingham, Jón Viðar Sigurðsson, M. Ní Mhaonaigh and E. A. Rowe, *Norse-Gaelic Contacts in a Viking World: Studies in the Literature and History of Norway, Iceland, Ireland, and the Isle of Man* (Turnhout, 2019), pp. 231–2.

[47] M. T. Flanagan, *The Transformation of the Irish Church in the Twelfth and Thirteenth Centuries* (Woodbridge, 2010), p. 14.

[48] Flanagan, *Transformation of the Irish Church*, pp. 118–68.

[49] P. P. Ó Néill, 'An Irishman at Chartres in the Twelfth Century: The Evidence of Oxford, Bodleian Library, MS Auct. F. III. 15', *Ériu* 48 (1997), 1–35; the discussion includes reference to one specific note in the manuscript in which Irish is found, alongside two different dialects of Old French (pp. 28–9). I am grateful to Keith Busby for drawing my attention to this.

writing intertwined. This is exemplified in the person of the main scribe of the earliest extant vernacular Irish manuscript, *Lebor na hUidre* (*The Book of the Dun Cow*).[50] Writing around the turn of the twelfth century, he compiled pseudo-historical and religious material in Irish in this codex, but also copied Boethius's *De re arithmetica*, a glossed version of which has survived in another manuscript from his hand, as Elizabeth Duncan has demonstrated.[51] Moreover, vernacular texts written in this period also show clear evidence for the close alignment of Irish scholars with current European thought.[52] The heroic biography of Brian Boru written in the first decade of the twelfth century already noted, for example, exhibits the creative use of up-to-date Latin rhetorical terminology in metatextual commentary. In approach, this bears comparison with that of leading centres of the period, such as the School of Chartres, with one significant difference: Irish scholars cast precise technical figures into their own vernacular in the process.[53] It was in the context of extensive and extended writing in Irish over centuries, as exemplified in the preceding, that this could be achieved. Cultivation of the vernacular was fostered in a bilingual, Latin-literate environment ensuring that medieval Irish scholars were in dialogue with learned contemporaries elsewhere. Such contacts mirrored engagement in political and ecclesiastical spheres which bound Ireland with Britain and beyond; illustrative examples of this interaction have been presented above.

Ireland's *Geste*

By the twelfth century, therefore, when writing in French was still in its infancy, Irish had become a vehicle for critical, conceptual written expression at a highly accomplished level, as we have seen. Thus, there is a marked contrast between the two languages in their literate form, though the position of written French became much more established as the twelfth century progressed.[54] Among the earliest glimpses of literary French, the *Chanson de Roland* survives

---

[50] For an introduction to the manuscript, see the collection of essays edited by R. Ó hUiginn, *Lebor na hUidre* (Dublin, 2015).

[51] E. Duncan, '*Lebor na hUidre* and a Copy of Boethius's *De re arithmetica*: A Palaeographical Note', *Ériu* 62 (2012), 1–32.

[52] M. Clarke and M. Ní Mhaonaigh, 'The Ages of the World and the Ages of Man: Irish and European Learning in the Twelfth Century', *Speculum* 95 (2020), 467–99.

[53] Clarke and Ní Mhaonaigh, 'The Ages of the World', pp. 485–7.

[54] S. Gaunt probed the beginnings of medieval French literature in his 'Romance Languages', in *How Literatures Begin: A Global History*, ed. J. B. Lande and D. Feeney (Princeton, 2021), pp. 239–60.

bound together with a copy of Calcidius's translation of *Timaeus* in Oxford, Bodleian Library, MS Digby 23. The cultivation of both Irish and French written vernaculars, therefore, took place within a similar intellectual milieu. And as writing in Irish was practised in centres outside and within Ireland, the development of literary French owes much to intellectual activity beyond northern France, including the Low Countries and England.[55] Indicative of this is the fact that Digby 23 came into being in an Anglo-Norman milieu of the first half of the twelfth century.[56] Ireland's Norman outpost contributed to this literary culture, as the verse chronicle concerning the adventures of English settlers in Ireland reveal.

Ireland's *Geste*, a term the author uses to describe his narrative,[57] survives in a single manuscript, London, Lambeth Palace Library, MS Carew 596. Material is missing both at the beginning and at the end, and there are some internal lacunae as well.[58] It is a thirteenth-century copy of a poem of 3,459 lines which has been dated to around the last decade of the twelfth century.[59] The format of octosyllabic rhymed couplets employed is standard for French verse-narrative (although unusually, they are here organised into *laisses*).[60] As a metrical chronicle, it bears resemblance to the history of the Dukes of Normandy, *Roman de Rou*, written by Wace in the 1160s and 1170s and dedicated to Henry II and his wife, Eleanor of Aquitaine.[61] It has been suggested that the Irish *Geste* also had a female patron, Isabel, daughter and granddaughter respectively of Strongbow and Diarmait Mac Murchada, two of the principal characters in the poem;[62] but evidence in support of this is

---

[55] See *MFLCA*.

[56] There is a brief discussion of the textual transmission of the *Chanson de Roland* in Gaunt, 'Romance Languages', pp. 246–8.

[57] *Geste*, ed. Mullally, ll. 6, 327, 2596; l. 1065 mentions 'la geste que lisum' ('the *geste* we are reading').

[58] M. R. James, *A Descriptive Catalogue of the Manuscripts in the Library of Lambeth Palace: the Medieval Manuscripts* (Cambridge, 1932), p. 778; and *Geste*, ed. Mullally, pp. 19–20, 37.

[59] *Geste*, ed. Mullally, p. 31; a reference to St Laurence O'Toole, an archbishop of Dublin canonised in 1225, has been taken as a later insertion, Mullally postulating 'a revision made around 1230' (*Geste*, p. 31).

[60] I. Short, 'Patrons and Polyglots: French Literature in Twelfth-century England', *Anglo-Norman Studies* 14 (1991), 229–49 (pp. 229, 234–5, 237).

[61] Short, 'Patrons and Polyglots', pp. 237–8.

[62] W. Sayers, 'The Patronage of *La conquête d'Irlande*', *Romance Philology* 21 (1967), 34–41; and J. Long, 'Dermot and the Earl: Who Wrote the Song?', *Proceedings of the Royal Irish Academy* 75 C (1975), 263–72.

lacking.[63] Part chanson de geste, part *estoire*, part romance, part epic,[64] this particular *Geste* is a vernacular literary narrative which draws on a range of motifs and approaches to present a version of events of the recent past highly favourable to King Diarmait and the Earl.[65]

In this way, Ireland's *Geste* forms part of the 'literary discourse of justification' that Simon Meecham-Jones has highlighted as a strand of twelfth-century ideological writing concerned with balancing conflicting loyalties and addressing tensions between king and an increasingly ambitious aristocratic class.[66] The text skilfully negotiates land grants and shifting political divisions to depict a landscape of power in Ireland's eastern region of Leinster in which steadfast allegiance is rewarded, while infidelity and alleged treason underpin disinheritance and defeat.[67] It accommodates settlers, *les Engleis*, and the enemy *Yrreis*, opponents of 'the noble king Diarmait' ('le gentilz reis Dermod') within a network of hybrid identities, best represented by the family of King Diarmait himself.[68] Diarmait's son Domnall Cáemánach acted as his military commander,[69] while his nephew, 'the felon' Muirchertach, opposed him.[70] After Diarmait's death, both allied with Earl Strongbow,[71] and were granted separate kingdoms, Uí Chennselaig (Diarmait's home territory) and 'the pleas of Leinster', respectively.[72] Such

---

[63] Short, 'Patrons and Polyglots', p. 240.

[64] As well as referring to his work as a *geste*, the author refers to it as *l'estorie* and *la chansun* (e.g. *Geste*, ed. Mullally, ll. 2, 7, 1910).

[65] S. Meecham-Jones has demonstrated the skill of the anonymous poet in drawing on a range of generic conventions, especially romance motifs: 'Romance Society and its Discontents: Romance Motifs and Romance Consequences in *The Song of Dermot and the Normans in Ireland*', in *Boundaries in Medieval Romance*, ed. N. Cartlidge (Cambridge, 2008), pp. 71–92 (pp. 73–4).

[66] S. Meecham-Jones, 'Introduction', in *Writers of the Reign of Henry II: Twelve Essays*, ed. R. Kennedy and S. Meecham-Jones (Basingstoke, 2006), pp. 1–24 (pp. 14–15).

[67] Meecham-Jones, 'Introduction', pp. 18–20; and Charles-Edwards, 'Ireland and its Invaders', pp. 10–11, 25–6.

[68] For this depiction of Diarmait, see *Geste*, ed. Mullally, l. 824; the narrative, as we have it, commences by praising him as the best king in Ireland in his day and 'very rich and magnificent/ he loved the generous, hated the mean' ('En Yrland a icel jor/ N'i out reis de tel valur./ Asez esteit manans e riches,/ Ama le[s] francs, haï les chiches'). *Geste*, ed. Mullally, ll. 12–15.

[69] For example, *Geste*, ed. Mullally, ll. 864–75, 944–7.

[70] 'le fel', *Geste*, ed. Mullally, l. 2281.

[71] *Geste*, ed. Mullally, ll. 3208–9.

[72] *Geste*, ed. Mullally, ll. 2181–8; see Charles-Edwards, 'Ireland and its Invaders', pp. 15–16.

shifting allegiances change the fabric of the political patchwork, Maurice de Prendergast (for example) leaving Diarmait to enter the service of Mac Donnchada, king of the south-eastern territory of Osraige, according to the poem.[73] As a result 'the Irish of this region' called him Morice Osseriath ('of Osraige'), an acquired identity embodied in a name.[74]

Structured around the activities of particular heroes,[75] the poem spans the events of ten consecutive years from 1166 when Diarmait Mac Murchada sought the assistance of Henry II and his magnates to regain his kingdom in Ireland, down to the activities of Strongbow and Hugh de Lacy there in the mid 1170s, five years after Diarmait's own death. Significant detail concerning the activities of the protagonists is related, some of which can be corroborated in the more laconic Irish annalistic entries of the period.[76] A different perspective is accorded by another account of these years, *Expugnatio Hibernica* (*The Conquest of Ireland*) written by Gerald of Wales, a relative of some of the settlers and who had visited Ireland in 1183 and 1185, on the latter occasion with King John.[77] His polemical, colourful narrative was completed in the summer of 1189 and so is broadly

---

[73] *Geste*, ed. Mullally, ll. 1066–151.

[74] 'Iloc resut le barun/ De Morice Osseriath le nun;/ Si l'apelouent tut dis/ Les Yrreis de cel païs/ Que en Osserie esteit venuz/ E od le rei remansçus' ('There the baron received the name of Maurice of Osraige; That is what the Irish of this region always called him, because he had come to Osraige and remained with the king'): *Geste*, ed. Mullally, ll. 1146–51.

[75] The author punctuates his poem with reference to the heroes in question, with connecting phrases such as 'Conter voil del rei Dermod...' ('I wish to tell how King Diarmait...'); 'Oiez, seignurs, del rei Henriz/ Que fiz esteit l'emperiz' ('Hear, lords, about King Henry fitz Empress'); 'Oiez, seignurs, baruns vaillant –/ Que Deus de[l] cel vus seit guarant! –/ Del reis engleis voil lesser/ Ki tant par est nobles e fer;/ Del gentil conte voil parler/ E de ses errures treiter' ('Listen lords, valiant barons – may God in heaven protect you! – I will leave off telling about the English king who is so noble and proud. I wish to tell of the noble earl and of his expeditions'); 'Dirrai vus de un chevalier,/ Reymund le Gros l'oï nomer' ('I shall tell you about a knight whom I heard called Raymond le Gros'): *Geste*, ed. Mullally, ll. 1392, 2577–8, 2982–7, 3354–5.

[76] Collections include *Annála Uladh, Annals of Ulster, Otherwise Annála Senait, Annals of Senat: A Chronicle of Irish Affairs, Vol. II, A.D. 1057–1131; 1155–1378*, ed. and trans. B. Mac Carthy (Dublin, 1893); 'The Annals of Tigernach: the Continuation A.D. 1088–1178', ed. and trans. W. Stokes, *Revue celtique* 18 (1897), 9–59, 150–97, 268–303; and the related *Chronicum Scotorum, A Chronicle of Irish Affairs, from the Earliest Times to A.D. 1135*, ed. and trans. W. M. Hennessy (London, 1866).

[77] Gerald of Wales, *Expugnatio Hibernica: the Conquest of Ireland by Giraldus Cambrensis*, ed. and trans. A. B. Scott and F. X. Martin (Dublin, 1978).

contemporary with the equally subjective Old French *Geste*.[78] Gerald's work too can be described as a 'literature of justification', legitimising the settlement by his colonial kinsmen with reference to the barbarism of the Irish, subjugation of whom is depicted as having a civilising intent.[79] Responding to a request by many persons to relate the recent conquest of Ireland, as he claims in various prefaces to the work, his intended audience were those observing developments rather than settlers on the ground. Dedicating a revised version to King John himself, Gerald was careful to highlight the monarch's role and that of his father Henry, while also glorifying his own Welsh kinsmen in the venture. Significantly, he suggests to the king that someone learned and skilled should be employed to translate his work into French, citing his contemporary, Walter Map, archdeacon of Oxford, in support.[80] But his wish that what he had related be better understood as a result, was less important to him, perhaps, than the reward increased familiarity would bring.[81]

Although entirely expected given his training as an ecclesiastic, writing in Latin was for Gerald nonetheless a conscious choice. French was likely to have been the language of his upbringing, the tongue of his Welsh mother leaving little linguistic trace.[82] He moved in aristocratic French-speaking circles and operated in a bilingual literary sphere. The quote attributed to Walter Map but in Gerald's own words reveals a view that writing in Latin was 'far more praiseworthy and permanent' than Walter's words 'delivered in everyday language' ('Et quanquam scripta vestra longe laudabiliora sint, et longeviora, quam dicta nostra, qui tamen hec aperta, communi quippe idiomate prolata').[83] Gerald may be peeved but is comfortable on what he

---

[78] For Gerald of Wales and his writing, see R. Bartlett, *Gerald of Wales: A Voice of the Middle Ages* (Stroud, 2006).

[79] R. Bartlett, *Gerald of Wales and the Ethnographic Imagination*, Kathleen Hughes Memorial Lectures 12 (Cambridge, 2013), pp. 10–11.

[80] Gerald of Wales, *Expugnatio Hibernica*, ed. Scott and Martin, p. 264. As J. B. Smith notes, the passage in question 'is less about Walter and more about Gerald's belief that the deck is always stacked against him': *Walter Map and the Matter of Britain* (Philadelphia, 2017), p. 155.

[81] Gerald of Wales, *Expugnatio Hibernica*, ed. Scott and Martin, p. 264.

[82] Busby discusses Gerald's use of and approach to languages, *French in Medieval Ireland*, pp. 19–28. See also Henley in this volume.

[83] Gerald of Wales, *Expugnatio Hibernica*, ed. Scott and Martin, pp. 264–5; see Smith, *Walter Map*, pp. 154–5.

perceives to be his own high ground, as Joshua Byron Smith explores.[84] Moreover, in the case of the *Expugnatio*, Latin reached the elevated audience to whom Gerald sought to appeal. By contrast, the 'knights, men-at-arms, and attendants' ('Chevaliers, serjanz e mechins'), addressed in the Irish *Geste* were more at home in what for them too was their everyday language, French.[85] The detailed account of the territorial advances, the military victories, as well as the valour of those supporting Diarmait Mac Murchada, his descendants and allies, resonated with the community of settlers who had been directly involved, making it likely 'that it was composed for performance before an audience of the English settlers in Leinster'.[86] Notwithstanding that practical linguistic dimension, composition in French constituted an ideological statement also, as Meecham-Jones has argued.[87] By choosing a vernacular idiom in which to recount his narrative, the author made his story part of a wider francophone literary culture, according it status as a result.[88]

The manner in which the *Geste* is claimed to have been transmitted similarly grants it authority. According to the narrator, it was related to him by Morice Regan, 'who composed the chronicle' ('ki cest jest' endita').[89] What's more, he was 'interpreter to King Diarmait, who held him very dear' ('Icil Morice iert latimer/ Al rei Dermot ke mult l'out cher').[90] He would appear to have been in Diarmait's service for some time, since within the body of the narrative it is recorded that the king sent him to Wales after he himself had returned from a sojourn seeking assistance there in 1166–7. Morice is said to have brought with him 'King Diarmait's letters' ('les brefs le rei Dermot'), addressed to 'earls, barons, knights, squires, men-at-arms, common soldiers, horse-men and foot-soldiers' ('Cuntes, baruns, chevaliers,/ Vallez, serjanz, soudeiers,/ Gent a cheval e a pé'), promising equipment and land in return for support.[91] The embassy had the desired effect, since 'when

---

[84] In Smith's words, 'Gerald ... believes he has taken the high road of writing in Latin, and it has cost him dearly': *Walter Map*, p. 155.

[85] *Geste*, ed. Mullally, l. 3353; on the text's audience see E. Mullally, 'Hiberno-Norman Literature and its Public', in *Settlement and Society in Medieval Ireland: Studies Presented to F. X. Martin, O.S.A.* (Kilkenny, 1998), pp. 327–43 (p. 329).

[86] Charles-Edwards, 'Ireland and its Invaders', p. 32.

[87] Meecham-Jones, 'Romance Society', pp. 82–3.

[88] See also Busby, *French in Medieval Ireland*, p. 84.

[89] *Geste*, ed. Mullally, l. 6; this is reinforced at various points throughout, e.g. 'Cum il me fud endité' ('as it was related to me') l. 177.

[90] *Geste*, ed. Mullally, ll. 8–9.

[91] *Geste*, ed. Mullally, ll. 425, 427–9.

the letters were read and the people had heard them' ('Quant les brefs esteient luz,/ E la gent les unt entenduz'), support was offered and reinforcements landed at Bannow Bay, Co. Wexford, on the east coast of Ireland in 1169.[92] After the arrival of Earl Strongbow the following year, Diarmait and his allies attacked Dublin, and it was Morice, according to the poem, who was sent in to demand that the city's inhabitants surrender.[93] Dublin's Hiberno-Norse ruler, 'the treacherous Asculf Mac Turcaill' ('Mac Turkil Esculf, le tricheür'), allegedly obeyed.[94] As latimer, Morice acted as political envoy also, negotiating various languages.[95] His position in Diarmait's retinue, as well as his name, Ua Riacáin (Regan), suggests that he was Irish; Morice may have rendered Irish 'Muirgius' into French.[96] The detailed information provided in the *Geste* concerning Diarmait's traitorous Irish opponents, as well as the incoming barons and knights, is likely to have emanated from a prominent figure whose experience and engagement with the events related was lengthy and deep.

That information includes the names of many peoples and places.[97] The orthography suggests that written sources may underlie some of them, since the spelling does not accord with contemporary pronunciation. These include Hathcleyth for Irish Áth Cliath (Dublin), the final *th* in spelling had already been reduced to the sound *h*. Confusion between 'th' and 'ch' in spelling may also indicate reliance on manuscript forms, the form of insular *t* and *c* being easily confused.[98] The various spellings of the name of Diarmait's ally, Mac Donnchaid, is a case in point, both Mac Donchid and Mac Donthid being attested.[99] However, the evidence is not clear-cut, since spellings with *h* for *th*

---

[92] *Geste*, ed. Mullally, ll. 439–40.

[93] *Geste*, ed. Mullally, ll. 1656–61.

[94] *Geste*, ed. Mullally, l. 1638; see also ll. 1668–73.

[95] See Busby, *French in Medieval Ireland*, pp. 70–5.

[96] Members of the Ua Riacáin dynasty were active in the midlands in the eleventh century: see *The Annals of Ulster (to A.D. 1131), Part I, Text and Translation*, ed. and trans. S. Mac Airt and G. Mac Niocaill (Dublin, 1983), pp. 490–1 (1053.4), 496–7 (1059.5).

[97] The majority of these are listed in T. F. O'Rahilly, 'Notes on Middle-Irish Pronunciation, I. The Irish Names in "The Song of Dermot and the Earl"', *Hermathena* 44 (1926), 152–95 (pp. 153–8).

[98] Note, for example, the spelling 'Mal Athlyn' for Máel Shechlainn; 'Glindelath' for Glenn Dá Locha 'Glendalough'; and 'Murtherdath', perhaps for Muirchertach: *Geste*, ed. Mullally, ll. 136, 887, 2181.

[99] *Geste*, ed. Mullally, ll. 595 and 640. Variant forms Mac Donnchada and Mac Donnchaid are attested in Irish, the French versions deriving from the latter.

are also found, including Mac Donehid, a form closer to the spoken word.[100] Spellings such as O Rageli (Ua Ragalaig), in which the final syllable has been reduced to a vowel, and Ins Tephene (Inis Temni), with a sound 'f' indicated by the spelling 'ph', representing a lenited *m*, also reflect pronunciation.[101] So too do the various forms of the name Amlaíb, Old Norse Áleifr, including Awelaf and Awelaph.[102] Similarly, the many spellings of 'Dublin' incorporate the pronunciation of lenited *b* as 'v' in the Irish form, such as Develin and Diviline.[103] Some of these names may have been transcribed in this way in written sources the author could have had at his disposal, though in some cases he may have recorded what he heard.[104] Notwithstanding the variance in the transcription of such names, the wealth of information provided on the people and places in question suggest that in creating his composition, however reliant he was on Morice Regan, the author was engrossed in the events he sought to relate.[105]

The nature of this engagement is manifest in the type of information provided. The terms used for the northern part and southern part of Ireland respectively are Leth Cuinn and Leth Moga, indicating familiarity with

[100] *Geste*, ed. Mullally, l. 1142; see also l. 1229; O'Rahilly, 'Notes', p. 156, repeats Orpen's observation that this particular name is written in thirteen different ways in the text.

[101] *Geste*, ed. Mullally, ll. 1786, 3013.

[102] *Geste*, ed. Mullally, ll. 225, 1787.

[103] *Geste*, ed. Mullally, ll. 1556, 1579.

[104] O'Rahilly did not give due credence to the possibility of scribal transmission, remarking that 'in reality there is no evidence that the author of the *chanson* was at all influenced by, or possessed any knowledge of Irish orthography. The variety of ways in which many of the Irish names are spelt, and the obvious difficulty which the author had in trying to represent unfamiliar Irish sounds, are inconsistent with the supposition that the author had anything to guide him in his spelling except the spoken Irish words': 'Notes', p. 153, but see Busby, *French in Medieval Ireland*, p. 98.

[105] On the level of detail reproduced, see Busby, *French in Medieval Ireland*, pp. 96–9. A detailed study of the orthography of the names in question (about 130 in O'Rahilly's list, 'Notes', pp. 153–8) remains a desideratum. They could profitably be compared with the spellings used by Anglo-Norman hands in the Annals of Inisfallen, the Annals of Boyle and the *Codex Salmanticensis*, for which see C. Breatnach, 'Irish Proper Names in the *Codex Salmanticensis*', *Ériu* 55 (2005), 85–101 (pp. 92–9). Other useful comparative material includes the forms of Irish names preserved in the thirteenth-century Old Norse text, *Konungs skuggsjá*, analysed in Etchingham, Sigurðsson, Ní Mhaonaigh and Rowe, *Norse-Gaelic Contacts*, pp. 66–83.

Irish concepts.[106] Reference to both the Norse and Irish names of Dublin and Waterford is included, 'Dublin, a greatly renowned city, which had formerly been called Áth Cliath ... the city of Waterford, which used to be called Port Láirge' ('Develine,/ Une cité mult loé,/ Que Hat Cleyth iert einz nomé./ E Watreford la cité,/ Que Port Largi esteit clamé').[107] And while Norse 'Wexford' is used most frequently, the Irish form Loch Garman also occurs,[108] and there is a similar alternation between Norse 'Wicklow' ('Wikinglo') and the Irish form 'Cill Mantáin'.[109] This is indicative of the milieu of Morice Regan who brought together both Leinster and settler strands of Diarmait Mac Murchada's evolving situation. However, the author's own voice is also present throughout the history, beginning with his remark that 'Here I will leave off telling about this man [Morice]; I wish to tell you about King Diarmait' ('Ici lirrai del bacheler,/ Del rei Dermod vus voil conter').[110] It seems likely, therefore, that Morice and his literary successor inhabited the same cultural world.

Keith Busby has done much to illuminate that intellectual context, as well as the nature of the *Geste*.[111] Of particular significance is his elucidation of the extent to which its author was immersed in the same kind of literary culture experienced by francophone communities in England and on the Continent and displayed the same familiarity with Latin writing and vernacular French texts, as well as being literate in Latin himself.[112] But equally important is Busby's consideration of the extent to which the author may have drawn on themes current in contemporary Irish writing. The evidence is elusive, but a reference to the division of Ireland by six brothers likely reflects an underlying Irish narrative.[113] An elaborate account of the pseudo-history of Ireland was shaped and reshaped in the eleventh

---

[106] Forms employed include 'Lethchoin' and 'Leth Muthe': *Geste*, ed. Mullally, ll. 22, 47; Orpen, *Song of Dermot*, p. 6, transcribes the latter form as 'Lethunthe'.

[107] *Geste*, ed. Mullally, ll. 2206–10.

[108] *Geste*, ed. Mullally, l. 3093; the various forms of 'Wexford' in the text include 'Weiseford' (l. 484), 'Weyseford' (l. 949), 'Weyseforde' (l. 1030) and 'Ueisseford' (l. 1967).

[109] *Geste*, ed. Mullally, l. 3090 ('Winkinglo'), l. 3092 ('Kyl Mantan').

[110] *Geste*, ed. Mullally, ll. 10–11.

[111] Busby, *French in Medieval Ireland*, pp. 77–107.

[112] Mullally (*Geste*, p. 33), had suggested that the author had no knowledge of Latin, and highlighted what she deemed to be his 'cultural isolation'; see also L. Ashe, *Fiction and History in England, 1066–1200* (Cambridge, 2007), pp. 164–6.

[113] Busby, *French in Medieval Ireland*, p. 99, n. 60; it is unlikely to refer to the division attributed to the prehistoric Fir Bolg, as Orpen claimed, *Song of Dermot*, p. 289.

and twelfth centuries, most notably in *Lebor Gabála Érenn* (*The Book of Invasions*). Material informing it had been discussed in Carolingian circles, as noted above,[114] and a Latin title, *captivitatis Hiberniae*, which appears to refer to the vernacular work, is used in later Irish manuscripts, so that it is likely that this legendary material circulated in Latin in scholarly circles in Ireland also. The Latin-literate author of the *Geste* could have had access to this material, as would his main informant, Morice Regan. The Irish-language sources on which the latter could draw might have been available to the author of the *Geste* as well, as the names in the poem and the use of a number of Irish words suggest.[115]

Whatever material informed the writing of the narrative, its overarching theme and tone would have resonated with audiences of vernacular Irish texts of the same period. The heroic biography of Brian Boru composed at the beginning of the twelfth century *Cogadh Gáedhel re Gallaibh*, noted in passing above, bears broad similarities to the glorified life of Diarmait that forms much of the *Geste*. In both cases, records such as annals and charters are combined with elements of romance to make heroic figures out of the Munster king and Leinster ruler in turn. Events are telescoped to highlight their greatness, encounters with Vikings merged within a single year in the case of Brian. In the *Geste*, Diarmait's abduction of Derbforgaill, wife of a rival leader, Tigernán Ua Ruairc, and the consequences that ensued, are presented as the immediate context to the quest for his kingdom around which the narrative is structured. The fourteen years which separated the encounter between Diarmait and Derbforgaill in 1152 and the Leinster king's banishment in 1166 are elided in the poem to dramatic effect.[116] In form and style, the two texts vary, the prosimetric *Cogadh* contrasting with the octosyllabic metre of the *Geste*. The language of this and other contemporary vernacular Irish texts is also more ornamented and alliterative than that employed in the French poem.[117]

---

[114] See Clarke, 'The *Leabhar Gabhála*'.

[115] These are *daingen* ('stronghold') and *longport* ('encampment'): *Geste*, ed. Mullally, 1. 176 ('dengin') and 1. 1000 ('langport'); see also Busby, *French in Medieval Ireland*, p. 98, and *Geste*, ed. Mullally, p. 32. In terms of the author's sources, J. Long allowed for both oral and written precedents, in Latin, French and Irish in his 'Dermot and the Earl'.

[116] Meecham-Jones, 'Romance Society', p. 80. The encounter is related in terms very favourable to Diarmait 'whom this lady loved so greatly' ('ki cel dame tant amout') in the poem: *Geste*, ed. Mullally, ll. 22–215 (1. 41). Drawing on historical sources, S. Ó Hoireabhárd probes Derbforgaill's role in 'Derbforgaill: Twelfth-Century Abductee, Patron and Wife', *Irish Historical Studies* 46:169 (2022), 1–24.

[117] This is not to suggest a lack of skill on the part of the author of the *Geste*, of which the text's editor has a low opinion: *Geste*, ed. Mullally, pp. 33–5; see also Mullally,

Moreover, while the *Geste* deals with near-contemporary events, comparable Irish texts deal with the history of the recent past in the case of the *Cogadh* and a related text, *Caithréim Chellacháin Chaisil* (*The Martial Career of Cellachán of Cashel*), and with the pre-Christian period in a third battle-narrative, *Cath Ruis na Ríg* (*The Battle of Rosnaree*).[118] In its focus on the present, the French chronicle is closer to poems extolling the deeds of contemporary rulers, such as those composed for Cathal Crobderg Ua Conchobair, younger half-brother of Ruaidrí who features in the *Geste*.[119] Underlying all these various texts, however, is the retrospective literary legitimisation of a political state of affairs.[120] A common truth is being constructed, and emphasis is thereby placed on the veracity of the word. Appeal to authoritative, personal testimony, the chronicler, Morice Regan, 'who conversed with him [Diarmait] face to face' is a significant strand in this discourse.[121] What is being recounted is 'according to the statement of history' ('Solum le dit [de] l'estorie'), as claimed in the *Geste*.[122] In theme and approach, therefore, this versified account of English settlers in Ireland bears comparison with vernacular literature in Ireland being produced around the same time. Moreover, the subject-matter of the poem, both in orthography and content, indicates direct engagement with an Irish social and literary milieu. This cross-cultural product of an emerging colony can indeed be described as Ireland's *Geste*.

'Hiberno-Norman Literature', p. 329. This view is shared by Short, for whom he is 'an outstandingly mediocre poet' ('Patrons and Polyglots', p. 240); see also Ashe, *Fiction and History*, p. 163 and p. 191. But for a different assessment, see J. F. O'Doherty, 'Historical Criticism of the *Song of Dermot and the Earl*', *Irish Historical Studies* 1 (1938), 4–34.

[118] *Caithréim Chellacháin Chaisil: The Victorious Career of Cellachán of Cashel, or the Wars between the Irishmen and the Norsemen in the Middle of the 10th Century*, ed. and trans. A. Bugge (Oslo, 1905); and *Cath Ruis na Ríg for Bóinn*, ed. and trans. E. Hogan, Todd Lecture Series 4 (Dublin, 1892).

[119] *Geste*, ed. Mullally, l. 3236. See, for example, 'A Poem Composed for Cathal Croibhdhearg Ó Conchubhair', ed. and trans. B. Ó Cuív, *Ériu* 34 (1983), 157–74.

[120] For this theme in the *Geste*, see Meecham-Jones, 'Introduction', pp. 18–20.

[121] 'Morice Regan iert celui/ Buche a buche parla a lui/ Ki cest jest' endita' ('This man was Maurice Regan. He who composed this chronicle conversed with him face to face'): *Geste*, ed. Mullally, ll. 4–6. For a discussion of the various interpretations of this passage, see Meecham-Jones, 'Romance Society', pp. 74–6.

[122] *Geste*, ed. Mullally, l. 2401.

Conclusion

The Irish cultural milieu within which the *Geste* was enmeshed had long been well connected, informing and benefitting from intense engagement with a wider European intellectual world, as has been illustrated above. Vernacular Irish writing was well-established within that literary space, and it was also characterised by productive co-existence of various languages, among which French became increasingly prominent as the twelfth century progressed. These circumstances shaped the writing of an Old French verse-chronicle somewhere in Leinster, within a generation of English settling there. Its expression of a version of recent history from a specific ideological stance is articulated with reference to the conventions of the evolving genre of romance.[123] Many other influences were also at play. Access to written Irish sources is indicated by the form of some of the names in the *Geste*, and figures such as Morice Regan who inhabited dual literary worlds, exemplify the considerable potential for interaction and influence in an area in which French and Irish were in close contact. The wider web of learned connections of which such contact formed part facilitated transmission of approaches and ideas, motifs and generic forms in both directions. The development of romance in a vernacular Irish context, for example, has been associated with a lengthy, complex narrative roughly contemporary with the *Geste, Acallam na Senórach* (*The Colloquy of the Ancients*).[124] Themes in the *Acallam* could and would have been shaped by those of contiguous literary cultures, including French, though the precise nature of that influence is not always clear-cut.[125] Irish scholars whose extensive writing reflected and also informed wider literary fashions, were undoubtedly open to ideas percolating in new religious houses in Ireland or at French-speaking

---

[123] This has been argued cogently by Meecham-Jones, 'Romance Society'; by contrast, in Mullally's view (*Geste*, p. 34), 'he [the author] appears to be untouched by the new genre of romance'.

[124] A. Dooley, 'The European Context of *Acallam na Senórach*', in *In Dialogue with the Agallamh: Essays in Honour of Seán Ó Coileáin*, ed. A. Doyle and K. Murray (Dublin, 2014), pp. 60–75, at pp. 61–2. For a translation of the narrative, see *Tales of the Elders of Ireland: A New Translation of* Acallam na Senórach, trans. A. Dooley and H. Roe (Oxford, 1999); for the text (with partial translation), see 'Acallamh na Senórach', ed. W. Stokes, in *Irische Texte mit Wörterbuch*, ed. E. Windisch and W. Stokes, 4 vols. (Leipzig, 1900), IV, 1–438. There is an introduction to the *Acallam* in K. Murray, *The Early Finn Cycle* (Dublin, 2017), pp. 21–49.

[125] At the 'French without Borders' conference underlying the papers in this volume, A. Connon and G. Parsons argued persuasively for specific aspects of *Acallam na Senórach* being shaped by contact with French literary culture, connections with *Tractatus de Purgatorio de Sancti Patricii* being highlighted by Connon, and Parsons postulating tentative links with the Francophone centre of New Ross, Co. Wexford.

settler courts, even if tangible evidence for such contacts is tantalizingly scarce.[126] This makes faint but audible echoes of French-Irish dialogue resounding in textual products of the twelfth and thirteenth centuries all the more precious, among which the Old French verse-chronicle detailing the deeds of the English in Ireland takes pride of place.

[126] Evidence from hagiography and thirteenth-century poetry is among the material discussed by P. P. Ó Néill, 'The Impact of the Norman Invasion on Irish Literature', *Anglo-Norman Studies* 20 (1998), 171–85. The extant material is comprehensively discussed in Busby, *French in Medieval Ireland* which negates what had been a prevailing view, expressed most strongly by E. Mullally, 'The native Irish were never influenced by French language or literature', 'Hiberno-Norman Literature', p. 339; and see also 'such influences as there were must have been minimal': W. A. Trinidade, 'History and Fiction in the *Song of Dermot and the Earl*', *Parergon* 8:1 (1990), 123–30 (p. 128).

5

The Presence of French in German Courtly Literature *c*.1200

Mark Chinca

1. The German reception of French and Occitan courtly literature: an overview

In the second half of the twelfth century, a courtly literature emerged in German-speaking lands that took its models from French (including Anglo-Norman) and Occitan. Romances and chansons de geste, trouvère and troubadour lyrics were imitated and reworked by German authors for a public situated in the highest ranks of the secular aristocracy.[1] The reception of these products of French and Occitan literary culture reached its peak around the turn of the thirteenth century – a period that literary historians have grown accustomed to call the *Blütezeit* or 'time of flowering' of medieval German literature.[2] In the case of the narrative genres of romance and chanson de geste, the process of transfer was oriented to the work as a discrete unity and preserved its identity, so that Hartmann von Aue's *Erec* or Konrad's *Rolandslied*, for example, are recognizable as German retextualizations of their respective French models, Chrétien de Troyes' *Erec et Enide* and the *Chanson de Roland*.[3] By contrast, the transfer of

---

[1] For an account of this literary transfer in the wider context of Franco-German intellectual, cultural, commercial, and dynastic relations see J. Bumke, *Höfische Kultur: Literatur und Gesellschaft im hohen Mittelalter* (Munich, 1986), pp. 83–136; English version: *Courtly Culture: Literature and Society in the High Middle Ages*, trans. T. Dunlap (Berkeley, 1991), pp. 61–101.

[2] A comprehensive literary history of the period is L. P. Johnson, *Die höfische Literatur der Blütezeit (1160/70–1220/30)* (Tübingen, 1999), which is vol. II, pt. 1, of *Geschichte der deutschen Literatur von den Anfängen bis zum Beginn der Neuzeit*, ed. J. Heinzle, 5 parts of 3 vols. published to date (Tübingen, 1984–2004; Berlin, 2020–). An excellent concise account in English is N. F. Palmer, 'The High and Later Middle Ages (1100–1450)', in *The Cambridge History of German Literature*, ed. H. Watanabe-O'Kelly (Cambridge, 1997), pp. 40–91, esp. pp. 43–72.

[3] Various terms have been coined to capture the dynamics of literary transfer into German; two with contemporary currency are 'renarration' (*Wiedererzählen*) and 'retextualization' (*Retextualisierung*). The former emphasizes that German romances

138   Mark Chinca

lyrics was not work-oriented or work-preserving, since it was generally not specific songs that were taken over into German but rather melodies and their allied metrical patterns and strophic forms (so-called contrafacta) along with the repertoire of themes, roles, scenarios, and stereotyped ways of speaking that combined to make the 'code' of *fin'amor* or courtly love service.[4]

The German reception of French and Occitan literature in the decades on either side of 1200 was highly selective. Interest in narrative literature focused on the courtly romance, with all three of its major subgenres, *romans d'antiquité*, *romans bretons*, and *romans d'aventure*, established in Germany by the 1220s;[5] by contrast, the *matière de France* held little appeal for a German-speaking audience, since only a small number of chansons de geste attracted retextualizations.[6] In the case of the lyric, the uptake was centred on the courtly *canso* and *grand chant*

---

and epics are not translations but retellings of their French narrative models, whereas the latter foregrounds the medium of written textuality, as authors worked with a French pre-text or pre-texts to create a German re-text. See F. J. Worstbrock, 'Wiedererzählen und Übersetzen', in *Mittelalter und frühe Neuzeit: Übergänge, Umbrüche und Neuansätze*, ed. W. Haug (Tübingen, 1999), pp. 128–42; J. Bumke and U. Peters, 'Einleitung', in *Retextualisierung in der mittelalterlichen Literatur*, special issue of *Zeitschrift für deutsche Philologie* 124 (2005), 1–5.

[4] Bumke, *Höfische Kultur*, pp. 129–31; *Courtly Culture*, trans. Dunlap, pp. 96–8. Because minnesang is overwhelmingly transmitted without musical notation, the positive identification of contrafacta is difficult and generally relies on metrical and formal correspondences alone. See J. Stevens, 'Medieval Song', in *The Early Middle Ages to 1300*, ed. R. Crocker and D. Hiley, 2nd edn (Oxford, 1990), vol. II of *The New Oxford History of Music*, 10 vols. (Oxford, 1957–2001), pp. 357–451, esp. pp. 381–7; R. Luff, 'Zum Problem der Verifizierbarkeit romanischer Einflüsse in der deutschen Minnelyrik des Hochmittelalters', *Beiträge zur Geschichte der deutschen Sprache und Literatur* 124 (2002), 250–60; A. Touber, 'Lyrische Strophenformen', in *Sprache und Verskunst*, ed. R. Pérennec (Berlin, 2014), pp. 267–302, which is vol. II of *Germania Litteraria Mediaevalis Francigena: Handbuch der deutschen und niederländischen literarischen Sprache, Formen, Motive, Stoffe und Werke französischer Herkunft (1100– 1300)*, 7 vols., ed. G. H. M. Claassens, F. P. Knapp, and R. Pérennec (Berlin, 2010– 2015); H. Brunner, 'Melodien zu Minneliedern', in *Handbuch Minnesang*, ed. B. Kellner, S. Reichlin, and A. Rudolph (Berlin, 2021), pp. 218–32, esp. pp. 220–2.

[5] Bumke, *Höfische Kultur*, pp. 126–8; *Courtly Culture*, trans. Dunlap, pp. 94–6. For a comprehensive survey of German and also Dutch reception of *romans d'antiquité* see *Historische und religiöse Erzählungen*, ed. G. H. M. Claassens, F. P. Knapp, H. Kugler, and N. Borgmann (Berlin, 2014), pp. 21–174, which is vol. IV of *Germania Litteraria Mediaevalis Francigena*, ed. Claassens et al.; for *romans bretons* and *romans d'aventure* see *Höfischer Roman in Vers und Prosa*, ed. R. Pérennec and E. Schmid (Berlin, 2010), which is vol. V of *Germania Litteraria Mediaevalis Francigena*, ed. Claassens et al.

[6] Bumke, *Höfische Kultur*, pp. 125–6; *Courtly Culture*, trans. Dunlap, pp. 92–3. For details of German and Dutch retextualizations of specific chansons de geste, see Claassens et al., *Historische und religiöse Erzählungen*, pp. 175–378.

THE PRESENCE OF FRENCH IN GERMAN COURTLY LITERATURE 139

courtois; except for a few dawnsongs, there are no German songs from the so-called *genres objectifs* – pastourelles (songs about the love of shepherdesses) or *chansons de toile* (songs of women pining for their lovers), for example – nor are there any *tensos* or *partimens* (types of debate poem) from this period.[7] The selectiveness of the transfer suggests that German authors and their aristocratic patrons and publics were overwhelmingly interested in those French or Occitan works and genres that combined formal virtuosity with the thematics of courtliness.[8]

Two further points can be made about the nature of the transfer. First, the intense reception of French and Occitan courtly literature in the late twelfth and early thirteenth centuries did not create a permanent dynamic of borrowing. As the subsequent history of German literature shows, it is not the case that every significant literary innovation in the French-speaking world appears in German a few decades later. Many of the major landmarks of French literature of the thirteenth to fifteenth centuries – the *Roman de la Rose* and the works of Christine de Pizan, for example – have no reception in Germany. And narrative prose, which became an established form in French literature from the early thirteenth century, had only a limited uptake in Germany before the fifteenth century; the *Prosa-Lancelot*, adapted from several books of the Old French Lancelot-Grail (or Vulgate) Cycle between the middle of the thirteenth century and the beginning of the fourteenth, is a real outlier.[9] The waning influence of French and Occitan literature after the

[7] Bumke, *Höfische Kultur*, pp. 131–3; *Courtly Culture*, trans. Dunlap, pp. 98–9. On German poets' concentration on the *canso* see also S. Seidl, 'Altokzitanische Lyrik', in *Handbuch Minnesang*, ed. Kellner, Reichlin, and Rudolph, pp. 103–12, esp. pp. 109–11; and R. Bauschke, 'Kanzone', in the same volume, pp. 509–21. The adoption into German minnesang of at least traits and motifs from Romance pastourelle has a long history of scholarly discussion; see P. Wapnewski, 'Walthers Lied von der Traumliebe (74,20) und die deutschsprachige Pastourelle', *Euphorion* 51 (1957), 113–50; S. C. Brinkmann, *Die deutschsprachige Pastourelle: 13. bis 16. Jahrhundert* (Göppingen, 1985); C. Edwards, 'Von Archilochos zu Walther von der Vogelweide: Zu den Anfängen der Pastourelle in Deutschland' in *Lied im deutschen Mittelalter: Überlieferung, Typen, Gebrauch. Chiemsee-Colloquium 1991*, ed. C. Edwards, E. Hellgardt, and N. H. Ott (Tübingen, 1996), pp. 1–25; and I. Kasten, 'Die Pastourelle im Gattungssystem der höfischen Lyrik', in the same volume, pp. 27–41. For the possibility that the melodies and strophic forms of *sirventes, partimen, tenso* etc. may have influenced German creators of 'Sangspruchdichtung' – poetry on religious, political, and moral themes – see M. Shields, 'Spruchdichtung und Sirventes', in Pérennec, *Sprache und Verskunst*, pp. 275–306. On dawnsongs see J. Mohr, 'Tagelied', in *Handbuch Minnesang*, ed. Kellner, Reichlin, and Rudolph, pp. 534–42.

[8] Bumke, *Höfische Kultur*, pp. 133–4; *Courtly Culture*, trans. Dunlap, pp. 99–100.

[9] See F. Brandsma and F. P. Knapp, 'Lancelotromane', in *Höfischer Roman in Vers und Prosa*, ed. Pérennec and Schmid, pp. 393–457, esp. pp. 415–24.

1220s coincides with a shift in the literary tastes of German-speaking elites, who increasingly sponsored works with religious and historical themes; in this changed landscape, it is not surprising if patrons and authors no longer sought out their models in a literature strongly associated with courtly refinement.[10]

The other point is that French and Occitan courtly genres and works were not received in a vacuum. Written literature in the German vernacular has a continuous tradition reaching back to the middle of the eleventh century, and there was a vibrant production in all kinds of genre: bible epic and commentary, verse homily, saint's life, also natural history, imperial chronicles, and secular narratives of love and kingship.[11] The French-derived courtly literature which appeared from the middle of the twelfth century did not supplant these already established genres, which continued to be cultivated, through ongoing copying and recension as well as through the creation of new works in the same genres.[12] Moreover, it is not the case that the two traditions were maintained in entirely separate and complementary environments. In a pattern that was already observable in the late twelfth century and continued into the fourteenth,

---

[10] K. Bertau, *Über Literaturgeschichte: Literarischer Kunstcharakter und Geschichte in der höfischen Epik um 1200* (Munich, 1983), pp. 107–8, diagnosed a 'historischer Diskurswechsel von den Feinen zu den Frommen' ('historical change from the discourse of the refined to the discourse of the pious') in German vernacular literature of the 1220s, as artistically ornate representations of the concerns of a courtly elite gave way to the existential thematics of the human person and her relation to God. J. Heinzle, *Wandlungen und Neuansätze im 13. Jahrhundert (1220/30–1280/90)*, 2nd edn (Tübingen, 1994), pp. 105–6 (which is vol. II, pt. 2 of *Geschichte der deutschen Literatur*, ed. J. Heinzle), notes a new desire among patrons and publics for the certainties of history and religion, reflected in the rise of chronicle and hagiography as dominant narrative genres in the thirteenth century. This change did not mean that there was no ongoing retextualization of French romances in the later thirteenth century; some impulses from French and Occitan lyric also continued to be reflected in German minnesang; see *Wandlungen und Neuansätze*, pp. 16–17, 39–40, 91, 106–7.

[11] Literary histories of this period are D. Kartschoke, *Geschichte der deutschen Literatur im frühen Mittelalter* (Munich, 1990); G. Vollmann-Profe, *Wiederbeginn volkssprachiger Schriftlichkeit im hohen Mittelalter (1050/60–1160/70)*, 2nd edn (Tübingen, 1994), which is vol. I, pt. 2 of *Geschichte der deutschen Literatur*, ed. J Heinzle. For a survey in English see M. Chinca and C. Young, 'German', in *Literary Beginnings in the European Middle Ages*, ed. M. Chinca and C. Young (Cambridge, 2022), pp. 179–202.

[12] The standout example is the *Kaiserchronik* (*c.*1140/50), which was redacted and updated twice in the thirteenth century and is transmitted in fifty surviving witnesses from the late twelfth to the late sixteenth century. See M. Chinca, H. Hunter and C. Young, 'The *Kaiserchronik* and its Three Recensions', *Zeitschrift für deutsches Altertum* 148 (2019), 141–208.

French-derived romances and epics were included in manuscript anthologies alongside works from genres that were already established in Germany.[13]

The original reception of French and Occitan courtly literature in Germany in the decades either side of 1200 is connected with a sociological phenomenon: the emergence of literary patronage at the courts of high-ranking secular nobles.[14] For these aristocratic grandees, sponsoring German versions of French romances and chansons de geste in particular was a means of exhibiting a cultural status to match their wealth and political power; the narrative works that resulted from their acts of patronage evidently counted as prestige projects, and it is striking that very few French romances or chansons de geste are transferred into German more than once.[15] The salient example of multiple retextualization is Chrétien de Troyes' Arthurian romance of *Erec*

[13] A text of the *Alexanderroman*, retextualized *c.*1150 by an author called 'the cleric [*pfaffe*] Lamprecht' from a Franco-Provençal source, the *Alexandréide* by Albéric de Pisançon, is transmitted in two manuscript collections of bible epics and verse homilies: Vorau, Stiftsbibliothek Cod. 276 (last quarter of the twelfth century; the anthology also includes a text of the *Kaiserchronik*) and the Strasbourg-Molsheim Codex, formerly Strasbourg, Bibliothèque du Séminaire Protestant Cod. C. V. 16.6 4° (early thirteenth century; the codex was destroyed in 1870). Bible narratives in the early Middle High German tradition are combined in St Gallen, Stiftsbibliothek Cod. 857 (second third of the thirteenth century) with the *Nibelungenlied* and *Klage*, heroic tales ultimately descended from Germanic oral tradition, and works derived directly or indirectly from French: *Parzival* and *Willehalm* by Wolfram von Eschenbach, renarrated from Chrétien de Troyes' grail romance *Perceval* and a chanson de geste from the Guillaume d'Orange cycle respectively; Der Stricker's *Karl der Große*, a reworking of Konrad's *Rolandslied* and thus a retextualization of the *Chanson de Roland* at one remove. Finally two Arthurian romances, Hartmann von Aue's *Iwein* (based on Chrétien de Troyes' *Yvain*) and Heinrich von dem Türlin's *Diu Crône* (an account of Gawain's successful quest for the grail) are included in the anthology Vienna, Österreichische Nationalbibliothek Cod. 2779 (second quarter of the fourteenth century) along with the *Kaiserchronik*, heroic epics about the Germanic warrior Dietrich von Bern, legends of the Holy Cross and Seven Sleepers of Ephesus, and moral didactic exempla. For further details of the anthologies and associated scholarship, along with links to digital facsimiles, where available, see the entries in the online resource *Handschriftencensus: Eine Bestandsaufnahme der handschriftlichen Überlieferung deutschsprachiger Texte des Mittelalters*, accessed 7 October 2023: https://handschriftencensus.de/1432 (Vorau); https://handschriftencensus.de/3680 (Strasbourg-Molsheim); https://handschriftencensus.de/1211 (St Gallen); https://handschriftencensus.de/2693 (Vienna).

[14] Bumke, *Höfische Kultur*, pp. 638–74; *Courtly Culture*, trans. Dunlap, pp. 458–87. See also J. Bumke, *Mäzene im Mittelalter: Die Gönner und Auftraggeber der höfischen Literatur in Deutschland, 1150–1300* (Munich, 1979).

[15] L. P. Johnson, 'Die Blütezeit und der neue Status der Literatur', in *Literarische Interessenbildung im Mittelalter*, ed. J. Heinzle (Stuttgart, 1993), pp. 235–56, esp. pp. 249–50.

142   MARK CHINCA

et Enide; in addition to the canonical version by Hartmann von Aue, we have fragments of a second version that differs from Hartmann and stays closer to Chrétien's text.[16] The general absence of multiple transfers of the same work suggests both a desire on the part of sponsors to possess something unique as well as the existence of an information network that kept everyone in the loop about which French works had been, or were being, retextualized in German.[17]

The focus of this chapter will, however, not be on the patrons, but on the authors; more specifically, on the authors of French-derived romances and epics and on the ways in which they made French present to their audiences. By 'presence' I do not mean the references their works contain to their French models (although the ways in which German authors name and describe their treatment of their French sources make for an interesting subject in itself).[18]

[16] The manuscript fragments in question, W I/II and Z, are mid thirteenth century and in so-called 'Central German-Low German', a variety of literary High German characteristic of the written transmission of courtly texts in Low German-speaking regions of northern Germany. Four further surviving fragments of W (nos. III–VI) are of Hartmann's text, indicating that W transmitted a composite *Erec* text drawn from both versions. See Hartmann von Aue, *Erec*, ed. A. Leitzmann and L. Wolff, 7th edn, rev. K. Gärtner (Tübingen, 2006), pp. xiv–xviii, xxii–xxiii; also S. Glauch, 'Zweimal "Erec" am Anfang des deutschen Artusromans? Einige Folgerungen aus den neugefundenen Fragmenten', *Zeitschrift für deutsche Philologie* 128 (2009), 347–71.

[17] Johnson, 'Blütezeit', p. 250.

[18] They are interesting from a documentary and a poetological point of view. Two authors give an unusually detailed description of the paths by which their French (in these cases Anglo-Norman) models reached them. Ulrich von Zatzikhoven, author of a Lancelot romance in verse (*c*.1195), informs his public that he has followed 'daz welsche buoch von Lanzelete' ('the French book of Lancelot'), an unidentified source, considerably different from Chrétien de Troyes' *Chevalier de la charrette*, brought to Germany by 'Hûc von Morville', one of the noblemen who stood hostage for the captured English king Richard I; *Lanzelet*, ed. and trans. F. Kragl (Berlin, 2006), ll. 9323–49. Pfaffe Konrad, the author of the *Rolandslied* (*c*.1170), states that he renarrated 'daz bůch ... gescriben ze den Karlingen' ('the book written in France') at the instigation of a certain Duke Henry and also to fulfill the wish of his wife 'di edele herzoginne, / aines richen chůniges barn' ('the noble duchess, daughter of a powerful king'); he also describes his way of working as first 'pressing' (*bedwingen*) the French text into Latin before 'turning' (*kêren*) his Latin version into German; *Rolandslied*, ed. C. Wesle, rev. P. Wapnewski (Tübingen, 1985), ll. 9017–25, 9079–83. The circumstances in which Ulrich came by his French source were undoubtedly unique, and Konrad's laborious method of retextualization may have been idiosyncratic; the reference to the duchess, however, reflects something more general: the role played by aristocratic intermarriage in the mediation of French literature to German-speaking audiences. The duke named by Konrad was almost certainly Henry the Lion, Duke of Saxony and Bavaria (d. 1180), which means that the duchess would have been Matilda (d. 1189), daughter of Henry II of England and Eleanor of Aquitaine; her connections to Anglo-Norman literary culture must have been instrumental in facilitating the project of a German retextualization of the *Chanson de*

Rather I will be concerned with mentions of the French language and actual uses of French words and phrases in German courtly narratives. My argument is that by the early thirteenth century, French had become part of the repertoire of German courtly literature, a literary resource available to authors for exploitation in a number of ways. The inclusion of references to the French language or even words in French may, for example, have the effect of suddenly and unpredictably forcing upon a German audience's attention the hitherto unnoticed or unreflected fact that French is being spoken; such 'aspectual switches' may be deployed by authors to procure effects of humour and irony (sections 2 and 3 below). Or again, French words and phrases may be included in a German text to highlight the operation of language as a system which overdetermines and

---

Roland. Further examples of patrons of German literature married to French speakers with literary interests are the dukes of Zähringen, the likely sponsors of Hartmann von Aue's versions of Chrétien's romances *Erec et Enide* and *Yvain*: Berthold IV (d. 1186) was married to Ida of Boulogne, a relative of Chrétien's patrons Philip of Flanders and Marie de Champagne; his successor Berthold V (d. 1218) married Clementia of Auxonne, who is attested as the patron of a vernacular legend of St Margaret of Antioch; Emperor Frederick Barbarossa, who had trouvères perform at the Mainz Court Diet of 1184, was married to Beatrice of Burgundy, an acknowledged patron of Gautier d'Arras's romance of *Ille et Galeron*. See Bumke, *Mäzene*, pp. 21, 23, 148–9, 172, 239.

Source references are poetologically interesting for the ways in which German authors proliferated languages and pre-texts and interposed them between their French models and the resulting German retextualizations. Heinrich von Veldeke states that he read up on the story of his *Eneasroman* (*c*.1175/85) in 'welschen büchen' ('French books'), i.e. the *Roman d'Eneas*, but adds that his French model was in its turn 'von latine getichtet': 'composed from the Latin' books of the *Aeneid* 'div Virgilius da uon schreip, / von dem vns div rede beleip' ('which Vergil wrote, from whom we have the story'); *Eneasroman*, ed. and trans. H. Fromm (Frankfurt am Main, 1992), 354,17–23. Gottfried von Strassburg (*c*.1210) declares that he is telling the story of Tristan and Isolde in accordance with 'die rihte und die wârheit' ('the right and true version') of Thomas of Britain, but only after researching 'in beider hande buochen / walschen und latînen' ('in both kinds of book, French and Latin') until he found one single book containing everything as Thomas told it; *Tristan und Isold*, ed. and trans. W. Haug and M. G. Scholz (Frankfurt am Main, 2011), ll. 149–66. Wolfram von Eschenbach suggests that 'von Troys meister Cristjân' – 'master Chrétien de Troyes', whose unfinished *Conte du Graal* was the main pre-text for *Parzival* (*c*.1205) – failed to do full justice to the story, which was completely and correctly brought 'von Provenz in tiuschiu lant' ('from Provence to German lands') by one 'Kyôt', also known as 'laschantiure' ('the magician'), who discovered the ultimate Arabic source of the Grail romance in Toledo and renarrated it in a French version which Wolfram claims to be putting into German; *Parzival*, ed. E. Nellmann, trans. D. Kuhn (Frankfurt am Main, 1994), 416,21–30, 453,11–14, 827,1–11. The question of the truth or inventedness of these accounts is secondary to their poetological function: they displace the authority of the identifiable French pretext onto a plethora of unidentifiable books in Latin, French, and Arabic, thereby dispersing any notion of a single origin of the story under renarration.

144 MARK CHINCA

exceeds the intentions of speakers who believe they master its codes (section 4). If these presences of French involve an appropriation of linguistic foreignness by authors exercising sovereignty over their story matter and also over their audience – by mentioning or using French they make their public perceive the irony or humour of a situation, or appreciate a thesis about language and the speaking subject – there is also a way of making Frenchness present that does not encourage feelings of sovereignty; for, as my final example will show, a French story and French words can be accommodated in a German text in a way that renders the hosts strangers in their own language (section 5).

2. Hartmann von Aue, *Iwein*

Hartmann von Aue's *Iwein* (*c*.1200) is a retextualization of Chrétien's romance of *Yvain*, the knight with the lion.[19] The passage in question is from the episode where Iwein comes across an enchanted castle, known as 'Pesme-Aventure' according to Chrétien, but without a name in Hartmann's version. Iwein, searching for the lord of this castle, stumbles upon an idyllic scene: in an orchard by the palace an elderly lord and lady are entertained by their daughter, who reads to them.

> und vor in beiden saz ein magt,
> diu vil wol, ist mir gesagt,
> wälsch lesen kunde:
> diu kurzte in die stunde.
> ouch mohte si ein lachen
> lîhte an in gemachen:
> ez dûhte si guot swaz si las,
> wande si ir beider tohter was.
> ez ist reht, daz man si krœne
> diu zuht unde schœne,
> hôhe geburt unde jugent,
> gewizzen unde ganze tugent,
> kiusche unde wîse rede hât.
> daz was an ir, unde gar der rât
> des der wunsch an wîbe gert.
> ir lesen was et dâ vil wert.[20]

(In front of them both sat a girl who, I am told, was adept at reading French. She made the time pass for them pleasantly. Indeed, she was easily able to

---

[19] For a comparison of Hartmann's re-text with Chrétien's pre-text see E. Schmid, 'Chrétiens "Yvain" und Hartmanns "Iwein"', in *Höfischer Roman in Vers und Prosa*, ed. Pérennec and Schmid, pp. 135–67.

[20] Hartmann von Aue, *Iwein*, ed. and trans. V. Mertens (Frankfurt am Main, 2004), ll. 6455–70.

THE PRESENCE OF FRENCH IN GERMAN COURTLY LITERATURE   145

put a smile on their faces: they liked anything she read, because she was their daughter. It is right that a crown should be awarded to a woman who possesses breeding and beauty, noble birth and youth, intelligence and perfect virtue, restraint and wise speech. She had all these qualities and an abundance of everything one could wish for in a woman. Truly her reading there was highly esteemed.)

This scene is considerably remodelled by comparison with Chrétien, who (unlike Hartmann) emphasizes not the daughter's paradigmatic courtliness, but her attractions for a lover: she is so beautiful and charming, Chrétien says, that the god of love would have assumed human form and shot himself with his own arrow in order to serve her.[21] The change that interests me however is this: whereas Chrétien describes the girl as reading 'en un romans, ne sai de cui' ('in a romance, I don't know about whom [*or* by whom?]') (*Yvain*, l. 5360), Hartmann replaces this coy reference to what might be the author's own work with an indicator of courtly accomplishment which supplements all the other attributes the girl possesses in abundance: in addition to being well bred, beautiful, nobly born, young, intelligent, virtuous, and so on, the daughter can read French. In one respect, then, the detail does not stand out; it is just another item on the list of qualities to be wished for in a courtly young woman. In another respect, however, the mention of the daughter's facility in reading French is salient. In the whole of the romance of *Iwein*, it is the only reference to the language or languages spoken and used by the characters.

The detail seems to be intentional, because Hartmann has gone out of his way to modify his exemplar Chrétien; the effect is that the audience are suddenly obliged to consider the narrated world under an aspect they have not previously entertained. Up until now, there has never been any reference to linguistic otherness that would prompt the audience to ask themselves: what language do the characters in the narrated world speak? Although the world they inhabit is located in 'Britain',[22] the language spoken there is never specified, and we cannot be sure what assumptions the original German audience might have made on that score – or indeed whether they entertained any assumptions at all. Moreover, the author Hartmann never so much as mentions that he is reworking a romance originally written in French, either directly or indirectly: Chrétien is never mentioned by

---

[21] Chrétien de Troyes, *Le Chevalier au Lion (Yvain)*, ed. M. Roques (Paris, 1971), ll. 5369–78. Subsequent line references to this edition are included parenthetically in the text.

[22] 'Britânje' (l. 1182); other toponyms are 'Karidôl' (l. 52; = Carlisle?) and 'Breziljân' (ll. 263, 925; = Broceliande, the forest in Brittany associated with adventure in Arthurian romances). It is not clear how many of Hartmann's public would have recognized the latter two as locations in Britain or Brittany.

146   MARK CHINCA

name.[23] The mention of the girl reading from a French book forces the question of language upon the audience's consciousness. And once it has been posed, it gives rise to further questions. Is French the native language of the girl and her parents, or is it a foreign language? If it is a foreign language, does the whole family know French, or just the daughter? Does the narrator's remark 'they liked anything she read, because she was their daughter' imply that the parents may not understand the language? These questions, triggered by the mention of the French language, produce what we may call an 'aspectual switch': suddenly a scene that is ostensibly a vignette of perfect courtliness – the orchard setting with its sweet-scented flowers and grass, the father reclining on a bed while his wife sits next to him, the beautiful daughter entertaining the parents with her reading – demands to be considered under the aspect of possible lack and deficiency: the parents may have no idea what their daughter, whose reading they hold in high esteem, is reading to them about. Through this switch, the scene of leisured reading from a French book is rendered double-aspected and ironic, since the consummate possession of courtliness it advertises may, for some of the participants at least, consist in little more than knowing when and where to bestow a smile.

3. Wolfram von Eschenbach, *Parzival*

An aspectual switch of a different kind is produced by the inclusion of a French word in Wolfram von Eschenbach's *Parzival* (*c.*1205), a version of Chrétien de Troyes' romance of *Perceval* or (in its alternative title) *Le Conte du Graal* (1180s).[24] The word occurs in a scene in which the protagonist Parzival encounters a lady who recognizes him: her name is Jeschute, and Parzival had previously forced

---

[23] Hartmann's only source acknowledgment, apart from 'so I was told' remarks from his narrator, is an oblique reference at the conclusion of the romance to 'the person from whom I have the story'. By contrast, Chrétien is named in Hartmann's earlier romance *Erec*, ed. Gärtner, l. 4629[12] (text of fragment W IV): 'alse uns Crestiens saget' ('as Chrétien tells us'). It is unlikely that Hartmann omitted to mention Chrétien's name in *Iwein* because he was working from a defective exemplar which was missing the epilogue, the only place in the French romance where the author is named: 'Del *Chevalier au lyeon* fine / Crestïens son romans ensi; / n'onques plus conter n'en oï / ne ja plus n'en orroiz conter / s'an n'i vialt mançonge ajoster' (*Yvain*, ed. Roques, ll. 6805–8; 'Chrétien ends his romance of the Knight of the Lion thus; I never heard more narrated, nor will you hear more narrated unless one wishes to add lies'). The same concluding idea ('I cannot narrate what I have not been told') forms the core of Hartmann's ending, indicating that the epilogue, along with its author's name, was known to him: 'ichn weiz aber was ode wie / in sît geschæhe beiden. / ezn wart mir niht bescheiden / von dem ich die rede habe' (*Iwein*, ed. Mertens, ll. 8160–3; 'But I do not know what happened to them since or how they fared. I have no information from the person from whom I have the story').

[24] For a comparison of *Parzival* with *Perceval* see the plot analysis by J. Bumke, *Wolfram von Eschenbach*, 8th edn (Stuttgart, 2004), pp. 40–124.

THE PRESENCE OF FRENCH IN GERMAN COURTLY LITERATURE   147

himself upon her, embraced and kissed her and stolen a ring and brooch from her.
Nothing else happened, but Jeschute's husband, Duke Orilus de Lalande, suspects
her of infidelity and punishes her by suspending sexual relations with her, refusing
to provide her with any clothes other than the shift she is wearing, and forcing
her to ride a horse starved of fodder. Now, when her path and Parzival's cross for
the second time, the horse is near collapse and her shift, which she is still wearing,
has been torn by thorns and branches into so many shreds that nothing remains
but a collection of knots and threads exposing her bare skin to view (*Parzival*,
ed. Nellmann, 136,24–138,1; 256,17–257,22). After painting this picture of a
distressed noblewoman (her status is underlined by the fourfold repetition of
the label *vrouwe* ('gentlewoman, lady') in the space of just over twenty lines), the
narrator comments to his public:

> nantes iemen vilân,
> der het ir unreht getân ....

> (*Parzival*, 257,23–4)

(Anyone who called her a *vilaine* [Middle High German *vilân* < Old French
vilain, -e 'commoner, peasant, uncourtly person'] would have done her an
injustice ....)

The immediately following line, which explains the nature of the injustice,
switches the aspect from social class to the state of Jeschute's clothing, and
reveals that the French loanword is in fact a bilingual pun:

> nantes iemen vilân,
> der het ir unreht getân:
> wan si hete wênc an ir.

> (*Parzival*, 257, 23–5)

(Anyone who called her a *vilaine* / anyone who called her 'lots on' [MHG
vil an] would have done her an injustice, because she had little on.)

The *vilân* / *vil an* pun effects a double dislocation. The first is a linguistic
dislocation between French and German. Not only does the loanword *vilân*
remind a German audience of the story's Frenchness – it opens with the
disinheritance of Parzival's father according to 'welhsch gerihte' (4,28; 'French
law') – and of the fact that it has crossed the border into another language, the
dislocation raises the question: who is the hypothetical 'anyone' (*iemen*) who calls
Jeschute *vilân*? Is it a German speaker using a French word? Might it even
be Wolfram, making a joke about his competence in French? He knows *vilân*
('peasant') is not the right French word to describe the courtly lady Jechute,
but for the wrong reason: he professes to believe it means something else
(*vil an*). Or is that hypothetical 'anyone' a French speaker, perhaps Chrétien?
The French author does not call the lady (in his version she has no name)

148   MARK CHINCA

(a) *vilaine* anywhere in the text of the *Conte du Graal*, but Wolfram might be disingenuously insinuating that he does. In that case, we would have Wolfram making a humorous dig at his model who, he would be suggesting, does not have the true measure of one of his own characters.

The second dislocation is between the acoustic and the optical medium. In spoken language (narrative verse was intended to be read aloud) the pun will not work, because the rhyme words have different vowel quantities in their final syllables: *vilân* meaning 'peasant' has a long *a* – confirmed by its rhyme with *getân* in the next line – whereas *vil an* 'lots on' has a short *a*.[25] Wolfram's bilingual play on words works fully only in the optical medium of writing, because unlike modern philological editors, who regularly indicate a long MHG vowel with a circumflex, medieval German scribes generally did not distinguish long vowels from short with any diacritic or symbol: both meanings were written as the same sequence of letters *v-i-l-a-n*. It is an eye-pun, if one can use the term, and it has a significance beyond the episode. Previously in *Parzival* Wolfram had presented himself as an illiterate author, ostentatiously declaring 'ine kan decheinen buochstap' (115,27; 'I don't know the alphabet [*lit.* don't know letters]'); at the same time, he indicates that these words are intended ironically, because he goes on to say that he would rather be caught naked in a steam-bath without a towel than for *Parzival* to be taken for a book – provided, he adds, that he had not forgotten to bring his whisk with him (116,1–4). So he would have something to cover his nakedness after all. The subsequent creation of an eye-pun picks up on and continues the earlier ironic claim to be illiterate, for here we have a self-declared unlettered author making a play on words in the medium of written letters. It has been suggested that the pun is not Wolfram's but a scribal interpolation. Karl Lachmann, Wolfram's nineteenth-century editor, declared it 'albern' ('imbecilic') and bracketed the lines in his critical text.[26] If the pun is not Wolfram further highlighting the irony in his own self-stylization, the person who introduced it into the text was no imbecile, but a highly astute reader who was alive to Wolfram's irony and enhanced it.[27]

---

[25] Even if the difference of vowel quantity might in theory be neutralized in an ambivalent spoken realization, there remains a suprasegmental and also a prosodic difference, neither of which is easily negotiated. MHG *vilân* 'peasant' has open first syllable *vi-*, whereas *vil* 'lots, much' is closed; *vi-* cannot bear metrical stress, so that the cadence is x͙x, matching its rhyme *getân* (and also necessitating reversal of the clitic pronoun in *nantes* > *nante si* – in fact the reading of most manuscripts – to maintain a four-beat line); *vil* can be stressed, giving the cadence x̍x, which clashes with the rhyme.

[26] *Wolfram von Eschenbach*, ed. K. Lachmann (Berlin, 1833), p. ix.

[27] Gesa Bonath, the authority on the transmission of *Parzival*, considered the pun more likely to be authorial than scribal; see her *Untersuchungen zur Überlieferung des Parzival Wolframs von Eschenbach*, 2 vols. (Lübeck, 1970–71), I, 67. The lines are in all the complete manuscripts of *Parzival* except one; see the synopsis of variants in the digital edition of the *Parzival-Projekt*, accessed 7

4. Gottfried von Strassburg, *Tristan und Isold*

If Hartmann's *Iwein* is a text where highlighting language difference is the exception rather than the rule, Gottfried's *Tristan und Isold* (*c.*1210) is the polar opposite.[28] His text projects a narrative world where language differences and the ability to negotiate them are constantly emphasized. The protagonist Tristan is a wunderkind who masters numerous foreign languages as part of his courtly education: Breton, Welsh, Latin, French, Norwegian, Irish, German, Scots Gaelic, Danish – all these tongues are in his repertoire (*Tristan und Isold*, ed. Haug and Scholz, ll. 2056–63, 2094–5, 3626–8, 3691–703). His lover Isolde also has a gift for languages: we are told that besides Irish, her native language, she speaks Latin and French (ll. 7985–6).

Among the languages spoken by the lovers, French stands out because it is not only mentioned but also used in the text. Tristan greets and converses in polite French with various representatives of courtly society: pilgrims, King Marke's huntsmen, the king himself (ll. 2681, 2685–6, 2962, 3137–9, 3160, 3259, 3269–70, 3353–5, 3363–4, 3613, 3616). Tristan also addresses Isolde in French, for example when his true identity as the killer of her uncle Morold is revealed and he begs her to show mercy: 'merzî, bêle Îsôt', he cries, 'â bêle Îsôt, merzî, merzî' (ll. 10202, 10229). French is conspicuous in Gottfried's text as the lingua franca of the courtly world, and mastery of French is an attribute of courtliness.[29] But French is also conspicuous as a means of illustrating one of Gottfried's great themes: how the lovers, who master language, not only by being able to speak several foreign tongues but also by skilfully deploying words to convey or conceal their passions according to the circumstances, are ultimately mastered by language. During his exile in Arundel (a location which Gottfried places 'between Brittany and England', l. 18687), Tristan entertains his hosts with displays of linguistic and musical artistry.

October 2023, https://parzival.unibe.ch: https://www.parzival.unibe.ch/parzdb/parzival.php?page=verssyn&dreissiger=257&suffix=23&zusatz=.

[28] For a comparison of Gottfried with his French pre-text, to the extent that one is possible given the former's incompleteness and the latter's fragmentary transmission, see U. Wyss, 'Tristanromane', in *Höfischer Roman in Vers und Prosa*, ed. Pérennec and Schmid, pp. 49–94, esp. pp. 75–86.

[29] It also functions as a tool for differentiating degrees of courtliness. King Marke's huntsmen are able to converse with Tristan in French, but they reveal their cultural deficit when they declare themselves unfamiliar with the French terms for the new and superior hunting techniques that Tristan demonstrates to them: *furkie* < OF *fourchie*, *curie* < *cuiriee*, *prisant* < *presant* (ll. 2924–3071).

150 MARK CHINCA

ofte unde dicke ergienc ouch daz:
sô daz gesinde in ein gesaz,
er unde Îsôt und Kâedîn,
der herzog und diu herzogîn,
vrouwen und barûne,
sô tihtete er schanzûne,
rundate und höfschiu liedelîn
und sanc ie diz refloit dar în:
'Îsôt ma drue, Îsôt m'amie,
en vûs ma mort, en vûs ma vie!'
und wan er daz sô gerne sanc,
sô was ir aller gedanc
und wânden ie genôte,
er meinde ir Îsôte.

...

daz er daz alsô gerne sanc:
'Îsôt ma drue, Îsôt m'amie,
en vûs ma mort, en vûs ma vie!'
daz lockete ir herze allez dar;
daz was, daz ir die liebe bar.

(*Tristan und Isold*, ll. 19205–18, 19408–12.)

(Often and frequently it happened that when the household were sitting together, Tristan and Isolde and Kaedin, the duke and duchess, ladies and barons, he would compose chansons, rondeaux, and courtly ditties, always singing this refrain in them: 'Îsôt ma drue, Îsôt m'amie, en vûs ma mort, en vûs ma vie!' And because he so liked to sing this, they all thought and firmly believed that he meant their Isolde. ... That he so liked to sing 'Îsôt ma drue, Îsôt m'amie, en vûs ma mort, en vûs ma vie!' – that was what enticed her heart to him, that was what caused love to be born in her.)

The duke and duchess, their son Kaedin and their daughter, who is fatefully also named Isolde, listen to the 'chansons, rondeaux, and courtly ditties' (ll. 19210–11) which Tristan composes and sings for them, and which always contain the refrain 'Îsôt ma drue, Îsôt m'amie, / en vûs ma mort, en vûs ma vie!' (ll. 19213–14; 19409–10; 'Isolde my love, Isolde my lover, in you my death, in you my life').[30]

---

[30] The words of the refrain appear to be derived from Thomas, who narrates how Tristran laments the absence of Yseult 'la bele raïne, s'amie, / en cui est sa mort e sa vie' ('the beautiful queen, his lover, who holds his death and his life in her') and how he addresses a message to her 'cum a dame, cum a s'amie, / en qui maint sa mort e sa vie' ('as to his lady and lover, in whom his death and his life repose'); Thomas,

THE PRESENCE OF FRENCH IN GERMAN COURTLY LITERATURE 151

The words are intended to express Tristan's enduring desire for his lover Isolde, from whom he is separated, but Tristan gives no sign of having reckoned with the multiple reference of the name; his hosts assume he means their daughter Isolde, and she too believes the refrain refers to her (ll. 19215–39, 19403–12). The consequence is that she develops feelings for him and he for her until the two are married in an unconsummated union that will produce misery for her and death for Tristan and his first love Isolde.

The lovers' unhappy end is already presaged by the French word through which they declare their love for each other. This is the famous passage which follows the scene in which Tristan and Isolde drink a love potion with fateful consequences. Isolde sets the avowal in train by revealing to Tristan that she is afflicted by something she calls (in French) *lameir*:

Der Minnen vederspil Îsôt,
'lameir', sprach si, 'daz ist mein nôt,
lameir daz swæret mir den muot,
lameir ist, daz mir leide tuot.'
dô si lameir sô dicke sprach,
er bedâhte unde besach
anclîchen unde cleine
des selben wortes meine.
sus begunde er sich versinnen,
lameir daz wære 'minnen',
lameir 'bitter', la meir 'mer':
der meine der dûhte in ein her.
...
dô er des wortes z'ende kam,
'minne' dar inne vernam,
er sprach vil tougenlîche z'ir:
'entriuwen schœne, als ist ouch mir,
lameir und ir, ir sît mîn nôt.
herzevrouwe, liebe Îsôt,
ir eine und iuwer minne
ir habet mir mîne sinne
gar verkêret unde benomen"
...
Îsôt sprach: 'hêrre, als sît ir mir.'

(*Tristan und Isold*, ll. 11985–95, 12011–19, 12028)

Le Roman de Tristan, ed. F. Lecoy, with notes, presentation, and translation by E. Baumgartner and I. Short (Paris, 2003), ll. 1215–16, 2861–2.

(Love's falcon Isolde said: '*Lameir* is my distress, *lameir* oppresses my thoughts, *lameir* is what afflicts me.' When she said *lameir* so often, he considered and reviewed closely and minutely that same word's meaning. Thus he realized that *lameir* might be 'love', *lameir* 'bitter', *la meir* 'sea'; it seemed to him the meanings were legion. ... When he had got to the bottom of the word and detected 'love' in it, he said to her most privily: 'In truth, my beauty, I feel the same. *Lameir* and you are my affliction. Mistress of my heart, dear Isolde, you alone and your love have turned my senses upside down and robbed me of them.' ... Isolde said: 'My lord, you do the same to me.')

The French word means 'love', 'the sea', and 'bitterness'. The lovers believe they are in control of the word's meanings, but in fact its meanings will overdetermine them. Isolde avows her love discreetly by uttering a polysemous foreign word that she knows Tristan will understand, and Tristan arrives at his understanding by reducing the word's polysemy to the one intended meaning 'love'. The lovers' display of semantic control – as if the word can have only the meaning they agree upon – is laden with dramatic irony, because the meanings of *lameir* that the lovers discard as irrelevant to their situation will return in the course of the story to afflict them. They will experience the bitterness of separation on more than one occasion, and during their last period apart it will be the sea that divides them and a storm at sea that prevents Isolde from rejoining her lover in time to save him from death.

The word *lameir* and the refrain 'Îsôt ma drue' owe their ability to portend catastrophe or even bring it about to the fact that they are polysemous and polyreferential, not to the fact that they are French. Yet their Frenchness, so conspicuous in a text written in German, enables Gottfried to foreground and intensify a feature of his French pre-text, the Tristan romance of Thomas of Britain. There too the word *lamer* is an object of linguistic analysis as the lovers reduce its spread of potential meanings to just one; there too the multiple reference of the personal name is brought into focus when Tristran sings his refrain in the presence of a second woman called Yseult.[31] But because in Gottfried's text the French words are additionally set off from the German ones that surround them, their object status as specimens of language with reference and meaning is enhanced; as foreign words, they stand out even more starkly as elements of a language system which is independent of its speaking subjects and their controlling intentions.

[31] For *lamer* see Thomas, *Tristan*, ed. Lecoy, ll. 39–73. Tristran's singing to the second Yseult is not preserved among the fragments of Thomas's romance, but the Old Norwegian renarration of it relates that Tristram sings for his hosts in exile 'ok nefndi í söngunum optliga at atkvæðum Ísönd' ('and in the songs he often used the name Ísönd'); *Tristrams saga ok Ísöndar*, ed. and trans. P. Jorgensen, chapter 69, in *Norse Romance*, vol. 1, *The Tristan Legend*, ed. M. E. Kalinke (Cambridge, 1999), pp. 168, 169.

THE PRESENCE OF FRENCH IN GERMAN COURTLY LITERATURE 153

5. Wolfram von Eschenbach, *Willehalm*

Willehalm (*c*.1210/20) is based on a version of the *Bataille d'Aliscans*, one of the cycle of chansons de geste about Guillaume d'Orange.[32] Wolfram constantly draws attention to the Frenchness of the story he is retelling for a German audience as well as to the Frenchness of the German in which the retelling is conducted. In the *Willehalm* prologue, he describes the relationship of French to German through the metaphor of hosting:

> er ist en franzois genant
> kuns Gwillâms de Orangis.
>
> …
>
> unsanfte mac genôzen
> diutscher rede deheine
> dirre, die ich nû meine,
> ir letze und ir beginnen.
> swer werdekeit wil minnen,
> der lât dise âventiure
> in sînem hûse zu viure:
> diu vert hie mit den gesten.
> Franzoiser die besten
> hânt ir des die volge lân,
> daz süezer rede wart nie getân
> mit wirde noch mit wârheit.
> underswanc noch underreit
> valschete dise rede nie:
> des jehent si dort – nû hoert se ouch hie![33]

(He is called in French kuns Gwillâms de Orangis. … Any German narrative will struggle to be the equal of this one, on which I am now intent, its end and its beginning. Whoever calls himself a friend of good repute will open home and hearth to this adventure: it travels here as a stranger. The best Frenchmen are agreed that no sweeter narrative was ever made in respect of worth or truth. No stroke or twist ever intervened to falsify this narrative: so they say there, now hear it here as well!)

There is nothing in German, Wolfram says, to compare with the narrative of the valiant knight who 'is called kuns Gwillâms de Orangis in French'; this Guillaume's foreign – one could even say outlandish – story travels in

---

[32] For a comparison of Wolfram's German re-text with its French pre-text see the plot analysis by Bumke, *Wolfram von Eschenbach*, pp. 276–320.

[33] Wolfram von Eschenbach, *Willehalm*, ed. J. Heinzle (Frankfurt am Main, 1991), 3,10–11; 4,30–5,14. Subsequent references are included parenthetically in the text.

154 MARK CHINCA

Germany 'mit den gesten' ('as a stranger'). As such it imposes a demand on the locals: those of Wolfram's compatriots who care about their good repute will uphold the obligation to show hospitality to strangers by opening their homes and their hearths to the story. What follows is difficult to understand, but it illustrates how the hosting metaphor also defines the relationship between the French and German languages in Wolfram's text. Just as the hosting of strangers involves both the suspension and the maintenance of boundaries – the host admits the guest into her home, but the guest is required to abide by the conditions on which hospitality is offered – Wolfram's hosting of a foreign language in his native German similarly mediates division while maintaining and even creating it.[34]

The difficulty of the passage arises from the nouns *underswanc* and *underreit*. These compound nouns appear to be neologisms of Wolfram's, formed from the prefix *under-* ('inter-') and the nouns *swanc* ('swing, stroke' – for example, of a sword) and *reit* ('twist' – for example, of a swordblade), so: 'intervening swordstroke' and 'intervening twist of a swordblade'. Scholarship has generally interpreted these compounds as poetological metaphors referring to the acts of textual abridgment and interpolation; accordingly, the gist of the passage would be that the French assert the supreme sweetness of this true and worthy narrative, whose qualities have never been falsified through abridgment or through the interpolation of extraneous material.[35] This interpretation is not convincing: the context is not obviously poetological, and the nouns are not attested elsewhere in Middle High German as metaphors for processes of text redaction.[36] In order to reach a more adequate understanding of the

[34] The paradox of hospitality – that it inevitably involves compliance with the heterogeneous yet indissoluble demands to suspend boundaries while at the same time defining and enforcing them – is the constant theme of Jacques Derrida's writings and statements on the subject. See J. Derrida, *De l'hospitalité: Anne Dufourmantelle invite Jacques Derrida à répondre* (Paris, 1997); English version: *Of Hospitality: Anne Dufourmantelle Invites Jacques Derrida to Respond*, trans. R. Bowlby (Stanford, 2000); J. Derrida, 'Hospitality, Justice and Responsibility: A Dialogue with Jacques Derrida', in *Questioning Ethics: Contemporary Debates in Philosophy*, ed. R. Kearney and M. Dooley (London, 1999), pp. 65–83; J. Derrida, 'Le principe d'hospitalité', in *Papier Machine: le ruban de machine à écrire et autres réponses* (Paris, 2001), pp. 273–7; English version: 'The Principle of Hospitality', in *Paper Machine*, trans. R. Bowlby (Stanford, 2005), pp. 66–9.

[35] For references see Heinzle's commentary in his edition of Wolfram's *Willehalm*, p. 828; cf. also W. Haug, *Literaturtheorie im deutschen Mittelalter*, 2nd edn (Darmstadt, 1992), p. 193.

[36] According to word searches in the *Mittelhochdeutsche Begriffsdatenbank* database, *underreit* is otherwise attested only as the preterite indicative of the strong verb *underriten* ('to ride between, prevent'), and all occurrences of the noun *underswanc*

passage, a first thing to note is that the words *underswanc* and *underreit* refer to the actions of a sword, and so can stand metonymically for the contents of a chanson de geste which is all about deeds of martial prowess. Thus the Frenchmen's assertion, which Wolfram is relaying to his German public, would seem to consist in the claim that the story's contents do not give the lie to its sweetness, truth, and worth. A second thing to emphasize about the words is that the prefix *under-* expresses both mediation and division: a stroke or twist of the sword that goes between, in the sense of interconnecting, but also comes between, interposes itself. Mediation and division are precisely what Wolfram's neologisms perform. They mediate, because they are coined by him to convey in German what the French say in praise of their incomparable story; they divide, not only because the act of mediation marks the difference between the 'here' of Wolfram and his fellow German speakers on the one hand and the 'there' of the story's French admirers on the other, but also and especially because they distinguish Wolfram's German from the rest of German. His neologisms are a hybridized and idiosyncratic 'German for French' which, in hosting the message of the foreigner, is a stranger itself to its native idiom.[37]

Wolfram was completely aware of the idiosyncratic character of his German, and how it is defined in a relation of mediation with, and division from, the French language that it hosts. In a much-quoted passage of *Willehalm*, Wolfram's narrator comments on the distinctiveness of his style,

---

('obstruction, curtailment') are in sources later than *Willehalm* and never in contexts where it could mean 'textual abridgment'. *Mittelhochdeutsche Begriffsdatenbank*, accessed 7 October 2023, http://mhdbdb.sbg.ac.at.

[37] The hybridity of Wolfram's German in this passage has been highlighted in previous scholarship and interpreted in different ways. According to M. Curschmann, 'The French, the Audience, and the Narrator in Wolfram's "Willehalm"', *Neophilologus* 59 (1975), 548–62, esp. pp. 557–8, Wolfram is passing humorous comment on the literary situation in early thirteenth-century Germany: satisfying his patron's and his public's desire for fashionable French story matter will, Wolfram jokes, cost them all time. Conversely, C. Kiening, *Reflexion – Narration: Wege zum "Willehalm" Wolframs von Eschenbach* (Tübingen, 1991), pp. 120–2, argues that Wolfram's 'crooked' German makes serious demands of the public, who must develop a tolerance for unevennesses, obscurities, and ruptures of narration. Finally, U. Wyss, '*Herbergen ist loischieren genant*: Zur Ästhetik der fremden Wörter im "Willehalm"', in *Blütezeit*, ed. M. Chinca, J. Heinzle, and C. Young (Tübingen, 2000), pp. 363–82, esp. pp. 376–7, regards Wolfram's incorporation of French vocabulary as a technique of aesthetic estrangement through which his German becomes literary and thus affords an experience of exile from the language of home. My account presses this insight further, arguing that the presence of French in *Willehalm* effects a radical estrangement as the consequence of hosting the foreign language in German.

which he describes as *krump* ('crooked, twisted, tortuous').[38] Once again, the commentary is stimulated by the French and their language. The context is as follows: Willehalm returns from the court of King Louis with an army of Frenchmen to relieve Orange, which is under siege from the Saracens. The army set up camp in sight of the besieged fortress (the first three lines of the quotation) and are joined by Willehalm's brother Bernart and his men (this leads into the second part, after the ellipsis, the narrator's commentary).

> Franzoiser loitschierten.
> die vürsten sunder zierten
> ir ringe, als ez in tohte.
>
> ...
>
> »herbergen« ist »loischieren« genant:
> sô vil hân ich der sprâche erkant.
> ein ungevüeger Tschampâneis
> kunde vil baz franzeis
> dann ich, swie ich franzois spreche.
> seht, waz ich an den reche,
> den ich diz maere diuten sol!
> den zaeme ein tiutschiu sprâche wol.
> mîn tiutsche ist etswâ doch sô krump,
> er mac mir lîhte sîn ze tump,
> den ich's niht gâhes bescheide:
> dâ sûme wir uns beide.

(Willehalm, 234,1–3; 237,3–14)

(The Frenchmen *loitschierten*. Each prince adorned his circle of tents as befitted him. ... *Loischieren* is the word for 'encamp'; that much of the language I have learned. An uncouth native of Champagne could speak far better French than I do, no matter how I speak French. See what punishment I inflict on people for whom I must translate this story! They could do with some German language. My German however is so tortuous in places that people may be too slow-witted for me when I can explain none of it to them quickly: then we both lose time.)

The word that triggers Wolfram's commentary, *loischieren* ('to encamp'), is neither fully German nor fully French. It is not fully German, because it is a loan formation, derived from Old French *logier* ('to dwell under canvas'), and moreover an apparent neologism of Wolfram's; there are no known examples

---

[38] For references to scholarship see Heinzle's commentary to his edition of Wolfram's *Willehalm*, pp. 988–9.

THE PRESENCE OF FRENCH IN GERMAN COURTLY LITERATURE   157

predating him.[39] It is not fully French, because *logier* has been integrated phonologically and morphologically into German: the spellings <sch> and <tsch> indicate that the voiced sounds [ʒ] and [dʒ] have become devoiced [ʃ] and [tʃ]; the verb conjugates like a regular MHG weak verb with infinitive *-en* and past tense *-ten*. This 'neither quite French nor quite German' status is fully acknowledged by Wolfram. The word defines his French: it is possibly the only word of the language he has learned, making his French permanently inferior to that of even the most ill-educated native speaker – so his French, no matter how good it may become, will always be a German speaker's not-quite-French.[40] At the same time it defines his German as not quite German – a tortuous German which is a punishment (*rechen*, 'to avenge, punish') for his fellow German-speakers, who would understand more quickly if the author simply used the German word *herbergen* ('to encamp'), and also something of a trial for Wolfram himself, who has to expend time explaining his usage.

There is, Jacques Derrida said, 'no hospitality, in the classic sense, without sovereignty of oneself over one's own home, but since there is also no hospitality without finitude, sovereignty can only be exercised by filtering, choosing, and thus by excluding and doing violence'.[41] And 'the first act of violence' perpetrated by a host exercising sovereignty over who or what has the right of sojourn in her home is a violence of language: the imposition of the host's own language on the stranger, who 'has to ask for hospitality in a language which by definition is not his own, the one imposed on him by the master of the house, the host, the king, the lord, the authorities, the nation, the State, the father, etc.'[42] Wolfram's hosting of French in *Willehalm* certainly displays the violence of a linguistic imposition: it is as if the French word *logier* may be granted house room in Wolfram's German only on condition that it bends

---

[39] The *Mittelhochdeutsche Begriffsdatenbank* gives no attestations earlier than Wolfram's *Parzival*.

[40] The formulation 'swie ich franzois spreche' is susceptible of more than one translation: 'no matter how [well] I speak French; 'although I speak French / and yet I do speak French.' However one chooses to translate it, the message remains the same: Wolfram's French will never be that of a native speaker. Cf. Heinzle's commentary to his *Willehalm* edition, pp. 988–9.

[41] Derrida, *Of Hospitality*, p. 55; *De l'hospitalité*, p. 53: 'Pas d'hospitalité, au sens classique, sans souveraineté du soi sur le chez-soi, mais comme il n'y a pas non plus d'hospitalité sans finitude, la souveraineté ne peut s'exercer qu'en filtrant, choisissant, donc en excluant et en faisant violence.'

[42] Derrida, *Of Hospitality*, p. 15; *De l'hospitalité*, p. 21: 'Il doit demander l'hospitalité dans une langue qui par définition n'est pas la sienne, qui lui impose le maître de la maison, l'hôte, le roi, le seigneur, le pouvoir, la nation, l'État, le père, etc. ... c'est la première violence.'

to the phonological and morphological requirements of his language. Yet the remarkable thing in this case is that the violence rebounds: on Wolfram, on his own language, on his audience. On Wolfram, because using the foreign word *loischieren* in place of native *herbergen* imposes the labour of explanation on him; and also because *loischieren*, as possibly the only word of French he knows, exposes his own lack of linguistic mastery. On his own language, because hosting the unfamiliar French word does violence to German, warping it and bending it out of shape. On his audience, because the resulting 'crooked' German, which severely taxes their powers of understanding, is a punishment for them.

This rebounding of linguistic violence is what sets *Willehalm* apart from the hostings of French in the other German narratives that I have discussed, including Wolfram's own *Parzival*. The violence in those examples consists in the appropriation of references to, or words in, the foreign language for the sake of demonstrating mastery over the story matter: ironizing it (*Iwein*), raising a laugh from it (*Parzival*), exploiting it as evidence for a thesis (*Tristan und Isold*). Here, in *Willehalm*, the effect of hosting the foreign language is to raise a barrier between the native language and its speakers, since Wolfram's crooked German, his mediating German for French, is an idiom that Germans do not speak and, without the help of time-consuming glosses, do not comprehend. Extending the hospitality of their German firesides to the adventure of 'kuns Gwillâms d'Orangis', the hosts will be latecomers to their own language, in which they are not at home.[43]

[43] I would like to record thanks to friends and colleagues for discussion and advice during the writing of this chapter: to Sarah Kay and Keith Busby, my co-panellists at the conference 'Medieval French Across Borders' (Fordham University, 20–21 March 2021), without whose encouragement I would never have gathered my ideas about the subject in the first place; to the editors Thomas O'Donnell, Jane Gilbert, and Brian Reilly for careful and sympathetic reading of the chapter in draft; and to Jelmar Hugen for thoughtful comments on the same draft. His recent essay 'Vernacular Multilingualism: The Use of French in Medieval Dutch Literature', *Neophilologus* 106 (2022), 181–98, which shows how French was used by Dutch authors to produce effects ranging from authority to satire and ridicule, is a model of the investigation of vernacular multilingualism in medieval literature.

6

Marco Polo and the Multilingual Middle Ages

Sharon Kinoshita

In the prologue to Marco Polo's *Le Devisement du monde* (*The Description of the World*), commonly if erroneously known in English translation as 'The Travels', his co-author, the Arthurian romance writer Rustichello of Pisa, tells us that when the young Marco, aged about twenty, first arrived at the court of Qubilai Khan, he 'enprant si bien le costume de Tartars et lor langajes et lor leteres que c'estoit mervoille' (learned the Tartars' customs, languages, and writing so well that it was a marvel). Moreover,

> avant grament de tens puis qu'il vint en la cort dou grant segnor, il soit de quatre langaies et de quatres letres et scriture. Il estoit sajes et proveanç outre mesure e molt li voloit gran bien le gran kaan.

> (not long after coming to the great lord's court, he learned to read and write [four] languages. He was wise and prudent beyond measure, and the Great Khan was very well-disposed toward him.)[1]

Frustratingly for us, Rustichello does not identify what these four languages were, and his phrasing leaves it uncertain whether 'Tartar' (the name commonly used for the Mongols) is one of them or in fact counts as a fifth. Even allowing for some exaggeration, however, the fact that it is Marco's linguistic prowess that first attracts Qubilai's favor illustrates how highly multilingualism was prized across the medieval world; in fact, Mongol princes in particular routinely recruited or conscripted 'multilingual individuals with commercial backgrounds, people like Polo', into their service.[2] In this essay, I take *Le Devisement du monde* (1298) as a frame for exploring the linguistic diversity of late thirteenth- and early fourteenth-century Eurasia. Composed at almost the exact midpoint of the remarkable century chronicled in Janet Abu-Lughod's landmark book *Before European Hegemony*, when the Mongol conquests had

---

[1] Marco Polo, *Milione/Le Divisament dou monde. Il Milione nelle redazioni Toscana e franco-italiana*, ed. G. Ronchi (Milan, 1982), XVI.1–2 (p. 318); Marco Polo, *The Description of the World*, trans. S. Kinoshita (Indianapolis, 2016), p. 10.

[2] T. T. Allsen, 'The Cultural Worlds of Marco Polo', *The Journal of Interdisciplinary History* 31 (2001), 375–83 (p. 378).

produced a world of unprecedented contact and exchange stretching from the Mediterranean to the Pacific, Marco's text reflects the linguistic diversity of this world.[3] For beneath the block of the great cosmopolitan languages like Latin, Arabic or Classical Chinese, strongly linked to the transregional religions and cultures through which we tend to view the distant past, lay a welter of local or regional languages and trade vernaculars that have left little trace in the historical record but would have mattered a great deal to a merchant and administrator like Marco Polo.[4]

This essay on Marco Polo's multilingualism draws on my larger project of taking the *Devisement du monde* as a matrix for sketching a connected literary and cultural history of the late thirteenth-century world.[5] To begin, we will consider what the *Devisement du monde* has to tell us about the diffusion of French as a lingua franca across the thirteenth-century Latin Mediterranean.[6] Part two examines, first, the multilingualism of the *Devisement* itself, as manifested in its citation of foreign terms, and, second, Marco's comments on those regions and kingdoms with 'a language of their own'. Part three turns to the world beyond the text, briefly outlining the multilingualism of some of the sites mentioned in the *Devisement* and speculating on candidates for the four languages that Marco is said to have learned with such impressive alacrity.

[3] J. L. Abu-Lughod, *Before European Hegemony: The World System A.D. 1250–1350* (Oxford, 1989).

[4] On the specificity of cosmopolitan languages, see K. Mallette, *Lives of the Great Languages: Arabic and Latin in the Medieval Mediterranean* (Chicago, 2021).

[5] My notion of connected history is inspired by the work of historian Sanjay Subrahmanyam. See his 'Connected Histories: Notes towards a Reconfiguration of Early Modern Eurasia', *Modern Asian Studies* 31 (1997), 735–62.

[6] 'Latin' here signifies those lands ruled by Christians who acknowledge the pope as their spiritual head and whose liturgical language is Latin. See R. Bartlett, *The Making of Europe: Conquest, Colonization and Cultural Change 950–1350* (Princeton, 1993), pp. 18–20. Throughout this essay, I use the term 'lingua franca', at the risk of causing some confusion with the later, poorly documented Italian-based pidgin found in the Mediterranean; on which, see K. Mallette, 'Lingua Franca', in *A Companion to Mediterranean History*, ed. P. Horden and S. Kinoshita (Oxford, 2014), pp. 330–44. In contrast to cosmopolitan languages that are 'formally difficult, with abstruse grammar that must be studied at school [and] complex, with a deep literary history' (Mallette, *Lives of the Great Language*, p. 13), French as a lingua franca – while not a native language for many of its users – is not necessarily 'learnèd' nor even written. 'Lingua franca' also resonates with 'Franks' in the sense of 'westerners as settlers or on aggressive expeditions far from home' (Bartlett, *The Making of Europe*, p. 105).

The most delightful language in the world

Counter-intuitively for modern readers, the *Devisement du monde*, fruit of a collaboration between a Venetian and a Pisan, was composed not in a dialect of Italian but in French. In the half-century before Dante's *Commedia* established Tuscan as a reputable literary language, French – which had emerged as a written vernacular in the first half of the twelfth century – became the language of choice for Italians writing for a non-clerical audience.[7] About five years before the seventeen-year-old Marco left home on his journey to Asia, his compatriot Martin da Canal set out to write *Les Estoires de Venise* (1266), a history of Venice meant to exalt the city and the deeds of its citizens. As he explains:

> [P]orce que lengue franceise cort parmi le monde et est la plus delitable a lire et a oïr que nule autre, me sui je entremis de translater l'anciene estoire des Veneciens de latin en franceis, et les euvres et les proeces que il ont faites et que il font.

> (Because the French language has spread all over the world, and is the most delightful to read and hear above any other, I have undertaken to translate the ancient history of the Venetians from Latin into French, and the works and deeds that they have accomplished and are accomplishing.)[8]

This was not an isolated case. At about the same time, Dante's mentor, Brunetto Latini – best remembered today for his appearance in Canto XV of the *Inferno* – then in exile from Florence, composed an encyclopedic work in three parts called *Le Livre dou tresor* (*The Book of Treasure*). Justifying his choice of language in terms nearly identical to Martin's, he wrote:

> Et se aucun demandoit por quoi ceste livre est escrit en roman selonc le patois de France, puis que nos [so]mes ytaliens, je diroie que ce est par .ii. raisons: l'une que nos [so]mes en France, l'autre por ce que la parleure est plus delitable et plus comune a touz languaiges.[9]

> (And if someone should ask why this book is written in the vernacular according to the dialect of France, since we are Italians, I would say that

---

[7] On the emergence of Italian translations of Latin texts in Marco Polo's half-century, see A. Cornish, *Vernacular Translation in Dante's Italy: Illiterate Literature* (Cambridge, 2011).

[8] Martin da Canal, *Les Estoires de Venise: Cronaca veneziana in lingua francese dalle origini al 1275*, ed. A. Limentani (Florence, 1972), I.5 (p. 2). Translation from Martin da Canal, *Les Estoires de Venise*, trans. L. K. Morreale (Padua, 2009), p. 3.

[9] Brunetto Latini, *Tresor*, ed. P. G. Beltrami, P. Squillacioti, P. Torri and S. Vetteroni (Turin, 2007), I.1.7 (p. 6).

this is for two reasons: one, that we are in France; the other, because the language is more pleasing and more widespread than all languages.)

Their praise of the aesthetic value of French notwithstanding, the fact that it 'cort parmi le monde' and is 'plus comune a touz languaiges' goes a long way in explaining the choice of both writers. A century and a half after the First Crusade, French had become the lingua franca of Outremer (the Latin states of the eastern Mediterranean);[10] French epics and romances were popular among the secular nobility across northern Italy (as Rustichello's own Arthurian Compilation attests);[11] and at no moment would the political expediency of writing in French have been more obvious than in the decade when Charles of Anjou, younger brother of King Louis IX of France, was flexing his military power in the Italian peninsula on his way to claiming the crown of Sicily.

Known to scholars as 'Franco-Italian', the 'French of Italy' had become the vehicle of a vibrant culture that today regularly falls between the cracks of the discrete 'national' traditions into which modern literary studies are segmented.[12] Genoa, the site of Marco and Rustichello's collaboration, actively contributed to the transmission of works in Franco-Italian. While the city's own literary culture remained Latin – notably in the writings of its archbishop, Jacopo da Varagine (also known as Jacobus or Jacob of Voragine), and in the Latin dictionary (the *Catholicon*) compiled by his fellow Dominican Giovanni Balbi in 1286 – the Genoese put Pisan prisoners (some of them notaries) to work copying manuscripts, including many in French:[13] histories (three copies of the *Histoire ancienne jusqu'à César*); encyclopedic material (such as Latini's *Trésor*); and, especially, Arthurian romances – the *Prose Tristan* and the *Prose Lancelot* (four copies each), *Guiron*

[10] For a recent overview, see L. Minervini, 'What We Know and Don't Yet Know about Outremer French', in *The French of Outremer: Communities and Communications in the Crusading Mediterranean*, ed. L. K. Morreale and N. L. Paul (New York, 2018), pp. 15–29. On its influence on the French of Pisa, see F. Zinelli, 'The French of Outremer Beyond the Holy Land', in *The French of Outremer*, ed. Morreale and Paul (New York, 2018), pp. 221–46.

[11] *MFLCA*, 58–83. On the popularity of Old French epics among northern Italian princes resisting both imperial and papal aggression, especially in the fractious period *c.*1250–1350, see L. Sunderland, *Rebel Barons: Resisting Royal Power in Medieval Culture* (Oxford, 2017), pp. 14–5.

[12] Happy exceptions to this neglect are the online journal edited at the Università degli Studi di Padova *Francigena: Rivista sul franco–italiano e sulle scritture francesi nel Medioevo d'Italia*, accessed 16 March 2022, https://www.francigena-unipd.com/index.php/francigena/index; and the archived Fordham University site *French of Italy*, accessed 19 May 2022, https://frenchofitaly.ace.fordham.edu.

[13] S. A. Epstein, *The Talents of Jacopo da Varagine: A Genoese Mind in Medieval Europe* (Ithaca, 2016), p. 176.

le Courtois (two copies) and Rustichello of Pisa's own Arthurian Compilation.[14] This informal scriptorium, of course, provides a vivid context for imagining the milieu in which *Le Devisement du monde* was composed.[15]

Medieval multilingualism and the Mongols

As widespread as French may have been across the Latin Mediterranean, its utility would hardly have extended beyond the borders of Outremer and its immediate Christian neighbours. In taking service with Qubilai Khan, Marco Polo found himself at the center of a vast empire, populated by diverse peoples both sedentary and nomadic, that was multilingual by necessity and design. Following their first wave of expansion, Mongol became the 'official' language of Yuan China, Ilkhanid Iran and the Golden Horde; within short order, however, the Mongols – never interested in imposing their language or culture on the peoples they conquered – responded to the task of ruling their vast empire by cultivating a corps of administrators versed in various languages. This situation created 'unique opportunities for interpreters and translators ... coming from different walks of life: merchants and diplomats, polyglot travellers and adventurers, as well as fervent missionaries of different confessions and scribes of the chancelleries, all of whom could find a place in this colourful stratum of medieval intelligentsia'.[16] Under Qubilai (ruled 1260–94), these *semu ren* or 'varied peoples' from West and Central Asia – including Turks (especially Uighurs), Persians and Arabs – composed the second of the four 'permanent legal definitions' of peoples within the Yuan (Chinese) empire, subordinate only

---

[14] These manuscripts have been identified by their combination of Genoese *mise-en-page* and artistic features in the illuminations with Pisan scribal hands. For the role of Pisan prisoners-of-war, see D. Delcorno Branca, 'Lecteurs et interprètes des romans arthuriens en Italie', in *Medieval Multilingualism: The Francophone World and Its Neighbours,* ed. C. Kleinhenz and K. Busby (Turnhout, 2010), p. 161. For a list of the manuscripts, see F. Cigni, 'Manuscrits en français, italien, et latin entre la Toscane et la Ligurie à la fin du XIIIe siècle', in *Medieval Multilingualism*, pp. 211–12 and, on their shared characteristics, pp. 194–7.

[15] The same scriptorium also produced a copy (Milan, Biblioteca Ambrosiana, MS M 76 sup.) of the *Legenda Aurea* collection of saints' lives, in Latin, compiled by Jacopo da Varagine *c.*1260–80 before he became archbishop of Genoa, as well as the earliest Italian translation of Latini's *Tresor* (Florence, Biblioteca Medicea Laurenziana, MS XLII, 23). F. Cigni, 'Copisti prigionieri (Genova, fine sec. XIII)', in *Studi di filologia romanza offerti a Valeria Bertolucci Pizzorusso*, ed. P. G. Beltrami, M. G. Capusso, F Cigni and S. Vatteroni, 2 vols. (Pisa, 2007), I, 425–39 (pp. 430, 434–5).

[16] I. Vásáry, 'The Role and Function of Mongolian and Turkic in Ilkhanid Iran', in *Turks and Iranians: Interactions in Language and History*, ed. E. A. Csató, L. Johanson, A. Róna-Tas and B. Utas (Wiesbaden, 2016), pp. 141–52 (p. 142).

to the Mongols themselves.[17] It is not difficult to imagine the Polos (Marco, his father and uncle) integrated into this multiethnic, multiconfessional and multilingual corps in Qubilai's service (especially since merchants frequently played more prominent roles in some Asian and Islamic cultures than in Latin Europe).[18] Elsewhere in the Mongol world, the Persian court historian Rashid al-Din (a convert from Judaism) credited Qubilai's great grand-nephew the Ilkhan Ghazan (who took power in 1295, just as the Polos were arriving back in Venice) with a knowledge of 'Arabic, Persian, Hindi, Kashmiri, Tibetan, Chinese, Frankish, and a smattering of other languages' along with his native Mongolian;[19] this places him in the company of other medieval rulers who flaunted their multilingualism as a mark of imperial prestige.[20]

Accounts written by two of Latin Europe's first official envoys to the Mongols suggest the kind of *ad hoc* negotiations that must have characterised early communications throughout the empire. As the Franciscan friar John of Plano Carpini, attending the enthronement (1246) of the Great Khan Güyük (Chinggis's grandson), later reported to Pope Innocent IV:

> We picked up many ... bits of private information about the Emperor from men who had come with other chiefs, a number of Russians and Hungarians knowing Latin and French and Russian clerics and others, who had been among the Tartars, some for thirty years, through wars and other happenings and who knew all about them, for they knew the language and had lived with them continually some twenty years, others ten, some more, some less. With the help of these men we were able to gain a thorough knowledge of

[17] The others were (3) the population of the former Jin territories of Northern China (including Khitans, Jurchens and Koreans); and (4) Nanren, or 'southerners' (the Chinese inhabitants of the recently conquered Southern Song empire). F. Mote, *Imperial China, 900–1800* (Cambridge MA, 1999), pp. 489–90.

[18] On the prominence of merchants in Asian cultures, see S. Kinoshita, 'Reorientations: The Worlding of Marco Polo', in *Cosmopolitanism and the Middle Ages*, ed. J. Ganim and S. Legassie (New York, 2013), pp. 39–57 (pp. 43–4). For the reconstruction of the life of an eighth-century merchant plying a circuit between Samarqand and the T'ang capital of Chang'an, see S. Whitfield, 'The Merchant's Tale', in *Life Along the Silk Road*, 2nd edn (Oakland, 2015), pp. 14–37.

[19] T. Allsen, 'The Rasûlid Hexaglot in its Eurasian Cultural Context', in *The King's Dictionary. The Rasûlid Hexaglot: Fourteenth Century Vocabularies in Arabic, Persian, Turkic, Greek, Armenian and Mongol*, ed. P. B. Golden (Leiden, 2000), pp. 25–48 (p. 29).

[20] Compare Emperor Frederick II (d. 1250), brought up in the multilingual court of Palermo, Sicily, who liked to fire off philosophical questions to Muslim intellectuals in Arabic. D. Abulafia, *Frederick II: A Medieval Emperor* (London, 1988), p. 258.

everything. They told us about everything willingly and sometimes without being asked, for they knew what we wanted.[21]

Less than a decade later, another Franciscan, William of Rubruck, came better prepared. Reporting on his 1253 meeting with Sartaq (son of Batu, khan of the Golden Horde) to French king Louis IX, he writes:

> I presented your letter to him, with copies in Arabic and Syriac, as I had had translations made at Acre into each language and script. There were Armenian priests here who knew Turkish and Arabic and the companion of David's sons who knew Syriac, Turkish and Arabic.

At this point, he concludes, secretaries 'had a translation made up' which was then read to Sartaq.[22]

Except for these secretaries (*scriptores*), these informants, far from the world of official or scholarly translators, are recognisably medieval 'fixers' – the modern term for those typically anonymous intermediaries on whom journalists, the military or aid workers so heavily rely.[23] In his early fourteenth-century *Libro di divisamenti di paesi* (whose title resonates closely with Marco Polo's *Devisement du monde*), the Florentine merchant Francesco Pegolotti advised readers setting out on the overland route to 'Cathay' from Tana (a trading emporium frequented by Italian merchants, located near where the Don River flows into the Sea of Azov) to:

> vuolsi fornire ... di turcimanni, e non si vuole guardare a rispiarme dal cattivo al buona, chè il buono non costa quello d'ingodo che l'uomo non – s'ene megliori via più.[24]

---

[21] *Mission to Asia*, trans. C. Dawson (New York, 1966; repr. Toronto, 1980), p. 66.

[22] William of Rubruck, *The Mission of Friar William of Rubruck: His Journey to the Court of the Great Khan Möngke, 1253–55*, trans. P. Jackson (Indianapolis, 2009), p. 118. David was a Christian from Mosul who had served as part of a Mongol embassy to Louis IX when the French king was on Cyprus; see William of Rubruck, *Mission*, trans. Jackson, pp. 33, 37. I retain the familiar name 'Golden Horde' for the entity that for the Mongols themselves was simply 'the Horde'. M. Favereau, *The Horde: How the Mongols Changed the World* (Cambridge MA, 2021), pp. 2, 10–12. Sartaq succeeded his father as khan in 1256.

[23] See Z. Stahuljak, *Les Fixeurs au Moyen Âge: Histoire et littérature connectées* (Paris, 2021).

[24] Francesco Balducci Pegolotti, *La Pratica della mercatura*, ed. A. Evans (Cambridge MA, 1936; repr. New York, 1970), p. 21. Often used as a generic name for Pegolotti's and similar texts, 'pratica della mercatura' (usually translated as 'merchant's manual') was an eighteenth-century invention. R. S. Lopez, 'Stars and Spices: The Earliest Italian Manual of Commercial Practice', in *Economy, Society, and Government in*

(furnish yourself with a dragoman. And you must not try to save money in the matter of dragomen by taking a bad one instead of a good one. For the additional wages of the good one will not cost you so much as you will save by having him.)[25]

Frequently used for contacts in the eastern Mediterranean, the term 'turcimanni' (dragoman) comes from *tarjuman*, the Arabic for 'translator'; its use here – in contrast to 'latinier' (translator, interpreter, one who knows several languages)[26] – signals on its own that we are outside the familiar bounds of the Latin Christian world.

Linguistic diversity in the *Devisement du Monde*

What traces did the multilingualism of the Mongol world leave in the *Devisement du monde*? At several places in his book, Marco makes a point of noting Mongol terms for certain distinctive institutions or customs with no western equivalent: *quecitain* for the Great Khan's imperial guard; *bularguci* for the Mongols' lost-and-found officer; *ianb* for stations in their famed long-distance postal service.[27] Elsewhere, he offers translations of proper names: the Georgian ruler 'Davit Melic, que v[a]ut a dir en fransois Davit roi' (Davit Melic, which means 'David king' in French); the 'un caustaus qui est appelés Cala Ataperistan, que vaut a dir en fransois castiaus de les aoraor do feu' (castle called Cala Ataperistan, which means 'castle of the fire worshippers' in French); the kings of Badakhshan, who 's'apelent tuit … Çulcarnein, en saraisin lor langajes, que vaut a dire en frascois Alixandre (all … are named Zulkarnein in their Saracen language, meaning 'Alexander' in French); or the 'tre nobilisime cité qui est apellé Quinsai, que vaut a dire en franchoit la cité dou ciel' (very noble city called Quinsai, which in French means the 'City of Heaven').[28] 'Yogi', he notes, is the name for the regular clergy among the

---

Medieval Italy. Essays in Memory of Robert L. Reynolds, ed. D. Herlihy, R. S. Lopez and V. Slessarev (Kent OH, 1969), pp. 35–42 (p. 36).

[25] Francesco Balducci Pegolotti, 'Notices of the Land Route to Cathay', in H. Yule, *Cathay and the Way Thither*, rev. H. Cordier, new edn, 3 vols.(London, 1914; repr. Liechtenstein, 1967), III, 137–73 (p. 151).

[26] See 'latinier' in A.-J. Greimas, *Dictionnaire de l'ancien français jusqu'au milieu du XIVe siècle* (Paris, 1988).

[27] Polo, *Description*, trans. Kinoshita, pp. 80, 83, 89.

[28] Polo, *Milione*, XIII.1 (p. 127), XXXI.7 (p. 339), XLVII.3 (p. 360), CLII.3 (p. 513); Polo, *Description*, trans. Kinoshita, pp. 17, 25, 38, 133. The fact that we are told the equivalent for all of these names 'in French' helps confirm that French, not Latin or Italian, was the original language of composition.

brahmins of India.[29] Despite this exactitude in reporting the use or meaning of foreign words and phrases, however, Marco (in contrast to William of Rubruck) includes no scenes of encounter with speakers of other languages that necessitate the intervention of bi- or multilingual fixers.[30]

When it comes to his geographical descriptions, in fact, Marco does not seem overly interested in languages *per se*. His entry on Mosul, for example, describes it as:

> un grant roiames qui l'habitent plusors jenerasion de jens ... une jens ki est apellé Arabi que orent Maomet; ... un autre generation de jens ke tent la loy cristiane, mes non as selo[n]c que comande l'eglise de Rome, car il failent en plusors couses... en les montagnes de ceste regne demorent jens ke sunt appelés C[u]rd, que sunt de cristiens nestorin et jacopit. Le une partie sunt sarain, que aorent Maomet; il sunt prodomes [d'armes] et mauveise jens; et robent voluntere les mercaant.[31]

> (a great kingdom inhabited by many races of people[:] ... a people called Arabs who worship Mohammad; ... another race of people who hold the Christian law, but not the way the church of Rome commands, for they fall short in several things. ... In the mountains of this kingdom live people called Kurds, who are Nestorian and Jacobite Christians; some are Saracens, who worship Mohammad. They are valiant men-at-arms and bad people; and they willingly rob merchants.)[32]

For Marco and Rustichello, the salient categories are, first, religious affiliation; and second, merchants (of various faiths), along with those who either protect or rob them. In fact, Mosul (near the ancient city of Nineveh in northern Iraq) was founded as a garrison during the seventh-century Muslim conquest; its name comes from the Arabic for 'point of junction' and, in Marco Polo's day, it remained a crossroads town with speakers of Arabic, Persian, Turkic, Kurdish, Aramaic, Syriac and Hebrew. As Arabist Li Guo writes, 'The Tower of Babel, metaphorically and physically, was just a stone's throw away'.[33]

---

[29] Polo, *Description*, trans. Kinoshita, p. 167.

[30] This absence may be explained, I think, in two ways. First, it may reflect the ease with which a multilingual Marco was able to move through Mongol-ruled lands; second, since the *Devisement* is not a travel narrative, references to Marco's first-hand experiences are the exception rather than the rule. See Polo, *Description*, trans. Kinoshita, p. xvi.

[31] Polo, *Milione*, XXIV.1–3, 8–9 (p. 328–9).

[32] Polo, *Description*, trans. Kinoshita, p. 19.

[33] L. Guo, *The Performing Arts in Medieval Islam: Shadow Play and Popular Poetry in Ibn Daniyāl's Mamluk Cairo* (Leiden, 2012), pp. 5–6.

Though Mosul's ethnic and linguistic plurality leaves little to no trace in the *Devisement*, Marco does occasionally comment or (more rarely) render judgment on a local language: in Anatolia, the Turcomans, 'que aurent Maom[e]t et tenent sa loy' (who worship Muhammad and hold to his law) are described as 'sinple jens' (a simple people) with 'brut lengajes' (a rough language);[34] in Qarajang (the kingdom of Dali in the modern-day Yunnan), ruled by Qubilai Khan's grandson, the people 'on lengajes por elz et est m[ou]t gref a entendre' (have a language of their own, which is very harsh to listen to).[35] Otherwise, numerous regions and kingdoms throughout the *Devisement* are said to have 'a language of their own', with no further comment. These are presumably local and regional vernaculars – some preliterate and others with some form of writing – in contrast to the cosmopolitan and administrative languages, the lingua francas and trade vernaculars, that those in Mongol service would have employed in their travels throughout Asia. Many of these are clustered in the Book of India: the islands of today's Indonesian archipelago (§§164–6; 168); the port cities on the west coast of India (§§180, 182–8); and the Zanzibar coast in East Africa (§182).[36] Others are sited in the mountainous region of the Pamirs, the Karakorum range and Himalayas. The province of Tangut (the former Tibeto-Burman kingdom of Xi Xia, conquered by the Mongols in 1227) is populated, Marco tells us, by idolators, Nestorians and Saracens (Muslims); of these, the idolators (in this context, Buddhists) 'have their own language' (§58, p. 45) – including, we now know, a script comprising almost 6000 ideograms (in inscriptions not discovered until the turn of the twentieth century and not yet completely deciphered).[37]

Cosmopolitan languages and lingua francas

Those parts of the world not noted as having 'a language of their own' are presumably places where it was possible to communicate in one of the cosmopolitan languages or lingua francas used across Mongol Eurasia. What might those languages have been? Arabic is an obvious candidate for Islamicate territories, though there are few, if any, indications that it is one of Marco's four languages. If he did know some written or, more likely, oral Arabic, this would have opened to him the mix of information and lore on the Indian Ocean world,

[34] Polo, *Milione*, XXI.2 (p. 325); *Description*, p. 16.

[35] Polo, *Milione*, CXVIII.3 (p. 469); *Description*, p. 104.

[36] The title 'Le Livre de Indie' [Book of India], comprising chapters 158–233 of the *Devisement*, appears in the rubric to chapter 158.

[37] D. Sinor, 'Languages and Cultural Interchange Along the Silk Roads', *Diogenes* 171 (1995), 1–14 (pp. 3–4).

recorded in surviving sources such as the *Akhbār al-Sīn wa-l-Hind* (*Accounts of China and India*), an Arabic text in two parts (the first composed by Abū Zayd al-Sīrāfī, from the Persian Gulf port of Siraf, in the mid ninth century, the second by an anonymous continuator in the late ninth or early tenth) and the tenth-century *Kitāb 'Ajā'ib al-Hind* (*Book of the Wonders of India*).[38] Scholarly consensus is that Marco Polo never learned Chinese:[39] despite our modern fascination with his accounts of China, for Marco and his contemporaries, his experiences would have been significant for what they revealed of the interconnected Mongol imperium on the one hand and the Indian Ocean world on the other. But if Arabic and Chinese were unlikely to have figured among Marco's languages, what were some of the other Asian lingua francas he might have known? One, as we shall see, is a world language that deserves to be better known among scholars of the medieval and modern West; but we begin with two others that have left even less imprint on the modern imagination.

Turkic

In his chapter on Ghinghintalas (an unidentified site in northwestern China, perhaps near the Qaidam Basin), Marco explains to his readers that 'salamander' (what we recognise from his description to be asbestos) is not an animal at all but a mineral that must be mined and laboriously processed. How does he know?

> [J]e voç di que je ot un compagnons, que avoit a nom Çurficar, un turs que mout estoit saje, qui demoroit trois anz por le grant can en celle provence por fair traire celle salamander … mun conpains me dist le fait et je meisme le vi.
>
> (I tell you that I had a companion named Çurficar, a very wise Turk, who on the Great Khan's behalf stayed in this province for three years to extract this salamander… my companion told me about it and I saw it myself.)[40]

Marco's assurance in overturning the authoritative knowledge of his day is based on first-hand experience: 'I saw it myself'. Just as crucially, however, he insists on

---

[38] Abū Zayd al-Sīrāfī, *Accounts of China and India*, trans. T. Mackintosh-Smith (New York, 2017); Buzurg ibn Shahriyar of Ramhormuz, *Book of the Wonders of India: Mainland, Sea and Islands*, ed. and trans. G. S. P. Freeman-Grenville (London, 1981).

[39] D. Morgan, 'Persian as a *Lingua Franca* in the Mongol Empire', in *Literacy in the Persianate World: Writing and the Social Order*, ed. B. Spooner and W.L. Hanaway (Philadelphia, 2012), pp. 160–70 (p. 161). For a counter-opinion, see S. G. Haw, 'The Persian Language in Yuan-Dynasty China: A Reappraisal', *East Asian History* 39 (2014), 5–32.

[40] Polo, *Milione*, LX.7–8 (p. 376); Polo, *Description*, §60 (p. 48).

the testimony of a 'very wise Turk' appointed by the Great Khan to a three-year term as governor of the province. Çurficar, then, belongs to the ranks of the *semu ren*: the 'varied peoples', predominantly Central and West Asians (Turks, Persians and Arabs) who constituted the second tier of the Mongol political hierarchy, just below the Mongols themselves and who featured prominently in their imperial administration;[41] it is to this group that the Polos too would have likely belonged during their years in Qubilai's service. Two things about this passage stand out. First, while a more mainstream writer like Brunetto Latini includes salamanders in his chapter on lizards – 'sachiez que salemandre vit enmi les flambés dou feu sens dolor et sens damaige de son cors, neis ele estaint le feu par sa nature' (know that the salamander lives amidst the fire's flames with neither pain nor harm to its body, but it extinguishes fire by its nature) – drawn from a reputable source, *De bestiis et aliis rebus* (a composite Latin translation of the second- or third-century Greek bestiary, the *Physiologus*),[42] Marco relies on a living informant who is not a scholar but an administrator, whose expertise comes from practical experience – one of the 'authoritative men of truth' that, Rustichello tells us in his opening chapter, constitute an important, if secondary, source for the diversities of the world contained in their book.[43] Even more striking is the sense of intimacy with which Marco refers to Çurficar, making a point of mentioning his proper name (a distinction usually reserved in the *Devisement* for rulers, high-ranking administrators, generals and saints), twice calling him his 'companion'.

In what language might Marco and Çurficar have communicated? Given the prestigious post that the latter occupied, he could plausibly have been a Uighur, member of a Turkic group that had established a nomadic empire in the eighth and ninth centuries, later settling down in the area of modern-day Xinjiang. Crucially, they had adapted an alphabet from Syriac script (used by Nestorian Christians along with Buddhists) – an alphabet that the Mongols adopted in turn after the Uighurs.[44] Writing to Pope Innocent IV in 1247, the Franciscan friar John of Plano Carpini reported that after Chinggis Khan defeated the Uighurs in battle (in fact, they voluntarily submitted to him in 1209), 'the Mongols took their alphabet, for formerly they had no written characters', making this acquisition sound almost like a spoil of war.[45] A decade later, fellow Franciscan William of Rubruck likewise wrote to King Louis IX of France that

---

[41] F. W. Mote, 'Chinese Society Under Mongol Rule', in *The Cambridge History of China*, 15 vols., VI, *Alien Regimes and Border States, 907–1368*, ed. H. Franke and D. Twitchett (Cambridge, 1994), pp. 616–64 (pp. 630–2).

[42] Latini, *Tresor*, I.144.2 (p. 250).

[43] Polo, *Description*, §1 (p. 1)

[44] Mote, 'Chinese Society Under Mongol Rule', p. 630.

[45] *Mission to Asia*, trans. C. Dawson (New York, 1966; repr. Toronto, 1980), p. 21.

the Mongols had adopted the Uighur alphabet and writing system: 'They begin writing at the top and carry the line downwards, reading in the same way and the lines succeed each other from left to right'. He further alerts the king that the Great Khan Möngke 'is sending you a letter which is in the Mo'al [Mongol] language but in their [the Uighurs'] script'.[46] In the Mongol Ilkhanate (sub-khanate), the Persian historian Juvayni (d. 1283) famously grumbled about the prominence and prestige the Uighur language had recently attained in Khurāsān (eastern Iran).[47] All these factors make Uighur a strong candidate to be one of the languages that Marco learned at Qubilai's court.

As Venetians doing business in West Asia, however, the Polos may already have been familiar with another Turkic language, Cuman. The Cumans, called Qipchaq in Muslim sources, were a loose confederation of originally distinct nomadic tribes that had fused in the process of their westward migration in the face of the political turmoil occasioned by the rise of the Jin dynasty in northern China, then of Mongol expansion.[48] In the twelfth and early thirteenth centuries, this Qipchaq-Cuman realm of 'loosely connected tribal units' stretched from modern-day Kazakhstan to the lower Danube on the western shores of the Black Sea. Across this vast region, they became 'deeply enmeshed in the politics of their neighbours. Women of the Qipchaq elite often married Russian, Hungarian, Georgian and Bulgarian princes', while the men served in their cavalries.[49]

This world was violently disrupted by the Mongols' westward drive in the 1220s and 1230s. The Mongols specifically targeted the Cumans for having given shelter to their enemies the Merkits. For William of Rubruck, writing in the early 1250s, the steppes of the Crimean Peninsula (which he calls Gazaria) and current-day southern Ukraine, formerly 'the grazing ground of the Comans', present a landscape of complete devastation, 'all laid waste by the Tartars' (that is, the Mongols) under the leadership of Chinggis Khan's eldest

---

[46] William of Rubruck, *Mission* trans. Jackson, pp. 154–5.

[47] Morgan, 'Persian as a *Lingua Franca*', p. 164.

[48] On their five original tribal zones, see D. Korobeinikov, 'A Broken Mirror: The Kipçak World in the Thirteenth Century', in *The Other Europe in the Middle Ages: Avars, Bulgars, Khazars and Cumans*, ed. F. Curta (Leiden, 2007), pp. 379–412 (p. 381). On the ethnogenesis, its complicated nomenclature and original homelands of the confederated tribes, see I. Vásáry, *Cumans and Tatars: Oriental Military in the Pre-Ottoman Balkans, 1185–1365* (Cambridge, 2005), pp. 4–7. On the flight from Mongol aggression, see Favereau, *The Horde*, pp. 46–7.

[49] Favereau, *The Horde*, p. 47. For example, Elizabeth, the wife of the Hungarian king Steven V (ruled 1270–72), was the daughter of a Cuman chieftain.

son Jochi, who established the khanate of the Golden Horde.[50] All that can be seen are 'great numbers of Coman graves', some 'visible to us two leagues off, owing to their practice of burying members of the family all together'.[51] For William, the former 'Qipchaq steppes' are haunted by the vanquished and vanished Cumans.

Writing over four decades later, Marco Polo modifies this portrait of genocide to one of diaspora. Before Jochi's conquest, he writes, the lands which would come to constitute the khanate of the Golden Horde were 'all ... subject to the Cumans but they were not held together, nor were they a unit; therefore [the Cumans] lost their lands and were chased all over the world. Those who were not expelled and are still there are all in servitude' to the Horde.[52] This picture of dispersion, as far westward as Hungary and eastward to the heart of the Mongol empire, is borne out in William's own experience. In the camp of Batu, khan of the Golden Horde, William is surprised to meet a Cuman who greets him in Latin and explains that he had been baptised in Hungary. In the Mongol capital of Qaraqorum, he meets 'the daughter of a Lorrainer but who was born in Hungary and who is quite familiar with French and Coman' as well as 'Basil, the son of an Englishman, who had been born in Hungary and who knows these same languages'.[53] These bi- and trilingual speakers – not important functionaries but ordinary people randomly encountered – demonstrate the extent to which Cuman had become a lingua franca over a vast swathe of the Eurasian steppes. Like medieval French, it was a language without borders, and the two languages together were spoken by two of William's three interlocutors. Of course, moving deeper into Mongol-held lands, one could not count on being able to converse in French or Latin. Thus Francesco Pegolotti, the Florentine merchant we earlier quoted underscoring the importance of securing a reliable translator, goes on to specify that:

> oltre a' turcimanni si conviene menare per lo meno due fanti buoni che sappiano bene la lingua cumanesca. E se il mercatante vuole menare dalla Tana niuna femmina con seco, ... conviene che sappia la lingua cumanesca come il fante.[54]

---

[50] William of Rubruck, *Mission*, trans. Jackson, pp. 105–6.

[51] William of Rubruck, *Mission*, trans. Jackson, pp. 99, 108.

[52] Polo, *Description*, p. 214 (§221).

[53] William of Rubruck, *Mission*, trans. Jackson, pp. 135–6, 212. On Hungary as 'undoubtedly the most ethno-religiously diverse kingdom in Latin Christendom' between the eleventh and thirteenth centuries, see B. A. Catlos, *Muslims of Medieval Latin Christendom, c. 1050–1614* (Cambridge, 2014), pp. 231ff.

[54] Pegolotti, *Pratica della mercatura*, pp. 21–2.

(besides the dragoman it will be well to take at least two good men servants, who are acquainted with the Cumanian tongue. And if the merchant likes to take a woman with him from Tana, ... it will be well that she be acquainted with the Cumanian tongue as well as the men.)[55]

Now, the administrative language of the Golden Horde was Chagatay – an eastern Turkic tongue that had become a literary language – that is, a written language that served as a vehicle of culture.[56] Pegolotti's insistence on acquiring servants or slaves familiar with Cuman (a western Turkic language) demonstrates that it is the spoken vernacular, not the written language of the chancery, that Italian merchants needed to make their way through West Asia beyond the bounds of Outremer.[57]

The connectivity of the Cumans in the western Eurasian steppe is graphically materialised in the grave goods from the Chungul Kurgan, an early thirteenth-century princely tomb excavated in 1981, goods 'likely accumulated through trading and raiding or through diplomatic and marriage gifts of this Qïpčaq leader, and his tribal confederation, with the neighboring Rus', Georgian, Armenian, Hungarian, Byzantine, Crusader and Islamic polities'.[58] These include: amphorae and albarello vessels likely used for the import of wine and *materia medica*, subsequently reused for local purposes; a gilded covered cup of Rhine-Meuse area manufacture; and burial caftans combining imitations of or reused pieces from Byzantine ceremonial robes with furs from the Russian fur trade.[59]

This connectivity is confirmed by an 'Interpreter's Book', part of a remarkable compilation known to modern scholars as the Codex Cumanicus (Venice, Biblioteca Marciana, Cod. Mar. Lat. DXLIX). A trilingual glossary in Latin, Cuman and Persian, scholars conjecture it was assembled by Genoese merchants

---

[55] Pegolotti, 'The Land Route to Cathay', pp. 151–2.

[56] Vásáry, 'Mongolian and Turkic', p. 148. Chagatay, one of Chinggis Khan's sons, gave his name to the Central Asian khanate given to him in appanage and to the language spoken there, which became the court language of Chagatay's direct and indirect successors. See N. Ostler, *Empires of the Word: A Language History of the World* (New York, 2005), p. 106.

[57] In any case, Crusader Acre fell to the Mamluks in 1291, leaving Lusignan Cyprus as the lone Francophone outpost in the eastern Mediterranean.

[58] R. Holod and Y. Rassamakin, 'Imported and Native Remedies for a Wounded "Prince": Grave Goods from the Chungul Kurgan in the Black Sea Steppe of the Thirteenth Century', *Medieval Encounters* 18 (2012), 339–81 (p. 339).

[59] For the containers and their contents, see Holod and Rassamakin, 'Imported and Native Remedies', pp. 356–81. For the clothing and belts, see W. T. Woodfin, Y. Rassamakin and R. Holod, 'Foreign Vesture and Nomadic Identity on the Black Sea Littoral in the Early Thirteenth Century', *Ars Orientalis* 38 (2010), 155–86.

in the Crimea in the 1290s.[60] Of the three languages, the first is 'a Vulgar Italo-Latin' (as opposed to the more standard Latin of the 'Missionaries Book', the other main text in the Codex, dating to *c.*1330–40); the Persian appears to be 'a kind of simplified koine', representing its status as a mercantile lingua franca; and the Cuman shows errors in grammar, syntax, phonetics and translation, suggesting a lingua franca as transcribed by non-Turkic (in this case, Genoese or possibly Venetian) speakers.[61] The glossary itself begins with a long list of conjugated verbs, in alphabetical order (in Latin), followed by adverbs, nouns and pronouns, words pertaining to spiritual matters (God, angel, peace, charity, paradise, hell, etc.), the four elements (air, water, earth, fire), the four humors, expressions of time (year, month, day, night, the canonical hours, the days of the week, the months of the year, etc.), the five senses, terms related to weather (cloud, dew, wind) and the directions, antonyms, qualities (goodness, beauty, length, health, etc.), a long list of spices, items related to various trades, colors, precious stones, body parts, kinship terms, things pertaining to war, the home, horses; and concluding with trees, animals, birds and miscellaneous foodstuffs.[62] The sheer scope of this word list affords a tantalising hint of the richness and complexity of the world of expatriate Italian merchants in West Asia.

Persian

In her provocatively titled book *Did Marco Polo Go To China?*, sinologist Frances Wood concluded that 'Marco Polo himself probably never traveled much further than the family's trading posts on the Black Sea and in Constantinople'.[63] This

[60] On the composition and dating of the compilation, see P. B. Golden, 'Codex Cumanicus', in *Central Asian Monuments*, ed. H. B. Paksoy (Istanbul, 1992), accessed 7 October 2023, http://vlib.iue.it/carrie/texts/carrie_books/paksoy-2/cam2.html, pp. 2–3. See also B. Grévin, *Le Parchemin des cieux: essai sur le Moyen Âge du langage* (Paris, 2012), pp. 347–51.

[61] Golden, 'Codex Cumanicus', p. 5. For analogous cases of written sources reflecting spoken dialects or vernaculars, see C. Aslanov, *Le Français au Levant, jadis et naguère: à la recherche d'une langue perdue* (Paris, 2006), pp. 37–51. Based on the phonetic transliteration of French words into Armenian, Coptic and Arabic, Aslanov argues for Norman dialectal influence on the French of Antioch (originally ruled by Bohemond of Hauteville) and Walloon influence on the kingdom of Jerusalem. Moreover, since Armenian forms seem to reflect forms preceding some identifiable sound shifts, Aslanov further argues for their relatively early (perhaps twelfth century) assimilation into Armenian. The Armenian texts examined are translations of crusader legal texts, whereas the Coptic and Arabic occur in multilingual glossaries.

[62] *Codex Comanicus. Édition diplomatique avec fac-similés*, ed. V. Drimba (Bucharest, 2000), pp. 35–109.

[63] F. Wood, *Did Marco Polo Go To China?* (Boulder, 1996), p. 150. This view has been roundly refuted by (for example) I. de Rachewiltz, 'Marco Polo Went to China',

is based in part on an argument from silence – why is there no mention of such quintessentially Chinese phenomena as tea, foot-binding and the Great Wall? – but in part because many of the names that Marco Polo uses for places or things reflect Persian terminology or pronunciation.[64] Far from being the indictment that Wood intends it to be, the proliferation of Persianate terms in the *Devisement* has an easy explanation: since Marco's cohort, as I have suggested, would have been West Asian *semu ren* speaking Persian, Arabic or Turkic, his use of their version of place names is no more indicative than saying 'Florence' rather than 'Firenze' would prove that an American's knowledge of that city was faked from a British or French guidebook.

In Marco Polo's day, Persian was on its way to becoming 'a language of governance or learning in a region that stretched from China to the Balkans, and from Siberia to southern India … a lingua franca promoted by multiethnic and multi-religious states, and aided further by education and diplomacy'.[65] Though the importance of religious difference in the Middle Ages predisposes us to focus on the predominance of Arabic across Islamicate Asia, Persian had emerged as a literary and cultural language under the Samanid and Ghaznavid rulers of ninth- and tenth-century Khorasan (in present-day northeastern Iran), culminating in Ferdowsi's vast historical epic, the *Shahnameh* (completed 1010).[66] It was subsequently adopted as the court language of the Great

---

Zentralasiatische Studien 27 (1997), 34–92 and H. U. Vogel, *Marco Polo Was in China: New Evidence from Currencies, Salts and Revenues* (Leiden, 2013). In the Afterword to the American Edition, Wood walks back her own claim, explaining that, 'in using modern versions of the text, cobbled together from a great variety of versions, [she] was laying something of a false trail. … The late appearance of some of the "best" material must suggest that it was added by later copyists or publishers (like Ramusio) [and] careful comparisons of the earliest versions reveal a far slimmer account than is popularly assumed. Crediting Polo himself with all these later additions has helped to create the myth of the great observer which is simply not tenable on the basis of early versions of *The Description of the World*'; Wood, *Did Marco Polo Go To China?*, pp. 154–5.

[64] For place names, she cites Chemeinfu for Kaipingfu (§14); Pianfu for Pingyangfu (§107), Quengianfu for Xi'anfu (§111), Taianfu for Tiayuanfu (§107) Tandinfu for Dongpingfu (§134), Yangiu for Yanzhou (§144), Giogiu for Zhuozhou (§106), Fugiu for Fuzhou (§155), Singui matu for Xinzhou matou (§135) and Taidu for Dadu (§85). Wood, *Did Marco Polo Go To China?*, p. 61.

[65] This is Nile Green's characterisation of the fifteenth century, just before the zenith of Persian's 'geographical and social reach between the sixteenth and eighteenth centuries'. N. Green, 'Introduction', in *The Persianate World: The Frontiers of a Eurasian Lingua Franca*, ed. N. Green (Oakland, 2019), pp. 1–71 (p. 1).

[66] On the *Shahnameh* and its place in Persian Tradition and in 'the World Literature Polysystem', see F. D. Lewis, 'A Book of Kings as the King of Books: The *Shahnameh*

Seljuqs, an Oghuz Turkic confederation that established an empire centred in Persia in the mid eleventh century; then, following their victory over the Byzantine emperor at the battle of Manzikert in 1071, they extended their rule over central and eastern Anatolia as the Seljuq sultanate of Rūm.[67] The Seljuq capital at Konya became a magnet for Persian scholars who served as administrators and religious figures who were central to the Islamicisation of Anatolia. What began in the late twelfth and early thirteenth centuries as 'a steady trickle of ... peripatetic individuals seeking patronage at the small Muslim courts of Anatolia ... bec[a]me a mighty torrent of refugees' as the Mongols swept westward in Asia.[68] Among these exiles was the mystic and poet Jalāl al-Din Rūmī, whose family had fled their home near Balkh (in present-day Afghanistan) sometime ahead of its sack by the Mongols (1220), with stays in Mecca, Damascus and Aleppo before eventually settling in Konya.[69] Composing verses (notably his *Masnavi*) in Persian and founding what would become the Mevlevi Sufi order, he attracted a fervent following, including Gürcü Hatun ('the Georgian lady'), born Princess Tamar of Georgia, who married the Seljuq sultan Kaykhusraw II and, after his death (1246), Mu'in al-Din Süleyman, the Ilkhanid-appointed governor of Rūm – thus bridging the 'before' and 'after' of the Mongol defeat of the Seljuqs in 1243.[70] In his *Devisement* chapter on the province of 'Turcomanie,' Marco Polo mentions Konya, Caeseria (modern Kayseri) and Sebastea (modern Sivas) together as 'nomé cité' (notable cities) subject to the Ilkhanate.[71] Given the importance of the trade route linking these three cities to the Anatolian coast in the southwest

---

of Ferdowsi', in *A Companion to World Literature*, vol. 2, ed. C. Chism (Hoboken, 2020), pp. 1255–67.

[67] Like the Byzantines, the Seljuqs thought of their land as 'Roman'. On the Persianisation of culture under the Seljuqs, see A. C. S. Peacock, 'Introduction: The Great Age of the Seljuqs', in *Court and Cosmos: The Great Age of the Seljuqs*, ed. S. R. Canby, D. Beyazit, M. Rugiadi, and A. C. S. Peacock (New York, 2016), pp. 2–44 (pp. 30–3).

[68] C. Hillenbrand, 'Rāvandī, the Seljuk Court at Konya and the Persianization of Anatolian Cities', *Mésogeios* 25–6 (2005), 157–69 (pp. 162–3).

[69] A. Schimmel, *The Triumphal Sun: A Study of the Works of Jalāloddin Rumi* (London, 1978), pp. 12–4. On images in Rūmī's poetry derived from everyday life in Konya, see ibid., p. xv.

[70] A. C. S. Peacock, 'Georgia and the Anatolian Turks in the 12th and 13th Centuries', *Anatolian Studies* 56 (2006), 127–46. Rūmī's modern biographer credits him with a knowledge of Arabic, Turkish and Greek in addition to Persian. See F. Lewis, *Rumi: Past and Present, East and West. The Life, Teaching and Poetry of Jalāl Al-Din Rumi* (Oxford, 2000), pp. 315–17.

[71] Polo, *Milione*, XXI.7 (p. 325).

and the overland 'Silk Road' in the east, the Polos may well have had first- (or at least second-)hand knowledge of this centre of Persian cultural influence.

In the meantime, among the ethnically and religiously mixed populations of eastern Anatolia and the Caucasus, Persian had become a prestige literary culture that, through a 'constellation of adaptive practices', helped generate new texts and genres in Georgian, Armenian and Turkish.[72] 'Perhaps counterintuitively', Michael Pifer writes, 'the development of cosmopolitan literary codes across multiple languages thus provided a baseline for poetic *differentiation* to occur, as diverse authors folded heterogeneity back into widely circulating literary genres, styles, and forms'.[73] In late twelfth- or early thirteenth-century Georgia, long narratives proved especially popular, like the prose translation of the Middle Persian romance *Vīs and Rāmin*, or Shota Rustaveli's *The Knight in the Panther Skin*, which its author describes as '[a]n ancient Persian tale' retold 'in the Georgian tongue'.[74] In Armenian, shorter verse forms prevailed, as in the work of Frik (second half of the thirteenth century), whose most famous poem includes a quatrain from a well-known Persian poem (transliterated in Armenian script).[75] Such examples, illegible from the perspective of nationalist literary historiographies, remind us of the dense cross-confessional, cross-linguistic and cross-cultural interplay that constituted business as usual across Marco Polo's world.[76]

[72] M. Pifer, *Kindred Voices: A Literary History of Medieval Anatolia* (New Haven, 2021), p. 19.

[73] Pifer, *Kindred Voices*, p. 23. The nearest equivalent might be the way translations of French romance material might keep or incorporate French vocabulary and expressions, as, for example, in Gottfried von Strassburg's Middle High German translation of the *Tristan*.

[74] S. Rustaveli, *The Knight in the Panther Skin*, trans. L. Coffin (Tblisi, 2015), 9.1, p. 12. On the *Visramiani*, see D. Rayfield, *The Literature of Georgia: A History*, 2nd edn (Richmond, 2000), pp. 72–5, and on *Vepkhistqaosani* (*Knight in the Panther Skin*), ibid., pp. 76–86.

[75] Frik is one of the two earliest 'vernacular' poets in Armenian; Pifer, *Kindred Voices*, p. 141. On the complexities of Frik's citation, translation and re-reading/adaptation of the poem's themes, see ibid., pp. 154–62.

[76] For example, Ganja (in present-day Azerbaijan), home to Nezami Ganjavi (1141–1209), author of the celebrated quintet of romances (*Khamsa*) in Middle Persian, was also the birthplace of the Armenian historian Kirakos Gandzaketsi (*c*.1200/2–71), author of a *History of the Armenians* that begins with Gregory the Illuminator and continues through the war between the Ilkhanate and the Golden Horde that first prompted the elder Polos to journey deeper into Asia. A corollary to this literary influence across religious 'boundaries' is the way these texts similarly travel across scriptworlds – David Damrosch's term for the shared literary culture created across languages written in the same script.

Mongol multilingualism, revisited

Compiled shortly after the Codex Cumanicus but with a direct connection to the Mongols was the Rasulid Hexaglot. It takes its name from the lone surviving copy, in a manuscript made *c.*1370 under al-Malik al-Afdal, the Rasulid sultan of Aden (the Arabian port at the southern entrance to the Red Sea, a centre for the Indian Ocean trade).[77] It comprises a wordlist in three core languages – Arabic, Persian and Turkish – juxtaposed in one part of the manuscript with Greek and Armenian and in another with Mongol – all recorded or transliterated in Arabic script. These combinations point to the consolidation of at least two prior sources, with Tabriz, capital of the Ilkhanate of Persia, as the likely place of assemblage. The Hexaglot's Turkish entries present a mixture of Cuman-Qipchaq and Anatolian elements, similar to the scripta found in Mamluk Egyptian sources; its Armenian is the western variant found in Cilicia (Marco Polo's 'Petite Armenie' [Lesser Armenia] [§20]); and its Greek is the demotic vernacular of Anatolia.[78]

While the Codex Cumanicus and the Rasulid Hexaglot are certainly exceptional documents, their choice of languages and vocabularies offers us a glimpse of the mosaic of languages informing the commercial centers of medieval West Asia. Overlapping with regions in which French would have served as a lingua franca for Latin Christian kings, nobles, crusaders, missionaries and pilgrims as well as merchants, the world of Marco Polo's *Devisement du monde* invites us to explore the linguistic and cultural complexities of the multilingual Middle Ages. Understanding the reach of medieval French as a language not yet constrained by national borders or treated as a vehicle for linguistic nationalism further opens our eyes to variety and interplay of languages beyond the bounds of Latin Christendom.

---

[77] See Polo, *Description*, §194. In the thirteenth century, the sultans of Aden exercised patronage over the expatriate Muslim trade communities of several port cities on the west coast of India. See E. Lambourn, 'India from Aden: *Khutba* and Muslim Urban Networks in Late Thirteenth-Century India', in *Secondary Cities and Urban Networks in the Indian Ocean Realm, c. 1400–1800*, ed. K. R. Hall (Lanham MD, 2008), pp. 55–97.

[78] Grévin, *Le parchemin des cieux*, pp. 352–3, 356. The same codex also contains an Arabic-Ethiopian lexicon. See also É. Vallet, 'La Grammaire du monde: Langue et pouvoir en Arabie occidentale à l'âge mongole', *Annales: histoire, sciences sociales* 70 (2015), 637–66.

7

Romancing Allegory:
Theories of the Vernacular in Outremer

Uri Zvi Shachar

The title of this chapter pays deliberate tribute to Gabrielle Spiegel's 1993 seminal monograph, *Romancing the Past*.[1] In this book Spiegel investigates the blossoming of Old French prose historiography in the context of the struggle between a northern French aristocracy that felt imminently marginalised and an increasingly sophisticated and ambitious Capetian crown. Baronial chroniclers forged a glorious past as a tool to provide patrons with moral reassurance and political justification. But for Spiegel the turn to prose romance also marks a profound shift in how these authors generated truth value. She asks what it meant for them to turn to prose as a vehicle for historical truth and through which to perform an efficacious self-fashioning. Why, in other words, had Latin writing become insufficient for their political needs? I invoke Spiegel's legacy not to suggest that a similar tension between francophone barons and the crown existed in the eastern Mediterranean. It is rather because Spiegel's concern with 'the social function of prose' is a reminder that there are always urgent intellectual stakes involved in these generic and linguistic choices and that, therefore, it is likely that authors are looking for ways to map out these stakes in their prose.

The use of vernacular languages became more widespread in the thirteenth century both in the number of works authored in local dialects and in the range of fields where the vernacular was seen to be appropriate.[2] We find the first translations of scripture into Old French in the twelfth century and into Castilian in the middle of the thirteenth century.[3] Later in the fourteenth

---

[1] G. Spiegel, *Romancing the Past: The Rise of Vernacular Prose Historiography in Thirteenth-Century France* (Los Angeles, 1993).

[2] On the vernacular revolution in the later Middle Ages, see: A. Minnis, *Medieval Theory of Authorship: Scholastic Literary Attitudes in the Later Middle Ages*, 2nd edn (Philadelphia, 1988), pp. ix–xxvi; A. Minnis, *Translations of Authority in Medieval English Literature: Valuing the Vernacular* (Cambridge, 2009), pp. 1–16.

[3] P. Nobel, 'La traduction biblique', in *Translations médiévales. Cinq siècles de traductions en français au Moyen Âge (XIe-XVe siècles). Étude et répertoire, Volume 1:*

and fifteenth centuries contemplative philosophy and natural philosophy are translated into Middle English and other European vernaculars.[4] Some world histories were translated from Latin to vernacular and others were authored originally in the vulgar tongues.[5] It is then, too, that authors of major allegorical literary works turned to the vernacular as the linguistic vehicle of their choice.[6] In other words, this shift took place in resolutely authoritative areas, where the stakes were extraordinarily high. The choice to turn away from Latin was controversial, even provocative, and the need to justify it inescapable. This was true of most European traditions, but perhaps even more so in the case of Outremer, or Mediterranean, French.[7]

In many ways the use of the vernacular posed a profound question: how could a dialect that had formerly been used to conduct mostly local, ephemeral affairs be seen as sufficient to encompass matters of widespread importance?[8] Authors rejected the conventional expectation that associated Latin with the learned and the universal and vernacular with the opposite. As a result, the turn to the vernacular demanded an appeal to a new kind of authority, or demanded the use of new strategies to justify its own rhetorical presumptions.

De la translatio studii *à l'étude de la* translatio, ed. C. Galderisi (Turnhout, 2011), pp. 207–23; E. Fracomano, 'Castilian Vernacular Bibles in Iberia, *c.*1250–1500', in *The Practice of the Bible in the Middle Ages: Production, Reception, and Performance in Western Christianity*, ed. S. Boynton and D. Reilly (New York, 2011), pp. 315–37.

[4] C. Burnett, 'Arabic into Latin: The Reception of Arabic Philosophy into Western Europe', in *The Cambridge Companion to Arabic Philosophy*, ed. P. Adamson and R. Taylor (Cambridge, 2005), pp. 370–404.

[5] M. Ailes, 'Ambroise's *Estoire de la guerre sainte* and the Development of a Genre', *Reading Medieval Studies* 34 (2008), 1–19; Spiegel, *Romancing the Past*, pp. 214–68.

[6] On the rise of vernacular allegory in the thirteenth century, see: S. Gibbs Kamath and R. Copeland, 'Medieval Secular Allegory: French and English', in *Cambridge Companion to Allegory*, ed. R. Copeland and P. Struck (Cambridge, 2010), pp. 136–47; and M. Zink, *La subjectivité littéraire: autour du siècle de saint Louis* (1985), pp. 127–270.

[7] J. Rubin, *Learning in a Crusader City: Intellectual Activity and Intercultural Exchanges in Acre, 1191–1291* (Cambridge, 2018), pp. 62–83; *MFLCA*, 122–57.

[8] T. Hinton, 'Translation, Authority, and the Valorization of the Vernacular', in *A Companion to Medieval Translation*, ed. J. Beer (Amsterdam, 2019), pp. 97–105; R. Copeland, 'Language Frontiers, Literary Form, and the Encyclopedia', in *Frontiers in the Middle Ages: Proceedings of the Third European Congress of the Medieval Studies*, ed. O. Merisalo (Turnhout, 2006), pp. 507–24; S. Nichols, 'Global Language or Universal Language? From Babel to the Illustrious Vernacular', *Digital Philology: A Journal of Medieval Cultures* 1 (2012), 73–109; K. Busby and A. Putter, 'Introduction: Medieval Francophonia', in *Medieval Multilingualism: The Francophone World and its Neighbours*, ed. C. Kleinhenz and K Busby (Turnhout, 2010), pp. 1–14.

This chapter will argue that in attempt to justify the use of Old French, various authors in the late medieval Mediterranean articulated a theory which sought to reconcile the particularistic quality of the vulgar idiom with an ambition to devise a non-exclusive and sometimes universal register. It traces the contours of a theory of French vernacular found in several late medieval works that saw in French the capacity to bear the dialectic between the particular and universal because of – not *despite* – its development over time and its contact with other linguistic traditions.

To show that this theory informed compositions in several genres, this chapter draws on three Old French works: the *Book of Sidrac*; Pierre de Paris's French translation and commentary of *De consolatione philosophiae*; and Philippe de Mézières's *Le songe du viel pelerin*. Finally, the chapter turns to a popular contemporary work in Arabic – *Sīrat al-Ẓāhir Baybars* – to suggest that there is a larger context in which the question of the use of vernacular idioms should be considered. All four works involve an attempt to theorise the conditions that make the vernacular efficacious. All four seek to show that this efficacy – thanks to which they are capable of bearing an encyclopaedic, philosophical or prophetic ambition, respectively – is achieved not by drawing on a sense of a universal grammar or some other constant. Rather, the four authors standing behind these works show that French or Arabic was, for them, an adequate vehicle to discuss virtuous government and personal perfection precisely thanks to their ability to make their linguistic imperfection and dependence manifest.

The question that the use of the vernacular posed speaks to a key rhetorical principle in medieval literary theory, namely the expectation that there be an agreement between the scope of the matter or the theme that is englobed in a text and the capacity of the language that presumes to convey it to the reader.[9] This mimesis was achieved in part through the prestige that Latin enjoyed thanks to its perceived antiquity and its ability, in the words of Rita Copeland, to propose 'a structure of organic, evolutionary continuity with ancient texts'.[10] The other, of course, relies on theological arguments which go back to Jerome, according to which Latin is not only a privileged descendent of Hebrew and Greek, but is the language of scripture in its own right.

---

[9] Rita Copeland addresses this principle in the context of translations, see: R. Copeland, *Rhetoric, Hermeneutics, and Translation in the Middle Ages: Academic Traditions and Vernacular Texts* (Cambridge, 1991), pp. 21–36.

[10] Copeland, *Rhetoric, Hermeneutics, and Translation*, p. 105; E. Auerbach, *Mimesis: The Representation of Reality in Western Literature*, trans. W. Trask (Princeton, 1953), pp. 23–49; E. Auerbach, *Literary Language and its Public in Late Latin Antiquity and in the Middle Ages*, trans. R. Manheim (Princeton, 1965), pp. 25–66 ('Sermo Humilis').

Commenting on the most important prooftext on the matter, John 19:20, which states that the *titulus* on Jesus's cross was trilingual, Agobard of Lyon contended that the translations of scripture to Greek (the Septuagint) and Latin (Vulgate) share in the sacral quality of the Hebrew original.[11] The *titulus*, Agobard explains, 'communicated the numinous character of Hebrew and Greek to Latin'.[12] Authors in late medieval academic discourses employed Latin within an ideological framework, which bore a dialectic between the movement that is inherent in the practice of exegesis and interpretation and the divine stability of ecclesiastical languages like Greek, Hebrew and Arabic. It is clear from this way of posing the problem that any attempt to justify the use of the vernacular to convey the sublime must be thought to achieve this by rejecting metaphors regarding the timelessness and transparency of language and instead exploiting notions of its movement and corporeality. The turn to the vulgar tongue involved the use of a language that embodies the division and confusion which characterises the fallen (or post-Babel) world, and therefore is inherently incapable of conveying historical facticity or theological truth. To borrow from Peter Haidu, the attempt to narrativise Truth must use the profanity – the ideological contradictions of political, anthropological and linguistic divisiveness – that characterises the postlapsarian world as its foundational hermeneutical device.[13]

The eastern Mediterranean at the turn of the fourteenth century was indeed a place in which this multiplicity was particularly pronounced. Cyprus, for example, after the final demise of the Kingdom of Jerusalem in 1291, had come to accommodate a tremendously diverse collection of communities. With its francophone ruling elite, Greek-speaking population, Italian merchant colonies and Arabic-speaking Christian communities, Cyprus during the Lusignan (1192–1489) period was a true site of multilingualism, multi-ethnicity and multi-confessionalism.[14] For short time-periods the island came to house, in addition, small communities of Greek- and German-speaking Jews, as well as Ethiopian and Jacobite/Syriac Christians.[15] Many of

---

[11] Agobard of Lyon, *Liber contra objectiones Fredigisi abbatis*, PL 104, 162d–5D.

[12] I. Resnick, 'Lingua Dei, Lingua Hominis: Sacred Language and Medieval Texts', *Viator* 21 (1990), 51–74 (pp. 63–4).

[13] P. Haidu, 'Au début du roman, l'ironie', *Poétique* 36 (1978), 443–66; I thank Sharon Kinoshita for this reference.

[14] N. Coureas, 'Religion and Ethnic Identity in Lusignan Cyprus', in *Identity/Identities in Late Medieval Cyprus*, ed. T. Papacostas and G. Saint-Guillain (Nicosia, 2014), pp. 13–25.

[15] K. Ciggaar, 'Le royaume des Lusignan: terre de littérature et des traductions, échanges littéraires et culturels', in *Les Lusignans et l'Outre-Mer. Actes du colloque*

these communities were not indigenous to the island in that they cultivated a sense of having come from elsewhere, and the memory of their immigration was still part of their liturgies and mythologies. Differences in language were both signs of their distinct identities and marks of displacement, even if this displacement were centuries old. Together Cyprus and the eastern Mediterranean functioned as a contact zone where language choice took into account the idea that one's one idiom was defined by the history of its movement and contact with other, similarly itinerant idioms.[16] It is perhaps no wonder that in this setting in which languages were both in motion and in contact, authors appealed not to some inherent quality of their respective vernaculars – such as sublime beauty and therefore the capacity to engage in poetry – in search for legitimacy, but instead drew on their genealogy.[17] The theory of vernacular that this essay attempts to trace in works of Old French and Arabic, then, is also a manifestation of the hermeneutical strategies that the contact between cultures in the eastern Mediterranean made possible.

One striking example of this strategy is found in the preamble of *The Book of Sidrac* – an anonymous encyclopaedic compendium that was composed in the late thirteenth century in Outremer, most likely in Cyprus.[18] The work survives in two versions, one long and another short, in over fifty medieval manuscripts, the earliest from the turn of the fourteenth century.[19] The vast knowledge that the work presumes to generate is framed as a conversation between a philosopher-prophet and the king of a fictitious oriental kingdom.

Poitiers–Lusignan, 20–24 octobre 1993, auditorium du Musée Sainte-Croix Poitiers, ed. C. Mutafian (Poitiers, 1994), pp. 89–98.

[16] M. L. Pratt, 'Arts of the Contact Zone', *Profession* (1991), 33–40; M. L. Pratt, 'Introduction', in *Engaging Transculturality: Concepts, Key Terms, Case Studies*, ed. L. Abu-Er-Rub, C. Brosius, S. Meurer, D. Panagiotopoulos and S. Richter (New York, 2019), pp. xxiii–xliv.

[17] For a socio-linguistic approach toward the notion of linguistic contact zones, see: C. Aslanov, 'Languages in Contact in the Latin East: Acre and Cyprus', *Crusades* 1 (2002), 155–81; and S. Lusignan, 'French Language in Contact with English: Social Context and Linguistic Change (mid-13th–14th centuries)', in *Lang Cult*, pp. 19–30.

[18] Langlois was among the first to study the *Sidrac* in depth, and he asserts on the basis of philological observations the eastern origins of the work, see: C.-V. Langlois, *La vie en France au moyen âge: la connaissance de la nature et du monde* (Paris, 1927), pp. 198–275; see more recently, P. Waffner, *Der Livre de Sidrac: die Quelle allen Wissens: Aspekte zur Tradition und Rezeption eines altfranzösischen Textes* (Milano, 2019), pp. 19–28.

[19] B. Weisel, 'Die Überlieferung des *Livre de Sidrac* in Handschriften und Drucken', in *Wissensliteratur im Mittelalter und in der Frühen Neuzeit*, ed. H. Brunner and N. Wolf (Wiesbaden, 1993), pp. 53–66.

The frame story relates that 847 years after the death of Noah a pagan king called Boctus (the ruler of Boctria, 'a kingdom between Persia and India'),[20] sought to conquer a neighbouring land. He turns to an ally king for help, having been told that he possesses a book 'from the time of Noah' and an all-knowing philosopher, called Sidrac, who knows how to interpret it. The kind ally agrees to send Sidrac and the book to Boctus, who is impressed by the proofs the philosopher provides for the superiority of his god, and soon thereafter converts to Christianity.[21]

Having been graced with the knowledge that is invested in Noah's book, Sidrac is capable of teaching not only about the creation and the Trinity, but also about the future. He answers the king's questions on a wide range of matters, including: 'on love, on hate, on prowess, on cowardice ... on the wise, on the foolish, on man, on woman, on the deaf, on the mute, on taking, on giving, on going, on coming, on war, on peace ... on friends, on enemies ... on law, on faith, on dreaming, on sighing, on almsgiving, on sin, on other visible and invisible things'.[22] The philosopher, furthermore, prophesies centuries in advance, as it were, the success of the crusades, the rise of the Mongols and multiple other contemporaneous events. Because the answers please King Boctus he compiles them in a book he names 'The Fountain of all Knowledge'.

The encyclopaedic ambition of the work is apparent not only from the scope of its material, but also from its prefatory claim that, having descended from Japheth son of Noah, Sidrac was graced with knowledge on the universe from the creation until his own lifetime. The narrative, then, conflates the anthropological myth of Noah's sons inhabiting the entire world with an epistemological one. In keeping with the biblical reference to and the division of the world 'according to clans and languages, by their lands and nations' (referring to Gen 10:5), the book itself is conspicuously preoccupied with questions of the origin and spread of language. For example, Boctus asks the philosopher 'from which one of Noah's sons are we descended?' to which Sidrac answers: 'We are descended from Noah, and so do the Hebrews [*Ebreu*],

---

[20] *Sydrac le philosophe: le livre de la fontaine de toutes sciences*, ed. E. Ruhe (Wiesbaden, 2000), p. 39. The Kingdom of 'Boctorie' is mentioned in the Alexander legend as the place whence princess Roxane hails. The choice to place the pivotal affair of the *Sidrac* plot in Boctria may be an attempt to gesture toward this authoritative tradition.

[21] *Sydrac*, ed. Ruhe, pp. 46–7.

[22] *Sydrac*, ed. Ruhe, p. 3: 'd'amor, de hayne, de prouesce, de couardise ... de sage, de fol, d'ome, de feme, de sort, de muet, de prendre, de doner, d'aler, de venir, de guerre, de pais ... d'amis, d'anemis ... de loi, de foi, de songier, de sospir, d'aumone, de pechié, d'autres choses assés visibles et non visibles.'

Chaldeans [*Caldeu*] and Greeks [*Grifon*]. The French, Italian [*Roumain*], English and the Spanish are descended from Japhet'.[23] The author, in other words, chronicles the spread of languages and divides them into two branches, of which the protagonists belong to the first – together with other classical languages and peoples – while the work itself, written in French, belongs to the second.

Elsewhere the king asks what language Adam spoke and why we speak a different one than he did. Sidrac explains that God created all things, and that then Adam named them in his language, which was Hebrew. He then continues to say that '540 years after the time of Noah, a sage named Maton discovered [*trouva*] through his wisdom the language that we speak in a country called Mogar, between Persia and India. And other languages will come after us in the future'.[24] While it is unclear to which language this foundational myth refers, and what it means that it was 'discovered' (*trouva* can also mean 'invented'), the author repeatedly looks to justify his vernacular (or the idea of one) by imagining it through a fictional prehistory that places it in contact with ancient and contemporaneous idioms. He then invokes the famous biological thought experiment to explain how the process of linguistic growth works: in the same way that a tree that is grafted from a different seed grows fruits that are consistent with the one from which it was

---

[23] *Sydrac*, ed. Ruhe, p. 420: 'Nous sonmes de la semence Noe et li Ebreu et li Caldeu et li Grifon: de Japhet sont ne li Francois, li Romain, li Englois et li Espaignol'; *Roumain* or *Rommain* denotes 'Roman' in Outremer French. See, for example, in the *Histoire ancienne jusqu'à César*: 'ore a presence vos dirais de Pirrus et des Roumains' (I will speak to you of Pirrus and of the Romans). *Histoire ancienne jusqu'à César*, ed. C. Gaullier-Bougassas (Turnhout, 2012), p. 196. Some versions of *Sidrac* contain an astrological *translatio imperii* which employs the same terminology: 'comme par les diz des astronomiens, et aussy appert par les ystoires, que les Juyfs qui furent au premier climat, en la premiere partie d'Orient orent la premiere seignerie soubz Saturne [...] Apres regnerent les Massodoniens soubz Mars, apres regnerent les Troyens soubz le Soleil apres regnerent les Griex soubz Venuz apres les Roumains souz Mercure et apres les Francoys qui sont ocidentel soubz la Lune.' ('According to what is found in works of astronomy and history, the Jews who were in the first climate in the first part of the orient possessed the first lordship under Saturn, then the Macedonians ruled under Mars, then the Trojans ruled under the Sun, then the Greeks ruled under Venus, then the Romans under Mercury, and then the French, who are occidental, [ruled] under the moon.') Paris, BnF MS fr. 1094, fol. 06v, in Waffner, *Der Livre de Sidrac*, p. 77 n. 60.

[24] *Sydrac*, ed. Ruhe, p. 274: 'Et depuis Noe de .v. cens et .lv. ans fu uns sages homs qui out a non Maton qui trouva par son sens cest language que nous parlons en une contree entre Ynde et Persse qui s'apelle Mogar. Et autres languages vendront aprés nous au temps qui est a venir.'

grafted, so we speak a language different from that of our forefather Adam. But if one were to take a small child, no older than forty days, and raise it in complete linguistic isolation, then when it grows this child would speak Hebrew, 'for he would turn to the language of his first father [i.e. Adam], like a tree that is not grafted, which turns to its own nature.'[25] This is to say that individuals (and by extension communities) preserve a biological memory of their linguistic essence, from which subsequent offshoots sprout. What these various meditations have in common is the choice to view language through genealogy and pre- and post-history. The author places the philosopher-protagonist in a privileged moment in the past, halfway between Noah and the present, between India and the West, to make a pseudo-prophetic case for the linguistic choice of the encyclopaedist.

This preoccupation with the conditions that make vernacular languages possible also informs the way the work justifies its own universal scope in space, time and theme, and the presumption to deploy this knowledge in Old French. The prologue of the work traces the book's prehistory, which consists of a long series of linguistic and cultural transformations. After King Boctus compiled *The Book of the Fountain of All Knowledge*, we are told, it found its way into the hands of a Chaldean king, but it was almost lost due to the recklessness of its subsequent owner, the prince of the knights of the king of Syria. Thanks to divine intervention the work was consigned to the Greek archbishop of Sebastia, whose helper, a priest called Demitre, travelled with the book to Muslim Spain in order to preach the Christian faith. The first identifiable chapter of this story outside of the Near East, then, takes us to ninth-century Iberia with the famous episode of the martyrs of Córdoba. And indeed we are told that Demitre was soon martyred, but his collaborators in Toledo translated the book from Greek to Latin, a feat that came to the attention not only of the king of Spain but also of his ally the emir of Tunis. At the latter's request the book was translated to Arabic and dispatched for the use of subsequent rulers of Tunis. Some time later the emperor Frederick II, impressed by the breadth of the knowledge of the emirs, and having been told about the wondrous book, sent a bilingual Friar Minor to translate the work

---

[25] *Sydrac*, ed. Ruhe, p. 126: 'car il tourneroit au language de son premier pere, comme la nature de l'arbre qui ne est entez qui torne a sa nature.' For a history of this thought experiment, see: R. Campbell and R. Greaves, 'Royal Investigations of the Origins of Language', *Historiographia Linguistica* 9 (1982), 43–74; and S. Ebbesen, 'Psammetichus's Experiment and the Scholastics: Is Language Innate?', in *The Language of Thought in Late Medieval Philosophy*, ed. J. Pelletier and M. Roques (Cham, 2017), pp. 287–302.

back into Latin.[26] In the imperial court a philosopher from Antioch smuggled a copy of the book to his patriarch, Aubert. The prologue then states that the book was finally transferred back to Toledo yet again, and ends with a prayer to 'God the creator that it might come into the possession of such a people [*gent*] who can truly understand and maintain what it says and put it into action for the salvation of body and soul'.[27] This Old French encyclopaedia, then, is presented to the reader as the product of a great journey which encompasses the multiple Mediterranean languages and encounters that serve as the linguistic condition which makes its universal ambition possible. As the prologue takes the book and the reader on a journey that crosses through some of the key stations in the intellectual history of the Mediterranean, the theory of the vernacular that informed its author becomes manifest. Both the frame-story and the various meditations on language in *The Book of Sidrac* indicate that the author looks to justify the use of Old French as a vehicle (or fountain) of 'all sciences' by reflecting on its defining movement over time and its contact with other authoritative languages. What is more, the author deploys the rhetorical ideology of the book by consolidating two vectors that together underlie the language of the book. The first draws on the image of the philosopher who prophesies the linguistic lineage that will yield its idiom, and the second is the 'book' itself that is imagined as a physical object which undergoes multiple translations. Together, both vectors articulate a theory of French universality that is inflected, or made possible, through its history of contact and transfer.

Another work that was produced in Outremer and demonstrates a similar concern with the conditions that make French an adequate vehicle for a philosophically universal inquiry is the translation and commentary of Boethius's *De consolatione philosophiae* made by Pierre de Paris.[28] The work survives in one manuscript, Vatican, Biblioteca Apostolica Vaticana, MS Vat.

---

[26] Several attempts have been made to identify this monk as well as other seemingly historical figures that the prologue mentions, see: E. Langley, 'The Extant Repertory of the Early Sicilian Poets', *PMLA* 28 (1913), 454–520 (p. 471); K. Mallette, 'Terra Recognita: Excursus on the Literary History of Sicily', *Mediaevalia* 24 (2003), 137–58; C. H. Haskins, 'Science at the Court of the Emperor Frederick II', *American Historical Review* 27 (1922), 673–89.

[27] *Sydrac*, ed. Ruhe, p. 3: 'nous prions Dieu le Creator que il puisse venir en povoir de tele gent que il puissent entendre et retenir ce que il dit et metre le en heuvre a salvation du cors et de l'ame.'

[28] Not much is known about the translator, see: A. M. Babbi, 'Pierre de Paris traducteur de la *Consolatio Philosophiae*', in *La traduction vers le moyen français: Actes du IIe colloque de l'AIEMF, Poitiers, 27–29 avril 2006*, ed. C. Galderisi and C. Pignatelli (Turnhout, 2007), pp. 23–32.

lat.4788, that was copied in 1309 for a Cypriot patron, Johan Coqueriau.[29] The prefatory note features conventional remarks on the attempt to render French as clear and accurate as possible.[30] In addition, both in the preface and throughout the commentary, Pierre is strikingly careful to make the classical past of his base text tangible. He does so, for example, by devising fictitious etymologies of words and names and by drawing on apocryphal narratives about Boethius's multilingual intellectual experiences in Athens.[31]

The *De consolatione* itself is a work of immense complexity and philosophical depth, but there is a clear overarching theme; namely, that the consoling path on which Lady Philosophy leads Boethius from agony to a spiritual appreciation of the world in its created harmony involves not only a series of analytical arguments on nature and God, but also a willingness to cultivate a new attitude toward the language that the protagonist chooses to employ.[32] Philosophy teaches Boethius to find reassurance in recognizing the harmonizing force of nature through God, as he oscillates between a despairing recognition of vectors that pull in various directions and the ability to cultivate a more cohesive (if usually momentary) understanding of the creation. This process, however, includes various cycles where the Boethius-protagonist agrees to redefine key terms in which his character seems at first to be deeply invested, such as honour, freedom, virtue etc. Key to the literary method of the allegory is the fact that instead of deploying a linear argumentative structure, Philosophy allows for multiple twists in which the protagonist lapses back to old semantic habits, spiralling the dialogue into a confusing aporia that only later becomes resolved.[33]

---

[29] C. Concina, 'Boethius in Cyprus? Pierre de Paris's Translation of the *Consolatio Philosophiae*', in *MFLCOF*, pp. 168–72; C. Concina, 'Traduzione e rielaborazione nel 'Boece' di Pierre de Paris', in *Francofonie medievali: lingue e letterature gallo-romanze fuori di Francia (sec. XII–XV)*, ed. A. M. Babbi and C. Concina (Verona, 2016), pp. 45–73; A. Thomas, 'Notice sur le manuscrit 4788 du Vatican', *Notices et extraits des manuscrits de la Bibliothèque nationale et autres bibliothèques* 41 (1917), 29–90.

[30] C. Concina, 'Le Prologue de Pierre de Paris à la traduction du *De Consolatione Philosophiae* de Boèce', *Le Moyen Français* 74 (2014), 23–46.

[31] Vatican, Biblioteca Apostolica Vaticana, MS Vat.lat.4788, fols. 6r–7r.

[32] S. Lerer, *Boethius and Dialogue: Literary Method in the 'Consolation of Philosophy'* (Princeton, 1985), pp. 125–66; on the use of the topos of the therapeutic power of language in the *Consolatio*, see A. Donato, 'Boethius's 'Consolation of Philosophy' and the Greco-Roman Consolatory Tradition', *Traditio* 67 (2012), 1–42.

[33] This dynamic speaks to the Neoplatonist principle that lies behind philosophical allegory, namely that language devises an ascending vector of increased clarity, see: A. Hughes, *The Texture of the Divine: Imagination in Medieval Islamic and Jewish*

Without a doubt the most pronounced of these instances is found in Book 3:12 prose. First Philosophy convinces Boethius that only a supreme being that is completely self-sufficient and entirely good could govern the entire world in its endless diversity. But just when Boethius thanks her both for the conclusion and 'for the words [she] used', Philosophy decides to bring up the problem of evil. 'You are playing with me, aren't you, by weaving a labyrinth of arguments from which I cannot find the way out', Boethius complains, but Philosophy insists that from this collision of arguments 'some beautiful spark of truth might leap forth'.[34] As an example of the way in which the resolution of such conflicts restores, or achieves a higher harmony, she invokes the myth of the giants who 'began attacking the heavens and, as was right, they too were kindly but firmly set to order'.[35] Drawing out the reference to the biblical Tower of Babel, Pierre glosses this pivotal passage in a highly revealing manner.

Pierre relates that the giants (inhabitants of Hebron)[36] started to build a tower in order to reach the skies ('se penserent d'avenir au ciel').[37] Seeing this, God sent a lightning bolt that struck down the large bricks: 'with one blow [the work] of six months was demolished'. The fools, however, as if deliberately looking to act against the will of God, began the construction of the tower again, and again God sent a lightning bolt that demolished the tower. The third time this happened God sent lightning but the tower remained intact, even after the second and third bolts. The misguided giants thought that this marked the limit of God's power, and that therefore they would be able to execute their plans. But just then God confounded their words: 'for whoever asked for water instead was brought lime, and he who asked for lime was given stones; they spoke one to another and the one did not understand what the other was saying'.[38] Because the workers were unable to communicate, their attempt to complete the tower failed soon thereafter.

Thought (Bloomington, 2004), pp. 48–61; and P. Struck, 'Allegory and Ascent in Neoplatonism', in *Cambridge Companion to Allegory*, ed. R. Copeland and P. Struck (Cambridge, 2010), pp. 57–69.

[34] Boethius, *The Consolation of Philosophy*, trans. V. Watt (London, 1969), p. 81.

[35] Boethius, *The Consolation of Philosophy*, trans Watt, p. 81.

[36] A reference to Joshua 15:13–14, which associates the giants in the Tower narrative with the conquest of Canaan by Joshua.

[37] MS Vat.lat. 4788, fol. 67r: 'si qu'elle trebucha del tout en .i. cop se que il avoient fait en .i. demi an.'

[38] MS Vat.lat. 4788, fol. 67r: 'car celuy qui demandoit l'aigue, l'en li portoit la chaus, et qui demandoit chaus, l'on li donoit pierres, se parloyent les uns as autres et l'un nen entendoit pas ce que l'autre disoit.'

The obvious conclusion, for Pierre, is that whoever looks to ignore or disobey the will of God is likely to incur punishment and damage. But he further explains that it is a mistake to think that God was unable simply to tear down the tower. The purpose of the successive lightning bolts, instead, was to make the foolishness of the giants apparent: 'so that they [the giants] would perceive that they had been deceived and ensnared by their own wicked will, God let them work [to rebuild the tower time and again] … They were compelled to abort their work … since the one could not understand at all what the other was saying, and this is how the seventy-two languages were founded'.[39] That is to say, the decision to generate a multiplicity of languages and to hamper the ability of men to understand those who speak another tongue, was of course intended as an obstacle, but it is one that was meant to help the giants, and the reader, notice and appreciate the work of the harmonizing God in the endlessly diverse world. Fallen languages in their multiplicity, then, are a living testament to the harmonizing beauty that governs creation, of which Philosophy speaks. Pierre's insistence on highlighting the translatability of his text – its Latin and Greek prehistory – therefore, is not meant to boast of his own erudition or to contribute toward a more accurate understanding of the text. Rather, it is a way of expressing what for him allegorical French is supposed to do and how it works: namely, to exhibit the harmony that nature achieves through endless (in this case, linguistic) diversity by making manifest the particularity of French vis-à-vis its neighbouring and preceding idioms.

While it seems that all medieval allegories to some extent draw on the Boethian paradigm, no other work is more closely modelled on the *De consolatione* than the fourteenth-century allegory *Le songe du viel pelerin* by Philippe de Mézières, the Chancellor of Cyprus during the reign of Peter I. No other work employs more powerfully this theory of allegorical French in a philosophical and literary investigation,[40] and it is one of most ambitious works of Old French literature and philosophy of the late Middle Ages.[41] Completed in 1389, the *Songe* is a sophisticated allegory that, like the *De consolatione*, rises from a sense of spiritual and literary anguish, and investigates

---

[39] MS Vat.lat. 4788, fol. 67r: 'Et ensi Dieu, voillant qu'il en la fin se trovassent deceus et engingnes de leur felonesse volente si les laissa bien travailler… si covint que il partissent de l'euvre… come soit chose que l'un n'entendoit de riens se que l'autre disoit, et illeuques furent troves les .lxxii. lengues.'

[40] A. Strubel, 'Le *Songe du vieil pèlerin* et les transformations de l'allégorie au quatorzième siècle', *Perspectives médiévales* 6 (1980), 54–73.

[41] N. Jorga, *Philippe de Mézières (1327–1405) et la croisade au XIVe* (Paris, 1896), pp. 76–91.

the conditions necessary for moral, religious and political reform.[42] In the story, the eponymous hero takes Queen Truth on a journey in order to convince her to suspend her reclusion in the Holy Mountain and return to the world. The two visit every country in the known world in an attempt to find a land suitable for the fabrication of holy currency – an allegory for the universal emanation of charity and grace in the world. But as the prologue clarifies, more than that, the dream vision chronicles the search for a language that could be a sufficient vehicle for a discourse on the desired return of mercy to Christendom. Many authors, Philippe famously says, had already penned works in Hebrew, Greek and Latin deploring the overabundance of vice and the absence of charity.[43] The *Songe* does not presume to devise a language of equal or superior scope. The allegory in French, rather, is presented as appropriate to bear the ascent to divine truth – crossing as it does through every region – precisely thanks to its imperfections.[44] Philippe invokes the metaphor of a simple bread, easier to digest, which if presented in a new way may 'whet the appetite' of the pious 'for the word of truth' ('aguisier l'appetit de dire verité').[45] It is through the distinctly Mediterranean dream journey, in which the travellers come in contact with interlocutors of all possible backgrounds, that these constructive limitations of vernacular allegory are played out.

The currency metaphor famously appears at the very beginning of the prologue and then again in the preambles of the two subsequent books in which Philippe glosses the Parable of the Talents from Matthew 25. But its linguistic underpinning unfolds in several revealing moments throughout the work, where the author fleshes out the stakes of his own rhetorical strategy. One such occasion takes place right after the entourage reaches Avignon and, in a performance of what Daisy Delogu calls auto-exegesis,[46] some of the subsidiary characters disclose their own allegorical meanings. In her turn, Pride

---

[42] A. Tarnowski, 'The Consolations of Writing Allegory: Philippe de Mézières' *Le songe du viel pèlerin*', in *Philippe de Mézières and His Age: Piety and Politics in the Fourteenth Century*, ed. R. Blumenfeld-Kosinski and K. Petkov (Leiden, 2012), pp. 237–54.

[43] Philippe de Mézières, *Songe du viel pelerin*, ed. J. Blanchard (Geneva, 2015), p. 23.

[44] B. Grévin, 'L'Europe des langues au temps de Philippe de Mézières', in *Philippe de Mézières et l'Europe: Nouvelle histoire, nouveaux espaces, nouveaux langages*, ed. J. Blanchard and R. Blumenfeld-Kosinski (Geneva, 2017), pp. 95–113.

[45] Philippe de Mézières, *Songe du viel pelerin*, p. 23.

[46] D. Delogu, 'Allegory, Semiotics, and Salvation: The Parable of the Talents in the *Songe du viel pèlerin*', in *Philippe de Mézières, rhétorique et poétique*, ed. J. Blanchard (Geneva, 2019), pp. 163–85; and D. Delogu, *Allegorical Bodies: Power and Gender in Late Medieval France* (Toronto, 2015), pp. 19–44.

(*Orgueil*) confesses that her sin is particularly harmful, for her impure forge has amply supplied 'the sagacious alchemists of the other capital sins' with currency (besants) necessary for their exploits.[47] Pride recalls that she used 'to forge [her] besants through the help of the giants, before the flood, and then of Nimrod who constructed the tower of Babel thanks to which I was planning to reach the heavens'.[48] She continues that indeed the world was subsequently subjected to her currency through the work of Alexander, Antioch and even of Saul the first king of Israel. But her attempt ultimately failed with the coming of Jesus Christ, 'who destroyed my forge and subjected all my besants to his disciples'.[49] The attempt to achieve uniformity of currency and language, then, proved both misguided (hence sinful) and deficient. The very particularity of the pure currency issued by the 'disciples of the crucified' is designed to remind the pious not only of the sin of pride and its consequences, but also of the word of Jesus in the world.

Another defining moment in the plot, where the consequences of salvation and language are staked out, takes place in the second book, where Queen Truth orchestrates a discussion on the merits of pious government and its many pitfalls. The discussion becomes consequential when Righteousness turns to speak about the danger that courtiers pose to the pious ruler. Righteousness explains that, like a living body, each part of a governing organism must match the whole in both size and character. This healthy ecosystem, however, is disrupted by the conniving courtiers, especially a *mahomet* ('courtier') whose religious identity, it is insinuated, is Muslim or at least different from that of his political master.[50] Through flattery and insincerity the *mahomet* effects the complete dependence of his lord, and very soon becomes the true master of the realm. What is worse, Righteousness says, 'the *mahomet* possesses the language so that with spies and agents he is able to [communicate] with all the other lords who come to court' and therefore effects an irreparable imbalance

---

[47] Philippe de Mézières, *Songe du viel pelerin*, p. 349: 'Par mes poissans besans et par ma monnoie fine tous les sages alkemistes des autres mortelx pechiés aprendent a ma forge et a mes besans sont subgiés.'

[48] Philippe de Mézières, *Songe du viel pelerin*, p. 349: 'Dame royne, dit la vielle, il vous souvient quelx besans jadis je forgoye par les jayans devant le deluge, et apres par Nemproth edifiant la thour de Babel, par laquelle monter ou ciel je desiroye.'

[49] Philippe de Mézières, *Songe du viel pelerin*, p. 349: 'c'est la foy de vostre Pere, le benoit Crucefis, qui ma forge quant a lui a destruicte et a ses disciples tous mes besans sousmis.'

[50] Philippe de Mézières, *Songe du viel pelerin*, p. 687–9.

in the regional bodies politic.[51] But then a *maḥomet* joins the discussion and subverts the accusations: 'since the reign of Nimrod, builder of the tower of Babel, first tyrant to rule by force over men, emperors, kings, princes of Jews, pagans and Christians, have had the power to promote those whom they please, for their own pleasure and relief'.[52] He, then, associates tyranny with the confusion of language and capricious government which appoints officials on the basis of personal interest instead of the public good. The *maḥomet* provides several examples of rulers, such as Pharaoh in the Exodus narrative and Nebuchadnezzar in the Book of Daniel, who appointed officials that belonged to a faith different from their own. In accepting this position, Queen Truth, like Pierre de Paris earlier, rejects the notion that linguistic and cultural division was simply a punishment that was meant to match the pride of the Giants. Ideal government, rather, is one that is reminded of its imperfection partly through the acknowledgement that its language is incapable of universal unity. It is this characteristic that makes French an ideal vehicle for a reflection on the possibility of virtuous government, insofar as its allegorical usage is able to make its dependence on and contact with other idioms manifest.

The final section of this chapter seeks to show that a similar dynamic can be observed in processes that took place at the turn of the fourteenth century not only in Old French but also in Arabic. The term 'vernacular' is not easily applied to Arabic, in which the dynamic between an authoritative idiom and local dialects is thought of in terms of registers of the same language. But a closer look shows that a colloquial register of Middle Arabic underwent a process very similar to Outremer French, and that these two Mediterranean traditions have much in common.

The second half of the fourteenth century marks a major turning-point in the history of the Mamluk sultanate. After decades of economic decline, social unrest and political fragmentation, al-Ẓāhir Barqūq took the throne and became the first ruler of Egypt who belonged to the so-called Burji cadre of the Mamluk army.[53] Scholars of Mamluk literature agree that it is in this context of regime change that one of the most popular narratives of its day

---

[51] Philippe de Mézières, *Songe du viel pelerin*, p. 687: 'cestui mahommet a ses espies et faitours pour acointer et hounourer tous les seigneurs qui viendront a la court.'

[52] Philippe de Mézières, *Songe du viel pelerin*, p. 688: 'depuis que Nemproth, qui edifia la tour de Babel et fut le premier tirant qui prist seignourie efforcie sur les hommes et resgna, les empereurs, roys, et grans princes, des Juifs, des payens, et de Crestiens, sont en possession de eslever, essaucier, et faire grans ceulx qui leur plaist, voire pour leur plaisance et consolacion.'

[53] A. Levanoni, *A Turning Point in Mamluk History: The Third Reign of al-Nasir Muhammad Ibn Qalawun* (Leiden, 1995); and J. Van Steenbergen, 'Mamluk Elite

coalesced, a story that traces the birth and ascent to power of Sultan al-Ẓāhir Baybars (d.1277).[54] The impending threat by a rival political party may have motivated storytellers to devise a narrative to celebrate the triumphant rise of the Baḥri Mamluks, led by Baybars, in their victorious succession to the Ayyubids. This epic, *Sīrat Baybars*, certainly does not capture the hegemonic voice of the increasingly dominant Circassian emirs, nor was it espoused by the intellectual and religious elite. But the work was nevertheless widespread among people from all walks of life.

That an increasingly disenfranchised military aristocracy would seek to boost its value by banking on an exalted figurehead and projecting an illustrious past, is to be expected. Far more surprising, however, is the choice to deploy this political propaganda – the illustrious ascent of Baybars and the Baḥri Mamluks – on a pan-Mediterranean fantasy that involves curious crossings and multiple contacts between protagonists of various faiths and backgrounds. Unlike most medieval Arabic epics that revolve around an iconic confrontation between the eponymous hero and a rival tribe or kingdom, *Sīrat Baybars* features many 'Others'. While much of the plot unfolds in the centres of Mamluk rule and trade – Cairo, Alexandria, and Damascus – the story includes multiple excursions across the Mediterranean, including pivotal episodes that take place in Italy, Provence, Byzantium and Iberia. What is more, all the key protagonists, including Baybars, undertake transformative voyages across the sea, in which their true identity, and oftentimes calling, is revealed. In fact, the very principle of the story's narrativity – the way in which the fiction presumes to unfold the past in a meaningful way – is revealed in arguably the most important of these crossings, in which al-Salih, the last Ayyubid Sultan, and his retinue are imagined to travel to Italy in order to release Baybars who had been kidnapped by the King of Genoa.

This episode is pivotal also because it marks the transition from the first part of the *Sīra*, which relates Baybars's childhood and early military career, to the second part which touches more directly on his ascent to the sultanate. The circumstances that lead to the important episode start when the king of Genoa (al-Rīn Ḥanna') decides to send his ill daughter, Maryam al-Zunāriyyah ('the girded', or 'girdler'), to Alexandria in order to seek medical treatment. [55] Not long after her health is restored, however, Maryam meets and falls in love with Maʿruf, Baybars's chief political collaborator. She converts to Islam and

---

on the Eve of al-Nasir Muhammad's Death (1341): A Look Behind the Scenes of Mamluk Politics', *Mamluk Studies Review* 9 (2005), 192–9.

[54] T. Herzog, 'The First Layer of the *Sirat Baybars*: Popular Romance and Political Propaganda', *Mamluk Studies Review* 7 (2003), 137–48.

[55] *Sīrat al-Ẓāhir Baybars*, no named editor (Cairo, 1996), p. 874.

conceives a child, who later in the story becomes an important hero. Hearing of this, the king of Genoa is of course enraged and looks to bring his daughter back home. He seeks out the help of the arch villain Juwan, who devises a ploy that involves kidnapping Baybars to Genoa.

What ensues is one of the most action-packed episodes of the *Sīra*: al-Salih assembles an army to liberate Baybars from captivity. The Mamluk forces conquer the port of Genoa, the sultan then miraculously splits open the walls of the city, they storm in and after a short battle both Baybars and King Ḥanna are snatched and shipped back to Egypt.[56] Significantly, as a result of these dramatic events key protagonists reveal their true identity. We learn, for example, that the kind and merciful prince who saved Baybars is in fact Shiḥa, the helpful trickster who throughout the *Sīra* takes on multiple identities and always shows up at the right moment to save the day.[57] Baybars is indeed released, and on the way back Shiḥa, the helpful trickster, reveals the most astonishing story: in ancient times, Shiḥa says, there was a soothsayer (*Kahin*) called al-Yūnān (literally, the Greek). He wrote a prophecy based on the information that his loyal jinns received from the angels. He predicted the arrival of the prophet Muhammad, whose followers would engage in battle against the leader of the Greeks, Juwan. The prophecy, in other words, predicted the war between Baybars, who al-Yūnān said will be 'the future sultan of the Muslims', and the Christian Genoese, being the fulfilment of the 'Greeks'.[58] In order to protect Juwan, the soothsayer recorded on golden plates all the *mahālik* ('pitfalls') of the Muslims and the *masālik* ('pathways') of Juwan over the course of his entire lifetime. He then sent the jinns to circulate this record in all the places where Juwan will eventually be, so that this useful knowledge would reach him. However, Shiḥa continues to explain, after al-Yūnān's death his son Aynān converted to Islam and he sent the jinn to the heavens in order to steal all the foreknowledge and put it to the opposite use. Aynān turned all the pitfalls of the Muslims into acts of salvation (*najāh*), and inscribed them on silver plates which he then bound together with his father's book. The 'Book of Yūnān', then, foresaw the battle between Juwan, fighting on behalf of

---

[56] *Sīrat al-Ẓāhir Baybars*, pp. 934–45.

[57] On the trickster in siyar literature see, M. C. Lyons, *The Man of Wiles in Popular Arabic Literature: A Study of a Medieval Arab Hero* (Edinburgh, 2012). During the first part of the *Sīra* the key trickster is Uthman. After this episode he all but disappears and instead Shiḥa comes to the fore.

[58] *Sīrat al-Ẓāhir Baybars*, pp. 958–9.

the Christian-Greeks, and Baybars the follower of the Prophet of Islam, and cast it as the battle between the forces of salvation and evil.[59]

The focus of the *Sīra* from this point returns to Egypt as soon thereafter al-Salih meets his death and Baybars eventually succeeds him. But the detour to Genoa proves transformative not only for the key protagonists – Juwan, Shiḥa, Baybars etc. – but for the narrative itself. The *Sīra* had to cross the Mediterranean, as it were, in order for us to know that in truth what it does is chronicle the fulfilment of the ancient prophecy. What is more, the prophecy functions as a hermeneutical allegory, for it not only reveals the true nature of the narrative, but also supplies the reader with instructions on how to discern its meaning: reading only the 'golden plates', as Juwan did, would yield only a misguided understanding of how to maintain a righteous path and to avoid 'pitfalls'. A proper understanding of the divine command requires reading both the gold and silver plates, which is to say, recognizing that the moralizing prose has a 'Greek-Christian' past that was superseded by an Arabic-Muslim present. In other words, what underwrites the *Sīra*'s claim for truth is the notion that the travel to Genoa and back mimics the facing-page translation – Gold facing Silver, Greek facing Arabic.

The travel of the *Sīra* across spaces and languages in search for a way to achieve intelligibility brings this chapter, too, back to its point of departure. The *Sīra* and *The Book of Sidrac* seek literary or intellectual perfection (respectively) not by imagining the language they employ as perfect in itself. Their epistemic strategy involves a rejection of the mimetic model, which presumes to convey universal truths by turning to canonical idioms whose claim for authority lies on the notion that they are eternal and immutable. Our works, instead, are predicated on the claim that, in its tangible imperfection, the vernacular too proves to be an appropriate vehicle to convey the sublime. The Neo-Platonist logic that lies at the heart of allegory fuels the theory that it is precisely the time-boundedness of the local idiom that provides a continuous opportunity for reflection on the harmonizing forces that work on and in Nature. For authors at the turn of the fourteenth century, Outremer French was a site of contact: as the material of allegory and through the material historicizing of their own language, it became a literary and epistemic vehicle.

---

[59] T. Herzog, 'Francs et Commerçants à Alexandrie dans le roman de Baybars', *Alexandrie médiévale* 1 (2002), 181–94; T. Herzog, *Geschichte und Imaginaire: Entstehung, Überlieferung und Bedeutung der Sirat Baibars in ihrem sozio-politischen Kontext* (Wiesbaden, 2006), pp. 873–4.

8

'Dize en la estoria francesa':
The Circulation of Francophone Matter of
Antiquity in Medieval Castile (*c.*1200–1369)

Clara Pascual-Argente

French, it is well known, never served as a full-blown literary language in the Iberian kingdom of Castile: we do not know of any books produced in this vernacular there, nor of any compositions in French primarily intended for a Castilian public. Yet francophone works and books remained an important building block in some key areas of Castile's literary culture, broadly understood, and they often contributed to the process of cultural homogenisation that Robert Bartlett has described as the 'Europeanization of Europe'.[1] One such area was the remaking of ancient, pagan history in the vernacular. This phenomenon was instrumental in creating the sense of a shared past among lay elites across Latin Christendom. Its earliest manifestations were the francophone *romans d'antiquité* composed in the second half of the 1100s, which became the object of interpolations, amplifications and rerenderings into prose that circulated widely throughout the 1200s and 1300s.[2] Furthermore, the genre soon spread to other vernaculars, whether through adaptations of francophone romances or through a process of direct adaptation of Latin models like the one that gave rise to the early *romans d'antiquité.* The romances of antiquity's sprawling, multilingual tradition also became integrated into another key point of access to the classical past: vernacular universal chronicles that used these romances

---

[1] R. Bartlett, *The Making of Europe: Conquest, Colonization, and Cultural Change, 950–1350* (Princeton, 1993).

[2] The three works traditionally labelled as *romans d'antiquité* are the *Roman de Thèbes*, *Roman de Troie* and *Roman d'Eneas*. However, most scholars now have a more expansive understanding of the term that also includes vernacular romances on Alexander the Great or Apollonius of Tyre, among others; see C. Baswell, 'Marvels of Translation and Crises of Transition in the Romances of Antiquity', in *The Cambridge Companion to Medieval Romance*, ed. R. L. Krueger (Cambridge, 2000), pp. 29–44; and the synthesis by F. Mora-Lebrun, *'Metre en romanz'. Les romans d'antiquité du XIIe siècle et leur postérité (XIIIe–XIVe siècle)* (Paris, 2008).

as historiographical sources.[3] In the Castilian case, vernacular narratives on the matter of antiquity first appear in the early thirteenth century and, until the violent dynastic change that took place in 1369, they remain closely tied to monarchic environments.

Between the 1200s and 1369, the Castilian royal court was a multilingual space, where the languages used for cultural and documentary production experienced significant shifts. The first half of the thirteenth century, which spans the reigns of Alfonso VIII (r.1158–1214), Enrique I (r.1214–17), Berenguela (r.1217) and Fernando III (r.1217–52), witnessed a momentous change from the use of Latin to the use of Castilian as the main language for documents created in the royal chancery.[4] Official historiography commissioned by the monarchs of this period was still composed in Latin, while some forms of vernacular engagement with the past in epic or romance form started to emerge around the royal court in the early part of the 1200s. By the mid-century, Castilian was established as the language for works of moral instruction for the nobility, which were often translated from Arabic.[5] In the second part of the century, Alfonso X (r. 1252–84) sponsored and directed a wide-ranging cultural programme to establish Castilian as the language of historiographic and scientific discourses, taking over, respectively, from Latin and Arabic.[6] As for the languages used for lyric production, the Castilian royal court was an important hub for Occitan lyric during the reign of Alfonso VIII, while Galician-Portuguese remained the main lyric language throughout the 1200s and early 1300s, although by the mid fourteenth century it was taking

---

[3] A recent overview of universal chronicles, including vernacular ones, with relevant contributions can be found in M. Campopiano and H. Bainton, ed., *Universal Chronicles in the High Middle Ages* (York, 2017).

[4] This phenomenon has been the object of numerous studies; see the synthesis in I. Fernández-Ordóñez, 'La lengua de los documentos del rey: del latín a las lenguas vernáculas en las cancillerías regias de la Península Ibérica', in *La construcción medieval de la memoria regia*, ed. P. Martínez Sopena and A. Rodríguez (València, 2011), pp. 323–62 (pp. 328–33).

[5] See F. Gómez Redondo, *Historia de la prosa medieval castellana*, 4 vols. (Madrid, 1998), I, 78–9, 180–3, 214–18.

[6] See I. Fernández-Ordóñez, 'De la historiografía fernandina a la alfonsí', *Alcanate* 3 (2003), 93–133; and F. Márquez Villanueva, *El concepto cultural alfonsí* (Barcelona, 2004). Within Alfonso X's cultural project, Arabic is the main authoritative language for scientific (rather than historical) knowledge, as was the case across medieval Europe; see R. Szpiech, 'Latin as a Language of Authoritative Tradition', in *The Oxford Handbook of Medieval Latin Literature*, ed. R. J. Hexter and D. Townsend (Oxford, 2012), pp. 63–85 (pp. 72–9).

a more Castilianised form.[7] Within the context of multilingual cultural and documentary production sketched above, French became one of the languages used in sources from which Castilian-language works drew. It shared this role with other supralocal languages such as Latin, Arabic or, to a lesser extent, Hebrew.

Francophone books on the matter of antiquity were present within the Castilian monarchy's orbit throughout the period under discussion. Not by chance, the francophone works on ancient history that we may trace to Castile's royal court belong to the three textual traditions that enjoyed the widest circulation throughout Latin Christendom: those originating in two romances of antiquity – the *Roman d'Alexandre* (before 1180), recounting the life of Alexander the Great, and Benoît de Sainte-Maure's groundbreaking version of the Trojan narrative, the *Roman de Troie* (*c.*1165) – and the universal history usually known as the *Histoire ancienne jusqu'à César* (*c.*1214). In every case, the specific exemplars present in the Iberian kingdom are lost to us. Nonetheless, we know of their presence because they served as sources for works produced at or around the royal court – all of them part of a Castilian tradition of narratives that refashioned ancient, pagan history to think through the kingdom's ongoing territorial expansion and give monarchs a spiritual genealogy populated with figures such as Hercules or Alexander the Great.[8]

This essay is organised around the three different moments during which these francophone books appeared at the Castilian royal court: the first third of the 1200s, when production of classically-themed narratives in Castilian starts with the composition of the earliest known romance of antiquity, the *Libro de Alexandre*; 1270–84, the period of composition of historiographical works paying particular attention to Gentile history, sponsored and supervised by King Alfonso X; and the 1340s through 1360s, with the development of several versions of the Trojan narrative at the courts of Alfonso XI (r.1312–50) and Pedro I (r.1350–69). For each of these moments, I explain how Castilian works about ancient history used sources in French and review what we know about circulation patterns in the relevant francophone traditions. With this information in hand, I lay out some hypotheses about the intellectual, family and political networks through which these francophone books could have reached Castile, considering what we may infer about the perception of francophone matter of antiquity, and of French as a literary language, in a Castilian courtly context.

---

[7]   See V. Beltran, *La corte de Babel. Lenguas, poética y política en la España del siglo XIII* (Madrid, 2005).

[8]   C. Pascual-Argente, *Memory, Media, and Empire in the Castilian Romances of Antiquity: Alexander's Heirs* (Leiden, 2022).

Between courts and schools: the *Libro de Alexandre* and the *Roman d'Alexandre*

The earliest traces of the presence of a francophone work on ancient history in Castile are found in the first romance of antiquity composed in Castilian, the *Libro de Alexandre*. An anonymous cleric, probably connected to the royal chancery and writing for the court, created this work, which would go on to become enormously influential, at some point in the first three decades of the thirteenth century.[9] The Iberian poem recounts in detail the life and exploits of Alexander the Great, drawing from a variety of sources. The main one is Walter of Châtillon's *Alexandreis*, a Latin epic about the Macedonian created around 1180 and dedicated to William, Archbishop of Reims. The *Alexandreis* quickly achieved an enormous success beyond the ecclesiastical courts we can assume to have been its initial reception milieu, becoming a staple of university curricula.[10]

The *Libro de Alexandre* is also related to the francophone romances of antiquity, as it draws from the textual tradition of the *Roman d'Alexandre*: a group of texts composed at different times and environments, connected by their subject matter (Alexander the Great), which were combined through addition, interpolation or rewriting to produce a variety of textual configurations.[11] Among them, the most widely diffused was the compilation and rewriting of earlier poems carried out by an Alexander of Paris, or Alexander of Bernay, in the 1180s, often called the vulgate version. However, the Castilian cleric who composed the *Libro de Alexandre* worked with a different form of the *Roman d'Alexandre*, close to the one found in Venice, Museo Correr, MS Correr 1493. This northern Italian codex, dating from the late thirteenth century, compiles a set of poems similar to those employed in the vulgate version to tell Alexander's story, but the rewriting that characterises the vulgate version is not carried out.[12] As Raymond Willis has shown, the *Libro de Alexandre* draws from a

---

[9]   Although not yet the object of consensus, the argument for the chancery origin and courtly destination of the *Libro de Alexandre* has been persuasively made in A. Arizaleta, 'El *Libro de Alexandre*: el clérigo al servicio del rey', *Troianalexandrina* 8 (2008), 73–114.

[10]   See A. Grondeux, 'L'*Alexandréide* dans le cursus grammatical médiéval', in *Poesía latina medieval (siglos V–XV): Actas del IV Congreso del 'Internationales Mittellateinerkomitee', Santiago de Compostela, 12–15 de septiembre de 2002*, ed. M. Díaz y Díaz and J. M. Díaz de Bustamante (Florence, 2005), pp. 825–50.

[11]   See M. Gosman, *La légende d'Alexandre le Grand dans la littérature française du 12e siècle. Une réécriture permanente* (Amsterdam, 1997).

[12]   The text contained in the Venice manuscript has been edited in *The Medieval French* Roman d'Alexandre. *Vol. I: Text of the Arsenal and Venice Versions*, ed. M. S.

version very similar to MS Correr 1493 in the sections that concern the hero's birth and childhood; his induction into knighthood and the establishment of the Twelve Peers; his famous aerial and submarine trips; the descriptions of his tent and the city of Babylon; and his death and testament.[13]

Despite this significant use of the *Roman d'Alexandre*, the *Libro de Alexandre* never refers to it as a source. By contrast, the narrator acknowledges the *Alexandreis* as his primary model on several occasions, including once where his source is the francophone *roman d'antiquité*, the description of Babylon. A veiled reference to the limitations of Walter of Châtillon's work in this passage is the closest that the Castilian poem gets to mentioning the *Roman d'Alexandre*: 'Que todas sus noblezas vos queramos dezir/ antes podrién tres días e tres noches trocir,/ ca Galter non las pudo, maguer quiso, complir' ('If we wished to tell you of all its fine features/ three days and three nights would first pass by,/ for, though he sought to, Walter could not complete it') (st. 1501abc).[14] The treatment of the *Roman d'Alexandre* thus contrasts with the way in which other secondary or indirect sources, such as Homer (in the form of the *Ilias latina*), Ovid or Isidore are readily invoked.[15]

How and where did the Iberian poet encounter the *Roman d'Alexandre*? We do not know much about the circulation patterns of the francophone poem – whether in the vulgate version or in alternative ones – before the mid to late 1200s, a period in which many surviving manuscripts of Alexander of Paris's version were produced in northern France. The creation of shorter Alexander narratives, designed for interpolation into the story, in the northeastern parts of the French kingdom from the late twelfth century and throughout the first half of the thirteenth, suggests that the narrative was already popular in the area.[16] Furthermore, two out of three extant codices with non-vulgate versions of the *Roman d'Alexandre* were produced or circulated in northern Italy in the

---

La Du (Paris, 1937); a facsimile version is available in R. Benedetti, ed., *Le roman d'Alexandre: riproduzione del ms. Venezia, Biblioteca Museo Correr, Correr 1493* (Tricesimo, 1998).

[13] R. S. Willis, *The Debt of the Spanish* Libro de Alexandre *to the French* Roman d'Alexandre (Princeton/Paris, 1935); see also M. Materni, 'Il *Libro de Alexandre* e il *Roman d'Alexandre* veneziano (con un'appendice sulle fonti del poema iberico)', *Medioevo europeo* 1.2 (2017), 61–105.

[14] All quotations and translations from the poem are taken, respectively, from *Libro de Alexandre*, ed. J. Casas Rigall (Madrid, 2014), and *Book of Alexander (Libro de Alexandre)*, ed. and trans. P. Such and R. Rabone (Oxford, 2009).

[15] *Libro de Alexandre*, ed. Rigall, p. 17.

[16] See S. Gaunt, et al., *Medieval Francophone Literary Culture Outside France*, accessed 25 August 2023, www.medievalfrancophone.ac.uk.

second part of the 1200s, and one of them may have been created there much earlier.[17] The first is Correr 1493, already mentioned in connection with the *Libro de Alexandre*, and the second is Paris, Bibliothèque de l'Arsenal, MS 3472, dating from the first quarter of the thirteenth century and traditionally linked to Poitou, although an origin in Bologna or Padua is now considered more likely. At any rate, Arsenal MS 3472 was in northern Italy at the turn of the fourteenth century, when it was partially restored.[18]

Given that the *Libro de Alexandre* was probably composed in the royal chancery and for the royal court, it would seem logical to think that its francophone counterpart may have reached Castile through the web of relationships around Queen Leonor, daughter of Eleanor of Aquitaine and Henry II of England and wife of King Alfonso VIII of Castile. The Angevin princess was queen of Castile from 1170 to 1214, maintaining strong ties to her family of origin and their cultural worlds, in which the *Roman d'Alexandre* appears likely to have figured.[19] The Castilian court itself was a lively centre of transnational courtly culture during the reign of Leonor and Alfonso, especially for Occitan lyric, although we do not have any specific evidence about the presence there of other kinds of courtly literary artifacts, such as francophone romances.[20] Yet there is a different, if complementary, possibility: the creator of the *Libro de Alexandre* may have enjoyed access to the *Roman d'Alexandre* through the same scholarly networks that made possible his encounter with the *Alexandreis*. Indeed, the intertwining of lay and ecclesiastical – including

[17] The third one, Paris, BnF, MS fr. 789, can be connected to Amiens in the late thirteenth or early fourteenth century; see A. Stones, 'Les manuscrits du *Roman d'Alexandre* en vers français et leurs contextes artistiques', in *Alexandre le Grand à la lumière des manuscrits et des premiers imprimés en Europe (XIIe–XVIe siècle): matérialité des textes, contextes et paratextes: des lectures originales*, ed. C. Gaullier-Bougassas (Turnhout, 2015), pp. 269–84 (pp. 270–2).

[18] See A. Stones, 'The Illustrated *Alexander* in French Verse: The Case of Italy', *Francigena* 5 (2019), 229–55 (pp. 231–2); and C. Gaullier-Bougassas, 'Les manuscrits italiens des *Romans d'Alexandre* français en vers et de l'*Histoire ancienne jusqu'à César* (XIIIe et XIVe siècles): lectures originales et créations inédites', in *Alexandre le Grand*, ed. C. Gaullier-Bougassas, pp. 49–80 (pp. 55–8).

[19] For possible links of texts in the *Roman d'Alexandre* tradition (and present in Correr 1493) to the Angevins, see *La fascination pour Alexandre le Grand dans les littératures européennes (Xe-XVIe siècle): réinventions d'un mythe*, ed. C. Gaullier-Bougassas, 4 vols. (Turnhout, 2015), pp. 1751–2.

[20] For an overview of the kinds of cultural production connected with Leonor and her court, see J. M. Cerda, 'Leonor Plantagenet y la consolidación castellana en el reinado de Alfonso VIII', *Anuario de Estudios Medievales* 42 (2012), 629–52 (pp. 638–40).

academic – environments is key to the creation and circulation of Alexander narratives during the twelfth and thirteenth centuries.

The overlap between ecclesiastical and lay courts seems to have been crucial to the emergence of the *Alexandreis* around 1180. While we might think of Walter of Châtillon as someone moving mostly in ecclesiastical courts and academic settings, he may also have been present in lay courts steeped in both Latin and vernacular literature, such as that of the counts of Champagne.[21] Venetia Bridges and Jean-Yves Tilliette have proposed that the Latin poem was created partly as a reaction to the success of the *Roman d'Alexandre* and other *romans d'antiquité*.[22] The vernacular poems not only broadened access to Gentile history but also used it to 'release themselves – for the sake of intellectual play and ethical inquiry – from the teleological interests of Christian morality'.[23] The *Alexandreis* shows both an interest in such precedents and strong reservations toward the vernacular genre's investment in shaping ancient, pagan characters as models for non-Latinate audiences. While the poem imitates set pieces characteristic of the *romans d'antiquité* (such as tomb descriptions), it also returns to the traditional form to retell heroic narratives set in the ancient past, Latin dactylic hexameters, and insists on Alexander's limitations. In short, it appears that the *Roman d'Alexandre* and the *Alexandreis* shared some of their reception environments, where they were part of a debate about the promises and dangers of increased access to Gentile history for medieval Christian audiences.

Those common reception environments may have been ecclesiastical courts, such as the one headed by the *Alexandreis*'s dedicatee, William of Reims; lay courts, like those of the counts of Champagne; and perhaps also the academic milieus in which Walter of Châtillon's poem soon circulated. We have long assumed that the creator of the *Libro de Alexandre* encountered the *Alexandreis* in the course of his education in one or several universities or cathedral

---

[21] V. Bridges, *Medieval Narratives of Alexander the Great: Transnational Texts in England and France* (Cambridge, 2018), pp. 69–72.

[22] See V. Bridges, "'L'estoire d'Alixandre vos veul par vers traitier […]": Passions and Polemics in Latin and Vernacular Alexander Literature of the Later Twelfth Century', *Nottingham Medieval Studies* 58 (2014), 87–113; and J.-Y. Tilliette, 'L'*Alexandréide* de Gautier de Châtillon: Enéide médiévale ou "Virgile travesti"?', in *Alexandre le Grand dans les littératures occidentales et proche-orientales*, ed. L. Harf-Lancner, C. Klapper and F. Suard (Nanterre, 1999), pp. 275–88. The question of access is only one aspect of a wider polemic about whether, and how, to reshape ancient, pagan history.

[23] B. Nolan, *Chaucer and the Tradition of the* Roman Antique (Cambridge, 1992), p. 9.

schools, which he may have pursued in Castile, abroad, or both.[24] The Iberian poet was certainly at pains to highlight key centres of learning in the Iberian Peninsula, France and Italy in the description of Europe within a world map represented in one of the panels of Alexander's tent. The passage constructs what Amaia Arizaleta has called 'a scholarly pilgrimage route' that follows academic centres with cathedral schools or universities such as Soria, Toledo, León, Lisbon, Tours and Pavia, highlighting Paris, where 'de toda clerezía avié grant abundançia' ('there was a rich abundance of all kinds of learning') and Bologna, which 'de lëys e decretos (...) es la fontana' ('is the fount of all laws and decrees').[25] The Castilian cleric may also have happened upon the *Roman d'Alexandre* in one of the stops of this route, since there are signs of the tradition's presence in academic environments: non-vulgate MS Arsenal 3472, mentioned above, appears to have circulated among jurists, perhaps in that 'fount of all laws and decrees', Bologna, as early as the first quarter of the 1200s.[26] If this is true, the *Roman d'Alexandre* would have been present in the Italian city at a time when there is a well-documented presence of masters and students from the Iberian Peninsula.[27]

Whether in Bologna or a different academic or courtly environment, it is likely that the Castilian poet encountered the *Roman d'Alexandre* in the context of the debate about the access to, and interpretation of, ancient, pagan history, described above. The two competing paradigms for the reshaping of classical history, vernacular romance of antiquity and Latin epic, are each represented in the *Libro de Alexandre*'s sources. Yet rather than following one of these models, the Iberian poem found a middle ground between them, offering an alternative path for narratives about the classical past: while composed in a vernacular, the *Libro de Alexandre* employs a Latinised stanza (monorhymed alexandrine quatrains) closely associated with religious instruction; it combines its deep admiration for Alexander with a grudging but unequivocal critique; and it is infused with open Christian moralisation, a trait absent from both

---

[24] See F. Rico, 'La clerecía del mester', *Hispanic Review* 53 (1985), 1–23, 127–50; and A. Arizaleta, *La translation d'Alexandre: recherches sur les structures et les significations du* Libro de Alexandre (Paris, 1999), pp. 209–18.

[25] Arizaleta, *La translation*, pp. 216–18; *Libro de Alexandre*, st. 2582b, 2583d.

[26] See Stones, 'The Illustrated *Alexander*', pp. 231–2; Gaullier-Bougassas, 'Les manuscrits italiens', pp. 56–7.

[27] See A. García y García, 'El *studium bononiense* y la Península Ibérica', in *Chiesa, diritto e ordinamiento della 'societas christiana' nei secoli XI e XII* (Milan, 1986), pp. 45–64.

the *Alexandreis* and the *Roman d'Alexandre*.[28] The lack of acknowledgement of the francophone poem's use in the *Libro de Alexandre* may be related to the difficult balance between competing models that the Iberian poet was trying to achieve. Perhaps the use of Castilian to retell ancient history – an absolute novelty in the context of the royal court – needed to be compensated for by foregrounding Latinate sources and hiding their vernacular counterparts.

The *estoria francesa*: Francophone sources in the *General estoria*

Around 1270, work started on the *General estoria*, a universal chronicle composed on the initiative and under the supervision of King Alfonso X, in parallel with an Iberian counterpart, the *Estoria de España*.[29] The *General estoria* aspires to produce the definitive narrative account of all known history, drawing from as many sources as possible and often incorporating within the text itself contrasts between and evaluations of different narratives of the same event. Gentile history has as much, if not more, weight as Biblical history in the *General estoria*, and it is precisely within the Gentile sections that two francophone works play a fundamental role, namely in the retelling of the stories of Thebes and Troy. The *Roman de Troie* is the main source for the narrative of the Greek *nostoi* after the Trojan War, while the *Histoire ancienne* provides the basis for the stories of Thebes and the Trojan conflict itself.[30] Furthermore, as Paloma Gracia has cogently argued, the francophone universal chronicle, in combining Gentile and biblical history in the vernacular, may

---

[28] For more details, see Pascual-Argente, *Memory, Media, and Empire*, pp. 126–31; and Pascual-Argente, 'The Matter of Meter: *Cuaderna Vía* and the Castilian Romance of Antiquity', in R. Bower and M. V. Desing, *A Companion to the Mester de Clerecía* (Leiden, forthcoming).

[29] The best introduction to these two works remains I. Fernández-Ordóñez, *Las estorias de Alfonso el Sabio* (Madrid, 1992).

[30] The use of the *Histoire ancienne* for the Trojan story in the *General estoria* was first noted in A. Punzi, *Sulla sezione troiana della* General estoria *di Alfonso X* (Roma, 1995); it is studied in detail, alongside the employ of the *Roman de Troie* in the third part, as well as other sources, in J. Casas Rigall, *La materia de Troya en las letras romances del siglo XIII hispano* (Santiago de Compostela, 1999), pp. 113–207. For the Theban section, see A. Punzi, *Oedipodae confusa domus: la materia tebana nel Medioevo latino e romanzo* (Roma, 1995); and P. Gracia, 'Actividad artística y creadora en la *General estoria*: la sección tebana de la *Histoire ancienne jusqu'à César* reescrita por Alfonso X', *Bulletin of Hispanic Studies* 81 (2004), 303–17; and P. Gracia, 'Singularidad y extrañeza en algunos lugares de la "Estoria de Tebas" (*General estoria*, Parte II), a la luz de la *Histoire ancienne jusqu'à César*', *Bulletin hispanique* 105 (2003), 7–17.

also have served as an overall model for its Castilian counterpart, alongside Latin works such as Peter Comestor's *Historia scholastica*.[31]

The creators of the *General estoria*, who generally make a point of citing their sources, acknowledge their use of the *Histoire ancienne*, treating its language as the work's identifying feature. The francophone chronicle is mentioned at the beginning of the *General estoria*'s Theban section, for which it serves as the main source, to mark a correction to it: 'Dize en la estoria francesa que (Cadmo) ovo dos fijos, mas non fue assí' ('The French history says that Cadmo had two sons, but it was not so');[32] and at the very end, where the compilers note that 'lo que fasta aquí es dicho contámoslo nós segunt que lo fallamos en la estoria del lenguaje francés e otras' ('what has been retold up to now, we have recounted as we found it in the history written in French and in others').[33] The *Histoire ancienne* is also mentioned at the beginning of the *General estoria*'s Trojan section, for which it is also the main source. In this case, the compilers refer to it to justify a deviation from the model it represents: 'fallamos que comiença la estoria francesa del destruimiento de Troya en el fecho de Jasón (…), mas por seer aún la razón más complida començaremos en su lugar las razones del fecho d'esta estoria en los infantes Frixo e Elle' ('we find that the French history about the destruction of Troy begins with Jason's deeds, but to provide a fuller narrative, we will instead begin our history with the princes Frixo and Elle').[34]

Nonetheless, when the *General estoria*'s compilators announce that they are going to retell the story of Thebes, they seem to point to a different source: 'un grant libro d'esta estoria' ('a great book about this story') that 'fizo (…) Estacio en latín por viessos' ('Statius made in Latin verse').[35] It would be logical to assume, therefore, that Statius's *Thebaid* served as the main source for this narrative – at least until the *Histoire ancienne* is identified as such at the end. Similarly, the Trojan narrative, whether it draws from the *Histoire ancienne* or

---

[31] P. Gracia, 'Hacia el modelo de la *General estoria*: París, la *translatio imperii et studii* y la *Histoire ancienne jusqu'à César*', *Zeitschrift für romanische Philologie* 122 (2006), 17–27.

[32] *General estoria*, 2.1, 459. Once the inaccuracy in the *Histoire ancienne* is explained and corrected, the return to it is also noted: 'E empós estos, assí como dize essa estoria del francés, reinó ý el rey Layo' ('And after those [Cadmo's descendants], as that same history in French says, King Laius reigned there [in Thebes]'). All quotations are taken from Alfonso X el Sabio, *General estoria: segunda parte*, ed. B. Almeida, 2 vols. (Madrid, 2009).

[33] *General estoria*, 2.1, 547–8.

[34] *General estoria* 2.2, 123.

[35] *General estoria* 2.1, 113.

the *Roman de Troie*, is repeatedly attributed to Dares (or Dares and Dictys). Benoît's poem is never singled out as a separate, francophone work.[36] Within the *General estoria*, then, the two francophone works are valued as a conduit for the Latin authorities that they claim as their sources, and Latin remains the language of authoritative sources on Gentile history.

It is difficult to pinpoint the origin of the exemplar(s) of the *Roman de Troie* used in the *General estoria*, since the circulation of Benoît's poem was widespread: by the 1270s, when the Castilian historians began their work, it was being copied beyond the Angevin domains where it first emerged, in central and northeastern France as well as in northern Italy.[37] The creators of the *General estoria* might have been using an illustrated copy coming from the Capetian court, a possibility to which I will return below. If this is true, the *Roman de Troie* may have reached Castile as a result of the close relationship between the Capetian and Castilian royal houses, fostered by two powerful sisters, Queens Berenguela (in Castile) and Blanche (in France), during the first part of the 1200s and further cemented, around the time the *General estoria*'s creators began their task, by the marriage between Alfonso X's son and heir, Fernando de la Cerda, and Blanche, daughter of Louis IX, in 1269. The union was meant to help advance the Castilian monarch's candidacy to head the Holy Roman Empire, smoothing his relationship with the Pope, as well as facilitate the resolution of territorial conflicts with France.[38] The existence of these 'close family and political bonds linking the king (Alfonso X) with the French crown, which resulted in strong cultural ties', is also the route that Gracia has suggested for the *Histoire ancienne*.[39] Yet what we know about the production patterns of the *Histoire ancienne* does not suggest its circulation at the French royal court in the 1260s, the decade before work started on the *General estoria*, or even in the 1270s.

[36] Casas Rigall, *La materia de Troya*, pp. 126–35, 176–99; see also Almeida's observations in *General estoria* 2.1, li–lii.

[37] See the list and detailed description of extant manuscripts and fragments in M.-R. Jung, *La légende de Troie en France au Moyen Age. Analyse des versions françaises et bibliograhie raisonnée des manuscrits* (Basel, 1996), pp. 78–330.

[38] A rich account of the ties fostered by Queens Blanche and Berenguela during the reign of Alfonso X's father and the beginning of Alfonso's own reign can be found in F. J. Hernández, 'La corte de Fernando III y la casa real de Francia: documentos, crónicas, monumentos', in *Fernando III y su tiempo (1201–1252): VIII Congreso de Estudios Medievales* (Ávila, 2003), pp. 103–56. For details on the political advantages of the marriage between Fernando and Blanche, as well as the succession woes and conflict with France caused by Fernando's untimely death, see F. J. Hernández, 'Relaciones de Alfonso X con Inglaterra y Francia', *Alcanate* 4 (2004–2005), 167–242 (pp. 193–219).

[39] Gracia, 'Hacia el modelo', p. 25.

No early manuscripts of the *Histoire ancienne* have reached us, which may indicate a limited initial diffusion, but copying of the universal chronicle appears to have accelerated in the middle of the 1200s. During the third quarter of the thirteenth century, two distinct geographical areas emerged as the main centres of production for manuscripts of the *Histoire ancienne*: the county of Flanders (possibly the area around Lille, where the work was first composed in the early part of the century), on the one hand; on the other, the most important city within the fragile remains of the Latin Kingdom of Jerusalem, Acre, which is not surprising given the prominence of Flemish aristocrats in the Crusades.[40] Indeed, there are reasons to believe that the historians working for Alfonso X had access to a copy of the *Histoire ancienne* connected to the group of codices created in Acre, which share certain textual features as well as their visual programme.

In his fundamental study of Trojan matter in the *General estoria*, Juan Casas Rigall has noted the close correspondence, both in terms of textual variants and chapter divisions, between the Trojan sections of the Castilian work drawn from the *Histoire ancienne* and the manuscript used in all modern editions of the *Histoire*: Paris, BnF, MS fr. 20125.[41] The exact provenance of this codex, dated to the late 1280s, is still in dispute, but it seems clear that it was created either in Acre or in northern France from an Acre exemplar.[42] What is more, Rosa Rodríguez Porto has argued for a connection between the manuscripts of the *Histoire ancienne* produced in the Holy Land and the presentation copy of the *Estoria de España* – the *General estoria*'s twin work – produced in Alfonso X's *scriptorium*.[43] According to Rodríguez Porto, the size and proportions of this volume, the extension of its visual cycle and the layout of its images, which

[40] On the provenance of thirteenth-century manuscripts of the *Histoire ancienne*, see D. Oltrogge, *Die Illustrationszyklen zur* Histoire ancienne jusqu'à César *(1250–1400)* (Frankfurt, 1989); Jung, *Légende de Troie*, pp. 340–57; M. L. Palermi, 'Histoire ancienne jusqu'à César: forme e percorsi del testo', *Critica del testo* 7 (2004), 213–56 (pp. 222–31).

[41] Casas Rigall, *La materia de Troya*, p. 126; see also P. Gracia, 'A vueltas con el modelo subyacente o lo que los originales franceses pueden aportar a la edición de sus derivados españoles: el caso de la sección tebana de la II parte de la *General Estoria*', in *La fractura historiográfica: las investigaciones de Edad Media y Renacimiento desde el Tercer Milenio*, ed. F. J. Burguillo, L. Mier and J. San José Lera (Salamanca, 2008), pp. 331–40 (pp. 336–7).

[42] See the summary of different positions about the provenance of MS fr. 20125 in *MFLCA*, pp. 137–8.

[43] Madrid, Real Biblioteca del Monasterio de San Lorenzo de El Escorial, MS Y.I.2. Despite a planned visual program of over 100 miniatures, only the first six were completed.

inaugurate a new typology for royal codices, may all be inspired by the Acre group of manuscripts.[44]

If this is true, an eastern Mediterranean *Histoire ancienne* would have served as a structural model, whether in textual or visual terms, for Alfonso X's two historiographical projects. The book may have joined the royal historiographical workshop and *scriptorium* through the conduit of family relationships: Alfonso was first cousin to Marie of Brienne, daughter of John of Brienne, king of Jerusalem and then Latin emperor of Constantinople, and wife to his successor, Baldwin II. Marie travelled to Castile around 1358 in search of funds to recover her son, mortgaged to Venetian merchants, while her three brothers, Alphonse, Louis and Jean of Brienne – or of Acre, where they had been born – were frequently present in the Castilian court from 1255 to 1274.[45] These close connections make the arrival of an eastern Mediterranean copy of the *Histoire ancienne* in the Castilian monarch's hands very plausible.

The importance of the *Histoire ancienne* for Alfonso X's historiographical projects may have stemmed not only from the work's status as a pioneer world history in a vernacular but also from the meaning that its provenance had in the Castilian political context. A book from Acre may have seemed especially valuable to Alfonso because of his own intense interest in the Levant around that time. Indeed, a planned invasion of North Africa – already underway when he acceded to the throne in 1252 – was framed as creating an alternative way of recovering the lost crusader territories; despite the lack of success of those plans, the Holy Land continued to be on the monarch's mind until the end of his days, when he asked for his heart to be buried on Jerusalem's Mount Calvary.[46] Furthermore, the *Histoire ancienne*'s Levantine copies, created in the final and chaotic years of Acre as a Christian-controlled city, presented ancient history as a useful frame to

---

[44] R. M. Rodríguez Porto, '*Thesaurum*: La *Crónica troyana de Alfonso XI* y los libros iluminados de la monarquía castellana (1284–1369)' (unpublished Ph.D. dissertation, Universidade de Santiago de Compostela, 2012), I, 107–8.

[45] R. L. Wolff, 'Mortgage and Redemption of an Emperor's Son: Castile and the Latin Empire of Constantinople', *Speculum* 29 (1954), 45–84. See also Hernández, 'Relaciones', pp. 191–2, 196–7.

[46] See P. Linehan, *Spain, 1157–1300: A Partible Inheritance* (Oxford, 2011), pp. 147–8. See Alfonso's will, in which he asks for his heart to be buried in the holy city, as were some of his ancestors, in M. González Jiménez, *Diplomatario andaluz de Alfonso X* (Sevilla, 1991), doc. 521.

make sense of the hopes, perils and precariousness of colonial power.[47] This approach was directly relevant to the Castilian kingdom, which had rapidly expanded its size during Fernando III's reign, leaving Alfonso to grapple with the fraught process of colonizing the lands conquered from Muslim rulers in the south of the Iberian Peninsula.

'De francés en castellano': The *Roman de Troie* in fourteenth-century Castile

Alfonso X's reign came to an end in 1284, as his rule was being challenged by his son Sancho. During the latter's reign as Sancho IV (r. 1284–95) and that of his immediate successor, Fernando IV (r. 1295–1312), the matter of antiquity ceased to be a central object of attention for the Castilian monarchs and was not to return in full force to the royal court until the reign of Alfonso XI. The 1340s saw the rise of two different Castilian versions of the Trojan narrative, both based on a now-lost prosification of the *Roman de Troie* in Galician-Portuguese or Galician-Leonese.[48] The first of them is a *prosimetrum*, the *Historia troyana polimétrica*, whose dating remains in dispute but may reasonably be related to an environment close to the Castilian royal court in the 1340s. The second is a lavishly illuminated manuscript commissioned by the monarch and completed shortly after his unexpected death from plague in 1350, the *Crónica troyana de Alfonso XI*.[49] Not much later, in the 1360s, the *Crónica troyana*'s text formed the basis for a more extensive version of the Trojan story through which Alfonso XI's son and heir, Pedro I, sought to outdo his father's project. The *Historia troyana de Pedro I* was planned as a textual and visual amplification of that work, using materials related to the *General estoria* and an Italian copy of the *Roman de Troie* (on which more presently) to that end.[50] This version

---

[47] See the contextualisation and interpretation of the *Histoire ancienne*'s Acre manuscripts in *MFLCA*, pp. 137–57.

[48] The western Iberian prosification of Benoît's poem might have existed before these projects took shape, but it could also have been created at Alfonso XI's court as part of the composition process for the Trojan works under discussion here, as proposed in C. Pascual-Argente, "De francés en castellano": La tradición manuscrita de la *Crónica troyana de Alfonso XI*', *Troianalexandrina* 20 (2020), 23–58.

[49] The *Crónica troyana* is Madrid, Real Biblioteca del Monasterio de San Lorenzo de El Escorial, MS h.I.6. The *Polimétrica* has reached us in fragmentary form, in two fourteenth-century manuscripts, where it was completed with the text of the *Crónica troyana*. There is a growing consensus about its composition in the first half of the 1300s. For details and bibliography, see Pascual-Argente, 'De francés'.

[50] For the *Historia troyana*'s amplificatory work, see R. Pichel, '"Lean por este libro que o acharam mays complidamente": del *Libro de Troya* alfonsí a la *Historia troyana* de

8.1. Santander, Biblioteca de Menéndez Pelayo, M-558, fol. 22r, c.1360–1380, detail. *Historia troyana de Pedro I*. Alfonso XI orders the translation of the *Roman de Troie* from French into Castilian, as specified in the minature's caption: 'De cómo el rey don Alfonso, que Dios perdone, mandó tornar este libro de francés en castellano' (How King don Alfonso, may God have him in his glory, ordered this book translated from French into Castilian). © Biblioteca de Menéndez Pelayo, Ayuntamiento de Santander. Image courtesy of Ricardo Pichel.

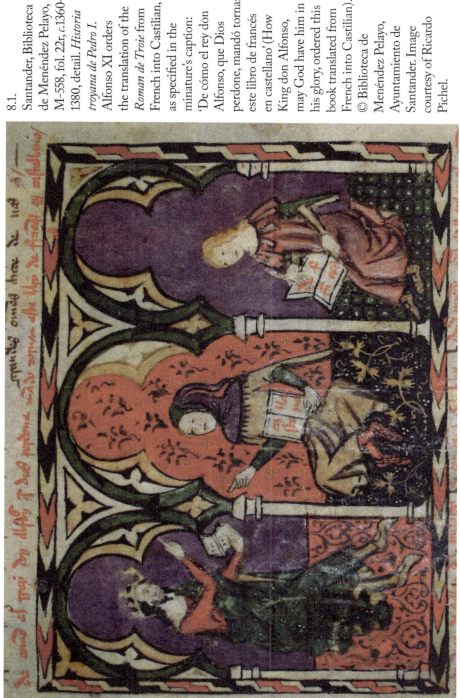

remained unfinished owing to the civil war that ended in Pedro's deposition and murder at the hands of his illegitimate half-brother, Enrique, in 1369, a date after which the strong link between the Castilian monarchy and the refashioning of ancient, pagan history also comes to an end.

In stark contrast with the treatment of the *Roman de Troie* in the *General estoria*, the Castilian Trojan narratives created in the 1300s acknowledge and foreground their origins in Benoît's work; instead, they gloss over the intermediate Galician-Portuguese or Galician-Leonese prosification of the poem that served as their immediate source.[51] Although the prologue to the *Polimétrica* is unfortunately lost to us, its counterpart in the *Crónica troyana* transforms Benoît's long prologue, which sets up a lineage of clerks, into a short overview that transforms them into faithful translators, from Dares's accurate transcription of what he saw in the Trojan War, to Cornelius, who 'sabía todos los lenguajes' ('knew every language') and translated Dares's book from Latin into Greek, to Benoît de Sainte-Maure who 'fue el que lo trasladó de latín en francés' ('was the one who translated it from Latin into French'), to the anonymous person who tells the audience, 'pues que todo esto sabedes, quiero començar a trasladar la estoria de francés en castellano' ('now that you know all this, I would like to start translating this history from French into Castilian').[52] Taking this prominent acknowledgement of its francophone origins further, the amplified *Historia troyana* visually represents the translation process in an illustration in which King Alfonso XI sets the process in motion, represented through two books marked with the words 'de francés' and 'castellano' (Plate 8.1).

The foregrounding of French as the language of the Trojan story should be understood in the context of Castilian cultural politics during Alfonso XI's reign. During this period, chivalric culture and institutions take centre stage in a bid to engage courtly aristocrats – in Castile and beyond – in a monarchic political project, as well as to create a space for a lay, monarchic culture independent of ecclesiastical interventions.[53] Thus, the founding of a

---

Pedro I', *Troianalexandrina* 16 (2016), 55–180; and Rodríguez Porto, '*Thesaurum*', II, 719–88.

[51] The significance of this silencing depends on whether the western Iberian version circulated independently or was created as part of the process that led to the *Crónica troyana* and the *Polimétrica* (in which case it would not have been perceived as an independent work).

[52] C. D'Ambruoso, 'Edición crítica y estudio de la *Crónica troyana* promovida por Alfonso XI' (unpublished Ph.D. dissertation, Universidade de Santiago de Compostela, 2012), p. 3.

[53] See P. Linehan, *History and the Historians in Medieval Spain* (Oxford, 1993), pp. 560–616; J. Rodríguez-Velasco, *Ciudadanía, soberanía monárquica y caballería: Poética del*

lay chivalric order, the Orden de la Banda, by the Castilian king; his public chivalric investiture, after which he knighted noblemen from Castile and other kingdoms; and the proliferation of Arthurian, Carolingian and especially Trojan narratives in the monarchy's environment are all part of the same effort. Although circulating in Castilian, most of those narratives (as well as many shorter chivalric tales also in circulation) had francophone origins, which may have contributed to a perception of French as a supralocal language closely tied to transnational chivalric culture. This could explain why the creators of the fourteenth-century Trojan narratives are eager to highlight the language of their ultimate source.

At the same time, these works – the earliest standalone narratives about the Trojan War in Castilian – are part of a renewed interest in the matter of Troy in Latin Europe during the fourteenth century. The Italian peninsula plays a key role in this renewal: extensive, lavishly executed image cycles for the *Roman de Troie* appear in northern Italy during the early part of the century;[54] in Naples, the court of King Robert of Anjou is the site where the second redaction of the *Histoire ancienne*, with a fully refashioned Trojan section, emerges;[55] and Giovanni Boccaccio remakes the episode of Trojan lovers Troilus and Briseis into the *Filostrato*.[56] The designers and artists working

---

orden de caballería (Madrid, 2009); and C. Pascual-Argente, "'En las corónicas antiguas de los grandes fechos que pasaron': La historia antigua en el proyecto cultural de Alfonso XI', *Revista de Literatura Medieval* 34 (2022), 133–61.

[54] See C. Cipollaro, 'Invenzione e reinvenzione negli esemplari miniati del *Roman de Troie* tra Francia e Italia. Dal ms. ambrosiano D 55 Sup. al Cod. 2571 di Vienna', in *Allen Mären ein Herr/Lord of all Tales: Ritterliches Troja in illuminierten Handschriften/Chivalric Troy in illuminated Manuscripts*, ed. C. Cipollaro and M. V. Schwarz (Vienna, 2017), pp. 19–66.

[55] All known copies of the *Histoire ancienne*'s second redaction derive from the Neapolitan codex now London, British Library, Royal MS 20 D I, which has recently been the subject of much critical attention; for a recent interpretation that also provides a full overview of current scholarship about this book, see *MFLCA*, pp. 174–93. It is very unlikely that the codex ever reached Castile; see R. M. Rodríguez Porto, 'Review of *Le 'epistole delle dame di Grecia' nel* Roman de Troie *in prosa: La prima traduzione francese delle* Eroidi *di Ovidio and* Les Epistres des Dames de Grece: Une version médiévale en prose française des *Heroïdes d'Ovide*, by L. Barbieri', *Troianalexandrina* 8 (2008), 311–18.

[56] For an introduction to the *Filostrato*, see G. Natali, 'A Lyrical Version: Boccaccio's *Filostrato*', in *The European Tragedy of Troilus*, ed. P. Boitani (Oxford, 1989), pp. 49–73. On possible francophone sources for Boccaccio's Neapolitan works, see M. Barbato and G. Palumbo, 'Fonti francesi di Boccaccio napoletano?', in *Boccaccio angioino: Materiali per la storia culturale di Napoli nel Trecento*, ed. G. Alfano, T. D'Urso and A. Perriccioli Saggese (Brussels, 2012), pp. 127–48.

on the *Crónica troyana*'s illustration programme were, as Rodríguez Porto has masterfully shown, intimately familiar with French and, especially, Italian cycles illustrating Benoît's poem. At a minimum, the Castilian creators had at their disposal an illustrated copy of the *Roman de Troie* that would have been very close to that found today in Venice, Biblioteca Marciana, MS fr. Z. XVII, a manuscript that is part of a group of lavishly illuminated exemplars of Benoît's work created in northern Italy *c.* 1320–45.[57] Unfortunately, the paths through which the Italian manuscript may have reached the Castilian royal court have yet to be retraced.

The designers of the *Crónica troyana* focused their reading of the Trojan narrative on its military aspects, making a selective use of the extensive illustration cycle in their Italian model. In contrast, the unillustrated *prosimetrum*, the *Polimétrica*, employs the inserted verse passages to highlight a wider variety of interests, including not only battles but also mourning, prophecy and the love triangle between Briseis, Troilus and Diomedes that figured prominently in Italian cycles. Whether this may reflect some contact with the Italian copy of the *Roman de Troie* present at the royal court is impossible to tell. There is no doubt, nonetheless, that the Italian codex remained in the Castilian royal court in the 1360s, where the designers working on Pedro's *Historia troyana* planned on following it closely in their attempt to create an extensive visual rendition of the Trojan story.[58]

There are also some reasons to believe that the designers of the *Crónica troyana* may have found inspiration in a French illustrated *Roman de Troie* that would have been closely related to Paris, BnF, MS fr. 1610. This manuscript, dated to 1264 and created, according to Elizabeth Morrison, in Paris for a Capetian environment, may be the oldest illustrated version of Benoît's poem. Its sophisticated illustration programme offers a coherent, selective retelling of the *Roman de Troie* as a tale focused on military events and makes use of

---

[57] The group also includes Vienna, Österreichische Nationalbibliothek, Cod. 2571; Saint Petersburg, Rossiyskaya natsional'naya biblioteka, MS fr. F.v.XIV.3; and Paris, BnF, MS fr. 782. See S. L'Engle, 'Three Manuscripts of the *Roman de Troie*: Codicology, Pictorial Cycles and Patronage', in *Allen Mären Ein Herr*, ed. Cipollaro and Schwarz, pp. 67–128; and the descriptions and commentary in Jung, *Légende de Troie*, pp. 177–80, 253–70, 287–91, 297–307. For the *Crónica troyana*'s relationship to these codices, see Rodríguez Porto, '*Thesaurum*', II, 545–63; and R.M. Rodríguez Porto, 'Dark and Elusive Fortune: Affectionate Readings of the *Roman de Troie* in Fourteenth-Century Castile', in *Allen Mären Ein Herr*, ed. Cipollaro and Schwarz, pp. 159–78.

[58] Rodríguez Porto, '*Thesaurum*', II, 759–66.

full-page miniatures that maximise visual impact.[59] These features make MS fr. 1610 an outlier among French visual renditions of the work but they connect it to the *Crónica troyana*, with which it also shares the composition of specific miniatures. The similarities between the two codices, noted by Rodríguez Porto, have led her to raise the possibility that the Castilian book's designers had access to a copy of the poem close to the Capetian manuscript. Given the date and creation environment of MS fr. 1610, it seems possible that such a codex would have reached the Castilian royal court by the 1270s, where it would have been used as a source for the *General estoria*.[60] If this is the case, the *Roman de Troie*, rather than the *Histoire ancienne*, would have indeed arrived at Alfonso X's court as a consequence of the king's close relationship with the Capetian monarchy, detailed above.

French at the Castilian royal court

The information presented above, however incomplete and tentative, can serve as the basis for some preliminary observations about the circulation and reception of francophone matter of antiquity in Castile and, more importantly, about the role of French as a vehicle for ancient history at the Castilian royal court. In this respect, I would argue that the treatment of francophone sources, and perhaps the perception of French, tracks the cultural politics of the Castilian royal court during each of the periods under consideration. In the first one, during the reigns of Alfonso VIII and, especially, Fernando III, ecclesiastical figures remain in charge of historiographical writing, in Latin, at the Castilian royal court, as well as of the chancery, where the production of vernacular documents was nonetheless becoming increasingly common.[61] Probably working at the chancery, the *Libro de Alexandre*'s creator sets out to revise the model of lay access to the classical past provided by the *romans d'antiquité*. The use of a Latinised Castilian (among other features) in the poem represents a bid for a higher degree of clerical control over the ancient past, influenced by the debate about the recreation and interpretation of the pagan past that gave rise to the *Alexandreis*; it is likely that the Iberian poet encountered the *Roman d'Alexandre* in the context of this debate. Thus, the

---

[59] E. Morrison, 'Linking Ancient Troy and Medieval France: Illuminations of an Early Copy of the *Roman de Troie*', in *Medieval Manuscripts, Their Makers and Users: A Special Issue of Viator in Honor of Richard and Mary Rouse* (Turnhout, 2011), pp. 77–102.

[60] Rodríguez Porto, '*Thesaurum*' II, 539–45.

[61] Juan Díaz, bishop of Osma, and Rodrigo Jiménez de Rada, archbishop of Toledo, serve as both historians and royal chancellors during the first half of the 1200s.

French vernacular may have been associated with an insufficiently mediated lay access to pagan history, representing a flawed, and therefore unacknowledged, model for the Castilian writer's own task. The clerical poet prefers instead to claim sources written in what remained the language of historiography at the royal court, Latin.

During the second of the periods under review, Alfonso X's cultural project consolidates Castilian as the language of historiography (as well as law and science). The monarch goes one step beyond his predecessors, fashioning himself as the main teacher to his subjects and taking a personal involvement, and ownership, in the vast array of works he sponsors, in a way that bypasses the clerical establishment's authoritative role.[62] Within this context, the *General estoria* has no qualms referring to the *Histoire ancienne* as a francophone source (although the *Roman de Troie* remains unacknowledged); still, the Castilian historians usually point to the two works' Latin antecedents (Statius, Dares and Dictys) to identify them. This suggests that – unlike the poet of the *Libro de Alexandre* – the Iberian creators consider French a reliable vehicle for the transmission of pagan history. Nonetheless, in the *General estoria*'s retelling of Gentile narratives, Castilian takes over Latin's authority and prestige; French does not enjoy a comparable standing in this realm. By contrast, I have hypothesised that the possible Levantine provenance of copy of the *Histoire ancienne* present at Alfonso X's court may have endowed it with additional interest and prestige, perhaps playing a role in its use as structural model for the *General estoria*.

Finally, the cultural production tied to Alfonso X's great-grandson, Alfonso XI, is characterised by the deployment of chivalric narratives as a way of incorporating courtly nobility into the monarch's political project. After the sudden death of the king in 1350, his successor, Pedro I, continued to promote these narratives. During this period, works deriving from the *Roman de Troie*, created for the two monarchs, prominently display their francophone origins. French seems now to have acquired a measure of prestige at the Castilian royal court, absent from the earlier uses of francophone matter of antiquity in the same environment. I have suggested that this development may stem from an association between French and the lay, chivalric culture promoted by the Castilian monarchy through narratives of mostly francophone origins. Yet additional information about the specific provenance of the *Roman de Troie*'s Italian exemplar used as a model for illustrating the Trojan narratives

---

[62] Márquez Villanueva, *El concepto cultural*, pp. 133–40.

commissioned by Alfonso XI and Pedro I would no doubt allow us to enrich or nuance this picture.[63]

At the beginning of this essay, I stated that, during the period under consideration, French was comparable to Latin or Arabic as one of the supralocal languages that were used as sources for the growing number of works in Castilian produced at the royal court. If Latin had long been dominant as the source of narratives about ancient, pagan history, starting in the twelfth century French became increasingly important throughout Latin Europe, where much of the 'canon of francophone texts' in active circulation 'were concerned with the narration of history and an understanding of the relation of the present to the past'.[64] Yet at the Castilian royal court, French did not enjoy the same level of authority as those languages, at least during the thirteenth century: Castilian works on the matter of antiquity are explicitly shaped after Latin models (even when, as in the *General estoria*, a francophone work may have played a major role in its structure) and claim Latin's authority for themselves. It is only in the 1300s that we see French acquire a higher standing, probably as the language of transnational, lay, chivalric culture.

Considering the possible provenance and paths through which francophone works on the matter of antiquity reached Castile also shows that the notions of centre and periphery that have traditionally underpinned medieval studies are not useful for understanding such connections (or even relevant). Instead, it is more helpful to think of the Castilian royal court as a node connected to a series of courtly and scholarly networks spanning francophone areas in the French kingdom, the Italian peninsula and the crusader states. Once they reach Castile, these books are used as purveyors of ancient matter in textual and visual form. Their differing modes of engagement with the classical past enter into a dialogue with the ambitious reshaping of vernacular ancient history taking place in the cultural environment that surrounds the monarchs of Castile. Yet even as they carry out elaborate transformations of their source materials that speak directly to local preoccupations, the Castilian works on the matter of antiquity often seem aware of the stakes and uses of ancient

---

[63] I remain intrigued by the parallel uses of the Trojan narrative in Castile and Naples as part of imperial political projects. Although the Italian codex closest to the one that served as a model for the *Crónica troyana*'s creators was thought to be Neapolitan, a northern Italian origin seems now more likely. It will be necessary to come back to this question once we know more about the northern Italian environments in which the *Roman de Troie* was illustrated, as well as about these codices' possible circulation in the southern Italian Peninsula.

[64] *MFLCA*, p. 19.

history specific to their francophone sources' places of provenance, as we have seen throughout this essay. What this means is something perhaps obvious but that is often forgotten: these books do not travel alone but through people who share them with one another, providing additional context and meaning for each of them. The networks through which the francophone matter of antiquity circulated made these books thick with meaning, in a way that we may be able partially to recover.

9

Anxiety in the Contact Zone: The Debate of the Body and the Soul in late-medieval French and Occitan poetry[1]

Catherine Léglu

Introduction

This chapter explores the possible contact zone between French and Occitan literature in late medieval Occitania.[2] Many cultures since Antiquity have explored another, metaphorical contact zone between the world of the living and that of the dead through a dialogue or encounter between an individual's body and its soul or spirit. One expression of this idea, popular in European Christian contexts, was defined as a discrete literary tradition in the late nineteenth century.[3] In a cluster of medieval poems the body and the soul argue over their respective responsibility for the fate of the dead person. A first ('particular') judgement leading to Purgatory anticipates that of the Last Judgement, at which the reunited soul and body are to be assigned to Heaven or Hell. Most of the poems that fall into this group derive from a dream poem known as the *Visio Philiberti* that circulated widely in Latin as well as in several vernacular translations and adaptations.[4]

The three texts at the centre of this study build on this shared tradition but also reveal important facets of the contact between French and Occitan within

---

[1] My thanks to the editors as well as to Sophie Oosterwijk, Laurent Ungeheuer and Beatrice Fedi for advice and comments on parts of this paper.

[2] For a general overview of contact between French and Occitan literatures in late medieval Occitania, see C. Léglu, 'Toulouse', in *Europe: A Literary History, 1348–1415*, ed. D. Wallace, 2 vols. (Oxford, 2016), I, 140–55.

[3] T. Batiouchkof, 'Le débat du corps et de l'âme', *Romania* 20 (1891), 1–55, 513–78; E. J. Richards, 'Body-Soul Debates in English, French and German Manuscripts, *c.*1200–*c.*1500' (unpublished Ph.D. thesis, University of York, 2009), pp. 21–30. Description and bibliography of the French tradition, 'Le débat du corps et de l'âme', in *ARLIMA, Archives de littérature du Moyen Age*, ed. L. Brun, accessed 17 February 2024, https://arlima.net/no/5657.

[4] D. Baker and N. Cartlidge, 'Manuscripts of the Medieval Latin Debate Between Body and Soul (*Visio Philiberti*)', *Notes and Queries* 61 (2014), 196–201.

the kingdom of France during the later Middle Ages. One of the most successful Debate poems in French was a *dit* entitled *L'altercacion et disputation entre l'ame et le corps*, which survives in twenty-two manuscripts as well as in print in Guyot Marchant's *Miroer salutaire* (1486).[5] Nothing is known of its authorship or original context, but it is probably from the fourteenth century, exclusively preserved in continental manuscripts. Two copies of the *Altercacion* survive in Occitan-speaking contexts: one printed, the other in manuscript, discussed below. In parallel, there are two poems composed in Occitan in the fourteenth century that have no explicit connection with this or any other poem in French. The first of these, the Occitan Debate poem, survives in a single copy produced after *c.*1350, possibly in a Catalan-speaking region.[6] It is echoed in the second poem, *Lo cocir de la mort (Anxiety about Death)*, which survives in one copy of a treatise on poetic composition, the *Leys d'Amors*, copied in Toulouse before 1355.[7]

Every linguistic and geographical variation on the *Visio Philiberti* offers a different interpretation. Neil Cartlidge disagrees with Michel-André Bossy's suggestion that these works should be read as 'forensic comedies', arguing that the Latin version is a solemn text.[8] Nataša Golob and Jessica Brantley have suggested that the poem was adopted by Carthusian monks for meditative purposes in Slovenia and England, respectively. J. Justin Brent argues that English and insular French versions are more exercises in rhetoric than tools for meditation.[9] The context of the Occitan poems is secular, as is the printed *Altercacion* from Toulouse.

---

[5]   *Danse macabre. Ce present livre est appellé Miroer salutaire pour toutes gens, et de tous estaz, et est de grant utilitez et recreacion, pour pleuseurs ensengnemens tant en latin comme en françoys lesquex il contient, ainsi composé pour ceulx qui desirent acquerir leur salut et qui le voudront avoir* (Paris, 1486), pp. 55–68.

[6]   Paris, BnF MS fr. 14973, fols. 1–26. *Le débat provençal de l'âme et du corps (texte critique)*, ed. B. Sutorius (Fribourg, 1916). The manuscript includes two other works, the *Song of the Sybil* and a life of Saint George, that point to a connection with Catalonia.

[7]   Toulouse, Bm, MS 2884, fols. 29v–31v, reproduced in *Rosalis. Bibliothèque numérique patrimoniale de Toulouse*, accessed 17 February 2024, https://rosalis.bibliotheque.toulouse.fr/ark:/12148/btv1b10560254h?rk=193134;0 ; *Las leys d'amors. Redazione lunga in prosa*, ed. B. Fedi (Florence, 2019), ii, 72, pp. 299–310.

[8]   N. Cartlidge, 'In the Silence of a Midwinter Night: A Re-evaluation of the *Visio Philiberti*', *Medium Ævum* 75 (2006), 24–46 (p. 28); M.-A. Bossy, 'Medieval Debates of Body and Soul', *Comparative Literature* 28 (1976), 144–163 (p. 155).

[9]   N. Golob, 'Charterhouse Readings: Dialogue between the Soul and the Body', *IKON* 4 (2011), 151–62; J. Brantley, *Reading in the Wilderness: Private Devotion and Public Performance in Late Medieval England* (Chicago, 2007), 27–78 (devotional and meditative practice), and 121–66 (the importance of lyric poetry and performance contexts); J. J. Brent, 'From Address to Debate: Generic Considerations in the *Debate between Soul and Body*', *Comitatus* 32 (2001), 1–18.

A comparative study of these poems draws attention to the multilingual contact zone that developed in the literature of Occitan-speaking regions once they were part of the French crown (from 1279). These regions had a distinctive Death culture that was often associated with heresy, and it marks one of the key distinctions between Northern and Southern French regions. Some of the more colourful narratives and practices regarding revenants, notably the revenant at Alès (discussed below) were incorporated by Jean-Claude Schmitt into his synthesis of Western European beliefs.[10] It is useful to treat them also as a distinctive cultural tradition that found expression in different ways. For example, late medieval Occitania lacked enthusiasm for the *Danse Macabre* or Dance of Death that flourished in the art and literature of French-, Castilian-, Catalan-, Italian- and German-speaking regions. The one surviving example, in Albi, pits Death against Nature, changing the focus towards an exchange that echoes that of the Debate.[11]

Occitan and French interacted in a shared space as distinct literary traditions expressed in mutually intelligible languages. The circulation of books may differ from the reading and listening habits of their users, a point that has been made recently by Lisa Demets in relation to late medieval Bruges.[12] By contrast with Demets's treatment of Bruges as a civic trading zone where monolingual books were produced in a space built on exchange, the linguistic asymmetries between Latin, French, and Occitan were an important source of friction, especially in terms of sacred expression.[13] In her influential articles of the 1990s, Mary Louise Pratt used the term 'contact zone' in order 'to refer to social spaces where cultures meet, clash, and grapple with each other, often in contexts of highly asymmetrical relations of power'.[14] She challenges the idea of the 'speech community' as a stable and discrete group defined by shared grammatical and other competences. Instead, a multilingual contact zone offers the possibility of creative mingling, but also that of setting up barriers between languages.

Recent research has challenged the idea that there was a stark opposition between body and soul in medieval culture, favouring nuanced beliefs that

---

[10] J.-C. Schmitt, *Les revenants. Les vivants et les morts dans la société médiévale* (Paris, 1994).

[11] I discuss the macabre and the *Cocir* in more detail in C. Léglu, 'Imagining Death in late-medieval Occitania', forthcoming. Richards declines to study the Occitan tradition on the grounds of its cultural distinctiveness; Richards, 'Body-Soul Debates', p. 30.

[12] L. Demets, 'Bruges as a Multilingual Contact Zone: Book Production and Multilingual Literary Networks in Fifteenth-Century Bruges', *Urban History* 50 (2023), 1–20.

[13] M. Banniard, 'La langue des esclaves peut-elle parler de Dieu? La langue occitane à la conquête de son acrolecte religieux', in *La parole sacrée – formes, fonctions, sens (XIe–XVe s.)*, Cahiers de Fanjeaux 47 (Toulouse, 2012), pp. 195–214.

[14] M. L. Pratt, 'Arts of the Contact Zone', *Profession* (1991), 33–40, quotations at pp. 33, 37.

changed with language and region.[15] The nature of the soul was hotly disputed in the early fourteenth century. The debates at the Council of Vienne (1311–12) encouraged the development of new theories, and these are echoed in the rise of interest in the Debate during the fourteenth century.[16] For example, the four last things (death, judgement, Hell and Heaven) acquired a controversial addition around the year 1300, the concept of beatitude (enduring happiness of body and soul). Beatitude in this life was condemned as a heresy at the Council of Vienne and attributed to the Languedoc-based movement of the Franciscan Peter John Olivi. In the 1330s, the suggestion of a Beatific Vision at the Last Judgement, postponing purgatorial fires, was made by the Quercy-born Pope John XXII (1316–34), and it was also condemned as heretical.[17] There was a new field of reference around the transition between life and death. The fact that it had an unorthodox flavour and seemed to arise in Occitan-speaking regions points to a more localized concern with the transition between life and death.

In late medieval wills from Provence, the lexis for death expresses anxiety (*anxietas, orrendum*) but also liberation: 'cum anima mea fuerit a carnis nexibus liberata seu rellaxata' ('as my soul has been liberated or set free from the bonds of the flesh').[18] The two Occitan poems emphasise the soul's fear, whereas the French poem does not. They introduce the particular judgement but not the weighing of the soul. Instead, the soul is condemned to either Hell or Purgatory after a formal trial (in the Debate) or arbitrarily (in the *Cocir*). The particular judgement, a contest between the angel and devil immediately after death for possession of the soul and the weighing of that soul (psychostasis), is found early in Occitan-speaking regions, sculpted in the tympanum at Sainte-Foy-de-Conques (Aveyron) (*c.*1100).[19]

---

[15] J. Baschet, *Corps et âmes. Une histoire de la personne au Moyen Âge* (Paris, 2016); N. M. Mandeville Caciola, *Afterlives: The Return of the Dead in the Middle Ages* (Ithaca NY, 2016), pp. 48–57, 72–4.

[16] W. Duba, 'The Souls after Vienne: Franciscan Theologians' Views on the Plurality of Forms and the Plurality of Souls, ca. 1315–30', in *Psychology and the Other Disciplines: A Case of Cross-Disciplinary Interaction (1250–1750)*, ed. P. J. J. M. Bakker, S. W. De Boer and C. Leijenhorst (Leiden, 2012), pp. 171–272.

[17] C. J. Mews and T. Zahora, 'Remembering Last Things and Regulating Behaviour in the Early Fourteenth Century: From the *De Consideratione Novissimorum* to the *Speculum Morale*', *Speculum* 90 (2015), 960–94 (pp. 965, 975).

[18] J. Chiffoleau, *La comptabilité de l'au-delà. Les hommes, la mort et la religion dans la région d'Avignon à la fin du Moyen Âge (vers 1320–vers 1480)* (Rome, 1980), pp. 112–15, quotations at pp. 112, 114.

[19] V. Brilliant, 'Envisaging the Particular Judgment in Late-Medieval Italy', *Speculum* 84 (2009), 314–46; J. Baschet, 'Une image à deux temps. Jugement Dernier et jugement des âmes au Moyen Age', *Images Re-vues* 1 (2008), accessed 17 February

A fine example of the northern and southern contact zone occurs in a psalter-hours from Avignon produced in the mid fourteenth century for secular owners by a Northern French scribe, possibly from Arras, and an artist from Provence who blended local, Parisian and Italian styles. It depicts a huge Devil rushing to claim the soul of a dying cleric as the Virgin, showing her breast, attempts to intercede, and the Crucifixion hovers overhead, with God dominant at the top of the frame.[20] The scene is depicted as a dramatic exchange, with French verse and prose scrolling from several protagonists. The speech scrolls are numbered, indicating how the scene could be read as a narrative. The first speaker is the dying monk, whose prayer to the Virgin is answered by the Devil. The Virgin speaks to Jesus, who addresses a plea to God. God sends his messenger to pronounce the fate of the soul. This scene replicates in part the content of the Occitan poems, with the major difference that both poems omit the Virgin from the judgement. This Avignonese image seems to reflect a strong focus on the deathbed. Before 1300, the deathbed administration of the Cathar *consolamentum* and the more arduous self-starvation known as the *endura* were scrutinized by inquisitors in the Languedoc, but they had disappeared, one exception being the Autier revival in the diocese of Pamiers.[21]

Heresy is inextricable from this enquiry, for in the centuries after the Albigensian Crusade (1209–49), Occitania, especially the Languedoc, was in a paradoxical situation with respect to mainstream Christianity as well as to the increasingly dominant linguistic and political presence of Northern France. Not colonised in any modern sense, the regions that were absorbed into the French crown were marked as, to quote modern scholars, 'a hot bed of heresy', but they also became the seat of almost permanent inquisition tribunals in Languedoc, and of the papal court in Provence.[22] They were simultaneously a seat of orthodoxy and of dissent, both authoritative and disruptive. In terms of Pratt's view of the asymmetries that produce a contact zone, the literature produced in these regions reflects what she terms 'a bifurcated universe of meaning', where

---

2024, https://doi.org/10.4000/imagesrevues.878; B. Williamson, 'Site, Seeing and Salvation in Fourteenth-Century Avignon', *Art History* 30 (2007), 1–25.

[20] Avignon, Bm Ceccano, MS 121, fol. 73v; C. Voyer, 'Voir et entendre: des paroles dans l'image. À propos d'une enluminure du manuscrit 121 de la Bibliothèque municipale d'Avignon', in *La parole sacrée – formes, fonctions, sens (XIe–XVe s.)*, Cahiers de Fanjeaux 47 (Toulouse, 2012), pp. 383–402 (pp. 386–8, and fig. 1). The manuscript's original owners are unknown but it contains the arms of the Clermont de Nesle family. Partial reproduction of the manuscript, in *Initiale, catalogue de manuscrits illuminés*, IRHT, 2012–22, accessed 17 February 2024, https://initiale.irht.cnrs.fr/codex/542/1729.

[21] C. Sparks, *Heresy, Inquisition and Life Cycle in Medieval Languedoc* (York, 2014), pp. 123–50.

[22] L. A. Burnham, *So Great a Light, So Great a Smoke: The Beguin Heretics of Languedoc* (Ithaca NY, 2008).

224 CATHERINE LÉGLU

the words reflected self-understanding and survival but also presented an official image to the gaze of those who might view them with suspicion.[23]

Literary traditions derived from the troubadours were preserved through strategies that were presented in terms of survival. From its foundation in 1323, Toulouse's civic poetry association, the *Concistori de la Gaya Sciencia de Tholoza*, held lyric poetry contests that were intended to *mantener* (maintain) the legacy of the troubadours while adapting it to Marian and other devotional traditions.[24] This was not the brutal imbalance of power between early modern and modern colonizer and indigenous cultures, but there are strong signs that belief systems were analysed and compared with each other.

The *Altercacion*

The *Altercacion* is a dream vision in which the hermit Philibert witnesses the whispered exchanges between a dead body and its soul. I quote from Guyot Marchant's edition of 1486 with reference to Emily Richards' transcription:[25]

> La nuit quant le corps dort: et lame souuent veille.
> Aduint ad le prudome tres grande merueille
> Car ung corps murmurant sentoit a son oreille.
> Et lame daultre part que du corps sesmerueille
>
> (Richards, lines 9–12).

(At night when the body sleeps and the soul is awake, a great marvel befell the wise man, because he heard a body murmur into his ear, and on the other side, the soul that was wondering at the body).

The soul deplores the body's loss of its social and material identity and criticises the body for tainting the soul's initial purity with its sinful actions. The body responds that it has been created by God as a servant of the soul: 'il t'a faicte ma dame et a toy m'a donnée/ Ta chambrière suis, par toy suis gouuvernée' ('He made you my lady and gave me to you. I am your chambermaid, I am governed by you'; Richards, lines 127–8). The body suggests that it is an innocent vehicle for the soul: 'La char qui doit pourrir ne scet point de malice./ On la demenne tout comme une beste nice' ('Flesh that must rot knows no malice, it is led like a simple beast'; Richards, lines 141–2). The soul replies that the body is making a dishonest claim, for it has ignored the soul's virtuous leanings and given in to appetites and pleasures (lines

---

[23] M. L. Pratt, 'Apocalypse in the Andes: Contact Zones and the Struggle for Interpretive Power', *Encuentros* 15 (1996), 1–16.

[24] *Leys*, ed. Fedi, pp. 77–9.

[25] Richards compares the printed version with two manuscript copies. She gives the poem the title based on its incipit, 'Une grante vision en ceste livre est escripte'. Richards, 'Body-Soul Debates', pp. 80–121, transcription, pp. 274–93.

169–88). While the soul admits that it repented too late and will probably suffer for it, it insists that the body is guiltier and will be condemned accordingly at the Last Judgement (lines 201–24). Three devils carry the soul to the gates of Hell and ignore its cries for intercession, because it waited too long to repent (lines 285–308).

For all its diatribes and occasional introduction of macabre elements such as the arrival of an army of ravenous worms (lines 155–60), the French poem narrates an orderly, coherent exchange. The body defends itself against the soul's complaints, and they agree in the end that they both deserve to be punished for the sins that they committed during their union. At the close of the *Altercacion*, the body must lie in its narrow coffin awaiting the Last Judgement, while the soul purges their sins in Purgatory.

There is no such confidence in the Occitan *Cocir*, which consigns the soul to Hell under the gaze of the body. The Occitan Debate poem stages a particular judgement of both the body and the soul, after which the soul is sent to Purgatory. Both poems place great emphasis on the soul's terror (*espaven*) at her vulnerability once she has left the body, something that is absent from the *Altercacion*. These subtle but important differences underline the importance of debate. As Abe Davies comments in a recent article: 'The debate format, with its capacity to accommodate scepticism and indeterminacy, and even a degree of the carnivalesque, has seemed the optimal formal expression of this complex theological and philosophical heritage'.[26]

The *Altercacion* in Occitan regions

The *Altercacion* in French appears in a manuscript from Avignon, as well as in a printed copy from Toulouse (dated 1540).[27] Nicolas Vieillard's printed book production was mostly in French,[28] but it existed in a multilingual context.[29] In 1402, a prominent city consul of Toulouse owned a copy of Brunetto Latini's

---

[26] A. Davies, '"Wite Þu Me, Werga": The Old English *Soul & Body* in Literary-Historical Context', *Modern Language Review* 116 (2021), 226–44 (pp. 227–8, 231).

[27] Avignon, Bm Ceccano, MS 344, fols. 40r–45r; and Aix-en-Provence, Bibliothèque Méjanes, MS S Res. 95, 3, 'S'ensuyt le debat du corps et de l'ame, tresutile et proffitable à ung chascun bon chrestien qui desire le proffit de son ame'. É. Aude, '*III. Les plaintes de la Vierge au pied de la croix et les quinze signes de la fin du monde,* d'après un imprimé toulousain du XVIe siècle', *Annales du Midi* 17 (1905), 365–85 (p. 366).

[28] See the recent edition of his unique *Letres des ysles et terres nouvellement trouvées par les Portugalois. Un voyage imaginaire à Sumatra à la Renaissance*, ed. G. Berthon and R. Cappellen (Geneva, 2021).

[29] H. Lieutard and P. Sauzet, 'D'une diglossie à l'autre: observations linguistiques et sociolinguistiques sur deux textes toulousains de 1555: *Las Ordenansas e coustumas del libre blanc* et *Las nompareilhas receptas*', in *Autour des quenouilles. La parole des femmes (1450–1600)*, ed. J.-F. Courouau, P. Gardy and J. Koopmans (Toulouse, 2010), pp. 109–146.

226   Catherine Léglu

Livre du Trésor 'in romanzo' with the *Distichs of Cato* in Latin, French and Occitan.[30] After 1475, migration from Castile made Toulouse increasingly Spanish-speaking. The first German printer in the city moved there from Segovia at the same time as woad merchants from Castile, especially Burgos. Jean-François Courouau's survey of Toulousain incunables shows that most (eighty-three percent) were in Latin, but of twenty-four titles in a vernacular, fourteen are in Castilian, seven in French, two in Catalan and only one in Occitan. The contents of the printed books reflect a connection with universities south of the Pyrenees, as well as printers in Burgos (Castile) and Zaragoza (Aragon). They include a translation by Fr. Vincente de Maçuelo of Guillaume de Digulleville's poem, as *El pelegrino de la vida humana* (1490).[31]

Books entered the Castilian and Catalan markets from Languedoc via the thriving import routes for woad, but the target audience also included Toulousain residents, notably merchant families, students, and other members of the university.[32] Many of the new arrivals (and new readers) were *conversos* fleeing religious intolerance. However, Toulouse's intellectual culture was dominated by the inquisition tribunal as well as the university, which had been founded in the context of the Albigensian Crusade; book production centered on the university.[33] The context of the printed *Altercacion* in Toulouse was a contact zone between several language communities and political as well as religious agendas.

The manuscript copy of the *Altercacion* in Avignon reflects a similar context in Provence, as it is inside a monolingual compilation of devotional texts written for the laity, including works by Jean Gerson, copied *c.*1420–50.[34] Marie-

---

[30] V. Lamazou-Duplan, 'Lire et écrire chez les notables toulousains à la fin du Moyen Âge: quelques pistes sur la culture des élites laïques avant 1450', in *Toulouse, une métropole méridionale. Vingt siècles de vie urbaine*, ed. B. Suau, J.-P. Amalric and J.-M. Olivier (Toulouse, 2009), pp. 145–62.

[31] J.-F. Courouau, 'Langues et incunables à Toulouse (1475–1500)', *Atalaya* 13 (2013), accessed 17 February 2024, https://doi.org/10.4000/atalaya.1036; F. M. Bango de la Campa, '*Le pèlerinage de vie humaine* versus *El pelegrino de la vida humana*', *Cahiers d'études hispaniques médiévales* 30 (2007), 85–108.

[32] L. Baquedano, 'Le pouvoir du livre: stratégies des imprimeurs dans les seuils de *l'Historia de la linda Melosina* (1489)', *Cahiers d'études hispaniques médiévales* 35 (2012), 233–42.

[33] C. Daydé, 'Un unicum méconnu: la *Repetitio de inquisitione hereticorum* de Nicolas Bertrand (1512)', in *Le livre dans la région toulousaine et ailleurs au Moyen Âge*, ed. S. Cassagnes-Brouquet and M. Fournié (Toulouse, 2010), pp. 121–34; M. J. Vega, 'El *De Iudaica Arbore* (1517) de Étienne Chenu y los conversos españoles en Tolosa y el Languedoc', *Atalaya* 13 (2013), accessed 17 February 2024, https://journals.openedition.org/atalaya/1065.

[34] See M.-L. Savoye, 'Notice de "AVIGNON, Bibliothèque municipale, 0344"', in *Jonas-IRHT/CNRS*, accessed 17 February 2024, https://jonas.irht.cnrs.fr/manuscrit/5196.

Rose Bonnet has noted that the council of the nearby city of Arles produced documents alternating between Latin and Occitan until around 1450, when Latin gave way to more Occitan.[35] Around the year 1500, French began to replace Occitan, a process that culminated around 1550.[36] Yet Arles had long had a significant Italian community, many of whom were the city scribes.[37] The French-language *Altercacion* illustrates the hardening of linguistic boundaries in Provence as well as the importance of secular devotion.

Cultural specificity

Written a century earlier, the two Occitan poems do not reflect French literary sources. The *Cocir* points to sensitive questions around the fate of the separated body-soul dyad, and the Debate resolves them by narrating the particular judgement, a belief that had more success in this part of Europe than elsewhere.[38]

Such features of both poems echo the major studies of death in Occitan-speaking regions. Jacques Chiffoleau identified original views of the body-soul relationship in wills from late medieval Provence, a study developed also for the Toulouse region by Marie-Claude Marandet, while Michèle Fournié studied the development in these regions during the late Middle Ages of an alms-giving practice with dedicated clergy and confraternities known as the *bacino ex Purgatorio* (basin of Purgatory).[39] Several dioceses in the Languedoc supplemented the Autumn feasts of the dead (All Souls and Michaelmas) with *festas d'armas* (feasts of souls) in the Spring, a further sign that there was distinctive ritual practice.[40] The stronger focus on the post-mortem journey of the soul may explain why funeral mass in these regions was often performed during, rather than after, the interment.[41]

[35] M. R. Bonnet, 'Arles du XVe au XVIe siècle, entre latin, provençal et français: deux siècles d'histoire, trois langues en contact', *Revue des langues romanes* 123 (2019), 23–44.

[36] Bonnet, 'Arles', pp. 27–3.

[37] Bonnet, 'Arles', pp. 31–2.

[38] Brilliant, 'Envisaging the Particular Judgment'; Baschet, 'Une image à deux temps'; Williamson, 'Site, Seeing and Salvation'.

[39] Chiffoleau, *La comptabilité de l'au-delà*; M.-C. Marandet, *Le souci de l'au-delà. La pratique testamentaire dans la région toulousaine (1300–1450)* (Perpignan, 1998); M. Fournié, *Le ciel peut-il attendre? Le culte du purgatoire dans le Midi de la France* (Paris, 1997).

[40] M. Fournié, 'L'au-delà dans le midi de la France et dans le Languedoc à la fin du Moyen Age', in *Le pays cathare. Les religions médiévales et leurs expressions méridionales*, ed. J. Berlioz (Paris, 2000), pp. 245–63 (pp. 255–8); Schmitt, *Les revenants*, p. 201.

[41] P.-M. Gy, 'La liturgie de la mort en France méridionale (XIIe–XVe siècle)', in *La mort et l'au-delà en France méridionale (XIIe–XVe siècle)*, Cahiers de Fanjeaux 33

The 'basins of Purgatory' may have been an attempt to insert into mainstream Christianity the activities of the *armiers* (messengers of souls), individuals who communicated with the souls of the recently-deceased that roamed the outskirts of villages and churches and who helped them to enter a 'place of rest' at the feast of All Saints.[42] Daniel Fabre suggested that *armiers* endured until the early modern era despite only one documented investigation into their activities by Jacques Fournier, the future pope Benedict XII (Pamiers, 1318–21).[43] A confession manual mentions that people would leave food out overnight for the souls of their neighbours, and that it was believed that souls left Purgatory on feast days.[44] The *armier* was one of a number of similar traditions found in Southern European regions.[45] Such beliefs and rituals differed from Northern French and Anglo-Norman beliefs and customs.

Medieval Provence produced two well-known descriptions of revenants, the first at Beaucaire (Gard) (*c.*1211, as narrated by Gervase of Tilbury), and the second sixty-five kilometres away in at Alès (Gard) (*c.*1324). Both narratives focus on the soul's continuing relationship after death with the living.[46] At Beaucaire, a girl was visited by the spirit of a murdered male cousin.[47] He entrusted visitors with political advice as well as an endorsement of the Albigensian crusade. A century later, the revenant at Alès, a middle-aged married man, did not engage in political comment, but the case was reported to Pope John XXII.[48] The revenant reported that he spent his days in a 'common Purgatory' and his nights in the 'particular Purgatory' of his home, and the civic authorities joined forces

---

(Toulouse, 1998), pp. 65–75 (pp. 67, 69); Marandet, *Le souci*, pp. 187–239.

[42] Fournié, *Le ciel*, pp. 356–91; J.-P. Albert, 'Croire et ne pas croire. Les chemins de l'hétérodoxie dans le Registre d'Inquisition de Jacques Fournier', *Heresis* 39 (2003), 91–106.

[43] D. Fabre, 'Le retour des morts', *Études rurales* 105/106 (1987), 9–34. Caciola, *Afterlives*, pp. 266–301.

[44] Marandet, *Le souci*, pp. 243–89, para. 117.

[45] Fabre, 'Le retour', pp. 24–5, cites the Pyrenees, Galicia and Corsica, while Caciola cites Provence and the Alps, *Afterlives*, pp. 268–71.

[46] Schmitt, *Les revenants*, pp. 175–9; Jean Gobi, *Dialogue avec un fantôme*, ed. and trans. M.-A. Polo de Beaulieu (Paris, 1994). Also in Chiffoleau, *La comptabilité de l'au-delà*, pp. 399–408. Caciola classifies the two cases as examples of *armiers*, *Afterlives*, pp. 261–301.

[47] Gervase of Tilbury, *Otia imperialia: Recreation for an Emperor*, ed. and trans. S. E. Banks and J. W. Binns (Oxford, 2002), iii.103, pp. 758–79; Schmitt, *Les revenants*, pp. 106–13, 140–4.

[48] M.-A. Polo De Beaulieu, 'De la rumeur aux textes: échos de l'apparition du revenant d'Alès (après 1323)', in *La circulation des nouvelles au Moyen Âge. XXIVe Congrès de la SHMES (Avignon, juin 1993)* (Rome, 1994), pp. 129–56; Schmitt, *Les revenants*, p. 207.

to ease him out of the house and into the collective afterlife.[49] This clashed with the new version of the Beatific Vision that was promulgated a few years later by John XXII and defended by the Minister General of the Franciscan Order, Geraldus Odonis, who came from the same region as the pope and had taught in Toulouse.[50] The Florentine merchant Giovanni Villani (d. 1343) commented anxiously on the papal suggestion that the torments of Hell would only take place after the Last Judgement, apparently dismissing Purgatory and the intercession of the saints.[51] It seems that an Occitan-speaking pope, his Minister General, the rural *armiers* and the local bishop who investigated them (and who later also became pope) were connected by anxiety around the process of separation between the living and the recently dead.

The two poems in Occitan diverge from the *Altercacion* in their focus on death as a traumatising process of separation, first of the soul from the body and second of the person from his or her past life. They also differ from the short Catalan poem entitled the *Qüestio de la Ànima ab lo Cors*.[52] While it is important to stress that too few poems survive to allow us to generalise, there seems to be a common thread. Indeed, a play entitled *Lo Contrach de l'arma e del cors* was commissioned and staged in 1424 by the town council of Digne (Alpes-de-Haute-Provence), a further sign of a tradition.[53]

The Debate: 'L'autrier ausiy une tenson'

The Occitan Debate of the Body and the Soul survives in a single unillustrated copy produced after *c.*1350.[54] The poem of 1165 octosyllables omits the framing dream vision and does not identify its narrator. Where the most diffused Latin versions open with an evocative scene, such as 'Noctis sub silentio tempore brumale' ('By

[49] Polo de Beaulieu, 'De la rumeur', pp. 136–7, 142; texts at pp. 149–50.

[50] Polo de Beaulieu 'De la rumeur', pp. 138–41; W. Duba. 'The Beatific Vision in the Sentences Commentary of Gerald Odonis', *Vivarium* 47 (2009), 348–63; J. Rabiot, 'La culture théologique d'un grand marchand florentin: échos de la controverse sur la vision béatifique dans la *Nuova cronica* de Giovanni Villani (XIVe siècle)', *Mélanges de l'École française de Rome – Moyen Âge* 125 (2013), accessed 17 February 2024, https://journals.openedition.org/mefrm/1143.

[51] Rabiot, 'La culture théologique', sections 8–10.

[52] R. Aramon i Serra, 'Un debat de l'ànima i el cos en versos catalans', in *Recueil de travaux offerts à M. Clovis Brunel par ses amis, collègues et élèves,* 2 vols. (Paris, 1955), I, 38–52.

[53] *Le débat*, ed. Sutorius, p. 10.

[54] Paris, BnF MS fr. 14973, fols. 1–26. Fol. 4 has a marginal drawing of a snake. All quotations are from *Le débat*, ed. Sutorius. Sutorius discusses Batiouchkof's interpretation of this poem, pp. 7–12; see Batiouchkof, 'Le débat du corps et de l'âme', pp. 532–42.

night, in silence, during midwinter…'), the Occitan Debate sets up a completely different expectation. The incipit 'l'autrier…', 'the other day' (here: 'The other day I heard a dispute') is the traditional opening of a *pastorela*, a comic, erotic debate poem based on the attempted seduction of a shepherdess by a knight or a cleric. The genre is described in the *Leys d'Amors* as a song with a lively melody in which 'amusing mockery' and bawdy jokes are exchanged between a man and a woman. It is noted that 'en aquest se peca hom mays que en los autres' ('in this [genre], one sins more than in others').[55] The Debate is an overheard dialogue, something that is also typical of the *pastorela*. Further undermining its seriousness, the Debate's narrator is not sure that the audience will listen, throwing in bitter comments about scattering pearls before swine (lines 5–9).

The narrator presents the feminine soul and the masculine body as a couple who are separating after their lifetime of cohabitation (lines 33–8). The allusion in the incipit to the *pastorela* invites the reader (or listener) to identify the feminine soul with a sharp-tongued working woman who holds her own against a libidinous male speaker. Although the scenario of pre- and post-mortem negotiation is anything but one of seduction, there is the expectation of mockery and jokes, and the clever soul does seem to defeat the earthy body. Yet the emotion that dominates in the speeches of the soul is fear. She expresses her terror at being taken by the devil (lines 44–7), and her fear of the decisions of the devil and the angel (lines 81 and 92):

> Cor, tant suy [yeu e]spaventada
> C'am penas puesc ma rason dire
> Tall paor ay que non me tire
> L'enemic all pa[r]tir de te.
>
> (lines 526–9).

(Body, I am so terrified that I can barely state my argument, I am so frightened of the Enemy taking me once I leave you.)

In another divergence from its standard model, the soul and body are treated as equals in the reckoning of their actions. The soul can see a devil coming with his written list of the dead man's transgressions, as well as an angel carrying a letter that records his good behaviour (lines 52–70, 85–90). The body reminds the soul that they are mutually dependent:

---

[55] 'E deu tractar d'esquern per donar solas… quar trufar se pot hom am femna e far esquern la .i. a l'autre ses dire e ses far viltat e dezonestat', *Leys*, ed. Fedi, ii, 153, p. 376; D. Billy, 'L'autrier cuidai aber druda (BdT 461.146),' *Lecturae tropatorum* 8 (2015), 1–30.

The Debate of the Body and the Soul   231

Ni ieu pogra far nullya re
Enans que fosas dedins me.
E non sabes tu que vers es
Que cors ses arma ren non es,
E obs es que no s'en desliure
Que cos ses arma non pot viure?

(lines 127–33).

(Nor could I do anything until you were inside me. Do you not know that it is true that the body without the soul is nothing, and it must not unbind from it because a body without a soul cannot live?)

Arguing that the limbs and bones can do no harm once the soul has left them, the body claims that the soul is wholly responsible for its words and deeds: 'Arma, fis anc ren negun dia/ Ses tu, pus fuy en ta paria?' (lines 157–8) ('Soul, did I ever do a single thing without you, since I was in a couple with you?'). Challenged by the soul to remember that they make up a single creature, the body insists that the soul was the helmsman of its ship, and the limbs were merely the crew. The ship has no aims or objectives, these are set by its captain (lines 229–59).

The disintegration of the unified self continues. The ears, eyes, nostrils, tongue, hands and feet are angered by the body's arguments, and they reply that the body had a choice between good and evil and that they merely obeyed its orders (lines 289–432). The soul is not pleased at the body's division of the man into legislative soul, executive body and subordinate limbs, but its terror at seeing the Devil draw near and the prospect of lying in Hell robs it of any further appetite for debate (lines 525–64).

The debate shifts from the body and soul to an exchange between the Devil and an angel. The devil, while deploying his rhetoric, accuses the angel of *contrastar* (debating) (lines 633, 637, 661, 675). They wrangle over which of them will win the soul (lines 565–799). The angel rejects the Devil's written evidence of sin on the grounds that all creatures can repent (lines 613–30). The Devil replies that the dying man's career as a usurer erases his penance (lines 631–48). The angel retorts that almsgiving, baptism and penance can erase sins (lines 695–734).

The duel moves to a higher level still when they invite Jesus to judge the outcome (lines 741–800). The narrative returns to its original protagonists, for the soul and body contemplate a dolorous Christ on the Cross, running with blood and pale-faced (lines 822–3, 832–40). The Devil and the angel show their written evidence to Christ who also listens to the arguments of the soul, the body and the limbs (lines 875–998). Surprisingly, Christ tells the body to reflect that his family will move on, his wife will remarry, and his children will spend his money and commit crimes (lines 998–1045). The body will become food for worms, returning to the earth (lines 1049–82). Neither the Devil nor the angel win the contest. Christ upbraids the soul for its poor management of the body and condemns it to the fires and the freezing waters of Purgatory. Once it has purged its sins it will be taken to Heaven by the angel, 'without a dispute' (*ses tensson*) (lines 999–1165). With a hint of its initial invocation of the earthy comedy of the *pastorela*, the poem ends with an uneven mixture of domestic advice to the body and spiritual sentencing for the soul.

Turning the particular judgement into a debate was attested a century earlier, in one of the best-known songs of the troubadour Peire Cardenal (active *c.*1216–75).[56] Its speaker proposes, before his judges, that God should dispossess the devils, thereby gaining more souls and more popularity, and then absolve himself of that deed (lines 17–22). He suggests that St Peter should admit every soul that reaches the gates of Heaven, for a good court should be above reproach. He concludes by proposing to establish an agreement with God:

> E farai vos une bella partia:
> Que'm tornetz lai don moc lo premier dia
> O que.m siatz de mos tortz perdonans.
> Qu'ieu no-ls fora si non fos natz enans.
>
> (lines 37–40)

> (And I will offer you a good deal: either take me back to where I came from on the first day or forgive me my sins – for I would never have committed them had I not been born.)

This song ends with a conventional appeal to the Virgin and St John as intercessors, lessening the suggestion that the speaker should return to the moment of his birth, which hints at the Cathar belief in the transmigration of souls.[57] The negotiation with God points to tensions between conventional piety and the religiously motivated conflict that profoundly changed society in the Languedoc.[58]

Lo cocir de la mort

The Occitan Debate is related to *Lo cocir de la mort* ('Anxiety about Death'), a lyric poem copied in Toulouse (*c.*1324–55). The new Consistory laid down

---

[56] 'Un sirventes novel vueill comensar', Peire Cardenal, *Il trovatore Peire Cardenal*, ed. S. Vatteroni, 2 vols. (Modena, 2013), II, poem 67; PC 335.67.

[57] G. Valenti, 'Riflessioni attorno alle citazioni mariane nelle liriche dei trovatori', *Cognitive Philology* 11 (2018), 1–19 (p. 14); Albert, 'Croire et ne pas croire'.

[58] J. M. Moreau, *Eschatological Subjects: Divine and Literary Judgment in Fourteenth-Century French Poetry* (Columbus, 2014), pp. 34–7; Marandet, *Le souci*, pp. 243–89.

its rules of poetic composition in the tradition of the troubadours in a treatise entitled the *Leys d'Amors* that was first compiled between 1324 and 1355, then revised and republished (with the approval of university masters and of the inquisitor) in 1356.[59] The development of a Marian poetry contest modelled on the Northern *puys* maintained the connection between poetry, prayer and intercession.[60] The *Cocir* is in the first, longer redaction completed before 1355.

The *Cocir* is a pre-mortem monologue by a family man who imagines what his fate might be after his death. It narrates the Soul's separation from the Body and its vulnerability before its fate is decided. It includes elements familiar from the Debate, but there is neither a debate nor a judgement. Instead, the speaker remains grounded in his emotional and material anxieties, while his soul is left to fend for itself. He ruminates on the selfishness of his loved ones and the possible suffering of his children at their hands. Beyond his worldly concerns, he fears that his soul has failed to make proper preparation for the afterlife. Indeed, he imagines that it is caught by the Devil and thrown into hellfire. The speaker takes pre-emptive action, ending the poem with prayers.

The poem divides each section with a rubric that describes a specific *cocir*. '[Del] cocir del deslassamen de l'arma' ('On the anxiety of the soul's departure') presents the body's terrifying loss of control over its soul. This time *espaven* is expressed by the dying man, rather than the soul:

Mays es al mieu cor
Le pas dezagradables
Qu'amarors de tor
E plus espaventables;
Quar mentre.l cors mor
Ades ve le diables
Cochos, de gran trot;
L'arma vol al clot
Cabussar [tro.l pot]
Et als focz perdurablas
Enpenher, si pot.

(2.1–11)

---

[59] The redaction of 1356, now Toulouse, Bm, MS 2883, is edited as *Las leys d'amors. Manuscrit de l'Académie des jeux floraux*, ed. J. Anglade, 3 vols. (Toulouse-Paris, 1919–20). A digital reproduction is available in *Rosalis. Bibliothèque numérique patrimoniale de Toulouse*, accessed 17 Februart 2024, https://rosalis.bibliotheque.toulouse.fr/ark:/12148/btv1b105602532/f1.item. C. Léglu, 'Languages in Conflict in Toulouse: *Las Leys d'Amors*', *Modern Language Review* 63 (2008), 388–96.

[60] Moreau, *Eschatological Subjects*, pp. 57–60.

234   Catherine Léglu

(The passage is more unpleasant to my heart than ox gall, and it is more frightening. Because while the body is dying, I can see the Devil rush over, at a trot. He wants to throw the soul into the hole and to push it in the eternal fires, if he can.)

At this point, the dead man's voice and tongue will have no power to respond to the accusations that the Devil will level at him. Nor can he ask the soul to assist him:

> E la lengua parlar
> No pot ni mot far
> Ni dir ni cridar.
> Bela companha cara,
> Venetz m'aiudar.
>
> (2.29–33)

(His tongue cannot speak nor utter a word, nor say, nor shout: 'Lovely, dear companion, come to my aid!')

The meditation ends with a definitive parting of soul from body, and of the dead from the living:

> Le cors es a part,
> L'arma se.n vay dolenta;
> Volontiers se.n part
> Cascus e se n'absenta.
>
> (2.45–8)

(The body has separated, the soul goes away, sorrowing. Everyone willingly draws away and leaves them.)

The section entitled 'Del cocir de l'arma qu'es fora del cors' ('On the anxiety of the soul that is outside the body') describes the plight of the soul. Expelled from her *escorsa* (shell, or bark), the soul is helpless as the Devil circles around her (6.1–10):

> L'arma de dolor
> E d'engoyssha languida,
> Can ve lo Trachor
> Plora, sospir'e crida.
> Va se.n de paor
> Coma cauza faydida.
> Cuia li fugir,
> Et el al esguir.
> No sab on se vir;
> Tant es trist'e marrida
> Que res no pot dir.
>
> (6.11–22)

(The Soul, exhausted by sorrow and anguish, when she sees the Traitor, weeps, sighs and screams. She carries on out of fear like a lost thing. She thinks she can run away from him, and he follows her. She does not know where to turn. She is so sad and distraught that she cannot say a word.)

We return to the speaker, who urges the soul to pray and to repent. The soul makes no reply (6.56–66). In the absence of the observer-narrator of the *Visio Philiberti*, the *Cocir* depicts the self as a consciousness that remains in the body, starkly separated from its soul. Far from the Debate's dialogue between equals, this soul is a passive, vulnerable creature that seems unable to understand its situation.

The grounding of the self so firmly in the body and its lack of communication with the soul are some of the most striking aspects of this profoundly pessimistic poem. It is very interesting that the revised *Leys d'Amors* of 1356 replaced the *Cocir* with a short meditation on Death followed by a long poem entitled the 'Contemplation of the Cross'.[61] As survivors of the Black Death, the Consistory might have had good reason to exclude the *Cocir*, but its replacement also implies that it was problematic in theological terms. The 'Contemplation' is in fact an Hours of the Cross that exists in other sources. Pope John XXII was reputed to be the author of a 'short office of the Cross' that may be related to this poem. Some psalters and books of hours noted as early as 1324 that John XXII granted an indulgence to anyone who recited his new Office.[62] A short poem later in the same section of the first redaction of the *Leys* leaves the reader in no doubt about the early Consistory's contempt for such spiritual investments:[63]

Qui sab de Santa Crotz l'ufici
Leu pot enpetrar benefici.
Quis fenh a donar mut ni sort
Atrobara corta la cort.
Qui servir sab als cardenals
Empetra rendas avesquals.

---

[61] Toulouse, Bm, MS 2884, fol. 29v. The original rubric was erased and rewritten in a less formal hand. Toulouse, Bm, MS 2883, fols. 82–92v. The short poem on Death is on fol. 82. Study and edition in J. Anglade, 'Poésies religieuses inédites du XIVe siècle en dialecte toulousain tirées des *Leys d'Amors,*' *Annales du Midi* 29 (1917), 1–48.

[62] K. A. Smith, *Art, Identity and Devotion in Fourteenth-Century England: Three Women and their Books of Hours* (London, 2003), pp. 58, 303, 'Incipit officium per Johannem papam xxii' (the De Bois Hours, *c.*1325–30 and the De Lisle Hours); L. Freeman Sandler, 'An Early Fourteenth-Century English Psalter in the Escorial', *Journal of the Warburg and Courtauld Institute* 42 (1979), 65–80 (pp. 71–2); G. Passerat, 'Les prières du pape Jean XXII', in *Jean XXII et le Midi*, Cahiers de Fanjeaux 45 (Toulouse, 2012), pp. 439–57.

[63] *Leys*, ed. Fedi, ii, 132, p. 361.

(He who knows the Office of Holy Cross can easily obtain a benefice. He who pretends to be deaf or dumb to Giving will find his time in court to be short. He who knows how to serve the cardinals will obtain a bishop's revenue.)

This squib against cynical careerism is a rare example of political protest within the Consistory in its early years. It also points to an underlying polemic in the choice of the 'Contemplation' over the *Cocir* in the new redaction of 1356, over twenty years after the death of a pope who had sponsored the tale of the revenant at Alès and sought to rethink the terms of postmortem judgement.

Conclusion

The *Altercacion* and the two Occitan poems are fragments of a linguistic and religious contact zone in which questions of death, post-mortem judgement and purgation were debated. Barbara Peklar has argued that the *Visio Philiberti* was not 'dualist' in the Manichean (Cathar) sense but set equivalences between the carnal and emotional flaws of a fallible human being.[64] There are no signs of Cathar dualism in the Occitan Debate, but the *Cocir*'s depiction of a lost, frightened soul expelled from its protective husk echoes the reported beliefs of the *armiers*. The anxiety of the secular man in both Occitan poems, fretting over his widow and his children, echoes the 'domestic' Purgatory of the bourgeois revenant at Alès. The Debate of the Body and the Soul allows the expression of multiple viewpoints as well as of theological ideas that might not have been voiced openly. Most striking is the insistence in the Occitan tradition on anxiety, an emotion that the French poem does not evoke. Anxiety, therefore, may mark the friction between French, the incoming idiom of prestige and power, and an Occitan-speaking culture that could address the theme but still grappled with the suspicion of heresy.

---

[64] B. Peklar, 'Discussing Medieval Dialogue between the Soul and the Body and the Question of Dualism', *Ars & Humanitas* 9 (2015), 172–99 (pp. 179–81).

10

The Uses of French in Medieval Wales

Georgia Henley

In this chapter, I offer a survey of the use of French as a language of spoken and written communication by elite laypeople in medieval Wales, particularly in the thirteenth and fourteenth centuries. Wales, a country made up of several kingdoms that were slowly conquered by Anglo-Norman and English kings over several centuries, was home to its own culture and language (Welsh), but also had ties to England, Normandy, Ireland, Brittany and Flanders. Its elites were often both Welsh- and French-speaking, and their chronicles referred to the Anglo-Norman conquerors (who were in fact Norman, Flemish, English and Hiberno-Norman in their ethnic makeup) as 'French'. The long period of the conquest of Wales, and its attendant political, cultural and military interactions between different cultures along a border zone known as the March of Wales, was characterised by the use of French as a spoken language of communication between Welsh and Anglo-Norman nobility. By 'Welsh', I mean people who were raised in or had substantial connections to the region of *pura Wallia*, had a Welsh identity and were Welsh-speaking. I will discuss the use of French in medieval Wales with a particular focus on examples of political communications among these elites and the intermarriage of Welsh and French nobility. I also discuss French as a significant literary language in Wales, evident in the translations of French texts into Middle Welsh. In doing so, I offer a corrective to the historical neglect of French in favour of the Welsh language in surveys of literature from medieval Wales. I also offer brief comment on the use of French in the March of Wales, a significant zone of contact between cultures and languages that was ruled by nobility of Norman, Welsh and Breton descent. In both Wales and the March of Wales, French was a medium through which literature and ideas were transmitted between the different peoples of these regions. I conclude by problematising the recent shift in terminology used to describe the French dialect in medieval Britain away from 'Anglo-Norman French' to 'the French of England', given that so much French literature in the Anglo-Norman dialect was produced and read outside England's borders. 'Insular French' or perhaps 'the French of Britain' are more appropriate terms that encompass these regions. Additionally, as a corrective to the assumption that Welsh was the only literary language

238   GEORGIA HENLEY

of medieval Wales (or, the only one worth studying), one hopes that future studies will consider at least three languages (Welsh, French and Latin) in concert as the literary languages of Wales.[1] Only then can their interactions in this multilingual society be better understood.

The evidence for French in Wales

French was both a spoken language of communication and a widespread written language in Wales, and examination of the evidence draws attention to the further need for the study of multilingualism and the interactions between the different vernacular languages there. First, French was a language of political diplomacy and written record among the Welsh nobility, a phenomenon which probably emerged because of their need to interact with the Norman and Anglo-Norman population of South Wales and the March. In this environment, French was not being used by choice as a marker of cultural prestige, as is often perceived, but out of necessity and for political survival. The Norman and Anglo-Norman nobility who colonised Wales in the late eleventh, twelfth and thirteenth centuries spoke French,[2] and some Welsh nobility had a long record of communicating with them in French throughout the medieval period, at least since the Norman advance into Wales in the late eleventh century brought French as a language of communication to the fore.[3] Whether this communication occurred through clerics and translators or through direct knowledge of French on the part of Welsh people probably varied. Marie Surridge writes, 'Many documents concerning Wales are written in French, some of them in Wales itself. The majority of such documents were presumably products of the Norman administration ... amongst them, however, are letters which must have been written in Wales and for, if not by, Welshmen ... they show at least that the Welsh leaders had access to clerks who could write French.'[4] In other words, along with Latin and Welsh, French

---

[1]   Several scholars have already worked to correct these assumptions. See, for example, C. Lloyd-Morgan, 'French Texts, Welsh Translators', in *The Medieval Translator II*, ed. R. H. Ellis (London, 1991), pp. 45–63 (p. 46).

[2]   See I. Short, 'On Bilingualism in Anglo-Norman England', *Romance Philology* 33 (1980), 467–79.

[3]   Documents in French from Wales are preserved in *Calendar of Ancient Correspondence concerning Wales*, ed. J. G. Edwards (Cardiff, 1935) and *Calendar of Ancient Petitions Relating to Wales*, ed. W. Rees (Cardiff, 1975), and discussed by D. Trotter, 'L'anglo-français au pays de Galles: une enquête préliminaire', *Revue de linguistique romane* 58 (1994), 461–87 (pp. 463–9).

[4]   M. Surridge, 'Romance Linguistic Influence on Middle Welsh: A Review of Some Problems', *Studia Celtica* 1 (1966), 63–92 (p. 66); L. B. Smith, 'The Welsh Language

was a language of record in Wales.[5] Llinos Beverley Smith, for example, points out the example of Llywelyn ap Llywelyn of Chirk giving his wife dower rights using a document written in French.[6]

French was also the dominant language spoken by clergy, particularly in South Wales where many personnel were Anglo-Norman or Flemish, or came directly from France, in the case of the continental monastic orders (particularly the Savigniacs and Cistercians in their early years).[7] In addition to employing multilingual clerics, Welsh nobility would have learned French from instruction, or perhaps more likely, from parents and nursemaids, given the degree to which Welsh and Norman nobility intermarried in the medieval period, and how many mothers and fathers of Welsh nobility would have spoken French in the household.[8] Much that was the case for Normans in Ireland is the case here.[9]

Among the more well-researched and prominent examples of the use of French by nobility in Wales are the writings of Gerald of Wales (*c.*1146–1223), a prolific author and cleric raised at Manorbier Castle in Pembrokeshire by a Welsh-Norman mother (Angharad, daughter of the Norman baron Gerald

---

before 1536', in *The Welsh Language before the Industrial Revolution*, ed. G. H. Jenkins (Cardiff, 1997), 15–44 (pp. 16, 28–9).

[5] Discussed by Smith, 'Welsh Language', pp. 28–9.

[6] Smith, 'Welsh Language', p. 28.

[7] Surridge, 'Romance Linguistic Influence', p. 71. For background, see D. H. Williams, *The Welsh Cistercians* (Leominster, 2001); F. G. Cowley, *The Monastic Order in South Wales, 1066–1349* (Cardiff, 1977).

[8] For intermarriage, see E. Cavell, 'Welsh Princes, English Wives: The Politics of Powys Wenwynwyn Revisited', *Welsh History Review* 27 (2014), 214–52; E. Cavell, 'Aristocratic Widows and the Medieval Welsh Frontier: The Shropshire Evidence', *Transactions of the Royal Historical Society* 17 (2007), 57–82; B. Holden, 'The Making of the Middle March of Wales, 1066–1250', *Welsh History Review* 20 (2000), 207–26 (pp. 219–23); Surridge, 'Romance Linguistic Influence', p. 70. Prominent examples of these marriages include Nest, daughter of Gruffudd ap Llywelyn, and Osbern fitz Richard (*fl.*1066–88); Nest, daughter of Rhys ap Tewdwr (d.*c.*1130), and Gerald of Windsor (d.1116x36); Margaret Corbet and Gwenwynwyn ab Owain (d.1216); Joan, daughter of King John (d.1237), and Llywelyn ab Iorwerth (*c.*1173–1240); Isabel de Braose and Dafydd ap Llywelyn (*c.*1215–46); Gwladys Ddu, daughter of Llywelyn ab Iorwerth (d.1251), and Reginald de Braose (d.1227/8), then Ralph Mortimer (d.1246); Emma d'Audley and Gruffudd Maelor II (d.1269); Isabel Marshal and Maredudd ap Rhys Grug (d.1271); Eleanor de Montfort (d.1282) and Llywelyn ap Gruffudd (d.1282); Hawise Lestrange and Gruffudd ap Gwenwynwyn (d.1286); and Ada Hastings and Rhys ap Maredudd (d.1292).

[9] See M. Ní Mhaonaigh in this volume; K. Busby, *French in Medieval Ireland, Ireland in Medieval French: The Paradox of Two Worlds* (Turnhout, 2017).

of Windsor and the Welsh princess Nest ferch Rhys) and a Norman father, William fitz Odo de Barry.[10] Gerald was fluent in French and Latin and may have spoken Welsh in childhood and some English.[11] While preaching the crusade in Wales with Baldwin, archbishop of Canterbury, he spoke French and Latin. In fact, Gerald remarks that his eloquence in these languages is so great that even listeners who could not speak those languages were moved to tears.[12] While Gerald and Baldwin's French and Latin speeches to the public were almost always translated into Welsh for the crowd by interpreters, Gerald and Baldwin also communicated regularly on their journey with the Lord Rhys ap Gruffudd, prince of Deheubarth (a kingdom of South Wales). These conversations were not interpreted. H. E. Butler, editor of Gerald's autobiography, quotes a story from Gerald's *Speculum ecclesiae* that he judges to be from the same time period. Gerald is sent into Wales by Henry II to deliver a message to Rhys ap Gruffudd, in residence at his castle of Llandovery in Cantref Bychan. Rhys comes out of his castle to greet Gerald and they have a detailed conversation.[13] This conversation, the contents of which are not important for present purposes, would have taken place in French. There is no mention of an interpreter or a language barrier in this scene. Gerald's exposure to and use of French and Latin is a prime example of the language ability of a highly educated marcher noble in this period.[14]

Gerald's fluency in French was not unusual for a noble raised in Wales in a Norman-Welsh family. To find other examples of knowledge of French on the part of Welsh people, we look to the translators who worked for people

---

[10] For discussion, see R. Bartlett, *Gerald of Wales, 1146–1223* (Oxford, 1982) and *Gerald of Wales: New Perspectives on a Medieval Writer and Critic*, ed. G. Henley and A. J. McMullen (Cardiff, 2018).

[11] For discussion, see A. Putter, 'Multilingualism in England and Wales, *c.* 1200: The Testimony of Gerald of Wales', in *Medieval Multilingualism: The Francophone World and its Neighbours*, ed. C. Kleinhenz and K. Busby (Turnhout, 2010), 83–105; S. Zimmer, 'A Medieval Linguist: Gerald de Barri', *Études celtiques* 35 (2003), 313–52.

[12] Gerald of Wales, *De rebus a se gestis* I.xviii, trans. H. E. Butler, *The Autobiography of Gerald of Wales*, new edn (Woodbridge, 2005), p. 101; Gerald of Wales, *Giraldi Cambrensis Opera*, ed. J. S. Brewer, vol. 1 (London, 1861), p. 76.

[13] Gerald of Wales, *Speculum ecclesiae* II.xxxii, ed. J. S. Brewer, *Giraldi Cambrensis Opera*, vol. 4 (London, 1873), pp. 100–01; Gerald of Wales, *Autobiography of Gerald of Wales*, trans. Butler, p. 85.

[14] In 'Multilingualism', pp. 88–9, Putter argues further that Gerald's remarks on the purity of the continental French language by comparison to the insular dialect of French indicate that French was still a living language in Britain in his time.

like Gerald and Baldwin.[15] For example, the Welsh nobleman Iorwerth Goch, half-brother of Madog ap Maredudd,[16] assumed the duties of royal interpreter (*latimarius*) for Henry II in the late 1150s during Henry's campaigns in Powys and remained in the king's service afterwards.[17] How he learned French is unknown, but he served as an intermediary between French and Welsh speakers. He married an Englishwoman, Maude, daughter of Roger of Manley. His son, Gruffudd ab Iorwerth Goch (d.1221), was also paid for work as a royal interpreter in 1211.[18] Gruffudd married an Anglo-Norman woman, Matilda Lestrange, heiress of the Shropshire lord Ralph Lestrange of Knockin. The need for translators would indicate that some of the Welsh- and French-speaking people in Wales and the March of Wales required language specialists for matters of communication and administration. It also indicates that access to French education on the part of Welsh nobility was possible, either formally or through French-speaking family members, and that this ability gave them some financial and political advantages.[19] In addition, the diplomatic missions sent to the English royal court to negotiate on behalf of Welsh princes (such as Ednyfed Fychan and Einion Fychan for Llywelyn ab Iorwerth, and Einion ap Caradog and Dafydd ab Einion for Llywelyn ap Gruffudd) presumably involved communication in French.[20] Finally, letters in French survive by Hywel ap Meurig (1274), Gruffudd ap Gwenwynwyn (1282), Rhys ap Maelgwn and Cynan ap Maredudd (1284 and 1286), among other Welsh princes, probably written (either transcribed or translated) by clerks and secretaries.[21]

---

[15] For general discussion, see C. Bullock-Davies, *Professional Interpreters and the Matter of Britain: A Lecture Delivered at a Colloquium of the Departments of Welsh in the University of Wales at Gregynog, 26 June, 1965* (Cardiff, 1966), pp. 15–17.

[16] Madog ap Maredudd (d.1160) was the last ruler of the Welsh kingdom of Powys, and uncle of Owain Cyfeiliog and Owain Fychan, erstwhile rulers of Powys.

[17] Discussed by F. C. Suppe, 'The Career and Subsequent Reputation of Iorwerth Goch, Bi-Cultural Denizen of the Medieval Welsh Marches', *North American Journal of Celtic Studies* 2 (2018), 133–54 (pp. 137–8), citing *Antiquities of Shropshire*, ed. R. W. Eyton, 12 vols. (London, 1854–60), II, 109–12.

[18] Discussed by D. Stephenson, 'Welsh Lords in Shropshire: Gruffydd ap Iorwerth Goch and his Descendants in the Thirteenth Century', *Transactions of the Shropshire Archaeological Society* 77 (2002), 32–7 (p. 32), citing *Antiquities of Shropshire*, ed. Eyton, II, 112–14.

[19] See E. J. Jones, *Education in Wales during the Middle Ages: Inaugural Lecture of the Professor of Education delivered at the College on 2 December 1947* (Swansea, [n.d.]).

[20] Smith, 'Welsh Language', pp. 29 and 29 n. 44.

[21] Discussed by Trotter, 'Anglo-français', p. 466.

Similar patterns of communication are reflected in literary works such as the romance of *Fouke le Fitz Waryn*, a French-language romance set in the March of Wales, surviving in a fourteenth-century manuscript, where dialogue between the Norman baron Fouke fitz Waryn and the Welsh princes Gwenwynwyn ab Owain of Powys and Llywelyn ab Iorwerth of Gwynedd is depicted as seamless.[22] These characters have no trouble communicating with one another, and presumably their dialogue was imagined as taking place in French (the language of the text), particularly as the narrator mentions that Llywelyn was brought up in the court of Henry II. This reflects the reality on the ground: that French was used in spoken communication between Welsh and Anglo-Norman people. The use of French by Welsh people therefore was not marked as unusual in literature.

French was also used in letters, petitions and other documents by Anglo-Norman bourgeoisie in Welsh towns, including Haverford, Llanfaes, Carmarthen, Welshpool, Caernarfon, Conwy, Denbigh and Rhuddlan.[23] To take a specific example, at the beginning of the fourteenth century, in 1307, the canonisation proceedings of Thomas Cantilupe, bishop of Hereford, indicate that laypeople including cooks and burgesses from the town of Conwy in North Wales spoke French and gave testimony in French. This suggests that 'in the new colonial foundation of Conwy French was used as a true lingua franca at the end of the thirteenth century and knowledge of French may even have been, in practice, a precondition for professional or occupational advancement.'[24] This evidence also indicates that French as a language of record was not as separated by class as one might assume and challenges the assumption that French in Wales was the purview of the gentry only.

Another oft-cited example of a Welshman knowing French is the Welsh poet Ieuan ap Rhydderch ab Ieuan Llwyd (*fl.*1430–70), a gentleman from Rhydderch Park in Llanbadarn, Ceredigion. He may have been trained at a

---

[22] *Fouke le Fitz Waryn*, ed. E. J. Hathaway, P. T. Ricketts, C. A. Robson and A. D. Wilshere (Oxford, 1975), p. 33; *Two Medieval Outlaws: Eustace the Monk and Fouke Fitz Waryn*, trans. G. S. Burgess (Cambridge, 1997), p. 159.

[23] Trotter, 'Anglo-français', pp. 464–8. For French as the language of petitions, see M. W. Ormrod, 'The Language of Complaint: Multilingualism and Petitioning in Later Medieval England', in *Lang Cult*, pp. 31–43.

[24] Smith, 'Welsh Language', p. 28; M. Richter, 'Collecting Miracles Along the Anglo-Welsh Border in the Early Fourteenth Century', in *Multilingualism in Later Medieval Britain*, ed. D. A. Trotter (Cambridge, 2000), pp. 53–61; S. Lusignan, 'French Language in Contact with English: Social Context and Linguistic Change (mid-13th–14th centuries)', in *Lang Cult*, pp. 19–30 (p. 20).

university, probably Oxford, and achieved a 'doctor of laws'.[25] In one of his poems, he states, 'Dysgais yr eang Ffrangeg – / doeth yw ei dysg, da iaith deg' ('I have learned the expansive French tongue / wise is its teaching, a fine, pretty language').[26] This quotation would suggest that knowledge of French, as well as (in this case) its prestige, persisted into the fifteenth century in Wales. There is also evidence of French influence on Welsh orthography (particularly the letter 'k' to represent the phoneme /k/), a further indication of the significant role that French played in Welsh documentary culture.[27] Finally, one result of the interaction between Welsh and French in the medieval period is documented borrowings of French words into Welsh, a matter worthy of further study.[28]

French literature in Wales

In this section, I discuss indirect evidence for knowledge of French in Wales, which comes in the form of romances and other texts translated from French into Middle Welsh. This practice fed an explosion of literary activity in fourteenth-century Wales, particularly South Wales, that has been the focus of

---

[25] L. Smith, 'Rhydderch ab Ieuan Llwyd (*c.* 1325–1392x8)', *ODNB*, accessed 17 February 2022, https://doi.org/10.1093/ref:odnb/48651; D. Jenkins, 'Ieuan ap Rhydderch ab Ieuan Llwyd (fl. 1340–1470), gentleman and poet, of Cardiganshire', *Dictionary of Welsh Biography*, accessed 17 February 2022, https://biography.wales/article/s-IEUA-APR-1430.

[26] *Cywyddau Iolo Goch ac Eraill*, ed. H. Lewis, T. Roberts and I. Williams (Cardiff, 1937), p. 228. My translation.

[27] See S. Rodway, 'Cymraeg vs. Kymraeg: Dylanwad Ffrangeg ar Orgraff Cymraeg Canol?', *Studia Celtica* 43 (2000), 123–33.

[28] See Trotter, 'Anglo-français', 475–7; M. E. Surridge, 'Words of Romance Origin in the Works of the Gogynfeirdd', *Bulletin of the Board of Celtic Studies* 29 (1981), 528–30; Surridge, 'Romance Linguistic Influence', pp. 63–8; M. Watkin, 'The French Linguistic Influence in Mediaeval Wales', *Transactions of the Honourable Society of Cymmrodorion* (1918–19), 146–222. A further layer of linguistic interaction that will not be discussed here is the influence of vulgar Latin in the sub-Roman period on the proto-Brythonic language that became Welsh. For discussion, see A. Harvey, 'Cambro-Romance? Celtic Britain's counterpart to Hiberno-Latin', in *Early Medieval Ireland and Europe: Chronology, Contacts, Scholarship. A Festschrift for Dáibhí Ó Cróinín*, ed. P. Moran and I. Warntjes (Turnhout, 2015), pp. 179–202; P. Russell, 'Latin and British in Roman and Post-Roman Britain: Methodology and Morphology', *Transactions of the Philological Society* 109 (2011), 138–57; P. Schrijver, 'Pruners and Trainers of the Celtic Family Tree: The Rise and Development of Celtic in the Light of Language Contact', in *Proceedings of the XIV International Congress of Celtic Studies, held in Maynooth University, 1–5 August 2011*, ed. L. Breatnach, R. Ó hUiginn, D. McManus and K. Simms (Dublin, 2015), pp. 191–219.

a great deal of scholarship in Welsh literary studies. Most of this scholarship has focused on the adaptation of three of Chrétien de Troyes's romances into Middle Welsh, but it is important to note that the bigger picture includes a wide array of texts adapted from French into Welsh, designed for the literary appetites of Welsh gentry households. Kristen Lee Over argues that in Wales the 'normative and hegemonic French vernacular culture' was 'inextricably linked to foreign overlordship', but this does not seem to have deterred interest in French texts, but rather to have influenced some of the adaptive decisions the translators made.[29]

The three romances by Chrétien de Troyes translated into Welsh are *Owain or Chwedyl iarlles y ffynnawn* ('The Tale of the Lady of the Fountain'), adapted from *Yvain ou le chevalier au lion*; as well as *Ystorya Geraint fab Erbin* ('The Story of Geraint son of Erbin'), adapted from *Erec et Enide*; and *Historia Peredur ab Efrawg* ('The Story of Peredur son of Efrawg'), adapted from *Perceval ou le conte du graal*.[30] These three romances were translated by different authors and are now considered to be part of the (post-medieval) literary collection known as the *Mabinogion*. Their earliest extant manuscripts are late thirteenth- and early fourteenth-century. As is so often the case with medieval translations, Lloyd-Morgan observes that these romances are more 'retellings' than translations, adapting the narrative from Chrétien into a form that would satisfy the cultural and literary conventions of a Welsh audience.[31]

---

[29] K. L. Over, 'Transcultural Change: Romance to *Rhamant*', in *Medieval Celtic Literature and Society*, ed. H. Fulton (Dublin, 2005), pp. 183–204.

[30] For general overviews, see R. Reck, '*Owain* or *Chwedyl Iarlles y Ffynnawn*', in *Arthur in the Celtic Languages: The Arthurian Legend in Celtic Literatures and Languages*, ed. C. Lloyd-Morgan and E. Poppe (Cardiff, 2019), pp. 117–31; E. Poppe, '*Ystorya Geraint fab Erbin*', in *Arthur in the Celtic Languages*, ed. Lloyd-Morgan and Poppe, pp. 132–44; C. Lloyd-Morgan, '*Historia Peredur ab Efrawg*', in *Arthur in the Celtic Languages*, ed. Lloyd-Morgan and Poppe, pp. 145–57; C. Lloyd-Morgan, 'Medieval Welsh Tales or Romances? Problems of Genre and Terminology', *Cambrian Medieval Celtic Studies* 47 (2004), 41–58; *The Arthur of the Welsh: The Arthurian Legend in Medieval Welsh Literature*, ed. R. Bromwich, A. O. H. Jarman and Brynley F. Roberts (Cardiff, 1991). For editions, see *Ystorya Gereint uab Erbin*, ed. R. L. Thomson (Dublin, 1997); *Historia Peredur vab Efrawc*, ed. G. W. Goetinck (Cardiff, 1976); *Owein, or, Chwedyl iarlles y ffynnawn*, ed. R. L. Thomson (Dublin, 1968). For translation, see *The Mabinogion*, trans. S. Davies (Oxford, 2007).

[31] Lloyd-Morgan, 'French Texts', pp. 49–51. The theory that Chrétien's romances and the Welsh tales share a common Celtic origin has been debunked. See discussion in C. Lloyd-Morgan and E. Poppe, 'The First Adaptations from French: History and Context of a Debate', in *Arthur in the Celtic Languages*, ed. Lloyd-Morgan and Poppe, pp. 110–16; P. Sims-Williams, 'Did Itinerant Breton *Conteurs* Transmit the *Matière de Bretagne*?', *Romania* 116 (1998), 72–111.

She writes, 'Although the names of the main characters correspond to those of their counterparts in the French, in terms of behaviour and reactions they have far more in common with the older Welsh heroes, whose names they bear, than with the *chevaliers* who people Chrétien's fictional world.'[32] To give one characteristic example, in Chrétien's *Perceval*, the young knight's Welsh clothing, javelins and boorish manners mark him as Welsh, in need of refinement at King Arthur's court; in *Peredur*, the title character is of noble lineage, fulfilling his destiny by reclaiming his patrimony. Kristen Lee Over argues, 'Rather than a tale of stereotyped ethnic distinction and failed assimilation [as in *Perceval*], *Peredur* is a story of noble destiny, a destiny of regained patrimony and reacquired sociopolitical status.'[33] In line with the practice of translators working in other medieval languages, Welsh translators deliberately adapted their source material to fit an audience with different cultural norms and expectations of literary narrative.[34] Most scholarship on the 'three romances', as they are conventionally but anachronistically called in Welsh Studies, has focused on comparing the Welsh and French texts to tease out the decisions made by the Welsh translators to fit Welsh culture.[35] With the exception of *Peredur*, which is often discussed in terms of postcolonial theory, the 'three romances' have been considered almost exclusively through the lens of comparative philology.[36] While the comparative lens is essential

[32] Lloyd-Morgan, 'French Texts', p. 49.

[33] Over, 'Transcultural Change', p. 200.

[34] C. Buridant, 'Esquisse d'une traductologie au Moyen Âge', in *Translations médiévales. Cinq siècles de traductions en français au Moyen Âge (XIe–XVe siècles). Étude et répertoire, Volume 1: De la* translatio studii *à l'étude de la* translatio, ed. C. Galderisi (Turnhout, 2011), pp. 325–81.

[35] E.g. L. Cordo Russo, 'Adaptation and Translation in Medieval Wales: *Chwedyl Iarlles y Ffynnawn* and *Cân Rolant*', *Keltische Forschungen* 7 (2016), 91–104; Over, 'Transcultural Change'; Lloyd-Morgan, 'Medieval Welsh Tales'; Lloyd-Morgan, 'French Texts', pp. 56–9; H. A. Roberts, 'Court and *Cyuoeth*: Chrétien de Troyes' *Erec et Enide* and the Middle Welsh *Gereint*', *Arthurian Literature* 21 (2004), 53–72; H. Fulton, 'Individual and Society in *Owein/Yvain* and *Gereint/Erec*', in *The Individual in Celtic Literatures*, ed. J. Falaky Nagy, CSANA Yearbook 1 (Dublin, 2001), pp. 15–50; S. Echard, 'Of Parody and Perceval: Generic Manipulation in *Peredur* and *Sir Perceval of Galles*', *Nottingham Medieval Studies* 40 (1996), 63–79; R. Middleton, 'Chwedl Geraint ab Erbin', in *The Arthur of the Welsh*, ed. Bromwich et al., pp. 147–57; R. L. Thomson, 'Owain: Chwedl Iarlles y Ffynnon', in *The Arthur of the Welsh*, ed. Bromwich et al., pp. 159–69; I. Lovecy, 'Historia Peredur ab Efrawg', in *The Arthur of the Welsh*, ed. Bromwich et al., pp. 171–82; *Historia Peredur vab Efrawc*, ed. Goetinck; *Owein*, ed. Thomson.

[36] E.g. C. Lumbley, 'The "Dark Welsh": Color, Race, and Alterity in the Matter of Medieval Wales', *Literature Compass* 16 (2019), 1–19; S. Aronstein, 'Becoming

246   GEORGIA HENLEY

for understanding the motivations and outcomes of the work of the author-translators of these texts, more work could be done on audience, impact, reception and the nature of the multilingual exchange at work in the translations and other historicist approaches.

A range of other texts is also extant, though rather less well-studied than the 'three romances'.[37] The Charlemagne cycle was translated into Middle Welsh: *Cân Rolant* is translated from the *Chanson de Roland*; *Pererindod Siarlymaen* from the *Pèlerinage de Charlemagne*; and *Rhamant Otuel* from the *Roman d'Otinel*.[38] *Y Seint Greal* is an adaptation of *La Queste del Saint Graal* and *Perlesvaus*;[39] and *Ystorya Bown o Hamtwn* is a translation from the Anglo-Norman *Geste de Boeve de Haumtone*.[40] Richart de Fornival's *Bestiaire d'Amour* was also translated into Welsh.[41] There is a fragmentary text known as *The Birth of Arthur* that translates sections of the *Prose Merlin*, and a prophetical text, *Darogan yr Olew Bendigaid* ('The Prophecy of the Holy Oil'), that translates parts of the French Vulgate Cycle of Arthurian prose romances.[42] In contrast to the *Mabinogion* romances, these texts have been comparatively neglected in scholarship.

Welsh: Counter-Colonialism and the Negotiation of Native Identity in *Peredur vab Efrawc*', *Exemplaria* 17 (2005), 135–68; Over, 'Transcultural Change'; S. Knight, 'Resemblance and Menace: A Post-Colonial Reading of *Peredur*', in *Canhwyll Marchogyon: Cyd-destunoli Peredur*, ed. S. Davies and P. Wynn Thomas (Cardiff, 2000), pp. 128–47.

[37] For the term 'three romances', see Lloyd-Morgan, 'Medieval Welsh Tales', pp. 41–4.

[38] *Cân Rolant: The Medieval Welsh Version of the 'Song of Roland'*, ed. and trans. A. C. Rejhon (Berkeley, 1984); *Ystorya de Carolo Magno o Lyfr Coch Hergest*, ed. S. J. Williams, 2nd edn (Cardiff, 1930); *Cân Rolant* is discussed in Cordo Russo, 'Adaptation'.

[39] *Ystoryaeu Seint Greal, Rhan 1: Y Keis*, ed. T. Jones (Cardiff, 1992); discussed in C. Lloyd-Morgan, '*Y Seint Greal*', in *Arthur in the Celtic Languages*, ed. Lloyd-Morgan and Poppe, pp. 158–69.

[40] *Selections from Ystorya Bown o Hamtwn*, ed. E. Poppe and R. Reck (Cardiff, 2009); discussed in E. Poppe and R. Reck, 'A French Romance in Wales: *Ystorya Bown o Hamtwn*: Processes of Medieval Translations', *Zeitschrift für celtische Philologie* 55 (2006), 122–80, and 56 (2008), 129–64.

[41] *A Welsh Bestiary of Love*, ed. G. C. G. Thomas (Dublin, 1988).

[42] Discussed in C. Lloyd-Morgan, 'Later Hybrid Narrative Texts in Middle Welsh', in *Arthur in the Celtic Languages*, ed. Lloyd-Morgan and Poppe, pp. 203–13; C. Lloyd-Morgan, 'Blending and Rebottling Old Wines: The Birth and Burial of Arthur in Middle Welsh', in *Adapting Texts and Styles in a Celtic Context: Interdisciplinary Perspectives on Processes of Literary Transfer in the Middle Ages: Studies in Honour of Erich Poppe*, ed. A. Harlos and N. Harlos (Münster, 2016), pp. 155–75.

Lloyd-Morgan argues that translators were clergy working for noble lay patrons.[43] Clergy, particularly in south-east Wales, where most of the translations are from, would be familiar with French. These texts constitute powerful evidence of contact between French and Welsh literature. They are also the only proof of knowledge of Chrétien de Troyes in Wales, since there are no surviving manuscripts of Chrétien's works in Wales. Lloyd-Morgan observes, 'The existence of *Peredur*, *Owein*, and *Gereint* is our only evidence that his works were known in Wales and cannot be taken as proof, for a Welsh redactor adapting them into Welsh could have gained access to the French texts outside Wales.'[44] But this is a very cautious stance. We would assume that a Middle English translation of a French text was a result of a copy of that text being in England – why not Wales, given the presence of the French language in the contexts described above? Why does Wales require a higher standard of proof than England for the use of French? We assume too little of Welsh book culture, perhaps because so little survives. In general, contact between France and Wales was both direct and indirect, with Anglo-Norman England and the French-speaking March of Wales functioning as intermediaries.[45] Most of the adaptations of French texts come from South Wales, where the Norman presence was the most pervasive.[46] The use of French in the March of Wales might hold the key to the transmission of French texts to Welsh centres of manuscript production, as well as to individuals.

I will conclude this chapter with brief discussion of French in the March of Wales, which, as mentioned above, was very likely an important conduit of transmission of French literary texts into Wales. In the medieval period, the March of Wales encompassed a patchwork of marcher lordships such as Glamorgan and Brecon, as well as English shires like Herefordshire, Shropshire and Gloucestershire. Sine the Norman Conquest, it was ruled by a French-speaking Anglo-Norman elite. It was also populated by English-speaking and Welsh-speaking people, with the Welsh people clustered in Herefordshire and Shropshire in areas such as Archenfield and Oswestry. The mixing of different peoples (Welsh, Norman, Flemish, Irish, English) in the region led to a high degree of multilingualism as well as literary contact between different languages.[47] Without question, the March of Wales was a significant

---

[43] Lloyd-Morgan, 'French Texts', p. 52.

[44] Lloyd-Morgan, 'Medieval Welsh Tales', pp. 43–4.

[45] Lloyd Morgan, 'French Texts', p. 47; Surridge, 'Romantic Linguistic Influence', pp. 77–9.

[46] As noted by Lloyd-Morgan, 'French Texts', p. 53.

[47] For discussion, see M. Lampitt, 'Networking the March: A History of Hereford and its Region from the Eleventh through Thirteenth Centuries', *Journal of the*

area of literary production in medieval Britain (home to, for example, the influential Latin writers Gerald of Wales and Geoffrey of Monmouth), and its multilingual character may have contributed to this.

There is considerable evidence for French speakers in Herefordshire, a region on the Welsh border that was often referred to in documentary culture as being *in Waliis*.[48] The Thomas Cantilupe trial of 1307 again attests to this, with around a hundred witnesses in Hereford giving testimony in French.[49] In addition to this evidence on the ground, there are literary examples. One significant French-language author who may have been from North Wales, but who lived near Hereford, is Hue de Rotelande, twelfth-century author of the octosyllabic parodic romances *Ipomedon* (set in southern Italy) and its sequel *Protheselaus* (set in Sicily), dedicated to Gilbert fitz Baderon (d.1191), lord of Monmouth. Hue takes his name from the town of Rhuddlan in Flintshire, but in adulthood seems to have been based near Hereford in Credenhill.[50] He says he knew Walter Map, another Norman-Welsh author associated with Hereford. Hue's works, particularly *Ipomedon*, are better studied than other works from the region and often interpreted through the lens of queer theory and sexuality studies as well as border literature.[51] Though Hue de Rotelande is

---

Mortimer History Society 1 (2017), 55–72; J. B. Smith, *Walter Map and the Matter of Britain* (Philadelphia, 2017).

[48] G. Henley, *Reimagining the Past in the Borderlands of Medieval England and Wales* (Oxford, 2024), Introduction.

[49] See discussion in Lusignan, 'French Language', p. 20; Richter, 'Collecting Miracles'.

[50] T. Hunt, 'Hue de Rotelande (*fl. c.* 1175–1185x90)', *ODNB*, https://doi.org/10.1093/ref:odnb/24146, accessed 5 April 2022; M. D. Legge, *Anglo-Norman Literature and its Background* (Oxford, 1963), pp. 85–96; J. Wogan-Browne, T. Fenster and D. W. Russell, 'Hue de Rotelande, *Ipomedon* [Dean 162], Prologue: London, British Library, MS Cotton Vespasian A.VII, f. 39ʳ', in *Vernacular Literary Theory from the French of Medieval England: Texts and Translations, c. 1120–c. 1450*, ed. and trans. J. Wogan-Browne, T. Fenster and D. W. Russell (Cambridge, 2016), pp. 36–40.

[51] E.g. D. Reeve, 'Queer Arts of Failure in Alan of Lille and Hue of Rotelande', in *Medieval Thought Experiments: Poetry, Hypothesis, and Experience in the European Middle Ages*, ed. P. Knox, J. Morton, and D. Reeve (Turnhout, 2018), 273–96; S. Kocher, 'Desire, Parody, and Sexual Mores in the Ending of Hue de Rotelande's *Impomedon*: An Invitation Through the Looking Glass', in *Sexuality in the Middle Ages and Early Modern Times: New Approaches to a Fundamental Cultural-Historical and Literary-Anthropological Theme*, ed. A. Classen (Berlin, 2008), pp. 429–47; C. Véran-Boussaadia, 'Hue de Rotelande, le jeu de la frontière et la frontière en Je', in *L'Expérience des frontières et les littératures de l'Europe médiévale*, ed. S. Lodén and V. Obry (Paris, 2019), pp. 45–55; S. Crane, 'Knights in Disguise: Identity and Incognito in Fourteenth-Century Chivalry', in *The Stranger in Medieval Society*,

not cited by his contemporaries, the popularity of *Ipomedon* is attested in three Middle English adaptations of the romance.[52]

Another French-language author from twelfth-century Hereford is Simund de Freine, canon of Hereford, who wrote two surviving poems in Anglo-Norman French addressed to Gerald of Wales, an adaptation into French of Boethius's *Consolation of Philosophy* (*Roman de Philosophie*) and a life of St George (*Vie de saint Georges*).[53] The latter two works, Jocelyn Wogan-Browne suggests, were written for William de Vere, bishop of Hereford (1186–98). The *Roman de Philosophie* is the first insular vernacular retelling of the text since the Old English Boethius, and the first retelling in French.[54] In the thirteenth century, the March was also home to Jean, the author of the French biography of William Marshal, who worked in the southern March, possibly lower Gwent.

The March of Wales was also important to English literature, as the place of origin of the earliest recensions of the Middle English Prose *Brut* and *Ancrene Wisse*, and the location of *Piers Plowman* (in the Malvern Hills on the Herefordshire border) by William Langland, who was probably from Ledbury in Herefordshire.[55] In addition, a range of historical and genealogical texts were written in French for Marcher families.[56] The March was also home to the prolific Harley scribe, working in or near the market town of Ludlow in the

---

ed. F. R. P. Akehurst and S. Cain Van D'Elden (Minneapolis, 1997), pp. 63–79; Lampitt, 'Networking the March'.

[52] Wogan-Browne et al., 'Hue de Rotelande', p. 37.

[53] For discussion of his adaptation of Boethius, see A. M. Babbi, 'La réception en Angleterre de la *Consolatio philosophiae*. Le *Roman de Philosophie* de Simund de Freine', in *Boèce au fil du temps: Son influence sur les lettres européennes du Moyen Age à nos jours*, ed. S. Conte, A. Oïffer-Bomsel and M. E. Cantarino-Suñer (Paris, 2019), pp. 369–82; Wogan-Browne et al., 'Simund de Freine, *Roman de philosophie* [Dean 243], Prologue: London, British Library, MS Add. 46,919, f. 107^{ra-b}', in *Vernacular Literary Theory*, ed. and trans. Wogan-Browne et al., pp. 352–4.

[54] J. Wogan-Browne, 'Simund de Freine (*d.* before 1228?)', *ODNB*, https://doi.org/10.1093/ref:odnb/25570, accessed 5 April 2022; Wogan-Browne et al., 'Simund de Freine', p. 352. Though sometimes he is referred to as Simund de Carmarthen, I have not been able to trace the reference to him being from Carmarthen.

[55] L. M. Matheson, *The Prose* Brut: *The Development of a Middle English Chronicle* (Tempe AZ, 1998), pp. 47–9; E. J. Dobson, *The Origins of* Ancrene Wisse (Oxford, 1976), pp. 299–31; J. Wogan-Browne, '"Cest livre liseez ... chescun jour": Women and Reading, c.1230-c.1430', in *Lang Cult*, pp. 239–53 (pp. 245–53); S. Horobin, '"In London and Opelond": The Dialect and Circulation of the C Version of "Piers Plowman"', *Medium Ævum* 74 (2005), 248–69.

[56] Henley, *Reimagining the Past*, pp. 120–30, 135–84.

mid fourteenth century, who produced three major manuscript compilations containing French, Middle English and Latin literature.[57] Keith Busby writes, 'Any notion of the West Midlands/Welsh Marches area as culturally isolated necks of the woods is belied by some of the "classic" French texts included in both Harley 2253 and the somewhat earlier Digby 86.'[58] The Harley scribe's French texts include *Ami et Amile*, Richard de Fournival's *Bestiaire d'amour*, William of Waddington's *Manuel des péchés*, the *Purgatoire saint Patrice*, the *Plainte d'amour*, the *Miroir de sainte église*, and the romance of *Fouke le fitz Waryn*. The multilingual contents of the Harley scribe's compilations provide a sense of the interests of a noble household in the March in the fourteenth century: their interests were in contemporary compositions, not preservations of an older literary culture, and show an impressive network of connections with scribes and texts further afield.

Despite the geographically peripheral position of the March of Wales in relation to perceived 'centres' of literary production in England, such as London, the region was actually central to Anglo-French literature (as well as to Middle English and Welsh literature, given that much surviving literature in Middle Welsh comes from the marcher lordships of Gower and Glamorgan). The centrality of Geoffrey Chaucer and others to the English literary canon has contributed to the traditional focus on London and other English metropolitan centres, while the reality is that these geographic peripheries made substantial contributions to literary production in several languages.

In terms of the study of the French of medieval England, the last several decades have brought a range of new studies of French in England that have questioned long-held assumptions and refined our views of the use of the language in England from the late eleventh to the fifteenth centuries.[59] Wales and the March of Wales are a necessary part of this conversation. Accounting for how much of the literature of the 'French of England' was produced in this supposedly peripheral region destabilises the term. Matthew Lampitt writes, 'It would be a very different picture of French in the British Isles that would emerge were locales like twelfth-century Hereford and fourteenth-century Ludlow to

---

[57] See C. Revard, 'Scribe and Provenance', in *Studies in the Harley Manuscript: The Scribes, Contents, and Social Contexts of British Library MS Harley 2253*, ed. S. Fein (Kalamazoo, 2000), pp. 21–110.

[58] K. Busby, 'Multilingualism, the Harley Scribe, and Johannes Jacobi', in *Insular Books: Vernacular Manuscript Miscellanies in Late Medieval Britain*, ed. M. Connolly and R. L. Radulescu (Oxford, 2015), pp. 49–60 (pp. 59–60).

[59] *Lang Cult*; Wogan-Browne, Fenster, and Russell, ed., *Vernacular Literary Theory*; T. Fenster and C. P. Collette, ed., *The French of Medieval England: Essays in Honour of Jocelyn Wogan-Browne* (Cambridge, 2017).

be extricated from the "French of England". It would, apart from anything else, force a radical rerouting of literary history ... imagine if manuscripts and corpora as central to Middle English studies – and to arguments in favour of emergent English nationalism – as the Ludlow-based Harley 2253 were no longer assimilable to England and English literary history.'[60] To put it another way, the 'French of England' is a limiting term that does not account for distinct regions of Anglo-Norman literary production outside of England. If the texts in the Harley scribe's hand are not claimed as English, or at least not *only* English, then they are something else—perhaps Marcher – and English hegemony over the canon is destabilised. English becomes, much earlier than usually supposed in the usual nationalistic narratives, a language detached from English identity and nationalism, and the 'French of England' label is complicated by the production of some of the texts under its purview in a third space, the March of Wales, which is not entirely English in its identity. The use of French in Wales and the March of Wales, furthermore, constitutes an important case of language being decoupled from national identity, in the sense that users of the language did not consider themselves to be French because they used that language.

Examining French in Wales also helps to decentre the prominence of Middle English literature in the study of the literatures and languages of medieval Britain. Lampitt notes the 'political expediency of a "French of Wales". As a short-hand term, the phrase has a decentring power: it enables a marginalised region of the 'Celtic Fringe' to rival the 'French of England', and it recalibrates a number of the cultural products attributed to the latter.'[61] Furthermore, in the case of Wales, scholars are not burdened by the false model of an inexorable progress towards Middle English heights with a corresponding decline of French, because Wales has a completely different vernacular situation and zone of contact with French: in England, the standard narrative is that French was the language of literature and aristocracy after the Norman conquest until it was replaced by English, while in Wales, Welsh remained the language of literature and aristocracy through the early modern period (though, as I discuss in this chapter, French was in fact used actively as well). French had less influence on Middle Welsh than it did on Middle English, and French loan words in Welsh are scattered and infrequent.[62] From this contrast, we can conclude that French was a dominant language among the elite (including

---

[60] Lampitt, 'Networking the March', p. 42.
[61] Lampitt, 'Networking the March', pp. 42–3.
[62] For loan words, see Trotter, 'Anglo-français', pp. 475–7. These are typically legal words.

lay households and clergy), and among the urban bourgeoisie, particularly the towns settled by Anglo-Normans, but it was not the dominant language in the majority of native Wales, where Welsh remained the principal language of communication, literature, law, medicine and praise poetry. It seems to be mostly as a language of administrative record that French was used in native Wales (Anglo-Norman or Cambro-Norman Wales is a different case). An important facet of this usage is that in Wales, French did not have the cultural prestige that it had in England.[63] As discussed previously, it was not used as a marker of cultural prestige but out of necessity.

An open question that deserves further study, but exceeds the scope of this chapter, is whether the patterns of French and English language usage in the March followed those of England. We cannot assume that the linguistic situation in the March is the same as in the rest of England, for the March was its own contact zone with Wales and other cultures. While the use of French by the elite may track with that in England, it seems that common people in the March spoke French into the fourteenth century, as discussed above, as well as other vernaculars, such as Welsh, that came into contact with French in particular ways, such as in the development of legal terminology. In this sense, the decoupling of Anglo-French from the standard narrative of the rise of English in the thirteenth and fourteenth centuries with a corresponding French decline allows for new perspectives on the use of French as a documentary and literary language in the medieval insular world. The 'French of Britain' is a more appropriate term to encompass the literature in French produced in England, Wales and the March of Wales, given how much of Anglo-French literature was produced outside England's borders.

---

[63] In this sense, the marcher lords are similar to the Normans and Angevins in Sicily and southern Italy, where they did not broadly impose French literary culture even though they brought French with them. I am grateful to Tom O'Donnell and Joshua Byron Smith for pointing out these points of comparison to me. See K. Mallette in this volume.

11

In Between Dutch and French: Multilingual Literary Patronage of the Flemish Nobility in the Fifteenth Century[1]

Bart Besamusca and Lisa Demets

The medieval county of Flanders was multilingual, as residents of the region spoke or wrote in Dutch, French and Latin. The role of French, in particular, both as an omnipresent vernacular in the south of the county and as a bureaucratic and political lingua franca in the overall Dutch-speaking north, has been pertinent in studies on Burgundian rule over Flanders (1384–1482).[2] Historians and literary historians have tried to trace the implications of this remarkable situation for the literary culture of Flanders. Some scholars have defined the French and Dutch literary writing culture in Flanders as 'transcultural', meaning the region is shaped by the interaction of different languages, cultures and communities.[3] Others deny that the presence of two different vernacular languages resulted in a simple exchange between two separate cultures, but argue that both languages were in fact part of one

---

[1] This article results from the research project 'The Multilingual Dynamics of the Literary Culture of Medieval Flanders, *c*.1200–*c*.1500' (https://multilingualdynamics.sites.uu.nl/), funded by the Dutch Research Council, and from the project 'Multilingual Encounters in the Late Medieval Town. Rewriting History in Multilingual Social and Political Contexts in Late Medieval Flanders and Brabant, 1380–1500', funded by the Research Foundation Flanders (FWO). We would like to thank the editors of this volume for their careful reading of the first draft of our contribution.

[2] M. Boone, 'Langue, pouvoirs et dialogue: Aspects linguistiques de la communication entre les ducs de Bourgogne et leurs sujets flamands (1385–1505)', *Revue du Nord* 379 (2009), 9–33; C. A. J. Armstrong, 'The Language Question in the Low Countries: The Use of French and Dutch by the Dukes of Burgundy and their Administration', in *Europe in the Late Middle Ages*, ed. J. R. Hale and J. R. Highfield (London, 1965), pp. 386–409.

[3] *The Multilingual Muse: Transcultural Poetics in the Burgundian Netherlands*, ed. A. Armstrong and E. Strietman (Cambridge, 2017).

and the same reading culture.[4] Margriet Hoogvliet, for instance, identifies a 'cultural continuity' in the Southern Low Countries and Northern France, as people with different mother tongues were reading the same texts, translations or very similar works.[5] Seen from this perspective, medieval Flanders was a 'contact zone' between the French and Dutch languages, and the literary culture within the Flemish contact zone was shared by French- and Dutch-speakers alike. In this contribution, we focus on the social profile and literary patronage of some Flemish readers who actively invested in both French and Dutch literature. We will show that they were 'at the intersection' not only of French and Dutch literature (even though their mother tongue was Dutch), but also, in a social perspective, of court, city and rural life.[6]

According to Mary Louise Pratt, the interaction of two or more languages in one social and physical space results in clashes and struggles between languages, related to the cultural and/or political hegemony of one dominant group.[7] However, in more recent research, scholars tend to see the concept of a multilingual contact zone in a less conflictual light: as a place or space where different languages interact in an enriching way, stimulating social exchange. Literary scholar Jonathan Hsy, for example, describes a 'multilingual contact zone' as 'any venue that facilitates ongoing interactions between people and exchange among languages'.[8] The question whether multilingualism has negative or positive implications is not solely related to our modern globalizing world. In the Middle Ages, multilingualism was characterised in both negative and positive terms. On the one hand, medieval people feared the consequences of

[4] M. Hoogvliet, 'Religious Reading in French and Middle Dutch in the Southern Low Countries and Northern France (c.1400–c.1520)', in *MFLCOF*, pp. 323–48 (p. 333). See also: M. Hoogvliet, '"Mez puy que je le enten, je suy conten": Bilingual Cities of Readers in the Southern Low Countries and Northern France (c.1400–c.1550)', in *Mittelalterliche Stadtsprachen*, ed. M. Selig and S. Ehrlich (Regensburg, 2016), pp. 45–61.

[5] Hoogvliet, 'Religious Reading', p. 338.

[6] Margriet Hoogvliet uses the terms 'intercultures' and 'in-betweenness'. Hoogvliet, 'Religious Reading', p. 333.

[7] M. L. Pratt, 'Arts of the Contact Zone', *Profession* 91 (1991), 33–40. In sociolinguistic research, this 'inequality' between languages is also stressed from a socio-cultural perspective, see for instance: R. Rindler Schjerve and E. Vetter, 'Historical Sociolinguistics and Multilingualism: Theoretical and Methodological Issues in the Development of a Multifunctional Framework', in *Diglossia and Power: Language Policies and Practice in the 19th Century Habsburg Empire*, ed. R. Rindler Schjerve (Berlin, 2003), pp. 35–68 (p. 47).

[8] J. Hsy, *Trading Tongues: Merchants, Multilingualism, and Medieval Literature* (Columbus, 2013), p. 4. See also S. Gaunt, *Marco Polo's 'Le Devisement du Monde': Narrative Voice, Language and Diversity* (Cambridge, 2013).

the multilingual melting pot: the use of different languages in a specific space or context could prevent communication and understanding and result in problems and conflicts (Tower of Babel).[9] On the other hand, medieval religious writers were intrigued by the miracle of the Pentecost: the empowerment by God to speak in different tongues. Medieval polyglot translators, who could bridge the gap between languages, were therefore held in high esteem.

Language may reflect asymmetrical relations of power. In the case of Flanders, French operated as a high-status lingua franca spoken by its social, bureaucratic and political elite. Particularly eminent during the rule of the Burgundian dukes (1384–1482), this social distinction between Dutch- and French-language users created political conflicts related to language and led to the demand for the use of Dutch in administration and juridical courts in the early fifteenth century.[10] In this context, bilingualism or trilingualism served the social and cultural capital and ambitions of certain social climbers. The institutionalisation and bureaucratisation of the Flemish administration under the last Flemish counts and first Burgundian dukes resulted in a new community of multilingual civil servants. Many of these freshly appointed bailiffs and state officials stemmed from the Flemish Dutch-speaking lower nobility, who actively invested in French-Dutch bilingualism.[11] Moreover, these state officials did not only play a role as intermediaries between French and Dutch, but also between urban and rural life, and between city and court.[12] Hanno Wijsman has categorised the new administrative and noble officials inspired by the Burgundian court's literary patronage as 'new men at court'.[13] Indeed, the Burgundian princes invested in a new bureaucratic and noble elite. However, their court identity is just one factor in the many networks in which these families played an important political, social and economic role. These noble officials are genuine go-betweens

[9] A. Classen, 'Multilingualism in the Middle Ages: Theoretical and Historical Reflections: An Introduction', in *Multilingualism in the Middle Ages and Early Modern Age: Communication and Miscommunication in the Premodern World*, ed. A. Classen (Berlin, 2016), pp. 1–46 (p. 5).

[10] Armstrong, 'The Language Question in the Low Countries'; Boone, 'Langue, pouvoirs et dialogue'.

[11] J. Dumolyn, *Staatsvorming en vorstelijke ambtenaren in het graafschap Vlaanderen (1419–1477)* (Leuven, 2003), p. 62. See also F. Buylaert, *Eeuwen van ambitie: de adel in laat-middeleeuws Vlaanderen* (Brussels, 2010).

[12] C. Cannon, 'Class Distinction and the French of England', in *Traditions and Innovations in the Study of Middle English Literature: The Influence of Derek Brewer*, ed. C. Brewer and B. Windeatt (Cambridge, 2013), pp. 48–59.

[13] H. Wijsman, *Luxury Bound: Illustrated Manuscript Production and Noble and Princely Book Ownership in the Burgundian Netherlands (1400–1550)* (Turnhout, 2010), pp. 481–3. On De Baenst see p. 493.

between court, urban and rural society: they appear as bailiffs in the countryside, as aldermen in the city and as administrators, valets and councillors at court.

Identifying this distinctive community within the larger group of the Flemish nobility allows us to contextualise the writing contexts of literary manuscripts and texts in various languages commissioned or written by these middle social strata of Flemish nobility in the fifteenth century. In our contribution, we scrutinise the literary manuscripts and texts of some of these noble 'state officials' who played an important role in the bureaucratisation under Burgundian rule. We present three case studies: Jan van den Berghe, the De Baenst family and the Van Gistel family. The Burgundian court included men and women from various regions within the Burgundian realm, and the peculiarity of the Flemings at the Burgundian court has been well addressed by several researchers in studies of politics, economic wealth, lordship, land-holding and social networks, precisely because of their Dutch-French bilingualism.[14] However, the relation between the literary patronage and language skills of this elite has never been fully scrutinised in comparison. The Van den Berghe, De Baenst and Van Gistel families were all Dutch native speakers stemming from the rural elite of Flanders, and – once involved in Burgundian politics and francophone administration – founded a complex social network in the most important Flemish cities.[15] We will show that these noble families not only invested in French-language proficiency for pragmatic reasons, but were also mediating between the extensive literary cultures in French and Dutch. In particular, their varied social networks are important, not only in connecting people, but also in sharing and inspiring literary culture, both in French and Dutch.[16]

Jan van den Berghe, Lord of Watervliet

Jan van den Berghe (d.1439) is our most atypical case study. First, only two extant manuscripts can be attributed to his library. Second, although his political career was remarkably successful, unlike the other individuals presented here he was unable to ensure the same position for his offspring.

---

[14] The multilingual capabilities of the Flemish nobility and administrators have been addressed on political and diplomatic levels, in particular as functionaries in Zeeland and Holland. See for example M. Boone, 'Une famille au service de l'Etat bourguignon naissant: Roland et Jean d'Uutkerke, nobles flamands dans l'entourage de Philippe le Bon', *Revue du Nord* 77 (1995), 233–56. See also M. Damen, *De staat van dienst: De gewestelijke ambtenaren van Holland en Zeeland in de Bourgondische periode (1425–1482)* (Hilversum, 2000).

[15] F. Buylaert, 'Sociale mobiliteit bij stedelijke elites in laatmiddeleeuws Vlaanderen: Een gevalstudie over de Vlaamse familie De Baenst', *Jaarboek voor Middeleeuwse Geschiedenis* 8 (2005), 201–51.

[16] Hoogvliet, 'Religious Reading', p. 325

And third, Van den Berghe was not only a patron, but also the author of a literary work.

Van den Berghe was born in the third quarter of the fourteenth century in Handzame, a small rural estate in the centre of the county of Flanders. Van den Berghe belonged to the lower rural nobility of Flanders. His father, Joos, was a local lord of Watervliet, in Handzame, and of Booitshoeke, in Veurne. Joos was frequently appointed alderman of the Liberty of Bruges, the rich rural district surrounding the medieval metropole Bruges, and he became burgomaster of the Liberty in 1386. Jan's mother Germaine of Lichtervelde had important connections at the Flemish court: she was a daughter of Roger of Lichtervelde, councillor to the Flemish count Louis of Male (1346–84). Van den Berghe married Margaret van Rooden in 1398, and in 1399, he was named alderman of the Liberty of Bruges for the first time, launching his political career.

Shortly thereafter, Van den Berghe was appointed bailiff and viscount of Wijnendale as substitute for Jan of Namen, brother of Willem II, Count of Namen. He maintained good relations with the comital family and carried on an extensive correspondence with Jeanne de Harcourt, widow of Count Willem II, who lived on her dower estate and castle in Béthune after the death of her husband in 1418.[17] A selection of this French letter collection (1420–37) was bound with all sorts of administrative (and mostly Dutch) family documents in a fifteenth-century register concerning the loans of the Van den Berghe family, now partially preserved in the Archives départementales du Nord in Lille.[18] The correspondence in the register offers a unique insight into the noble networks and political involvement of Jan van den Berghe. He frequently informed the dowager countess about the whereabouts and policies of the Burgundian duke. The letters also included concerns of a personal nature. Jan van den Berghe asked the dowager countess, for example, to welcome his son, Joos, to her court in Béthune. In her reply, she referred to the reason for his stay, which was to learn the French language ('de le voloir recepvoir deleis moy en mon hosteil pour aprendre le langage franchoy').[19] According to Egied Strubbe, Jan van den Berghe also hoped to educate his son into the 'noble manners' of the Burgundian court. Indeed, as mentioned in the court manual of Éléonore de Poitiers, viscountess of Veurne, 'Madame de Namur'– as Jeanne

---

[17] E. I. Strubbe, 'De briefwisseling tussen Jan van den Berghe en Johanna van Harcourt (1420–1437)', *Bulletin de la Commission Royale* 125 (1959), 511–60 (p. 523). The article includes an edition of the letter collection.

[18] Lille, Archives départementales du Nord, reg. B 4025. On the Dutch family record book of Jan of Dadizele, bailiff of Ghent, see also F. Buylaert and J. Haemers, 'Record-keeping and Status Performance in the Early Modern Low Countries', *Past and Present* 230 (2016), 131–50.

[19] Strubbe, 'De briefwisseling', p. 531.

de Harcourt is called – was known for having educated and instructed in court manners various Burgundian duchesses, among them Isabel of Portugal, the wife of Philip the Good (1419–67).[20] Despite his francophone and courtly education, however, Joos would not have the same regional administrative career as his father, but ruled as a local lord in Watervliet in Handzame.[21]

On 15 August 1401, the Burgundian Duke Philip the Bold (1384–1404) appointed Jan van den Berghe as bailiff of Vier Ambachten (the rural district around Ghent). From then on, Van den Berghe was established in the Burgundian administration. In 1405, he became bailiff in Kortrijk, and in 1407 in Veurne. During or shortly after his office in Kortrijk, he wrote *Protocole in Vlaemssche*, a Dutch formulary book of standard charters and deeds.[22] In 1411, in the midst of a political crisis, Duke John the Fearless (1405–19), Philip's successor, appointed Van den Berghe as *schout* (sheriff) of Bruges. A year earlier, the craft guilds of Bruges had openly contested the implications of the *Calfvel*, a charter imposed by the bailiff at the time, who was forced to flee the town.[23] In 1411, Van den Berghe picked up the charter from the archives in Lille and delivered it to the Bruges citizens. Shortly thereafter, it was publicly destroyed and torn to pieces by the craft guilds. However, the Bruges privileges stipulated that the sheriff of Bruges could not be an inhabitant of the Liberty of Bruges, so Van den Berghe could not remain in this role. Therefore a few months later in 1411, Van den Berghe became water bailiff of the port city of Sluis, an important strategic position at the time. As a reward for his services during the Bruges crisis, John the Fearless sold the 'foresterie' of the large forest in Houthulst, including the rights to hunt and the fining of poaching, to Van den Berghe in 1414. Between 1412 and 1414, he became a councillor in the Council of Flanders, the highest juridical court in the county, a position he held for the rest of his life. Since

[20] Éléonore de Poitiers noted that Jeanne de Harcourt, 'la plus sçachante' ('the cleverest'), wrote everything down in her own court manual: 'Madame de Namur comme j'ouys dire estoit la plus sçachante de touts estats que dame qui fut au royaume de France, et avoit un grand libvre où tout estoit escrit' ('Madame de Namur, as I heard tell, was the cleverest lady of any estate who was in the kingdom of France and had a large book where everything was written down'). See J. Paviot, 'Éléonore de Poitiers: les états de France (Les Honneurs de la Cour)', *Annuaire-Bulletin de la Société de l'histoire de France* 1996, 75–118 (p. 89).

[21] The fact that the Van den Berghe family did not consolidate a firm position at the court might be due to their close relations with the Van Uutkerke family: the literary society hosted by the Burgundian nobleman Roeland van Uutkerke in Bruges probably inspired Van den Berghe to write his *Kaetspel ghemoralizeert*. In 1441, Jan van Uutkerke was executed on grounds of sodomy, which caused a huge scandal and forced Roeland and his wife to sell most of their properties.

[22] Brussels, Algemeen Rijksarchief, reg. 1243.

[23] See J. Dumolyn, *De Brugse opstand van 1436–1438* (Heule, 1997).

complaints about the francophone Council in Lille were addressed to Countess Margaret of Flanders in 1404 and then to John the Fearless in 1405, the Council moved its seat to Dutch-speaking Ghent in 1407.[24] These lower or new noble elites who already held local or regional services on behalf of the Duke were quite commonly recruited by the Council of Flanders.[25] Although most – like Jan van den Berghe – were not university-schooled, these noblemen had an excellent knowledge of the local customary law as a result of their experience.

Van den Berghe's juridical career inspired him to write two additional Dutch works: one technical juridical treatise and one literary work with a juridical content. The *Jurisdictien van Vlaenderen* deals with contemporary juridical and legal questions, problems and controversies.[26] The *Kaetspel ghemoralizeert*, written around 1431, is an allegorical description of a trial by means of the popular medieval ballgame ('jeu de paume', a version of tennis). The text consists of moralizing anecdotes ('exempel') drawn from his own experience in the courtroom. Interestingly, in the epilogue of the text, Van den Berghe refers to a literary society hosted by a well-respected nobleman in his Bruges residence.[27] Van den Berghe dedicated his work to this noble host who has been identified as Roeland van Uutkerke by modern scholars. Van Uutkerke also came from a family of rural nobility in the Liberty of Bruges.[28] Thanks to his successes on the battlefield in the service of John the Fearless, Van Uutkerke was held in high esteem by the Burgundian duke and became one of the most important military captains of John's successor, Philip the Good. Owing to his bilingual skills, he played an important role in the diplomatic and military conquest of Holland and Zeeland in 1425–8.[29] In 1430, he joined the esteemed knightly order of the Golden Fleece founded by the duke.

---

[24] The language issues and in particular the exclusively francophone council and administration of the counts was a recurrent topic in the negotiations between the representatives of the Flemish cities with Margaret of Male (1384–1405) and later John the Fearless: W. Prevenier, *Handelingen van de Leden en van de Staten van Vlaanderen (1384–1405)* (Brussels, 1959), p. 320; A. Zoete, *Handelingen van de Leden en van de Staten van Vlaanderen (1405–1419)* 2 vols. (Brussels, 1981–1982), I, 10–11, 21–3.

[25] Dumolyn, *Staatsvorming*, p. 62.

[26] E. I. Strubbe, 'Jean van den Berghe, écrivain et juriste flamand (13..–1439)', *Bulletin de la Commission royale des anciennes lois et ordonnances de Belgique* 12.3 (1926), 174–201 (p. 183). In a sixteenth-century manuscript, now preserved in the University Library of Ghent (MS 1627), the *Jurisdictien van Vlaenderen* is bound together with a legal treatise by Philip Wielant (*Tractaat van den leenrechten na den hove van Vlaenderen*).

[27] Jan van den Berghe, *Dat kaetspel ghemoralizeert*, ed. J. Roetert Frederikse (Leiden, 1915), p. 110.

[28] Boone, 'Une famille au service', p. 236.

[29] Boone, 'Une famille au service', p. 244; Damen, *Staat van dienst*, p. 256.

His social network of (noble) literary enthusiasts inspired Van den Berghe's first steps into literature in the last years of his life. These details on the literary society offer an indirect insight into Van den Berghe's literary interests and cultural activities. In *Kaetspel ghemoralizeert* he attributes his inspiration to a group discussion on 'the moralised chess game'; this might refer to the *Ludus scaccorum* by Jacobus de Cessolis (*c.*1250–*c.*1322), or to one of the French or Dutch translations.[30] Subsequently, the group discussed which other games would be suitable for such a moralised allegory. Furthermore, the description points to the fact that this informal literary society frequently gathered to read new poems, rondels, ballades and other sorts of poetry to each other. Unlike the institutionalised all-male Chambers of Rhetoric in the Low Countries,[31] this literary group was mixed-gender, as a 'young lady' performed an 'excellent new poem' the night they discussed the moralised chess game. It is not explicitly mentioned whether the literary group jointly read Dutch or French poems and literature. The first is probable, but it is not unlikely that the participants read both languages. Coincidentally or not, only a few years later, in 1435, an anonymous Bruges shearer finished a French *Jeu de la paulme*. The content of this French version does not compare to Van den Berghe's *Kaetspel*, as it is not an allegorical treatise on the juridical system but a work in spiritual-moralizing mode.[32] It may be that the shearer was inspired by the same discussion. This could imply that the informal literary society was open to other social classes, including those of the urban middle classes, and that the group read, wrote and performed both Dutch and French texts.

The De Baenst family in Bruges and Ghent

Belonging to the lower nobility of Cadsant in the fourteenth century, the De Baenst family appears in Flanders around 1300 among the aldermen of the Liberty of Bruges. They became one of the most influential noble families in the fifteenth-century urban communities of Bruges, Sluis and Ghent, as well

---

[30] It is likely that Van den Berghe refers to a Middle Dutch version. In the early fifteenth century, the *Ludus scaccorum* was translated into Dutch by Franconis, probably a Fleming. Around 1434, a certain A. Drubbel copied a manuscript with the Middle Dutch *Scaecspel* in Bruges. See *Dat Scaecspel*, ed. G. Van Schaick Avelingh (Leiden, 1912).

[31] Chambers of Rhetoric were literary societies with a guild structure typical of the Low Countries. See A.-L. Van Bruaene, *Om beters wille: rederijkerskamers en de stedelijke cultuur in de Zuidelijke Nederlanden (1400–1650)* (Amsterdam, 2008).

[32] Two fifteenth-century manuscripts are preserved in the Royal Library (KBR) in Brussels: MS 9390 and MS 11120–22. See L. Schepens, 'Le Livre du jeu de la paulme moralisé', *Revue belge de philologie et d'histoire* 40.3 (1962), 804–14.

as the countryside and the Burgundian court.[33] The De Baenst family is known for its literary patronage, and a multilingual collection of manuscripts related to members of this family is still extant today. Three cousins had a particular interest in books: Jan III (d.1486), Roeland I (d.1484) and Guy II (d. before 1502).[34] Each represents a different branch of the De Baenst family: Jan was most active in Bruges, Roeland in Ghent and Guy in Sluis.[35] Additionally, Jan III's nephew Paul de Baenst (d.1497), son of his brother Louis, was interested in humanistic works.[36] The literary interests of Jan III de Baenst and Roeland I de Baenst are particularly relevant for understanding the relation between French and Dutch. Not only their local environment, but also their political and social interests shaped the languages of their books.

Jan III de Baenst is well known as a literary patron. As the eldest son of Jan II de Baenst, he stemmed from the senior branch of the family.[37] He settled in Bruges where he established the *Sint-Jorishof* (St. George Court, later 'Hof van Watervliet') as his residence. This made him a near-neighbour of

[33] Buylaert, 'Sociale mobiliteit'.

[34] C. Van Hoorebeeck, 'La ville, le prince et leurs officiers en Flandre à la fin du Moyen Âge: livres et lectures de la famille de Baenst', *Le Moyen Âge* 113 (2007), 45–67. There are no manuscripts preserved which can be linked to Guy II de Baenst, but a confiscation list of his goods, drawn up between 1484–1485 during the Flemish revolt that targeted pro-Habsburg politicians, gives insight into some of his books. The first manuscript mentioned is a missal which was bought by the Saint George guild of Ghent. The second book was probably a print (or a manuscript copy) of the Dutch *Fasciculus temporum*. A third book in his collection was a printed edition of *De proprietatibus rerum* by Bartholomeus Anglicus.

[35] Buylaert, 'Sociale mobiliteit', pp. 204–14.

[36] Paul de Baenst was the first of the De Baenst family to attend university (in Leuven). He obtained a doctorate in law in Padua in 1474 and was appointed rector there. In 1479, he became president of the Council of Flanders, the highest juridical court in the county. Paul de Baenst acquired a second hand two-volume work, originally written under the patronage of the influential Ten Duinen abbot, Jan Crabbe. The manuscripts (now Wells-next-the-Sea, Holkham Hall, Library of the Earl of Leicester, MS 311) contain several works by Virgil: *Bucolica*, *Georgica* and *Aeneid*. The last text was based on a 1428 edition by the Italian humanist Maffeo Vegio. The manuscripts also contain texts to help understanding Virgil's works, such as a commentary by the Latin author Servius, a Latin glossary by Mico Grammaticus and a rarer text, the *Interpretationes Vergilianae*, a rhetorical commentary on Virgil's *Aeneid* by the Roman author Donatius. See: Van Hoorebeeck, 'La ville', p. 59; N. Geirnaert, 'Classical Texts in Bruges around 1473: Cooperation of Italian Scribes, Bruges Parchment Rulers, Illuminators and Bookbinders for Johannes Crabbe, Abbot of Les Dunes Abbey', *Transactions of the Cambridge Bibliographical Society* 10 (1992), 173–81.

[37] Buylaert, 'Sociale mobiliteit', pp. 204–9.

the famous Bruges bibliophile, Louis de Gruuthuse.[38] Like his predecessors, he started his career as bailiff and alderman in the Liberty of Bruges, but he quickly became involved in Bruges city politics, first as alderman and later as burgomaster. He was also a courtier and councillor at the court of Philip the Good (1419–67) and Charles the Bold (1467–77). In 1466, he intervened on behalf of Anthonis de Roovere, one of the most productive Dutch poets in Bruges, with the Burgundian prince Charles and the Bruges city government, which resulted in a yearly allowance for the Bruges poet. Five extant manuscripts can be traced to Jan III's library, which must have been much more substantial during his lifetime.[39]

The first volume is a Latin Book of Hours (Use of Rome), probably ordered around 1440–50 before his marriage to Margareta de Fever, as her coat of arms is absent.[40] Typical Bruges patron saints such as Saint Donatian are missing from the calendar. Jan de Baenst started building St George Court only after his marriage. The Book of Hours was therefore copied before his definite settling in Bruges. The manuscript holds traces of at least six pilgrim badges and *insignes* probably added by Jan III de Baenst himself after one of his journeys to Jerusalem.[41] A second manuscript was written around 1470–5 in Bruges and is a French multi-text codex including the *Histoire de la vraie croix* and the *Pénitence d'Adam* in the prose versions written by the Bruges stationer and printer Colard Mansion for Louis de Gruuthuse.[42] Was this manuscript inspired by the example of Gruuthuse? Jan III de Baenst's literary interests were clearly francophone: he also owned two volumes of Augustine's *De civitate Dei* in a French translation by Raoul de Presles.[43] In addition to these francophone manuscripts, he also commissioned a unique Dutch translation of Christine de Pizan's *Cité des dames*.[44] It has been suggested the translation was made by Anthonis de Roovere.[45] The only extant manuscript was copied around 1475,

---

[38] Van Hoorebeeck, 'La ville', p. 50.

[39] Van Hoorebeeck, 'La ville', p. 50.

[40] Brussels, KBR, MS IV 746.

[41] H. van Asperen, *Pelgrimstekens op perkament: originele en nageschilderde bedevaarts-souvenirs in religieuze boeken (ca. 1450–ca. 1530)* (Edam, 2009), p. 313.

[42] Paris, Bibliothèque de l'Arsenal, MS 5092.

[43] Lille, Médiathèque Jean Levy, MS 647–8.

[44] London, British Library, MS Additional 20698. It has been suggested that the work was written for his daughters. See O. S. H. Lie, M. Meuwese, M. Aussems and H. Joldersma, *Christine de Pizan in Bruges:* Le Livre de la Cité des Dames *as* Het Bouc van de Stede der Vrauwen *(London, British Library, Add. 20698)* (Hilversum, 2015).

[45] J. Oosterman, 'Anthonis de Roovere. Het werk: overlevering, toeschrijving en plaatsbepaling', *Jaarboek De Fonteine* (1995–1996), 29–140, here pp. 33–4.

but the miniatures were never completed, because in 1477, during an uprising after the death of Duke Charles the Bold, Jan III de Baenst was arrested and tortured for his involvement in the pro-Burgundian city governments.[46]

The De Baenst family was not only inspired by the literary endeavours of Burgundian courtiers such as Gruuthuse, but also by local and urban literary practices, as is shown by Jan III de Baenst's cousin, Roeland I de Baenst. He was the son of Antoine de Baenst, the brother of Jan II de Baenst. Roeland was the first of this branch of the De Baenst family who left the Liberty of Bruges in order to settle in Ghent. As many members of the De Baenst family were already involved in the Liberty of Bruges, Antoine de Baenst aimed at Ghent and married many of his children to important Ghent families.[47] Roeland and his sister were married to members of the Utenhove family, one of the most prominent Ghent patrician families.

Little is known about Roeland's literary patronage, but we do have one autograph manuscript partially written by him and continued by his son Antoine and other relatives. Roeland probably started writing around 1476 and continued until his death in 1486.[48] This so-called 'memory book' is a typical Ghent genre of local history-writing, where a list of the Ghent aldermen was provided with additional historical notes.[49] This memory book is highly personal: the list of aldermen (1301–1487) in the De Baenst memory book was written by Roeland, and the historical notes were provided by Antoine. With this 'memory book', this Ghent branch of the De Baenst family adopted the historiographical and literary customs of the Ghent political elite.[50] As far as we know, neither the Bruges nor the Sluis branches of the family held similar family records.

The manuscript contains other texts as well, most related to fiefs of the De Baenst family. Almost all the texts were written in Dutch, but the codex includes one French text. This is a short summary of the twelfth-century *De multro traditione et occisione gloriosi Karoli comitis Flandriarum* by Galbert of Bruges, which narrates the murder of the Flemish count Charles the Good and thus refers back to the history of Bruges. According to Jeff Rider, the fragment was

---

[46] J. Haemers, *For the Common Good: State Power and Urban Revolts in the Reign of Mary of Burgundy (1477–1482)* (Turnhout, 2009).

[47] Buylaert, 'Sociale mobiliteit', 209–12.

[48] Bruges, Openbare Bibliotheek, MS 442; A.-L. Van Bruaene, *De Gentse memorieboeken als spiegel van stedelijk historisch bewustzijn (14de tot 16de eeuw)* (Gent, 1998), 359–65.

[49] Van Bruaene, *De Gentse memorieboeken*, 78.

[50] Many Ghent patricians owned personal memory books, such as the Borluuts. See Van Bruaene, *De Gentse memorieboeken*, p. 299.

written by Roeland or Antoine,[51] but Anne-Laure Van Bruaene has suggested that another author is at work here: perhaps Jan or Jacob de Baenst, sons of Antoine.[52] The so-called *Résumé de Baenst* is the only medieval witness of Galbert of Bruges's text. Nevertheless, the exact motivations for writing the *Résumé* and its place in the memory book remain food for discussion.[53]

The Van Gistel family

Like the De Baenst family, the Van Gistel family were highly respected aristocrats in late medieval Flanders.[54] They held important fiefs in the countryside, were involved in Bruges city politics as burgomasters and were loyal servants of the comital family, as by tradition they held the office of chamberlain to the counts. Two of the most influential individuals were Jan VI (d.1417) and Jacob II (d.1488). Jean Froissart called Jan 'le grant seigneur de Ghistelles'.[55] He was the last chamberlain to the count and was appointed the first governor and captain-general of Flanders by Philip the Bold when the latter inherited the county in 1384. Jacob was Lord of Dudzeele and Straten. From 1477, he served as councillor to Mary of Burgundy (1477–82) and later as chamberlain to her widower Maximilian of Austria. As a pro-Habsburg party member, Jacob had much to endure during the uprising against the regency of the Habsburg Archduke after Duchess Mary's death (1482–92). On 23 February 1484, for instance, militias destroyed his castle in Dudzele. Finally, shortly after Maximilian was imprisoned, Jacob was beheaded on the Bruges marketplace on 8 March 1488.[56]

---

[51] J. Rider, *The Murder, Betrayal, and Slaughter of the Glorious Charles, Count of Flanders* (New Haven, 2013), p. xix.

[52] Van Bruaene, *De Gentse memorieboeken*, pp. 79–80.

[53] The memory book was written and compiled in a turbulent political period, the so-called Flemish revolt (1482–1492) against the regency of the Habsburg archduke Maximilian of Austria. As a result, the inclusion of the 'Résumé de Baenst' has been interpreted as an anti-Habsburg statement. Nevertheless, as Frederik Buylaert has shown, the attitude of the De Baenst family (with the exception of Jan Zegerszoon de Baenst) was more pragmatic in this conflict. They remained on good terms with the rebel regime as well as with supporters of the archduke. See Buylaert, 'Sociale mobiliteit', p. 225.

[54] See F. Buylaert, *Repertorium van de Vlaamse adel (ca. 1350–ca. 1500)* (Ghent, 2011); Wijsman, *Luxury Bound*, pp. 350–5. See also E. Warlop, *The Flemish Nobility before 1300* (Kortrijk, 1976), II, 1, 840–8.

[55] *Corpus Catalogorum Belgii: The Medieval Booklists of the Southern Low Countries*, vol. 1, *Province of West Flanders*, ed. A. Derolez and B. Victor (Brussels, 1997), p. 183.

[56] J. Haemers, *De strijd om het regentschap over Filips de Schone: opstand, facties en geweld in Brugge, Gent en Ieper (1482–1488)* (Ghent, 2014), pp. 118, 273.

Members of the Dutch-speaking Van Gistel family were involved in the French-oriented literary culture of the Flemish court. The evidence for their participation includes a manuscript that is now housed in Ghent (Universiteitsbibliotheek, MS 6).[57] It is a copy of the French *Prose Tristan*, produced between 1470 and 1480 for Jacob, whose coat of arms appears in the lower margin of the frontispiece. The codex is connected to the courtly milieu in two ways. First, the *Prose Tristan* was a favourite in circles of the highest nobility. Secondly, the illustration is attributed to Loyset Liédet, who illustrated a series of manuscripts at the request of Philip the Good.[58]

Additional evidence of the cultural interactions between the Van Gistel family and the Flemish court is provided by the book ownership of two other family members: Margareta and Gerard van Gistel. Margareta (d.1495) and her husband Pierre de Roubaix possessed a manuscript of *Le Mesnagier de Paris*, a treatise on household management, written in French and made after 1440 (Paris, BnF, n.a.f. 6739). The scribe's exemplar was a manuscript owned by Philip the Good (Paris, BnF, MS fr. 12477).[59] The other member of the Van Gistel family, Gerard, was Lord of Beveren and married to Alix de Wancourt. They, or one of their children, owned a manuscript which was produced around 1445 and contains four French texts: the *Chronique de France et de Flandre*, *Les Voeux du héron*, the *Chronique normande abrégée* and *Les Sept Articles de la foy* (Brussels, Koninklijke Bibliotheek van België, MS 10432–5). The connection with the ducal court is established by the fact that the codex entered the Burgundian book collection before 1469.[60]

Jan VI van Gistel is a prime example of a Flemish nobleman mediating between the literary cultures in French and Dutch. This can be deduced from the inventory of his estate which was made in 1417 and lists his twenty-seven books and three scrolls.[61] Even though the list is limited in its specification of the languages of the texts, it offers valuable insights into what exactly Jan read.

---

[57] See A. Derolez, H. Defoort and F. Vanlangenhove, *Medieval Manuscripts: Ghent University Library* (Ghent, 2017), p. 23. See also the description on the website of 'Medieval Francophone Literary Culture Outside France'.

[58] Wijsman, *Luxury Bound*, p. 354; M. Smeyers, *Vlaamse miniaturen van de 8ste tot het midden van de 16de eeuw: De middeleeuwse wereld op perkament* (Leuven, 1998), pp. 313–16.

[59] See *Corpus Catalogorum Belgii: The Medieval Booklists of the Southern Low Countries*, vol. 5, *Dukes of Burgundy*, ed. T. Falmagne and B Van den Abeele (Leuven, 2016), nos 5.102, 8.127. See also Wijsman, *Luxury Bound*, p. 354.

[60] See *Corpus Catalogorum Belgii*, ed. Falmagne and Van den Abeele, V, nos 5.98 and 8.290. See also Wijsman, *Luxury Bound*, pp. 354–5.

[61] See *Corpus Catalogorum Belgii*, ed. Derolez and Victor, I, 183–5.

Like the family members just mentioned, he appreciated French literature. Three items of the list mention that a text was 'in waelsch' ('in French'): a 'bouc van Renaere ende van Ysengeny' (no. 7), a 'bouc van der bibelle' (no. 11) and a 'bouc van Romilis ende van Rome' (no. 13). The *Roman de Renart* (no. 7) is particularly interesting for our purposes, more so than the French biblical text (no. 11) and the chronicle about Romulus and Rome (no. 13), because we know that the Reynardian stories were highly popular in Flanders, both in French and Dutch.[62] Jan participated in this bilingual literary tradition.

Four items on Jan's list are specified as being in 'vlaemsche' or 'dietsch' (which, we think, both refer to Dutch): a 'dietsch bouc' (no. 3), a 'bouc [...] van den spighel storiael' (no. 8), a 'rollekin van groetenesse van Onser Vrouwen' (no. 23) and a 'bouc sprekende van ystorien van Ingeland ende van den ruddere metten leeuwe ende andren' (no. 25). Here it is interesting to note that Jan shared his appreciation of the *Spiegel historiael* (no. 8), the Middle Dutch adaptation of Vincent of Beauvais' *Speculum historiale*, with many other Dutch-speaking Flemish individuals from various social-cultural milieus, as indicated by the manuscript transmission and notes of ownership.[63] It is also noteworthy that he possessed a multi-text codex containing a chronicle about the history of England and a chivalric romance (no. 25). The chronicle (probably a Dutch rendition of the *Roman de Brut*) fits in very well with the strong Flemish economic, social and cultural ties with England. The 'ruddere metten leeuwe', the Dutch version of Chrétien de Troyes's *Chevalier au lion*, which has not come down to us, links Jan's literary interests to those of the Flemish court, where the romances of Chrétien, and in particular his *Perceval* and its Continuations, were very popular.[64] In this context, it is highly relevant that Jan owned, according to the inventory, a 'bouc van Perchevaul', in French or Dutch, and that he had a bastard son called Perchevale.[65]

The last book on Jan's list is a 'bouc gheheeten Mandeville' (no. 26). This must be a copy of the mid fourteenth century *Voyages* of Jean de Mandeville,

---

[62] See P. Wackers, 'The Dutch Reynaert Tradition in National and European Perspective', in *Literature without Frontiers: Transnational Perspectives on Premodern Literature in the Low Countries 1200–1800*, ed. C. van der Haven, J. Bloemendal, Y. Desplenter and J.A. Parente, Jr. (Leiden, 2023), pp. 79–95.

[63] See J. A. A. M. Biemans, *Onsen Speghele Ystoriale in Vlaemsche. Codicologisch onderzoek naar de overlevering van de* Spiegel historiael *van Jacob van Maerlant, Philip Utenbroeke en Lodewijk van Velthem, met een beschrijving van de handschriften en fragmenten*, 2 vols. (Leuven, 1997).

[64] See K. Busby and M. Meuwese, 'French Arthurian Literature in the Low Countries', in *The Arthur of the Low Countries: The Arthurian Legend in Dutch and Flemish Literature*, ed. B. Besamusca and F. Brandsma (Cardiff, 2021), pp. 31–44.

[65] *Corpus Catalogorum Belgii*, ed. Derolez and Victor, I, 184 note.

either in Dutch or French.[66] Jan's interest in Mandeville's travels were shared by his family member Joos (d.1520), the only son of Gerard van Gistele, Lord of Axel and Moere, and Isabelle de Wilde. Born in 1446 and raised in Burgundian circles, Joos travelled to the Middle East from 1481–5. His travel notes were written out by a certain Ambrosius Zeebout around 1490, *Tvoyage van Mher Joos van Ghistele*.[67] Three Flemish copies of this text, dating from around 1500, 1535 and somewhere in the sixteenth century, have come down to us.[68] They were followed in the sixteenth century by printed editions, published in Ghent (1557, 1563, 1572). This textual transmission shows that the Van Gistel family was still firmly embedded in Flemish culture at the end of the Middle Ages.

Conclusion: Mediating between French and Dutch?

Our three case studies illustrate the different appearances of bilingual literary interests. Additionally, three general observations can be made. First and foremost, it should be underlined that these families are not socially isolated and that their Dutch and French literary patronage should be interpreted against the background of their complex social networks.[69] The Van Gistel family was inspired by the literary taste of the Burgundian dukes and vice versa: some of their manuscripts ended up in the ducal collection. Like Jacob van Gistel, Jan III de Baenst was mostly influenced by the Burgundian libraries and the literary aspirations of other courtiers such as Louis de Gruuthuse. His literary interests were therefore mostly French-orientated, influenced by the francophone book culture in Bruges. Nevertheless, like Louis de Gruuthuse, Jan III de Baenst commissioned a Middle Dutch manuscript, in this case a translation of the *Cité des dames* of Christine de Pizan. There is, furthermore, additional evidence of Dutch literary patronage, as De Baenst felt confident enough as a courtier to express his literary interests in his native language when he intervened on behalf of one the most important Dutch-language poets in Bruges, Anthonis de Roovere. Similarly, although the French correspondence between Jan van den Berghe and Jeanne de Harcourt reflected Jan's noble and political ambitions as a social climber, his social connections with equally

---

[66] Wijsman, *Luxury Bound*, p. 353, suggests that this manuscript is still extant: Chantilly, Musée Condé, MS 699 (1414). This codex shows the arms of the Van Gistel family.

[67] See Ambrosius Zeebout, *Tvoyage van Mher Joos van Ghistele*, ed. R. J. G. A. A. Gaspar (Hilversum, 1998).

[68] Brussels, Egyptologische Stichting Koningin Elisabeth, MS 55.473; Brussels, KBR, MS IV 330; Namur, Bibliothèque universitaire, MS R.Mn B46.

[69] Hoogvliet, 'Religious Reading', p. 332.

prestigious Dutch-speaking nobility, such as the nobleman Roeland van Uutkerke, and his informal (Dutch or bilingual?) literary society spurred him to start his own literary work in his native tongue.

Second, our case studies show the importance of collective reading practices and textual communities sharing the same texts.[70] For instance, Roeland I de Baenst invested in his image as a Ghent patrician by imitating a 'Ghent historiographical trend': the memory book. Most of the texts in the record were written in Dutch with the exception of the so-called *Resumé de Baenst*, which shows both the French literary interests of the family and the importance of Bruges for the history of the family, even to their Ghent branch. Furthermore, these textual communities could bring together different social classes. The allegory of the medieval ballgame 'kaatsen' was not only used by Van den Berghe in his Dutch work, but also by an anonymous Bruges shearer, albeit in a different literary project and in French. The manuscript containing a *Chronique de France et de Flandre, Les Voeux du héron*, the *Chronique normande abrégée* and *Les Sept Articles de la foy*, probably owned by Gerard van Gistel, his wife Alix de Wancourt or one of their children, ended up in the Burgundian library before 1469. As such, Flanders can be defined as a multilingual contact zone with a shared literary culture in French, Dutch and even Latin.

Third and last, literary and manuscript patronage are closely connected to the 'noble lifestyle' to which this new elite aspired (the so-called *vivre noblement*).[71] The role of language in the noble ambitions of these families is more complex. At first glance, they mirrored the francophone literary culture of the Burgundian court, but at the same time, almost all these cases show an equal interest in Dutch literature. These noble families are true intermediaries between French and Middle Dutch, on the level of politics as of literary patronage. Clearly, they cannot be characterised as Dutch native speakers with exclusively francophone ambitions. In fact, they were 'recruited' by the Burgundian court because of their bilingual capabilities which added in all these cases – Van den Berghe, De Baenst and Van Gistel – to their administrative and political roles, importance and authority. As a result, their bilingualism was crucial also in their role as literary patrons.

[70] Hoogvliet, 'Religious Reading', p. 333.

[71] F. Buylaert, W. De Clercq and J. Dumolyn, 'Sumptuary Legislation, Material Culture and the Semiotics of *"vivre noblement"* in the County of Flanders (14th–16th Centuries)', *Social History* 36 (2011), 393–417.

12

Sicilian Multilingualism and Cosmopolitan French[1]

Karla Mallette

In the history of cosmopolitan French, Italy (using that word, anachronistically, to include Sicily along with the peninsula) is anomalous in two ways. In northern Italy, during the twelfth and thirteenth centuries, writers adopted French as a literary language despite the absence of northern French settlement. In this sense, the Franco-Italian literature of northern Italy distinguishes itself from the French of England or of the eastern Mediterranean, areas occupied by French-speaking settlers, and French in the Low Countries, adjacent to francophone territories. Sicily was unique in a different way: although the island was ruled by francophone populations twice during the late Middle Ages, Sicilians did not adopt French as a language of literature. Rather, during the twelfth and thirteenth centuries, Sicilians wrote in other cosmopolitan languages – in particular, Arabic and Latin – and pioneered the use of an Italianate vernacular as literary language. During the fourteenth century, as the fledgling Italian vernacular flourished in northern Italy, Sicilians wrote poetry in their own vernacular – a variety of Italian with distinct morphology, grammar and vocabulary – and histories in both Sicilian and Latin, a cosmopolitan language used on the island since the days of Roman settlement. They did not write in French, and Sicilian literature shows no discernible trace of French influence. That is, despite the presence of Norman and Angevin settlers and administrators, who likely spoke a regional version of *vernacular* French, Sicily saw virtually no uptake of *cosmopolitan* French: the French used with equal proficiency by native speakers and those who learned it as a literary register; the French attached, not to territory, but rather to texts, which moved freely along the paths of trade and transit in western Europe and the Mediterranean region.

In this essay, I will reflect on the second of these historical anomalies. The Norman conquest of the eleventh century and Norman rule during the twelfth century brought French-speaking settlers to the island. The (brief) period

---

[1] I am grateful for the editors' thoughtful reading of an earlier draft of this essay. Their suggestions caught oversights and infelicities; errors that remain are my own.

of Angevin rule at the end of the thirteenth century linked Sicily again to transregional French-language culture. Networks of trade and travel connected the island to centres of French literary and manuscript production in the Veneto and northern Italy, the eastern Mediterranean, and the Angevin Kingdom of Naples (the *Regno*, as it is often termed in anglophone scholarship). Why, despite this sustained contact with populations who left a lasting literary trace in other parts of the Mediterranean world, did French letters have so little impact in Sicily? I will summarise the history that entangled Sicily and speakers of French, both Norman and Angevin, and Sicilian literary production between the twelfth and fourteenth centuries. I will then narrow my focus to a single genre – histories – and to a brief period, between 1287 and 1358. As we will see, histories written in Sicily, in Sicilian and about Sicily address the periods of conquest and rule by Normans and Angevins. Another 'history' written by a Sicilian drew directly on a French-language source and addressed a topic dear to the hearts of readers of French: the matter of Troy. Yet even here, where we might expect to see the transfer of French themes and styles, there is no trace of French literary models. Sicily, I will argue, provides an important counterexample to the uptake of French elsewhere, from the wild west of Britain to the Babelian tableau of the eastern Mediterranean. Even in the adjacent Kingdom of Naples, courtiers and copyists (to a limited extent) embraced French. In Sicily, however, by the fourteenth century, the linguistic palette had been reduced to two: the local vernacular paired with Latin.[2] For reasons that are impossible to reconstruct, given the absence of contemporary sources, French did not take root. Even the French historiographical practices and historical legends that proved popular in northern Italy did not establish themselves in Sicily. In this sense, Sicily demonstrates the wide *but discontinuous* valence of French as a cosmopolitan language in the medieval Mediterranean. Textual French might knit together the eastern Mediterranean and Britain; writers in the Veneto or the Kingdom of Naples might opt into cosmopolitan French; at the same time, Sicilian litterateurs chose a third way, looking away from French and the access it granted them and using a local vernacular (Sicilian) and a familiar cosmopolitan (Latin) to express the home truths of Sicilian history.[3]

---

[2] For a brief discussion of Sicilian letters at the end of the fourteenth and beginning of the fifteenth century that captures the ephemeral survival of other languages in Sicily (including Arabic, spoken by Sicilian Jews, and Greek, present in manuscripts preserved in Sicilian libraries), see K. Mallette, 'Palermo', in *Europe: A Literary History, 1348–1418*, ed. D. Wallace, 2 vols.(Oxford, 2016), II, 12–24.

[3] For discussion of the territorial range of the cosmopolitan language, see K. Mallette, *Lives of the Great Languages: Arabic and Latin in the Medieval Mediterranean* (Chicago, 2021), pp. 26–31, 45–57.

When the Normans arrived in Sicily, Sicily's two languages were Greek and (mainly) Arabic. Muslim warriors had conquered Byzantine Sicily in 833. In 1061, a Byzantine general invited two Norman brothers to participate as mercenaries in raids against Muslim Sicily. Raids matured into conquest, and in 1139, at Mignano, Pope Innocent II issued a privilege designating Roger II (the son of one of the Norman warriors) King of Sicily, Duke of Puglia and Prince of Capua. Norman monarchs ruled the Kingdom of Sicily through the twelfth century.[4] Following the death of the last of the male heirs of the Norman rulers in 1194, the crown passed to Constance, daughter of Roger II, and her husband, Henry VI of Hohenstaufen. Their child, Frederick II, would rule as King of Sicily from 1198 until his death in 1250. He would be succeeded by his son, Conrad. On Conrad's death in 1254, his son Conradin, the last of the Hohenstaufen dynasty, and Manfred, the illegitimate son of Frederick II, vied for power in Sicily. The advance of Charles of Anjou, tapped by the pope to rule the Kingdom of Sicily – which still at this point included Naples and the southern portion of the peninsula – ended both Manfred's and Conradin's lives, and with them the Norman dynasty in Sicily. Manfred died in battle against the Angevins in 1266. The Angevins defeated Conradin in battle, and Charles ordered him beheaded in 1268.[5]

Charles of Anjou was now nominal king of Sicily. However, the Sicilians resented the extractive foreign rule of a sovereign with ambitions throughout the Adriatic and the central and eastern Mediterranean, and the Angevins did not establish a presence on the island that might influence hearts and minds or impose tyranny. The 1282 uprising known as the Sicilian Vespers toppled Angevin rule. The Vespers represented the culmination of a movement of urban bourgeoisie and militias, the emphatic rejection of excessive Angevin taxation, and the attempt to reassert Sicilian autonomy.[6] At the invitation of

---

[4] On the Norman conquest of Sicily, see S. Davis-Secord, *Where Three Worlds Met: Sicily in the Early Mediterranean* (Ithaca, 2017), pp. 174–212. On the peace of Mignano, see H. Wieruszowski, 'Roger II of Sicily, Rex-Tyrannus, in Twelfth-Century Political Thought', *Speculum* 38 (1963), 46–78.

[5] For thirteenth-century Sicilian history, see D. Abulafia, 'The kingdom of Sicily under the Hohenstaufen and Angevins', in *The New Cambridge Medieval History*, ed. D. Abulafia (Cambridge, 1999), pp. 498–522.

[6] In the absence of contemporary Sicilian records, the historiography struggles to account for the sudden, decisive violence of the Vespers revolt; F. Renda compares it to the eruption of Etna, *Storia della Sicilia dalle origini ai giorni nostri* (Palermo, 2003), p. 448. Certainly, the impulse to expel the Angevin regime was stronger than any vision of what was to replace it. To some extent, what played out in Sicily was a preview of the proxy wars that would convulse the Italian peninsula during the first half of the fifteenth century. In this case, Sicilians contended for autonomy in the

the Sicilians, Peter III of Aragon was installed on the Sicilian throne. A 1295 treaty negotiated between the pope and Aragonese and Angevin claimants ceded the island to the Angevins; fierce Sicilian resistance resulted in the naming of a new Aragonese king and, in repudiation, papal excommunication of that king and interdict of the island. The 1302 Treaty of Caltabellotta resolved the impasse and gave Sicily to the Aragonese and the mainland to the Angevins.[7] The treaty specified that Sicily would be ceded to the Angevins following the death of Frederick III of Sicily, but the Aragonese flouted the agreement, resulting in intermittent outbreaks of hostility until in 1372 a treaty negotiated with papal oversight brought peace between Sicily and Naples – and affirmed Aragonese possession of the island.[8]

Even considered in telegraphic brevity – focusing on relations between the island and the mainland and on angles of the history that concern French-speaking populations, and ignoring the internal debates that motivated Sicilian actions – this is a stormy and eventful history. Two elements of this history are particularly relevant to the topic at hand. First, the Guelf-Ghibelline hostilities and standoffs that drove so much northern Italian history during this same period also informed the competition between Angevins and Aragonese in southern Italy and in Sicily.[9] Certainly, a fierce Sicilian desire for independence and self-rule (coupled with a sense that Aragonese rule would be more hands-off than Angevin rule had proved to be), controversy over how best to achieve autonomy, and debates about the

---

face of Angevin and Aragonese ambitions in the central and eastern Mediterranean. See Renda, *Storia della Sicilia*, pp. 436–49; V. D'Alessandro, 'Società e potere nella Sicilia medievale: Un profilo', *Archivio Storico Italiano* 174 (January–March 2016), 31–80, pp. 50–2; Abulafia, 'The Kingdom of Sicily under the Hohenstaufen and Angevins', pp. 513–16.

[7] See S. Péquignot, 'Treaty of Caltabellotta (1302)', in *The Encyclopedia of Diplomacy*, ed. G. Martel, 3 May 2018, accessed 29 December 2022, https://doi-org.proxy.lib. umich.edu/10.1002/9781118885154.dipl0488.

[8] Renda, *Storia della Sicilia*, pp. 546–8.

[9] For details concerning the Guelf and Ghibelline ideologies of the contenders for the Sicilian throne and their allies in Sicily, see Renda, *Storia della Sicilia*, pp. 435–6; and d'Alessandro, 'Società e potere', p. 50. For discussion of the Guelf ideology of the Florentine histories influenced by French-language historiography, see L. K. Morreale, 'French Literature, Florentine Politics, and Vernacular Historical Writing, 1270–1348', *Speculum* 85 (2010), 868–93, especially pp. 868–70, 881–2. For an overview of the struggles between Guelfs (supporters of the temporal rule of the Church) and Ghibellines (supporters of the temporal rule of an Emperor) in Italy, see J. Koenig, 'Guelphs and Ghibellines' in *Dictionary of the Middle Ages*, ed. J. R. Strayer, accessed 8 August 2022, link.gale.com/apps/doc/BT2353201309/ WHIC?u=umuser&sid=bookmark-WHIC&xid=67c0a460.

structure of rule on the island were more important to Sicilians themselves.[10] From an international perspective, however, the jockeying for power in Sicily unfolded as a proxy war. As in northern Italy, the Angevins had the support of Italian Guelfs and the popes; the Aragonese, aligned with Italian Ghibellines, hoped to claim the imperial throne. This fact will be important to the histories written in Sicilian and about Sicily. Second, the two periods of rule by French-speaking populations – the twelfth century and 1268–82 – did not translate into an enduring French cultural presence on the island. The period of Angevin rule during the late thirteenth century was too ephemeral to leave a mark on Sicilian language or literature. The 'Normans' who settled Sicily during the eleventh and twelfth centuries did not necessarily share a language (many came from non-French-speaking parts of France, especially Brittany) and were not particularly bookish.[11] Gallo-romance elements in the Sicilian dialects indicate the linguistic influence of French-speaking settlers.[12] But French literature did not have a comparable impact on Sicilian letters, for the simple reason that Sicilians did not write in any vernacular during the twelfth century at the height of Norman settlement of the island.

Rather, Sicilian literature indicates other linguistic affiliations and a distinct trajectory. During the twelfth century, the Norman monarchs sponsored works in Arabic by court poets (like al-Atrabanishi) and the geography of al-Idrisi.[13] Sicilians also translated philosophy from Greek into Latin. Henricus Aristippus translated Plato's *Meno* and *Phaedo*, and an anonymous translation of Ptolemy's *Almagest* from the same period survives. A courtier by the name of Eugenius wrote poetry in Greek and translated Ptolemy's *Optics* from Arabic into Latin.[14] A Greek translation of the Arabic *Kalila wa-Dimna* dedicated to Eugenius would serve as one of the primary conduits that brought that narrative tradition into the languages of western Europe.[15]

---

[10] See D'Alessandro, 'Società e potere' for a discussion of governance and debate in Sicily from the Norman era through the Aragonese rule.

[11] See C. Lee, 'That Obscure Object of Desire: French in Southern Italy', in *MFLCOF*, pp. 73–100, p. 76; L.-R. Ménager, 'Pesanteur et étiologie de la colonisation normande de l'Italie', in *Roberto il Guiscardo e il suo tempo. Atti delle prime giornate normanno-sveve (Bari, 28–29 May 1973)* (Bari, 1975 repr. 1991), pp. 189–214.

[12] Lee, 'That Obscure Object of Desire', pp. 73–8.

[13] For al-Atrabanishi, see K. Mallette, *The Kingdom of Sicily, 1100–1250: A Literary History* (Philadelphia, 2011), pp. 25–7, 140–1. For al-Idrisi, see Mallette, *The Kingdom of Sicily*, pp. 30, 146–8.

[14] Mallette, *The Kingdom of Sicily*, p. 30.

[15] On this translation, see B. Krönung, 'The Wisdom of the Beasts: The Arabic *Book of Kalila and Dimna* and the Byzantine *Book of Stephanites and Ichnelates*', trans. A.

This literary activity drew on linguistic traditions that had been present in Sicily. Sicilians had written in Arabic during the two centuries of Muslim rule (Ibn Hamdis, the greatest Arabic poet of Sicily, left for al-Andalus during the years of Norman conquest and died in Majorca in 1133).[16] Greek was not an important language of literature in Sicily during the centuries of Muslim rule; but poets still wrote in Greek at Otranto (in Puglia, on the mainland) during the thirteenth century.[17] The Normans also introduced Latin as both bureaucratic language and language of record. Hugo Falcandus wrote a Latin history of the Norman conquest of Sicily between 1154 and 1169, during the reigns of William I and William II.[18] Peter of Eboli (fl. 1196–1220) wrote poetic panegyrics for Henry IV – the Hohenstaufen king whose marriage to Constance, daughter of Roger II, made him King of Sicily – and Henry and Constance's son, Frederick II.[19]

Thus, while French literature began to establish itself in northern Italy; while Gaimar, Marie de France and Benoît de Sainte-Maure were active in Britain; the Normans of Sicily sponsored works in Arabic, Latin and Greek. What is missing from this picture is vernacular composition. Sicilians would not create a vernacular literature until the first half of the thirteenth century, when Sicilian poets wrote the first corpus of lyric poetry in an Italian vernacular. This body of poetry aligns itself explicitly and self-consciously with the vernacular traditions of western Europe. Modern scholarship has taken a translation from Occitan to Italian, appearing in an important manuscript preserving the Sicilians' poetry, as the iconic example of the Sicilians'

Kinney, in *Fictional Storytelling in the Medieval Eastern Mediterranean and Beyond*, ed. C. Cupane and B. Krönung (Leiden, 2016), pp. 427–60 (pp. 453–6). On its transmission in Italy, see J.-T. Papademetriou, 'The Sources and the Character of *Del governo de' regni*', *Transactions and Proceedings of the American Philological Association* 92 (1961), 422–39.

[16] On Ibn Hamdis, see W. Granara, *Ibn Hamdis the Sicilian: Eulogist for a Falling Homeland* (London, 2021).

[17] See M. Gigante, *Poeti italobizantini del secolo XIII* (Naples, 1953).

[18] See Mallette, *The Kingdom of Sicily*, pp. 32, 51–2, 158–60; Hugo Falcandus, *La Historia o Liber de Regno Sicilie et la Epistola ad Petrum Panormitane Ecclesie Thesaurarium*, ed. G. B. Siragusa (Rome, 1897); and Hugo Falcandus, *History of the Tyrants of Sicily by 'Hugo Falcandus'*, trans. and annotated G. A. Loud and T. Wiedemann (Manchester, 1998).

[19] See Mallette, *The Kingdom of Sicily*, pp. 95, 161–2 and Petrus Ansolini de Ebulo, *De rebus siculis carmen*, ed. E. Rota, in *Rerum Italicarum Scriptores*, gen. ed. L. A. Muratori, 34 vols., XXXI, pt. 1 (Castello, 1904).

recognition of previous lyric traditions.[20] A *canzoniere* of Italian lyric held today in the Vatican Library (Vatican, Biblioteca Apostolica Vaticana, MS Vat. lat.3793) opens with an anthology of Sicilian poetry, beginning with poems by Giacomo da Lentini, the most prolific and most talented of the Sicilians. The first of his poems in this manuscript, 'Madonna dir vo voglio', is a translation of Folquet de Marselha's Occitan-language 'A vos, midontç, voill retrair'en cantan' (PC 155.4). Giacomo's translation presaged the *volgarizzamenti*, or vernacular translations that Italians produced especially between 1250 and 1350, typically from Latin and French prose originals. Together with the copyist's thoughtful, deliberate product placement of that poem at the head of a collection of Italian verse, Giacomo's poem suggests that response to the Occitan lyric tradition was a conscious part of the Sicilians' poetic practice.[21] Indeed, given the delayed appearance of Italian as literary language – a full century after the flowering of Occitan lyric and the spread of francophone letters to northern Italy and Britain – these translations should be seen as a gracious recognition of literary antecedents.

This burst of lyric poetry is associated with the reign of Frederick II. Frederick himself wrote poetry; several poems are ascribed to him in the extant manuscripts, and two of them (most scholars agree) quite likely were his work.[22] After Frederick's death, the activity of the Sicilian poets seems to come to an abrupt halt. From the turbulent fourteenth century, Sicilian literary production consists of a small handful of poems in the Sicilian vernacular, very different in tone and topic from the work of the early thirteenth-century poets. The few extant poems from the fourteenth century address religious topics (including a 'Pianto di Maria', 'Mary's Lament', and a *sonetto caudato* on free

---

[20] I use the undifferentiated 'Italian' here to refer to the Tuscanised manuscripts in which almost all of the Sicilians' poetry has been preserved. Copied by Tuscan scribes, these poems have lost most of the Sicilian dialect markers that would distinguish them from the compositions of later Tuscan poets. Only rhymes that do not quite work and the occasional unassimilated Sicilian word indicate the linguistic provenance of the poetry.

[21] See A. Roncaglia, 'De quibusdam provincialibus translatis in lingua nostra', in *Letteratura e critica: Studi in onore di Natalino Sapegno*, ed. W. Binni (Rome, 1975), pp. 1–36 (pp. 25–36); A. Varvaro, 'Il regno normanno-svevo', in *Letteratura Italiana. Storia e Geografia*, ed. A. Asor Rosa (Turin, 1987), 3 vols., Vol. 1: L'età medievale, I, 79–99 (pp. 92–3); and F. Brugnolo, 'La Scuola poetica siciliana', in *Storia Della Letteratura Italiana*, ed. E. Malato (Rome, 1995), pp. 265–337 (pp. 302–3).

[22] S. Rapisardo, 'Federico II, attività poetica', in *Treccani.it – Enciclopedie on line*, Istituto dell'Enciclopedia Italiana, accessed 17 June 2022, https://www.treccani.it/enciclopedia/federico-ii-attivita-poetica_%28Federiciana%29/.

will) and the misfortunes of Sicilian history.[23] Each of these works survives in a single manuscript. They seem to be the occasional compositions of amateur poets, rather than the work of polished professionals paying deliberate homage to literary history, like the poets of Frederick's era.

Between 1250 and 1400, Sicilians also wrote prose histories. Two of these, written in the Sicilian vernacular, recounted important episodes in the Sicilian past that involved colonisation or settlement by French-speaking populations: the Norman conquest and the Sicilian Vespers. Meanwhile, Sicilian Guido delle Colonne produced a Latin translation of Benoît de Sainte-Maure's French history of Troy. These historical works will be discussed in more detail below. But the sense of literary productivity that characterises the century of Norman rule and the era of Frederick II ends abruptly following Frederick's death. In the absence of contemporary records to explain either the intensification or the abatement of literary activity, this shift has led some historians to attribute agency to the monarchs themselves: to assume that their patronage, along with the sense of order and prosperity associated with the periods of their rule, inspired literary activity during the twelfth and first half of the thirteenth century. This explanation seems plausible but not exhaustive and does not fully account for the most interesting details in the literary life of the period: for instance, the explosion of Sicilian vernacular poetry during the thirteenth century and the absence of composition in French. To be sure, my emphasis on the period from the twelfth through to the fourteenth century, and exclusion of the fifteenth and sixteenth, emphasises the sense of literary collapse. We have many more poems (most of them devotional or historical works that survive in a single manuscript) from the fifteenth century, and during the sixteenth, the great poet Antonio Veneziano (1543–93) revived the reputation of the Sicilian vernacular and was read on the mainland as well as in Sicily.[24] But extending the archive to include the fifteenth and sixteenth centuries will not provide more detail to think about the focus of this essay: the surprising absence of cosmopolitan French and the persistent importance of two languages, Sicilian and Latin, in late medieval Sicily.

Sicilians did not write in French; but did they *read* French? French-language books from medieval Sicilian libraries do not survive. However,

---

[23] For the 'Pianto di Maria', see G. Cusimano, *Poesie siciliane dei secoli XIV e XV*, 2 vols.(Palermo, 1951), I, 31–5; for the 'Sonicium di libero arbitrio', see Cusimano, *Poesie siciliane*, I, 36. A *sonetto caudato* – or 'tailed' sonnet – has additional three-line stanzas appended at the end. Later Italian *sonetti caudati* are typically comic; this sonnet decidedly is not.

[24] For the poems of the fifteenth century, see Cusimano, *Poesie siciliane*; for Antonio Veneziano, see A. Veneziano, *Ottave*, ed. A. Rigoli (Turin, 1967).

given the deplorable survival rate of medieval manuscripts in general, this is not conclusive evidence that Sicilians did not write or read French. Parchment retrieved from the bindings of books made in Sicily provides (admittedly meagre) evidence of consumption of literary French in Sicily: fragments of a fourteenth-century copy of Guillaume de Machaut's *Livre du Voir-Dit* and an anonymous prose *Roman de Merlin*, now lost.[25] A French translation of a Latin lapidary treatise has been tentatively identified as Sicilian.[26] Furthermore, the documentary record supplies evidence of the limited presence of French books in Sicily. Henri Bresc, who studied the inventories of fourteenth- and fifteenth-century Sicilian libraries left in wills and correspondence, points out that vernacular books are often difficult to identify, because notaries might enumerate 'books in vernacular' without identifying them or even specifying in which vernacular they were written; the exceptions were the well-known authors, especially Dante.[27] A small number of French books appear in the libraries of foreigners resident in the island. Some are identified as vernacular translations of Latin works (specifically, Lucan and the *Decades* of Livy).[28] Bresc's inventories suggest that the Aragonese resident in Sicily during this period read (and, presumably, spoke) Catalan, rather than Castilian. The library of the Aragonese nobleman Giovanni de Cruyllas, inventoried in 1423, details the habits of an exceptional reader. Of the eighteen items listed, only one is in Latin. The others are in Catalan, French and Sicilian, with a single book of Occitan poetry ('unu canzuneri in lemosini'). Three French romances appear on the list: a 'Merlinu', a 'Galeoctu' and a 'Lanziloctu'.[29] But Giovanni's library was not typical. Catalan books were more common than French in Sicily – not surprising, given Sicilian history and demographics.

Fragmentary material evidence suggests the presence of French story cycles in the Kingdom of Sicily, including the southern tip of the mainland. A mosaic on the floor of the cathedral of Brindisi (1178?) depicts an episode

---

[25] L. Ingallinella, 'Un frammento di un volgarizzamento siciliano trecentesco delle Vite dei Santi Padri', *Bollettino del Centro di Studi filologici e linguistici siciliani* 25 (2014), 47–111 (pp. 51–2).

[26] This work (in Paris, BnF MS latin 14470) is described in M. Careri, C. Ruby and I. Short, *Livres et écritures en français et en occitan au XIIe siècle: Catalogue illustré* (Rome, 2011), pp. 188–9.

[27] H. Bresc, *Livre et société en Sicile (1299–1499)* (Palermo, 1971), pp. 55–7.

[28] Bresc, *Livre et société en Sicile*, p. 58; document 37, p. 135; document 65, p. 154.

[29] H. Bresc, 'La bibliothèque de Giovanni de Cruyllas (1423)', *Bollettino del Centro di Studi filologici e linguistici siciliani* 10 (1969), 414–19 (pp. 418, 419).

from Arthurian legend.[30] Gervase of Tilbury reports having heard legends of Arthur while in Sicily.[31] Textile wall-hangings made in Sicily in the third quarter of the fourteenth century for a Tuscan patron illustrate scenes from the romance of Tristan and include captions in Sicilian.[32] This evidence suggests the reception of French chivalric stories in Sicily, quite possibly as oral literature and in Sicilian. The Sicilian *opera dei pupi*, the marionette theatre inducted into the UNESCO Representative List of the Intangible Cultural Heritage of Humanity in 2008, features stories ultimately derived from the *Chanson de Roland* and other medieval French chanson de geste cycles. However, these tales had been circulating throughout western Europe for centuries – and filtered through early modern Italian epics by Boiardo, Ariosto and many others – before they reached the puppet theatres of Sicily, likely in the third decade of the nineteenth century.[33]

One topic seemed to attract Sicilian authors even during the century following the death of Frederick II, when Sicilian literary activity ebbed: history. In 1287, Guido delle Colonne created a Latin translation – a reverse *volgarizzamento* – of Benoît de Sainte-Maure's *Roman de Troie*. Guido's *Historia destructionis Troiae* would become the standard prose history of the Trojan War in western Europe, considered authoritative until the eighteenth century. During the first half of the fourteenth century, probably between 1337 and 1350, an anonymous author translated a Tuscan history of the Sicilian Vespers into Sicilian. This work is known in the scholarship as *Lu rebellamentu di Sichilia*. In 1358, Simone da Lentini, a Franciscan monk, wrote a Sicilian vernacular translation of portions of Geoffrey Malaterra's Latin history of the Norman conquest of Sicily: *La conquesta di Sichilia fatta per li Normandi*. These two local histories, both in the Sicilian vernacular, would continue to circulate

---

[30] Lee, 'That Obscure Object of Desire', pp. 78–9; Varvaro, 'Il regno normanno-svevo', p. 82.

[31] Varvaro, 'Il regno normanno-svevo', p. 82.

[32] P. Rajna, 'Intorno a due antiche coperte con figurazioni tratte dalle storie di Tristano', *Romania* 42 (1913), 517–79; Ingallinella, 'Un frammento di un volgarizzamento siciliano trecentesco', p. 53.

[33] A. Carocci, *Il poema che cammina: La letteratura cavalleresca nell'opera dei pupi* (Palermo, 2019), p. 29. For the UNESCO designation as Intangible Cultural Heritage of Humanity, see *Opera dei Pupi, Sicilian Puppet Theatre*, accessed 29 December 2022, https://ich.unesco.org/en/RL/opera-dei-pupi-sicilian-puppet-theatre-00011.

SICILIAN MULTILINGUALISM AND COSMOPOLITAN FRENCH 279

in manuscript, typically copied alongside Latin histories of Sicily, until the eighteenth century.[34]

In the absence of evidence of French-language influence on Sicilian poetic or epic traditions, these three histories provide a superb opportunity to scan Sicilian historiography for covert French influence. In a provocative recent essay, Laura Morreale argued that Florentine histories demonstrate evidence of French influence in style and structure. After the arrival of Charles of Anjou, with papal support, in northern Italy in the late 1260s, Florence – with its Guelf leanings and mercantile links to Angevin Naples – developed strong pro-Angevin sympathies. Soon after, a short list of new thematic elements began to appear in Florentine histories, themes common in French-language histories that had not been prevalent in earlier Florentine (or northern Italian) histories. These include the *translatio imperii* motif (in this case, a transfer of power from Rome to Florence); the perils of treachery and the importance of loyalty to the stability of the state; first-person authorial statements that present history both as entertaining and as a way to preserve the community's past; rubrics as aids to the reader; first-person and second-person authorial asides addressing the reader; the role of love as motivating factor in history; and the importance of friendship between warriors.[35] The history of the Trojan War, too, emerged as an important template for historical narratives. In particular, the disruptive force of love as motivation for civil upheaval – so central to medieval accounts of the Trojan War – appeared in Florentine histories of the late thirteenth and fourteenth centuries.[36] Can we identify any of these characteristics in the two Sicilian histories of the fourteenth centuries? Does Guido's translation indicate that Benoît's *Troie* was known in Sicily and that Benoît, Guido, or both might have served as a conduit for French-language historical models in Sicily as in Tuscany?

Of these historical works, Simone da Lentini's *Conquesta* functions like a control: though it is the latest of the three, it can easily be eliminated because it falls outside any possible Angevin sphere of influence. The Latin work that Simone translated – Geoffrey Malaterra's *De rebus gestis Rogerii Calabriae comitis et Roberti Guiscardi ducis fratris eius* – was written during the eleventh century, long before there were Angevin claimants to thrones in the Italian peninsula. Simone translated the work in Sicily in 1358, during a period of

---

[34] Bresc's inventories (*Livres et société*) do not indicate whether the vernacular histories were read in Sicily during the fourteenth and fifteenth centuries (see below, n. 70). However, as noted above, those inventories provide scant evidence about the content and nature of the vernacular books in Sicilian libraries.

[35] Morreale, 'French Literature, Florentine Politics', pp. 873–8.

[36] Morreale, 'French Literature, Florentine Politics', pp. 876–8.

intransigent anti-Angevin sentiment. No Angevin histories circulated in Sicily at the time to influence him; nor did Simone travel to the mainland to encounter French histories and be influenced by them. Indeed, the elements that Morreale identified in Florentine history are in short supply in Simone's translation. No introduction in the author's voice explains the entertainment value or ethical importance of local history. The narrative begins without fanfare, with only a few short lines to situate the translation: for the sake of his Sicilian public, Simone will translate those portions of Malaterra's history that address the conquest of Sicily itself, 'leaving out the conquest of other lands outside of Sicily'.[37] No rubrics punctuate the narrative. The author does occasionally address an aside to the reader in the first person to explain difficult passages or voice an opinion. However, these asides are functional. Rather than establish an informal communication between author and reader (like the passages discussed by Morreale), these comments typically explain or update the source text, written two and a half centuries earlier.[38] The Sicilian people love their rulers and Count Roger loves his wife, but love is not a motivating force in the history. Indeed, when Simone mentions love, in its romantic or feudal expressions, he is translating Malaterra's words – and often compressing or simplifying a more detailed passage from the Latin as he translates.[39] Simone's *Conquesta* was the work of a patriotic Sicilian, created

[37] Simone da Lentini, *La conquesta di Sichilia fatta per li normandi*, ed. G. Rossi-Taibbi (Palermo, 1955), p. 3.

[38] When Simone is describing the bite of the tarantula and how to cure it, for instance, he takes issue with the practice of placing the patient inside a furnace or some other heated place: 'Eu criyu beni chi una chiraulu curaria sucandu killu tossicu fridu, vininosu et dotusu, sencza furnu' (I believe that a surgeon could cure him sucking this cold, poisonous, and dangerous toxin, without an oven; Simone da Lentini, *La conquesta di Sichilia*, p. 68).

[39] For instance, Simone describes the love that Count Roger feels for his wife with the phrase 'Illu amava chista donna di ardentissimu amuri' (He loved this woman with a most ardent love; Simone da Lentini, *La conquesta di Sichilia*, pp. 94–5). Here, he condenses Malaterra's 18-line poem celebrating the nuptials and the love between Roger and his wife: Geoffrey Malaterra, *De Rebus gestis Rogerii Calabriae et Siciliae comitis et Roberti Guiscardi ducis fratris eius*, ed. L. A. Muratori (Bologna, 1927), pp. 70–1). Later, when the Pope arrives at Salerno to meet with Count Roger, Malaterra tells us that he feels 'amicabilem venerationem' for the Count (Malaterra, *De Rebus Gestis Rogerii Calabriae*, p. 107, l. 2); Simone translates that as 'grandi amuri' (Simone da Lentini, *La conquesta di Sichilia*, p. 146). A few lines later, Malaterra describes the Count's zeal for the Church with the somewhat florid phrase 'in omnibus negotiis ecclesiasticis exequendis zelo divini ardoris effervescentem' (overflowing in the execution of all ecclesiastical affairs with the zeal of divine ardour; p. 107, ll. 9–10). Simone renders this, once again, as 'grandi

during a period of turmoil. The Sicilians had defeated the Angevin fleet in the Gulf of Catania in May 1357, and the Aragonese King Frederick and his court were in residence at Cefalù in March of 1358 – the start of Lent – when Simone, Frederick's confessor, started this translation.[40] The ongoing popularity of Simone's *volgarizzamento* of Malaterra is a question that I will discuss later.

Lu rebellamentu di Sichilia is a more plausible candidate for French influence. This anonymous work, which describes the Sicilian Vespers, has a tangled history. The Sicilian version of the work is preserved in nine manuscripts; three histories of the Vespers related to the *Rebellamentu* in Tuscan Italian survive. Marcello Barbato, who edited the modern edition, proposes that all extant versions descend from a Tuscan original that does not survive. Furthermore, he suggests that the original was pro-Angevin and anti-Aragonese, and that the Sicilian translation downplayed the anti-Aragonese sentiment of the original for a Sicilian audience. Barbato dates the Sicilian translation to between 1337 and 1350, and he reckons that the Tuscan original was created earlier in the fourteenth century.[41] If the original were touched by the Angevin influence that Morreale describes, a glimmer of this structure might have been transplanted with the translation to Sicilian soil, and might create its own offshoots – second- and third-generation histories influenced by French-language models – in Sicilian historiography.

At first blush, the *Rebellamentu* looks nothing like the Florentine histories that interest Morreale. The author does not situate his work as entertaining or ethically improving. There are no rubrics or authorial asides to the reader. Love plays no role in the story. The *Rebellamentu* is fascinating first and foremost because it treats the story of the Vespers as a bureaucratic procedural. Giovanni da Procida – in all Sicilian accounts, the hero of the Vespers – flits from one end of the Mediterranean to the other, securing the support he needs to throw the Angevins out of Sicily. Without explaining his opposition to the Angevins, he travels first to Constantinople, where – after patient diplomatic preparation – he enlists the aid of the Palaeologus. He travels to Sicily and convinces the Sicilian barons to invite Peter of Aragon to oppose the Angevins. He goes next to the pope. Here, too, careful diplomatic spadework is necessary before he wins papal favour. And so on: the history reads like

---

amuri': 'per lu grandi amuri chi portava ferventimenti a la Ecclesia' (for the great love that he carried fervently for the Church; Simone da Lentini, *La conquesta di Sichilia*, p. 146).

[40] See Rossi-Tabbi's introduction, Simone da Lentini, *La conquesta di Sichilia*, pp. viii–ix.

[41] *Lu rebellamentu di Sichilia*, ed. M. Barbato (Palermo, 2010), pp. vii–ix.

a primer in fourteenth-century Mediterranean diplomacy, showing how to build consensus and military support, from Constantinople to Sicily to Rome to Catalonia.

Nothing could appear less 'Florentine' (in Morreale's sense) or less 'Trojan' – influenced by contemporary narratives of the Trojan War – than the bureaucratic realism of the *Rebellamentu*, until we reach the spark that lights the Sicilian conflagration. Giovanni da Procida has tapped every potential ally and has lined up the support he needs to overthrow Angevin rule. An armada is in place off the coast; Charles and his son are far away. Giovanni addresses his allies in a rousing speech that would not be out of place in a classic Hollywood war movie.[42] The next chapter begins with a dramatic call-out:

> Eccu ki fu vinutu lu misi di apprili l'annu di li milli e due chentu octanta dui, lu martidii di la Pascua di la Resurreccioni. Eccu ki misser Palmeri Abati e mmisser Alaimu di Lintini et misser Galteri di Calatagiruni et tucti li altri baruni di Sichilia, tucti accordati ad un voliri per loru discretu consiglu, viniru in Palermu per fari la ribellacioni.

> (Lo, the month of April of the year 1282 had come, the Tuesday of Easter week. Lo, Sir Palmeri Abati and Sir Alaimu of Lentini and Sir Galteri of Caltagirone and all the other barons of Sicily, all agreed on a single desire through their discreet counsel, came to Palermo to carry out the rebellion.)

What sets the rebellion in train, however, is not a signal from Giovanni da Procida, the revolutionary who has so carefully arranged this event from the beginning of the narrative, but rather an act of disrespect toward a Sicilian woman. At a Palermo church, a Frenchman touches a Sicilian woman 'disonestamenti, comu ià eranu usati di fari' (with disrespect, as they were wont to do).[43] The woman screams. Outraged, the barons rush to avenge the woman's honour. They slaughter all the 'franchiski' present.[44] The Sicilian Vespers – so called because they began at the Vespers prayers on the Tuesday of Easter week – have begun. Perhaps most remarkable, this narrative detail elides the agency of Giovanni da Procida entirely. He is not mentioned in this episode; indeed, he reappears only eleven chapters later, in Tunisia.[45]

Of course, this episode of a woman wronged and avenged is not a story of love (or of lust), like the story of Paris and Helen that sparked the Trojan War. But because of the situation – the tensions between Sicilians and Angevins;

[42] This is the beginning of chapter 43, pp. 38–9.
[43] *Rebellamentu*, chapter 44, p. 39.
[44] *Rebellamentu*, chapter 44, p. 40.
[45] *Rebellamentu*, chapter 55, pp. 51–3.

the carefully laid plans to revolt against the Angevin occupation – rather than end in a duel between two men, this dispute escalates into an uprising that will drive all the French out of the island by the end of 1282. The Sicilian versions of the *Rebellamentu* double down on this message by including a paragraph at the end of the narrative – not included in the continental manuscripts – that recalls the vendetta and reinscribes Giovanni da Procida in this key plot element by identifying the woman insulted as his daughter.

> La raxuni perchì miser Iohanni di Prochita si misi a ctractari et ordinari quista rebellioni contra di lu re Carlu, sì fu chi unu grandi baruni di lu re Carlu fichi forza ad una figla di misser Iohanni et illu si 'ndi fichi plena iusticia comu a mmiser Iohanni si convinia. Et misser Iohanni si propossi in cori comu potissi distrudiri lu re Carlu et viniarisi di la iniuria la quali avia richiputa, di ki l'ordinau quistu tracctatu comu tucti aviti intisu.[46]

> (The reason why Sir Giovanni di Procida began to plan and organise this rebellion against King Charles was that a great baron of King Charles used force against a daughter of master Giovanni and for that reason he sought full justice just as was fitting for him. And Sir Giovanni deliberated in his heart how he could destroy King Charles and avenge himself for the injury which he had received, for which reason he organised this plan, as you have all heard.)

The information given here is not mentioned earlier in the narrative and seems to be an effort to magnify readers' outrage against the Angevin oppressors and the justice of the Sicilian revolutionaries' cause.

Giovanni's failed attempt to restore justice by asking King Charles to avenge the violence against his daughter – while it contradicts everything else we read about Giovanni's actions in the *Rebellamentu* – foreshadows the dynamics of another Sicilian legend: the tale of three brothers, Osso, Mastrosso and Carcagnosso. This story starts in Spain in 1412, where a sister of the three brothers is raped by a wealthy, well-connected man. The brothers go to the Aragonese king, who refuses their pleas for vengeance. Enraged, they avenge their sister by killing the man who violated her. They are convicted of murder and banished to a prison on the island of Favignana (just off the Sicilian coast). When they are released from prison, each sets off for a different destination: Osso goes to Sicily, where he founds the Cosa Nostra; Mastrosso goes to Calabria, where he founds the 'Ndrangheta; and Carcagnosso goes to

---

[46] *Rebellamentu*, pp. 65–6.

Naples, where he founds the Camorra.[47] There is no reason to believe that this tale goes back to the fifteenth century. Rather, it encodes elements of nineteenth-century mafia history. Mafiosi sometimes trace the origin of their organisation to the period of Aragonese rule of Sicily, which is assuredly not true. However, prisons – including Ustica, an island prison in the Tyrrhenian Sea, about fifty kilometres north of Palermo – were incubators for the mafia during the nineteenth century.[48] Giovanni Verga's short story 'Cavalleria rusticana' ('Rustic Chivalry', published in 1880), and the opera based on that story by Pietro Mascagni (music) and Giovanni Targioni-Tozzetti and Guido Menasci (libretto), first performed in 1890, established the notion in the European imagination of the vendetta as the quintessential Sicilian myth. The use of the opera in movies like *Rocky* and *The Godfather III* demonstrates the power of this image well into the twentieth century.[49] But the legend of the three brothers as charter myth of the mafia, and its similarity to the revenge plot folded into the fourteenth-century Sicilian *Rebellamentu*, suggests that the vendetta motif may have deep roots in Sicilian folk myths. And it hints at the enduring resonance in Sicily of tales that use violence against women to justify violence against a state, and even revolution (or the creation of predatory pseudo-governmental organisations within the state).

In other words, the *Rebellamentu* reads like a distinctly Sicilian narrative of an event of key importance to Sicilian history. Although it apparently derives from a work that can be tracked to Tuscany during the early fourteenth

---

[47] For online versions of this popular myth, see e.g., G. Tantillo, 'Tre fratelli e un "fattaccio": Osso, Mastrosso e Carcagnosso, fondatori di tutte le mafie', *Balarm*, 28 June 2021, accessed 2 October 2023, https://www.balarm.it/news/tre-fratelli-e-un-fattaccio-osso-mastrosso-e-carcagnosso-fondatori-di-tutte-le-mafie-124279; E. Tonni, 'La fonte battesimale di mafia e massoneria', *La verità di Ninco Nanco*, 29 June 2015, accessed 29 December 2022, https://laveritadininconaco.altervista.org/la-fonte-battesimale-di-mafia-e-massoneria/. The legend of Osso, Mastrosso and Carcagnosso inspired a modern spinoff, *A Classic Horror Story* dir. R. de Feo and P. Strippoli (Italy, 2021). A Netflix Italia trailer interlaces two dimensions of the myth: legends about the origin of organized crime in southern Italy and Sicily, and a twenty-first century twist that reframes the legends as modern folk horror. See 'La leggenda di Osso Mastrosso e Carcagnosso spiegata in A Classic Horror Story', *Youtube*, accessed 14 August 2023, https://www.youtube.com/watch?v=P7AIPpfy7D4.

[48] See J. Dickie, *Cosa Nostra: A History of the Sicilian Mafia* (New York, 2004), p. 81.

[49] The 'Interlude' from *Cavalleria rusticana* plays during the opening credits of the original *Rocky* (dir. J. G. Avildsen, USA, 1976). *The Godfather III* (dir. F. F. Coppola, USA, 1990) ends with an attack on the reigning family boss on the steps of the Teatro Massimo in Palermo following a performance of *Cavalleria rusticana*; the scene is scored with the 'Interlude' from the opera.

century, it does not suggest that French influence (of the sort that coloured Florentine histories) extended to Sicily. None of the narrative elements borrowed from French historical narratives show up in the *Rebellamentu*. The vendetta plot placed at the heart of a bureaucratic procedural to explain the motivations for the Sicilian Vespers, like motifs borrowed from the narratives of the Trojan War in the Florentine narratives discussed by Morreale, uses gendered personal relations and emotions to explain political history and social movements. However, it is an entirely Sicilian motif. There is no structural similarity between the tangled webs of romantic intrigue at the heart of the Trojan narratives and this brief tale of a Sicilian woman wronged.

In fact, we do not have evidence that the romance narrative of the Trojan war circulated in Sicily – unless Guido delle Colonne's *Historia destructionis Troiae* was written in Sicily. Guido delle Colonne was the name of a poet active at the court of Frederick II. Like most Sicilian poets of Frederick's age, he was also a court functionary. Documentary evidence shows that he was a judge at Messina. The name Guido delle Colonne is also associated with a Latin reworking of Benoît de Sainte-Maure's *Roman de Troie*, which was dedicated to a patron at Salerno in 1287 (long after Frederick's death in 1250). It is not clear whether the poet and the historian were two men or one (exceptionally long-lived) polymath.[50] The *Historia* is not precisely a translation; the text presents itself as an independent history of Troy, based on two late antique accounts supposedly written by eyewitnesses, Dares Phrygius and Dictys Cretensis. Guido did, indeed, consult several Latin authors on the characters and history he describes.[51] However, much of his narrative follows Benoît's *Roman*, at times word for word. The translator of the *Roman* was either the Sicilian poet and a very old man when he finished that work, or a different man with the same name. Given how little we know about him, it's impossible to know whether he found Benoît's *Roman de Troie* in Sicily or (given the dedication) in southern Italy, or where he got his French.

Benoît's *Roman de Troie* brought together the Latin histories of the Trojan War attributed to the Trojan Dares and Cretan Dictys, and proved an irresistible poetic confection, one of the most-copied works of the thirteenth century in Italy, France, and England. The histories of Dares and Dictys themselves, received in the Latin Middle Ages as eyewitness accounts of the

---

[50] See C. Calenda, 'Guido delle Colonne', in *I poeti della scuola siciliana. Poeti della corte di Federico II*, ed. C. Di Girolamo (Milan, 2008), pp. 53–108 (p. 54) for discussion of the case made for both opinions and further bibliography.

[51] See M. E. Meek's introduction to her translation of the *History* for a discussion of Guido's sources; Guido delle Colonne, *Historia Destructionis Troiae*, trans. M. E. Meek (Bloomington, 1974), pp. xix–xvii.

Trojan War, date to the Second Sophistic: a period when Greek historians looked for strategies to mine distant historical sources, even literary sources, for plausible information about a storied past.[52] In a fascinating recent essay, Valentina Prosperi places Dares and Dictys among a trend of writers who parodied this fad, purposefully trampling the line between poetic fiction and historical fact for comedic effect.[53] When they were translated into Latin, however – Dictys during the fourth century, Dares likely during the fifth century – they proved useful to Latin Christian authors generating universal histories, who needed sources to talk about the distant past. Thus, the Latin Middle Ages received them at their word as factual eyewitnesses of the events they described.[54] Benoît, a French-language writer from Tours at the court of the Anglo-Norman king Henry II, drew on Dictys and Dares's accounts to create a rambunctious poetic epic telling the story of the Trojan War (and so much more). Benoît's *Roman de Troie* would become the most-copied literary work in French of the twelfth century and inspired scores of abridgements, versifications, translations and imitations.[55]

Benoît's narrative is a groaning board of events, as tangled and improbable as a telenovela. In the *Historia* (based on Benoît, although he claims to be drawing directly on Dares and Dictys), Guido kept the density of event that characterises the *Roman de Troie*, but he wrote in prose and stripped the narrative surplus – the excess of precious detail – that appealed to Benoît's readers.[56] Guido's *Historia*, like Benoît's *Roman* before it, also proved popular,

[52] For discussion of Dares and Dictys in the context of the Second Sophistic, and what we know and can't know about the dates of composition of the two works, see F. Clark, *The First Pagan Historian: The Fortunes of a Fraud from Antiquity to the Enlightenment*, pp. 54–65.

[53] V. Prosperi, 'Strategie di autoconservazione del mito: La guerra di Troia tra Seconda Sofistica e prima età moderna', *Materiali e discussioni per l'analisi dei testi classici*, 71 (2013), 145–75 (pp. 153–4).

[54] Prosperi, 'Strategie di autoconservazione del mito', pp. 163–4. On the complexity of medieval historians' and poets' 'belief' in histories of antiquity, see Clark, *First Pagan Historian*, pp. 23–32.

[55] For the twelfth-century manuscripts in particular, see M.-R. Jung, *La légende de Troie en France au Moyen Age. Analyse des versions françaises et bibliographie raisonnée des manuscrits* (Basel, 1996), pp. 19–39. For updates on medieval manuscripts containing the late antique Troy legends, see N. Kıvılcım Yavuz, *Transtextual Networks*, 1 November 2020, accessed 29 December 2022, https://www.transtextual. net/.

[56] In fact, Guido seems to have acquired a copy of Dares's narrative before he finished his translation and to have had a fleeting *pentimento*, a moment of doubt about the source he worked from: did Benoît really know his Trojan history? This resulted in contradictions between Guido's prologue and epilogue. (See Meek, 'Introduction'

but for different reasons. As Prosperi argues, if the Latin reception of Dares and Dictys blurred the distinction between fiction and history – neither were intended to be read as history, yet as such the Latin translations presented them – with Guido's translation, the difference between fancy and fact evident to readers of the original Greek versions was restored: for late medieval readers, Benoît's *Roman* would be seen as poetic fantasy, Guido's *Historia* as sober historical account.[57] What the two had in common was the centrality to their plots of the same device, the same *diabolus ex machina*: in both narratives, violence against women is the engine that drives the plot. Guido, appreciably more misogynistic than Benoît, is more prone to interpret his female characters' victimisation, somehow, as culpability. To cite two examples presented by both Benoît and Guido as *casus belli*, turning points that build ineluctably to war, when he introduces Hesione – a Trojan maiden who has been raped and abducted by Greek Telamon – Guido blames her for the massacre of the Trojans and the destruction of Troy to come.[58] Later, when he introduces Helen, she inspires a meditation on the wickedness of women and (again) a lament for those to die at Troy.[59] Benoît, in contrast, presents both Hesione and Helen as paragons of feminine beauty and virtue, and lays blame for their mistreatment at the feet of the men who rape and/or abduct them.[60]

None of these Sicilian historical works – the *Historia*, the *Rebellamentu* or the *Conquesta* – supplies evidence of French influence on Sicilian letters. The *Conquesta* treats the topic of Norman conquest in Sicily but relies entirely on a Latin Sicilian source. Neither the *Conquesta* nor the *Rebellamentu* shows traces of the influence of French histories comparable to what Morreale describes

---

to the *Historia Destructionis Troiae*, pp. xix–xxi.) The reception history of Benoît's *Troie* is as complex as the story he tells; for discussion of the place of Guido's Latin translation in that history, see Jung, *Légende de Troie*, pp. 563–80. Jung reckons Guido's Latin prose translation to be roughly contemporary to the first prose versions in French (ibid., p. 563); but the history is murky, and Guido may have relied upon French prosifications of Benoît that also, like Guido, intensified the anti-feminist messages of the *Roman*.

[57] Prosperi, 'Strategie di autoconservazione del mito', p. 167.

[58] Guido delle Colonne, *Historia Destructionis Troiae*, ed. N. E. Griffin (Cambridge MA, 1936).p. 42; Guido delle Colonne, *Historia*, trans. Meek, p. 41.

[59] Guido delle Colonne, *Historia*, ed. Griffin, pp. 70–1; Guido delle Colonne, *Historia*, trans. Meek, pp. 68–9.

[60] For Hesione, see Benoît de Sainte-Maure, *Le Roman de Troie de Benoît de Sainte-Maure*, ed. L. Constans, 6 vols.(Paris, 1904–12), I, ll. 2793–824; Benoît de Sainte-Maure, *The Roman de Troie*, trans. G. S. Burgess and D. Kelly (Cambridge, 2017), pp. 77–8. For Helen, see *Le Roman de Troie*, ed. Constans, I, ll. 4315–72; *The Roman de Troie*, trans. Burgess and Kelly, pp. 94–5.

in Florentine histories. Even the *Historia*, largely translated from a French-language source, reframes Benoît's spin on the Troy narrative in a way that presages the Sicilian histories that would be written in the subsequent century. By translating the *Roman* from French to Latin and from poetry to prose, by stripping poetic detail and emphasising its anti-feminism, Guido's *Historia* turns Benoît's *Roman* into something that would not be out of place on a Sicilian bookshelf, next to the *Rebellamentu* and the *Conquesta*: a bureaucratic procedural leading the reader through a series of military engagements and negotiations between power brokers, rather than a sequence of entwined narratives of love and lust.

The reception histories of these three works, though they play out on very different scales, indicate that they found a readership both in Sicily and beyond. Guido's *Historia* would prove to be the most popular version of the Troy story during the late Middle Ages. It survives in roughly 240 manuscripts and would generate vernacular translations (*rivolgarizzamenti*, as it were), including an Italian vernacular translation made in *c.*1350 in Angevin Naples.[61] Henri Bresc's survey of Sicilian library inventories records four works on Trojan history, although it is not clear which works these were or even in what language; in one case alone does an inventory specify that it refers to Guido's history.[62] The *Historia* remained popular in printed editions and would not be debunked and discredited until the eighteenth century.[63] The *Rebellamentu* and the *Conquesta* would have a modest success in Sicily (mainly later than the fourteenth- and fifteenth-century library inventories surveyed by Bresc); the *Rebellamentu* survives in nine manuscripts and the *Conquesta* in sixteen. Neither would appear in printed editions until the patriotic enthusiasm for tracing the history of vernacular traditions drew scholars' attention to such works. An edition of the *Conquesta* was printed in 1865 and again in 1954, and the *Rebellamentu* in 1917 and again in 2010.

Given the topic of this essay – the fates of French in Sicily – the linguistic surround of the vernacular histories in their transmission history (each copy or translation was negotiated against a backdrop of linguistic actualities as intricate as those I am describing in this essay, a fractal complexity) and the passages between languages of all three of these works may be as revealing as their content. Guido's Trojan history began in Greek with Dares and Dictys. It found new life in Latin, then provided raw material for Benoît's

---

[61] Jung, *Légende de Troie*, p. 565; *Libro de la destructione de Troya: Volgarizzamento napoletano trecentesco da Guido delle Colonne*, ed. N. De Blasi (Rome, 1986), p. 11.

[62] Bresc, *Livre et société en Sicile*, p. 57.

[63] See Guido delle Colonne, *Historia*, trans. Meek, p. xi.

French romance and its prosifications. Guido translated it (back) into Latin, and that version generated imitations and retranslations in vernaculars across western Europe. This recursive translation history shows how entangled Latin and vernaculars were in western Europe during the late Middle Ages. It's tempting to think that the translation movement moved in one direction only: from Latin to the vernaculars. In fact, texts might bounce between languages. Guido's Latin history of Troy also demonstrates the advantages of Latin over the vernaculars. Benoît's *Roman* found a public in England, northern Italy and France, but Guido's *Historia* was read everywhere. Its linguistic dressing is (at least in part) to thank for its success. In late medieval and early modern Europe, Latin still was able to cross linguistic frontiers in a way that the vernaculars could not – not even a *cosmopolitan vernacular*, like French.

The *Rebellamentu* and the *Conquesta*, too, emerged from and were transmitted in a complex linguistic environment – but, again, on a much smaller scale, entirely internal to Sicily. Born as a *volgarizzamento* of a Latin original, the *Conquesta* would be (like Guido's *Historia*) retranslated into Latin. This translation, made in Sicily by Renaissance polymath Francesco Maurolico (1494–1575), did not have the same success as Guido's *Historia*; it survives in a single manuscript.[64] The *Rebellamentu* was a Sicilian version of a Tuscan account of Sicilian history. It's difficult to know exactly what to call such language work: is the *Rebellamentu* a translation or a *volgarizzamento*? (Modern Italian scholars, for the record, have no difficulty using the word 'traduzione' to describe it.) It did not generate subsequent translations.

As stated above, my focus on a period when little happened in the Sicilian literary record, roughly 1250–1400, creates a sense of literary collapse that belies both preceding and subsequent eras in Sicilian literature. Yet at the same time it provides an intriguing tableau for thinking about the trajectory of cosmopolitan French. In the closing pages of this essay, I shall survey the afterlife of the *Rebellamentu* and the *Conquesta* and make some observations about what this tells us not only about the fates of French in Sicily but more pointedly about the languages that *did* thrive in late medieval Sicily. Both the *Rebellamentu* and the *Conquesta* circulated (often together) in the company of a short list of Latin works about Sicily and its history. Five manuscripts (of the sixteen extant manuscripts of the *Conquesta* and the nine extant manuscripts of the *Rebellamentu*) include both vernacular histories.[65] All five manuscripts

---

[64] See Simone da Lentini, *La conquesta di Sichilia*, pp. 167–8. On Maurolico, see G. Lipari, 'Per una storia della cultura letteraria a Messina', *Archivio storico messinese* 40 (1982), 65–188 (pp. 132–41).

[65] For the extant manuscripts of the *Conquesta*, see Rossi-Taibbi's survey (Simone da Lentini, *La conquesta di Sichilia*, pp. 153–82). For the *Rebellamentu*, see Barbato's

also include a Latin history known as *De acquisicione insule Sicilie per Archadium facta rebellione Maniachii* (although that title only describes the content of the first chapter of the work).[66] Three of the five include a Latin geography of Sicily that has not been published or discussed in the scholarship.[67] This short shelf of Sicilian history and geography circulated together in manuscripts copied between the fifteenth and seventeenth centuries. The vernacular works did not appear in print until they came to the attention of modern philologists. *De acquisicione* has not appeared in print since the eighteenth century;[68] the Latin geography has never been printed.

What to make of this tradition: straddling Latin and vernacular, carried forward exclusively in manuscripts, well into the era of print? Like the vernacular-to-Latin translations, it bucks our preconceived notions of the forward progress of late medieval literary history and book history. We see these succession histories – Latin to vernacular and manuscript to print – as mono-directional and inevitable. However, as so often happens, the facts on the ground are more networked and entangled than that. Sicilian histories provide a superb example of an alternative to a more common trend, with the endurance of Latin and the persistence of manuscript transmission (alongside an emergent vernacular and print tradition within Sicily).

Indeed, we might add cosmopolitan French to the list of literary trends with weak uptake in Sicily. Sicily had its vernacular revolution in the first half of the thirteenth century. During the second half of that century, while French manuscript production was trending in northern Italy, Sicilian vernacular composition recedes; Guido's *Historia* shows that Latin remained relevant. French manuscripts were created and read in Angevin Naples during the fourteenth century. Sicilians, in the fourteenth century, wrote in Sicilian and Latin. That is, through the thirteenth and fourteenth centuries, the Sicilian tradition preserved what had long been at the heart of Sicilian letters: a combination of languages, engineered to speak to different constituencies, or

---

survey (*Rebellamentu*, pp. 75–99).

[66] On this work, see P. Colletta, 'La cronaca *De acquisicione insule Sicilie* e il suo volgarizzamento: appunti di ricerca', *Bollettino del Centro di Studi filologici e linguistici siciliani* 21 (2007), 215–42.

[67] This geography appears in Naples, Biblioteca Nazionale, MS XIII D 104, fols. 39r–94v (for Rossi-Taibbi's discussion, see Simone da Lentini, *La Conquesta*, p. 160); Barcelona, Biblioteca de Catalunya, MS 1034, fols. 95r–124v (see ibid., p. 162); and Naples, Biblioteca Nazionale, MS V G 29, fols. 7r–38r (see ibid., p. 163).

[68] For a list of the eighteenth-century print editions of *De acquisicione*, see Colletta, 'La cronaca *De acquisicione*', p. 215, n. 1. Colletta is now working on an edition of the work.

SICILIAN MULTILINGUALISM AND COSMOPOLITAN FRENCH 291

perhaps in this case speaking to the same constituency to tell different stories. More remarkable is the topic of these works: directed entirely inward, they spoke about Sicily, in many cases in Sicilian, and to Sicilians. The *Rebellamentu* was regularly accompanied by a historical appendix written in the Sicilian vernacular, a timeline of events in Sicilian history following the Vespers uprising discussed in the work itself.[69] Together, these historical narratives in Latin and Sicilian and the timeline bringing us up to the present became something like a journaling exercise, affective history and affective manuscript production used by bookish Sicilians to absorb and think through their history and its lineage to the present.

Bresc's library inventories of the fourteenth and fifteenth centuries note very few works of Sicilian history, and it may be the case that Sicilians' interest in local history intensified in later centuries.[70] Only two extant manuscripts of the *Rebellamentu* and the *Conquesta* date to the fifteenth century. Eight manuscripts date to the sixteenth century, seven to the seventeenth century, and two to the eighteenth century. Between the nineteenth century and the present, an interest in early vernacular texts and in local histories has guided our focus on these works and encouraged philologists to track them down on the paths followed by Sicilians during the years of Aragonese domination. Almost all the extant manuscripts of the *Rebellamentu* and the *Conquesta* are held in libraries in Sicily, Naples, and Barcelona.[71]

It seems appropriate that in the compound Latin-vernacular manuscript tradition that I'm describing, the vernacular works describe conquest and revolt, while the Latin works record geography and *longue durée* histories.

---

[69] This timeline appears in Piacenza, Biblioteca Comunale, MS 7 Pall. 225, fols. 74v–76v (for Rossi-Taibbi's discussion, see Simone da Lentini, *La Conquesta*, p. 153); Barcelona, Biblioteca de Catalunya, MS 990, fols. 66r–179r (this is a *volgarizzamento* of the *Historia Sicula di Nicolò Speciale*; see ibid., p. 157); Naples, Biblioteca Nazionale, MS XIII D 104, fols. 108v–109v (see ibid., p. 161); and Naples, Biblioteca Nazionale, MS V G 29, fols. 158v–159r (see ibid., p. 163).

[70] See Bresc, *Livre et société*, p. 57 for the few works of Sicilian history in Sicilian library inventories. He notes the 'very interesting' case of a library that includes just four volumes: a *Troyanus*, *Liber Alexandri*, the chronicle of Martin de Troppau and the *Conquesta*: 'romance and history are closely associated' (ibid.; document 10, page 118).

[71] One manuscript consulted for both Barbato's edition of the *Rebellamentu* and Rossi-Taibbi's edition of the *Conquesta* is held at Piacenza (Rossi-Taibbi, in Simone da Lentini, *La conquesta*, pp. 153–6; Barbato, *Rebellamentu*, pp. 78–81). There are manuscripts of the *Conquesta* in Paris (Simone da Lentini, *La conquesta*, p. 168) and Modena (ibid., p. 169). All other copies of the works are held in libraries in Sicily, Naples or Barcelona.

Latin was the language of ancient history (like Guido's *Historia*) or histories with a wide temporal scope. Vernacular gave voice to those upheavals and uprisings seen as generative of a uniquely Sicilian identity. French letters – received with enthusiasm in northern Italy, and over time transformed into thoroughly Italian products: Florentine histories and the glorious chivalric epics of the Renaissance – did not speak to Sicilians. In the nineteenth century, those chivalric epics, in a naturalised Italian form and updated by authors like Boiardo and Ariosto, arrived in (or perhaps returned to) Sicily, to be repackaged as the *opera dei pupi*. But during the centuries that stretched between the late Middle Ages and early modernity, Sicilians resisted cosmopolitan French, and opted for a compound Latin-vernacular literary culture. Only with these two voices in concert – and only these two voices – it seems, could Sicilian history be sung.

Bibliography

Manuscripts

Aix-en-Provence, Bibliothèque Méjanes, MS S Res. 95, 3.
Auxerre, Bm, MS 212 (179).
Avignon, Bm Ceccano, MSS 121; 344.
Avranches, Bibliothèque patrimoniale, MS 236.
Barcelona, Biblioteca de Catalunya, MSS 990; 1034
Bern, Burgerbibliothek, MS 207.
Bruges, Openbare Bibliotheek, MS 442.
Brussels, Algemeen Rijksarchief, reg. 1243.
Brussels, Egyptologische Stichting Koningin Elisabeth, MS 55.473.
Brussels, KBR, MSS 9390; 10432–5; 11120–22; IV 330; IV 746.
Cambrai, Bm, MS 679.
Chantilly, Musée Condé, MS 699 (1414).
Copenhagen, Det Kongelige Bibliotek, MS GKS 487.
Ghent, Universiteitsbibliotheek, MS 6.
Laon, Bm, MSS 442; 447.
Lille, Archives départementales du Nord, reg. B 4025.
Lille, Médiathèque Jean Levy, MS 647–648.
London, BL, Additional MS 20698; Harley MS 4487; Royal MS 20 D I.
London, Lambeth Palace Library, MS Carew 596.
Madrid, Real Biblioteca del Monasterio de San Lorenzo de El Escorial, MSS h.I.6; Y.I.2.
Namur, Bibliothèque universitaire, MS R.Mn B46.
Oxford, Bodleian Library, MSS Auct. F. III 15; Digby 23.
Paris, Bibliothèque de l'Arsenal, MSS 3472; 5092.
Paris, BnF, MSS fr. 782; fr. 789; fr. 1094; fr. 1610; fr. 12477; fr. 14973; fr. 15101; fr. 20125; fr. 24376; lat. 6400B; n.a.f. 6739.
Piacenza, Biblioteca Comunale, MS 7 Pall. 225.
Saint Petersburg, Rossiyskaya natsional'naya biblioteka, MS fr. F.v.XIV.3.
Santander, Biblioteca de Menéndez Pelayo, M-558.
Toulouse, Bm, MSS 2883; 2884.
Vatican, Biblioteca Apostolica Vaticana, MSS Reg.lat.165; Vat.lat.3793; MS Vat.lat.4788.
Venice, Biblioteca Marciana, MS fr. Z. XVII.
Venice, Museo Correr, MS Correr 1493.
Vienna, Österreichische Nationalbibliothek, Cod. 2571.
Wells-next-the-Sea, Holkham Hall, Library of the Earl of Leicester, MS 311.

294   BIBLIOGRAPHY

Primary sources

'Acallamh na Senórach', ed. with partial trans. W. Stokes, in *Irische Texte mit Wörterbuch*, ed. E. Windisch and W. Stokes, 4 vols. (Leipzig, 1900), IV, 1–438.

Adelard of Bath, *Adelard of Bath's Conversations with His Nephew*, ed. and trans. C. Burnett (Cambridge, 1998).

Adémar of Chabannes, *Ademari Cabannensis Chronicon*, ed. P. Bourgain, Corpus Christianorum Continuatio mediaevalis 129 (Turnhout, 1999).

Agobard of Lyon, *Liber contra objectiones Fredigisi abbatis*, *PL* 104, 162–5.

Aimon de Varennes, *Florimont: Ein altfranzösischer Abenteuerroman*, ed. A. Hilka [and A. Risop] (Gottingen, 1932).

Albertus Magnus, *Alberti Magni opera omnia*, ed. A. Borgnet, 38 vols. (Paris, 1890–5).

Alfonso X el Sabio, *General estoria: segunda parte*, ed. B. Almeida, 2 vols. (Madrid, 2009).

al-Idrisi, *Opus Geographicum*, ed. E. Cerulli (Leiden, 1970).

al-Jurjānī, ʿAbd al-Qāhir ibn ʿAbd al-Raḥmān n. *Kitāb asrār al-balāgha* [Arabic], ed. H. Ritter (Istanbul, 1954).

al-Sīrāfī, Abū Zayd, *Accounts of China and India*, trans. T. Mackintosh-Smith (New York, 2017).

al-Washshāʾ, Muḥammad ibn Isḥāq ibn Yaḥyā, *El Libro del Brocado* [*Kitāb al-muwashshā*], trans. T. Garulo (Madrid, 1990).

al-Washshāʾ, Muḥammad ibn Isḥāq ibn Yaḥyā, *Kitāb al-muwashshā* [Arabic] (Beirut, 1965).

Ambrosius Zeebout, *Tvoyage van Mher Joos van Ghistele*, ed. R. J. G. A. A. Gaspar (Hilversum, 1998).

Anna Comnena, *Annae Comnenae Alexias*, ed. D. R. Reinsch and A. Kambylis, 2 vols. (Berlin, 2001).

Annála Uladh, Annals of Ulster, Otherwise Annála Senait, Annals of Senat: A Chronicle of Irish Affairs, Vol. II, A.D. 1057–1131; 1155–1378, ed. and trans. B. Mac Carthy (Dublin, 1893).

The Annals of Inisfallen (MS. Rawlinson B. 503), ed. and trans. S. Mac Airt (Dublin, 1951).

'The Annals of Tigernach: The Continuation A.D. 1088–1178', ed. and trans. W. Stokes, *Revue celtique* 18 (1897), 9–59, 150–97, 268–303.

The Annals of Ulster (to A.D. 1131), Part I, Text and Translation, ed. and trans. S. Mac Airt and G. Mac Niocaill (Dublin, 1983).

Antiquities of Shropshire, ed. R. W. Eyton, 12 vols. (London, 1854–60).

Aucassin et Nicolette and Other Tales, trans. P. Matarasso (Harmondsworth, 1971).

Aucassin et Nicolette, ed. M. Roques (Paris, 1977).

BIBLIOGRAPHY 295

Ben Elʿazar, Jacob, 'Sipure ha-ahava shel Yaʿaqov ben Elʿazar' [Hebrew], ed. J. Schirmann, *Studies of the Research Institute for Hebrew Poetry in Jerusalem* 5 (1939), 247–66.

Ben Elʿazar, Jacob, *Sipure ahava shel Yaʿakov ben Elʿazar* [Hebrew], ed. Y. David (Tel Aviv, 1992).

Benoît de Sainte-Maure, *Le roman de Troie de Benoît de Sainte-Maure*, ed. L. Constans, 6 vols. (Paris, 1904–12).

Benoît de Sainte-Maure, *The Roman de Troie*, trans. G. S. Burgess and D. Kelly (Cambridge, 2017).

Berekhiah Ha-Naqdan, *Dodi ve-Nechdi (Uncle & Nephew)*, ed. and trans. H. Gollancz (Oxford, 1920).

Biographies des troubadours: textes provençaux des XIIIe et XIVe siècles, ed. J. Boutière and A.-H. Schutz (Paris, 1964).

Boethius, *The Consolation of Philosophy*, trans. V. Watt (London, 1969).

Book of Alexander (Libro de Alexandre), ed. and trans. P. Such and R. Rabone (Oxford, 2009).

Buzurg ibn Shahriyar of Ramhormuz, *Book of the Wonders of India: Mainland, Sea and Islands*, ed. and trans. G. S. P. Freeman-Grenville (London, 1981).

Caithréim Chellacháin Chaisil: The Victorious Career of Cellachán of Cashel, or the Wars between the Irishmen and the Norsemen in the Middle of the 10th Century, ed. and trans. A. Bugge (Oslo, 1905).

Calendar of Ancient Correspondence concerning Wales, ed. J. G. Edwards (Cardiff, 1935).

Calendar of Ancient Petitions Relating to Wales, ed. W. Rees (Cardiff, 1975).

Cân Rolant: The Medieval Welsh Version of the 'Song of Roland', ed. and trans. A. C. Rejhon (Berkeley, 1984).

Cath Ruis na Ríg for Bóinn, ed. and trans. E. Hogan, Todd Lecture Series 4 (Dublin, 1892).

La chanson de Girart de Rousillon, ed. M. de Combarieu du Grès and G. Gouiran (Paris, 1993).

Chrétien de Troyes, *Le Chevalier au Lion (Yvain)*, ed. M. Roques (Paris, 1971).

The Chronicle of Morea, ed. J. Schmitt (London, 1904).

Chronicum Scotorum, A Chronicle of Irish Affairs, from the Earliest Times to A.D. 1135, ed. and trans. W. M. Hennessy (London, 1866).

Codex Comanicus. Édition diplomatique avec fac-similés, ed. V. Drimba (Bucharest, 2000).

Cogadh Gaedhel re Gallaibh: The War of the Gaedhil with the Gaill, or the Invasions of Ireland by the Danes and Other Norsemen, ed. and trans. J. H. Todd (Dublin, 1867).

A Commentary on the Book of Job, ed. W. A. Wright and trans. S. A. Hirsch (London, 1905).

Constantine Manasses, *Constantini Manassis breviarium chronicum*, ed. O. Lampsides, 2 vols. (Athens, 1996).

Constantine VII Porphyrogenitus, *De ceremoniis aulae byzantinae libri duo*, ed. J. J. Reiske, 2 vols. (Bonn, 1829–40).

Corpus Catalogorum Belgii: The Medieval Booklists of the Southern Low Countries, vol. 1, *Province of West Flanders*, ed. A. Derolez and B. Victor (Brussels, 1997).

Corpus Catalogorum Belgii: The Medieval Booklists of the Southern Low Countries, vol. 5, *Dukes of Burgundy*, ed. T. Falmagne and B. Van den Abeele (Leuven, 2016).

Cywyddau Iolo Goch ac Eraill, ed. H. Lewis, T. Roberts and I. Williams (Cardiff, 1937).

Danse macabre. Ce present livre est appellé Miroer salutaire pour toutes gens, et de tous estaz, et est de grant utilitez et recreacion, pour pleuseurs ensengnemens tant en latin comme en françoys lesquex il contient, ainsi composé pour ceulx qui desirent acquerir leur salut et qui le voudront avoir (Paris, 1486).

de Feo, R. and P. Strippoli, directors, *A Classic Horror Story* (Italy, 2021).

Le débat provençal de l'âme et du corps (texte critique), ed. B. Sutorius (Fribourg, 1916).

'Edición crítica y estudio de la *Crónica troyana* promovida por Alfonso XI', ed. C. D'Ambruoso (unpublished Ph.D. dissertation, Universidade de Santiago de Compostela, 2012).

Falaquera, Shem Tov ben Joseph ibn, *The Book of the Seeker (Sefer Ha-Mebaqqesh)*, trans. M. H. Levine (New York, 1976).

Fouke le Fitz Waryn, ed. E. J. Hathaway, P. T. Ricketts, C. A. Robson and A. D. Wilshere (Oxford, 1975).

Fulcher of Chartres, *Historia Hierosolymitana (1095–1127)*, ed. H. Hagenmeyer (Heidelberg, 1913).

Geoffrey Malaterra, *De rebus gestis Rogerii Calabriae comitis et Roberti Guiscardi ducis fratris eius*, ed. L. A. Muratori (Bologna, 1927).

Geoffroy de Villehardouin, *La conquête de Constantinople*, ed. J. Dufournet (Paris, 2004).

Gerald of Wales, *De rebus a se gestis*, ed. J. S. Brewer, *Giraldi Cambrensis Opera*, vol. 1 (London, 1861).

Gerald of Wales, *De rebus a se gestis*, trans. H. E. Butler, *The Autobiography of Gerald of Wales*, new edn (Woodbridge, 2005).

Gerald of Wales, *Expugnatio Hibernica: the Conquest of Ireland by Giraldus Cambrensis*, ed. and trans. A. B. Scott and F. X. Martin (Dublin, 1978).

Gerald of Wales, *Speculum ecclesiae*, ed. J. S. Brewer, *Giraldi Cambrensis Opera*, vol. 4 (London, 1873).

Gervase of Tilbury, *Otia imperialia: Recreation for an Emperor*, ed. and trans. S. E. Banks and J. W. Binns (Oxford, 2002).

La geste des Engleis en Yrlande: The Deeds of the Normans in Ireland: A New Edition of the Chronicle Formerly Known as the Song of Dermot and the Earl, ed. and trans. E. Mullally (Dublin, 2002).

Le Glossaire de Leipzig, ed. M. Banitt, 4 vols. (Jerusalem, 1995–2005).

Gottfried von Strassburg, Tristan und Isold, ed. and trans. W. Haug and M. G. Scholz (Frankfurt am Main, 2011).

Guido delle Colonne, Historia Destructionis Troiae, ed. N. E. Griffin (Cambridge MA, 1936).

Guido delle Colonne, Historia Destructionis Troiae, trans. M. E. Meek (Bloomington, 1974).

Handelingen van de Leden en van de Staten van Vlaanderen (1384–1405), ed. W. Prevenier (Brussels, 1959).

Handelingen van de Leden en van de Staten van Vlaanderen (1405–1419), ed. A. Zoete (Brussels, 1981–82).

Hartmann von Aue, Erec, ed. A. Leitzmann and L. Wolff, 7th edn, rev. K. Gärtner (Tübingen, 2006).

Hartmann von Aue, Iwein, ed. and trans. V. Mertens (Frankfurt am Main, 2004).

Heinrich von Veldeke, Eneasroman, ed. and trans. H. Fromm (Frankfurt am Main, 1992).

Histoire ancienne jusqu'à César, ed. C. Gaullier-Bougassas (Turnhout, 2012).

Historia Peredur vab Efrawc, ed. G. W. Goetinck (Cardiff, 1976).

Homer, Iliad, ed. and trans. A. T. Murray and W. F. Wyatt, 2 vols. (Cambridge MA 1999).

Hugo Falcandus, History of the Tyrants of Sicily by 'Hugo Falcandus', trans. and annotated G. A. Loud and T. Wiedemann (Manchester, 1998).

Hugo Falcandus, La Historia o Liber de Regno Sicilie et la Epistola ad Petrum Panormitane Ecclesie Thesaurarium, ed. G. B. Siragusa (Rome, 1897).

Ibn Ezra, Abraham, El Comentario de Abraham Ibn Ezra al Libro de Job: Edición Crítica, Traducción y Estudio Introductorio, ed. and trans. M. Gómez Aranda (Madrid, 2004).

Ibn Ezra, Moses, Kitāb al-muḥāḍara wa-l-mudhākara, ed. M. Abumalham Mas, 2 vols. (Madrid, 1986).

Ibn Sahula, Isaac, Meshal ha-qadmoni, ed. and trans. R. Loewe (Oxford, 2004).

Ibn Ṣaqbel, Solomon, 'Asher in the Harem', trans. R. P. Scheindlin, in Rabbinic Fantasies: Imaginative Narratives from Classical Hebrew Literature, ed. D. Stern and M. J. Mirsky (New Haven, 1998), pp. 253–67.

Ibn Ṣaqbel, Solomon, Ha-shira ha-'ivrit bi-Sfarad uvi-Provans, ed. J. Schirmann [Hebrew] (Jerusalem, 1954).

Isidore of Seville, The Etymologies of Isidore of Seville, trans. S. A. Barney (Cambridge, 2006).

Jan van den Berghe, *Dat kaetspel ghemoralizeert*, ed. J. Roetert Frederikse (Leiden, 1915).

Jean Gobi, *Dialogue avec un fantôme*, ed. and trans. M.-A. Polo de Beaulieu (Paris, 1994).

Jean Renart, *Le roman de la rose ou de Guillaume de Dole*, ed. F. Lecoy (Paris, 2005).

Jean Renart, *The Romance of the Rose, or, Guillaume de Dole*, trans. P. Terry and N. V. Durling (Philadelphia, 1993).

Joffroi de Waterford, *The French Works of Joffroi de Waterford: A Critical Edition*, ed. K. Busby (Turnhout, 2020).

John Cinnamus, *Ioannis Cinnami epitome rerum ab Ioanne et Alexio Comnenis gestarum*, ed. A. Meineke (Bonn, 1836).

John of Garland, *Parisiana poetria*, ed. and trans. T. Lawler (Cambridge, 2000).

John Scottus Eriugena, *Glossae divinae historiae: The Biblical Glosses of John Scottus Eriugena*, ed. J. J. Contreni and P. P. Ó Néill (Florence, 1997).

Lanfranc, Archbishop of Canterbury, *The Letters of Lanfranc, Archbishop of Canterbury*, ed. and trans. H. Clover and M. Gibson (Oxford, 1979).

Latini, Brunetto, *Tresor*, ed. P. G. Beltrami, P. Squillacioti, P. Torri and S. Vetteroni (Turin, 2007).

'La leggenda di Osso Mastrosso e Carcagnosso spiegata in A Classic Horror Story', *Youtube*, accessed 14 August 2023, https://www.youtube.com/watch?v=P7AIPpfy7D4.

Letres des ysles et terres nouvellement trouvées par les Portugalois. Un voyage imaginaire à Sumatra à la Renaissance, ed. G. Berthon and R. Cappellen (Geneva, 2021).

Las leys d'amors. Manuscrit de l'Académie des jeux floraux, ed. J. Anglade, 3 vols. (Toulouse-Paris, 1919–20).

Las leys d'amors. Redazione lunga in prosa, ed. B. Fedi (Florence, 2019).

Libro de Alexandre, ed. J. Casas Rigall (Madrid, 2014).

Libro de la destructione de Troya: Volgarizzamento napoletano trecentesco da Guido delle Colonne, ed. N. De Blasi (Rome, 1986).

The Life of St. Andrew the Fool, ed. L. Rydén, 2 vols. (Uppsala, 1995).

The Mabinogion, trans. S. Davies (Oxford, 2007).

Maimonides, Moses, *Maimonides' Treatise on Logic (Maqāla fī sinā'at al-mantiq)*, ed. and trans. I. Efros (New York, 1938).

Maimonides, Moses, *Mishna 'im perush Rabenu Moshe ben Maimon*, ed. and trans. Y. Qaʿfiḥ (Jerusalem, 1964).

Maimonides, Moses, *The Guide of the Perplexed*, trans. S. Pines (Chicago, 1963).

Marie de France, *Les Fables*, ed. C. Brucker, 2nd edn (Paris, 1998)

Martin da Canal, *Les estoires de Venise*, trans. L. K. Morreale (Padua, 2009).

Martin da Canal, *Les estoires de Venise: cronaca veneziana in lingua francese dalle origini al 1275*, ed. A. Limentani (Florence, 1972).

The Medieval French Roman d'Alexandre. *Vol. I: Text of the Arsenal and Venice Versions*, ed. M. S. La Du (Paris, 1937).

The Medieval French Roman d'Alexandre. *Vol. II: Version of Alexandre de Paris, Text*, ed. E.C. Armstrong, D.L. Buffum, B. Edwards, and L.F.H. Lowe (Princeton, 1938).

Michael Psellus, *Michaelis Pselli chronographia*, ed. D. R. Reinsch (Berlin, 2014).

Mikra'ot Gedolot 'Ha-Keter', 24 books in 21 volumes, ed. M. Cohen (Ramat Gan, 1992).

Mission to Asia, trans. C. Dawson (New York, 1966; repr. Toronto, 1980).

Nicetas Choniates, *Nicetae Choniatae historia*, ed. J. A. van Dieten, 2 vols. (Berlin, 1975).

Odo of Deuil, *De profectione Ludovici VII in orientem*, ed. and trans. V. G. Berry (New York, 1948).

Opera omnia Liudprandi Cremonensis, ed. P. Chiesa (Turnhout, 1998).

De Oorkonden der Graven van Vlaanderen (1191–Aanvang 1206), Part I, ed. W. Prevenier (Brussels, 1966).

Owein, or, Chwedyl iarlles y ffynnawn, ed. R. L. Thomson (Dublin, 1968).

Paulus Orosius, *Pauli Orosii Historiarum Adversum Paganos Libri VII*, I, ed. Karl Zangemeister, Corpus Scriptorum Ecclesiasticorum Latinorum 5 (Vienna, 1882).

Pegolotti, Francesco Balducci, 'Notices of the Land Route to Cathay', ed. H. Yule, *Cathay and the Way Thither*, rev. H. Cordier, new edn, 3 vols. (London, 1914; repr. Liechtenstein, 1967), III, 137–73.

Pegolotti, Francesco Balducci, *La pratica della mercatura*, ed. A. Evans (Cambridge MA, 1936; repr. New York, 1970).

Peire Cardenale, *Il trovatore Peire Cardenal*, ed. S. Vatteroni, 2 vols. (Modena, 2013).

Le pèlerinage de Charlemagne, ed. and trans. G. S. Burgess (Edinburgh, 1998).

Petrus Ansolini de Ebulo, *De rebus siculis carmen*, ed. E. Rota, in *Rerum Italicarum Scriptores*, gen. ed. L. A. Muratori, 34 vols., XXXI, pt. 1 (Castello, 1904).

Pfaffe Konrad, *Rolandslied*, ed. C. Wesle, rev. P. Wapnewski (Tübingen, 1985).

Philippe de Mézières, *Songe du viel pelerin*, ed. J. Blanchard (Geneva, 2015).

'A Poem Composed for Cathal Croibhdhearg Ó Conchubhair', ed. and trans. B. Ó Cuív, *Ériu* 34 (1983), 157–74.

Polo, Marco, *Milione/Le divisament dou monde. Il Milione nelle redazioni Toscana e franco-italiana*, ed. G. Ronchi (Milan, 1982).

Polo, Marco, *The Description of the World*, trans. S. Kinoshita (Indianapolis, 2016).

Повѣсть времѧньныхъ лѣтъ (*Povest' vremennych let*), trans. S. H. Cross and O. P. Sherbowitz-Wetzor (Cambridge MA, 1953).

Raimbaut de Vaqueiras, *The Poems of the Troubadour Raimbaut de Vaqueiras*, ed. J. Linskill (The Hague, 1964).

Raimon Vidal, *The* Razos de trobar *of Raimon Vidal and Associated Texts*, ed. J. H. Marshall (London, 1972).

Rashi (Solomon ben Isaac), *Commentary on Job*, trans. R. A. J. Rosenberg, *Job: A New English Translation* (New York, 1995).

Rashi (Solomon ben Isaac), *Pentateuch with Rashi's Commentary*, ed. and trans. M. Rosenbaum and A. M. Silbermann (London, 1929–34), *Sefaria*, accessed 25 August 2023, https://www.sefaria.org/Rashi_on_Genesis.1.1.1?lang=en.

Lu rebellamentu di Sichilia, ed. Marcello Barbato (Palermo, 2010).

Récits d'un ménestrel de Reims, ed. N. de Wailly (Paris, 1876).

Robert de Clari, *La conquête de Constantinople*, ed. J. Dufournet (Paris, 2004).

Le roman de Thèbes, ed. and trans. F. Mora-Lebrun (Paris, 1995).

Rustaveli, Shota, *The Knight in the Panther Skin*, trans. L. Coffin (Tblisi, 2015).

Dat Scaecspel, ed. G. Van Schaick Avelingh (Leiden, 1912).

Scriptores originum Constantinopolitanarum, ed. T. Preger, 2 vols. (Leipzig 1901–7).

Selections from Ystorya Bown o Hamtwn, ed. E. Poppe and R. Reck (Cardiff, 2009).

Simone da Lentini, *La conquesta di Sichilia fatta per li normandi*, ed. G. Rossi-Taibbi (Palermo, 1955).

Sīrat al-Ẓāhir Baybars, no named editor (Cairo, 1996).

The Song of Dermot and the Earl: An Old French Poem from the Carew Manuscript no. 596 in the Archiepiscopal Library at Lambeth Palace, ed. and trans. G. H. Orpen (Oxford, 1892).

Sydrac le philosophe: le livre de la fontaine de toutes sciences, ed. E. Ruhe (Wiesbaden, 2000).

Tales of the Elders of Ireland: A New Translation of Acallam na Senórach, trans. A. Dooley and H. Roe (Oxford, 1999).

Tibaut, *Le roman de la poire*, ed. C. Marchello-Nizia (Paris, 1984).

Thomas, *Le roman de Tristan*, ed. F. Lecoy, with notes, presentation, and translation by E. Baumgartner and I. Short (Paris, 2003).

Tristrams saga ok Ísöndar, ed. and trans. P. Jorgensen, in *Norse Romance*, vol. I: *The Tristan Legend*, ed. M. E. Kalinke (Cambridge, 1999).

Two Medieval Outlaws: Eustace the Monk and Fouke Fitz Waryn, trans. G. S. Burgess (Cambridge, 1997).

Ulrich von Zatzikhoven, *Lanzelet*, ed. and trans. F. Kragl (Berlin, 2006).

Urkunden zur älteren Handels- und Staatsgeschichte der Republik Venedig mit besonderer Beziehung auf Byzanz und die Levante vom neunten bis zum Ausgang des fünfzehnten Jahrhunderts, ed. G. L. F. Tafel and G. M. Thomas, 3 vols. (Vienna, 1856–7).

Veneziano, A., *Ottave*, ed. A. Rigoli (Turin, 1967).

Walter Map, *De nugis curialium*, ed. and trans. M. R. James, rev. R. Mynors (Oxford, 2002).

Warner of Rouen, *Moriuht, A Norman Latin Poem from the Early Eleventh Century*, ed. and trans. C. J. McDonough (Toronto, 1995).

The Way of Lovers: The Oxford Anonymous Commentary on the Song of Songs (Bodleian Library, MS Opp. 625), ed. and trans. S. Japhet and B. D. Walfish (Leiden, 2017).

A Welsh Bestiary of Love, ed. G. C. G. Thomas (Dublin, 1988).

Willelmi Tyrensis Archiepiscopi chronicon, ed. R. B. C. Huygens, 3 vols. (Turnhout, 1986).

The William Davidson Talmud, Sefaria, ed. and trans. A. Steinsaltz, accessed 25 August 2023, https://www.sefaria.org/texts/Talmud/Bavli.

William of Rubruck, *The Mission of Friar William of Rubruck: His Journey to the Court of the Great Khan Möngke, 1253–55*, trans. P. Jackson (Indianapolis, 2009).

[Wolfram von Eschenbach], *Wolfram von Eschenbach*, ed. K. Lachmann (Berlin, 1833).

Wolfram von Eschenbach, *Parzival*, ed. E. Nellmann, trans. D. Kuhn (Frankfurt am Main, 1994).

Wolfram von Eschenbach, *Willehalm*, ed. and trans. J. Heinzle (Frankfurt am Main, 1991).

Ystorya de Carolo Magno o Lyfr Coch Hergest, ed. S. J. Williams, 2nd edn (Cardiff, 1930).

Ystorya Gereint uab Erbin, ed. R. L. Thomson (Dublin, 1997).

Ystoryaeu Seint Greal, Rhan 1: Y Keis, ed. T. Jones (Cardiff, 1992).

Secondary works

Abulafia, D., *Frederick II: A Medieval Emperor* (London, 1988).

——, 'The Kingdom of Sicily under the Hohenstaufen and Angevins', in *The New Cambridge Medieval History*, ed. D. Abulafia (Cambridge, 1999), pp. 498–522.

Abu-Lughod, J. L., *Before European Hegemony: The World System A.D. 1250–1350* (Oxford, 1989).

Aerts, W. J., 'Froumund's Greek: An Analysis of fol. 12v of the Codex Vindobonensis Graecus 114, Followed by a Comparison with a Latin-Greek Wordlist in MS 179 Auxerre fol.137v ff.', in *The Empress Theophano*, ed. A. Davids (Cambridge, 1995), pp. 194–209.

——, 'The Latin-Greek Wordlist in MS. 236 of the Municipal Library of Avranches, fol. 97v', *Anglo-Norman Studies* 9 (1987), 64–9.

Ailes, M., 'Ambroise's *Estoire de la guerre sainte* and the Development of a Genre', *Reading Medieval Studies* 34 (2008), 1–19.

Albert, J.-P., 'Croire et ne pas croire. Les chemins de l'hétérodoxie dans le Registre d'Inquisition de Jacques Fournier', *Heresis* 39 (2003), 91–106.

Allsen, T. T., 'The Cultural Worlds of Marco Polo', *Journal of Interdisciplinary History* 31 (2001), 375–83.

——, 'The Rasûlid Hexaglot in its Eurasian Cultural Context', in *The King's Dictionary. The Rasûlid Hexaglot: Fourteenth Century Vocabularies in Arabic, Persian, Turkic, Greek, Armenian and Mongol*, ed. P. B. Golden (Leiden, 2000), pp. 25–48.

Amer, S., *Crossing Borders: Love between Women in Medieval French and Arabic Literatures* (Philadelphia, 2008).

Anderson, B., *Imagined Communities: Reflections on the Origin and Spread of Nationalism*, rev. edn (London and New York, 2006).

Anglade, J., 'Poésies religieuses inédites du XIVe siècle en dialecte toulousain tirées des *Leys d'Amors*,' *Annales du Midi* 29 (1917), 1–48.

Aramon i Serra, R., 'Un debat de l'ànima i el cos en versos catalans', in *Recueil de travaux offerts à M. Clovis Brunel par ses amis, collègues et élèves*, 2 vols. (Paris, 1955), I, 38–52.

Arizaleta, A., 'El *Libro de Alexandre*: el clérigo al servicio del rey', *Troianalexandrina* 8 (2008), 73–114.

——, *La translation d'Alexandre. Recherches sur les structures et les significations du* Libro de Alexandre (Paris, 1999).

Armstrong, A., and E. Strietman, ed., *The Multilingual Muse: Transcultural Poetics in the Burgundian Netherlands* (Cambridge, 2017).

Armstrong, C. A. J., 'The Language Question in the Low Countries: The Use of French and Dutch by the Dukes of Burgundy and their Administration', in *Europe in the Late Middle Ages*, ed. J. R. Hale and J. R. Highfield (London, 1965), pp. 386–409.

Aronstein, S., 'Becoming Welsh: Counter-Colonialism and the Negotiation of Native Identity in *Peredur vab Efrawc*', *Exemplaria* 17 (2005), 135–68.

Ashe, L., *Fiction and History in England, 1066–1200* (Cambridge, 2007).

Aslanov, C., *Evidence of Francophony in Mediaeval Levant: Decipherment and Interpretation (MS. Paris BnF copte 43)* (Jerusalem, 2006).

——, *Le français au Levant, jadis et naguère. A la recherche d'une langue perdue* (Paris, 2006).

——, 'Le français de Rabbi Joseph Kara et de Rabbi Eliezer de Beaugency d'après leurs commentaires sur Ezekiel', *Revue des études juives* 159 (2000), 425–46.

——, 'Languages in Contact in the Latin East: Acre and Cyprus', *Crusades* 1 (2002), 155–81.

——, 'The Old French Glosses of an Anonymous *Peshat* Commentary on Song of Songs', *Jewish Quarterly Review* 109 (2019), 38–53.

Aude, É., '*III. Les plaintes de la Vierge au pied de la croix et les quinze signes de la fin du monde*, d'après un imprimé toulousain du XVIe siècle', *Annales du Midi* 17 (1905), 365–85.

Auerbach, E., *Literary Language and Its Public in Late Latin Antiquity and in the Middle Ages*, trans. R. Manheim (Princeton, 1965).

——, *Mimesis: The Representation of Reality in Western Literature*, trans. W. Trask (Princeton, 1953).

Babbi, A. M., 'Pierre de Paris traducteur de la *Consolatio Philosophiae*', in *La traduction vers le moyen français. Actes du IIe colloque de l'AIEMF, Poitiers, 27–29 avril 2006*, ed. C. Galderisi and C. Pignatelli (Turnhout, 2007), pp. 23–32.

——, 'La réception en Angleterre de la *Consolatio philosophiae*. Le *Roman de Philosophie* de Simund de Freine', in *Boèce au fil du temps. Son influence sur les lettres européennes du Moyen Age à nos jours*, ed. S. Conte, A. Oïffer-Bomsel and M. E. Cantarino-Suñer (Paris, 2019), pp. 369–82.

Badel, P.-Y., 'Lire la merveille selon Marco Polo', *Revue des Sciences Humaines* 183 (1981), 7–16.

Baker, D. P., and N. Cartlidge, 'Manuscripts of the Medieval Latin Debate Between Body and Soul (*Visio Philiberti*)', *Notes and Queries* 61 (2014), 196–201.

Bango de la Campa, F. M., '*Le pèlerinage de vie humaine* versus *El pelegrino de la vida humana*', *Cahiers d'études hispaniques médiévales* 30 (2007), 85–108.

Banitt, M., 'La langue vernaculaire dans les commentaires de Raschi', in *Rashi 1040–1990. Hommage à Ephraim Urbach: congrès européen des études juives*, ed. G. Sed-Rajna (Paris, 1993), pp. 411–18.

Banniard, M., 'La langue des esclaves peut-elle parler de Dieu? La langue occitane à la conquête de son acrolecte religieux', in *La parole sacrée — formes, fonctions, sens (XIe–XVe s.)*, Cahiers de Fanjeaux 47 (Toulouse, 2012), pp. 195–214.

——, *Viva voce. Communication écrite et communication orale du IVe au IXe siècle en Occident latin* (Paris, 1992).

Baquedano, L., 'Le pouvoir du livre: stratégies des imprimeurs dans les seuils de *l'Historia de la linda Melosina* (1489)', *Cahiers d'études hispaniques médiévales* 35 (2012), 233–42.

Barbato, M., and G. Palumbo, 'Fonti francesi di Boccaccio napoletano?', in *Boccaccio angioino: materiali per la storia culturale di Napoli nel Trecento*, ed. G. Alfano, T. D'Urso and A. Perriccioli Saggese (Brussels, 2012), pp. 127–48.

Bartlett, R., *Gerald of Wales, 1146–1223* (Oxford, 1982).

——, *Gerald of Wales: A Voice of the Middle Ages* (Stroud, 2006).

——, *Gerald of Wales and the Ethnographic Imagination*, Kathleen Hughes Memorial Lectures 12 (Cambridge, 2013).

——, *The Making of Europe: Conquest, Colonization, and Cultural Change, 950–1350* (Princeton, 1993).

Baschet, J., *Corps et âmes. Une histoire de la personne au Moyen Âge* (Paris, 2016).

——, 'Une image à deux temps. Jugement Dernier et jugement des âmes au Moyen Age', *Images Re-vues* 1 (2008), accessed 17 February 2024, https://doi.org/10.4000/imagesrevues.878.

Baswell, C., 'Marvels of Translation and Crises of Transition in the Romances of Antiquity', in *Cambridge Companion to Medieval Romance*, ed. R. L. Krueger (Cambridge, 2000).

Baswell, C., C. Cannon, J. Wogan-Browne and K. Kerby-Fulton, 'Competing Archives, Competing Histories: French and Its Cultural Locations in Late-Medieval England', *Speculum* 90 (2015), 635–700.

Batiouchkof, T., 'Le débat du corps et de l'âme', *Romania* 20 (1891), 1–55, 513–78.

Bauschke, R., 'Kanzone', in Kellner, Reichlin and Rudolph, ed., *Handbuch Minnesang*, pp. 509–21.

Beihammer, A., 'Comnenian Imperial Succession and the Ritual World of Niketas Choniates's Chronike Diegesis', in *Court Ceremonies and Rituals of Power in Byzantium and the Medieval Mediterranean*, ed. A. Beihammer, S. Constantinou and M. Parani (Leiden, 2013), pp. 159–202.

Beit-Arié, M., ed., *The Only Dated Medieval Hebrew Manuscript Written in England (1189 CE) and the Problem of Pre-explusion Anglo-Hebrew Manuscripts*, with appendices by M. Banitt and Z. E. Rokéaḥ (London, 1985).

Beltran, V., *La corte de Babel. Lenguas, poética y política en la España del siglo XIII* (Madrid, 2005).

Benedetti, R., ed., *Le roman d'Alexandre: riproduzione del ms. Venezia, Biblioteca Museo Correr, Correr 1493* (Tricesimo, 1998).

Benjamin, W., 'The Task of the Translator', in *Illuminations. Essays and Reflections*, ed. H. Arendt, trans. H. Zohn (New York, 2007), pp. 69–82.

Berschin, W., 'Greek Elements in Medieval Latin Manuscripts', in *The Sacred Nectar of the Greeks: The Study of Greek in the West in the Early Middle Ages*, ed. S. A. Brown and M. W. Herren (London: King's College London, 1988), pp. 85–104.

——, *Greek Letters and the Latin Middle Ages: From Jerome to Nicholas of Cusa* (Washington, 1988).

Bertau, K., *Über Literaturgeschichte: Literarischer Kunstcharakter und Geschichte in der höfischen Epik um 1200* (Munich, 1983).

Bibring, T., 'Fairies, Lovers, and Glass Palaces: French Influences on Thirteenth-Century Hebrew Poetry in Spain — the Case of Yaʿakov ben Elʿazar's Ninth Maḥberet', *Jewish Quarterly Review* 107 (2017), 297–322.

Biemans, J. A. A. M., *Onsen Speghele Ystoriale in Vlaemsche. Codicologisch onderzoek naar de overlevering van de* Spiegel historiael *van Jacob van Maerlant*,

Philip Utenbroeke en Lodewijk van Velthem, met een beschrijving van de handschriften en fragmenten, 2 vols. (Leuven, 1997).

Biesterfeldt, H. H., and D. Gutas, 'The Malady of Love', *Journal of the American Oriental Society* 104 (1984), 21–55.

Billy, D., 'L'autrier cuidai aber druda (BdT 461.146)', *Lecturae tropatorum* 8 (2015), 1–30.

Bisagni, J., *From Atoms to the Cosmos: The Irish Tradition of the Divisions of Time in the Early Middle Ages*, Kathleen Hughes Memorial Lectures 18 (Cambridge, 2020).

——, 'Paris BnF MS Lat. 6400B', in J. Bisagni, ed., *A Descriptive Handlist of Breton Manuscripts, c. AD 780–1100*, accessed 3 February 2023, https://ircabritt.nuigalway.ie/handlist/catalogue/138.

Bischoff, B., 'Das griechische Element in der abendländischen Bildung des Mittelalters', *Byzantinische Zeitschrift* 44 (1951), 27–55.

Blakey, B., 'Aucassin et Nicolette XXIX, 4', *French Studies* 22 (1968), 97–8.

Bonath, G., *Untersuchungen zur Überlieferung des Parzival Wolframs von Eschenbach*, 2 vols. (Lübeck, 1970–1).

Bonnet, M. R., 'Arles du XVe au XVIe siècle, entre latin, provençal et français: deux siècles d'histoire, trois langues en contact', *Revue des langues romanes* 123 (2019), 23–44.

Boone, M., 'Une famille au service de l'État bourguignon naissant: Roland et Jean d'Uutkerke, nobles flamands dans l'entourage de Philippe le Bon', *Revue du Nord* 77 (1995), 233–56.

——, 'Langue, pouvoirs et dialogue: aspects linguistiques de la communication entre les ducs de Bourgogne et leurs sujets flamands (1385–1505)', *Revue du Nord* 379 (2009), 9–33.

Bossy, M.-A., 'Medieval Debates of Body and Soul', *Comparative Literature* 28 (1976), 144–63.

Bou, E., 'Catalan Poetry', in *The Princeton Encyclopedia of Poetry and Poetics*, 4th edn, ed. R. Greene, S. Cushman, C. Cavanagh, J. Ramazani, P. Rouzer, H. Feinsod, D. Marno and A. Slessarev, pp. 211–13 (Princeton, 2012).

Brand, C., *Byzantium Confronts the West* (Cambridge MA, 1968).

Brandsma, F., and F. P. Knapp, 'Lancelotromane', in Pérennec and Schmid, *Höfischer Roman in Vers und Prosa*, pp. 393–457.

Brann, R., *The Compunctious Poet: Cultural Ambiguity and Hebrew Poetry in Muslim Spain* (Baltimore, 1991).

——, *Iberian Moorings: Al-Andalus, Sefarad, and the Tropes of Exceptionalism* (Philadelphia, 2021).

Brantley, J., *Reading in the Wilderness: Private Devotion and Public Performance in Late Medieval England* (Chicago, 2007).

Breatnach, C., 'Irish Proper Names in the *Codex Salmanticensis*', *Ériu* 55 (2005), 85–101.

Bregman, D., *The Golden Way: The Hebrew Sonnet during the Renaissance and the Baroque*, trans. A. Brener (Tempe AZ, 2006).

Brent, J. J., 'From Address to Debate: Generic Considerations in the *Debate between Soul and Body*', *Comitatus* 32 (2001), 1–18.

Bresc, H., 'La bibliothèque de Guiovanni de Cruyllas (1423)', *Bollettino del Centro di Studi filologici e linguistici siciliani* 10 (1969), 414–19.

——, *Livre et société en Sicile (1299–1499)* (Palermo, 1971).

Bridges, V., '"L'estoire d'Alixandre vos veul par vers traitier …": Passions and Polemics in Latin and Vernacular Alexander Literature of the Later Twelfth Century', *Nottingham Medieval Studies* 58 (2014), 87–113.

——, *Medieval Narratives of Alexander the Great: Transnational Texts in England and France* (Cambridge, 2018).

Brilliant, V., 'Envisaging the Particular Judgment in Late-Medieval Italy', *Speculum* 84 (2009), 314–46.

Brinkmann, S. C., *Die deutschsprachige Pastourelle: 13. bis 16. Jahrhundert* (Göppingen, 1985).

Britnell, R., 'Uses of French Medieval English Towns', *Lang Cult*, pp. 81–9.

Bromwich, R., A. O. H. Jarman and B. F. Roberts, ed., *The Arthur of the Welsh: The Arthurian Legend in Medieval Welsh Literature* (Cardiff, 1991).

Brown, H. F., 'The Venetians and the Venetian Quarter in Constantinople to the Close of the Twelfth Century', *The Journal of Hellenic Studies* 40 (1920), 68–88.

Brugnolo, F., 'La scuola poetica siciliana', in *Storia della letteratura italiana*, ed. E. Malato (Rome, 1995), pp. 265–337.

Brunner, H., 'Melodien zu Minneliedern', in Kellner, Reichlin and Rudolph, ed., *Handbuch Minnesang*, pp. 218–32.

Bullock-Davies, C., *Professional Interpreters and the Matter of Britain: A Lecture Delivered at a Colloquium of the Departments of Welsh in the University of Wales at Gregynog, 26 June, 1965* (Cardiff, 1966).

Bumke, J., *Höfische Kultur: Literatur und Gesellschaft im hohen Mittelalter* (Munich, 1986), pp. 83–136; English version: *Courtly Culture: Literature and Society in the High Middle Ages*, trans. T. Dunlap (Berkeley, 1991).

——, *Mäzene im Mittelalter: Die Gönner und Auftraggeber der höfischen Literatur in Deutschland, 1150–1300* (Munich, 1979).

——, *Wolfram von Eschenbach*, 8th edn (Stuttgart, 2004).

Bumke, J., and U. Peters, 'Einleitung', in *Retextualisierung in der mittelalterlichen Literatur*, special issue of *Zeitschrift für deutsche Philologie* 124 (2005), 1–5.

Burgwinkle, W. E., *Love for Sale: Materialist Readings of the Troubadour Razo Corpus* (New York, 1997).

——, *Razos and Troubadour Songs* (London, 2019).

——, 'Utopia and its Uses: Twelfth-Century Romance and History', *Journal of Medieval and Early Modern Studies* 36 (2006), 539–60.

Buridant, C., 'Esquisse d'une traductologie au Moyen Âge', in *Translations médiévales. Cinq siècles de traductions en français au Moyen Âge (XIe–XVe siècles). Étude et répertoire, Volume 1: De la* translatio studii *à l'étude de la* translatio, ed. C. Galderisi (Turnhout, 2011), pp. 325–81.

Burnett, C., 'Arabic into Latin: The Reception of Arabic Philosophy into Western Europe', in *The Cambridge Companion to Arabic Philosophy*, ed. P. Adamson and R. Taylor (Cambridge, 2005), pp. 370–404.

Burnham, L. A., *So Great a Light, So Great a Smoke: The Beguin Heretics of Languedoc* (Ithaca NY, 2008).

Busby, K., *French in Medieval Ireland, Ireland in Medieval French: The Paradox of Two Worlds* (Turnhout, 2017).

——, 'Multilingualism, the Harley Scribe, and Johannes Jacobi', in *Insular Books: Vernacular Manuscript Miscellanies in Late Medieval Britain*, ed. M. Connolly and R. L. Radulescu (Oxford, 2015), pp. 49–60.

Busby, K., and M. Meuwese, 'French Arthurian Literature in the Low Countries', in *The Arthur of the Low Countries: The Arthurian Legend in Dutch and Flemish Literature*, ed. B. Besamusca and F. Brandsma (Cardiff, 2021), pp. 31–44.

Busby, K., and A. Putter, 'Introduction: Medieval Francophonia', in Kleinhenz and Busby, ed., *Medieval Multilingualism*, pp. 1–14.

Butterfield, A., *The Familiar Enemy: Chaucer, Language, and Nation in the Hundred Years War* (Oxford, 2009).

Buylaert, F., *Eeuwen van ambitie: de adel in laat-middeleeuws Vlaanderen* (Brussels, 2010).

——, *Repertorium van de Vlaamse adel (ca. 1350–ca. 1500)* (Ghent, 2011).

——, 'Sociale mobiliteit bij stedelijke elites in laatmiddeleeuws Vlaanderen: een gevalstudie over de Vlaamse familie De Baenst', *Jaarboek voor Middeleeuwse Geschiedenis* 8 (2005), 201–51.

Buylaert, F., W. De Clercq and J. Dumolyn, 'Sumptuary Legislation, Material Culture and the Semiotics of 'Vivre Noblement' in the County of Flanders (14th–16th Centuries)', *Social History* 36 (2011), 393–417.

Buylaert, F., and J. Haemers, 'Record-keeping and Status Performance in the Early Modern Low Countries', *Past and Present* 230 (2016), 131–50.

Bynum, C. W., 'Wonder', *American Historical Review* 102 (1997), 1–26.

Caciola, N. M., *Afterlives: The Return of the Dead in the Middle Ages* (Ithaca, 2016).

Calenda, C., 'Guido delle Colonne', in *I poeti della scuola siciliana. Poeti della corte di Federico II*, ed. C. Di Girolamo (Milan, 2008), pp. 53–108.

Cameron, A., 'The Construction of Court Ritual: The Byzantine Book of Ceremonies', in *Rituals of Royalty. Power and Ceremonial in Traditional Societies*, ed. D. Cannadine and S. Price (Cambridge, 1987), pp. 106–36.

Campbell, E., and R. Mills, 'Introduction: Rethinking Medieval Translation', in *Rethinking Medieval Translation: Ethics, Politics, Theory*, ed. E. Campbell and R. Mills (Cambridge, 2012), pp. 1–20.

Campbell, R., and R. Greaves, 'Royal Investigations of the Origins of Language', *Historiographia Linguistica* 9 (1982), 43–74.

Campopiano, M., and H. Bainton, ed., *Universal Chronicles in the High Middle Ages* (York, 2017).

Cannon, C., 'Class Distinction and the French of England', in *Traditions and Innovations in the Study of Middle English Literature: The Influence of Derek Brewer*, ed. C. Brewer and B. Windeatt (Cambridge, 2013), pp. 48–59.

Careri, M., C. Ruby and I. Short, with the collaboration of T. Nixon and P. Stirnemann, *Livres et écritures en français et en occitan au XIIe siècle. Catalogue illustré* (Rome, 2011).

Carocci, A., *Il poema che cammina. La letteratura cavalleresca nell'opera dei pupi* (Palermo, 2019).

Cartlidge, N., 'In the Silence of a Midwinter Night: A Re-Evaluation of the *Visio Philiberti*', *Medium Ævum* 75 (2006), 24–46.

Casas Rigall, J., *La materia de Troya en las letras romances del siglo XIII hispano* (Santiago de Compostela, 1999).

Catane, M., *Otsar Leazei Rashi* (Jerusalem, 1988).

Catlos, B. A., *Muslims of Medieval Latin Christendom, c. 1050–1614* (Cambridge, 2014).

Cavell, E., 'Aristocratic Widows and the Medieval Welsh Frontier: The Shropshire Evidence', *Transactions of the Royal Historical Society* 17 (2007), 57–82.

——, 'Welsh Princes, English Wives: The Politics of Powys Wenwynwyn Revisited', *Welsh History Review* 27 (2014), 214–52.

Cerda, J. M., 'Leonor Plantagenet y la consolidación castellana en el reinado de Alfonso VIII', *Anuario de Estudios Medievales* 42 (2012), 629–52.

Chalon, R., 'Trois bulles d'or des empereurs belges de Constantinople', *Revue de numismatique belge* 17 (1861), 384–8.

Charles-Edwards, T. M., 'Ireland and its Invaders, 1166–1186', *Quaestio insularis* 4 (2003), 1–34.

Chiffoleau, J., *La comptabilité de l'au-delà. Les hommes, la mort et la religion dans la région d'Avignon à la fin du Moyen Âge (vers 1320–vers 1480)* (Rome, 1980).

Chinca, M., H. Hunter and C. Young, 'The *Kaiserchronik* and its Three Recensions', *Zeitschrift für deutsches Altertum* 148 (2019), 141–208.

Chinca, M., and C. Young, 'German', in *Literary Beginnings in the European Middle Ages*, ed. M. Chinca and C. Young (Cambridge, 2022), pp. 179–202.

Chow, R., *Not Like a Native Speaker: On Languaging as a Postcolonial Experience* (New York, 2014).

Chun, W. H. K., 'Imagined Networks: Digital Media, Race, and the University', *Traces 5: Universities in Translation: The Mental Labour of Globalization*, ed. B. de Bary (Hong Kong, 2009), 341–54.

Chun, W. H. K., 'Networks NOW: Belated Too Early', *Amerikastudien / American Studies* 60 (2015), 37–58.

Ciggaar, K. N., 'Bilingual Word Lists and Phrase Lists: For Teaching or For Travelling?', in *Travel in the Byzantine World*, ed. R. Macrides (Aldershot, 2002), pp. 165–78.

——, 'Une description anonyme de Constantinople du XIIe siècle', *Revue des études byzantines* 31 (1973), 335–54.

——, 'Une description de Constantinople dans le Tarragonensis 55', *Revue des études byzantines* 53 (1995), 117–40.

——, 'Une description de Constantinople traduite par un pèlerin anglais', *Revue des études byzantines* 34 (1976), 211–68.

——, 'Le royaume des Lusignan: terre de littérature et des traductions, échanges littéraires et culturels', in *Les Lusignan et l'Outre-Mer. Actes du colloque Poitiers-Lusignan, 20–24 octobre 1993, auditorium du Musée Sainte-Croix Poitiers*, ed. C. Mutafian (Poitiers, 1994), pp. 89–98.

——, *Western Travellers to Constantinople: The West and Byzantium, 962–1204* (Leiden, 1996).

Cigni, F., 'Copisti prigionieri (Genova, fine sec. XIII)', in *Studi di filologia romanza offerti a Valeria Bertolucci Pizzorusso*, ed. P. G. Beltrami, M. G. Capusso, F. Cigni and S. Vatteroni, 2 vols. (Pisa, 2007), I, 425–39.

——, 'French Redactions in Italy: Rustichello da Pisa', *The Arthur of the Italians: The Arthurian Legend in Medieval Italian Literature and Culture*, ed. F. R. Psaki and G. Allaire (Cardiff, 2014), pp. 21–40.

——, 'Manuscrits en français, italien et latin entre la Toscane et la Ligurie à la fin du XIIIe siècle', in Kleinhenz and Busby, ed., *Medieval Multilingualism*, pp. 187–217.

Cipollaro, C., 'Invenzione e reinvenzione negli esemplari miniati del *Roman de Troie* tra Francia e Italia. Dal ms. ambrosiano D 55 Sup. al Cod. 2571 di Vienna', in Cipollaro and Schwarz, ed., *Allen Mären ein Herr*, pp. 19–66.

Cipollaro, C., and M. V. Schwarz, ed., *Allen Mären ein Herr/Lord of all Tales: Ritterliches Troja in illuminierten Handschriften/Chivalric Troy in Illuminated Manuscripts* (Vienna, 2017).

Claassens, G. H. M., F. P. Knapp, H. Kugler, and N. Borgmann, ed., *Historische und religiöse Erzählungen*, in Claassens, Knapp and Pérennec, ed., *Germania Litteraria Mediaevalis Francigena*, vol. IV (Berlin, 2014).

Claassens, G. H. M., F. P. Knapp and R. Pérennec, ed., *Germania Litteraria Mediaevalis Francigena: Handbuch der deutschen und niederländischen literarischen Sprache, Formen, Motive, Stoffe und Werke französischer Herkunft (1100–1300)*, 7 vols. (Berlin, 2010–15).

Clark, F., *The First Pagan Historian: The Fortunes of a Fraud from Antiquity to the Enlightenment* (New York, 2020).

Clarke, M., 'The *Leabhar Gabhála* and Carolingian Origin Legends', in *Early Medieval Ireland and Europe: Chronology, Contacts, Scholarship*, ed. P. Moran and I. Warntjes (Turnhout, 2015), pp. 441–79.

Clarke, M., and M. Ní Mhaonaigh, 'The Ages of the World and the Ages of Man: Irish and European Learning in the Twelfth Century', *Speculum* 95 (2020), 467–99.

Classen, A., 'Multilingualism in the Middle Ages: Theoretical and Historical Reflections: An Introduction', in *Multilingualism in the Middle Ages and Early Modern Age: Communication and Miscommunication in the Premodern World*, ed. A. Classen (Berlin, 2016), pp. 1–46.

Cohen, M. Z., 'Ibn Ezra vs. Maimonides: Argument for a Poetic Definition of Metaphor (Istiaʿāra)', *Edebiyāt* 2 (2000), 1–28.

Colletta, P., 'La cronaca *De acquisicione insule Sicilie* e il suo volgarizzamento. Appunti di ricerca', *Bollettino del Centro di Studi filologici e linguistici siciliani* 21 (2007), 215–42.

Concina, C., 'Boethius in Cyprus? Pierre de Paris's Translation of the *Consolatio Philosophiae*', in Morato and Schoenaers, ed., *Medieval Francophone Literary Culture Outside France*, pp. 168–72.

——, 'Le Prologue de Pierre de Paris à la traduction du *De Consolatione Philosophiae* de Boèce', *Le Moyen Français* 74 (2014), 23–46.

——, 'Traduzione e rielaborazione nel 'Boece' di Pierre de Paris', in *Francofonie medievali: lingue e letterature gallo-romanze fuori di Francia (sec. XII–XV)*, ed. A. M. Babbi and C. Concina (Verona, 2016), pp. 45–73.

Copeland, R., 'Language Frontiers, Literary Form, and the Encyclopedia', in *Frontiers in the Middle Ages: Proceedings of the Third European Congress of Medieval Studies (Jyväskylä, 10–14 June 2003)*, ed. O. Merisalo (Turnhout, 2006), pp. 507–24.

——, *Rhetoric, Hermeneutics, and Translation in the Middle Ages: Academic Traditions and Vernacular Texts* (Cambridge, 1991).

Copeland, R., and P. Struck, ed., *Cambridge Companion to Allegory* (Cambridge, 2010).

Cordo Russo, L., 'Adaptation and Translation in Medieval Wales: *Chwedyl Iarlles y Ffynnawn* and *Cân Rolant*', *Keltische Forschungen* 7 (2016), 91–104.

Cornish, A., *Vernacular Translation in Dante's Italy: Illiterate Literature* (Cambridge, 2011).

——, 'Translatio Galliae: Effects of Early Franco-Italian Literary Exchange', *Romanic Review* 97 (2006), 309–30.

Coureas, N., 'Religion and Ethnic Identity in Lusignan Cyprus', in *Identity/ Identities in Late Medieval Cyprus*, ed. T. Papacostas and G. Saint-Guillain (Nicosia, 2014), pp. 13–25.

Courouau, J.-F., 'Langues et incunables à Toulouse (1475–1500)', *Atalaya* 13 (2013), accessed 17 February 2024, https://doi.org/10.4000/atalaya.1036.

Cowley, F. G., *The Monastic Order in South Wales, 1066–1349* (Cardiff, 1977).

Crane, S., 'Knights in Disguise: Identity and Incognito in Fourteenth-Century Chivalry', in *The Stranger in Medieval Society*, ed. F. R. P. Akehurst and S. Cain Van D'Elden (Minneapolis, 1997), pp. 63–79.

Crick, J., '"The English" and "the Irish" from Cnut to John: Speculations on a Linguistic Interface', in *Conceptualizing Multilingualism in Medieval England, c. 800 – c. 1250*, ed. E. M. Tyler (Turnhout, 2011), pp. 217–37.

Curschmann, M., 'The French, the Audience, and the Narrator in Wolfram's "Willehalm"', *Neophilologus* 59 (1975), 548–62.

Curtis, E., 'Muirchertach O'Brien, High-king of Ireland, and his Norman Son-in-law, Arnulf de Montgomery, c. 1100', *Journal of the Royal Society of Antiquaries of Ireland* 6th ser., 11 (1921), 116–24.

Cusimano, G., *Poesie siciliane dei secoli XIV e XV*, 2 vols. (Palermo, 1951).

D'Alessandro, V., 'Società e potere nella Sicilia medievale: un profilo', *Archivio Storico Italiano* 174 (January–March 2016), 31–80.

Dagron, G., *Constantinople imaginaire: études sur le recueil des* Patria (Paris, 1984).

——, Priest and Emperor: The Imperial Office in Byzantium, trans. J. Birrell (Cambridge, 2007).

Damen, M., *De staat van dienst: De gewestelijke ambtenaren van Holland en Zeeland in de Bourgondische periode (1425–1482)* (Hilversum, 2000).

Davies, A., '"Wite Þu Me, Werga": The Old English *Soul & Body* in Literary-Historical Context', *Modern Language Review* 116 (2021), 226–44.

Davis-Secord, S., *Where Three Worlds Met: Sicily in the Early Mediterranean* (Ithaca, 2017).

Daydé, C., 'Un unicum méconnu: la *Repetitio de inquisitione hereticorum* de Nicolas Bertrand (1512)', in *Le livre dans la région toulousaine et ailleurs au Moyen Âge*, ed. S. Cassagnes-Brouquet and M. Fournié (Toulouse, 2010), pp. 121–34.

de Jong, F. P. C., 'Rival Schoolmasters in Early Eleventh-century Rouen with Special Reference to the Poetry of Warner of Rouen (fl. 996–1027)', *Anglo-Norman Studies* 39 (2016), 45–64.

de Rachewiltz, I., 'Marco Polo Went to China', *Zentralasiatische Studien* 27 (1997), 34–92.

DEAFpré Online, *s.v. foudrien*, ed. F. Möhren and T. Städtler, accessed 29 Jan 2023, https://deaf-server.adw.uni-heidelberg.de/lemme/foudre#foudrien

'Le débat du corps et de l'âme', in *ARLIMA, Archives de littérature du Moyen Âge*, ed. L. Brun, accessed 17 February 2024, https://arlima.net/no/5657.

Decter, J. P., 'Belles-Lettres', in *The Cambridge History of Judaism*, vol. 6, *The Middle Ages: The Christian World*, ed. R. Chazan (Cambridge, 2018), pp. 787–812.

——, *Dominion Built of Praise: Panegyric and Legitimacy among Jews in the Medieval Mediterranean* (Philadelphia, 2018).

——, 'A Hebrew "Sodomite" Tale from Thirteenth-Century Toledo: Jacob Ben El'azar's Story of Sapir, Shapir and Birsha', *Journal of Medieval Iberian Studies* 3 (2011), 187–202.

——, *Iberian Jewish Literature: Between al-Andalus and Christian Europe* (Bloomington, 2007).

——, 'Panegyric as Pedagogy: Moses ibn Ezra's Didactic Poem on the "Beautiful Elements of Poetry" (*maḥāsin al-shiʿr*) in the Context of Classical Arabic Poetics', in *'His Pen and Ink Are a Powerful Mirror': Andalusi, Judaeo-Arabic, and Other Near Eastern Studies in Honor of Ross Brann*, ed. A. Bursi, S. J. Pearce and H. M. Zafer (Leiden, 2018), pp. 65–93.

Delcorno Branca, D., 'Lecteurs et interprètes des romans arthuriens en Italie', in Kleinhenz and Busby, ed., *Medieval Multilingualism*, pp. 155–86.

Deleuze, G., and F. Guattari, *Kafka: Toward a Minor Literature*, trans. D. Polan (Minneapolis, 1986).

Delisle, L., 'Notes sur quelques manuscrits de la Bibliothèque d'Auxerre', *Le cabinet historique* 23 (1887), 11–15.

Delogu, D., *Allegorical Bodies: Power and Gender in Late Medieval France* (Toronto, 2015).

——, 'Allegory, Semiotics, and Salvation: The Parable of the Talents in the *Songe du viel pèlerin*', in *Philippe de Mézières, rhétorique et poétique*, ed. J. Blanchard (Geneva, 2019), pp. 163–85.

Demets, L., 'Bruges as a Multilingual Contact Zone: Book Production and Multilingual Literary Networks in Fifteenth-Century Bruges', *Urban History* 50 (2023), 1–20.

Derolez, A., H. Defoort and F. Vanlangenhove, *Medieval Manuscripts: Ghent University Library* (Ghent, 2017).

Derolez, R., 'Ogam, "Egyptian", "African" and "Gothic" Alphabets: Some Remarks in Connection with Codex Bernensis 207', *Scriptorium* 51 (1951), 3–19.

Derrida, J., 'L'autre cap: mémoires, réponses et responsabilités', in *L'autre cap; suivi de La démocratie ajournée* (Paris, 1991), pp. 11–101; English version: J. Derrida, *The Other Heading: Reflections on Today's Europe*, trans. P.-A. Brault and M. B. Naas (Bloomington, 1992).

——, *De l'hospitalité: Anne Dufourmantelle invite Jacques Derrida à répondre* (Paris, 1997); English version: *Of Hospitality: Anne Dufourmantelle Invites Jacques Derrida to Respond*, trans. R. Bowlby (Stanford, 2000).

———, 'Hospitality, Justice and Responsibility: A Dialogue with Jacques Derrida', in *Questioning Ethics: Contemporary Debates in Philosophy*, ed. R. Kearney and M. Dooley (London, 1999), pp. 65–83.

———, *Le monolinguisme de l'autre, ou la prothèse d'origine* (Paris, 1996); English version: *Monolingualism of the Other; or, The Prosthesis of Origin*, tr. P. Mensah (Stanford, 1998).

———, *Passions* (Paris, 1993); English version: 'Passions', trans. D. Wood, in *On the Name*, ed. T. Dutoit (Stanford, 1995), pp. 3–34.

———, 'Le principe d'hospitalité', in *Papier Machine. Le ruban de machine à écrire et autres réponses* (Paris, 2001), pp. 273–7; English version: 'The Principle of Hospitality', in *Paper Machine*, trans. R. Bowlby (Stanford, 2005), pp. 66–9.

Desimoni, C., 'I Genovesi ed i loro quartieri in Constantinopli nel secolo XIII', *Giornale ligustico di archeologia, storia, e belle arti* 3 (1876), 217–74.

Devereaux, R., *Constantinople and the West in Medieval French Literature: Renewal and Utopia* (Cambridge, 2012).

Dickie, J., *Cosa Nostra: A History of the Sicilian Mafia* (New York, 2004).

DigiFlorimont, accessed 13 April 2022, http://digiflorimont.huma-num.fr/flsite/florimont.html#.

Dobson, E. J., *The Origins of Ancrene Wisse* (Oxford, 1976).

Doggett, L. E., 'When Lovers Recount their Own Stories: Assimilating Text and Image Units in the Prologue of the *Roman de la Poire*, MS Paris BnF 2186', *Textual Cultures: Texts, Contexts, Interpretation* 11 (2019), 17–41.

Donato, A., 'Boethius's 'Consolation of Philosophy' and the Greco-Roman Consolatory Tradition', *Traditio* 67 (2012), 1–42.

Dooley, A., 'The European Context of *Acallam na Senórach*', in *In Dialogue with the Agallamh: Essays in Honour of Seán Ó Coileáin*, ed. A. Doyle and K. Murray (Dublin, 2014), pp. 60–75.

Dronke, P., *Verse with Prose from Petronius to Dante: The Art and Scope of Mixed Form* (Cambridge MA, 1994).

Drory, R., 'The Hidden Context: On Literary Products of Tri-Cultural Contacts in the Middle Ages' [Hebrew], *Pe'amim: Studies in Oriental Jewry* 46/47 (1991), 9–28.

———, 'The Maqāma', in *The Literature of Al-Andalus*, ed. M. R. Menocal, M. Sells and R. P. Scheindlin (Cambridge, 2000), pp. 190–210.

———, '"Words Beautifully Put": Hebrew versus Arabic in Tenth-Century Jewish Literature', in *Genizah Research after Ninety Years: The Case of Judaeo-Arabic*, ed. J. Blau and S. C. Reif (Cambridge, 1992), pp. 53–63.

Duba, W., 'The Beatific Vision in the Sentences Commentary of Gerald Odonis', *Vivarium* 47 (2009), 348–63.

———, 'The Souls after Vienne: Franciscan Theologians' Views on the Plurality of Forms and the Plurality of Souls, ca. 1315–30', in *Psychology and the Other*

Disciplines: A Case of Cross-Disciplinary Interaction (1250–1750), ed. P. J. J. M. Bakker, S. W. De Boer and C. Leijenhorst (Leiden, 2012), pp. 171–272.

Duffy, S., *Ireland in the Middle Ages* (Dublin, 1997).

Dumolyn, J., *De Brugse opstand van 1436–1438* (Heule, 1997).

——, *Staatsvorming en vorstelijke ambtenaren in het graafschap Vlaanderen (1419–1477)* (Leuven, 2003).

Duncan, E., '*Lebor na hUidre* and a Copy of Boethius's *De re arithmetica*: A Palaeographical Note', *Ériu* 62 (2012), 1–32.

The Dynamics of the Medieval Manuscript: Text Collections from a European Perspective, accessed February 24 2023, https://dynamicsofthemedievalmanuscript.eu/.

Ebbesen, S., 'Psammetichus's Experiment and the Scholastics: Is Language Innate?', in *The Language of Thought in Late Medieval Philosophy*, ed. J. Pelletier and M. Roques (Cham, 2017), pp. 287–302.

Echard, S., 'Of Parody and Perceval: Generic Manipulation in *Peredur* and *Sir Perceval of Galles*', *Nottingham Medieval Studies* 40 (1996), 63–79.

Edwards, C. 'Von Archilochos zu Walther von der Vogelweide: Zu den Anfängen der Pastourelle in Deutschland', in Edwards, Hellgardt and Ott, ed., *Lied im deutschen Mittelalter*, pp. 1–25.

Edwards, C., E. Hellgardt and N. H. Ott, ed., *Lied im deutschen Mittelalter: Überlieferung, Typen, Gebrauch. Chiemsee-Colloquium 1991* (Tübingen, 1996).

The Electronic Dictionary of the Irish Language, based on *Contributions to a Dictionary of the Irish Language* (Dublin: Royal Irish Academy, 1913–76), accessed 3 February 2023, http://www.dil.ie.

Epstein, S. A., *The Talents of Jacopo da Varagine: A Genoese Mind in Medieval Europe* (Ithaca, 2016).

Etchingham, C., Jón Viðar Sigurðsson, M. Ní Mhaonaigh and E. A. Rowe, *Norse-Gaelic Contacts in a Viking World: Studies in the Literature and History of Norway, Iceland, Ireland, and the Isle of Man* (Turnhout, 2019).

Fabre, D., 'Le retour des morts', *Études rurales* 105/106 (1987), 9–34.

Favereau, M., *The Horde: How the Mongols Changed the World* (Cambridge MA, 2021).

Fenster, T., and C. P. Collette, ed., *The French of Medieval England: Essays in Honour of Jocelyn Wogan-Browne* (Cambridge, 2017).

Fernández-Ordóñez, I., *Las estorias de Alfonso el Sabio* (Madrid, 1992)

——, 'De la historiografía fernandina a la alfonsí', *Alcanate* 3 (2003), 93–133.

——, 'La lengua de los documentos del rey: del latín a las lenguas vernáculas en las cancillerías regias de la Península Ibérica', in *La construcción medieval de la memoria regia*, ed. P. Martínez Sopena and A. Rodríguez (Valencia, 2011), pp. 323–62.

Flanagan, M. T., *Irish Society, Anglo-Norman Settlers, Angevin Kingship: Interactions in Ireland in the Late 12th Century* (Oxford, 1989).

———, *The Transformation of the Irish Church in the Twelfth and Thirteenth Centuries* (Woodbridge, 2010).

Flechner, R., and S. Meeder, ed., *The Irish in Early Medieval Europe: Identity, Culture and Religion* (London, 2016).

Fleischer, E., 'Studies in Liturgical and Secular Poetry' [Hebrew], in *Studies in Literature Presented to Simon Halkin*, ed. E. Fleischer (Jerusalem, 1973), pp. 183–204.

Flesher, P. V. M., and B. Chilton, *The Targums: A Critical Introduction* (Waco, 2011).

Fournié, M., 'L'au-delà dans le midi de la France et dans le Languedoc à la fin du Moyen Age', in *Le pays cathare. Les religions médiévales et leurs expressions méridionales*, ed. J. Berlioz (Paris, 2000), pp. 245–63.

———, *Le ciel peut-il attendre? Le culte du purgatoire dans le Midi de la France* (Paris, 1997).

Fraade, S. D., 'Rabbinic Views on the Practice of Targum and Multilingualism in Jewish Galilee of the Third–Sixth Centuries', in *The Galilee in Late Antiquity*, ed. L. I. Levine (Cambridge MA, 1992), pp. 253–86.

Fracomano, E., 'Castilian Vernacular Bibles in Iberia, *c.*1250–1500', in *The Practice of the Bible in the Middle Ages: Production, Reception, and Performance in Western Christianity*, ed. S. Boynton and D. Reilly (New York, 2011), pp 315–37.

Francigena: Rivista sul franco-italiano e sulle scritture francesi nel Medioevo d'Italia, *The Università degli Studi di Padova*, accessed 16 March 2022, https://www.francigena-unipd.com/index.php/francigena/index.

Franco Júnior, H., 'Entre la figue et la pomme: l'iconographie romane du fruit défendu', *Revue de l'histoire des religions* 223 (2006), 29–70.

Freeman Sandler, L., 'An Early Fourteenth-Century English Psalter in the Escorial', *Journal of the Warburg and Courtauld Institute* 42 (1979), 65–80.

French of England, accessed 4 April, 2023, https://frenchofengland.ace.fordham.edu.

French of Italy, accessed 24 February 2023, https://frenchofitaly.ace.fordham.edu.

French of Outremer, accessed February 24 2023, https://frenchofoutremer.ace.fordham.edu.

Freudenthal, G., 'Arabic and Latin Cultures as Resources for the Hebrew Translation Movement', in *Science in Medieval Jewish Cultures*, ed. G. Freudenthal (Cambridge, 2012), pp. 74–105.

Frugoni, C., *Historia Alexandri elevati per griphos ad aerem, origine, iconografia e fortuna di un tema* (Rome, 1973).

Fudeman, K., 'The Linguistic Significance of the Le'azim in Joseph Kara's Job Commentary', *Jewish Quarterly Review* 43 (2003), 397–414.

———, 'The Old French Glosses in Joseph Kara's Isaiah Commentary', *Revue des études juives* 165 (2006), 147–77.

———, *Vernacular Voices: Language and Identity in Medieval French Jewish Communities, Jewish Culture and Contexts* (Philadelphia, 2010).

Fulton, H., 'Individual and Society in *Owein/Yvain* and *Gereint/Erec*', in *The Individual in Celtic Literatures*, ed. J. F. Nagy, CSANA Yearbook 1 (Dublin, 2001), pp. 15–50.

Galvez, M., 'Review Essay', *H-France Forum* 16:4 (2021), accessed 24 February 2023, https://h-france.net/wp-content/uploads/2021/09/Stahuljak3.pdf.

———, 'Unthought Medievalism', *Neophilologus* 105 (2021), 365–89.

García y García, A., 'El *studium bononiense* y la Península Ibérica', in *Chiesa, diritto e ordinamiento della 'societas christiana' nei secoli XI e XII* (Milan, 1986), pp. 45–64.

Gaullier-Bougassas, C., ed., *Alexandre le Grand à la lumière des manuscrits et des premiers imprimés en Europe (XIIe–XVIe siècle): matérialité des texts, contextes et paratextes: des lectures originales* (Turnhout, 2015).

——— ed., *La fascination pour Alexandre le Grand dans les littératures européennes (Xe–XVIe siècle). réinventions d'un mythe*, 4 vols. (Turnhout, 2015).

———, 'Les manuscrits italiens des *Romans d'Alexandre* français en vers et de l'*Histoire ancienne jusqu'à César* (XIIIe et XIVe siècles). Lectures originales et créations inédites', in Gaullier-Bougassas, ed., *Alexandre le Grand*, pp. 49–80.

Gaunt, S., *Marco Polo's* Le Devisement du Monde: *Narrative Voice, Language and Diversity* (Cambridge, 2013).

———, 'Romance Languages', in *How Literatures Begin: A Global History*, ed. J. B. Lande and D. Feeney (Princeton, 2021), pp. 239–60.

———, 'Texte et/ou manuscrit? A propos de l'*Histoire ancienne jusqu'à César*', in *En français hors de France*, ed. Zinelli and Lefèvre, pp. 35–57.

Gautier, A., 'Vernacular Languages in the Long Ninth Century: Towards a Connected History', *Journal of Medieval History* 47:4–5 (2021), 433–50.

Geirnaert, N., 'Classical Texts in Bruges around 1473: Cooperation of Italian Scribes, Bruges Parchment Rulers, Illuminators and Bookbinders for Johannes Crabbe, Abbot of Les Dunes Abbey', *Transactions of the Cambridge Bibliographical Society* 10 (1992), 173–81.

Gibbs Kamath, S., and R. Copeland, 'Medieval Secular Allegory: French and English', in Copeland and Struck, ed., *Cambridge Companion to Allegory*, pp. 136–47.

Gigante, M., *Poeti italobizantini del secolo XIII* (Naples, 1953).

Gilbert, J., C. Keen and E. Williams, ed., *The Italian Angevins: Naples and Beyond, 1266–1343*, special number of *Italian Studies* 72 (2017).

Gilbert, J., S. Gaunt and W. Burgwinkle, *Medieval French Literary Culture Abroad* (Oxford, 2020).

Gillingham, J., 'Ademar of Chabannes and the History of Aquitaine in the Reign of Charles the Bald', in *Charles the Bald: Court and Kingdom*, ed. M. T. Gibson and J. L. Nelson (Oxford, 1981), pp. 3–14.

Glauch, S., 'Zweimal "Erec" am Anfang des deutschen Artusromans? Einige Folgerungen aus den neugefundenen Fragmenten', *Zeitschrift für deutsche Philologie* 128 (2009), 347–71.

Glessgen, M., 'La genèse d'une norme en ancien français au Moyen Âge: mythe et réalité du "francien"', *Revue de Linguistique Romane* 81 (207), 313–97.

Glessgen, M., and D. Trotter, ed., *La régionalité lexicale du français au Moyen Âge* (Strasbourg, 2016).

Glissant, É., *Introduction à une poétique du divers* (Paris, 1996); English version: *Introduction to a Poetics of Diversity*, trans. C. Britton (Liverpool, 2020).

Glissant, É., with A. Leupin, *Les entretiens de Baton Rouge* (Paris, 2008); English version: É. Glissant, *The Baton Rouge Interviews, with Alexandre Leupin*, trans. K. M. Cooper (Liverpool, 2020).

Golb, N., *The Jews of Medieval Normandy: A Social and Intellectual History* (Cambridge, 1998).

Golden, P. B., 'Codex Cumanicus', in *Central Asian Monuments*, ed. H. B. Paksoy (Istanbul, 1992), accessed 7 October 2023, http://vlib.iue.it/carrie/texts/carrie_books/paksoy-2/cam2.html

Golob, N., 'Charterhouse Readings: Dialogue between the Soul and the Body', *IKON* 4 (2011), 151–62.

Gómez Redondo, F., *Historia de la prosa medieval castellana*, 4 vols. (Madrid, 1998).

González Jiménez, M., *Diplomatario andaluz de Alfonso X* (Sevilla, 1991).

Gosman, M., *La légende d'Alexandre le Grand dans la littérature française du 12e siècle. Une réécriture permanente* (Amsterdam, 1997).

Gossen, C. T., *Grammaire de l'ancien picard*, rev. edn (Paris, 1976).

Gracia, P., 'A vueltas con el modelo subyacente o lo que los originales franceses pueden aportar a la edición de sus derivados españoles: el caso de la sección tebana de la II parte de la *General Estoria*', in *La fractura historiográfica: las investigaciones de Edad Media y Renacimiento desde el Tercer Milenio*, ed. F. J. Burguillo, L. Mier and J. San José Lera (Salamanca, 2008), pp. 331–40.

——, 'Actividad artística y creadora en la *General estoria*: la sección tebana de la *Histoire ancienne jusqu'à César* reescrita por Alfonso X', *Bulletin of Hispanic Studies* 81 (2004), 303–17.

——, 'Hacia el modelo de la *General estoria*: París, la *translatio imperii et studii* y la *Histoire ancienne jusqu'à César*', *Zeitschrift für romanische Philologie* 122 (2006), 17–27.

——, 'Singularidad y extrañeza en algunos lugares de la "Estoria de Tebas" (*General estoria*, Parte II), a la luz de la *Histoire ancienne jusqu'à César*', *Bulletin hispanique* 105 (2003), 7–17.

Granara, W., *Ibn Hamdis the Sicilian: Eulogist for a Falling Homeland* (London, 2021).

Green, N., 'Introduction', in *The Persianate World: The Frontiers of a Eurasian Lingua Franca*, ed. N. Green (Oakland, 2019), pp. 1–71.

Greimas, A. J., *Dictionnaire de l'ancien français jusqu'au milieu du XIVe siècle* (Paris, 1988).

Grévin, B., 'L'Europe des langues au temps de Philippe de Mézières', in *Philippe de Mézières et l'Europe. Nouvelle histoire, nouveaux espaces, nouveaux langages*, ed. J. Blanchard and R. Blumenfeld-Kosinski (Geneva, 2017), pp. 95–113.

Grévin, B., *Le parchemin des cieux. Essai sur le Moyen Âge du langage* (Paris, 2012).

Grondeux, A., 'L'*Alexandréide* dans le cursus grammatical medieval', in *Poesía latina medieval (siglos V–XV). Actas del IV Congreso del 'Internationales Mittellateinerkomitee', Santiago de Compostela, 12–15 de septiembre de 2002*, ed. M. Díaz y Díaz and J. M. Díaz de Bustamante (Florence, 2005), pp. 825–50.

Grosjean, F., *Life with Two Languages: An Introduction to Bilingualism* (Cambridge, Mass., 1982).

Grossman, A., 'The School of Literal Jewish Exegesis in Northern France', in M. Sæbo, ed., *Hebrew Bible/Old Testament: The History of Its Interpretation*, 3 vols. (Göttingen, 2000), I, 320–71.

Gruppo Guiron, *Il ciclo di Guiron le courtois*, accessed 24 February 2023, https://guiron.fefonlus.it/.

Guo, L., *The Performing Arts in Medieval Islam: Shadow Play and Popular Poetry in Ibn Daniyāl's Mamluk Cairo* (Leiden, 2012).

Gy, P.-M., 'La liturgie de la mort en France méridionale (XIIe–XVe siècle)', in *La mort et l'au-delà en France méridionale (XIIe–XVe siècle)*, Cahiers de Fanjeaux 33 (Toulouse, 1998), pp. 65–75.

Haemers, J., *For the Common Good: State Power and Urban Revolts in the Reign of Mary of Burgundy (1477–1482)* (Turnhout, 2009).

——, *De strijd om het regentschap over Filips de Schone: opstand, facties en geweld in Brugge, Gent en Ieper (1482–1488)* (Ghent, 2014).

Haidu, P., 'Au début du roman, l'ironie', *Poétique* 36 (1978), 443–66.

Handschriftencensus: Eine Bestandsaufnahme der handschriftlichen Überlieferung deutschsprachiger Texte des Mittelalters, accessed 7 October 2023, https://handschriftencensus.de.

Harb, L., *Arabic Poetics: Aesthetic Experience in Classical Arabic Literature* (Cambridge, 2020).

Harf-Lancner, L., 'Le *Florimont* d'Aimon de Varennes: un prologue du *Roman d'Alexandre*', *Cahiers de civilisation médiévale* 147 (1994), 241–53.

Harmann, S., 'St Fursa, the Genealogy of an Irish Saint – the Historical Person and his Cult', *Proceedings of the Royal Irish Academy* 112 C (2012), 147–87.

Harris, J., *Constantinople: Capital of Byzantium* (London, 2007).

Hartman, S., 'Venus in Two Acts', *Small Axe*, 12.2 (2008), 1–14.

Harvey, A., 'Cambro-Romance? Celtic Britain's counterpart to Hiberno-Latin', in *Early Medieval Ireland and Europe: Chronology, Contacts, Scholarship. A Festschrift for Dáibhí Ó Cróinín*, ed. P. Moran and I. Warntjes (Turnhout, 2015), pp. 179–202.

Harvey, R., 'Courtly Culture in Medieval Occitania', in *The Troubadours: An Introduction*, ed. S. Gaunt and S. Kay (Cambridge, 1999), pp. 8–27.

Haskins, C. H., 'Science at the Court of the Emperor Frederick II', *American Historical Review* 27 (1922), 673–89.

Haug, W., *Literaturtheorie im deutschen Mittelalter*, 2nd edn (Darmstadt, 1992).

Haw, S. G., 'The Persian Language in Yuan-Dynasty China: A Reappraisal', *East Asian History* 39 (2014), 5–32.

Heinrichs, W., 'Prosimetrical Genres in Classical Arabic Literature', in *Prosimetrum: Crosscultural Perspectives on Narrative in Prose and Verse*, ed. J. Harris and K. Reichl (Cambridge, 1997), pp. 249–75.

——, 'Takhyīl: Make-Believe and Image Creation in Arabic Literary Theory', in *Takhyīl: The Imaginary in Classical Arabic Poetics*, ed. G. J. van Gelder and M. Hammond (Cambridge, 2008), pp. 1–14.

Heinzle, J., ed., *Geschichte der deutschen Literatur von den Anfängen bis zum Beginn der Neuzeit*, 5 parts of 3 vols. published to date (Tübingen, 1984–2004; Berlin, 2020–).

——, *Wandlungen und Neuansätze im 13. Jahrhundert (1220/30–1280/90)*, 2nd edn, in Heinzle, ed., *Geschichte der deutschen Literatur*, vol. II, pt. 2 (Tübingen, 1994).

Hendrickx, B., 'Les institutions de l'empire latin de Constantinople (1204–1261). Le pouvoir impérial (L'empereur, les régents, l'impératrice)', *Βυζαντινά* 6 (1974), 85–154.

——, and C. Matzukis, 'Alexios V Doukas Mourtzouphlos: His Life, Reign and Death (?–1204)', *Ἑλληνικά* 31 (1979), 108–32.

Heng, G., *Empire of Magic: Medieval Romance and the Politics of Cultural Fantasy* (New York, 2003).

Henley, G., *Reimagining the Past in the Borderlands of Medieval England and Wales* (Oxford, 2024).

Henley, G., and A. J. McMullen, ed., *Gerald of Wales: New Perspectives on a Medieval Writer and Critic* (Cardiff, 2018).

Hernández, F. J., 'La corte de Fernando III y la casa real de Francia: documentos, crónicas, monumentos', in *Fernando III y su tiempo (1201–1252): VIII Congreso de Estudios Medievales* (Ávila, 2003), pp. 103–56.

——, 'Relaciones de Alfonso X con Inglaterra y Francia', *Alcanate* 4 (2004–2005), 167–242.

Herren, M., 'Ériugena, John Scottus', in *Medieval Ireland: An Encyclopaedia*, ed. S. Duffy (New York, 2005), pp. 157–9.

Herzog, T., 'The First Layer of the *Sirat Baybars*: Popular Romance and Political Propaganda', *Mamluk Studies Review* 7 (2003), 137–48.

——, 'Francs et Commerçants à Alexandrie dans le roman de Baybars', *Alexandrie médiévale* 1 (2002), 181–94.

——, *Geschichte und Imaginaire: Entstehung, Überlieferung und Bedeutung der Sirat Baibars in ihrem sozio-politischen Kontext* (Wiesbaden, 2006).

Hillenbrand, C., 'Rāvandī, the Seljuk Court at Konya and the Persianization of Anatolian Cities', *Mésogeios* 25–6 (2005), 157–69.

Hinton, T., 'Anglo-French in the Thirteenth Century: A Reappraisal of Walter de Bibbesworth's *Tretiz*', *Modern Language Review* 112 (2017), 855–81.

——, 'Translation, Authority, and the Valorization of the Vernacular', in *A Companion to Medieval Translation*, ed. J. Beer (Amsterdam, 2019), pp. 97–105.

Holden, B., 'The Making of the Middle March of Wales, 1066–1250', *Welsh History Review* 20 (2000), 207–26.

Holod, R., and Y. Rassamakin, 'Imported and Native Remedies for a Wounded "Prince": Grave Goods from the Chungul Kurgan in the Black Sea Steppe of the Thirteenth Century', *Medieval Encounters* 18 (2012), 339–81.

Hoogvliet, M., '"Mez puy que je le enten, je suy conten": Bilingual Cities of Readers in the Southern Low Countries and Northern France (*c.*1400–*c.*1550)', in *Mittelalterliche Stadtsprachen*, ed. M. Selig and S. Ehrlich (Regensburg, 2016), pp. 45–61.

Hoogvliet, M., 'Religious Reading in French and Middle Dutch in the Southern Low Countries and Northern France (*c.*1400–*c.*1520)', in Morato and Schoenaers, ed., *Medieval Francophone Literary Culture outside France*, pp. 323–48.

Horobin, S., '"In London and Opelond": The Dialect and Circulation of the C Version of "Piers Plowman"', *Medium Ævum* 74 (2005), 248–69.

Houtman, A. 'The Role of the Targum in Jewish Education in Medieval Europe', in *A Jewish Targum in a Christian World*, ed. A. Houtman, E. van Staalduine-Sulman and H.-M. Kirn (Leiden, 2014), pp. 81–98.

Hsy, J., *Trading Tongues: Merchants, Multilingualism, and Medieval Literature* (Columbus, 2013).

Hudson, B. T., 'The Family of Harold Godwinsson and the Irish Sea Province', *Journal of the Royal Society of Antiquaries of Ireland* 109 (1979), 92–100; republished in his *Irish Sea Studies 900–1200* (Dublin, 2006), pp. 100–8.

——, 'William the Conqueror and Ireland', *Irish Historical Studies* 29:114 (1994), 145–58; republished in his *Irish Sea Studies 900–1200* (Dublin, 2006), pp. 119–22.

Hugen, J., 'Vernacular Multilingualism: The Use of French in Medieval Dutch Literature', *Neophilologus* 106 (2022), 181–98.

Hughes, A., *The Texture of the Divine: Imagination in Medieval Islamic and Jewish Thought* (Bloomington, 2004).

Hunger, H., 'Zum Epilog der Theogonie des Johannes Tzetzes', *Byzantinische Zeitschrift* 46 (1953), 302–7.

Hunt, T., 'Hue de Rotelande (*fl. c.* 1175–1185x90)', *ODNB*, accessed 5 April 2022, https://doi.org/10.1093/ref:odnb/24146.

——, 'Precursors and Progenitors of *Aucassin et Nicolette*', *Studies in Philology* 74 (1977), 1–19.

Huot, S., 'From *Roman de la Rose* to *Roman de la Poire*: The Ovidian Tradition and the Poetics of Courtly Literature', *Medievalia et Humanistica* n.s. 13 (1985), 95–111.

Huss, M., 'Clarifications regarding the Time and Date of Composition of *Sefer HaMeshalim*' [Hebrew], in *Meir Benayahu Memorial Volume: Studies in Talmud, Halakha, Custom, Jewish History, Kabbala, Jewish Thought, Liturgy, Piyyut, and Poetry in Memory of Professor Meir Benayahu z'l*, ed. M. Bar-Asher, Y. Libes, M. Assis and Y. Kaplan (Jerusalem, 2019), pp. 1021–56.

——, 'The Status of Fiction in the Hebrew Maqama: Judah Alḥarizi and Immanuel of Rome' [Hebrew], *Tarbiṣ* 67 (1998), 351–78.

Ingallinella, L., 'Un frammento di un volgarizzamento siciliano trecentesco delle Vite dei Santi Padri', *Bollettino del Centro di Studi filologici e linguistici siciliani* 25 (2014), 47–111.

Initiale, catalogue de manuscrits illuminés, IRHT, 2012–22, accessed 17 February 2024, http://initiale.irht.cnrs.fr.

Jacoby, D., 'The Venetian Quarter of Constantinople from 1082 to 1261: Topographical Considerations', in *Novum millennium: Studies in Byzantine History and Culture, dedicated to Paul Speck*, ed. C. Sode and S. Takács (Aldershot, 2001), pp. 153–70.

Jager, E., *The Book of the Heart* (Chicago, 2000)

James, M. R., *A Descriptive Catalogue of the Manuscripts in the Library of Lambeth Palace: The Medieval Manuscripts* (Cambridge, 1932).

Janin, R., *Constantinople byzantine* (Paris, 1964).

Jastrow, M., *A Dictionary of the Targumim, The Talmud Babli and Yerushalmi, and the Midrashic Literature* (Philadelphia, 1883–1903).

Jenkins, D., 'Ieuan ap Rhydderch ab Ieuan Llwyd (fl. 1340–1470), gentleman and poet, of Cardiganshire', *Dictionary of Welsh Biography*, accessed 17 February 2022, https://biography.wales/article/s-IEUA-APR-1430.

Johnson, L. P., 'Die Blütezeit und der neue Status der Literatur', in *Literarische Interessenbildung im Mittelalter*, ed. J. Heinzle (Stuttgart, 1993), pp. 235–56.

——, *Die höfische Literatur der Blütezeit (1160/70–1220/30)*, in Heinzle, ed., *Geschichte der deutschen Literatur*, vol. II, pt. 1 (Tübingen, 1999).

Jones, E. J., *Education in Wales during the Middle Ages: Inaugural Lecture of the Professor of Education delivered at the College on 2 December 1947* (Swansea, [n.d.]).

Jorga, N., *Philippe de Mézières (1327–1405) et la croisade au XIVe siècle* (Paris, 1896).

Jung, M.-R., *La légende de Troie en France au Moyen Age. Analyse des versions françaises et bibliographie raisonnée des manuscrits* (Basel and Tübingen, 1996).

Kabir, A. J., and D. Williams, ed., *Postcolonial Approaches to the European Middle Ages* (Cambridge, 2005).

Kanarfogel, E., 'Schools and Education', in *Cambridge History of Judaism, Volume 6: The Middle Ages: The Christian World*, ed. R. Chazan (Cambridge, 2018), pp. 393–415.

Kartschoke, D., *Geschichte der deutschen Literatur im frühen Mittelalter* (Munich, 1990).

Kasten, I., 'Die Pastourelle im Gattungssystem der höfischen Lyrik', in Edwards, Hellgardt and Ott, ed., *Lied im deutschen Mittelalter*, pp. 27–41.

Kay, S., *Parrots and Nightingales: Troubadour Quotations and the Development of European Poetry* (Philadelphia, 2013).

Kellner, B., S. Reichlin and A. Rudolph, ed., *Handbuch Minnesang* (Berlin, 2021).

Kelly, D., 'The Composition of Aimon de Varennes' *Florimont*', *Romance Philology* 23 (1970), 277–92.

Khanmohamadi, S. A., *In Light of Another's Word: European Ethnography in the Middle Ages* (Philadelphia, 2014).

Kiening, C. *Reflexion – Narration: Wege zum 'Willehalm' Wolframs von Eschenbach* (Tübingen, 1991).

Kinoshita, S., *Medieval Boundaries: Rethinking Difference in Old French Literature* (Philadelphia, 2006).

——, 'Reorientations: The Worlding of Marco Polo', in *Cosmopolitanism and the Middle Ages*, ed. J. Ganim and S. Legassie (New York, 2013), pp. 39–57.

Kıvılcım Yavuz, N., *Transtextual Networks*, 1 November 2020, accessed 29 December 2022, https://www.transtextual.net/.

Kleinhenz, C., and K. Busby, ed., *Medieval Multilingualism: The Francophone World and its Neighbours* (Turnhout, 2010).

Knight, G., 'Bilingualism in the *Cambrai Homily*', in *Movement and Mobility: Ideologies of Translation III*, ed. J. Odstrčilík (Vienna, 2021), pp. 104–19.

Knight, S., 'Resemblance and Menace: A Post-Colonial Reading of *Peredur*', in *Canhwyll Marchogyon: Cyd-destunoli Peredur*, ed. S. Davies and P. Wynn Thomas (Cardiff, 2000), pp. 128–47.

Knirk, J. E., 'Runer i Hagia Sofia i Istanbul', *Nytt om runer 14* (1999), 26–7.

Knox, P., 'The English Glosses in Walter de Bibbesworth's *Tretiz*', *Notes and Queries* 60 (2013), 349–59.

Kocher, S., 'Desire, Parody, and Sexual Mores in the Ending of Hue de Rotelande's *Ipomedon*: An Invitation Through the Looking Glass', in *Sexuality in the Middle Ages and Early Modern Times: New Approaches to a Fundamental Cultural-Historical and Literary-Anthropological Theme*, ed. A. Classen (Berlin, 2008), pp. 429–47.

Koder, J., 'Liutprand von Cremona und die griechische Sprache', in *Liutprand von Cremona in Konstantinopel*, ed. J. Koder and T. Weber (Vienna, 1980), pp. 15–70.

Koenig, J., 'Guelphs and Ghibellines', in *Dictionary of the Middle Ages*, ed. J. R. Strayer, accessed 8 August 2023, link.gale.com/apps/doc/BT2353201309/ WHIC?u=umuser&sid=bookmark-WHIC&xid=67c0a460.

Korobeinikov, D., 'A Broken Mirror: The Kipçak World in the Thirteenth Century', in *The Other Europe in the Middle Ages: Avars, Bulgars, Khazars and Cumans*, ed. F. Curta (Leiden, 2007), pp. 379–412.

Kristol, A. M., 'Le début du rayonnement parisien et l'unité du français au moyen âge. Le témoignage des manuels d'enseignement du français écrits en Angleterre entre le XIIIe et le début du XVe siècle', *Revue de linguistique romane* 53 (1989), 335–67.

Kowaleski, M., 'The French of England: A Maritime *Lingua Franca*?' in *Lang Cult*, pp. 103–17.

Krönung, B., 'The Wisdom of the Beasts: The Arabic *Book of Kalīla and Dimna* and the Byzantine *Book of Stephanites and Ichnelates*', trans. A. Kinney, in *Fictional Storytelling in the Medieval Eastern Mediterranean and Beyond*, ed. C. Cupane and B. Krönung (Leiden, 2016), pp. 427–60.

Kullberg, C., and D. Watson, 'Introduction: Theorizing the Vernacular', in *Vernaculars in an Age of World Literatures*, ed. C. Kullberg and D. Watson (London, 2022), pp. 1–24.

L'Engle, S., 'Three Manuscripts of the *Roman de Troie*: Codicology, Pictorial Cycles and Patronage', in Cipollaro and Schwarz, ed., *Allen Mären ein Herr*, pp. 67–128.

Lamazou-Duplan, V., 'Lire et écrire chez les notables toulousains à la fin du Moyen Âge: quelques pistes sur la culture des élites laïques avant 1450', in *Toulouse, une métropole méridionale. Vingt siècles de vie urbaine*, ed. B. Suau, J.-P. Amalric and J.-M. Olivier (Toulouse, 2009), pp. 145–62.

Lambourn, E., 'India from Aden: Khutba and Muslim Urban Networks in Late Thirteenth-Century India', in *Secondary Cities and Urban Networks in the Indian Ocean Realm, c. 1400–1800*, ed. K. R. Hall (Lanham MD, 2008), pp. 55–97.

Lamma, P., 'Manuele Comneno nel panegirico di Michele Italico (Codice 2412 della Bibliotheca Universitaria di Bologna)', in *Atti dell'VIII congressio internazionale di studi bizantini*, 2 vols. (Palermo, 1951), I, 397–408.

Lampitt, M., 'Networking the March: A History of Hereford and its Region from the Eleventh through Thirteenth Centuries', *Journal of the Mortimer History Society* 1 (2017), 55–72.

Lang, H. R., 'The Relations of the Earliest Portuguese Lyric School with the Troubadours and Trouvères', *Modern Language Notes* 10 (1895), 104–16.

Langley, E., 'The Extant Repertory of the Early Sicilian Poets', *PMLA* 28 (1913), 454–520.

Langlois, C.-V., *La vie en France au moyen âge: la connaissance de la nature et du monde* (Paris, 1927).

Larison, D., 'Sanctions are Targeted Warfare, and They do Kill', *Responsible Statecraft*, September 16 2022, accessed 24 February 2023, https://responsiblestatecraft.org/2022/09/16/sanctions-are-targeted-warfare-and-they-do-kill/.

Larsson, M. G., 'Nyfunna runor i Hagia Sofia', *Fornvännen* 84 (1989), 12–14.

Leder, S., and H. Kilpatrick, 'Classical Arabic Prose Literature: A Researchers' Sketch Map', *Journal of Arabic Literature* 23 (1992), 2–26.

Lee, C., 'That Obscure Object of Desire: French in Southern Italy', in Morato and Schoenaers, ed., *Medieval Francophone Literary Culture Outside France*, pp. 73–100.

Lefèvre, S., and F. Zinelli, 'La France, jardin d'acclimatation pour la francophonie médiévale?', in *En français hors de France. Textes, livres, collections du Moyen Âge*, ed. F. Zinelli and S. Lefèvre (Strasbourg, 2021), pp. 1–31.

Legge, M. D., *Anglo-Norman Literature and Its Background* (Oxford, 1963).

Léglu, C., 'Imagining Death in late-medieval Occitania', forthcoming.

——, 'Languages in Conflict in Toulouse: *Las Leys d'Amors*', *Modern Language Review* 63 (2008), 388–96.

——, *Multilingualism and Mother Tongue in Medieval French, Occitan, and Catalan Narratives* (University Park, 2010).

——, 'Toulouse', in *Europe: A Literary History, 1348–1415*, ed. D. Wallace, 2 vols. (Oxford, 2016), I, 140–55.

Legrand, É., 'Description des œuvres d'art et de l'église des Saints Apôtres de Constantinople: poème en vers iambiques par Constantin le Rhodien', *Revue des études grecques* 9 (1896), 32–65.

Lerer, S., *Boethius and Dialogue: Literary Method in the* Consolation of Philosophy (Princeton, 1985).

Leupin, A., *Édouard Glissant, philosophe. Héraclite et Hegel dans le Tout-Monde* (Paris, 2016); English version: *Édouard Glissant, Philosopher: Heraclitus and Hegel in the Whole-World*, trans. A. Brown (Albany, 2021).

Levanoni, A., *A Turning Point in Mamluk History: The Third Reign of al-Nasir Muhammad Ibn Qalawun* (Leiden, 1995).

Levy, I., 'Hybridity through Poetry: *Sefer ha-meshalim* and the Status of Poetry in Medieval Iberia', in *A Comparative History of Literatures in the Iberian*

Peninsula, ed. C. Domínguez, A. Abuín González and E. Sapega, 2 vols. (Philadelphia, 2016), II, 131–7.

——, *Jewish Literary Eros: Between Poetry and Prose in the Medieval Mediterranean* (Bloomington, 2022).

Levy, I., and D. Torollo, 'Romance Literature in Hebrew Language with an Arabic Twist: The First Story of Jacob ben El'azar's *Sefer ha-meshalim*', *La Corónica* 45 (2017), 279–304.

Lewin, B., 'Ibn al-Mut'azz', in *Encyclopaedia of Islam*, 2nd edn (Leiden, first published online 2012), accessed 5 December 2022, http://dx.doi.org/10.1163/1573-3912_islam_SIM_3312.

Lewis, F. D., 'A Book of Kings as the King of Books: The *Shahnameh* of Ferdowsi', in *A Companion to World Literature*, vol. 2, ed. C. Chism (Hoboken, 2020), pp. 1255–67.

——, *Rumi: Past and Present, East and West. The Life, Teaching and Poetry of Jalâl Al-Din Rumi* (Oxford, 2000).

Leyser, K., 'Ends and Means in Liudprand of Cremona', in *Communications and Power in Medieval Europe*, ed. T. Reuter (London, 1994), pp. 125–42.

Lie, O. S. H., M. Meuwese, M. Aussems and H. Joldersma, *Christine de Pizan in Bruges:* Le Livre de la Cité des Dames *as* Het Bouc van de Stede der Vrauwen *(London, British Library, Add. 20698)* (Hilversum, 2015).

Lieutard, H., and P. Sauzet, 'D'une diglossie à l'autre: observations linguistiques et sociolinguistiques sur deux textes toulousains de 1555: *Las Ordenansas e coustumas del libre blanc* et *Las nompareilhas receptas*', in *Autour des quenouilles. La parole des femmes (1450–1600)*, ed. J.-F. Courouau, P. Gardy and J. Koopmans (Toulouse, 2010), pp. 109–46.

Linehan, P., *History and the Historians in Medieval Spain* (Oxford, 1993).

——, *Spain, 1157–1300: A Partible Inheritance* (Oxford, 2011).

Lipari, G., 'Per una storia della cultura letteraria a Messina', *Archivio storico messinese* 40 (1982), 65–188.

Lloyd-Morgan, C., 'Blending and Rebottling Old Wines: The Birth and Burial of Arthur in Middle Welsh', in *Adapting Texts and Styles in a Celtic Context: Interdisciplinary Perspectives on Processes of Literary Transfer in the Middle Ages: Studies in Honour of Erich Poppe*, ed. A. Harlos and N. Harlos (Münster, 2016), pp. 155–75.

——, 'French Texts, Welsh Translators', in *The Medieval Translator II*, ed. R. H. Ellis (London, 1991), pp. 45–63.

——, '*Historia Peredur ab Efrawg*', in Lloyd-Morgan and Poppe, ed., *Arthur in the Celtic Languages*, pp. 145–57.

——, 'Later Hybrid Narrative Texts in Middle Welsh', in Lloyd-Morgan and Poppe, ed., *Arthur in the Celtic Languages*, pp. 203–13.

——, 'Medieval Welsh Tales or Romances? Problems of Genre and Terminology', *Cambrian Medieval Celtic Studies* 47 (2004), 41–58.

——, 'Y Seint Greal', in Lloyd-Morgan and Poppe, ed., *Arthur in the Celtic Languages*, pp. 158–69.

Lloyd-Morgan, C., and E. Poppe, 'The First Adaptations from French: History and Context of a Debate', in Lloyd-Morgan and Poppe, ed., *Arthur in the Celtic Languages*, pp. 110–16.

—— ed., *Arthur in the Celtic Languages: The Arthurian Legend in Celtic Literatures and Languages* (Cardiff, 2019).

Long, J., 'Dermot and the Earl: Who Wrote the Song?', *Proceedings of the Royal Irish Academy* 75 C (1975), 263–72.

Longnon, J., 'Notes sur la diplomatique de l'empire latin de Constantinople', in *Mélanges dédiés à la mémoire de Félix Grat*, ed. É.-A. van Moé, J. Vielliard and P. Marot, 2 vols. (Paris, 1949), II, 3–18.

Lopez, R. S., 'Stars and Spices: The Earliest Italian Manual of Commercial Practice', in *Economy, Society, and Government in Medieval Italy. Essays in Memory of Robert L. Reynolds*, ed. D. Herlihy, R. S. Lopez and V. Slessarev (Kent OH, 1969), pp. 35–42.

Lovecy, I., 'Historia Peredur ab Efrawg', in Bromwich et al., ed., *The Arthur of the Welsh*, pp. 171–82.

Luff, R., 'Zum Problem der Verifizierbarkeit romanischer Einflüsse in der deutschen Minnelyrik des Hochmittelalters', *Beiträge zur Geschichte der deutschen Sprache und Literatur* 124 (2002), 250–60.

Lugli, E., *The Making of Measure and the Promise of Sameness* (Chicago, 2019).

Lumbley, C., 'The "Dark Welsh": Color, Race, and Alterity in the Matter of Medieval Wales', *Literature Compass* 16 (2019), 1–19.

Lusignan, S., *Essai d'histoire sociolinguistique. Le français picard au moyen âge* (Paris, 2012).

——, 'Le français médiéval: perspectives historiques sur une langue plurielle', in S. Lusignan, F. Martineau, Y.-C. Morin and P. Cohen, *L'introuvable unité du français. Contacts et variations linguistiques en Europe et en Amérique (XIIe–XVIIIe)* (Quebec, 2011), pp. 45–65.

——, 'French Language in Contact with English: Social Context and Linguistic Change (mid-13th–14th centuries)', in *Lang Cult*, pp. 19–30.

——, *La langue des rois au Moyen Âge. Le français en France et en Angleterre* (Paris, 2004).

Lynch, K. L., *The High Medieval Dream Vision: Poetry, Philosophy, and Literary Form* (Stanford, 1988).

Lyons, M. C., *The Man of Wiles in Popular Arabic Literature: A Study of a Medieval Arab Hero* (Edinburgh, 2012).

Machan, T. W., 'French, English, and the Late Medieval Linguistic Repertoire', in *Lang Cult*, pp. 363–72.

Macrides, R., 'Constantinople: The Crusaders' Gaze', in *Travel in the Byzantine World*, ed. R. Macrides (Aldershot, 2002), pp. 193–212.

Madden, T., *Enrico Dandolo and the Rise of Venice* (Baltimore, 2003).

Magdalino, P., 'The Bath of Leo the Wise and the "Macedonian Renaissance" Revisited: Topography, Iconography, Ceremonial, Ideology', *Dumbarton Oaks Papers* 42 (1988), 97–118.

Magdalino, P., and R. Nelson, 'The Emperor in Byzantine Art of the Twelfth Century', *Byzantinische Forschungen* 8 (1982), 123–83.

Malamut, E., *Les îles de l'empire byzantin, VIIe–XIIe siècles*, 2 vols. (Paris, 1988).

Mallette, K., 'Lingua Franca', in *A Companion to Mediterranean History*, ed. P. Horden and S. Kinoshita (Oxford, 2014), pp. 330–44.

——, *Lives of the Great Languages: Arabic and Latin in the Medieval Mediterranean* (Chicago, 2021).

——, 'Palermo', in *Europe: A Literary History, 1348–1418*, ed. D. Wallace, 2 vols. (Oxford, 2016), II, 12–24.

——, 'Terra Recognita: Excursus on the Literary History of Sicily', *Mediaevalia* 24 (2003), 137–58.

——, *The Kingdom of Sicily, 1100–1250: A Literary History* (Philadelphia, 2011).

Mango, C., 'Antique Statuary and the Byzantine Beholder', *Dumbarton Oaks Papers* 17 (1963), 53–75.

——, *Studies in Constantinople* (Aldershot, 1993).

Mango, C., G. Dagron and G. Greatrex, ed., *Constantinople and its Hinterland: Papers from the Twenty-Seventh Spring Symposium of Byzantine Studies, Oxford, April 1993* (London, 1995).

Marandet, M.-C., *Le souci de l'au-delà. La pratique testamentaire dans la région toulousaine (1300–1450)* (Perpignan, 1998).

Márquez Villanueva, F., *El concepto cultural alfonsí* (Barcelona, 2004).

Marroni, S., 'La meraviglia di Marco Polo: L'espressione della meraviglia nel lessico e nella sintassi del Milione', in *I viaggi del Milione: Itinerari testuali, vettori di trasmissione e metamorfosi del Devisement du monde di Marco Polo e Rustichello da Pisa nella pluralità delle attestazioni*, ed. S. Conte (Rome, 2008), pp. 233–62.

Martin, M. E., 'The Chrysobull of Alexius I Comnenus to the Venetians and the Early Venetian Quarter in Constantinople', *Byzantinoslavica* (1978), 19–23.

Martínez Manzano, T., *Konstantinos Laskaris. Humanist, Philologe, Lehrer, Kopist* (Hamburg, 1994).

Materni, M., 'Il *Libro de Alexandre* e il *Roman d'Alexandre* veneziano (con un'appendice sulle fonti del poema iberico)', *Medioevo europeo* 1.2 (2017), 61–105.

Matheson, L. M., *The Prose Brut: The Development of a Middle English Chronicle* (Tempe, 1998).

Mayr-Harting, H., 'Liudprand of Cremona's Account of his Legation to Constantinople and Ottonian Imperial Strategy', *English Historical Review* 116 (2001), 539–56.

McCormick, M., 'Analyzing Imperial Ceremonies', *Jahrbuch der österreichischen Gesellschaft für Byzantinistik* 35 (1985), 1–20.

——, Eternal Victory: Triumphal Rulership in Late Antiquity, Byzantium and the Early Medieval West (Cambridge, 1986).

Medieval Francophone Literary Culture Outside France, accessed 25 August 2023, www.medievalfrancophone.ac.uk.

Meecham-Jones, S., 'Introduction', in *Writers of the Reign of Henry II: Twelve Essays*, ed. R. Kennedy and S. Meecham-Jones (Basingstoke, 2006), pp. 1–24.

——, 'Romance Society and its Discontents: Romance Motifs and Romance Consequences in *The Song of Dermot and the Normans in Ireland*', in *Boundaries in Medieval Romance*, ed. N. Cartlidge (Cambridge, 2008), pp. 71–92.

Ménager, L.-R., 'Pesanteur et étiologie de la colonisation normande de l'Italie', in *Roberto il Guiscardo e il suo tempo. Atti delle prime giornate normanno-sveve (Bari, 28–29 May 1973)* (Bari, 1975 repr. 1991), pp. 189–214.

Menocal, M. R., *The Arabic Role in Medieval Literary History: A Forgotten Heritage* (Philadelphia, 1988).

Mews, C. J., and T. Zahora, 'Remembering Last Things and Regulating Behaviour in the Early Fourteenth Century: From the *De Consideratione Novissimorum* to the *Speculum Morale*', *Speculum* 90 (2015), 960–94.

Middleton, R., 'Chwedl Geraint ab Erbin', in Bromwich et al., ed., *The Arthur of the Welsh*, pp. 147–57.

Minervini, L., 'Le français dans l'Orient latin (XIIIe–XIVe siècles). Éléments pour la caractérisation d'une scripta du Levant', *Revue de linguistique romane* 74 (2010), 119–98.

——, 'What We Know and Don't Yet Know about Outremer French', in Morreale and Paul, ed., *The French of Outremer*, pp. 15–29.

Minnis, A., *Medieval Theory of Authorship: Scholastic Literary Attitudes in the Later Middle Ages*, 2nd edn (Philadelphia, 1988).

——, *Translations of Authority in Medieval English Literature: Valuing the Vernacular* (Cambridge, 2009).

Minnis, A. J., and A. B. Scott, ed., with the assistance of D. Wallace, *Medieval Literary Theory and Criticism c. 1100–c. 1375: The Commentary Tradition* (Oxford, 1988).

Mittelhochdeutsche Begriffsdatenbank, accessed 7 October 2023, http://mhdbdb.sbg.ac.at.

Mohr, J., 'Tagelied', in Kellner, Reichlin and Rudolph, ed., *Handbuch Minnesang*, pp. 534–42.

Monroe, J. T., 'Maimonides on the Mozarabic Lyric (A Note on the *Muwaššaḥa*)', *La Corónica* 17.2 (1989), 18–32.

Mora-Lebrun, F., *'Metre en romanz'. Les romans d'antiquité du XIIe siècle et leur postérité (XIIIe–XIVe siècle)* (Paris, 2008).

Morato, N., and D. Schoenaers, ed., *Medieval Francophone Literary Culture Outside France: Studies in the Moving Word* (Turnhout, 2018).

Moreau, J. M., *Eschatological Subjects: Divine and Literary Judgment in Fourteenth-Century French Poetry* (Columbus, 2014).

Morgan, D., 'Persian as a *Lingua Franca* in the Mongol Empire', in *Literacy in the Persianate World: Writing and the Social Order*, ed. B. Spooner and W. L. Hanaway (Philadelphia, 2012), pp. 160–70.

Morreale, L. K., 'French Literature, Florentine Politics, and Vernacular Historical Writing, 1270–1348', *Speculum* 85 (2010), 868–93.

Morreale, L. K., and N. L. Paul, ed., *The French of Outremer: Communities and Communications in the Crusading Mediterranean* (New York, 2018).

Morrison, E., 'Linking Ancient Troy and Medieval France: Illuminations of an Early Copy of the *Roman de Troie*', in *Medieval Manuscripts, Their Makers and Users: A Special Issue of 'Viator' in Honor of Richard and Mary Rouse* (Turnhout, 2011), pp. 77–102.

Mortara-Ottolenghi, L., 'The Illumination and the Artists', in *The Rothschild Miscellany*, ed. I. Fishof, 2 vols. (London, 1989), II, 127–251.

Mote, F. W., 'Chinese Society Under Mongol Rule', in *The Cambridge History of China*, 15 vols., VI, *Alien Regimes and Border States, 907–1368*, ed. H. Franke and D. Twitchett (Cambridge, 1994), pp. 616–64.

——, *Imperial China, 900–1800* (Cambridge MA, 1999).

Mufwene, S. S., 'L'émergence des parlers créoles et l'évolution des langues romanes. Faits, mythes et idéologies', *Études créoles* 33 (2016), n.p., accessed 24 February 2023, https://doi.org/10.4000/etudescreoles.525.

——, 'The Emergence of Creoles and Language Change', in *The Routledge Handbook of Linguistic Anthropology*, ed. N. Bonvillain (London, 2015), pp. 345–68.

Mullally, E., 'Hiberno-Norman Literature and Its Public', in *Settlement and Society in Medieval Ireland: Studies Presented to F. X. Martin, O.S.A.* (Kilkenny, 1998), pp. 327–43.

Multilingual Dynamics of Medieval Flanders, accessed 24 February 2023, https://multilingualdynamics.sites.uu.nl/.

Murphy, J. J., 'The Arts of Poetry and Prose', in *The Cambridge History of Literary Criticism. Vol. 2: The Middle Ages*, ed. A. Minnis and I. Johnson (Cambridge, 2005), pp. 42–67.

—— ed., *Three Medieval Rhetorical Arts* (Berkeley, 1985).

Murray, K., *The Early Finn Cycle* (Dublin, 2017).

Natali, G., 'A Lyrical Version: Boccaccio's *Filostrato*', in *The European Tragedy of Troilus*, ed. P. Boitani (Oxford, 1989), pp. 49–73.

Necipoğlu, N., *Byzantine Constantinople: Monuments, Topography and Everyday Life* (Leiden, 2001).

Ní Mhaonaigh, M., *Brian Boru: Ireland's Greatest King?* (Stroud, 2007).

——, '*Carait tairisi*: Literary Links between Ireland and England in the Eleventh Century', in *Adapting Texts and Styles in a Celtic Context: Interdisciplinary Perspectives on Processes of Literary Transfer in the Middle Ages, Studies in Honour of Erich Poppe*, ed. A. Harlos and N. Harlos (Münster, 2016), pp. 265–88.

——, 'The Date of *Cogad Gáedel re Gallaib*', *Peritia* 9 (1995), 354–77.

——, 'The Literature of Medieval Ireland, 800–1200: from the Vikings to the Normans', in *The Cambridge History of Irish Literature, Volume 1: to 1890*, ed. M. Kelleher and P. O'Leary (Cambridge, 2006), pp. 32–73.

——, 'Of Bede's 'Five Languages and Four Nations': The Earliest Writing from Ireland, Scotland and Wales', in *The Cambridge History of Early Medieval English Literature*, ed. C. A. Lees (Cambridge, 2012), pp. 99–119.

Nichols, S., 'Global Language or Universal Language? From Babel to the Illustrious Vernacular', *Digital Philology: A Journal of Medieval Cultures* 1 (2012), 73–109.

Nicol, D. M., *Byzantium and Venice: A Study in Diplomatic and Cultural Relations* (Cambridge, 1988).

Niiranen, S., 'Apothecary's Art as a Contact Zone in Late Medieval Southern France', in *Multilingualism in the Middle Ages and Early Modern Age: Communication and Miscommunication in the Premodern World*, ed. A. Classen (Berlin, 2016), pp. 207–32.

Nisse, R., *Jacob's Shipwreck: Diaspora, Translation, and Jewish-Christian Relations in Medieval England* (Ithaca, 2017).

Nobel, P., 'La traduction biblique', in *Translations médiévales. Cinq siècles de traductions en français au Moyen Âge (XIe–XVe siècles). Étude et répertoire, Volume 1: De la* translatio studii *à l'étude de la* translatio, ed. C. Galderisi (Turnhout, 2011), pp. 207–23.

Nolan, B., *Chaucer and the Tradition of the* Roman Antique (Cambridge, 1992).

Ó Cathasaigh, T., 'The Literature of Medieval Ireland to *c*. 800: St Patrick to the Vikings', in *The Cambridge History of Irish Literature, Volume 1: to 1890*, ed. M. Kelleher and P. O'Leary (Cambridge, 2006), pp. 9–31.

Ó Corráin, D., 'Foreign Connections and Domestic Politics: Killaloe and the Uí Briain in Twelfth-Century Hagiography', in *Ireland in Early Mediaeval Europe: Studies in Memory of Kathleen Hughes*, ed. D. Whitelock, R. McKitterick and D. N. Dumville (Cambridge, 1982), pp. 213–31.

——, 'Orosius, Ireland and Christianity', *Peritia* 28 (2017), 113–24.

Ó Hoireabhárd, S., 'Derbforgaill: Twelfth-Century Abductee, Patron and Wife', *Irish Historical Studies* 46:169 (2022), 1–24.

Ó hUiginn, R., ed., *Lebor na hUidre* (Dublin, 2015).

Ó Néill, P. P., 'The Background to the Cambrai Homily', *Ériu* 32 (1981), 137–48.

——, 'The Impact of the Norman Invasion on Irish Literature', *Anglo-Norman Studies* 20 (1998), 171–85.

——, 'An Irishman at Chartres in the Twelfth Century: The Evidence of Oxford, Bodleian Library, MS Auct. F. III. 15', *Ériu* 48 (1997), 1–35.

Ó Riain Raedel, D., 'The Travels of Irish Manuscripts: from the Continent to Ireland', in *A Miracle of Learning: Essays in Honour of William O'Sullivan*, ed. T. Barnard, D. Ó Cróinín and K. Simms (Aldershot, 1998), pp. 52–67.

O'Brien, B., *Reversing Babel: Translation Among the English During an Age of Conquests, c.800 to c.1200* (Newark DE, 2011).

O'Doherty, J. F., 'Historical Criticism of the *Song of Dermot and the Earl*', *Irish Historical Studies* 1 (1938), 4–34.

O'Donnell, T., 'Talking to the Neighbours', *High Medieval Literature*, ed. E. M. Tyler and J. Wogan-Browne (Oxford, forthcoming).

O'Rahilly, T. F., 'Notes on Middle-Irish Pronunciation, I. The Irish Names in "The Song of Dermot and the Earl"', *Hermathena* 44 (1926), 152–95.

Oliva, M., 'The French of England in Female Convents: The French Kitcheners' Accounts of Campsey Ash Priory', *Lang Cult*, pp. 90–102.

Olszowy-Schlanger, J., 'Hebrew Books', in *The European Book in the Twelfth Century*, ed. E. Kwakkel and R. Thomson (Cambridge, 2018), pp. 159–74.

——, 'Livre de Job avec le Commentaire de Berakhyah ben Natronai ha-Naqdan', in *Savants et croyants. Les juifs d'Europe du Nord au Moyen Age*, ed. N. Hatot and J. Olszowy-Schlanger (Ghent, 2018), pp. 134–5.

Oltrogge, D., *Die Illustrationszyklen zur* Histoire ancienne jusqu'à César *(1250–1400)* (Frankfurt am Main, 1989).

Oosterman, J., 'Anthonis de Roovere. Het werk: overlevering, toeschrijving en plaatsbepaling', *Jaarboek De Fonteine* (1995–96), 29–140.

Opera dei Pupi, Sicilian Puppet Theatre, accessed 29 December 2022, https://ich.unesco.org/en/RL/opera-dei-pupi-sicilian-puppet-theatre-00011.

Orlandini, G., 'Marco Polo e la sua famiglia', *Archivio veneto-tridentinio* 9 (1926), 1–68.

Ormrod, M. W., 'The Language of Complaint: Multilingualism and Petitioning in Later Medieval England', in *Lang Cult*, pp. 31–43.

Ostler, N., *Empires of the Word: A Language History of the World* (New York, 2005).

Over, K. L., 'Transcultural Change: Romance to *Rhamant*', in *Medieval Celtic Literature and Society*, ed. H. Fulton (Dublin, 2005), pp. 183–204.

Pagis, D., 'Variety in Medieval Rhymed Narratives', *Scripta Hierosolymitana* 27 (1978), 79–98.

Palermi, M. L., 'Histoire ancienne jusqu'à César: forme e percorsi del testo', Critica del testo 7 (2004), 213–56.

Palmer, N. F., 'The High and Later Middle Ages (1100–1450)', in The Cambridge History of German Literature, ed. H. Watanabe-O'Kelly (Cambridge, 1997), pp. 40–91.

Papademetriou, J.-T., 'The Sources and the Character of Del governo de' regni', Transactions and Proceedings of the American Philological Association 92 (1961), 422–39.

Parzival-Projekt, accessed 7 October 2023, https://www.parzival.unibe.ch.

Pascual-Argente, C., '"De francés en castellano": La tradición manuscrita de la Crónica troyana de Alfonso XI', Troianalexandrina 20 (2020), 23–58.

——, '"En las corónicas antiguas de los grandes fechos que pasaron": La historia antigua en el proyecto cultural de Alfonso XI', Revista de Literatura Medieval 34 (2022), 133–61.

——, 'The Matter of Meter: Cuaderna Vía and the Castilian Romance of Antiquity', in A Companion to the Mester de Clerecía, ed. R. Bower and M. V. Desing (Leiden, forthcoming).

——, Memory, Media, and Empire in the Castilian Romances of Antiquity: Alexander's Heirs (Leiden, 2022).

Passerat, G., 'Les prières du pape Jean XXII', in Jean XXII et le Midi, Cahiers de Fanjeaux 45 (Toulouse, 2012), pp. 439–57.

Paviot, J., 'Éléonore de Poitiers: les états de France (Les Honneurs de la Cour)', Annuaire-Bulletin de la Société de l'histoire de France 1996, 75–118.

Peacock, A. C. S., 'Georgia and the Anatolian Turks in the 12th and 13th Centuries', Anatolian Studies 56 (2006), 127–46.

——, 'Introduction: The Great Age of the Seljuqs', in Court and Cosmos: The Great Age of the Seljuqs, ed. S. R. Canby, D. Beyazit, M. Rugiadi and A. C. S. Peacock (New York, 2016), pp. 2–44.

Peklar, B., 'Discussing Medieval Dialogue between the Soul and the Body and the Question of Dualism', Ars & Humanitas 9 (2015), 172–99.

Penkower, J., 'The End of Rashi's Commentary on Job: The Manuscripts and the Printed Editions', Jewish Studies Quarterly 10 (2003), 18–48.

——, 'The Process of the Canonization of Rashi's Commentary on the Torah' [Hebrew], in Study and Knowledge in Jewish Thought, ed. H. Kreisel (Beer-sheva, 2006), pp. 123–46.

Péquignot, S., 'Treaty of Caltabellotta (1302)', in The Encyclopedia of Diplomacy, ed. G. Martel, accessed 25 August 2023, https://doi.org/10.1002/9781118885154.diplo488.

Pérennec, R. and E. Schmid, ed., Höfischer Roman in Vers und Prosa, in Claassens, Knapp and Pérennec, ed., Germania Litteraria Mediaevalis Francigena, vol. V (Berlin, 2010).

Pérennec, R., ed., *Sprache und Verskunst*, in Claassens, Knapp and Pérennec, ed., *Germania Litteraria Mediaevalis Francigena*, vol. II (Berlin, 2014).

Perros, H., 'Crossing the Shannon Frontier: Connacht and the Anglo-Normans, 1170–1224', in *Colony and Frontier in Medieval Ireland: Essays Presented to J. F. Lydon*, ed. T. B. Barry, R. Frame and K. Simms (London, 1995), pp. 177–200.

Phillips, J., *The Fourth Crusade and the Sack of Constantinople* (London, 2004).

Pichel, R. '"Lean por este libro que o acharam mays complidamente": del *Libro de Troya* alfonsí a la *Historia troyana* de Pedro I', *Troianalexandrina* 16 (2016), 55–180.

Pifer, M., *Kindred Voices: A Literary History of Medieval Anatolia* (New Haven, 2021).

Poe, E. W., *From Poetry to Prose in Old Provençal: The Emergence of the 'Vidas', the 'Razos', and the 'Razos de trobar'* (Birmingham AL, 1984).

——, 'The *Vidas* and *Razos*', in *A Handbook of the Troubadours*, ed. F. R. P. Akehurst and J. M. Davis (Berkeley, 1995), pp. 185–97.

Polak, L., 'Charlemagne and the Marvels of Constantinople', in *The Medieval Alexander and Romance Epic*, ed. P. Noble, L. Polak and C. Isoz (New York, 1982), pp. 159–71.

Pollock, S., 'The Cosmopolitan Vernacular', *Journal of South Asian Studies* 57 (1998), 6–37.

——, *The Language of the Gods in the World of Men: Sanskrit, Culture, and Power in Premodern India* (Berkeley, 2006).

Polo De Beaulieu, M.-A., 'De la rumeur aux textes: échos de l'apparition du revenant d'Alès (après 1323)', in *La circulation des nouvelles au Moyen Âge. XXIVe Congrès de la SHMES (Avignon, juin 1993)* (Rome, 1994), pp. 129–56.

Poppe, E., '*Ystorya Geraint fab Erbin*', in Lloyd-Morgan and Poppe, ed., *Arthur in the Celtic Languages*, pp. 132–44.

Poppe, E., and R. Reck, A French Romance in Wales: *Ystorya Bown o Hamtwn*: Processes of Medieval Translations', *Zeitschrift für celtische Philologie* 55 (2006), 122–80, and 56 (2008), 129–64.

Pratt, M. L., 'Apocalypse in the Andes: Contact Zones and the Struggle for Interpretive Power', *Encuentros* 15 (1996), 1–16.

——, 'Arts of the Contact Zone', *Profession* (1991), 33–40.

——, 'Introduction', in *Engaging Transculturality: Concepts, Key Terms, Case Studies*, ed. L. Abu-Er-Rub, C. Brosius, S. Meurer, D. Panagiotopoulos and S. Richter (New York, 2019), pp. xxiii–xliv.

Prosperi, V., 'Strategie di autoconservazione del mito: la guerra di Troia tra Seconda Sofistica e prima età moderna', *Materiali e discussioni per l'analisi dei testi classici*, 71 (2013), 145–75.

Psaki, F. R., and G. Allaire, ed., *The Arthur of the Italians: The Arthurian Legend in Medieval Italian Literature and Culture* (Cardiff, 2014).

Psichari, J., 'Le *Roman de Florimont*: contribution à l'histoire littéraire – étude des mots grecs dans ce roman', in *Études romanes dédiées à Gaston Paris le 29 décembre 1890 (25e anniversaire de son doctorat ès lettres)* ed. 'par ses élèves français et ses élèves étrangers des pays de langue française' (Paris, 1891), pp. 507–50.

Punzi, A., *Oedipodae confusa domus: la materia tebana nel Medioevo latino e romanzo* (Rome, 1995).

——, *Sulla sezione troiana della* General estoria *di Alfonso X* (Rome, 1995).

Putter, A., 'Multilingualism in England and Wales, *c.* 1200: The Testimony of Gerald of Wales', in Kleinhenz and Busby, ed., *Medieval Multilingualism*, pp. 83–106.

Queller, D. E., and T. E. Madden, *The Fourth Crusade and the Conquest of Constantinople* (Philadelphia, 1997).

Rabiot, J., 'La culture théologique d'un grand marchand florentin: échos de la controverse sur la vision béatifique dans la *Nuova cronica* de Giovanni Villani (XIVe siècle)', *Mélanges de l'École française de Rome – Moyen Âge* 125 (2013), accessed 17 February 2024, https://journals.openedition.org/mefrm/1143.

Rachetta, M. T., 'Evolving Texts and Evolving Witnesses', *The Values of French Blog*, April 24 2017, accessed 24 February 2023, https://tvof.ac.uk/blog/evolving-texts-and-evolving-witnesses.

Rajna, P., 'Intorno a due antiche coperte con figurazioni tratte dalle storie di Tristano', *Romania* 42 (1913), 517–79.

Rapisardo, S., 'Federico II, attività poetica', in *Treccani.it – Enciclopedie on line*, Istituto dell'Enciclopedia Italian, accessed 17 June 2022, https://www.treccani.it/enciclopedia/federico-ii-attivita-poetica_%28Federiciana%29/.

Rapp, C., 'A Medieval Cosmopolis: Constantinople and its Foreigners', in *Constantinople as Center and Crossroad*, ed. O. Heilo and I. Nilsson (Istanbul, 2019), pp. 100–15.

Rayfield, D., *The Literature of Georgia: A History*, 2nd edn (Richmond, 2000).

Reck, R., '*Owain* or *Chwedyl Iarlles y Ffynnawn*', in Lloyd-Morgan and Poppe, ed., *Arthur in the Celtic Languages*, pp. 117–31.

Reeve, D., 'Queer Arts of Failure in Alan of Lille and Hue of Rotelande', in *Medieval Thought Experiments: Poetry, Hypothesis, and Experience in the European Middle Ages*, ed. P. Knox, J. Morton, and D. Reeve (Turnhout, 2018), 273–96.

Regel, W., *Fontes rerum byzantinarum*, 2 parts (St Petersburg, 1892–1917).

Renda, F., *Storia della Sicilia dalle origini ai giorni nostri* (Palermo, 2003).

Resnick, I., 'Lingua Dei, Lingua Hominis: Sacred Language and Medieval Texts', *Viator* 21 (1990), 51–74.

Revard, C., 'Scribe and Provenance', in *Studies in the Harley Manuscript: The Scribes, Contents, and Social Contexts of British Library MS Harley 2253*, ed. S. Fein (Kalamazoo, 2000), pp. 21–110.

RIALFrI – Repertorio informatizzato antica litterature franco-italiana, accessed 7 October 2023, https://www.rialfri.eu/.

Richards, E. J., 'Body-Soul Debates in English, French and German Manuscripts, *c.*1200–*c.*1500' (unpublished Ph.D. thesis, University of York, 2009), pp. 21–30.

Richter, M., 'Collecting Miracles Along the Anglo-Welsh Border in the Early Fourteenth Century', in *Multilingualism in Later Medieval Britain*, ed. D. A. Trotter (Cambridge, 2000), pp. 53–61.

Rico, F., 'La clerecía del mester', *Hispanic Review* 53 (1985), 1–23, 127–50.

Ridel, E., *Les Vikings et les mots. L'apport de l'ancien scandinave à la langue française* (Paris, 2009).

Rider, J., *The Murder, Betrayal, and Slaughter of the Glorious Charles, Count of Flanders* (New Haven, 2013).

Rindler Schjerve, R., and Vetter, E., 'Historical Sociolinguistics and Multilingualism: Theoretical and Methodological Issues in the Development of a Multifunctional Framework', in *Diglossia and Power: Language Policies and Practice in the 19th Century Habsburg Empire*, ed. R. Rindler Schjerve (Berlin, 2003), pp. 35–68.

Risop, A., 'Ungelöste Fragen zum *Florimont*', in *Abhandlungen Herrn Prof. Dr. Adolf Tobler zur Feier seiner fünfundzwanzigjährigen Thätigkeit als ordentlicher Professor an der Universität Berlin von dankbaren Schülern in Ehrerbietung dargebracht* (Halle, 1895), pp. 430–63.

Roberts, H. A., 'Court and *Cyuoeth*: Chrétien de Troyes' *Erec et Enide* and the Middle Welsh *Gereint*', *Arthurian Literature* 21 (2004), 53–72.

Roberts-Zauderer, D. L., *Metaphor and Imagination in Medieval Jewish Thought: Moses ibn Ezra, Judah Halevi, Moses Maimonides and Shem Tov ibn Falaquera* (Cham, 2019).

Rodríguez Porto, R. M., 'A Crucial Episode in the History of Medieval Book Illustration: The *Histoire ancienne* in Italy', *The Values of French Blog*, December 19 2018, accessed 24 February 2023, https://tvof.ac.uk/blog/crucial-episode-history-medieval-book-illustration-histoire-ancienne-italy.

——, 'Dark and Elusive Fortune: Affectionate Readings of the *Roman de Troie* in Fourteenth-Century Castile', in Cipollaro and Schwarz, ed., *Allen Mären ein Herr*, pp. 159–78.

——, 'Review of *Le 'epistole delle dame di Grecia' nel* Roman de Troie *in prosa: La prima traduzione francese delle* Eroidi di Ovidio and *Les Epistres des Dames de Grece: une version médiévale en prose française des* Heroïdes d'Ovide, by L. Barbieri', *Troianalexandrina* 8 (2008), 311–18.

—, '*Thesaurum*: La *Crónica troyana de Alfonso XI* y los libros iluminados de la monarquía castellana (1284–1369)', 2 vols. (unpublished Ph.D. dissertation, Universidade de Santiago de Compostela, 2012).

Rodríguez-Velasco, J., *Ciudadanía, soberanía monárquica y caballería. Poética del orden de caballería* (Madrid, 2009).

Rodway, S., 'Cymraeg vs. Kymraeg: Dylanwad Ffrangeg ar Orgraff Cymraeg Canol?', *Studia Celtica* 43 (2000), 123–33.

Roncaglia, A., 'De quibusdam provincialibus translatis in lingua nostra', in *Letteratura e critica: Studi in onore di Natalino Sapegno*, ed. W. Binni (Rome, 1975), pp. 1–36.

Rosalis. Bibliothèque numérique patrimoniale de Toulouse, accessed 17 February 2024, https://rosalis.bibliotheque.toulouse.fr/rosalis/fr/content/accueil-fr.

Rosen, T., 'The Story of Maskil and Peninah by Jacob Ben El'azar: A Thirteenth-Century Romance', *Florilegium* 23 (2006), 155–72.

—, *Unveiling Eve: Reading Gender in Medieval Hebrew Literature* (Philadelphia, 2003).

Roth, C., 'Benjamin of Cambridge', in *Encyclopaedia Judaica*, ed. M. Berenbaum and F. Skolnik, 3 vols., 2nd edn (Farmington Hills, 2007), III, 362.

Roth, P., 'Rabbi Benjamin of Cambridge: First of the English Rabbis' [Hebrew], *Mehkere Talmud* 4, forthcoming.

Rothwell, W., 'Sugar and Spice and All Things Nice: From Oriental Bazar to English Cloister in Anglo-French', *Modern Language Review* 94 (1999), 647–59.

Rubin, J., *Learning in a Crusader City: Intellectual Activity and Intercultural Exchanges in Acre, 1191–1291* (Cambridge, 2018).

Russell, P., 'Latin and British in Roman and Post-Roman Britain: Methodology and Morphology', *Transactions of the Philological Society* 109 (2011), 138–57.

Rydén, L., 'The Andreas Salos Apocalypse: Greek Text, Translation and Commentary', *Dumbarton Oaks Papers* 28 (1974), 197–261.

Savoye, M.-L., 'Notice de "AVIGNON, Bibliothèque municipale, 0344"', in *Jonas-IRHT/CNRS*, accessed 17 February 2024, https://jonas.irht.cnrs.fr/manuscrit/5196.

Sayers, W., 'The Patronage of *La conquête d'Irlande*', *Romance Philology* 21 (1967), 34–41.

Scheindlin, R. P., 'Hebrew Poetry in Medieval Iberia', in *Convivencia: Jews, Muslims, and Christians in Medieval Spain*, ed. V. B. Mann, T. F. Glick and J. D. Dodds (New York, 1992), pp. 38–59.

—, 'Sipure ha-ahava shel Ya'aqov ben El'azar' [Hebrew], in *Proceedings of the Eleventh World Congress of Jewish Studies*, ed. D. Assaf (Jerusalem, 1994), pp. 16–20.

Schepens, L., 'Le Livre du jeu de la paulme moralisé', *Revue belge de philologie et d'histoire* 40.3 (1962), 804–14.

Schimmel, A., *The Triumphal Sun: A Study of the Works of Jalāloddin Rumi* (London, 1978).

Schippers, A., 'Hebrew Andalusian and Arabic Poetry: Descriptions of Fruit in the Tradition of the "Elegants" or ẓurafā'', *Journal of Semitic Studies* 33 (1988), 219–32.

Schirmann, J., 'L'Amour spirituel dans la poésie hébraïque du moyen âge', *Lettres Romanes* 15 (1961), 315–25.

——, 'Les contes rimés de Jacob ben Eléazar de Tolède', in *Études d'orientalisme dédiés à la mémoire de Lévi-Provençal*, ed. R. Brunschvig (Paris, 1962), pp. 285–97.

——, 'Poets Contemporaneous with Moses Ibn Ezra and Judah Halevi' [Hebrew], *Studies of the Research Institute for Hebrew Poetry* 2 (1936), 62–152.

Schirmann, J., and E. Fleischer, *Toledot ha-shira ha-ʿivrit bi-Sfarad ha-noṣrit uvi-drom Ṣarefat*, [Hebrew] (Jerusalem, 1997).

Schlumberger, G., F. Chalandon and A. Blanchet, *Sigillographie de l'Orient latin* (Paris, 1943).

Schmid, E., 'Chrétiens "Yvain" und Hartmanns "Iwein"', in Pérennec and Schmid, *Höfischer Roman in Vers und Prosa*, pp. 135–67.

Schmitt, J.-C., *Les revenants. Les vivants et les morts dans la société médiévale* (Paris, 1994).

Schrijver, P., 'Pruners and Trainers of the Celtic Family Tree: The Rise and Development of Celtic in the Light of Language Contact', in *Proceedings of the XIV International Congress of Celtic Studies, held in Maynooth University, 1–5 August 2011*, ed. L. Breatnach, R. Ó hUiginn, D. McManus and K. Simms (Dublin, 2015), pp. 191–219.

Seidl, S., 'Altokzitanische Lyrik', in Kellner et al., *Handbuch Minnesang*, pp. 103–12.

Selig, M., 'L'église et le passage à l'écrit du vernaculaire dans le Nord de la France au XIᵉ siècle', in *The Church and Vernacular Literature in Medieval France*, ed. D. Kullman (Toronto, 2009), pp. 15–34.

Shawcross, T., 'The City as an Archive of Speaking Statues: Language, Record-keeping and Memory in the Middle Byzantine Empire', in *Anekdota: Festschrift für Albrecht Berger*, ed. A. Riehle, I. Grimm-Stadelmann, R. Tocci and M. Vučetić (Boston and Berlin, 2023), pp. 661–81.

——, 'Conquest Legitimized: The Making of a Byzantine Emperor in Crusader Constantinople (1204–1261),' in *Byzantines, Latins, and Turks in the Eastern Mediterranean World after 1150*, ed. J. Harris, C. Holmes and E. Russell (Oxford, 2012), pp. 198–204.

——, 'The Seduction of Constantinople', *The French of Outremer: Communities and Communications in the Crusading Mediterranean*, accessed 13

April 2022, https://mvstconference.ace.fordham.edu/frenchofoutremer/conference-program/.

——, 'The Worldview of Marco Polo's *Devisament dou monde*: Commercial Marvels, Silk Route Nostalgia and Global Empire in the Late Middle Ages', in *Authorship, Worldview, and Identity in Medieval Europe*, ed. C. Raffensperger (Abingdon, 2022), pp. 142–70.

Shields, M., 'Spruchdichtung und Sirventes', in Pérennec, *Sprache und Verskunst*, pp. 275–306.

Short, I., *Manual of Anglo-Norman*, 2nd edn (Oxford, 2013).

——, 'On Bilingualism in Anglo-Norman England', *Romance Philology* 33 (1980), 467–79.

——, 'Patrons and Polyglots: French Literature in Twelfth-Century England', *Anglo-Norman Studies* 14 (1991), 229–49.

Simon, U., 'Abraham ibn Ezra' in M. Sæbo, ed., *Hebrew Bible/Old Testament: The History of Its Interpretation*, 3 vols. (Göttingen, 2000), I, 376–87.

Simons, P., 'Naming Names: Onomastics, Etymologies and Intertexts in Aimon de Varennes' *Florimont*', *Neuphilologische Mitteilungen* 113 (2012), 457–85.

Sims-Williams, P., 'Did Itinerant Breton *Conteurs* Transmit the *Matière de Bretagne*?', *Romania* 116 (1998), 72–111.

Sinor, D., 'Languages and Cultural Interchange along the Silk Roads', *Diogenes* 171 (1995), 1–14.

Small, A. M., 'Constantinopolitan Connections: Liudprand of Cremona and Byzantium', in *From Constantinople to the Frontier: The City and the Cities*, ed. N. S. M. Matheou, T. Kampianaki and L. M. Bondioli (Leiden, 2016), pp. 84–97.

Smeyers, M., *Vlaamse miniaturen van de 8ste tot het midden van de 16de eeuw: De middeleeuwse wereld op perkament* (Leuven, 1998).

Smith, J. B., *Walter Map and the Matter of Britain* (Philadelphia, 2017)

Smith, J. M. H., 'Writing in Britain and Ireland, *c.* 400–*c.* 800', in *The Cambridge History of Early Medieval English Literature*, ed. C. A. Lees (Cambridge, 2012), pp. 19–49.

Smith, K. A., *Art, Identity and Devotion in Fourteenth-Century England: Three Women and Their Books of Hours* (London, 2003).

Smith, L. B., 'The Welsh Language before 1536', in *The Welsh Language before the Industrial Revolution*, ed. G. H. Jenkins (Cardiff, 1997), 15–44.

Smith, L., 'Rhydderch ab Ieuan Llwyd (*c.* 1325–1392x8)', *ODNB*, accessed 17 February 2022, https://doi.org/10.1093/ref:odnb/48651.

Sokoloff, M., *A Dictionary of Jewish Palestinian Aramaic of the Byzantine Period*, 3rd edn (Ramat Gan, 2017).

Sokoloff, M., *Dictionary of Jewish Babylonian Aramaic*, 2nd edn (Ramat Gan, 2020).

Solterer, H., *The Master and Minerva: Disputing Women in French Medieval Culture* (Berkeley, 1995).

——, 'A Timely Villon: Anachrony and Premodern Poetic Fiction', *New Literary History* 52 (2021), 311–34.

Somerset, F., and N. Watson, 'Preface: On "Vernacular"', in *The Vulgar Tongue: Medieval and Postmedieval Vernacularity*, ed. F. Somerset and N. Watson (Philadelphia, 2003), pp. ix–xvi.

Sparks, C., *Heresy, Inquisition and Life Cycle in Medieval Languedoc* (York, 2014).

Spiegel, G., *Romancing the Past: The Rise of Vernacular Prose Historiography in Thirteenth-Century France* (Los Angeles, 1993).

Stahl, A., 'Coinage and Money in the Latin Empire of Constantinople', *Dumbarton Oaks Papers* 55 (2001), 197–206.

Stahuljak, Z., *Les Fixeurs au Moyen Âge. Histoire et littérature connectées* (Paris, 2021).

Stephenson, D., 'Welsh Lords in Shropshire: Gruffydd ap Iorwerth Goch and his Descendants in the Thirteenth Century', *Transactions of the Shropshire Archaeological Society* 77 (2002), 32–7.

Stevens, J. 'Medieval Song', in *The New Oxford History of Music*, vol. II: *The Early Middle Ages to 1300*, ed. R. Crocker and D. Hiley, 2nd edn (Oxford, 1990), pp. 357–451.

Stones, A., *Gothic Manuscripts, 1260–1320* (London, 2013).

——, 'Les manuscrits du *Roman d'Alexandre* en vers français et leurs contextes artistiques', in Gaullier-Bougassas, ed., *Alexandre le Grand*, pp. 269–84.

——, 'The Illustrated *Alexander* in French Verse: The Case of Italy', *Francigena* 5 (2019), 229–55.

Strubbe, E. I., 'De briefwisseling tussen Jan van den Berghe en Johanna van Harcourt (1420–1437)', *Bulletin de la Commission Royale* 125 (1959), 511–60.

Strubbe, E. I., 'Jean van den Berghe, écrivain et juriste flamand (13..–1439)', *Bulletin de la Commission royale des anciennes lois et ordonnances de Belgique* 12.3 (1926), 174–201.

Strubel, A., 'Le *Songe du vieil pèlerin* et les transformations de l'allégorie au quatorzième siècle', *Perspectives médiévales* 6 (1980), 54–73.

Struck, P., 'Allegory and Ascent in Neoplatonism', in Copeland and Struck, ed., *Cambridge Companion to Allegory*, pp. 57–69.

Subrahmanyam, S., 'Connected Histories: Notes towards a Reconfiguration of Early Modern Eurasia', *Modern Asian Studies* 31 (1997), 735–762.

Sunderland, L., *Rebel Barons: Resisting Royal Power in Medieval Culture* (Oxford, 2017).

Suppe, F. C., 'The Career and Subsequent Reputation of Iorwerth Goch, Bi-Cultural Denizen of the Medieval Welsh Marches', *North American Journal of Celtic Studies* 2 (2018), 133–54.

Surridge, M. E., 'Romance Linguistic Influence on Middle Welsh: A Review of Some Problems', *Studia Celtica* 1 (1966), 63–92.

——, 'Words of Romance Origin in the Works of the Gogynfeirdd', *Bulletin of the Board of Celtic Studies* 29 (1981), 528–30.

Svärdström, E., 'Runorna i Hagia Sofia', *Fornvännen* 65 (1970), 247–9.

Szerwiniack, O., 'D'Orose au *LGÉ*', *Études celtiques* 31 (1995), 205–17.

——, 'Un commentaire hiberno-latin des deux premier livres d'Orose, *Histoire contre les païens*', *Archivum Latinitatis Medii Aevi* 51 (1992–3), 5–137, and 65 (2007), 165–207.

Szpiech, R., 'Latin as a Language of Authoritative Tradition', in *Oxford Handbook of Medieval Latin Literature*, ed. R. J. Hexter and D. Townsend (Oxford, 2012), pp. 63–85.

Tantillo, G. 'Tre fratelli e un "fattaccio": Osso, Mastrosso e Carcagnosso, fondatori di tutte le mafie', *Balarm*, 28 June 2021, accessed 2 October 2023, https://www.balarm.it/news/tre-fratelli-e-un-fattaccio-osso-mastrosso-e-carcagnosso-fondatori-di-tutte-le-mafie-124279.

Tarnowski, A., 'The Consolations of Writing Allegory: Philippe de Mézières' *Le songe du vieil pèlerin*', in *Philippe de Mézières and His Age: Piety and Politics in the Fourteenth Century*, ed. R. Blumenfeld-Kosinski and K. Petkov (Leiden, 2012), pp. 237–54.

Thomas, A., 'Notice sur le manuscrit 4788 du Vatican', *Notices et extraits des manuscrits de la Bibliothèque nationale et autres bibliothèques* 41 (1917), 29–90.

Thomson, R. L., 'Owain: Chwedl Iarlles y Ffynnon', in Bromwich et al., ed., *The Arthur of the Welsh*, pp. 159–69.

Tilliette, J.-Y., 'L'*Alexandréide* de Gautier de Châtillon: Enéide médiévale ou "Virgile travesti"?', in *Alexandre le Grand dans les littératures occidentales et proche-orientales*, ed. L. Harf-Lancner, C. Klapper and F. Suard (Nanterre, 1999), pp. 275–88.

Tonni, E., 'La fonte battesimale di mafia e massoneria', *La verità di Ninco Nanco*, 29 June 2015, accessed 29 December 2022, https://laveritadininco-naco.altervista.org/la-fonte-battesimale-di-mafia-e-massoneria/

Touber, A., 'Lyrische Strophenformen', in Pérennec, ed., *Sprache und Verskunst*, pp. 267–302.

Trilling, J., 'Daedalus and the Nightingale: Art and Technology in the Myth of the Byzantine Court', in *Byzantine Court Culture from 829 to 1204*, ed. H. Maguire (Washington, 1997), pp. 217–30.

Trinidade, W. A., 'History and Fiction in the *Song of Dermot and the Earl*', *Parergon* 8 (1990), 123–30.

Trotter, D., 'L'anglo-français au pays de Galles: une enquête préliminaire', *Revue de linguistique romane* 58 (1994), 461–87.

——, '*Deinz Certeins Boundes*: Where Does Anglo-Norman Begin and End?', *Romance Philology* 67 (2013), 139–77.

——, 'Italian Merchants in London and Paris: Evidence of Language Contact in the Gallerani Accounts, 1305–8', in *On Linguistic Change in French: Socio-historical Approaches. Le changement linguistique en français: aspects sociohistoriques. Studies in Honour of R. Anthony Lodge. Études en hommage au Professeur R. Anthony Lodge*, ed. D. Lagorgette and T. Pooley (Chambéry 2011), pp. 209–26.

——, '*Oceano vox*: You Never Know Where a Ship Comes From: On Multilingualism and Language-Mixing in Medieval Britain', in *Aspects of Multilingualism in European Language History*, ed. G. Ferraresi and K. Braunmüller (Amsterdam, 2003), pp. 15–33.

——, '"Une et indivisible": Variation and Ideology in the Historiography and History of France', *Revue roumaine de linguistique* 51 (2006), 359–76.

Trouillot, M.-R., *Silencing the Past: Power and the Production of History* (Boston MA, 1995).

Tyerman, C., *The Debate on the Crusades, 1099–2010* (Manchester, 2011).

Valenti, G., 'Riflessioni attorno alle citazioni mariane nelle liriche dei trovatori', *Cognitive Philology* 11 (2018), 1–19.

Vallet, É., 'La grammaire du monde. Langue et pouvoir en Arabie occidentale à l'âge mongole', *Annales: histoire, sciences sociales* 70 (2015), 637–66.

The Values of French, accessed 24 February 2023, https://tvof.ac.uk.

van Asperen, H., *Pelgrimstekens op perkament: originele en nageschilderde bedevaartssouvenirs in religieuze boeken (ca. 1450–ca. 1530)* (Edam, 2009).

Van Bruaene, A.-L., *De Gentse memorieboeken als spiegel van stedelijk historisch bewustzijn (14de tot 16de eeuw)* (Ghent, 1998).

——, *Om beters wille: rederijkerskamers en de stedelijke cultuur in de Zuidelijke Nederlanden (1400–1650)* (Amsterdam, 2008).

Van Hoorebeeck, C. 'La ville, le prince et leurs officiers en Flandre à la fin du Moyen Âge: livres et lectures de la famille de Baenst', *Le moyen âge* 113 (2007), 45–67.

van Houts, E., 'The Date of Warner's *Moriuht*', in E. van Houts, *History and Family Traditions in England and the Continent, 1000–1200* (Aldershot, 1999), pp. 1–6 (IIIb).

——, 'The Norman Conquest through European Eyes', *English Historical Review* 110 (1995), 832–53.

Van Steenbergen, J., 'Mamluk Elite on the Eve of al-Nasir Muhammad's Death (1341): A Look Behind the Scenes of Mamluk Politics', *Mamluk Studies Review* 9 (2005), 192–9.

Varvaro, A., 'Il regno normanno-svevo', in *Letteratura Italiana. Storia e Geografia*, ed. A. Asor Rosa, 3 vols. (Turin, 1987), I, 79–99.

Vásáry, I., *Cumans and Tatars: Oriental Military in the Pre-Ottoman Balkans, 1185–1365* (Cambridge, 2005).

——, 'The Role and Function of Mongolian and Turkic in Ilkhanid Iran', in *Turks and Iranians: Interactions in Language and History*, ed. E. A. Csató, L. Johanson, A. Róna-Tas and B. Utas (Wiesbaden, 2016), pp. 141–52.

Veach, C., 'Conquest and Conquerors', in *The Cambridge History of Ireland, Volume 1, 600–1550*, ed. B. Smith (Cambridge, 2018), pp. 157–81.

Vega, M. J., 'El *De Iudaica Arbore* (1517) de Étienne Chenu y los conversos españoles en Tolosa y el Languedoc', *Atalaya* 13 (2013), accessed 17 February 2024, https://journals.openedition.org/atalaya/1065.

Véran-Boussaadia, C., 'Hue de Rotelande, le jeu de la frontière et la frontière en Je', in *L'expérience des frontières et les littératures de l'Europe médiévale*, ed. S. Lodén and V. Obry (Paris, 2019), pp. 45–55.

Viezel, E., 'Abraham Ibn Ezra's Commentary on Job 2:11', *Hebrew Union College Annual* 88 (2017), 113–57.

——, 'Targum Onkelos in Rashi's Exegetical Consciousness', *Review of Rabbinic Judaism* 15 (2012), 1–19.

Visi, T., 'Berechiah ben Natronai ha-Naqdan's *Dodi ve-Nekhdi* and the Transfer of Scientific Knowledge from Latin to Hebrew in the Twelfth Century', *Aleph* 14 (2014), 9–73.

——, 'Introduction', in *Berekhiah Ben Natronai Ha-Naqdan's Works and Their Reception*, ed. T. Visi, T. Bibring and D. Soukup (Brepols, 2019), pp. 7–28.

Vogel, H. U., *Marco Polo was in China: New Evidence from Currencies, Salts and Revenues* (Leiden, 2013).

Vollmann-Profe, G., *Wiederbeginn volkssprachiger Schriftlichkeit im hohen Mittelalter (1050/60–1160/70)*, in Heinzle, ed., *Geschichte der deutschen Literatur*, vol. I, pt. 2, 2nd edn (Tübingen, 1994).

Voyer, C., 'Voir et entendre: des paroles dans l'image. À propos d'une enluminure du manuscrit 121 de la Bibliothèque municipale d'Avignon', in *La parole sacrée – formes, fonctions, sens (Xie – XVe siècle)*, Cahiers de Fanjeaux 47 (Toulouse, 2012), pp. 383–402.

Wackers, P., 'The Dutch Reynaert Tradition in National and European Perspective', in *Literature without Frontiers: Transnational Perspectives on Premodern Literature in the Low Countries 1200–1800*, ed. C. van der Haven, J. Bloemendal, Y. Desplenter and J.A. Parente, Jr. (Leiden, 2023), pp. 79–95.

Wacks, D., *Double Diaspora in Sephardic Literature: Jewish Cultural Production Before and After 1492* (Bloomington, 2015).

Wadden, P., 'Some Views of the Normans in Eleventh- and Twelfth-Century Ireland', in *The English Isles: Cultural Transmission and Political Conflict in Britain and Ireland, 1100–1500*, ed. S. Duffy and S. Foran (Dublin, 2013), pp. 13–36.

——, '"The Beauty and Lust of the Gaels": National Characteristics and Medieval Gaelic Learned Culture', *North American Journal of Celtic Studies* 2 (2018), 85–104.

Waffner, P., *Der* Livre de Sidrac: *die Quelle allen Wissens: Aspekte zur Tradition und Rezeption eines altfranzösischen Textes* (Milan, 2019).

Wallace, D., ed., *Europe: A Literary History, 1343–1418*, 2 vols. (Oxford, 2017).

Wapnewski, P., 'Walthers Lied von der Traumliebe (74,20) und die deutschsprachige Pastourelle', *Euphorion* 51 (1957), 113–50.

Warlop, E., *The Flemish Nobility before 1300* (Kortrijk, 1976).

Warntjes, I., 'Die Verwendung der Volkssprache in frühmittelalterlichen Klosterschulen', in *Wissenspaläste: Räume des Wissens in der Vormoderne*, ed. G. Mierke and C. Fasbender (Würzburg, 2013), pp. 153–83.

Warren, M. R., *Creole Medievalism: Colonial France and Joseph Bédier's Middle Ages* (Minneapolis, 2011).

Waswo, R., *The Founding Legend of Western Civilization: From Virgil to Vietnam* (Hanover NH, 1997).

——, 'The History That Literature Makes', *New Literary History* 19 (1988), 541–64.

Waters, C. M., *Translating Clergie: Status, Education and Salvation in Thirteenth-Century Vernacular Texts* (Philadelphia, 2016).

Watkin, M., 'The French Linguistic Influence in Mediaeval Wales', *Transactions of the Honourable Society of Cymmrodorion* (1918–19), 146–222.

Weinreich, U., *Languages in Contact: Findings and Problems* (The Hague, 1979).

Weisel, B., 'Die Überlieferung des *Livre de Sidrac* in Handschriften und Drucken', in *Wissensliteratur im Mittelalter und in der Frühen Neuzeit*, ed. H. Brunner and N. Wolf (Wiesbaden, 1993), pp. 53–66.

Weiss, J., 'Thomas and the Earl: Literary and Historical Contexts for the *Romance of Horn*', in *Tradition and Transformation in Medieval Romance*, ed. R. Field (Cambridge, 1999), pp. 1–13.

Whitfield, S., 'The Merchant's Tale', in *Life Along the Silk Road*, 2nd edn (Oakland, 2015), pp. 14–37.

Wieruszowski, H., 'Roger II of Sicily, Rex-Tyrannus, in Twelfth-Century Political Thought', *Speculum* 38 (1963), 46–78.

Wijsman, H., *Luxury Bound: Illustrated Manuscript Production and Noble and Princely Book Ownership in the Burgundian Netherlands (1400–1550)* (Turnhout, 2010).

Williams, D. H., *The Welsh Cistercians* (Leominster, 2001).

Williamson, B., 'Site, Seeing and Salvation in Fourteenth-Century Avignon', *Art History* 30 (2007), 1–25.

Willis, R. S., *The Debt of the Spanish* Libro de Alexandre *to the French* Roman d'Alexandre (Princeton, 1935).

Wogan-Browne, J., '"Cest livre liseez ... chescun jour": Women and Reading, c.1230-c.1430', in *Lang Cult*, pp. 239–53.

——, 'Simund de Freine (*d.* before 1228?)', *ODNB*, accessed 5 April 2022, https://doi.org/10.1093/ref:odnb/25570.

Wogan-Browne, J., T. Fenster and D. W. Russell, ed., 'Hue de Rotelande, *Ipomedon* [Dean 162], Prologue: London, British Library, MS Cotton Vespasian A.VII, f. 39ʳ', in Wogan-Browne, Fenster and Russell, ed., *Vernacular Literary Theory*, pp. 36–40.

——, 'Simund de Freine, *Roman de philosophie* [Dean 243], Prologue: London, British Library, MS Add. 46,919, f. 107ʳᵃ⁻ᵇ', in Wogan-Browne, Fenster and Russell, ed., *Vernacular Literary Theory*, pp. 352–4.

Wogan-Browne, J., T. Fenster and D. W. Russell, ed., *Vernacular Literary Theory from the French of England: Texts and Translations, c.1120–c.1450* (Cambridge, 2016).

Wolff, R. L., 'Mortgage and Redemption of an Emperor's Son: Castile and the Latin Empire of Constantinople', *Speculum* 29 (1954), 45–84.

Wood, F., *Did Marco Polo go to China?* (Boulder, 1996).

Woodfin, W. T., Y. Rassamakin and R. Holod, 'Foreign Vesture and Nomadic Identity on the Black Sea Littoral in the Early Thirteenth Century', *Ars Orientalis* 38 (2010), 155–86.

Worstbrock, F. J., 'Wiedererzählen und Übersetzen', in *Mittelalter und frühe Neuzeit: Übergänge, Umbrüche und Neuansätze*, ed. W. Haug (Tübingen, 1999), pp. 128–42.

Wright, L., 'Bills, Accounts, Inventories: Everyday Trilingual Activities in the Business World of Later Medieval England', in *Multilingualism in Later Medieval Britain*, ed. D. A. Trotter (Cambridge, 2000), pp. 150–6.

Wright, R., *Late Latin and Early Romance in Spain and Carolingian France* (Liverpool, 1982).

Wyss, U., '*Herbergen ist loischieren genant*: Zur Ästhetik der fremden Wörter im "Willehalm"', in *Blütezeit*, ed. M. Chinca, J. Heinzle, and C. Young (Tübingen, 2000), pp. 363–82.

Wyss, U., 'Tristanromane', in Pérennec and Schmid, *Höfischer Roman in Vers und Prosa*, pp. 49–94.

Yúdice, G., 'We are *Not* the World', *Social Text* 31/32 (1992), 202–16.

Zimmer, S., 'A Medieval Linguist: Gerald de Barri', *Études celtiques* 35 (2003), 313–52.

Zinelli, F., 'The French of Outremer Beyond the Holy Land', in Morreale and Paul, ed., *The French of Outremer*, pp. 221–46.

——, 'Inside/Outside Grammar: The French of Italy Between Structuralism and Trends of Exoticism', in *Medieval Francophone Literary Culture Outside France*, ed. Morato and Schoenaers, pp. 31–72.

Zingesser, E., *Stolen Song: How the Troubadours Became French* (Ithaca, 2020).

Zink, M., *La subjectivité littéraire: autour du siècle de saint Louis* (Paris, 1985).

Index

Abū Zayd al-Sīrāfī 169
Acallam na Senórach 135
Acre 25, 165, 173 n. 57, 208–9
Adelard of Bath 28–29, 33, 40–41, 43–46
Aden 178
Agobard of Lyon 182
Agnes, empress 82
Adémar of Chabannes 121
Agobard of Lyon 182
Aimon de Varennes 68
Akhbār al-Sin wa-l-Hind (Abū Zayd
 al-Sīrāfī) 169
Al-Andalus 90–91, 111, 274
 Literature of 90–99, 101, 105, 111
Al-Din, Rashid 164
Al-Din Rūmī, Jalāl 176
Al-Din Süleyman, Mu'in 176
Al-Ḥarizi 92
Al-Washshā', Muḥammad ibn Isḥāq ibn
 Yaḥyā 101
Albertus Magnus 87
Albigensian Crusade 100 n. 42, 223, 226
Alexander of Paris (*alias*, Alexander of
 Bernay) 200, 201
Alexander the Great 199–200
Alexandreis 203, 215
Alexandria 194
Alexiad 69
Alexios I, emperor 69
Alfonso VIII, king 92, 198, 202, 215
Alfonso X, king 91–92, 198 n. 6, 199,
 205, 207–10, 215–16
Alfonso XI, king 199, 210 n. 48, 216–17
Alix de Wancourt 268
Alès 221, 228, 236
Allegory 98, 190–93, 196, 259–60
 in Phillipe de Mézières's
  Songe 190–93
 in poetry 98, 190
 in prophecy 196

Biblical 192–93
 Moralized 259–60
*L'altercacion et disputation entre l'ame et le
 corps* 220, 224–26, 227, 229, 236
Angevins 270, 272–73, 279–80
Anglo-French 12, 250, 252
Anna Komnene 69
Antapodosis (Liutprand of Cremona) 55,
 60
Antoine de Baenst 263–64
Anthonis de Roovere 262, 267
Ara·m conseillatz, seignor (PC 70.6) 111
Arabic
 Language 29, 40, 90–92, 101, 168–69,
  175, 193, 217, 273–74
 Literature 93, 95, 99, 105, 109, 114,
  181, 195
 Poetics 91, 97–98, 105–6, 108
  Allegory 194, 196
 Poetry 90, 91, 94, 98–99, 101, 105
  in Sicily 273–74
Aramaic language 30, 32–40, 42, 45–46
Aristippus, Henricus 273
Aristotle 93–94
Arnulf de Montgomery 122
Aucassin et Nicolette 89, 100, 104, 106–7,
 109, 111
Avianus 28

de Baenst Family 260–61, 264
Baldwin II, king 84–86
Baldwin, archbishop 240–41
Batu, khan 165, 172
Ben El'azar, Jacob 92, 98–99, 102, 106,
 109
Benedict XII, pope 228
Benoît de Sainte-Maure 199, 207, 212,
 214, 217, 274, 276, 278, 279, 285–88
Berekhiah Ha-Naqdan 27–30, 33–34,
 36–37, 39, 41–45

346 INDEX

Berenguela, queen 198, 207
Bernard of Clairvaux 123
Bernart de Ventadorn 111
Bertran de Born 112
Boccaccio, Giovanni 213
Boctus, king 184, 186
Boiardo 278, 292
Book of Sidrac 181, 183–86, 196
Bossy, Michel-André 220
Brian Boru 121–22, 124, 133
Bruges 221, 257–64, 267–68
 Elite of 259, 261–62
Burgundians, court of 255–57, 266, 268
 Culture of 265
Burgwinkle, William 110, 113
Busby, Keith 132, 250
Byzantium 67–69, 73, 77–82, 87
 Court of 68, 73
 Culture of 67, 77, 79, 85
 Monuments of 77–80, 82, 87

Calcidius 123, 125
Capetian monarchy 179, 207, 215
Castile
 Language of 91, 92, 197, 215, 226
 Crown of 197–99, 201–2, 207, 209–10, 213, 215–217
Cathal Crobderg Ua Conchobair 134
Cathars 223, 232, 236
Chagatay 173
Chanson de geste 75, 137–38, 141, 153, 155, 278
Chanson de Girart de Rouissillon 55, 69
Chanson de Roland 124, 137, 278
Charlemagne cycle 55, 69, 75, 118, 246
Charles I of Anjou 271, 279, 282–83
Charles Martel 55, 69
Charles the Bald 118
Charles the Bold 262–63
Chevalier au lion (Chrétien de Troyes) 266
Chinese language 169
Chinggis Khan 164, 170–71
Chivalry, cultures of 216–17
Chrétien de Troyes 137, 141, 143 n. 18, 244–45, 266

Christine de Pizan 139, 262, 267
Chronicle Writing 121, 127, 129–30, 132–36, 161, 179–80, 197, 205, 207, 210, 212, 214, 278, 281–83
Cligès (Chrétien de Troyes) 108
Lo cocir de la mort 220, 225, 227, 232–36
Code-Switching 32, 50
Codex Cumanicus 173–74, 178
Cogadh Gaedhel re Gallaibh 122, 133
Coins 83
Comestor, Peter 206
La conquesta di Sichilia fatta per li normandi 279–80, 287, 289, 291
Conqueste de Constantinoble (Robert de Clari) 49, 51, 69, 71, 73, 75, 78, 86
De consolatione philosophiae (Boethius) 181, 187–90
Constantinople 47, 49, 52, 55, 60, 71, 77, 87
Contact Zone 1–2, 4–5, 8, 16, 22, 221
 in the Castilian Royal Court 217
 in Constantinople 52, 88
 in Cyprus 183
 in Flanders 254, 268
 in Ireland 116
 in Jewish Literature 27, 38
 in the Kingdom of France 3, 13, 220
 in the March of Wales 237, 252
 in the Mediterranean 10
 in Occitania 219, 223, 227
 in Outremer French 162–63, 180, 183, 196
 in Persian Literature 177
 in Toulouse 226
 in Troyes 27, 31
Conrad IV, king 271
Conradin, king 271
Council of Vienne 222
Courtiers 192, 267
Courtliness 17, 55, 68, 86, 145–46, 150
Courtly literature 138–41, 143, 153, 156
Creation Narrative 184–86, 188–90
Créolisation 5, 7, 19
Cronica Troyana 215
Crusader Narrative 49, 51–52, 69, 73, 77–80, 82, 86, 127

INDEX 347

Cuman (language) 171, 174
Cuman (people) 172, 173
Cumtach na nIudiade nArd 120
Cyprus 182–83

Dares Phrygius 285–86
Debate poems 220, 225, 227, 229–32, 235–36
Derbforgaill, wife of Tigernan Ua Ruairc 133
Derrida, Jacques 3, 4, 9, 157
Le devisement du monde (Marco Polo) 159–61, 163, 166, 168, 176, 178
Diarmait Mac Murchada 127, 129–30
Dictys Cretensis 207, 216, 285–87
Domna, pos de mi no᾽ us cal (PC 80.12) 112
Donnchada, king of Osraige 127
Dream poems 219

Ecclesiastical courts 203
Egypt 44, 193, 195–96
Éléonore of Poitiers, viscountess 257
Eliezer of Beaugency 28
English (language) 116, 180, 220, 247, 249–52
England (people) 11, 15, 25, 52, 122, 125, 129, 134, 237
Enrique I, king 198, 212
Epic literature 194–96
Epistle to Can Grande della Scala 97
Érec et Énide (Chrétien de Troyes) 137, 141–42
Les estoires de Venise (Martin da Canal) 161
Eugenius (translator of the *Optics*) 273
Expugnatio Hibernica (Gerald of Wales) 127, 129

Ferdinand III, king 92
Fernando III, king 198, 210, 215
Fernando IV, king 210
Il filostrato (Giovanni Boccaccio) 213
Flanders 253–68
    Administration 255, 257–58

Chamberlains of 254
Elite families of 260–67
Multilingualism of 268
Florimont (Aimon de Varennes) 63
Folk myths 284
Fouke le Fitz Waryn 242
Frederick II, emperor 186, 271, 274–76, 278
Poetry of 275–76
French language
    in Britain 2, 124, 237, 247, 251–52, 270, 274–75
    in Cyprus 17, 180, 182–83, 187, 190, 196
    in England 4, 11–12, 15, 115, 121, 125, 132, 202, 237, 247, 250–51, 269
    in Flanders 17, 20, 208, 237, 253–57, 260, 266–68
    in Ireland 12, 14, 18, 22, 115–24, 128–29, 135
    in Italy 3, 15, 18, 162, 201, 202, 213–14, 269, 289, 292
    in the Kingdom of France 13, 220–23
    in Occitania 219–21, 224–27, 236
    in Sicily 269–70, 273–75, 277, 285–87, 288–89, 292
    in Wales 20, 128–29, 237–44, 247–48, 250–52
Froissart, Jean 264
Fudeman, Kirsten 30–32, 44
Fursa, saint 117

Gaimar 274
Galbert of Bruges 263–64
Galen 179
Gaucelm Faidit 112
Gaunt, Simon 15
Gazan, ilkhan 164
Gender 104–5, 230, 234–35, 285
    in histories 285
    in literature 230, 234–35
General Estoria (Alfonso X) 204–8, 210, 212, 215–16
Genoa 162, 195–96
Geoffrey of Malaterra 278–81
Geoffrey de Villehardouin 49, 80, 82, 86

348 INDEX

Geoffrey of Vinsauf 96
Gerald of Wales 127–28, 239–40
Gerald of Windsor 239–40
German
Language 148, 154, 157
Lyric poetry 137–40, 143, 147, 149, 156
Germain of Lichtervelde 257
La geste des Engleis en Yrlande 115–16,
125, 133–35
Ghent 258–61, 263, 265, 267–68
Giacomo da Lentini 275
Gilbert fitz Baderon, lord 248
Giovanni da Procida 281–83
Giovanni de Cruyllas 277
van Gistel Family 264–68
van Gistel, Gerard 265, 267–68
van Gistel, Jacob II 264
van Gistel, Jan VI 264–67
Glissant, Édouard 5–8, 12
Gottfried von Strassburg 143 n. 18, 149,
152, 177 n. 73
Greek Language 44–45, 51, 56, 274
Gruffudd ab Iorwerth Goch 241
Gruffudd ap Gwenwynwyn 241
Guelfs and Ghibellines 272–73
Guido delle Colonne 278, 285
Guillaume de Machaut 277
Guillaume d'Orange Cycle 141 n. 13
Guyuk, khan 164

Harold Godwineson 121
Hartmann von Aue 137, 141 f.13, 142,
144–45
Hebrew
Language 44–46, 89, 90, 92
Maqamat 91–92, 99, 105, 113
Poetics 27, 30, 90–92, 98, 101, 106–8,
110–11, 114
Poems 99–100
Prose 111
Henry I, king of England 122
Henry II, king of England 115–16, 125,
127, 240–41
Henry IV, king of Sicily 274
Histoire ancienne jusqu'à César 205–9,
213, 215, 216

Historia destructionis Troiae (Guido delle
Colonne) 285–90
La Historia (Hugo Falcandus) 274
Historiography
of French Chronicles 51, 206–7, 285
of Florence 279–81, 284, 292
of Sicily 272, 280–81, 288, 292
Vernacular 197, 203, 212, 214, 216–17,
281–83
Hue de Rotelande 248
Hugh de Lacy, earl 127

Ibn Ezra, Abraham 29, 31, 33, 37–39, 43
Ibn Ezra, Moses 93–95
Ibn Falaquera, Shem Tov 95–96, 114
Ibn Hamdis 274
Ibn Ṣaqbel, Solomon 89, 97, 99–100,
103, 105–6, 109 n. 70, 110
Ibn Sahula, Isaac 92
Ieuan ap Rhydderch ab Ieuan
Llwyd 242–43
Innocent II, pope 271
Innocent IV, pope 164, 170
Iorweth Goch 241
Ireland 122, 131–32
Irish (language) 117–18, 124, 130–32
Literature in 117–18, 123
Irish (people) 118, 120, 122, 127
Italian 25, 161, 269, 274–75, 281, 288
Italy 15, 194, 204, 248, 285, 290
North 9, 162, 201–2, 213–14, 269,
273–75, 279, 289
South 21, 248, 272, 276, 285
Iwein (Hartmann von Aue) 144

Jacobus de Cessolis 260
Jacopo da Varagine 162
Jan III de Baenst 261–63, 267
Jan of Namen 257
Jan van den Berghe 256–57, 260
Authorship of 258–59
Jeanne de Harcourt 257–58, 267
John of Brienne 209
John of Garland 96
John of Plano Carpini, Friar 164, 170

John the Fearless, duke of
  Burgundy 258–59
John, king of England 128
John XXII, pope 222, 228–29, 235–36
Joseph Kara, rabbi 28, 32–33, 44

Kallir, Eleazar 36
Kitāb al-muḥāḍara wa-l-mudhākara
  (Moses ibn Ezra) 93

La'az 31, 40, 44–45
Langland, William 249
Language
  Biblical 44, 105
  Communities 175, 182, 221, 227, 241,
    253
    French 248, 272–73
  Composite 6, 63–64, 83, 147, 251
  Cosmopolitan 168, 270, 292
  Derivation 45
  Networks 15, 17, 20, 52, 173
  of diplomacy 172, 238, 241, 252
  of learning 23, 118, 175
  of record 18, 239, 242, 252
  of trade 122
  Mixing 51, 60, 124, 143, 151, 154–56,
    158, 190, 254, 290
Latin
  and the Crusades 51, 55, 60, 64, 67, 79
  and Jewish Scholars 40, 43–46
  in instruction 96–97, 277
  Language 109, 174, 289, 291
    of elites 117–20, 123, 128, 132, 240
    of record 197–98
  Medieval Academic 179–82
  Histories 278–79, 285–86, 288, 290
  in the Mediterranean 160–62, 274,
    287, 292
Latini, Brunetto 161, 170
Lebor na hUidre 124
Leinster 116, 126
Les leys d'Amors (attributed to Guilhem
  Molinier) 96, 220, 230, 233, 235
Libro de Alexandre 199–202, 204, 215–16
Lille 259

Lingua Franca 118, 149, 160, 162, 168–69,
  172, 174–75, 178, 242
  French as 253, 255
Literature
  Adaptation 266
  Allegory 188, 190, 191–93
  Culture
    Castilian 197, 201, 213
    Welsh 244, 247
    Burgundian 253–54, 256
    Persian 177
    Sicilian 277
  Language 173, 177, 269
    French as 199, 237
    of Wales 238
  Patronage 254, 257, 261–63, 268
    in Flanders 256, 267
    in Germany 141–42
    in Sicily 275–76
  Society 259–61, 263
  Traditions 67, 221, 249, 266
  Transmission 67, 92, 270
Liutprand of Cremona 55, 65
Le livre du trésor (Brunetto Latini) 161,
  226
Louis de Gruuthuse, Bruges
  bibliophile 262–63
Louis IX, king 162, 165, 170, 207
Louis of Male 257
Love Poetry 98–99, 103–4
Lyric Poetry 89, 91, 100, 105, 113, 224

Maimonides 94
Malachy, saint 123
Manfred, regent of Sicily 271
Mamluk 193–95
Manuscripts 15, 39, 45, 67, 118–19, 141,
  162, 265–66
  Circulation 15
  Collection 141, 265
  Glosses 39, 45, 67, 118–19
  Production 162
  Transmission 266
Map, Walter 248
Marchant, Guyot 220, 224
Margaret, countess 259

350 INDEX

Margaret van Rooden 257
Martin de Canal 161
Matter of France 138
Matter of Troy 270
Maximilian I, emperor 264
Memory Book 263, 268
Menasci, Guido 284
Meshal ha-qadmoni 110
Metaphor 36
  in Poetry 96, 101
  Biblical 93, 95, 103, 110
Mongols
  Conquest 171–72, 176
  Court 164
  Languages of 170–74
Morice Regan 129–34
Moriuht (Warner of Rouen) 119–20
Morreale, Laura 279–82, 285, 287
Mosul 167–68
Multilingualism
  Biblical 193
  in texts 38, 41, 117, 178, 263, 266
  in Castile 197–98
  in Cyprus 182, 187
  in diplomacy 166–67, 240, 255
  in Eurasia 159–60, 163–64, 166–67,
    172, 175
  in German poetry 148–49
  in glosses 27, 30, 34–35, 44–45
  in literary culture 177, 253–55, 260,
    267
  of Occitania 221, 223, 225
  Welsh 129, 135, 239
Mythology 105, 284
  in film 284
  National 284

Ne' um Asher ben Yehuda (Solomon ibn
    Şaqbel) 97–98, 102, 105, 107–8, 111
Neoplatonism 43
Network Studies 16
Normans
  in Ireland 120, 121, 122, 124
  in Sicily 269–70, 273, 271, 278
Norse Language 132

Occitan
  Culture 226, 236
  Language 96, 110, 137, 139, 220–21, 223
  Literature 100, 138–39, 219–20, 222,
    224, 227–31, 231
  Poetry 100–1, 140, 220–21, 223, 225,
    229, 233, 236, 275
Occitania 221, 223, 225, 227–28
  French administration of 223
  Ritual practice in 227–28
Odonis, Geraldus 229
Oral Literature 7, 34, 131, 141 n. 13, 148,
    278

*Parisiana poetria de arte prosayca, metrica
    et rithmica* (John of Garland) 96
Parzival (Hartmann von Aue) 146–48,
    158
Patria (genre) 64–65, 78–79
Paul de Baenst 261
Pedro I, king 199, 210, 216–17
Pegolotti, Francesco 165
Peire Cardenal 232
Pèlerinage de Charlemagne 69, 75
Perceval (Chrétien de Troyes) 245, 266
Persian Language 175, 177
Peter I, king of Cyprus 190
Peter III, king of Aragon 272
Peter of Eboli 274
Peter John Olivi 222
Philip the Bold 258
Philip the Good 262, 265
Philippe de Mézières 181, 190–91, 193
Physiognomy 111, 219, 221–22, 224–25,
    229–31, 234–36
Picard 13–14
Pierre de Paris 181, 187–90
Pilgrimage, in Iberia 204
Poetria Nova (Geoffrey of Vinsauf) 96
Poetry
  as parody 107, 109, 114
  Metaphor in 96, 101
  Prosimetra in 100, 107, 110–11, 113,
    210, 214
Polo, Marco 159, 163–64, 167–70, 172,
    175–76

Postcolonial Literary Studies 16
Pratt, Mary-Louise 1, 2, 22, 221, 223, 254
Printing 220, 225, 226, 261, 267, 288, 290
Prose Histories 276, 281

Quaestiones naturales (Adelard of
  Bath) 28–29
Qubilai, khan 159, 163–64, 168, 170–71

Raimbaut de Vaqueiras 113
Raimon Vidal de Besalú 97
Rashi (Rabbi Solomon ben Isaac of
  Troyes) 30–31, 33–39, 42, 45, 164
Rasulid Hexaglot 178
Lu rebellamentu di Sichilia 281–84,
  287–89, 291
Récits d'un ménestrel de Reims 86
Rhetorical Devices 50, 56, 65, 77, 93,
  96–97, 148, 158, 181, 191–92, 297
Rhys ap Gruffudd 240
Richard Fitzgilbert de Clare
  (Strongbow) 116, 125–27, 130
Robert, count 280
Robert de Clari 49, 73, 75, 77–80, 83,
  86–87
Robert of Anjou, king 213
Roeland I de Baenst 263, 268
Roeland van Uutkerke 259–60, 267
Roger II, king 271, 274
Roger of Lichtervelde 257
Roman d'Alexandre (Bibliothèque de
  l'Arsenal MS 3472) 201–2, 204
Roman d'Alexandre (Vulgate cycle) 59,
  75, 199–204, 215
Romans d'antiquité 21, 75, 138, 197–98,
  201, 203, 204, 213, 215, 217
  French in 200, 212, 216, 217
Roman de Horn 116
Roman de la poire 89, 100, 103, 107, 111,
  114
*Roman de la rose ou de Guillaume de
  Dole* 100, 109
Roman de Philosophie (Simund de
  Freine) 249
Roman de Renart 266
Roman de Thebes 75

Roman de Tristan en prose 265
Roman de Troie (Benoît de Sainte-
  Maure) 205, 207, 210, 212–16, 278,
  285–87
Romance (languages) 97, 185
Poetics 93, 97, 99, 101–4, 108–10, 114, 154
Romance
  and Hebrew literature 91–92, 105–6
  and the Crusades 194–96, 209
  in Castilian 198–99, 205–6, 208, 210
  in English 116, 126, 138, 249
  in French 37, 100, 103, 108, 126, 162,
    179, 197, 242–44, 266, 288
  in Middle High German 137, 141,
    143–47, 149, 151–54, 158
  in Sicilian 273, 277–78, 285
  in Welsh 244–46
  Literature 91, 105–6, 108, 133, 135, 137,
    145, 149, 152, 162, 177, 179, 198–99, 202,
    204, 213, 242–43, 250–52
  Poetry 103, 113, 177
Rustichello of Pisa 11, 17, 26, 159, 162–63

Sancho IV, king 210
Sefer ha–Meshalim (Jacob ben
  El'azar) 92, 105 n. 57, 108, 110, 113
Sefer ha–Mevaqesh (Shem Tov ibn
  Falaquera) 95, 114
Seljuqs 176
Settler Colonialism 126, 128–29, 238
Sicilian
  History 271–72
  Language 269, 274–78, 282, 292
  Literature of 270, 278, 289
  Poetry in 269, 275, 279
  Vespers 271–72, 281–83, 291
Sicily 269, 272–73, 285, 289–90
  Aragonese rule of 272–73, 284
Simund de Freine 249
Sirat al-Ẓāhir Baybars 181, 193–96
Le songe du viel pelerin (Philippe de
  Mézières) 190–92
Spiegel, Gabrielle 179

Taḥkemoni (al-Ḥarizi) 92, 99, 101, 110
Tairdelbach Ua Briain 122–23

352 INDEX

Targum 33–36, 38–39, 42
Textual
  Adaptation 25, 145, 197, 219, 244–49, 266
  Reception 138–40, 287–88
  Transmission 129, 140, 157, 173, 187, 201–2, 204, 207–10, 214, 218, 247, 250, 262, 267, 289
Thomas of Cantilupe, bishop 242, 248
Toulouse 224, 226–27
  Intellectual culture in 226
Tower of Babel 189–90
Trade 21, 168, 176
Translatio imperii 185, 279
Translation 219
  Arabic 165
  French 45, 56, 63, 130, 179–80, 190, 212, 243, 254, 277
  German 142–48, 152, 177 n. 73
  Greek 57, 65, 273
  Hebrew 27, 29, 32, 36–38, 40, 40, 41, 43, 45
  Welsh 240, 244–47
  Latin 44, 51, 63, 65, 166, 186–87, 285–86, 290
  of Histories 278, 289
  Sicilian 274–77, 279, 281
Travel literature 63, 77, 159, 165–67, 169
Treatise on Logic (Maimonides) 95
Tretiz (Walter de Bibbesworth) 19, 20
Tristan und Isolde (Gottfried von Strassburg) 149–52, 288
Trojan History 288
Troubadours 89, 92, 103, 112, 137, 224, 232
Turkish Language 168–71

Uighurs 170–71
  Language 171
Uncle and Nephew (Berekhiah Ha-Naqdan) 27, 29, 38–39, 41, 43, 45–46

Veneziano, Antonio 276
Vernacular
  Language 22, 27, 31, 36, 167–68, 172, 178–80, 183, 186–87, 193, 270, 253
  Literary Tradition 126, 140, 203, 219, 224, 226, 288
  Writing 110, 115–18, 135, 140, 161, 173, 185, 200, 203, 216–17, 219, 224, 226, 251, 269–70, 277, 288
    Castilian 198, 208
    Sicilian 273, 274, 290, 292
  Texts in 118, 120, 124, 129, 133, 181–82, 196–97, 199, 249, 275, 277, 291
Villani, Giovanni 229
Visio Philiberti 219–20, 236
Voyages of Jean de Mandeville 266

Wales 129, 238–39, 242, 250–52
  Elite laypeople of 237–39, 244, 247, 252
  Literature of 244–45, 247–50
  March of 237–38, 242, 247–50, 252
  Poetry of 249, 252
Welsh (Language) 237, 245, 252
Walter de Bibbesworth 19–20
Walter of Châtillon 200–1, 203
Willehalm (Wolfram von Eschenbach) 153, 156–58
Willem II, count 257
William de Vere, bishop 240
William of Rubruck 165, 17
William fitz Odo de Berry 240
Wogan-Browne, Jocelyn 15, 249
Wolfram von Eschenbach 146, 148, 153, 155–58
Women 71, 98–99, 102, 104–5, 139, 147, 171, 256, 282, 287
  in Hebrew Maqama 98–99
  in histories 80, 282, 284, 287
  in romance 102, 104, 147

Zeebout, Ambrosius 267

Printed in the USA
CPSIA information can be obtained
at www.ICGtesting.com
JSHW051911150524
63207JS00004B/36